Oracle Press™

Oracle8*i* Networking 101

ORACLE®

Oracle Press™

Oracle8*i* Networking 101

Marlene L. Theriault

Osborne/**McGraw-Hill**

Berkeley New York St. Louis San Francisco
Auckland Bogotá Hamburg London Madrid
Mexico City Milan Montreal New Delhi Panama City
Paris São Paulo Singapore Sydney
Tokyo Toronto

Osborne/**McGraw-Hill**
2600 Tenth Street
Berkeley, California 94710
U.S.A.

For information on translations or book distributors outside the U.S.A., or to arrange bulk purchase discounts for sales promotions, premiums, or fund-raisers, please contact Osborne/**McGraw-Hill** at the above address.

Oracle8*i* Networking 101

1234567890 DOC DOC 019876543210

ISBN 0-07-212517-9

Publisher
Brandon A. Nordin

Vice President and Associate Publisher
Scott Rogers

Acquisitions Editor
Jeremy Judson

Project Editor
Madhu Prasher

Acquisitions Coordinator
Monika Faltiss

Technical Editor
Ian Fickling

Developmental Editor
Rachel Carmichael

Copy Editor
Judith Brown

Proofreader
Paul Tyler

Indexer
Jack Lewis

Computer Designers
Jani Beckwith
Lucie Ericksen

Illustrator
Michael Mueller

Series Design
Peter Hancik

This book was composed with Corel VENTURA™ Publisher.

I dedicate this book to

**My husband, Nelson J. Cahill, my son, Marc I. Goodman,
My mother, Lillian M. Siegel, my aunt, Mollie C. Robbins,
And to anyone who has ever spent more than one hour trying to
correct an Oracle networking problem.**

About the Author

Marlene Theriault has been an Oracle Database Administrator for over 18 years and began working with Oracle products at version 2.0 of the Oracle RDBMS. She is coauthor of *The Oracle8i DBA Handbook* with Kevin Loney for Osborne (Oracle Press), *Oracle DBA 101* with Rachel Carmichael and James Viscusi for Osborne (Oracle Press), and *Oracle Security* with William Heney. Ms. Theriault has presented at conferences throughout the world and received the "Best User Presentation" award at EOUG'99 for her presentation at EOUG'98, an "Outstanding Speaker" award at ECO'98, and "Distinguished Speaker" awards at ECO'95 and ECO'96. She is chair of the Mid-Atlantic Association of Oracle Professionals (MAOP) and writes an "Ask the DBA" column for their newsletter. Ms. Theriault is an avid recreational walker (Volksmarching) and has done at least one six-mile walk in each of the 50 United States. She can be reached at mtheriault@mindspring.com.

Contents at a Glance

PART III
Oracle Networking and the Internet

PART IV
Troubleshooting

Contents

PART III

Oracle Networking and the Internet

PART IV
Troubleshooting

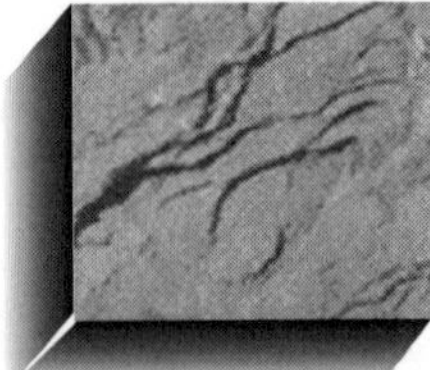

Acknowledgments

Oddly enough, books do not seem to write themselves. There are many people who work long hours to bring a book to market. Some of these people, I have never and probably will never meet. Whether I meet them or not, I'm very grateful for their help in making this book a reality.

There are many people I would like to recognize here for their efforts. The entire Osborne staff is absolutely first rate. You could not ask for or find a better acquisitions editor than Jeremy Judson, better chief editor than Scott Rogers, or better staff to work with than Madhu Prasher, Monika Faltiss, Judith Brown, and Denise Graab.

There are several people within Oracle Corporation who deserve special recognition for their help and support. Edward Montes, our Oracle sponsor for the MAOP DBA SIG, stands out for his willingness to answer my questions when no one else would and to point me to significant white papers and Oracle site URLs when I needed them most. Ed is one of the finest Oracle employees I've ever had the pleasure to know. He has been kind, patient, and always willing to go the extra distance to help Oracle customers. At the risk of gushing, I must say, "Ed, you have my deepest gratitude and friendship. You are *terrific*!" My thanks go, too, to Pierre Baudin, David L. Chen, and their associated groups at Oracle Corporation, with special thanks to Peter Povinec and Ashish Kolli, for their help in resolving problems that I encountered as I worked through configuring the Oracle Internet Directory and other Oracle8i

Net8 features. Because of their willingness to help, I was able to provide you, the reader, with much more accurate information about these products.

I would be completely remiss if I did not thank Barbara Pascavage for bringing the idea for this book to me. Barbara is always willing to provide insights into DBA issues and share her time and knowledge with fellow DBAs.

Circulating around email recently was a piece about different kinds of friends and their impact on our lives. There is no doubt in my mind that Rachel Carmichael is one of my "forever friends." Rachel was willing to take on the responsibilities of being my developmental editor and page proofer even after she assured me that she did not want to be involved with another book for at least a year. Thanks so much, Rachel, for helping to make this book both more readable and understandable with your comments like, "Marlene: I don't understand this at all! I'm confused!"

Speaking of comments and making the book much better, my technical reviewer, Ian Fickling, deserves a huge pat on the back for not only finding and helping me to correct errors but for contributing some of the text as well. With any luck, one of these days his name will be on a book cover.

Edwin Hart is a networking guru whom I had the pleasure of working with at the Johns Hopkins University Applied Physics Laboratory. Ed took the time and trouble to read through and help me iron out the rough spots in the first chapter of this book. I deeply appreciate our telephone conversations and Ed's contributions to help make Chapter 1 and a section of Chapter 13 both more understandable and technically accurate.

User groups play an important part in the life of any Oracle professional, so I must take a minute to thank some of the people who work tirelessly to bring information and solutions to all of us. I'd like to personally thank Stephen Vandivier, president of the Mid-Atlantic Association of Oracle Professionals. Craig and Keith Warman who put in long hours working with the Virginia Oracle User Group. Bert Spencer and Carl Dudley who help support the European OUG, Middle East OUG, and United Kingdom OUG, along with Joe Testa who supports the Ohio OUG, and Jim Lopatosky with the Northeast OUG. I love working with all of you and deeply value your friendships.

Friends play such an important role in our lives that I'd like to take the time to thank some people whom I am very proud to call my friends. To Sue Hornbuckle, Cathy Lockwood, Roslyn Croog, Susan St. Claire, Eyal Aronoff, Kevin Loney, Marty Rosman, Debbie Wong, Tony Ziemba, Pat and Steve Arnett, Ron and Fran Looper, Jim and Sandi Viscusi, Marty and Sharon Rosman, and all of you who are not mentioned here because of lack of space. Thank you so very much for being there when I've needed you. You all mean more to me than words convey.

I feel incredibly lucky that I have such a warm and loving family. Thanks to my son, Marc Goodman, who is never too busy to talk with me or make great suggestions on everything from stock purchases to new technologies. My nieces, Lynn Benade, Robin Delciappo, and Sharon Landy Fayad, are very special to me and show me steadily that I am a special part of their lives as well. So, thanks, ladies, from your "Auntie M." Thanks too to my sister, Judith Zieske, for just being herself.

In the *Oracle DBA 101* book, I acknowledged my (now) husband's "quiet patience." Since he felt I made it sound like he had slept through the writing of that book, I'd like to thank my husband, Nelson Cahill, for his patient, unwavering, devoted, unobtrusive, charming, and audible support during this venture. Without someone behind you helping to keep the household going and life on a fairly even keel, books just don't get written at all. Nelson has a fantastic imagination, and some of the ideas for scenarios within this book came from his suggestions. Mostly though, I'd like to thank Nelson for his willingness to join me in walking through life together.

Getting Started

net•work *n*
(net-wərk) 1 :NET 2 :a system of elements (as lines or channels) that cross in the manner of threads in a net 3 :a group or system of related or connected parts.

I want you to know immediately that I really have no particular reason for presenting you with a definition of the word "network" except that it seems like a great way to begin a book about Oracle Corporation's Oracle8i, Release 2 implementation of networking, known as Net8. I'm not going to go into great detail about how this definition ties into topics in this book. I'll let you determine the ties for yourself as you read the first and second chapters. I'm also not going to bore you with a bunch of technical jargon right off the top either. I guess I just really wanted to get you started thinking about networks in general. Hopefully, when you read the definition above, you'll begin to picture in your mind a collection of lines (cables), computers, and other hardware connected together to form a system over which people can obtain and disseminate information easily.

Do you have access to the Internet and the World Wide Web? Have you ever wondered how all of the underlying network technology works to bring you information about such diverse topics as beanbag toys, medieval history, and medical breakthroughs? Have you ever sat in a meeting at work or in a conference presentation and felt overwhelmed or just plain ignorant because someone was using networking terms that you didn't understand? Are you just starting out or considering a position that includes Oracle products and want to learn how Oracle handles networking or what you need to know to configure an Oracle network? Have you been working with Oracle products for many years but haven't needed to know a lot about Oracle's implementation of networks? If you answered "yes" to any of these questions, this book is a great way to enter the Oracle8i networking world. Even if I didn't happen to mention your particular reason for looking at this book, it's still a great way to round out your Oracle networking knowledge.

Basically, if you have not read the first book in the 101 line, *Oracle DBA 101*, this section should begin to give you a feel for my writing style and my approach to conveying information to you. I have tried very hard to find different ways to help you learn and understand technical concepts by relating them to everyday things. Don't misunderstand though. Just because I invite you to come play a game with me or wander off on a field trip, don't assume that this book treats heavy technical concepts in a "watered down" manner.

Using this book you will learn general networking terms and Oracle's approach to networking, as well as the following information:

- How to configure Oracle clients and servers to communicate using Net8
- How Oracle Names servers work and how to configure and use this feature
- What LDAP is and how to configure and use the Oracle Internet Directory server
- How to determine your company's Oracle networking needs and create an Oracle network plan
- How to use the Oracle-supplied configuration tools: Net8 Assistant, Net8 Configuration Assistant, and the Connection Manager
- Ways to help support a high-volume, high-connectivity system
- How to configure and use the WebDB listener
- What the Oracle Advanced Security features are
- How to troubleshoot problems in your Oracle network

Although this book is not intended as the be-all and end-all networking tome, it is intended to give you a working knowledge of how to configure Oracle networking features and make them work. So, without further ado, get ready to set sail for an Oracle network adventure.

PART I

Getting Down to Basics

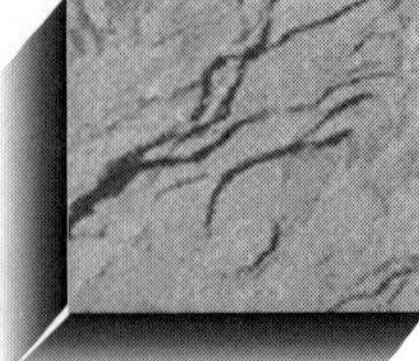

CHAPTER 1

Overview of Networking

A systems administrator I once worked with was fond of saying, "To understand the future, you must examine the past" because our current technology often reflects and encompasses the advances of the past.

This book is both an introduction and a guide to interacting with Oracle in a networked environment. However, I believe that to work effectively with the product set, you must know a little about how network components are assembled and, at the very least, understand some of the basic terminology involved. I spent many years hearing others using terms such as "token-ring" and "Ethernet" or "T1 line," without understanding exactly what they were talking about. (I would, of course, never admit that to them!) Therefore, this first chapter is devoted to some of the history of networking, elementary terminology, and network configurations. I'll also describe some of the hardware involved and the protocols used. Although this book is very Oracle networking centered, this chapter will not cover much Oracle-specific information.

If you already feel comfortable about your knowledge level of basic networking, you can move on to Chapter 2. Of course, you will be missing a review of networking basics, but you will have saved a bit of reading time.

A Brief History of Network Communications

In the mid-1860s, the following scene might have taken place. A sheriff's deputy comes running into the railroad station and hurries to the desk of the Western Union telegraph operator. "Quick," he shouts to the operator, "send a message to the sheriff of Bogus City. Tell him that Butch Blunder and his gang are headed towards his town. He needs to be prepared!" With due haste, the operator sends the message in Morse code. The method used to transmit the message consisting of letters and numbers is a series of timed on-and-off pulses of electricity. Each letter or number has a unique set of short and/or long pulses. The line over which the message is sent is a single wire. The mechanism used to send and receive the message is relatively rugged—to stand up to the rough-and-ready frontier life. Although very simplistic by today's standards, the telegraph provided eastern businesses with a way to communicate with the rugged West. Let's see where communications have gone since the time that early telegram might have been sent.

On February 14, 1876, Alexander Graham Bell patented the telephone—two hours before Elisha Gray, of Western Union, filed his patent. The timing on that patent filing is significant because, after a court battle, Bell was awarded not only the rights and patents to the telephone but the network of telephones that Western Union had established, including all enhancements that had been made to Bell's original designs. One hundred years later, Bell's company (later known as AT&T) was the largest company in the world.

Now, let's move our earlier scene forward in time to the late 1800s. Instead of a telegram, the deputy would just pick up a telephone headset consisting of a transmitter (the mouthpiece) and a receiver (the earpiece). He would call a central telephone operator who would then use a switchboard to transfer his call to the sheriff of Bogus City. In 1889, Almon Brown, a Kansas City undertaker, invented the Strowger switch and the telephone dial. These inventions enabled a person to dial a telephone number directly instead of having to go through an operator.

The third version of our story, taking place after the turn of the century, might have the deputy sending a written teletype warning to the sheriff of Bogus City. The original telegraph had some major drawbacks. Only one conversation at a time could cross the line. The wire used was handmade and very brittle. Installing the line was very time consuming, costly, and dangerous. The obvious solution was to develop a multiplex telegraph that would enable several operators to send and receive messages at the same time. The other goal was to create a telegraph system that did not require as much human intervention. A French inventor, Emile Baudot, made many of the necessary breakthroughs. His printing telegraph was the first to use a typewriter keyboard and enabled eight machines to share a single wire. Instead of Morse code, Baudot's machine used a five-level code that sent five pulses down the wire for each character. The machines did the encoding and decoding.

The reoccurring theme in these scenarios is, of course, our society's need to communicate information rapidly from one location to another. There's another, more important point to the three scenarios though. Have you figured it out yet? If you said, "They are all examples of networking," you'd be correct. We tend to think of electronic networks in relation to computers and cable companies that transmit radio and television broadcasts, but, as you can see from this brief history, electronic networks have been around since the mid-1800s.

At first glance, the telephone seems far removed from the computer. In reality, there is a strong interdependency between the two forms of equipment. Over the years, the telephone companies have come to rely on the computer to provide call processing, traffic routing, order tracking, and so on, while computer technology has come to rely on the telephone network to enable worldwide computer interconnection and communication.

For the most part, both the computer and the telephone rely on digital communications—those "on" and "off" pulses that Morse code relied on. However, the telephone still retains analog lines both to your home or office and to the telephone companies' switching equipment. The need to send digital signals over analog lines was the driving force in AT&T's successful invention of the telephone modem. AT&T employees also created the transistor at Bell Labs in 1948.

Looking back at our earliest example of networking, the telegraph, you see an example of point-to-point communications. The early telephone lines were also point-to-point. Today, however, you see a mass of telephone lines and central switching offices with the offices connecting to a complex system of cables, microwave towers, fiber-optic cables, and communications satellites. You might never realize how complex this system is until your telephone ceases to function properly, or your calls to the Internet are frequently disconnecting, or the speed is much less than you expect, and you have to contact a telephone company to diagnose and possibly repair the problem. (Dreaded thought!)

The Telephone Network

Now that you have a little background in the history of network communications, let's take a brief look at how a telephone network works. In Figure 1-1, you can see a very elementary graphic of telephone communications.

At its simplest level, making a telephone call involves taking your voice communication and translating it into electronic pulses that are transported across telephone lines through a central office and either back out of that office to a local number or forward through routing equipment to a destination. In Figure 1-1, the routing is done from a central office via satellite dishes to a remote receiver and on to the destination.

Let's say you are placing a telephone call from your house. Originally, a telephone required a pair of copper or iron wires leading from your home to the telephone company's central office. The wires were hung from huge wooden poles. Today, most homes have either the two-wire *twisted pair* or, more recently, a fiber-optic line to connect their home phone to the central office. To complete your call, especially if it's overseas, the central office uses digital switching equipment

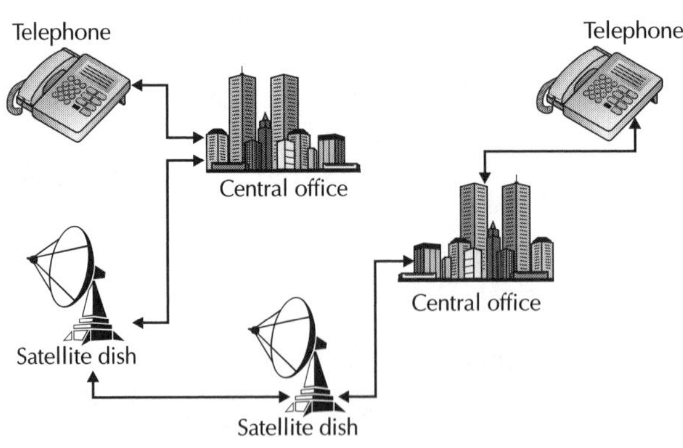

FIGURE 1-1. *A simple telephone network*

to route your call—again using fiber-optic lines, undersea cable, microwave radio, and/or satellite dishes. The telephone's central switching offices generally contain trunk lines that communicate using digital signals. I'll talk more about digital and analog signals later in this chapter. Between central switching offices, the signals that are sent are usually digital frequencies. Above these central offices is a hierarchy of other offices.

A fiber-optic cable can carry as many as 4,032 telephone conversations at once. Today, dedicated telephone lines are available in many areas to provide all-digital telephone service for voice and data communications. These lines, called *Integrated Services Digital Network* (ISDN) lines, provide two channels that can be used independently for voice or data transmission.

Although ISDN lines have made an incredible difference in the way you and I can transmit and receive information through our personal home computers, large companies often find that the lines are too restrictive and not cost effective for their needs. Many large companies use special, high-density digital T1 lines that provide 24 voice or 1.544 Megabits per second (Mbps) data communication channels. Each channel can have its own phone number. Partial T1 lines are available for companies that don't need 24 channels. Large companies that need even more speed can use T2 or T3 lines that are much faster. For example, a T2 line has a speed equal to 4 T1 lines for a rate of 6 Mbps, while a T3 line is equivalent to 28 T1 circuits for a total speed of 43.232 Mbps. However, most people just say 43 Mbps.

Okay, so we've established that telecommunications plays an important part in how we as individuals and as companies communicate and exchange information. Let's look now at the computer side of the equation and see how all of the technologies come together to implement networking.

The Computer Network

I can remember, when I was young, reading *Alice in Wonderland* by Lewis Carroll. Did you ever read that book? In the story, a girl named Alice starts out as a normal-sized person, and when she eats something like a cookie or a mushroom, she either shrinks or grows to an astounding degree. She never knows in advance how she will be affected by what she eats. She is always quite surprised to find herself growing or shrinking in a seemingly unbounded way.

In many respects, the computer has both shrunk and grown in a similar manner. You see, when the first computer was invented, it was huge, with minimal resources like memory or storage space. Today, computers have shrunk to very small sizes, with tremendous resources.

To begin our examination of the growth of computer technology, let's travel back to the early 1950s and work our way forward towards today's environment.

A Look at Early Computers

In the late 1950s and early 1960s, a single computer took up an entire room. Because the components within the computer had a tendency to overheat, the room was kept air-conditioned. The room was also kept dust free. The computers were fed information via punched cards, and all jobs were run in a batch mode. People did not directly interact with these computers as we do today with our PCs. In batch mode, there was a lot of wasted time as machines sat idle between jobs that could only be run one at a time.

The invention and use of tape drives and, later, disk storage units improved the input and output times, but the computers were still not using all of their processing resources. By the mid-1960s, the idea of multiprogramming was coming into play. Using multiprogramming, several jobs could be placed into the computer's memory at a time, and then the computer's processing time could be parceled out among the various jobs. In this scenario, each job had to be allotted its own area of memory and be protected from any other job that was being run at the same time. The computer's operating system had to be aware of all the jobs that needed to be run. Operating system software had to be redesigned to enable the computer to know how and when to switch from one job to another. The continuing drawback was that every time a program ran, the most seemingly insignificant error—even a single mistyped character—would cause the entire program to fail, or "bomb," and have to be rerun. The scheme of multitasking, however, led the way to time-sharing of resources. Memory was at a premium, and a "large" machine might have had about 8 megabytes—almost laughable compared to today's machines with 2–4 gigabytes of memory! Sometime during this period, the *modem* became available. A computer could now be accessed from remote locations by connecting it to a modem.

Moving Forward in Time

Towards the late 1960s, in a joint effort by General Electric, Bell Laboratories, and the Massachusetts Institute of Technology, the first time-sharing operating system (multiplexed information and computing service, called MULTICS) was developed. Although time-sharing also used a multiprogramming approach, the difference in this operating system was the introduction of user interaction through terminals that were directly connected to the computer. The terminals consisted of a keyboard for input and a terminal screen for output. Because these terminals had no actual resources of their own, they were referred to as *dumb terminals*. This was the first real computer network, and it enabled more work to be done in much less time than was previously possible.

In the 1970s, thanks to the earlier invention of the modem, which enabled machine-to-machine communications via our old friend the telephone, companies could support computer/human interfaces remote from the computer. The modem would convert information to and from the digital form needed by computers to the analog form that enabled it to travel over telephone lines, just as it does today.

But what was life really like for a programmer back then?

Working on an Early Computer Network

Let me reminisce a bit and describe what it was like to be a programmer working in the 1960s and 1970s. When I started as a programmer with the job title Programmer/ Analyst C (the lowest level programmer in my company's "food chain"), everything was run on a mainframe computer. All of our computing tasks were centralized. We had a sign-up sheet, and we scheduled the time that we were permitted to use the computer. At our scheduled time, my fellow employees and I would walk down the hall from our offices to a computer room in which there were several dumb terminals, as described earlier. We would log on to our accounts, perform the tasks that we had prepared to implement, and work until our allotted time was up and the next scheduled group arrived to take over. The terminals were wired directly to the computer, and there was no interaction with any computers outside of that room. In Figure 1-2, you can see this configuration. There are four terminals directly connected to a single mainframe computer.

In this environment, there was one point of failure and one point of information where everyone could call for support or status on what was happening with the system. There was a centralized support staff consisting of a single system administrator and, perhaps, a computer operator or two. (We all knew *who* to blame!) There was one set of software that everyone shared, and we all knew who had access to the computer at all times. Since you had to be physically in the same room as the terminals and the terminals were wired directly to the computer, there was little chance that someone from outside this network could gain access. Thus, security was easier to maintain.

There was also a problem or two involved with this configuration. We had very limited resources. Disk space and memory were minimal, and the cost of adding resources to a mainframe computer was extremely high. Each of us was allocated a small (by today's standards) amount of personal disk space in which to do our work. If I needed 200,000 bytes of space in which to compile my very intricate program and only had 150,000 bytes available, I'd have to bargain with you and other programmers to move your files off the disk to make room for my needs. In return, I'd have to remove my files to make room for you to do your work. There was a lot of time spent shuffling files on and off disks. We often used removable disks so that each group could have their own resources to work with and each group could maintain security and privacy of their data if necessary.

Because each of us could work with the computer for a limited amount of time, we had to plan our activities carefully and could only get a portion of our tasks done during each session. If I was working out of town, I would have to make a copy of my work to a nine-track tape and carry the tape back to my office or ship the tape to myself and hope that it got there in a timely manner. Often, the tape would be delayed, and I would have to wait several days to resume my work on a specific project.

Yes, by then, we did have modem communications available. These modems could carry 300 bytes per second, which was really much faster than the 110 bytes

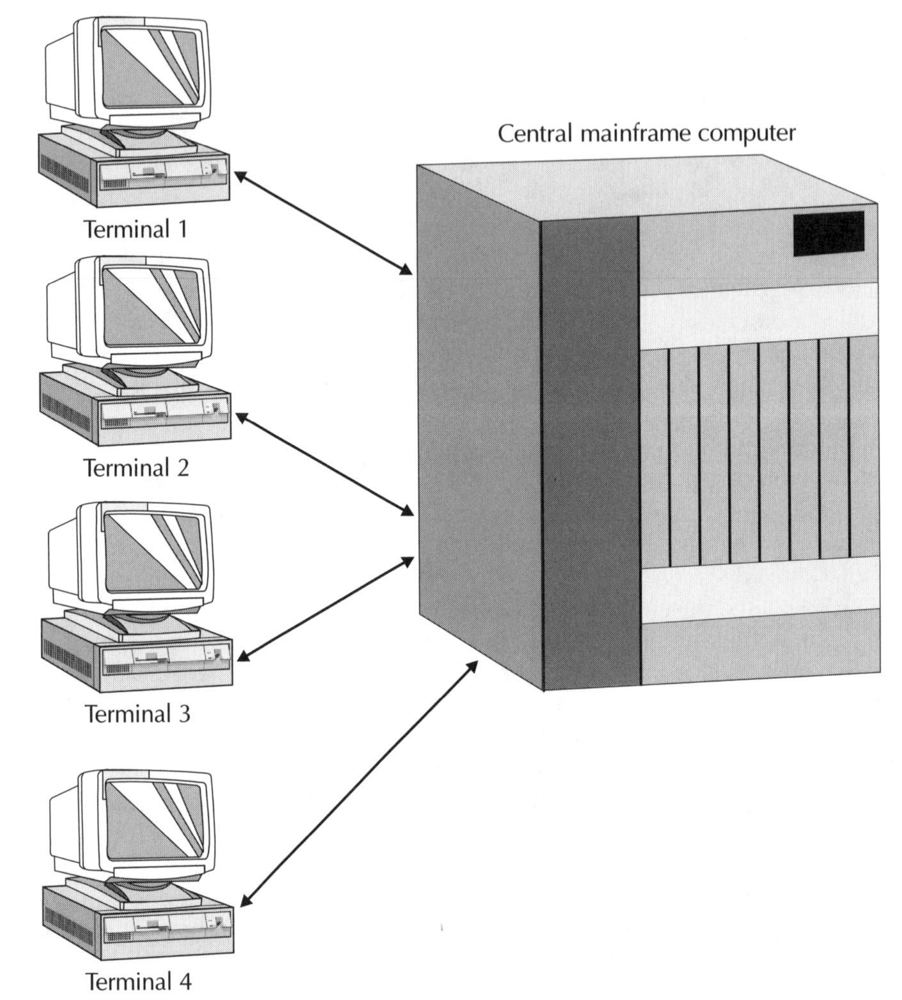

FIGURE 1-2. *Isolated computer with terminals connected*

per second obtained by the teletype machine. Remote batch computing was also done with a card reader, terminals, and a remote printer. For our purposes, however, modems were too slow, and the phone lines were not clean enough to ensure that even if the data got from point A to point B, it would arrive uncorrupted in some way. A loss of time became much more desirable than a loss of data through corruption.

By today's standards, our computing environment was archaic, cumbersome, and difficult.

The Network Begins to Mature

In an environment where computers were accessible using phone lines and modems, all of the processing still took place on a central server, with jobs being scheduled in a batch mode. The host machine accepted communications from the terminals but did not really communicate back.

In the 1970s, the reality of host-to-host communications was brought into being through the advent of the network known as ARPANET. ARPANET was named after its sponsors: the Advanced Research Projects Agency of the U.S. Department of Defense. ARPANET was used to link computers at universities and research labs around the country and provided a highway for military communications as well. The linking of computers in this way was referred to as a *peer-based network*. Figure 1-3 shows a basic peer-based network configuration. The protocols that were "sitting" on top of the ARPANET were FTP, telnet, electronic mail, and boxes that were called Terminal Access Protocol sets (TAPs).

The original idea had been to combine computers together. By making computers available over the network, researchers could share resources to cut costs and increase different kinds of computer availability. Once the computers were connected as an individual network, the networks were connected together to form an environment in which scientists could run both interactive and batch jobs.

With a mechanism called *packet switching*, you could break files into small, uniform pieces called packets and intersperse the packets to satisfy both large batch job processing and small, interactive tasks. For a more resilient network, you had software that would recognize that a portion of the network was unavailable and take an alternate route. The things that would usually fail were the Interface Message Processors (IMPs). IMPs were the predecessors of routers. A router, or gateway, connects one network to another network and forwards packets between the networks it interconnects. A router operates at level 3 of the ISO Open Systems Interconnect model, which I'll talk more about later in this chapter. Anyway, for networks back then, you had IMPs, TAPs, and lines to carry the electronic pulses from one computer to another.

Okay, so now you have the hardware side of these early networks, but how could you set up a system to enable each computer to communicate with all the other computers? You could assign each computer a unique name using some form of naming convention, or you could assign a unique number. And how would the information be moved from one computer to another, completely and accurately? Those are two questions that have been answered and refined over and over again in various forms. Let's take a look at what the developers of ARPANET used.

Each computer was (and still is) assigned a unique address. The numbers used today are referred to as *Internet Protocol* (IP) addresses and take the form of four

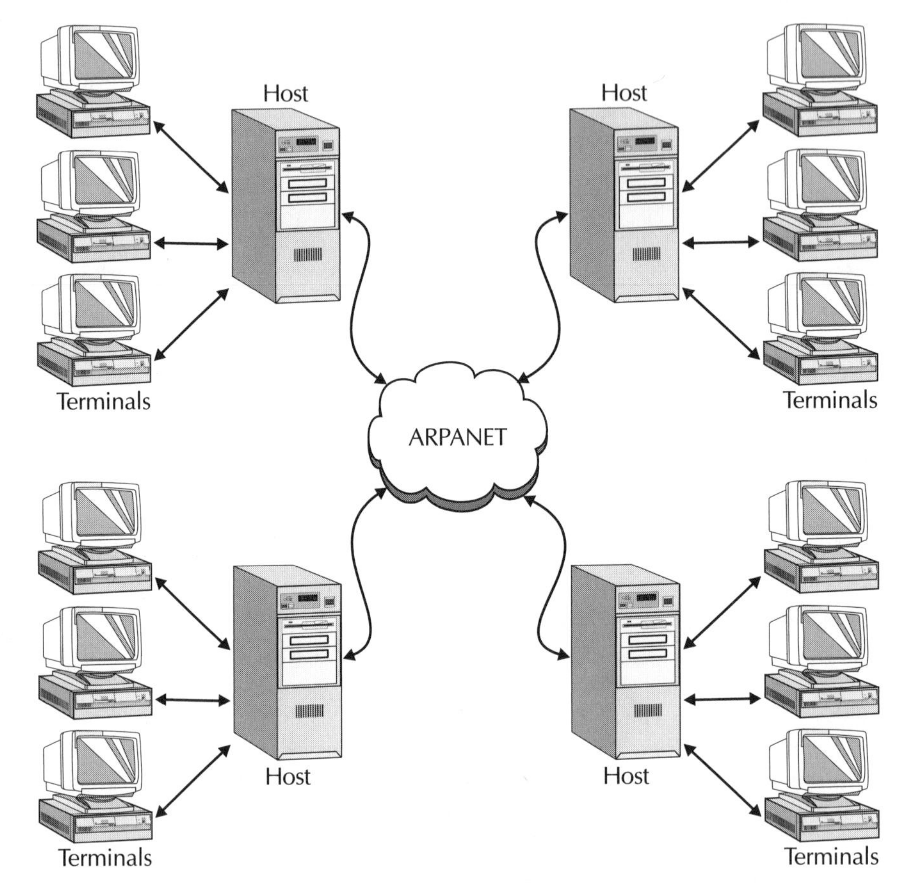

FIGURE 1-3. *Peer-based network*

groups of numbers between 0 and 255, with one to three digits in each group. This is known as *dotted octet* format. The groups of digits are separated with periods or dots in the form: ###.###.###.### or 111.122.233.254. This format is not very easy to remember but is the only "name" that computers use to recognize each other. I'll talk more about how human-related naming is also used for intercomputer communications in the section about the domain name system (DNS).

Personal Computers Join the Mix

In the late 1960s, minicomputers entered the computing scene. These computers had up to about a gigabyte of real memory and a relatively small footprint. *Footprint* refers to the amount of physical space on the computer room floor that a machine takes up. A mainframe computer had a huge footprint, while a minicomputer could be as small as one foot by three feet in size. Your notebook computer today might have a footprint of 13 inches by 18 inches (more like a handprint by comparison). Minicomputers paved the way for the personal computers that came next.

In 1975, the first personal computer was introduced as a hobbyist's machine. Known as the MITS Altair, it was a smallish box with about 256 bytes—not kilobytes or megabytes but *bytes*—of real memory. There were lights for output and switches for input to the device, and no terminal or keyboard or any standardized software until Gates and Allen created a BASIC programming language for it.

Within a few years, the original Apple and then the Apple II were on the market. In 1978, my son Marc and I went shopping for a computer for him. We looked carefully at various PCs that offered a keyboard, a monitor, and a floppy disk drive. Marc opted to purchase the Apple II because it had eight-color graphics and 64K of real memory. There wasn't much disk space either, but at that time, it was the most resource-intensive machine that we could afford. The price tag for that machine was about $1,200. Twenty-two years later, the same $1,200 can buy a machine with the processing power and speed of an early, huge machine! With its no-nonsense approach to computing and business applications written for it, the IBM PC, which burst on the scene in 1981, found its way fairly rapidly into the business world. The saying around this time was that minicomputers were not delivered, they were abandoned. This story was repeated with the early microcomputers.

The problem with the early personal computers was that they were *very* personal. There was you and there was a machine. Your computing world consisted of your data, your applications, your command files, and so on. The corporate world was slow in finding ways for these limited-resource machines to fit into the business environment. Programs like VisiCalc spreadsheet for the Apple, Lotus for the IBM PC, and dBase database software for the IBM PC really helped. Terminal emulation software was also developed to enable the microcomputer to talk to the mainframe or larger computers. Oracle Corporation released a version of its relational database products for the IBM PC as well.

Enter LANs and WANs

During the 1970s, the concept and implementation of the local area network (LAN) became a reality. Metcalf and Boggs first described Ethernet and the concepts of a local area versus a wide area network in a really cool paper in the July, 1976, *Communications of the Association for Computing Machinery (CACM) Journal.* Metcalf actually invented, described, and built a local area, high-speed network and differentiated between the wide area, low-speed network and the LAN. In those days, computing power was costly. Many companies and most universities could not justify the considerable cost for a high-speed wide area network. Metcalf, working at Xerox Palo Alto Research Center (Xerox PARC), hooked up not-very-powerful ALTOS computers to an Ethernet network, enabling print servers, file servers, and electronic mail to be shared with high speed. With a shared system available, you didn't need to have all that stuff on your PC. This was an awesome breakthrough that started a new industry. Metcalf, by the way, was one of the founders of 3Com.

With a LAN, separate computers could be linked over a short distance of hundreds of meters at high speed (3 Mbps). As the name implies, the computers had to be in fairly close proximity—in an office, on the same floor of a building, within several buildings of the same company campus, and so on. As is still true today, the computers, known as *nodes*, were linked together using cables and network interface cards (NICs). By using a network of computers, people could share information and resources such as printers or centralized software applications. The early networks consisted of a few computers located within about 600 feet of each other. That seemed to be the maximum cable length that would support effective connectivity.

As with all the computer-related technologies, network resources and capacities have grown and expanded rapidly. Today we have wide area networks (WANs) that span the globe.

Networks Become More Sophisticated

As I mentioned earlier in this chapter, the original, large-scale network created by the Department of Defense to link universities, research facilities, and military areas was the ARPANET. Many technologies that networks rely on today were developed for use within ARPANET. We can thank ARPANET for packet switching as well as a set of protocols, or rules, that have made our modern networks possible. Chief among these protocols are the Transmission Control Protocol (TCP), which defines the packaging, and the Internet Protocol (IP), which defines the routing of information. The combined protocol, TCP/IP, defines the way computers communicate over the Internet. The key concept of packet switching is that you break messages into smaller, uniform-sized groups called *packets* for transmission over the network. Because each packet is tagged with information that allows the complete message to be reassembled in its correct order, the packets can be sent mixed together or meshed. The ARPANET is a "mesh" network. Thus, you could have packets traveling in parallel through the network, intermeshed with each other.

The only way a university could interact with the ARPANET, which originally consisted of four nodes, was through a grant from the Department of Defense. The National Science Foundation, in 1986, began to form another, more open network that anyone could participate in. This network was known as the NSFNET. Where the ARPANET was a small cluster of computers, the NSFNET was formed on a backbone of several supercomputers to which regional computers connected. More and more computers and networks joined the NSFNET, and somewhere along the way, the name was changed to the Internet. By the 1990s, the Internet consisted of many high-speed backbones and more than one million computers. Around 1995, access to the Internet shifted to public, for-profit Internet Service Providers (ISPs). In 1997, over 30 million computers were connected to the Internet, with many different geographical and functional *domains* involved. Most likely, you are familiar with many of the functional and regional domains that currently exist. Some of the current domains, identified by their abbreviations, are listed here:

- .com for commercial
- .gov for national, state, and local governments
- .edu to identify an educational organization
- .net for networks
- .fr for France
- .uk for the United Kingdom
- .us for the United States

About the Web

Anyone who has ever connected to the Internet has probably used an address that included the initials "www". The World Wide Web (www) is a graphical, mouse-oriented part of the Internet that has a mind-boggling number of sites linked together. Commonly referred to as the *Web*, it was invented by Tim Berners-Lee in 1989 at the CERN particle physics laboratory in Switzerland. CERN's Web home page (http://www.cern.ch/Public/Welcome.html) even has the caption "where the Web was born."

The original Internet was text based and predominantly devoted to email, terminal emulation and terminal access, transferring of files, bulletin boards, and, later, news groups. The Web is devoted to browser usage, which enables people to communicate and share ideas and information through *hyperlinks* that include Universal Resource Locators (URLs). URLs are file locations on disks on specific computers, and a browser enables you to open and examine the file at the specified location. The files involved can be text, graphics, video, or sound files. You can even view movies or live action over the Web. Back when the Web began, email was addicting, and people who used it suffered withdrawal symptoms when they couldn't "get connected."

Today, the Web provides a way for people to move naturally from topic to topic using more and more sophisticated browsers that remember where you've been. You can access information much like a computer does—randomly, from disk location to disk location, except that rather than being on your computer, the data may be scattered over the Internet. So now, you can access data the way your mind naturally works—jumping from idea to idea in a "stream of consciousness" manner.

In the business world, the Web is providing a new way to do business. Called eCommerce, this form of conducting business brings with it a new set of resource requirements and greater reliance on the ability to successfully network your computer to the outside world while still retaining areas of privacy. In the next section, I'll look at some basic network configurations and terminology.

Basic Network Configurations and Features

Consider the different ways that you can hear a piece of music. You could go to a concert hall and experience a live performance of your favorite singer or orchestra. You could go to a store and buy a record, cassette tape, or CD and take it home to listen. Of course, if you really weren't in any hurry to hear a particular piece, you could just tune into a radio station and hope that it comes on. Like the approaches you can use to hearing music, there are several different ways that you can establish and use a computer network.

How many different basic types of networks would you guess there are today? One? Ten? Hundreds? In reality, there are only four basic types of networks: centralized, ring, bus, and distributed. We've already looked a bit at a centralized network in Figure 1-2 and a distributed network (the ARPANET configuration) in Figure 1-3. Take a minute to look back at these figures. I'll wait for you to come back.

While I'm waiting for you to look at the figures, I'll just think about the fact that there are different ways of looking at a network. Let's see. I could tell you about *topology,* which describes how you hook things together, or about *protocol stacks* that describe how you send things across the network, or, finally, about how you achieve *distributed computing.*

Ah, you're back. Good. You see, you need different kinds of protocols for different types of topologies. Most networks that we have today are a mix of different network types with different topologies controlled by different protocols. I'd like to tell you more about topologies and protocols and distributed computing next.

The Different Types of Networks

Now, in a centralized network, the terminals are connected to a mainframe computer. Resources are limited, and expanding the environment can be very costly since the central computer must be replaced with a larger, faster one. As I mentioned earlier, there's generally one central system administrator to decide who will work with what resources when.

In a peer-based network, computers are connected together, and, as the name implies, all are equal partners that can share resources. In other words, in a peer-to-peer network, a printer or disk farm that's physically connected to machine A will be available for use by machine A as well as machines B, C, and D. Peer-to-peer networks are usually best suited for small installations. They can be both easy to install and lower cost. As far as administration goes, each person controls the resources on her machine and controls who will access her resources.

A Look at a Client/Server Network

Let's take a look at the basic client/server network configuration, as shown in Figure 1-4.

Client/server networks are both more powerful and broader ranging than centralized or peer-to-peer networks. You can link many different computers with different operating systems to support hundreds of clients. Unlike a centralized network, there may be one or more minicomputer or high-end microcomputer servers linked together to provide a broad range of computer resources. The servers in this network configuration will have server-oriented operating systems. In the case of pure client/server networking, the clients have some independent processing power and resources of their own. Where peer-to-peer networks have the computers linked directly to one another via cables, client/server networks can also have the

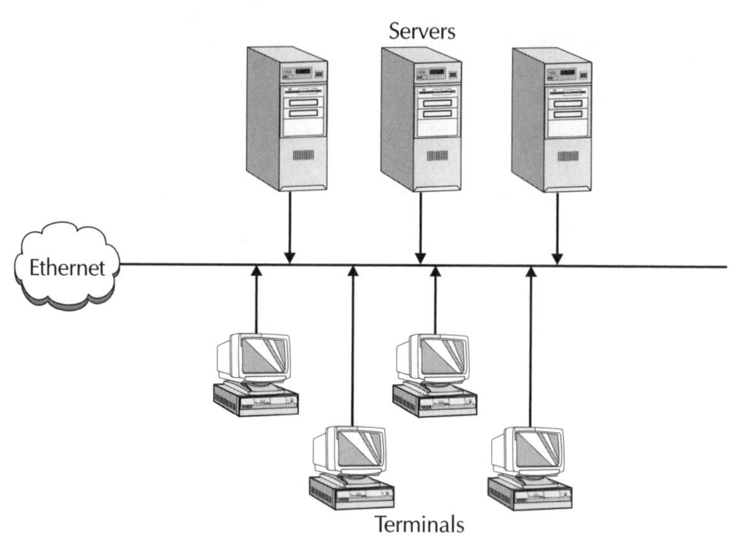

FIGURE 1-4. *Client/server network*

computers linked via cables to the server. A client can even connect to the server over a telephone line from a remote location. Where peer-based networks contain servers that are equal and powerful, client/server networks contain less powerful clients connected to servers. Client/server networks promote scalability because, as the connection requirements increase, more servers can be added to expand the system.

Generally, Windows NT servers, UNIX machines, or Novell NetWare systems are used to support a network operating system (NOS). Network operating systems are a way to link services to each other over a network. These server systems are more robust than your typical desktop computer and must offer fault tolerance, security, the ability to be backed up successfully, different levels of access by users and administrators, and the capacity for heavy communications traffic from messages and security information as well as user traffic. That's quite a lot to ask of a network operating system! The network software can be a separate product that you add to your system, such as Novell NetWare, or it might already be built into your system. Examples of systems with preinstalled network software are Windows 95, Windows 98, and Windows NT. Apple computers use AppleTalk network protocols to communicate with each other. Although Novell NetWare and Windows NT are geared to support PCs, they have optional services to support the Apple Macintosh computers as well.

About Clients and Servers

There are actually two types of client/server environments in use today: client/server and thin-client architecture. Hmm, what's the difference? Glad you asked! Client/server architecture includes a desktop PC with an amount of physical resource like memory and/or hard disk storage space. Normally, some application code is stored on this desktop PC and connects to the server to perform various tasks. The resources available can vary greatly from PC to PC, with some PCs unable to actually perform all of the work that their user needs to accomplish. So, there are resource-rich and resource-poor machines connecting to the server. There might be a printer installed locally to the client for printing purposes.

Now, let's look at a thin-client architecture. In this environment, three different machines are involved. Figure 1-5 shows an example of the thin-client architecture.

As you can see in Figure 1-5, client machines are connected to a middle-tier application server. The clients will usually have very limited resources. They must have a way to communicate with the middle tier to request actions and receive replies. Generally, the clients will have a browser to enable this communication but will not have any local storage. They must rely on the network server for applications, data storage, and any other resources needed to complete work. PCs have a high-speed, graphical display unit. One of the goals of thin-client architecture is to take advantage of the rapid response time between the application server and the PC's graphical display unit.

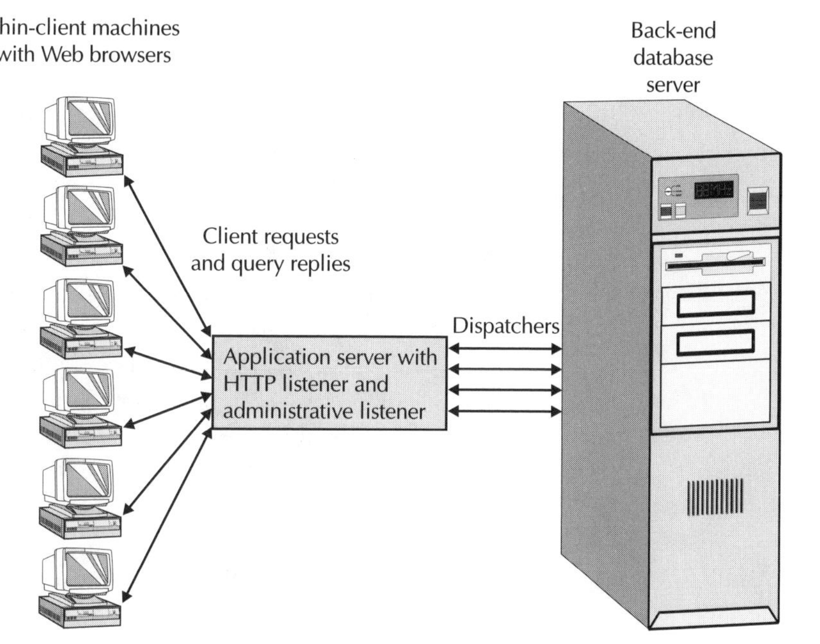

FIGURE 1-5. *Thin-client architecture*

Applications on the middle tier are often under the control of a Transaction Processing Monitor (TPM). The most commonly used TPMs are Tuxedo, Encina, CICS, NCR Top End, Microsoft Transaction Server, and Digital ACMSxp. TPMs usually come into play to support high transaction volumes that may interact with one or more databases. Table 1-1 shows the features that are guaranteed by a TPM.

The third computer in thin-client architecture, a back-end server, is a much more resource-rich machine than either of the other computers. In-depth processing power is provided by the back-end server. In the networking world, many different forms of servers provide different categories of support to an organization. You will find that servers tend to be categorized by the type of work they perform. Table 1-2 shows some different categories of servers. One or more of these server types will be used in a network.

Now that you know the basic types of networks, let's take a look at the hardware necessary to connect one computer to another.

The Necessary Hardware

All of the machines in a network must have a network adapter card or a network interface card (NIC) in order to communicate with each other. This card is usually

Feature	**Explanation**
Atomicity	All transactions are either performed completely—*committed*—or are not done at all; a partial transaction that is aborted must be rolled back.
Consistency	The effects of a transaction must preserve required system properties. For example, if funds are transferred between accounts, a deposit and withdrawal must both be committed to the database, so that the accounting system does not fall out of balance.
Isolation	Intermediate stages must not be made visible to other transactions. Thus, in the case of a transfer of funds between accounts, both sides of the double-entry bookkeeping system must change together. This means that transactions appear to execute serially (in order), even if the work is done concurrently.
Durability	Once a transaction is committed, the change must persist, except in the face of a catastrophic failure.

TABLE 1-1. *Features Offered by a Transaction Processing Monitor*

installed in one of the expansion slots inside the machine. In the case of a notebook computer, the card might be a PCMCIA card that slides into a slot on the side of the machine and provides a modem or network connection. The network card is used both to send messages and to listen for incoming messages addressed to the computer's network address.

Let's take a moment to look at the cabling involved in connecting a client to a server. The area of the network adapter that the cable connects to is called a *port*. If you look at the network adapter on a computer, you'll find that it supports one of several kinds of connectors. A connector plug might be round and will be known as a British Naval Connector (BNC), or it might be a 15-pin attachment unit interface (AUI) connector. An AUI will look the most like connectors usually used with computers. The network adapter could be an RJ-45 jack and look similar to a connector at the end of a telephone wire but will be larger.

WARNING
Do not plug your phone line into your local area network card. You could "blow" your network card if you do.

Server Type	Purpose
Dedicated servers	Provide network and user support exclusively. They do not perform any client tasks.
Nondedicated servers	Provide server resources and can do the work requested by client machines.
File servers	Store files that were created by application programs. They usually contain full documents and transfer those documents when they are requested. They provide the ability to simultaneously access the same file. An Oracle database is a classic example of a shared file system.
Print servers	Enable users to print to one or more attached printers. Print servers spool print requests to a file until each current job has completed. A print server reports the status of each print job and recognizes the priority of each job.
Application servers	Store information and enable back-end processing of that information.
Mail servers	Provide a centralized post office for message handling and storage. They can be configured to recognize aliases for people or collections of addresses.
Fax servers	Handle incoming and outgoing fax communications.
Communication servers	Provide dial-up access to the network, or provide a way that people can dial out from the network to other services.
Firewalls	Provide a secure gateway through which validated users can connect to private company servers. Firewall servers provide security and control to protect computers inside the firewall. They can be used to enable users within the network to communicate with the outside world as well. The server configuration is usually from the Internet to a firewall to another firewall to the company's private data.
Backup servers	Use backup and storage media to enable protection of data. They can be set up to run backup jobs automatically at a specified time each day, week, or month.

TABLE 1-2. *Types of Servers on a Network*

Network Topology

Let's play a guessing game. I'm holding something in my hand. It's perfectly round and completely white and very hard. Any idea what it is? Would it make it easier to guess if I told you that I'm standing in a room with a very large, rectangular table that's covered in green felt? Hmm. That makes the guessing easier, doesn't it? If you guessed that I'm holding a cue ball and standing next to a pool table, you'd be right. You see, when you are describing things, the shape is really important. So, let's take a look at some of the common shapes, or topologies, of networks. When you describe a network topology, you are actually describing how the various pieces are cabled together. The three basic topologies are bus or linear (straight line), token-ring, and star. Now, keep in mind that if you were to look at a collection of computers and terminals networked together, they might not resemble any of these shapes. In this case, I'm talking about logical rather than physical shape and describing the way network traffic travels from one machine to another—in a straight line, in a circle, or from a center point outward.

Bus or Linear Topology

This topology is the easiest to implement because everything connects to a single cable. This cable is often referred to as a *trunk* or *backbone* and has a terminator at each end to keep signals from bouncing back along the cable and wreaking havoc with the messages. The signals can travel either from left to right or from right to left. In reality, the *cable* is many cables that are connected from interface card to interface card. A thin Ethernet or linear bus cable is connected to a T-shaped coaxial connector at each interface card. A wiring hub provides a central point for the cables of each interface card. Fiber-optic, coaxial, and/or twisted-pair wires can be used to connect the interface cards to the wiring hub. Another form of frequently used connection, the Ethernet configuration using unshielded twisted-pair (UTP) wire, is known as 10BaseT. What in the world does that mean? Well, it means that 10 megabits per second (Mbps) signaling speed, direct current (or *baseband*) signaling and twisted-pair wire are being used. This configuration includes a central wiring hub with special circuitry to isolate malfunctioning segments. Even the newer, bigger 100BaseT and gigabit Ethernet signaling schemes use UTP cabling with upgraded hubs and adapters.

In a bus topology, all the nodes or participants are passive—that is, they have software installed that listens for messages with their address. They do nothing to help move messages from one node to another. Any node can send a message to any other node as often as it wants. The message is sent out from the sender's unique address to the receiver's unique address, but it's sent to the entire community. Only the recipient can actually read the message. Only one node can send a message at a time across the line. If other nodes want to send a message, they have to wait their turn. To avoid contention, the Ethernet standard is used. This standard manages contention by a technique known as *carrier sense multiple access with collision detection* (CSMA/CD), which says that a node must wait for the line to be free before attempting to transmit a message. If two nodes send a message at exactly the same time, both messages will be bounced back, and each node will have to wait a random amount of time before sending the message again.

Figure 1-6 shows an example of a bus or linear topology. As you can see, both terminals and servers reside on the same single cable line, and the communications path is bidirectional.

Although bus networks are easy to implement and lower cost (fewer cables needed), they can be hard to troubleshoot if a problem arises, and if the cable breaks, the entire network becomes unavailable. Keep in mind, too, that the more nodes that are added to this bus type, the slower message transfers may be, because each node must wait its turn to send a message.

Token-Ring Topology

Picture five children standing with their hands joined to form a circle. Each child can only touch the child on either side. If they want to whisper a message from the first child to the fourth child without letting go of each other's hands, each child in the circle must receive the message and pass it on to the next one. The path would either be from child 1 to child 2 to child 3 to child 4 or from child 1 to child 5 to child 4. From each node's perspective, a ring network—more commonly referred to as a token-ring—forms a circle. Token-ring topology functions in the same way as the circle of children whispering a message to each other, but the signal can only travel in one direction. Unlike a bus network, each node in a token-ring is an active participant generating, passing, and receiving messages. The node may even boost or enhance the signal as it passes that signal on to the next node in the ring.

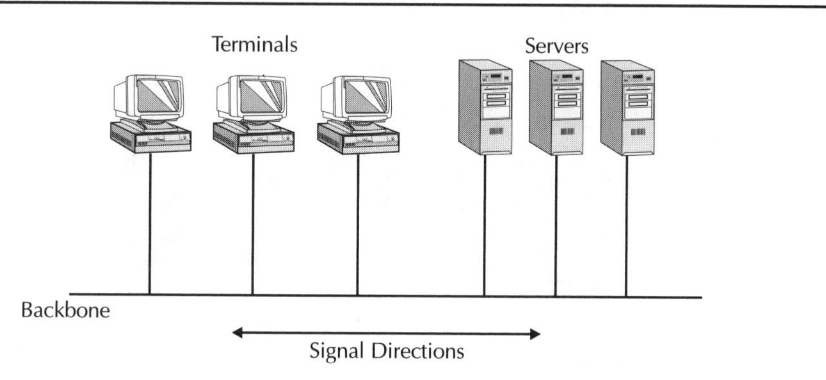

FIGURE 1-6. *Bus or linear topology*

Initially, a *token*, a small collection of bits, is passed from node to node around the ring. When a node wants to transmit information, it must first wait until it receives the token. The node modifies the token, *stamping* it to let the other nodes know that the token is in use, and passes the token with the added message to the next node. When the modified token, along with the message, is received by the recipient, an acknowledgment is sent, and the receiving node generates a new token telling the rest of the nodes that the token is again available for use.

Before talking about how a token-ring network is wired, let's take a look at the third form of topology, the star network.

Star Topology

This form of network topology takes its name from the fact that the cables stretch out from a central location in many different directions much like the points of a star. Figure 1-7 shows a star topology with the nodes connected to a central hub via cables.

The hub itself can be active or passive. As an active participant, it might boost a signal as the signal is passed on. As a passive participant, it might just pass signals through the network. You can have a star network composed of both active and passive hubs, with the passive hubs acting as plug-in points for groups of nodes. The active hubs act as central gathering points for servers, hubs, and nodes. Like a token-ring, the star configuration also uses token passing to maintain order. Since

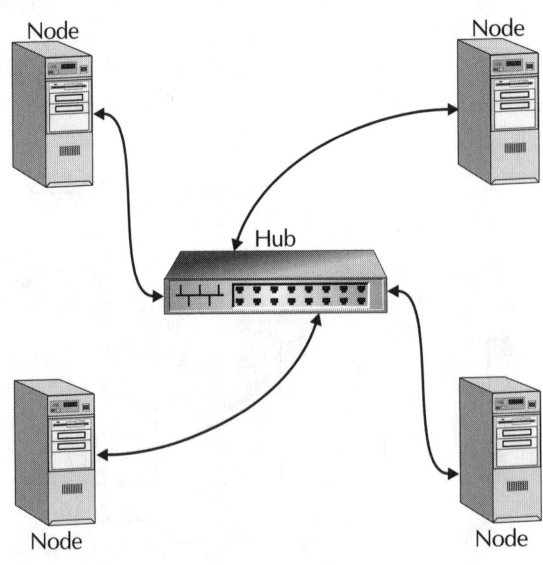

FIGURE 1-7. *Star topology*

the nodes are not arranged in a circle, there is a specific, preassigned order in which the token is passed from node to node.

You can use a star topology in a hybrid network and mix both active hubs and bus topology. Star networks are highly expandable because nodes can be added or removed easily. Hybrid hubs that support more than one kind of cable connection are also available. Because the cables extend from a central hub to each node, isolating a problem is much easier than in a ring configuration. Of course, if a network only has one hub and the hub breaks down, the network will go down as well.

Now, let's take a look at how the connections are configured in a star topology. To join two hubs, fiber-optic cable is used with lengths that can be thousands of feet. The computers or other devices are connected with either shielded or unshielded twisted-pair wires that must be within 100 feet of the wiring hub. The packages of data, which are called *frames,* move from one node to another in a circle, but the wiring is actually in a star formation. A token-ring network has the same wiring configuration as a star, but the actual ring exists within the wiring hub.

Network Data Packaging

Okay. So, now you know about the topology of a network and some types of networks that you may encounter. That's all very interesting, but how does that email message or data file you want to transfer to me actually get where it's supposed to go? After all, you might be in London, England, and I might be in Vienna, Virginia. That's a lot of area to cover! To begin the explanation of how data is transmitted across a network, we'll need to think about the potential limits that may exist for data transmission.

Life's a Highway

When I leave my house in the morning, I pull from my driveway on to a one-way street that has a lane for parked cars and a lane for cars to drive on. I go down to the corner of my street and on to a highway that has enough room for cars to park on either side of the street with two lanes available for driving. There is two-way traffic on this street. I proceed to the stop light at the end of that street and pull on to a divided highway that has three lanes of traffic each way and a divider in the center of the road. This road leads to a superhighway that can hold six lanes of traffic each way. The little one-way road I live on has a speed limit of 15 miles per hour, while the superhighway has a speed limit of 55 miles per hour. If I want to go to the local shopping mall, I take my street to the highway and then the superhighway until I get to the exit for the mall. If there's a big sale going on, many cars will be trying to exit at the same time that I am. Thus, there may be cars from six lanes of traffic trying to merge into one or two lanes to get to the mall. It's possible that I'll wait in traffic for quite a while trying to get from the superhighway exit to the mall parking lot. Of course, then I'm going to have to find a parking space, but that's another story.

A network can be much like my set of highways. Each cable can accommodate a different amount of traffic, so the rate at which my data will travel around the network will depend on how much data the smallest cable can carry. The speed at which a cable can carry data is referred to as its *bandwidth*. Parts of a network can have different bandwidths. Now consider the possibility that you might want to transfer a huge file across the network at the same time that I want to send a very small message. It would not be fair for you to hog the entire system to send your file while I wait to send mine.

Although networks function really quickly, it still takes time for each piece of information to be transferred across the network. How can we each get our specific pieces of information out at the same time? Quite simply, each message is divided into a succession of data packets or envelopes for transmission. Therefore, the large file becomes many small packets, and our files can both be transmitted at the same time. Because each packet has its own information to enable the file to be reassembled entirely and in the correct order at the receiving end, the packets can be interwoven to be sent across the network.

But, what's the composition of each packet? You now know that each packet contains a chunk of data. What else would a packet need to enable its reassembly on the receiving side? The packet would need to include information such as where it came from, where it's going, its sequence number for reassembly, and error-handling information. A packet is actually composed of three sections or parts: a header, a chunk of data, and a trailer. The header contains the source and destination addresses plus control and timing information. The data section contains the actual chunk of information being transmitted and is generally between 512 bytes and 4 kilobytes in size. The trailer contains the rest of the information required, such as error-handling information that helps ensure the data arrives intact.

How can one computer be sure that the information it's received is exactly the same as what was sent? A method known as *cyclical redundancy check* (CRC) is used. The computer that is transmitting the data calculates a value based on the contents of the data. This value is included in the packet. The receiving computer also calculates a value for the packet's contents and then compares the value it arrived at with the one that was sent by the transmitting computer. If both values match, the data is assumed to be intact. If the values do not match, the receiving computer will follow the error-handling information contained in the packet to resolve the problem. There are several standards that detail how the value for a packet is calculated and how errors are to be handled.

Chunking and Transmitting Data

What hardware or software, you might ask, is putting the data into packets and applying the header and trailer information? What is reassembling the data at the other end? The mechanism used must divide the data to be transmitted into neat chunks, attach the sending and receiving addresses to each individual piece, and transmit the packets. There must be a comparable mechanism at the receiving end to read each packet and reassemble all of them into a complete file. The network adapter or interface card, mentioned earlier in this chapter, performs most of the jobs listed here. Remember that each computer connected to the network must have an adapter card to enable connection to and communications over the network.

Earlier, I told you that bandwidth was the measure of maximum speed at which a mechanism can move data. The way bandwidth is measured depends on whether the signal being sent is analog or digital (voice as opposed to data). An analog signal travels in a continuous variable wave, while a digital signal travels in discrete on-and-off pulses. Figure 1-8 shows analog and digital wave patterns.

Look at the analog signal. The wave cycle is measured from wave top to wave top (referred to as crest to crest) or from dip to dip (referred to as trough to trough). The closer the cycles are to each other, the more frequently they will occur in a given amount of time. Analog bandwidth is measured in Hertz and is a count of the number of cycles that occur within a given space of time. If you look at the spectrum of frequencies, you'll find that they range from low, slow frequencies to very high, rapid ones. Analog bandwidth also refers to the spread between the lowest and highest frequencies in a communication channel.

A digital signal's bandwidth, on the other hand, is measured in bits per second (bps). Modems transmit digital signals, while radio, television, and telephone signals are analog. Keep in mind that the greater the number of bits per second, the greater the bandwidth will be. The latest high-speed communications lines like ISDN and ADSL carry data at rates that are so rapid they are measured in kilobytes per second (kbps), megabytes per second (mbps), or even gigabytes per second (gbps).

Baseband vs. Broadband Transmissions

What about the transmissions themselves? Well, there are actually two basic forms of transmission, baseband and broadband. Baseband transmissions send a single

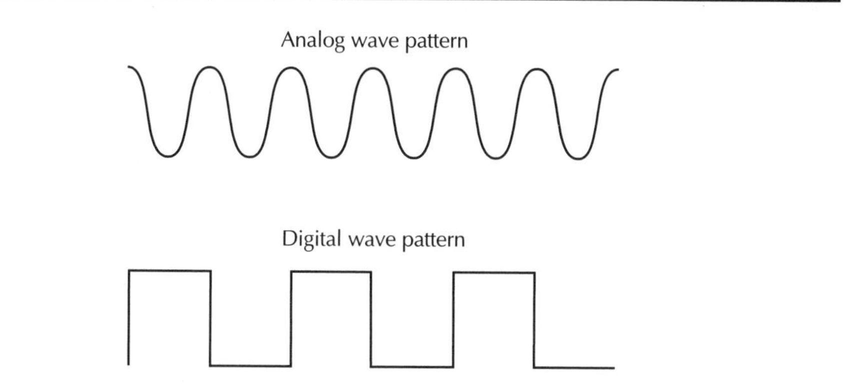

FIGURE 1-8. *Analog and digital wave patterns*

digital signal over a channel at a time. That sounds like one transmission will consume the entire bandwidth, doesn't it. Well, that's not quite the case. You see, a technique called *multiplexing* can be used to send multiple transmissions over the channel by intermixing the transmissions and separating them either by space or time. Thus, either space division multiplexing or time division multiplexing can be used to transmit multiple sets of information over the channel at a time.

There's a problem with baseband transmissions though. As a signal travels over a baseband channel, the farther it goes, the more it can degenerate. The solution is to have a mechanism that will boost or enhance the signal as it travels to ensure that the data does not degenerate enough to be useless on the receiving end. The equipment used to revitalize the signal is called a *repeater*. Baseband signals are commonly used in Ethernet and token-ring topologies. Remember, as I mentioned when discussing Ethernet transmissions earlier, a digital signal can be bidirectional.

Now, let's take a look at broadband transmissions and see how they differ from baseband. First of all, a broadband signal is an analog transmission that travels as a frequency over a communications medium like a coaxial cable or fiber-optic line. Coaxial cable carries electrical transmissions, while fiber-optic lines carry light transmissions. The cable can carry more than one unidirectional signal at once by dividing the transmissions into several channels that are separated by small bands of unused frequencies. In that way, one signal will not interfere with another. Since broadband signals can only travel in one direction, in order to both send and receive information, you need either two channels or two separate cables. You can also reserve separate channels to handle voice, data, and video signals at the same time. The most common uses for broadband transmissions are wide area networking and cable television.

A Look at Open Systems Interconnection

Hey, let's play a game. Which one should we choose? How about playing Whichwidget with me. What's that you say? You've never heard of it? Well, of course you haven't, since I just made it up! Here, let me describe it to you. The goal of this game is to guess the name of the everyday object I've written on this three-by-five-inch card. You can only ask three questions, and each question must be answered with a yes, no, or maybe. Okay?

Admittedly, it's too hard to play a game like this if you and I are not face-to-face or able to communicate in an immediate manner. The point is that in order to play any game, you must first understand the goal or object of the game and know the rules. From the description of my invented game, you know that you can only ask three questions and that they must be structured in a pretty specific way. I've given you two rules that you must follow.

So far, we've seen how a network is assembled physically. We've looked at the hardware involved, the topology, and how information is transmitted and received. A network can comprise many different pieces and parts, and they can be built on very different architectures. What controls how all of these pieces will fit together and be able to successfully form a usable network? The answer is *standards*, or the rules that must be followed in order to play the networking game.

Standards at Work

In 1978 (yep, here I go with a history lesson again), the International Organization for Standardization (ISO) developed a set of standards known as the Open Systems Interconnection reference model. The standards were revised and rereleased in 1984 and describe how all the disparate parts of a network will be designed and configured to ensure that they all work together. This set of standards is referred to as the ISO/OSI model. Hardware and software manufacturers follow this set of standards, which helps their products fit neatly together into a layered architectural approach.

Although the model describes a pattern for building components, it leaves the details of how those components will be built to the manufacturers. Keep in mind, too, that several different standards are available on which networks are built.

The architecture model in the OSI standard is based on seven protocol layers. Let's take a look at each layer in detail next, and then I'll walk you through some of the other standards and how they function.

Seven Layers of the OSI

The seven layers of the OSI are referred to as protocol layers, and each layer is responsible for a specific action or service to help prepare information to be sent over a network. The seven layers are sometimes referred to as a *protocol stack* since each layer "rides" upon the next one. Each layer can only interact with its immediate neighbor or neighbors on the stack. A clearly defined interface describes how each layer will offer its services to the layer above it and how it will access the layer below it.

At the very bottom, you have the physical hardware layer that deals in electronic pulses, while at the very top, you have the software application layer. The layers are usually said to define the successive *layers of abstraction* because each layer moves farther away from the physical hardware. Therefore, the higher up the stack you go, the more meaningful the communication will be to the end user. Table 1-3 shows the seven layers with a brief description of each one. I've numbered each layer in the table so that I can more easily reference them later.

Layer Number	Name	Description
7	Application layer	Provides network access to applications and follows standards that define look and feel.
6	Presentation layer	Ensures that information presented between computers is formatted in the same way for viewing and for use on specific equipment.
5	Session layer	Enables a communications session to be established and provides a standard way to move data between application programs.
4	Transport layer	Provides for reliable and transparent transfer of packets between stations; particularly important for local area networks.
3	Network layer	Provides the addressing and routing information services both within and between networks. Provides the interface between the physical and data-link layers and the higher-level software.
2	Data-link layer	Packages the data into frames and creates the actual network session. It synchronizes the blocks of data, recognizes errors, and controls the flow of data.
1	Physical layer	Defines the hardware and transfers data as a steady, serial bit stream over physical cables and wires. At this level, hardware and software deal with the types of connectors, signaling, and media-sharing network schemes.

TABLE 1-3. *Seven Layers of OSI*

Now that you've seen each layer, let's talk about them in a bit more detail. Whether I start at the top or seventh layer and work my way down the stack, or start at the bottom layer and work my way up the stack, the functions of each layer are the same. Arbitrarily, just because you and your users interact with the application layer most frequently, let's start with the seventh layer and work our way down.

Layer 7: The Application Layer

The application layer, as the "top layer on the cake," provides applications with network access and serves the user. It's where the application programs and network operating system code reside. The applications can be as varied as print-job spooling, electronic mail (Microsoft Outlook or Outlook Express, for example), file transfer software, database access software (SQL*Net or Net8 interacting with an Oracle database), or accounting software. Some applications, like the file transfer software, work from the application layer but really do jobs that are normally assigned to a lower level. Think of your manager performing data-entry tasks because the job has to get done, and there's no one else available to do it.

This layer also enables shared printers and file access as well as directory services like the domain names service I talked about earlier. Each program that uses the network follows specific program-level protocols. Many of these protocols, such as IBM's Systems Application Architecture (SAA), are quite new. For example, email follows the X.400 Message Handling specifications, while directory services follow X.500. Oracle follows several protocols and standards that I'll talk about in Chapter 2.

Layer 6: The Presentation Layer

If you were to look at this page of text on a computer screen, you'd see that the section title is displayed in bold type. Now, let's say you're looking at your computer screen and you see blinking characters or data-entry formats or graphics. What you're interacting with is the presentation layer.

The primary job of the presentation layer is to ensure that information gets formatted correctly so that the final product looks the way the programmer intended it to. The presentation layer is the home of graphics codes and character sets. Although most computers today use the American Standard Code for Information Interchange (ASCII, pronounced "askey") character set, some, like the IBM mainframe, still use Extended Binary Coded Decimal Interchange Code (EBCDIC, pronounced "ebsadic"). ASCII uses either 7 or 8 bits to represent up to 256 characters, while EBCDIC uses only 8 bits to represent the same 256 characters. However, ASCII uses a decimal 97 to represent the lowercase letter *a*, while EBCDIC uses a decimal 129. Quite a difference, huh? The Hypertext Transfer Protocol (HTTP), used to format information for Web sites, is another example of the presentation layer protocol at work.

Thus, it's the presentation layer's job to ensure that both computers use the same representation for data. The presentation layer is also responsible for encryption and compression of data as well as controlling output to printers, plotters, and other peripherals.

Layer 5: The Session Layer

Let's say that you and I are using an instant messaging service on our PCs, and I want to start a conversation with you. How am I going to do that? Well, first, I need to get your attention. I may have to present a password to begin sending a message to you. Then, once I've established a connection with you, we'll "talk" until one of us ends the conversation. This scenario assumes that you and I both have a way to ensure that the conversation runs smoothly. Enter the session layer.

Through the session layer, communications sessions are established between two parties known as application entities (AEs). Once a connection is established, the session layer takes care of any security issues and then monitors and synchronizes the data flow, controlling who transmits, when, and for how long. It's the session layer's job to ensure that, after the conversation is completed, both parties disconnect successfully. The session layer is also responsible for name recognition, logging, administration, and other similar functions.

One protocol involved in the session layer is the NetBIOS Extended User Interface (NetBEUI) protocol implemented by Microsoft-based networks. (The NetBIOS is an application program interface that enables application programs to request session connections.) However, the NetBIOS, and Named Pipes as well, often perform both transport layer and session layer functions. There doesn't seem to be one, pure session layer piece that is unique to this layer.

Layer 4: The Transport Layer

The transport layer does many of the same jobs as the network layer below it. However, the transport layer acts locally. Hmm, what happens if there's a problem with the network and it becomes unavailable? The transport layer will look for a different route to send the data over. The transport layer may save the data until the network connection is reestablished. When data is received, it's the transport layer's job to ensure that it's in the correct format and in the right order. This layer opens each packet to ensure that none of the contents are missing or broken.

Until the data reaches the transport layer, it's been passed from layer to layer in whatever-sized chunks it was originally created. When it gets to the transport layer, the data will be broken down into packets of a uniform size as required by the network layers below it to be sent across the network. When the transmitted packet is received, it's the transport layer's task to reassemble the packets in the original chunk of information. The transport layer will number each packet so that, should the packets arrive out of order at their destination, they'll be reassembled in the correct order. Another task of the transport layer is to notify the sending computer that a message has been received without error.

When data is transmitted, the receiving computer uses a temporary storage area called a *frame buffer* in which to order the message. If that buffer is full, the transport layer on the receiving machine will notify the transmitting machine to wait before sending more data. If multiplexing of messages or sessions is available, the transport layer is the area in which this activity will be controlled. The transport layer sits between the application layers above it and the network/hardware-related layers, called the *subnet,* below it and acts as the intermediary between the two levels.

Now, let's say two dissimilar computers need to communicate over the network. How is that action handled effectively? Well, several transport protocols can be used on one machine to resolve disparities. The Transmission Control Protocol (TCP) I talked about earlier, developed by the Department of Defense, is one that has been adopted by many companies as part of their TCP/IP protocol suite. Two other PC network transport layer protocols are NetBIOS, mentioned earlier, and NetWare's Internetwork Protocol Exchange (IPX).

Layer 3: The Network Layer

The network layer software usually resides in switches out on the network. The interface card in your PC must put each packet or frame together in a way that the network software can recognize and use its information to successfully route the message from one machine to another. As the topmost of the three subnet layers, the network layer

- Acts as the controller for routing and addressing messages within and between networks
- Decides which physical pathway the data should take based on the network conditions, the packet's priority, and other factors
- Guarantees reliability to the higher layers
- Removes the need for any of the higher levels to know anything about the actual transmission and routing technologies used by the subnet

By performing an evaluation of the network conditions, the network layer will determine which route to use in sending a message. The network layer can transmit a frame to a router if necessary. If the frame is larger than the maximum transmission unit (MTU) allowed by the receiving machine, the network layer will allow the router to break the frame into smaller units. Likewise, the receiving network layer takes responsibility for reassembling the smaller pieces.

In the list above, I mentioned that one of the network layer's tasks is to address messages. Let's talk a bit more about addressing now. When I was growing up, I had a friend named Lauren. For some strange reason or other, her mother started to call her "Pitsaritz" as a nickname. Well, the name "Pitsy" stuck, and throughout school, Lauren was known as Pitsy. Even the teachers used that name. My son, Marc, hates his middle name (which I won't reveal here since it would embarrass him), so he never uses it.

What's that got to do with networking and addressing, you might ask. Well, we all have one or more names. There's the name that appears on your birth certificate.

That's your "hardwired" name. Then there may be one or more other names that you use for business and social gatherings. Each computer has a physical address that is burned in, or hardwired, to its network adapter card. This is known as the Media Access Control address, or MAC.

The computer generally has one or more logical addresses. It will have an IP address that is in dotted octet format, as I described in the peer-based network section earlier. The computer may also have a Web-based address in a URL format. The IP and URL addresses are logical. The network layer must resolve and translate logical and physical network addresses. On every system there is a file somewhere that provides information allowing the network layer to resolve addresses.

Several protocols operate at the network layer. Among these are the Internet Protocol (IP) and the X.25 Protocol that is used to connect a computer to a packet-switching network.

Layer 2: The Data-Link Layer

Many years ago, I became interested in making mosaic pictures. To make a mosaic picture, you take small, odd-shaped materials and arrange them in an artistic way to form a picture. You then glue them together with a medium such as plaster. In the same way, the data-link layer, which resides between and communicates with the physical layer below it and the network layer above it, takes characters in a stream and forms them into a message. It then checks the message before moving it to the next level.

The data-link layer is responsible for creating and terminating links between network nodes and transmitting the packets over the physical layer. This layer may also get a verification notice from the receiving computer telling it that the message arrived successfully. The data-link layer will acknowledge transmission and, if necessary, retransmit frames that have been damaged en route.

Typically, the functions of the data-link layer are performed by special integrated circuits in the interface or adapter card. If you use FTP, Xmodem, or Crosstalk's DART protocol for error detection and retransmission during a file exchange, you are using software programs that act like a data-link protocol during the time that a file is being transferred.

Among the protocols that this layer uses are the High-Level Data Link Control (HDLC), bisynchronous communications, and Advanced Data Communications Control Procedures (ADCCP).

Layer 1: The Physical Layer

Well, we've finally arrived at the bottom of the OSI stack. What a trip! As the name implies, this layer deals with the physical hardware. All of the subsequent layers that we've looked at talk to the outside world through this layer. At the physical layer, a stream of zeros (0) and ones (1) are sent across the network from one computer to another. The physical layer is concerned with the cabling, connectors, and pins, adapter or interface cards, and electrical signals. Twisted-pair wiring, fiber-optic strands, and coaxial cable are all a part of this layer. As with the other layers, this one has numerous specifications to deal with each hardware element. There are specifications, for example, that cover

- The number and functions of pins in a connector, including the pin assignments
- The type and kind of cables to be used to make a connection between equipment
- How the cables are connected to the network adapter

As well as dealing with the hardware, the physical layer controls the encoding and decoding of the bit stream and the timing and synchronization methods used to ensure that each bit leaves and arrives exactly as it was at the transmitting end.

Of the specifications that are followed at this layer, three stand out. They are the Institute of Electrical and Electronic Engineers (IEEE, pronounced "eye-triple-e") 802.3 specification for Ethernet networks, the IEEE 802.5 specification for token-ring networks, and the Electronic Industries Association (EIA) RS-232-C standard for serial communications, which covers modem communications. The RS-232-C standard defines which pin on the connector does what, and when a voltage level on a wire indicates a 0 or 1. The European international standard V.24 is very like the RS-232-C standard.

About Protocols

Throughout the previous sections, I mentioned various protocols by their names without really explaining what a protocol is. Simply stated, a *protocol* is an agreement made among different parts of a network on how data is transferred. We've all watched our great nations arguing over how things will be done. Well, the arena of networking is not very different. At every layer, there are standards, and various committees are working hard to describe exactly how each specific piece within a layer will function. There are often arguments over whose ideas will prevail in each area. Sometimes, because a product gains overwhelming popularity, the protocol used by that product becomes the de facto standard and is almost universally used. Microsoft Windows in its several flavors is an excellent example of popularity (or monopoly) driving standards.

As with any language, protocol standards deal with syntax, semantics, and timing. Syntax defines how a signal level is to be used. Semantics describes how the data is structured for coordination among the various machines and for information handling. Timing encompasses the sequence, or proper ordering, of the data and how to match speeds between machines. Hmm, what does "match speeds" mean? Let's say your computer has a port with a 33.6 kbps speed, while my machine can talk at 54 kbps. How are they going to talk to each other? Timing standards will provide the definition to help enable communications between our machines.

Although standards define how things should be, in the real world of standards implementation where real products are built, the standards are not always implemented exactly to the full description of the OSI model. It's hard for an engineer to resist adding that one little extra modification to his product to make it "better" or faster or whatever the perceived advantage is.

The SNA and TCP/IP Reference Models

Although the OSI model is most commonly used and most often referenced, for completeness, I want to look at two other standards that are also layered and tend to be referenced in networking discussions. One of these models is the IBM networking architecture known as the System Network Architecture (SNA), and the other is an Internet-related model known as the TCP/IP reference model or the Internet reference model. Let's take a look at each of these standards separately and see what's the same and what's different about them that sets them apart from the OSI model.

The SNA Model

In 1970, IBM designed the SNA model to enable its products to communicate with each other. IBM, at that time, manufactured mainframes, printers, and terminals. Although the model originally was designed to define how terminals and mainframes talked to each other, the model was later modified to include microcomputers and PCs. The modified specification is known as the Advanced Program to Program Communications (APPC).

Because IBM defined the SNA model, it's mostly IBM specific. However, there are parallels between it and the later OSI model. The original version contained five layers, and the later version extends the model to round it out to seven layers that roughly equate to the OSI model. Let's take a look at the layers of the SNA model, as shown in Table 1-4. An asterisk is used to denote the two extended layers. I have added in parenthesis the corresponding OSI model layer or layers.

Since the SNA model was built around the IBM mainframe, the model is based on the premise that the mainframe is in charge of creating every communication session. If communication sessions extend beyond the mainframe, additional controllers known as Network Control Programs (NCPs) perform the routing and path control through intermediate nodes. The APPC enhancement I mentioned earlier in this section provides for two different kinds of nodes. End nodes (EN) connect to and use the network, while network nodes (NN) connect to the network and perform routing and management duties. There are many more abbreviations in the SNA model, but this should be enough to give you a taste of the IBM SNA networking model.

Layer	Description
Transaction services*	Provides the application-to-application communication protocols. (Corresponds to the application layer of the OSI model.)
Presentation services	Handles formatting, compression, and data translation. (Corresponds directly to the presentation layer of the OSI model.)
Data flow control	Describes the rules to follow during a communication session and defines whether data will be transmitted in two directions at the same time (full duplex) or in only one direction at a time (half duplex). (Corresponds partially to the session layer of the OSI model.)
Transmission control	Handles sessions between communications nodes; starts, stops, and maintains sessions; routes data over the network; ensures that data arrives correctly. (Corresponds in part to the session, transport, and network layers of the OSI model.)
Path control	Creates the links to nodes, manages the links, and routes data. (Corresponds to the transport and network layers of the OSI model.)
Data-link control	Ensures reliable data transfer over the physical, network hardware. (Corresponds directly to the data-link layer of the OSI model.)
Physical*	Encompasses the physical hardware structure and electrical signaling used in the network. It is not directly implemented in the SNA. (Corresponds to the physical layer of the OSI model.)

TABLE 1-4. *Layers of the IBM SNA Model*

Oh, by the way, TCP/IP can now run on mainframe machines, but it does not completely replace the SNA model. In a nutshell, the version of TCP/IP for the mainframe calls many of the services of the SNA layers.

The TCP/IP or Internet Reference Model

As its name implies, the TCP/IP or Internet reference model is based on and reflects the world of internetworking, where information is transferred between workstations and networks. Table 1-5 shows the layers of the TCP/IP reference model. As I did with the SNA model, I will identify in parentheses the associated OSI model layers. However, the internetworking layer has no corresponding OSI layer, and there is no physical layer shown, even though we all know that there must be hardware underlying all of the communications performed by and through this model.

Although different in definition, the TCP/IP, SNA, and OSI models are not mutually exclusive. It is not uncommon to find a network that runs one model based on an operating system that runs a different model. Thus, a local area network could run the TCP/IP protocols on an operating system that has been designed along the ISO/OSI model while conversing with an IBM-based SNA mainframe network. Pretty amazing, huh! Overall, though, the TCP/IP protocol has become the most prevalent model in use today.

Layer	**Description**
Application layer	Clearly equates to the application and presentation layers of the OSI model and performs the same functions as described in those sections. (Corresponds to the application and presentation layers of the OSI model.)
Transport layer	Ensures reliable end-to-end datagram delivery and helps to establish a connection known as a *virtual circuit*. *Datagrams* are packets that include data, header, and trailer information. A transmission may not require an actual connection, in which case it will be referred to as connectionless. (Corresponds to the session and transport layers of the OSI model.)
Internetworking layer	Includes the protocols responsible for routing messages from sender to receiver. This layer includes the routers and gateways used to move datagrams. (Does not correspond to any layer of the OSI model.)
Network access layer	Includes the protocols that define how data frames are transmitted and delivered. This layer relies on the hardwired address of the network adapter cards and interacts with the physical hardware. (Corresponds to the network and data-link layers of the OSI model.)

TABLE 1-5. *TCP/IP or Internet Reference Model*

Research information used for this chapter was obtained from the following books:

1. *How Networks Work,* by Frank J. Derfler, Jr., and Les Freed, Que Corporation, 1998.
2. *Step Up to Networking,* by JoAnne Woodcock, Microsoft Press, 1999.
3. *Using Networks,* by Frank Derfler, Que, 1998.

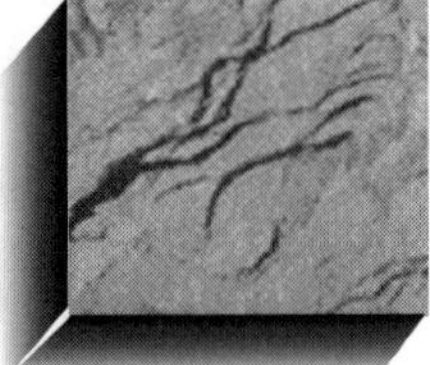

CHAPTER 2

Oracle Network Components

o begin this chapter, I'd like to quote from the Oracle Corporation documentation found in the *Net8 Administrator's Guide*, Release 8.1.5, in the Net8 Overview section. "Net8 is the foundation of Oracle's family of networking products, allowing services and their applications to reside on different computers and communicate as peer applications. The main function of Net8 is to establish network sessions and transfer data between a client machine and a server or between two servers." Sounds pretty simple and straightforward, doesn't it?

In some ways, Net8 *is* very simple and straightforward. In other ways, dealing with networking in the Oracle world can become very complex very quickly. I'll try to keep things simple and understandable as you and I examine Net8.

A Little Bit of Oracle History

Following the premise introduced in Chapter 1 that to understand the present and future, you must understand the past, let's first take a look at the computing environment when I started working with Oracle products. I'm going to give a brief overview of Oracle's general product history to help provide some perspective on where Oracle was, how far the product set has come, and what part networking has played both in Oracle's success and the growth of the computer industry in general.

Although Oracle Corporation first released its database software around 1979, in November of 1983 when I was hired as a Programmer/Analyst C to work as a developer on a "scientific application," my company was only using version 2.0 of the Oracle relational database management system (RDBMS). At that time, we were writing code to process collected data by using software to "drive" hardware. We wrote FORTRAN programs that processed the data stored in the database. The Oracle product set was very immature, and enhancements to the Oracle code were released very slowly.

We "talked" to our Oracle database using languages called User Friendly Interface (UFI) and Procedural UFI, the forerunners of SQL and PL/SQL. I was working on a Digital VAX system that supported screen displays. Our forms were actually graphical programs that used Oracle's Interactive Forms package (IAF). We created a source file with a .inp extension. We next compiled the forms using interactive graphics (IAG) commands and then ran the executable output (.iap) using the command **runform**.

We created our database using the create contiguous file command (**ccf**) with a file name and a size. When we began to run out of space in this file, we could unload the data using an export utility, re-create the file with a larger size, and import the data to the new file. We could use Oracle Data Loader (ODL) to load data to the database, and we could monitor the database using the Oracle Display System (ODS), which we generally referred to as "odious"! To start the database, we would issue the command **ior** (initialize Oracle). We had both a before image journal (BI) file and an after image journal (AI) file to keep track of the appearance of the data before and after changes were made. We used dumb terminals to interact with the database. We could not interact directly with the database from a remote computer.

As the product matured, we gained three utilities: a FASTFORM utility that became the default block generator in SQL*Forms; a utility called **crt** to control our screen display environment; and a report generator called **rpt**, later named Oracle Report, that let us display reports in a flexible format. The **rpt** utility was a command interpreter as opposed to a compiled executable program and was both slow and cumbersome to use. The report layout had to be predesigned and preformatted so that you knew exactly where on the page each element of the report would be displayed. If a column size was changed, the whole report might have to be completely recalculated.

The SCOTT account, identified by the password TIGER, has existed in the Oracle RDBMS since the early days. This account is a great way to learn Structured Query Language (SQL) and test your database/system for network connectivity. Originally, you had to create the account, declaring the well-known password yourself, and assign the access rights before you could run the procedures to create the demonstration objects. The scripts were (and still are) stored in the SQL*Plus/demo directory. In more recent versions, the SCOTT account is automatically installed with its password and associated objects.

During the early years, the database administrator (DBA) faced the challenge of just trying to keep the database running. There were database crashes that not only took the system down but sometimes corrupted the database as well and forced complete rebuilds. Tuning or influencing the performance of the system was almost impossible. Oracle was in its infancy, and DBAs were just trying to manage this new and very strange beast. There were no user groups with people available to turn to when you had questions. Today, there are a large number of wonderful groups available that you can turn to for advice and help with Oracle problems.

The common approach to upgrading an Oracle database was to install the complete new software system on top of the old one. When something broke, you were "just out of luck!" Most companies had a developer who performed both database administration and development tasks. Developers, working with rudimentary tools, were called upon to use a great deal of creative thinking to accomplish tasks that, by today's standards, seem simple. Today, the Oracle product set is both complex and robust. There is now a rich assortment of development tools that you can use to provide end users with effective solutions to their computing problems.

Enter SQL*Net

When version 5 of the RDBMS became available, we saw a few major advances in the product. Toward the end of version 4, the first Oracle version created to run on a personal computer was released, but it was incredibly unstable at best. We didn't seem to notice Oracle for DOS until versions 5.0.b and 5.0.c. In fact, almost everyone who worked with Oracle products around that time ended up with a copy of one of the PC versions of Oracle on their bookshelf (but not necessarily on their machine). Why? Because the PC version was inexpensive and was shipped with a complete set of hard-copy books—worth much more than the cost of the product alone!

The other significant event related to version 5 was the release of a networking product called SQL*Net (version 1.0), which helped to change the face of Oracle computing. However, before we look more carefully at SQL*Net, I'd like you to think for a moment about a train riding on a set of railroad tracks. If our train could think, it wouldn't care what material the tracks were made of or how far apart the spikes were placed to hold the tracks together. The only thing that our thinking train might care about is whether or not there was enough track available to continue running on. Now, with the train in mind, let's look at the earliest release of SQL*Net.

The first version of SQL*Net was very simplistic but very well written and effective. The software ran on several different machines, just as our train can run on many different tracks in many locations. There was a set of protocols that SQL*Net worked with and that Oracle could "ride" on. For all intents and purposes, the Oracle database software functioned in an environment that did not need to know what protocol was used, just as our train does not need to know the type of track it's running on.

The server ran a program that listened for connection requests from clients and passed those requests to the database. SQL*Net enabled chunks of information to be passed back and forth between the server and clients in a seamless manner.

The theme for the 1991 International Oracle User Week (IOUW) held in Miami, Florida, was "Client Surfer," and the logo was a guy on a surfboard riding an ocean wave. Oracle Card, a software package that was based on Apple's Hypertalk language, was introduced as the "wave of the future." This software let you easily build client applications that allowed interaction between a PC and your database on a server. In the keynote speech at that conference, we were told that centralized, mainframe computing was a thing of the past, and the only computing environment that would make sense in the future was client/server.

Suddenly, an effective networking approach was available, and a computing revolution was under way. Over the years, SQL*Net has evolved, and the product name has been changed to Net8.

Basic Architecture

At the beginning of this chapter, I quoted from the *Net8 Administrator's Guide*. Let's take a minute now to look at that quote again, sentence by sentence. "Net8 is the foundation of Oracle's family of networking products, allowing services and their applications to reside on different computers and communicate as peer applications." In a client/server environment, the applications are usually stored on the client PCs with just enough resources (memory, disk space, computing power) to perform their required tasks, and the database resides on a mainframe, mini-, or microcomputer that is much more resource rich. You need both computers to complete one data transaction.

"The main function of Net8 is to establish network sessions and transfer data between a client machine and a server or between two servers." Okay. We've already talked a little bit about transferring data between a client machine and a server, but what about the second part, "between two servers?" Along with the ability to communicate with one server database from a number of PCs, Oracle has also developed the technology that allows us to distribute databases on more than one machine and interact with them all as one logical database. Pretty cool! The mechanism used to support distributed databases is called a *database link*. Figure 2-1 shows a client performing a task that interacts with three separate databases. However, from the client's perspective, there exists only one database.

A database link is created within a database and supplies the information needed to enable Net8 to connect one database to another. I'll talk more about database links at the end of this chapter. For now, just keep in mind that Net8 can be used to perform both client-to-server and server-to-server connections.

Hardware Requirements

My sister-in-law, Joan, has a wonderful recipe for strawberry gelatin salad that I'd like to share. You use two small boxes or one large box of strawberry gelatin, two cups of boiling hot water, one container of frozen strawberries, eight bananas, one cup of walnuts broken or crushed into very small pieces, and two small cans of pineapple well drained. You mix the hot water in with the gelatin, and once it's dissolved, you add the other ingredients and refrigerate the mixture until it's set. Delicious!

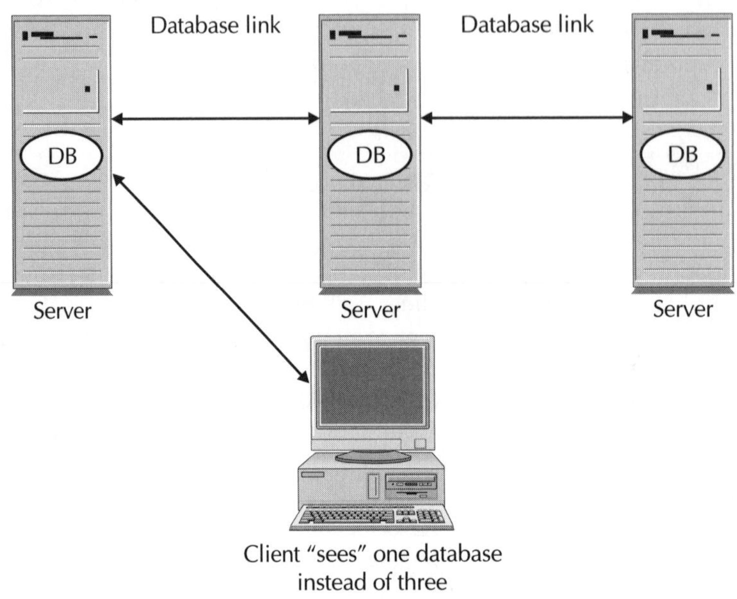

FIGURE 2-1. *Client using database links with multiple databases*

Hmm, what haven't I mentioned in this recipe? I've talked about the contents and the procedures, but nowhere have I told you about the "hardware" that is required to implement this tasty side dish. You are left to decide for yourself whether you want to heat the water on your stovetop or in a microwave oven or whether the water coming out of your tap is hot enough to dissolve gelatin. I also haven't said anything about what size or type of bowl or measuring or mixing tools you should use. Why? Because the recipe can be made successfully regardless of what method you use to heat the water or measure the ingredients. The only impact hardware might have on the mix is the size of the bowl you choose to use. Ideally, you will choose a bowl that's big enough to hold the ingredients without spilling any of the mixture.

Net8 and its predecessor SQL*Net are mostly platform independent. The only reference to the word "hardware" in the *Net8 Administrator's Guide*, Release 8.1.5, is the comment: "In fact, the number of networking protocols supported is limited only by those restrictions imposed by the specific node's hardware, memory and operating system." (I'll talk more about the networking protocols a bit later in this chapter.)

The primary concern that you should have with computer hardware when you are getting ready to install and configure Net8, therefore, is whether your computer is using a supported, compatible network software product. Your next concern is whether the version of that network software is correct for the version of Net8 that you are going to use. And, finally, you must ensure that the network port number that you intend to assign for Oracle is not currently in use by another product. I'll talk more about port numbers in Chapter 3.

Component Layers

In some of the Oracle Education classes that I have taken, the first view of Oracle that we, as students, were given was of the Oracle *onion*. Picture a target like the one you use when you play darts. There's a center circle with larger, evenly spaced circles around it. Figure 2-2 shows an example of this target with a few labels for the layers. If

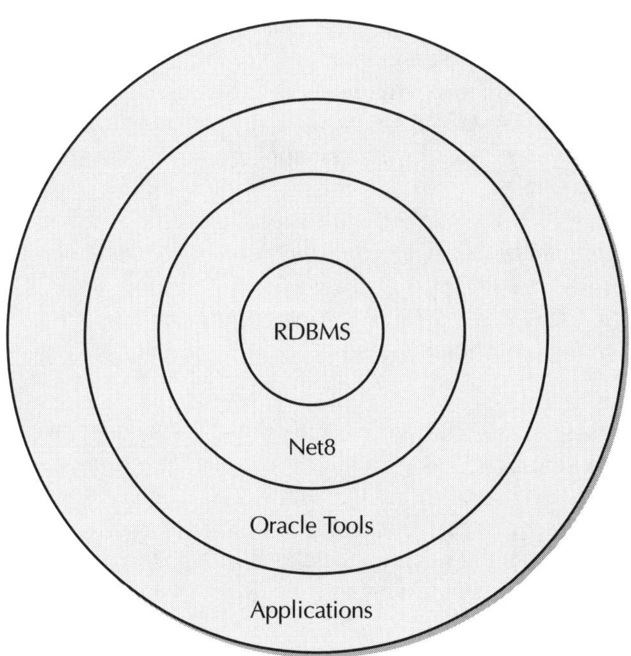

FIGURE 2-2. *The Oracle component layers*

you peel the layers of an onion, eventually, you reach the core or center layer. The heart of the Oracle onion is the RDBMS. Between the core and all other layers lies the networking protocol. You must have this second layer in order to interact with all other products in the Oracle suite.

So, let's peel back the layers and see how Oracle fits together with the underlying network protocols.

Oracle Protocols

In Chapter 1, I told you about the ISO/OSI protocol and about the communications layers. Just to review a bit, when one computer communicates with another, the request is sent through a set of individual communications layers called a stack. Remember how each layer of the stack performs a different function in translating a message into a series of electronic impulses as it's moved from the user's keyboard to the underlying physical hardware? Well, each different type of network-specific protocol will have a different but similar stack since the basic job at hand is to get the message from one computer through a wire to another computer.

Oracle uses the Transparent Network Substrate (TNS) and a set of industry-standard protocols as its basic technology. TNS is built into Oracle's networking to enable it to communicate with the underlying computer network protocol. Net8 is a stack of layers that sits on top of the network protocol.

Each machine that communicates with a database must have Net8 installed on it. Table 2-1 shows the Net8 layers that apply to an Oracle server.

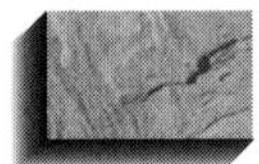

NOTE
If you are using the Internet Inter-Orb Protocol (IIOP) or Oracle's Java Database Connectivity Drivers (JDBC), the protocol stack will be slightly different from the one shown in Table 2-1.

From the client side, the stack is almost the same. The difference is seen in the top layer. Instead of the Oracle-side Programmatic Interface (OPI), on the client side, you have an application layer that has the Oracle Call Interface (OCI) built in. Through the application, the user makes a request that is processed on the server side. The response is sent back from the server to the client through the stacks. Unless a network problem occurs, your users will usually only be aware of and interact with their applications.

Following a Call down the Client Stack

Let's take a minute to walk through a request from the client to the server to be sure we understand how this works. We start out in the client application. The application provides the interface between the user and the database through the terminal displays. The application is built to identify database operations to send to the server.

Stack Layer	Description
Oracle-side Programmatic Interface (OPI)	Responsible for responding to each of the possible messages sent by the client-side Oracle Call Interface (OCI). For example, an OCI request to fetch 25 rows would have an OPI response to return the 25 rows once they have been fetched.
Two-Task Common	Resolves character set differences between the sender and receiver.
Net8 (consists of three layers)	Network Interface (NI)—Hides the underlying network protocol and media from the client application. Network Routing (NR)/Network Naming (NN)/ Network Authentication (NA)—Takes care of routing the data to its final destination. Transparent Network Substrate (TNS)—Takes care of generic communications such as sending and receiving data.
ORACLE Protocol Adapter	Thin layer of code that insulates Net8 from the underlying network protocol.
Network-Specific Protocol	Stack of layers that translates the SQL statement into packets to transmit across the network.

TABLE 2-1. *Net8 Server Components*

OCI Layer The OCI is used to initiate a dialogue between the client and server so that the server can process the request by first parsing the SQL statements for correct syntax. This layer was referred to as the User Program Interface (UPI) in SQL*Net V2, but the functions and purpose of this layer have not changed. A cursor or buffer area is opened for the SQL statement, and any client application variables are placed into the server's shared memory area. Placing a variable in a memory area for use within the SQL query is called *binding* it. Client application program variables used within SQL statements are stored in the stack space within the Process Global Area (PGA). The binding process involves placing references (pointers) to the values stored in the PGA. Since the binding is done by reference, a variable does not have to be re-bound before reexecuting the SQL statement; simply changing the value is sufficient.

The server's data dictionary is used to determine the composition of the fields being returned, and the SQL statements are executed within the cursor memory space. As the statements are being processed, one or more rows of data are sent to and displayed from the user's application. Once all of the information is retrieved, the cursor or memory buffer area is closed and released.

Depending on how the application is written, the calls to the server may be either bundled into a single message to the server or sent one at a time for processing. The goal, of course, is to minimize the number of calls to the server and, therefore, reduce the amount of network traffic. When a call is initiated, control passes from the OCI layer to the Net8 layers to establish the connection and transmit the request to the server.

Two-Task Common Layer In the ISO/OSI model, the presentation layer ensures that information presented between computers is formatted in the same way for viewing and for use on specific equipment. The Two-Task Common layer is Oracle's implementation of the presentation layer and provides character set and data type conversion between different character sets or formats on the client and server. To reduce the time and resources required for processing, this layer has been optimized to perform conversion only when it's required. Thus, it's the Two-Task Common layer's job to decide whether any conversions are required for two computers to communicate. It accomplishes its task by evaluating the differences in the internal data and character sets.

Net8 Layers Net8's job is to provide the session layer functionality. Through its three components, the Net8 layer establishes and maintains connections between the client and server and enables messages to be exchanged between them. As shown in Table 2-1, the three component layers are the NI, the combination component NR/NN/NA, and the TNS. The functionality each component provides is as follows:

- Network Interface (NI) handles the "break" and "reset" requests for a connection.
- Network Routing (NR) provides routing of the network session to the destination. This may include any intermediary destinations or "hops" on the route to the server destination.
- Network Naming (NN) resolves net service names to a Net8 destination address.
- Network Authentication (NA) negotiates any authentication requirement with the destination.
- Transparent Network Substrate (TNS) provides a common interface to the industry-standard protocols to open, close, send, and receive requests from Net8 and settle any generic machine-level connectivity issues.

The TNS component is of interest because it's the layer that interacts most directly with the underlying network protocols and determines

- The location of the server or destination and whether one or more protocols will be involved
- The handling of interrupts between the client and server
- When and how to pass control to an Oracle protocol to make a protocol-specific call

To protect data while it's in transit, the TNS supports encryption and sequenced cryptographic message digests.

Each layer is vitally important, for without all of these components in place, the client application will not successfully talk to the database server.

On the Server Side

Once the message is received on the server side, it's moved up the server stack to the database where the request is processed. The stack looks similar to the client stack, but the request travels in the reverse order from the TNS layer up through the Oracle Programmatic Interface to the Oracle server, where the SQL statement is resolved. Once the request has been processed, the data is passed back through the server stack, across the network to the client machine, and back through the client stack to the application.

In the case of server-to-server communications, the actions are the same. The only difference between server-to-server and client-to-server communications is that with server-to-server requests, instead of a client application, there's a server-specific OCI called the Network Program Interface (NPI). The NPI enables a server to construct SQL requests for interaction with other servers and is able to perform all the functions of the OCI layer if necessary.

Communications Stacks Used by Oracle

So far, we've looked at the general composition of the Oracle communications stack on both the client side and the server side. We've also looked at server-to-server communications. On the server side, there is a new presentation layer called the General Inter-Orb Protocol (GIOP) that Oracle supports. The nomenclature "Orb" actually stands for Object Request Broker. Oracle's version of GIOP is called the Internet Inter-Orb Protocol (IIOP) and works over both TCP/IP and TCP/IP with Secure Sockets Layer (SSL) lines. The IIOP option enables clients using Java to interact with an Oracle database.

IIOP Communications Stack

When a client uses the IIOP communications stack, there is no session layer involved. Thus, TNS is not used. Also, since GIOP is used as the presentation layer, there is no Two-Task Common layer present in the IIOP model. Table 2-2 shows the layers of the client-side IIOP stack.

As you can see, the IIOP stack is much more streamlined, with a potentially faster and less complicated interface that makes it well suited for Internet communications.

On the server side, the IIOP stack is also much more compact and less complicated. Table 2-3 shows the layers of the server-side IIOP stack as implemented with the Java option.

Since the IIOP stack is used for client interaction through Internet access using Java applications (applets or Java beans), let's look at the Java Database Connectivity (JDBC) stack next.

Java Database Connectivity stack

Let's say for conversational purposes that you are a Java developer working on an application and you need to connect to, insert into, update or delete from, and/or obtain information from an Oracle database. You have the choice of writing your application using one of two types of JDBC drivers. You can write your application as a Java-based client/server or thin-client application using either Java Web servers or Java application servers, or you can write your application using Java applets.

If you opt to use the Java-based client/server or thin-client approach, you'll use the JDBC/OCI driver. This driver converts JDBC code to calls to the Oracle Call Interface

Stack Layer	**Description**
Client Application	The same application layer that appears in the Net8 stack
GIOP	The presentation layer
Oracle TCP/IP or TCP/IP with SSL	The network protocol stack used to transport requests and responses from one machine to another

TABLE 2-2. *Client-Side IIOP Communications Stack*

Stack Layer	Description
Oracle Server	The layer that performs the request processing
TNS	Transparent Network Substrate
Oracle TCP/IP Protocol (with or without SSL)	Oracle's implementation of the transport protocol layer with or without the Secure Sockets Layer
TCP/IP Network-Specific Protocol	The network implementation of the transport protocol layer that carries requests and responses between the machines

TABLE 2-3. *Server-Side IIOP Communications Stack*

(OCI). Once the JDBC calls are converted to OCI, Net8 is used to send the converted calls to the Oracle database server.

For the Java applet developer, the thin JDBC driver is used to establish a direct connection to the Oracle database server over Java sockets. In this case, a lightweight implementation of Net8 and the Two-Task Common layers is used to access the database.

If you look at the layers of the JDBC/OCI client communications stack, you'll see that they are very similar to the standard Oracle communications stack. The only difference between the stacks is the client interface. In the standard Oracle stack, the top layer is shown as "Client Application." For the JDBC client application stack, there are really three layers, as shown in Table 2-4. The way these layers are implemented will vary based on whether the application is written in JDBC/OCI or Java applet thin JDBC code calls.

Stack Layer	Description
JDBC Client	Java application code
JDBC Driver	The JDBC/OCI driver or the thin JDBC driver
DBAccess Interface	The mechanism used to initiate SQL sessions (much like the OCI interface)

TABLE 2-4. *JDBC Client Application Stack Layers*

Now, for the thin JDBC communications stack, you'll see a very different set of layers. They are listed in Table 2-5.

As you can see from Table 2-5, information passes through the Java client applet to the server and back through several protocol layers with names that are very different from the standard Oracle communications layers. Let's take a look at each of these layers to better understand how they are used to process a request for information. Remember that the Java DBAccess Interface is used by both the JDBC/OCI and thin JDBC to initiate a SQL session.

JavaTTC Layer As a subset of the Two-Task Common layer, the JavaTTC layer is used to verify and negotiate the protocol version and data type. After determining whether the Java client character set needs conversion to be compatible with the server character set, the JavaTTC layer handles the actual SQL statement execution.

JavaNet Layer Divided into three functional layers, JavaNet is implemented to provide the same type of communications processing functionality that the NI, NR/NN/NA, and TNS layers do in Net8. The Communication Interface layer acts very much like the NI layer in the standard Oracle stack to provide an interface between the JavaTTC layer and the underlying network layers. The Addressing layer functions like the NN layer in the standard Oracle stack to process Net8 destination addresses. The JavaNS (Java Network Substrate) acts like the TNS to provide a common interface to TCP/IP with the open/close and send/receive functions and determines

- The location of the server or destination
- The number of protocols that will be involved to make the connection
- The handling of interrupts between the client and server depending on the capabilities of each

Stack Layer	**Description**
JavaTTC	Consists of a subset of the Two-Task Common layer to enable exchanges of information between the Java client and the database
JavaNet	Consists of three layers: Communication Interface, Addressing, and the Java Network Substrate
Network Protocol Layer	Consists of two layers: Java Sockets and TCP/IP

TABLE 2-5. *Thin JDBC Communications Stack Layers*

Network Protocol Layer The Network Protocol layer is divided into two functional layers: the Java Sockets that provides a connection between the JavaNS, and TCP/IP. Java Sockets will only work with and run on top of TCP/IP. Therefore, TCP/IP is the only protocol layer shown with this configuration.

On the Server Side

Although the communications protocol for a client using Java applets looks very different from the standard Oracle stack, the server-side stack looks and functions identically to the one shown in Table 2-1. You see, by the time the request is processed through the thin JDBC communications stack, it looks just like any other request that's received by the server through Net8.

Oracle-Compatible Protocols

Oracle Corporation has created a set of protocols that are Oracle's own implementation of the transport layer. To understand what that means, let's review very briefly the ISO/OSI model transport layer. Acting locally, the network transport layer does many jobs. Here is a list of tasks that the transport layer performs:

- Determines another route for a transmission if there's a problem within the network, or saves data until the network connection is reestablished.
- Ensures that received data is in the correct format and proper order by opening each packet to verify that none of the contents are missing or damaged.
- Breaks data into uniformly sized packets, as required by the network layers below it, to be sent across the network.
- Reassembles the packets in the original chunk of information when a transmission is received.
- Numbers each packet so that should the packets arrive out of order at their destination, they'll be reassembled in the correct order.
- Notifies the sending computer that a message has been received without error.
- Notifies the transmitting machine to wait before sending more information if the frame buffer on the receiving machine is full.
- If available, multiplexes messages or sessions.

Several transport protocols can be used on one machine to resolve disparities. The Transmission Control Protocol (TCP) has been adopted by many companies as a part of their TCP/IP protocol suite and has become the implicit Internet standard.

Okay, now that you have a good grasp of the actions that the network transport layer can take, let's think about what you need to do to make a secondary protocol compatible with the network transport layer. Since there are several different transport protocols available, you will want to ensure that your networking products work with the most commonly used underlying products, right? Well, that's what Oracle has done. Each of the Oracle protocols is responsible for mapping the equivalent functions between its transport network substrate and the specific protocol.

Table 2-6 lists some of the most frequently used protocols that Oracle has matched. In all cases, the assumption is that the Oracle database is running on a host system that supports network communications through the listed protocol.

NOTE
Table 2-6 is not a complete list of the supported protocols.

I'll tell you more about the bequeath protocol, often referred to as the bequeath listener, later in this chapter.

Dedicated Server Processes

By default, Net8 creates dedicated connections to a database. Each time a new client makes a database request, a new connection is established between the client machine across the network and a listener on the server. The listener assigns the client request to a specific operating system network port number and then connects that client through that port number to the database. We'll look more closely at all of this in Chapter 3 when I tell you about the listener. The point for now is that each request that's made requires a separate connection to the database via a different operating system network port number, and each dedicated connection remains until one of the following events occurs:

- The client disconnects the session through application software.
- The connection is timed out due to lack of activity (if it's configured to do so).
- The network, client machine, or server machine disconnects due to a shutdown or reboot of one or more parts of the system.

Note that a physical network failure does not always result in connections being closed. For example, if a network router in a TCP/IP network broke but was repaired within, say, 10 minutes, a client and server connection could appear to be hung until the router was repaired.

Figure 2-3 shows three separate client machines, each with a dedicated connection to the database.

So, now that you know about dedicated connections, do you see any problem with them? As long as there are enough system resources to support the number

Protocol	Description
TCP/IP	Enables client/server conversation over a network using TCP/IP.
TCP/IP with SSL	Enables client/server conversation over a network using TCP/IP and the Secure Sockets Layer (SSL). SSL stores authentication data, such as certificates and private keys, in an Oracle Wallet. When the client initiates a Net8 connection to the server, SSL performs a handshake between the two by using the private key and certificate.
SPX	Enables client/server conversation over a network using SPX/IPX. This protocol is predominantly used in Novell NetWare environments.
Named Pipes	A high-level interface providing interprocess communications between clients and servers (distributed applications). One process (the server side of the application) creates the pipe, and the other process (the client side) opens it by name. What one side writes, the other side can read, and vice versa. Named Pipes is specifically designed for PC LAN environments.
Logical Unit Type 6.2 (LU6.2)	Part of the IBM Advanced Program-to-Program Communication (APPC) architecture, which lets the client and host communicate over an SNA network without forcing the client to emulate a terminal (as in terminal-to-host protocols). APPC architecture allows peer-to-peer communication; the client can initiate communication with the server. An SNA network with the LU6.2 and Physical Unit Type 2.1 (PU2.1) protocols provides APPC. The LU6.2 protocol defines a session between two application programs; LU6.2 is a product-independent LU type. LU6.2 enables an Oracle application on a PC to communicate with an Oracle database. This communication occurs over an SNA network with the Oracle database on a host system that supports APPC.
Bequeath	Enables clients to retrieve information from the database without using the network listener. The bequeath protocol internally spawns a server thread for each client application. In a sense, it does the same operation locally that a remote network listener would do for your connection.

TABLE 2-6. *Oracle-Supported Protocols*

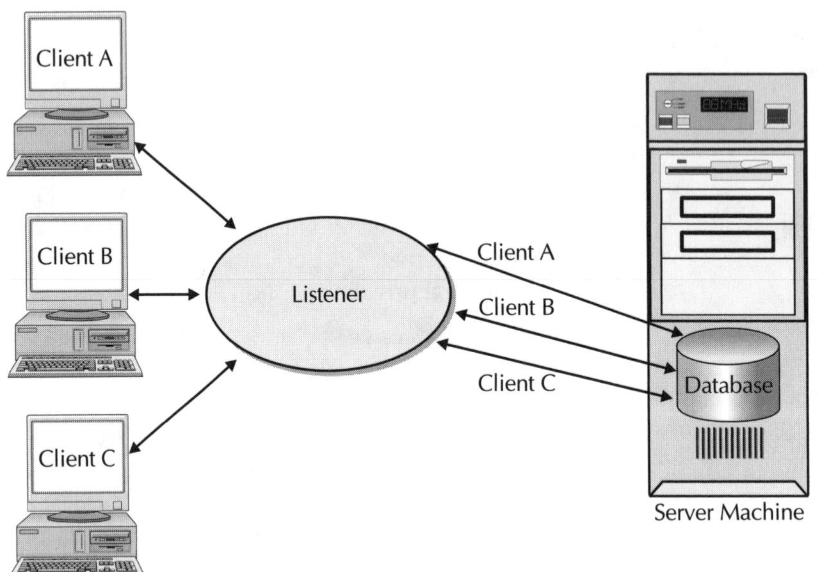
Client A
Client B
Client C
Listener
Client A
Client B
Client C
Database
Server Machine
The client's Net8 software contacts the listener and receives a port assignment. The Net8 software disconnects from the listener and connects through its listener-assigned port address to the database.

FIGURE 2-3. *Three clients with dedicated connections to the database*

of connections to the database, there really isn't a problem. However, since each connection does take some real system resources, if enough dedicated processes are created, eventually you're going to either hit an upper limit in the number of connections the server will allow or run out of resources and be unable to create another process. Oops!

Also, while a person is performing processing activities, the probability is that the person will not be constantly working. I know that when I'm typing a lot, I generally take breaks to get a cup of coffee or eat lunch or stop to ask a question or answer one. Okay, sometimes I do take a few minutes to visit with someone or step away from my desk to "smell the roses." The point is, unless the connection from a process to the database is an automated batch loading or processing job, there's going to be some amount of (wasted) time when each connection is sitting idle and no work is being performed.

Oracle has a multithreaded connection approach that you can use to take advantage of the idle time and enable more clients to be accommodated with less resource use. Let's take a look at this option now.

Multi-Threaded Server Processes

With a dedicated server process, only one client can talk over each connection. As mentioned in the previous section, that's not a bad situation if the machine being used has enough resources to effectively support the number of connections required in an acceptable amount of time. But what happens if the machine doesn't have the necessary resources? Well, if the number of allowable connections has been reached, any other client request will be refused.

Picture this, if you will. You go to make a connection and are refused because the maximum number of connections has been reached. You know for a fact that the person who shares your office space has a connection to the database that she's not using because you watched her log in this morning and know that she has gone to lunch without logging out of the database and terminating her connection. How frustrating!

What's the answer? Oracle has developed a Multi-Threaded Server (MTS) approach that allows one connection to be used by more than one client at a time through a mechanism called a *dispatcher.* A dispatcher handles and directs connections to the database so that less resource is used to support more users. Let's take a look at how MTS works.

Whether you're using dedicated or Multi-Threaded Server connections, the first action that you take when starting your system is to start the *listener*—a device used to listen for connection requests. It listens on either a default address, usually port 1521 or 1526, or the addresses that have been specified in its configuration file, listener.ora. Now that the listener is started, one or more databases are started. As each database starts, it registers itself with the listener. This is a departure from the earlier versions of the networking software in which the databases are started first, and then the listener is started and connects to each active database.

When the database starts, if the appropriate configuration parameters are present in the initialization file, init.ora, dispatchers are started. Each dispatcher then listens on the address that has been assigned to it. When the dispatcher is started, its address is registered with the listener. The dispatcher either will attempt to register with the listener at its default listener address or will use the listener's network name that is specified in the database init.ora file. The listener's network name can resolve to more than one address if multiple listeners are being used. Using this approach, once the dispatchers are registered, the listener can redirect incoming connection requests to the dispatchers.

Once the listener has been brought up and the database and Oracle dispatcher server have registered with it, incoming network sessions can be received. Hmm, what happens in Oracle8i if the databases are brought up before the listener? Well, in that case, the databases will not register successfully with the listener, MTS connections will be refused, and all connections will be made as dedicated connections.

To check which dispatchers have registered with the listener, you can issue a **services** command in the Listener Control Utility (lsnrctl). I'll talk more about this in Chapter 3.

Okay, so now we've got the listener, databases, and dispatchers all up and running and registered. What happens next? Well, let's see. Take a look at Figure 2-4. It shows the client making a connection to the shared server.

Using the listener network address, the client connects to the listener. The listener validates the connection request to determine whether the request may be serviced. If it can't be serviced, the listener refuses the network session. If it can, the listener issues a redirect message to the client. This message contains the network address of the least-used dispatcher for the shared server. Using the dispatcher

1. Client makes a request.
2. Listener determines the least-busy dispatcher address and passes it back to the client.
3. Client disconnects from listener and connects to dispatcher.
4. Dispatcher places request on Shared Server queue.
5. Shared server picks up request and connects to database to process client request.

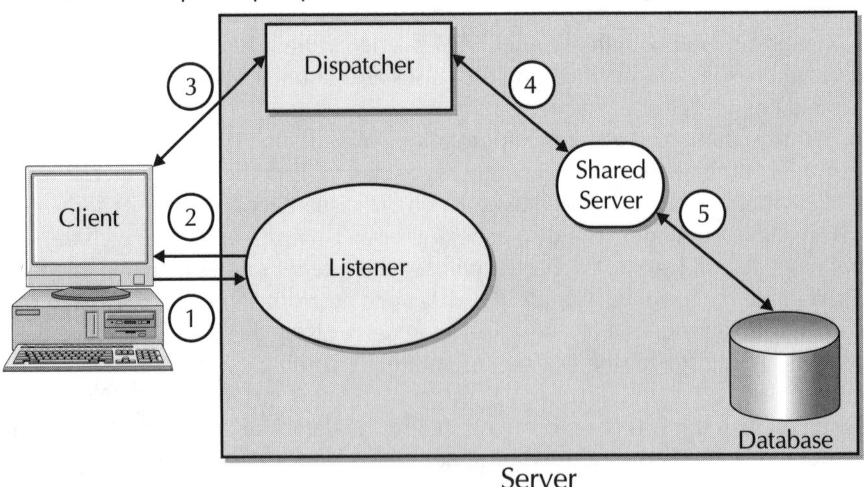

FIGURE 2-4. *Client using a dispatcher to make an MTS connection*

network address provided, the client dissolves the network session to the listener and establishes a network session to the dispatcher. Once the connection has been established, the dispatcher updates the listener with the new load value. In this way, the listener will be able to balance the incoming network session requests between dispatchers running on the same protocol. The dispatcher then places the client request on a queue to be picked up by a shared server.

If the listener refuses a connection because it is invalid, the listener just goes back to listening for new requests and processing them. Once a client disconnects from a dispatcher, the dispatcher remains available, and other incoming requests are processed by the shared server. In this way, it's possible for different requests from the same client to be processed by more than one shared server.

Connection Pooling and Load Balancing

Let's think about the process the listener goes through to determine to which dispatcher it will pass a client request. The listener evaluates each dispatcher load by the number of connections it is currently supporting. As each connection completes and disconnects, the dispatcher notifies the listener so that the current number of active connections for that dispatcher can be recalculated and tracked. This approach is known as *connection load balancing*. If there is more than one dispatcher or more than one node, the listener will take into consideration both the dispatcher load and the number of connections on the node to determine which node and dispatcher to use for a client request.

But how does a dispatcher support multiple users at the same time? Does the dispatcher maintain a physical connection to the database for each client? Well, no. That would reduce the amount of available resources just as much as dedicated servers do. The answer to both of these questions is that *connection pooling* is used. If a client's connection is idle for a specific length of time, a time-out mechanism is used to temporarily release the client's transport connection while still maintaining a logical connection between the dispatcher and the client. In the meantime, the dispatcher can make the now freed physical connection available for a new incoming request. When the idle client becomes active again, the dispatcher reestablishes a physical connection on the client's behalf.

Connection pooling and load balancing can only be used on the server and only if the Multi-Threaded Server option is configured and available. I'll talk more about MTS, connection pooling, and load balancing in Chapter 11.

Multiple Listeners

Earlier, I skimmed over the idea of having more than one listener available to process client requests. Why would you want to have more than one listener on a machine? Multiple listeners are used to help balance the connection load, whether you are using

MTS or not. Using multiple listeners will not reduce the amount of system resources required but can more effectively balance the number of connections that each listener is handling. If you have multiple network interface cards (NICs), you can use multiple listeners to load balance that way as well. I'll talk more about how to configure and use multiple listeners in Chapter 3.

Bequeath Connections

Now that you understand both dedicated and Multi-Threaded Server connections, let's look at a third, much more subtle form of connection. Many Oracle professionals do not realize that there are actually two different forms of listeners available on a system: the Net8 listener and the bequeath protocol or listener. The bequeath listener acts locally to provide the same functionality that the Net8 listener provides for a client to a remote server. It enables clients to retrieve information from the database without using the network listener by internally spawning a server client thread for each client application request.

When you are using a client machine and want to connect directly to a database on a server, you type

```
sqlplus username/password@service_name
```

The **@service_name** portion of the command line signals that you want to make your connection to the database via Net8. Now, let's say that you've connected to the server machine via a telnet session. From the telnet session, you want to use SQL*Plus. When you make your request to connect to the database this time, all you need to do at the operating system prompt is type

```
$ sqlplus
```

The bequeath listener acts on your behalf to make the connection. You don't need to do anything special to activate the bequeath process. It acts automatically. However, you can type the username or the username and password on the same line (if it's a password that you don't mind the world seeing). You do not use a connection string like "@mydatabase" to perform the connection because you're not connecting through the network listener. Also, since the bequeath protocol does not use a network listener, no network listener configuration is required and it's installed by default with the Net8 client software.

The bequeath protocol only works in dedicated server mode and cannot be used in a Multi-Threaded Server (MTS) mode. Oh, and it is supported on Windows NT for 32-bit applications or Windows 95 or 98 for connections to a Personal Oracle8i database for 32-bit applications.

Database Links

Until now, you've seen different forms of connections from client machines to servers that all had one thing in common: The connections were all initiated externally from the operating system level to a specific database. One form of connection that I mentioned earlier very briefly and promised to talk more about is created and initiated from inside the database. It's now time to talk about database links.

The concept of a database link is not hard to understand if you think about the different ways you can get information that you need. Let's say you want to know the names of Santa's reindeer. You can hunt through the house until you find a copy of the book *The Night Before Christmas*, do an Internet search, or either drive over to your local public library to find the book or go to a bookstore and buy the book. Hmm, better yet, you could call the library. That's much easier and much faster. When you make your telephone call, you pick up the telephone receiver and dial the library's number. The phone rings, and with any luck, a librarian answers. You explain that you are looking for the names of Santa's reindeer. Because the librarian doesn't have the information immediately available, he transfers your call to another librarian who supplies the names (Dasher, Dancer, Prancer, Vixen, Comet, Cupid, Donner, Blitzen, and, of course, Rudolph). You say "Thank you" and hang up.

Now, let's think about this scenario for a minute. You called and talked to one person, but another person actually answered your question. You may not have known or cared about the fact that the first person did not know the answer since the end result of your call was that you got the answer you needed. Essentially, a database link provides the same service. You see, a database link enables you to connect from one database to another to access the second database's objects just as though they were within the first database. A database link can be available to everyone who interacts with the database (public) or can be made available only to a person connecting directly to a particular schema (private). Keep in mind, too, that the listener does not supply the answers to your queries. Just as the first librarian passed your question to someone else, the listener passes your connection request through the database link to another database.

We'll look first at the basic architecture of a database link. Then we'll examine how a database link is created and the different objects you can access and actions you can take when using one.

Basic Database Link Architecture

In the world of Oracle databases, there's no rule that says you can't have databases with the same name on different machines. Hmm, if you can have a database called ORDDB on several different machines and you want to be able to create connections to all of the databases at the same time, how are you going to designate which database you're actually connecting to?

Although each database has its own individual name, you must ensure that each database on the system has a unique global name. Generally, the network domain name for each node is unique within your system. Therefore, putting the network domain name in front of the individual database name creates a database's global name. Let's say first that all of the databases we're dealing with in this example belong to the XYZ Company. The XYZ Company, by the way, manufactures a complete line of skingwaddles. Figure 2-5 shows the hierarchical chart for the company's offices and databases. There are four production databases in different parts of the United States that are used for specific tasks. The databases that reside in Vienna, Virginia, and Fresno, California, receive and store orders for the entire United States, while the two databases in Denver, Colorado, track the manufacturing and shipping information for

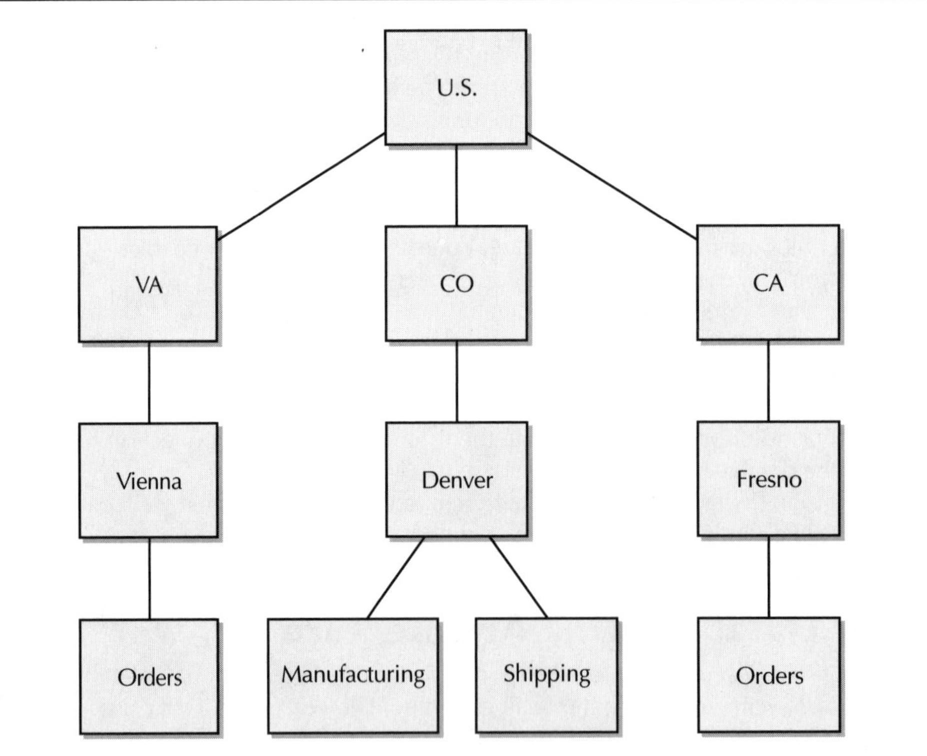

FIGURE 2-5. *Hierarchy chart for the XYZ Company, U.S. division*

the company. The domain names for these databases start with the nomenclature "us" to indicate that they all reside in the United States. The network global domain name for the database in Virginia is us.va.vienna.orders, while the database in California is us.ca.fresno.orders. There isn't an orders database in Denver, but the network global domain name for the shipping database is us.co.denver.shipping. Once you know the database name for an area, it's easy to put the database global name together by adding it to the global domain name. Therefore, the database global name you can create for Virginia's ORDDB database would be us.va.vienna.orders.orddb.

To let Oracle know that you are going to enforce global naming, you set the initialization parameter GLOBAL_NAMES to TRUE. Oracle then ensures that the name of the database link is the same as the global database name of the remote database. If you set GLOBAL_NAMES to FALSE, you don't have to use global naming. If you require more than one public database link to the same remote database, you will not be able to use global naming. However, Oracle Corporation strongly recommends that you use global naming whenever possible because many useful features, including Oracle Advanced Replication, require that global naming be enforced.

Now that you understand how to create and use global names, we can think about how a database link would help us to gather information about the total orders that have been taken and shipped. You see, database links are a wonderful way to hide the actual location of data. They enable users to obtain information from remote databases easily and transparently. Through a database link, users can insert, update, or delete information from both local and remote databases simultaneously.

Creating a Database Link

To create a database link, you must first decide whether the link is to be public, private, or global. If you create a public database link, anyone who can access the database, including PL/SQL subprograms, can access information through the link. If you create a private database link, only users or PL/SQL subprograms connected to the specific account that owns the link can access information through it. With a global database link, all of the users and PL/SQL subprograms in any database can access data and database objects in the corresponding remote database.

To create a private database link, you need the **create database link** privilege, while to create a public database link, you need the **create public database link** privilege. You must also have the **create session** privilege in the database you are going to connect to. Oh, and the Net8 software must be installed on both machines that are involved. It's possible to access non-Oracle databases through a database link from an Oracle database, but you'll need to have the Oracle Heterogeneous Services installed to do that. For global database links, you must use the Oracle Names software and define the global database link from that tool. I'll tell you more about global database links in Chapter 4.

Determining the Type of Link to Create

To determine the type of database links you need to employ in a distributed database, you must consider the specific requirements of the applications using the system. Let's look at an advantage of each type of database link:

- With a private database link, you have a more secure environment than with a public or global link, because only the owner of the private link, or subprograms within the same schema, can use the private link to access the specified remote database.
- If many users require an access path to a remote Oracle database, you can create a single public database link for all users in a database. By using a public database link, you enable many users to connect to a remote database transparently.
- If your Oracle network uses Oracle Names, you can conveniently manage global database links for all databases in the system and enable many users to access several databases seamlessly. This approach makes database link management centralized and simple.

The Create Database Link Syntax

Now, let's look at the syntax for creating a public database link. The minimum information you must supply to create this database link is

```
create public database link <DBLINK_NAME>
connect to <USER> identified by <PASSWORD>
using '<CONNECTION STRING>';
```

To create a public database link using the global naming shown earlier to connect the database in Vienna, Virginia, to the ORD schema in the California database, you'd use the following:

```
create public database link US.CA.FRESNO.ORDERS
connect to ORD identified by HAPPY_2B
using '@ORDDB';
```

Now, here's an example of how to create a private database link that does not use the global conventions. Let's say you want to connect the schema called NELSON in MYDB1 to the same schema in MYDB2. Logged in as NELSON, the syntax you'd use is

```
create database link MYLINK
connect to NELSON identified by OSOSILLY1
using '@MYDB2';
```

In this case, since the user is the same in both databases, you could also use the **current_user** parameter (explained in Table 2-7). Table 2-7 shows the complete set of parameters that you can use with the **create database link** command, along with an explanation of each. I'll tell you more about **current_user** a bit later in this chapter.

Before you look at Table 2-7, let's take a quick look at the syntax for the database link creation statement as shown in Oracle's documentation:

```
create [public|shared] database link <DBLINK>
[connect to [current_user|<USER> identified by <PASSWORD>]]
[authenticated by <SCHEMA> identified by <PASSWORD>]
using '<CONNECT STRING>';
```

Now, take a look at Table 2-7.

Some restrictions associated with naming a database link are

- You cannot create a database link in another user's schema. For example, SUE cannot create a database link in a schema owned by CATHY.
- Since periods are permitted in names of database links, you cannot qualify DBLINK with the name of a schema. For example, Oracle would see the name NELSON.ORDDB as the entire name of the link rather than seeing the name as ORDDB in the NELSON schema.
- The initialization parameter OPEN_LINKS determines and limits the number of different database links that can appear in a single statement.

How to Use a Database Link

Once you've created a database link, how do you actually use it? Let's say you want to determine the total orders for skingwaddles for the month of February across the entire country for the XYZ Company. Remember that the Fresno center takes orders for the Midwestern through western states, while the Vienna center takes all of the orders from the East Coast to the Midwest. Using the public link that was created in the previous section, the query would look like this:

```
select sum(TOTAL_ORDERS)
  from ORD.ORDER_TAB a,ORDER_TAB@US.CA.FRESNO.ORDERS b
 where a.ORDER_DATE between '01-FEB-2000' and '29-FEB-2000'
/
```

Database Link Connections

Let's stop and think for a moment about what's really going on when the database link you've created is used. You have defined a communication path from one database to another and enabled connections to be made from your local database to a remote one. When an application uses your database link to access the remote database, Oracle establishes a session in the remote database on behalf of the local application request using a username and password you have supplied for the connection. That

Parameter	Description
Link Type:	Defines the accessibility of the link to database users.
Shared	Uses a single network connection to create a public database link that can be shared among multiple users. This clause is available only with the Multi-Threaded Server configuration.
Public	Creates a public database link available to all users. If you omit this clause, the database link is private and is available only to you.
DBLINK	The complete or partial name of the database link.
Connection Clause (connect to):	Establishes a connection to the remote database.
current_user	Creates a current user database link. The current user must be a global user with a valid account on the remote database for the link to succeed. If the database link is used directly—that is, not from within a stored object—then the current user is the same as the connected user. When executing a stored object (such as a procedure, view, or trigger) that initiates a database link, **current_user** is the username that owns the stored object, not the username that called the object. For example, if the database link appears inside procedure NELSON.PROC (created by NELSON), and user ROZ calls procedure NELSON.PROC, the current user is NELSON. However, if the stored object is an invoker-rights function, procedure, or package, the invoker's authorization ID is used to connect as a remote user. For example, if the privileged database link appears inside procedure NELSON.PROC (an invoker-rights procedure created by NELSON), and user ROZ calls procedure NELSON.PROC, then **current_user** is ROZ and the procedure executes with ROZ's privileges.

TABLE 2-7. *Create Database Link Parameters*

USER identified by PASSWORD	Specifies the username and password used to connect to the remote database (fixed user database link). If you omit this clause, the database link uses the username and password of each user who is connected to the database (connected user database link).
Authenticated_clause	Specifies the username and password on the target instance. This clause authenticates the user to the remote server and is required for security. The specified username and password must be a valid username and password on the remote instance. The username and password are used only for authentication. No other operations are performed on behalf of this user. You must specify this clause when using the **shared** clause.
using 'CONNECT STRING'	Specifies the service name of a remote database.

TABLE 2-7. *Create Database Link Parameters* (continued)

information has to be stored somewhere in the local database, right? Maybe, or maybe not. You see, there are several different ways that you can create the database link and several parameters that you can use to determine whether you will have to specify and store a password.

In the case of a *fixed user* database link, you supply a username and password to enable the connection to be made. The sample **create database link** statements I used earlier were all fixed user links. When an application uses a fixed user database link, the local server always establishes the connection to a specific, fixed remote schema in the remote database, and the user's credentials are always sent across the network.

Another form of connection that you can create is a *connected user* database link. To create a connected user link, you merely omit the CONNECT TO clause in your **create database link** statement like this:

```
create database link US.CA.FRESNO.ORDERS
using 'ORDERS';
```

The other form of connection that you can use is called a *current user* database link. The syntax you use to create the link is as follows:

```
create database link US.CA.FRESNO.ORDERS
connect to current_user
```

To use a current user database link, the current user must be a global user that is authenticated by the Oracle Security Server.

NOTE
At the time of this writing, the global user utility is being rewritten and may not be available for use.

Security Problem with Database Links

Let's think about the possible problem involved with storing an account password in the data dictionary. There are five different ways that you can see information in the Oracle data dictionary about a database link. You can use DBA_DB_LINKS, ALL_DB_LINKS, USER_DB_LINKS, V$DBLINK, or LINK$. If you use either the DBA_DB_LINKS or ALL_DB_LINKS view, you will see the information displayed in Table 2-8. You will notice that there is no PASSWORD column included in either of these views.

So, there's no problem there.

Now we're ready to move on to the third way mentioned above to view a database link. The next view that can be used should really cause you concern. It's the USER_DB_LINKS view. Let's take a look at this view and the problem involved.

Column	Definition
OWNER	Owner of the database link
DB_LINK	Name of the database link
USERNAME	Name of user to log in as
HOST	Connect string
CREATED	Creation time of the database link

TABLE 2-8. *The DBA_DB_LINKS View*

Using Oracle 8.1.6., the **describe** command gives the following output for USER_DB_LINKS:

```
SQL*Plus: Release 8.1.6.0.0 - Production on Sun May 14 22:50:53 2000
(c) Copyright 1999 Oracle Corporation.  All rights reserved.

Connected to:
Oracle8i Enterprise Edition Release 8.1.6.0.0 - Production
With the Partitioning and Java options
JServer Release 8.1.6.0.0 - Production

describe USER_DB_LINKS
Name                                      Null?    Type
----------------------------------------- -------- ----------------------------
DB_LINK                                   NOT NULL VARCHAR2(128)
USERNAME                                           VARCHAR2(30)
PASSWORD                                           VARCHAR2(30)
HOST                                               VARCHAR2(2000)
CREATED                                   NOT NULL DATE
```

Oh dear, look! The column PASSWORD is clearly displayed in the view. You would immediately assume that the column will contain an encrypted password, right? Let's take a look and see how this column is displayed. The output from a private database link is

```
DB_LINK                              USERNAME   PASSWORD   HOST       CREATED
------------------------------------ ---------- ---------- ---------- ---------
MYLINK.US.ORACLE.COM                 IAN1       IAN1       avenger    16-JAN-00
```

The password is clearly displayed. Ugly!

Now, let's see the columns in V$DBLINK. Table 2-9 shows this view.

Well, there's no problem here. No password is displayed or available. By the way, this view is great. You can use it to describe all of the database links (links with IN_TRANSACTION = YES) that are opened by the session issuing the query (in this case, your session).

Okay, let's look at LINK$ now. The only way to see the columns in LINK$ is to connect to the database as SYS or INTERNAL. Here are the columns in LINK$:

```
Column Name                    Null?    Type
------------------------------ -------- ----------------
OWNER#                         NOT NULL NUMBER
NAME                           NOT NULL VARCHAR2(128)
CTIME                          NOT NULL DATE
HOST                                    VARCHAR2(2000)
USERID                                  VARCHAR2(30)
PASSWORD                                VARCHAR2(30)
FLAG                                    NUMBER
AUTHUSR                                 VARCHAR2(30)
AUTHPWD                                 VARCHAR2(30)
```

Column	**Definition**
DB_LINK	Name of the database link
OWNER_ID	Owner of the database link UID
LOGGED_ON	Whether the database link is currently logged on
HETEROGENEOUS	Whether the database link is heterogeneous
PROTOCOL	Communication protocol for the database link
OPEN_CURSORS	Whether there are open cursors for the database link
IN_TRANSACTION	Whether the database link is currently in a transaction
UPDATE_SENT	Whether there has been an update on the database link
COMMIT_POINT_STRENGTH	The value given a distributed transaction on the database link to control the order in which transactions are committed

TABLE 2-9. *The V$DBLINK View*

Oops! Not only can you see the password, you can also get the authorized user and authorized password. "Ah, but," you say, "you have to be a privileged user to get to this view and see these passwords." True. However, this is still a security hole that you must be aware of so that you can take measures to protect your database. Let's be a bit nosy and see what information is in this table.

```
column NAME format a15
column HOST format a10
column USERID format a10
column PASSWORD format a18
column OWNER# format 9999999
select OWNER#, HOST, USERID, PASSWORD
  from LINK$;

  OWNER# HOST       USERID     PASSWORD
-------- ---------- ---------- ------------------
       0 case       SYS        ONLY_FOR_A_MINUTE
      49 orcl.world HR         PUFFINSTUFF
```

Not much of a security breach here, huh!

Another security consideration is that you are sending the username and password over a network. If you are on an unsecured network to support your distributed database and you use fixed user database links, you should consider encrypting the login packets for your server-to-server connections.

About Shared Database Links

Earlier in this chapter, you learned about dedicated connections and Multi-Threaded Server connections. By default, each database link connection that you make is a dedicated connection. That means that if many users are running an application simultaneously, there can be a huge number of database link connections occurring at the same time.

Just as Multi-Threaded Server connections enable you to support many users connecting to a server over a limited number of network connections, shared database links let you limit the number of network connections from one server to another while supporting multiple users. To use shared database links, the local server must run in MTS mode. The remote server can run in either MTS mode or dedicated server mode.

This is not a cure-all, and it's possible to actually reduce rather than improve performance if you use shared database links incorrectly; so be sure to proceed with caution when using this feature.

When to Use a Shared Database Link

To determine whether a shared database link is appropriate, look at the total number of concurrent connections using each specific database link on your system. If only a few users are connecting at once, a shared database link is not appropriate. As the number of concurrent users increases, the need for shared database links will also increase.

In other words, if you've designed your application to use a standard public database link and 50 users simultaneously access the link, 50 direct network connections will be created and used. In the same situation, however, if you use shared database links and there are 10 shared servers in the local, Multi-Threaded Server mode, the 50 users will only require a maximum of 10 network connections (and possibly fewer). You see, each local shared server may only need one connection to the remote server to support more than one connection request from the local database.

Creating a Shared Database Link

Okay, so you've determined that a shared database link is necessary for your system. To create one, you must use the keyword **shared** in your **create database link** statement as follows:

```
create shared database link <DBLINK_NAME>
authenticated by <SCHEMA_NAME> identified by <PASSWORD>;
```

Those are the mandatory keywords. You can include the keywords **connect to**, **identified by**, **connect to current_user**, and **using** as well, but these keywords are optional. The only privilege required on the remote database account to which you are connecting is the **create session** privilege. Note that you must use the **authenticated by** clause, and there must be an account on the remote database with the specified username and password. However, the schema that you specify in the **authenticated by** clause is used strictly for security reasons, so it can be a dummy schema.

CHAPTER 3

Oracle Net8 Components

hen you make an operator-assisted phone call, you pick up a telephone receiver, dial zero, and you are connected to an operator who has been waiting to assist you. It is the operator's job to listen for requests and attempt to fulfill them. You tell him who you are calling and the telephone number. The operator, acting on your behalf, dials the number and then disconnects from your line. Once your call has been passed on to another line you remain connected to your party, even if the operator goes out to lunch. Whether you hang up or not, the operator is still at a switchboard waiting to receive and assist in connecting calls (if he hasn't gone to lunch, that is).

In the same way, after you've started the Oracle Net8 listener, it will be available to listen for incoming requests, to process those requests, and, even after you've disconnected, will remain available to process other clients' connections. You see, the Oracle Net8 listener is actually a detached process that runs from the time it's started until a listener shutdown request is received or the machine that it's on is shut down or crashes. Even if the listener is interactively started from the server and no one is logged on to the server, the listener will continue to run until something stops it. When an Oracle database starts, it will try to register itself to the listener by passing information such as its database service names and instance names.

In this chapter, you'll learn about the listener and the component files that support it. I'll give you an overview of the Oracle-supplied Net8 utilities and the Oracle Enterprise Manager so that you'll be ready to work with these tools in later chapters.

Net8 Components and Parameters

To begin our exploration of the Net8 components, let's concentrate on connections to the Oracle database since they are the most common forms of connection used. Keep in mind, though, that Net8 also supports connections to non-Oracle databases, gateways, and external procedures, such as functions that can be called from a PL/SQL program.

Before I begin talking about the listener and connections, I want to make sure that you understand the difference between a service name and a server name. A *server name* refers to a physical machine that contains one or more Oracle databases. Within a network, each server has a specific, unique address, as described in Chapter 1. You can use either the name or the network address to refer to a server. On the other hand, a *service name* is a logical representation of one or more instances and may contain a database name. Later in this chapter, I'll show you how to use the tnsnames.ora and init.ora files to identify a service. The service name is a string variable comprising the database name and domain name. You enter the values during installation or database creation, and they are held in memory to make them available during the initial network configuration operations.

Now, let's get on to making a connection.

Making a Connection

When you want to connect from your client machine to a database on a server, you use a connection string that contains a username, password, and net service connection information to tell Net8 how and where to make the connection. For example, if you want to connect to a net service named MYDB with the username NELSON and the password HOP_SCOTCH2, your connection string is

```
connect NELSON/HOP_SCOTCH2@MYDB
```

To perform the connection, the Net8 client software must resolve the connection string to the actual network route to the service, including the listener location through a protocol address and global database name, which generally contains the database and database domain names. Gee, that sounded impressive, but what does it mean? All I'm really saying is that the Net8 client software is written to go out and ask the system network software for the actual network address of the machine that you're trying to connect to. The client software decomposes the global database name into its subparts so that it knows which database it's attempting to connect to. Once the machine address and the database name are obtained, the client program goes to the listener on that machine to request the connection to the database. We've talked about network addresses in Chapter 1 and global database names in Chapter 2.

When a client initiates a request, via a specific protocol, the receiving listener verifies the information passed to it and matches the information that has been registered both in the database service and in the listener's own listener.ora file to determine whether the client request may be serviced. If everything is correct and verifiable and the client request can be serviced, the listener spawns a process or uses a prespawned process. Through the spawned or prespawned process, communication between the client and the database is enabled. After the client connection request is passed to a process, the listener is free to continue to listen for requests.

Several different configuration files are used to support connections between clients through a listener to an Oracle database. The files that you use to configure and support Net8 are shown in Table 3-1.

NOTE

If Net8 connections are going to be made from server to server, both the sqlnet.ora and tnsnames.ora files will need to be present on the server.

File Name	**Description**
listener.ora	Located on the server, this file includes addresses of all listeners on a server and various control parameters used by the listener.
tnsnames.ora	Located on the client(s), this file includes a list of net service names and their listener address and service descriptions.
sqlnet.ora	Located on the client(s), this file includes the names resolution method.
names.ora	Located on the Oracle Names server, this file includes the location, domain information, and optional configuration parameters for each Names server (assuming the Oracle Names server is used).

TABLE 3-1. *Net8 Configuration Files*

You will find the Net8 configuration files listener.ora, tnsnames.ora, and sqlnet.ora in the following directory locations:

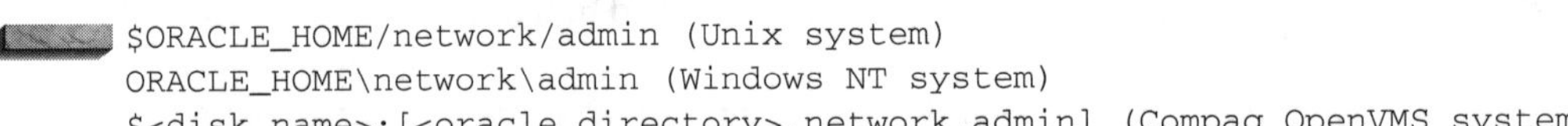

```
$ORACLE_HOME/network/admin (Unix system)
ORACLE_HOME\network\admin (Windows NT system)
$<disk_name>:[<oracle_directory>.network.admin] (Compaq OpenVMS system)
```

Let's take a look at each of the files and examine the composition and how the entries are used.

Listener.ora

Let's be honest right from the beginning. Configuring the listener is not always the easiest task that you will face. With years of practice, I don't always get it exactly right the first time myself. But, don't despair! The more you understand the composition and contents of the listener.ora file, the easier this task will be.

Each server that has an Oracle database must have a listener.ora file to enable a listener to run on that server. The listener.ora file contains the parameters that are used to configure the listener. The file is broken into four separate areas: the header information, the Listener Address section, the SID_LIST_<lsnr> Static Service section where the system identifier is described, and the Control Parameters section. Table 3-2 lists the different sections and describes what each one contains.

Let's walk through the sample listener.ora file that was delivered with my Oracle8i version 8.1.5 Windows NT distribution. The entire sample file is delivered

Section	Purpose
Header	Contains version and date-created information
Listener Address	Defines the listener protocol address and the presentation and session layers to use
SID_LIST_<lsnr>	Defines the system identifier (SID) of the database served by the listener
Control Parameters	Controls the behavior of the listener

TABLE 3-2. *Listener.ora Sections and Their Purpose*

with all of the lines commented out. The comment indicator is the pound sign (#) at the beginning of each line. I'll present a group of lines and then talk about them. I'll try to identify the sections as I go along since I've split the sample file into smaller pieces than the four sections listed above.

Header Section

```
# copyright © 1997 by the Oracle Corporation
#
# NAME
#   listener.ora
# FUNCTION
#   Network Listener startup parameter file example
# NOTES
#   This file contains all the parameters for listener.ora,
#   and could be used to configure the listener by uncommenting
#   and changing values.  Multiple listeners can be configured
#   in one listener.ora, so listener.ora parameters take the form
#   of SID_LIST_<lsnr>, where <lsnr> is the name of the listener
#   this parameter refers to.  All parameters and values are
#   case-insensitive.
```

This is the header section for the sample file. There's actually a lot of information in this little section. After the copyright date, you can see the name of the file and its purpose. Within the notes section, several important pieces of information tell you that

- You can use this file by uncommenting (removing the initial pound signs from) sections of the file and inserting your specific configuration information.

- You can configure more than one listener within this file.
- To identify each listener, you replace each occurrence of <lsnr> with the listener name that you want to use.
- There is no case sensitivity, so you can use upper- or lowercase or a mix of the two within the file.

The point about identifying a listener by replacing each occurrence of <lsnr> with the listener name is one that's tripped me up more than once. It's very easy to overlook an occurrence of the name and miss a parameter that must be set for a new listener.

In my Oracle8i listener file for a Windows NT system (shown below), the actual header information is only two comment lines without a copyright date or notes. Because of the length of the file name, the first line has wrapped and appears to be on two lines, but it really is only on one very long line. Both the full file name and the location of the file are listed on the first line, while the "creator" is listed on the second. When the Net8 product set is installed, the Oracle Net8 Assistant tool automatically generates a listener.ora file. The Net8 Assistant is a wonderful tool that you can use to set up your listener and configure the associated files. However, if you have to troubleshoot any of these files, you really must know the underlying code, or you probably won't stand a chance of fixing the problem. The tools are wonderful, and I'll tell you much more about them throughout the book, but you can't rely on them to do 100 percent of your work.

```
# D:\ORA8I\NETWORK\ADMIN\LISTENER.ORA Configuration
File:D:\ora8i\network\admin\listener.ora
# Generated by Oracle Net8 Assistant
```

Listener Address Parameters

By default, if you are running only one listener on a system, the listener's name is LISTENER. Pretty obvious, right? Well, no, not necessarily. If you don't realize that the listener's name is LISTENER and you try to configure a new one, you're probably going to miss some of the parameters that need to be changed. Oh, and by default, for earlier versions of SQL*Net and Net8, the password for the default listener is ORACLE.

Here's a sample piece of listener configuration code. Your task is to duplicate and modify this code to retain the existing LISTENER version and add a new listener named MYLIST1. See if you can identify all of the places where you need to substitute MYLIST1. I'll wait.

```
LISTENER =
  (ADDRESS_LIST =
```

```
          (ADDRESS=
            (PROTOCOL= IPC)
            (KEY= oracle.world)
          )
          (ADDRESS=
            (PROTOCOL= TCP)
            (Host= marlenes-pc)
            (Port= 1526)
          )
  )
STARTUP_WAIT_TIME_LISTENER = 0
CONNECT_TIMEOUT_LISTENER = 10
TRACE_LEVEL_LISTENER = 0
SID_LIST_LISTENER =
  (SID_LIST =
    (SID_DESC =
      (GLOBAL_DBNAME = marlenes-pc)
      (SID_NAME = ORCL)
    )
  )
PASSWORDS_LISTENER = (oracle)
```

If you looked ahead, you know that the very first line needs to be changed, as do five others. Here's my answer:

```
LISTENER =
  (ADDRESS_LIST =
          (ADDRESS=
            (PROTOCOL= IPC)
            (KEY= oracle.world)
          )
          (ADDRESS=
            (PROTOCOL= TCP)
            (Host= marlenes-pc)
            (Port= 1526)
          )
  )
STARTUP_WAIT_TIME_LISTENER = 0
CONNECT_TIMEOUT_LISTENER = 10
TRACE_LEVEL_LISTENER = 0
SID_LIST_LISTENER =
  (SID_LIST =
    (SID_DESC =
      (GLOBAL_DBNAME = marlenes-pc)
      (SID_NAME = ORCL)
    )
  )
```

```
PASSWORDS_LISTENER = (oracle)
#
# Here's the part that was added to define the second listener, MYLIST1
#
MYLIST1 =
  (ADDRESS_LIST =
        (ADDRESS=
          (PROTOCOL= IPC)
          (KEY= oracle.world)
        )
        (ADDRESS=
          (PROTOCOL= TCP)
          (Host= marlenes-pc)
          (Port= 1521)
        )
  )
STARTUP_WAIT_TIME_MYLIST1 = 0
CONNECT_TIMEOUT_MYLIST1 = 10
TRACE_LEVEL_MYLIST1 = 0
SID_LIST_MYLIST1 =
  (SID_LIST =
    (SID_DESC =
      (GLOBAL_DBNAME = marlenes-pc)
      (SID_NAME = MYDB)
    )
  )
PASSWORDS_MYLIST1 = (mypassword)
```

Of the many changes I made to configure the new listener, I think the most subtle change was in the SID_LIST_MYLIST1 where the new SID_NAME is defined.

Did you catch all of the needed changes? Good job! We'll talk more about the other parameters as we go along.

Listener Address Section Continued

Okay, let's continue to the next section of the listener.ora file.

```
# <lsnr>
#   This parameter specifies both the name of the listener, and
#   its listening address(es). Other parameters for this listener
#   use this name in place of <lsnr>.  When not specified,
#   the name for <lsnr> defaults to "LISTENER", with the default
#   address value as shown below.
#
# LISTENER =
#  (ADDRESS_LIST=
```

```
#       (ADDRESS=(PROTOCOL=tcp)(HOST=localhost)(PORT=1521))
#       (ADDRESS=(PROTOCOL=ipc)(KEY=PNPKEY)))
```

The comments in the first part of the Listener Address section reiterate what I said in the previous section and give you the beginning code for the **address_list** section as you saw in the previous example. The **protocol** being used in this example is TCP. The parameters used with TCP are **host** and **port**. The **host** value that you use is the network name of the server that your listener is going to be running on. If the network machine name is MARLENES-PC, that's the value that will go into the **host=** parameter.

By default, the **port** values that Oracle uses for a listener are 1521 and 1526. However, when you use a port designation, you can use any port number that is not assigned to another process. Oracle can use any port number from 1 to 65535, but port numbers below 1024 are usually reserved for privileged access on some systems. Table 3-3 lists some of the port assignments that Oracle commonly uses.

Port Number	Description
1521	Default listening port for client connections to a database service. In future releases, this port number may change to the officially registered port number of 2483 for TCP/IP and 2484 for TCP/IP with SSL.
2481	The recommended and officially registered listening port for client connections to the Java option using TCP/IP.
2482	The recommended and officially registered listening port for client connections to the Java option using TCP/IP with SSL.
1575	The default and officially registered listening port for an Oracle Names server using TCP/IP or TCP/IP with SSL.
1630	The default and officially registered listening port using TCP/IP for the Oracle Connection Manager CMGW gateway process.
1830	The default and officially registered listening port using TCP/IP for the Oracle Connection Manager CMADMIN administrative process.

TABLE 3-3. *Oracle Registered Port Numbers and Their Uses*

If you are using Two-Task Common or TNS, you do not need a **description_list** definition. However, in order to connect to the Java option in the database, you'll need to use the **protocol_stack**, **presentation**, and **session** description parameters as shown here:

```
LISTENER_NAME =
    (DESCRIPTION_LIST =
          (DESCRIPTION =
              (ADDRESS_LIST =
                (ADDRESS=
                      (PROTOCOL=IPC)
                      (KEY=EXTPROC0)
              )
            )
          )
          (DESCRIPTION =
               (PROTOCOL_STACK =
                      (PRESENTATION=GIOP)
                      (SESSION=RAW)
               )
              (ADDRESS_LIST =
                (ADDRESS =
                      (PROTOCOL=TCP)
                      (HOST=MARLENES-PC)
                      (PORT=2481)
                )
              )
          )
    )
```

In the listing, the area that shows

```
(PROTOCOL_STACK =
       (PRESENTATION=GIOP)
       (SESSION=RAW)
```

contains all new parameters for 8i.

I realize that the parentheses look like I'm wasting a lot of space, but I've learned over the years to be very careful about them, especially in a listener.ora file. You'll see samples and documentation that run them all together; but if you accidentally miss one, the listener won't start, and you can spend hours trying to figure out why. Often, that one missing parenthesis is what's kept the listener down. To help avoid the missing-parenthesis problem, you can insert a one-line comment after a closing brace to promote readability and comprehension. Having warned you sufficiently about parentheses, take a look at the **description_list** area of the Listener Address section.

Under the **description_list** are the listener protocol **address_list=** and **protocol_stack=** descriptions. The **address_list** parameter defines listener protocol addresses with one address per instance. Although you must specify the **address** parameter for each address, the **address_list** parameter is not necessary. However, the Net8 Assistant and Net8 Configuration Assistant tools create an **address_list** each time an address is specified. If you do use the **address_list** parameter, it will be embedded under the description or **description_list**. Within the **protocol_stack=** area, you list the **presentation** type and **session** values. The protocol_stack section of the description is new with Oracle8i and is used for IIOP descriptors to support the Java database connection option.

The choices for the presentation parameter are either TTC or GIOP, with TTC being the default value. IIOP clients require a presentation layer of GIOP. The options for the **session** parameter are either NS or RAW, with NS (Network Substrate) being the default value. IIOP clients require no session layer. Therefore, RAW, indicating that no additional protocol layering is needed, should be used for them.

Now, what about the **key** parameter? That's always paired with the Inter-Process Communications (IPC) protocol and is used as a way of identifying the server that's involved. Oracle Corporation recommends using the name of the service. In the example, EXTPROC0 is the machine or service name.

SID List Section

The next section of the listener.ora file contains the list of services, instances, and/or databases that the listener needs to know about. This is the area of the file in which you tell the listener where and how to locate a specific instance, service, or database.

```
# SID_LIST_<lsnr>
#   List of services the listener knows about and can connect
#   clients to.  There is no default.  See the Net8 Administrator's
#   Guide for more information.
#
# SID_LIST_LISTENER=
#   (SID_LIST=
#     (SID_DESC=
#      #BEQUEATH CONFIG
#          (GLOBAL_DBNAME=salesdb.mycompany)
#          (SID_NAME=sid1)
#          (ORACLE_HOME=/private/app/oracle/product/8.0.3)
#      #PRESPAWN CONFIG
#         (PRESPAWN_MAX=20)
#       (PRESPAWN_LIST=
```

```
#             (PRESPAWN_DESC=(PROTOCOL=tcp)(POOL_SIZE=2)(TIMEOUT=1))
#           )
#         )
#       )
```

An example of this section taken from my listener.ora file on a Windows NT system follows.

```
SID_LIST_LISTENER =
  (SID_LIST =
    (SID_DESC =
      (SID_NAME = PLSExtProc)
      (ORACLE_HOME = D:\ora8i)
      (PROGRAM = extproc)
    )
    (SID_DESC =
      (GLOBAL_DBNAME = orc1.world)
      (ORACLE_HOME = D:\ora8i)
      (SID_NAME = ORC1)
      (PRESPAWN_MAX = 99)
      (PRESPAWN_LIST =
        (PRESPAWN_DESC =
          (PROTOCOL = TCP)
          (POOL_SIZE = 10)
          (TIMEOUT = 2)
        )
      )
    )
  )
```

The first parameter encountered is the **SID_LIST_<lsnr>** descriptor used to identify the beginning of the list of system identification (SID) names. When you (or your database administrator) create a database, you tell Oracle what the SID for your database will be. If you're using Parallel Server, you'll probably have more than one distinct SID to identify each instance that will interact with the database. Therefore, there can be more than one SID within the **sid_list**= section for a single database, but each SID will be unique.

Below **sid_list=** is the **sid_desc**= followed by one or more actual parameters. If you are going to use any of the parameters that I discuss next, they must be placed within the **sid_desc=** area in order for the listener to understand them.

The **sid_name** parameter is used to describe the SID of a database. The value for the **sid_name** is operating-system specific.

There are two files in which you can specify a **service_name** value for a database. One is the init.ora file for the database. The other is specified as the **global_dbname**= database's global name in the listener.ora file.

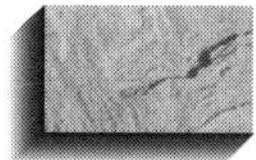

NOTE
If you are going to use the database's global database name, you must ensure that it matches exactly the entry for **service_name** *in the init.ora parameter file.*

To tell the listener the oracle_home directory for the database, you use the **oracle_home=** parameter with the fully qualified directory location. **Program=** is used to declare the service's executable program. In our example above, the program extproc.exe is listed without the file extension.

The next parameter in the example under the **sid_desc** area is **prespawn_max** with a value of 99. To explain this parameter, I'd like you to look back at the example under the **prespawn_list= prespawn_desc=** area. The protocol being described there is TCP (**protocol**=tcp), and a **pool_size** value of 10 is declared just below it. This set of parameters tells the listener that ten dedicated server processes should be precreated or prespawned for this protocol. **Prespawn_max** is the maximum number of dedicated server processes that can be precreated; so it should be set to a number at least as high as the sum of all the **pool_size** values declared. A high number, as shown in this example, is recommended to ensure that enough processes will be available for new client connections. There must be a separate **prespawn_desc=** section for each protocol you want to define.

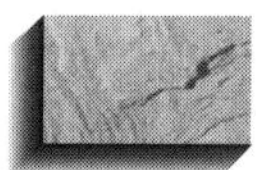

NOTE
Assigning too many dispatchers can have a detrimental effect on performance due to memory consumption factors.

The **timeout=** parameter tells the listener the number of minutes that an inactive prespawned dedicated server process should wait for the next connection. Since a value of 0 lets an inactive shadow process continue indefinitely, the timeout value should be set to a short timeout higher than zero. The timeout parameter is only used for prespawned processes that have had at least one connection; so if a prespawned dedicated server hasn't had any connections at all, it will not time out.

Control Parameters

There are many parameters that you can define for a listener. To more easily view and discuss them, I'm going to abandon displaying the sample listener.ora file and show them to you in Table 3-4.

As I mentioned earlier, by default there is no set listener password in Oracle8i. However, in earlier versions, the listener.ora default file will have the parameter

Parameter	Description/Default/Value/Example
PASSWORDS_<lsnr>	Specifies a password to authenticate stopping the listener. Both encrypted and plain text values can be set. Encrypted passwords can be set and stored using the lsnrctl utility. Default: NONE Example: PASSWORDS_LISTENER = 20A22647832FB454 "foobar"
SAVE_CONFIG_ON_STOP_<lsnr>	Tells the listener to save configuration changes to listener.ora when it shuts down. Changed parameter values will be written to the file while preserving formatting and comments. Default: OFF Values: ON/OFF Example: SAVE_CONFIG_ON_STOP_LISTENER = ON
USE_PLUG_AND_PLAY_<lsnr>	Tells the listener to contact an Onames server and register itself and its services with Onames. Default: OFF Values: ON/OFF Example: USE_PLUG_AND_PLAY_LISTENER = ON
LOG_FILE_<lsnr>	Sets the name of the listener's log file. The .log extension is added automatically. Default: <lsnr> Example: LOG_FILE_LISTENER = lsnr
LOG_DIRECTORY_<lsnr>	Sets the directory for the listener's log file. Default: <oracle_home>/network/log Example: LOG_DIRECTORY_LISTENER = /private/app/oracle/product/8.0.3/network/log
TRACE_LEVEL_<lsnr>	Specifies desired tracing level. Default: OFF Values: OFF/USER/ADMIN/SUPPORT/0-16 Example: TRACE_LEVEL_LISTENER = SUPPORT
TRACE_FILE_<lsnr>	Sets the name of the listener's trace file. The .trc extension is added automatically. Default: <lsnr> TRACE_FILE_LISTENER = lsnr

TABLE 3-4. *Listener.ora Control Parameters*

Parameter	Description/Default/Value/Example
TRACE_DIRECTORY_<lsnr>	Sets the directory for the listener's trace file. Default: <oracle_home>/network/trace TRACE_DIRECTORY_LISTENER=/private/app/oracle/product/8.0.3/network/trace
CONNECT_TIMEOUT_<lsnr>	Sets the number of seconds that the listener waits to get a valid database query after it has been started. Default: 10 CONNECT_TIMEOUT_LISTENER=10

TABLE 3-4. *Listener.ora Control Parameters* (continued)

passwords_<lsnr> automatically set to ORACLE with the default listener name LISTENER. Hmm, if there's no password set, do you want to set one? If you do, how are you going to set or change the password? Glad you asked!

Oracle supplies a utility called Listener Control (lsnrctl) that you can use to start and control the listener directly from the operating system level or through a command file. You can set or modify the password using lsnrctl. Let's take a look at this utility now.

The Listener Control Utility (lsnrctl)

The Listener Control utility is activated when you type **lsnrctl** at your operating system prompt. The command syntax is

```
lsnrctl command [listener_name] arguments
```

For instance, if you want to start a listener named LIST1, you can either type

```
lsnrctl start LIST1
```

or you can type **lsnrctl** at the command line, press ENTER to open the tool, and then type **start LIST1**.

After typing **lsnrctl**, a command line is displayed with header data that tells you which version of Oracle you're interacting with, a copyright date, and how to get help. If you type **help** at the command line prompt, you are presented with a list of command topics to choose from. Unfortunately, there's not much help supplied for each of these commands. For example, if you type **help start**, the utility displays

```
start [<listener_name>] : start listener
```

I'd be willing to wager that you would have guessed that yourself! The list of parameters that you can obtain help on is shown in Table 3-5, with the explanation that the utility provides. For commands and explanations that do not seem obvious or well explained, I'll give more details following Table 3-5 and Table 3-6.

If you've configured the Intelligent Agent (sometimes referred to as the db subagent) to provide an Oracle Enterprise Manager (OEM) listener on your system,

Parameter	Description
start	start [<listener_name>] : start listener
stop	stop [<listener_name>] : stop listener
status	status [<listener_name>] : get the status of the listener
services	service [<listener_name>] : get the service information of the listener
version	version [<listener_name>] : get the version information of the listener
reload	reload [<listener_name>] : reload the parameter files and SIDs
save_config	save_config [<listener_name>] : saves configuration changes to parameter file
trace	trace OFF : USER : ADMIN [<listener_name>] : set tracing to the specified level
dbsnmp_start	dbsnmp_start : start db subagent (otherwise known as the Intelligent Agent)
dbsnmp_stop	dbsnmp_stop : stop db subagent
dbsnmp_status	dbsnmp_status : status db subagent
change_password	change_password [<listener_name>] : changes the password of the listener
test	test the listener
quit/exit	quit : exit : exit LSNRCTL

TABLE 3-5. *lsnrctl Parameters*

<table>
<tr><th>Parameter</th><th>Description</th></tr>
<tr><td>password</td><td>set password : set the password for subsequent calls</td></tr>
<tr><td>rawmode</td><td>set rawmode ON : Off: set output mode for services and status commands</td></tr>
<tr><td>displaymode</td><td>set displaymode RAW | COMPAT | NORMAL | VERBOSE : output mode for listener display</td></tr>
<tr><td>trc_file|trc_directory|
trc_level</td><td>set|show trc_< > [<value>] : set|show trace parameters of current listener</td></tr>
<tr><td>log_file|log_directory|
log_status</td><td>set|show log_< > [<value>] : set|show log parameters of current listener</td></tr>
<tr><td>current_listener</td><td>set|show current_listener [<listener_name>] : sets|shows current listener</td></tr>
<tr><td>connect_timeout</td><td>set|show parm_name [<value>] : sets|shows current listener parm value</td></tr>
<tr><td>startup_waittime</td><td>set|show parm_name [<value>] : sets|shows current listener parm value</td></tr>
<tr><td>use_plugandplay</td><td>set|show parm_name [<value>] : sets|shows current listener parm value</td></tr>
<tr><td>direct_handoff</td><td>DIRECT_HANDOFF can be either ON or OFF</td></tr>
<tr><td>save_config_on_stop</td><td>set|show parm_name [<value>] : sets|shows current listener parm value</td></tr>
</table>

TABLE 3-6. *lsnrctl* ***set*** *and* ***show*** *Parameters*

the commands **dbsnmp_start**, **dbsnmp_stop**, and **dbsnmp_status** are important to learn. They provide a way for you to control and obtain the status of the Intelligent Agent both interactively and from a batch job, but they can only be run locally. I'll talk more about OEM at the end of this chapter.

When you issue the **reload** command, the listener rereads the listener.ora file. You can, therefore, add or change services without actually stopping the listener. If a password is associated with the listener, you must use the **set password** command before issuing the **reload** command. The **services** command provides detailed information about the services the listener is listening for. For example, the **services** command will tell you how many connections have been established and how many have been refused. The **services** command displays three different types of services: dedicated servers from listener.ora, dispatcher information, and prespawned shadow processes.

Two other parameters listed in the lsnrctl help output—**set** and **show**—are followed by an asterisk. The asterisk denotes that additional modifiers or extended commands are associated with the variable. Table 3-6 shows the additional **set** parameters. In many cases, when you type **help set** [<parameter>], the documentation for both **set** and **show** is shown. Table 3-6 reflects this information. You generally use the **show** command first, to see the current value for a parameter, and then use the **set** command to change that value. For example, if you have more then one listener on a node, before you begin to make changes to one of the listeners, you want to determine which listener the lsnrctl utility considers the current listener by issuing

```
show current_listener
```

If the listener displayed is not the one you need, you then issue

```
set current_listener <listener_name>
```

to modify the current listener value. If you're really paranoid, you can issue the **show** command again to verify that the change has been made. Now, take a look at Table 3-6 for the **set/show** command parameters as explained from the lsnrctl help output.

Many of the explanations really don't seem to explain anything, do they. How frustrating! Let's see how you actually use some of the commands or what the explanation is really trying to tell you.

A Closer Look at Some Commands

To start our exploration of nonobvious Listener Control utility commands, let's take a look at the password commands and how they work. There are two commands associated with the listener password: **change_password** and **set password**. The **change_password** command will prompt you for the old and new passwords, ask you to retype the new password, and then change the listener password. The utility will use encryption to match the old password and to set the new one. Here's an example of how the **change_password** parameter works for a listener named LISTENER connecting through an IPC protocol to a service named SRVR:

```
lsnrctl> change_password LISTENER
Old password:
New password:
Reenter new password:
Connecting to (ADDRESS=(PROTOCOL=ipc)(KEY=srvr))
```

```
Password changed for LISTENER
The command completed successfully
```

When you use the **change_password** parameter, you will be able to change the encrypted password for a listener. If there are unencrypted passwords in the listener configuration file (listener.ora), they will be unchanged. You can only create a new encrypted password or change an existing encrypted password through the lsnrctl utility.

At first glance, you would think that the **set password** command could be used to modify a listener password. However, this command is used to activate an already created password. When would you use this command? Let's say you are currently interacting with a listener named LIST1. You've made some changes to that listener, and now you want to make the same changes to another listener named LIST2. LIST2 has a password established in its listener.ora file using the parameter and value

```
passwords_list2 = MYPWD2
```

To switch over to LIST2, you'll first have to set the password for this listener and then make your changes. So, here's what you'll type from the lsnrctl utility:

```
set password <password>
```

Is that the only time you need to use the **set password** command? Well, no, not quite. The rules say that any time you use the **set** command and you have a password set for the listener, you'll have to use the **set password** command prior to using the **set** command. When won't you need to use the **set password** command? You won't need to use it when there is no password established for the listener.

What about the rest of the **set** commands? Here's a list of the others with a brief description of each one.

connect_timeout This command determines the amount of time in seconds the listener will wait for a valid connection request after a connection has been started.

current_listener If there is more than one listener on a node, any **lsnrctl** command acts on the default listener unless another listener has been set. Any subsequent **lsnrctl** commands, within the same **lsnrctl** session, will apply to the second listener, unless you reset **current_listener**. Let's see how that works. We'll say that you have three listeners on your production machine called LIST1, LIST2, and LIST3. To see which listener you're pointing to from the lsnrctl utility, you type

```
lsnrctl> show current_listener
```

If the listener is not the one you need to interact with, you can change the listener you're looking at by typing

```
lsnrctl> set current_listener <listener_name>
```

I know this is going to sound picky, but you must enter the command **set current_listener** from the utility; and once you exit the utility, the setting will be lost.

displaymode This command changes the output of the **lsnrctl service** and **lsnrctl status** commands based on the argument you use. The arguments are as follows: **raw**, which acts the same as **set rawmode**; **compat**, to set the compatibility mode for older versions; **normal**; and **verbose**, to provide more information for support if you are trying to troubleshoot a problem. A note in the Oracle 8.1.5 documentation says **normal** and **verbose** are not fully functional in the 8.1.5 release. The note is missing in the 8.1.6 documentation.

For 8.1.6, **compat** is used as the default value, and there is a note that **raw** should only be used if it is recommended by Oracle World Wide Support.

log_file, log_directory, and log_status The first two commands let you change the file name and directory location of the listener log file. The third command lets you display the log status and is either ON or OFF.

rawmode This command is used to change the output for the **services** and **status** commands. The arguments are either ON or OFF. By setting **rawmode** ON, you will obtain additional information about the listener state that can be helpful if you are trying to debug a problem. Normally, the **rawmode** is left OFF.

save_config_on_stop The arguments for this command are ON and OFF. If you've set this command to ON, any changes you made using the **lsnrctl set** command will be saved to the listener.ora file right after you type **exit** or **quit** but before the listener exits the utility. Saving all of the modified parameters occurs right before the listener exits, taking as much care as possible to preserve the formatting, comments, and capitalization. If you want to have all of the parameters that you've modified saved immediately, you use the **save_config** command.

startup_waittime You set this command to the amount of time, in seconds, that you want the listener to sleep before executing the **start** command. You can only set this parameter at the operating system level. You can set this parameter as follows:

```
lsnrctl set startup_waittime 10
```

trc_file, trc_directory, and trc_level Like the **log_** commands described earlier, the **trc_** commands let you set or show the trace file name, directory location, and level. The available levels are OFF, USER, ADMIN, SUPPORT, 0, 4, 10, and 16. OFF or 0 turns tracing off. USER or 4 displays user information, while ADMIN or 10 provides administration trace information, and SUPPORT or 16 gives you additional information to relay to the Oracle support group while you are performing troubleshooting or problem-solving activities. The higher the level, the more information you will obtain. If you use **set trc_level**, the command will override whatever level has been set in the listener.ora file.

use_plugandplay This command tells the listener to register its information with the Oracle Names server. The arguments for this parameter are ON and OFF.

More on the show Command

For completeness, here's the list of parameters for the **show** command. As you can see, they mirror the **set** command parameters.

- connect_timeout
- current_listener
- displaymode
- log_file, log_directory, log_status password
- raw_mode
- save_config_on_stop
- startup_waittime
- trc_file, trc_directory, trc_level
- use_plugandplay

Tnsnames.ora

The tnsnames.ora file is used to store the configuration information for the Transparent Network Substrate local names. Well, that sounds really fancy, but what does it mean? To more clearly understand what's stored in the tnsnames.ora file, think for a moment about the following names: Bill, Jim, Peg, and Marty. What do they have in common? If you said that they could all be nicknames, you'd be right. Bill can be a nickname for William, and Jim can be a nickname for James. Peg could actually be used in place of either Peggy or Margaret, while Marty could be Martin or Martha. Now, is a nickname the same as an alias? Well, according to my little dictionary, the word "alias" means "otherwise called," so I guess alias and nickname mean about the same thing.

Now, why all this fuss about alias and nickname? You see, on a client machine the tnsnames.ora file defines or describes the names that you use to connect from that machine to the database. On the server, they're the names that the listener uses to enable a connection to the database. When you start the listener in versions earlier than 8.1.5, the listener reads the tnsnames.ora file to look up the name and location of each database that is listed in its listener.ora file. In version 8.1.5 and higher, the database will register its information with the listener when the database is started. Periodically, the listener polls to register databases; so if the database is started first, you'll still get registration with the listener when the listener has started. It might take a bit of time though.

A Sample Tnsnames.ora File in Oracle

Here's the sample tnsnames.ora file that came with my Windows NT version 8.1.5 Net8 installation:

```
# This file contains the syntax information for
# the entries to be put in any tnsnames.ora file
# The entries in this file are need based.
# There are no defaults for entries in this file
# that Sqlnet/Net3 use that need to be overridden
#
# Typically you could have two tnsnames.ora files
# in the system, one that is set for the entire system
# and is called the system tnsnames.ora file, and a
# second file that is used by each user locally so that
# he can override the definitions dictated by the system
# tnsnames.ora file.
```

In the header, you can see that this file must be pretty old because it lists SQL*Net and Net3 (the original name for Net8) but makes no mention of Net8.

As the second paragraph tells you, you can have more than one tnsnames.ora file on a system. The problem, as you'll see in the next chapter when I talk about the Oracle Names server, is that you can get into a real hornet's nest when trying to maintain a large number of tnsnames.ora files to support application developers and end users.

```
# The entries in tnsnames.ora are an alternative to using
# the names server with the onames adapter.
# They are a collection of aliases for the addresses that
# the listener(s) is(are) listening for a database or
# several databases.
```

This section is pretty straightforward. It's just saying that you use the tnsnames.ora file if you are not using the Names server. The entries within the tnsnames.ora file are a collection of aliases for the listener to use to make database connections.

```
# The following is the general syntax for any entry in
# a tnsnames.ora file. There could be several such entries
# tailored to the user's needs.

<alias>= [ (DESCRIPTION_LIST =  # Optional depending on whether u have
                    # one or more descriptions
                    # If there is just one description, unnecessary ]
          (DESCRIPTION=
           [ (SDU=2048) ]      # Optional, defaults to 2048
                    # Can take values between 512 and 32K
           [ (ADDRESS_LIST=    # Optional depending on whether u have
                    # one or more addresses
                    # If there is just one address, unnecessary ]
             (ADDRESS=
             [ (COMMUNITY=<community_name>) ]
             (PROTOCOL=tcp)
             (HOST=<hostname>)
             (PORT=<portnumber (1521 is a standard port used)>)
             )
             [ (ADDRESS=
               (PROTOCOL=ipc)
               (KEY=<ipckey (PNPKEY is a standard key used)>)
             )
             ]
             [ (ADDRESS=
               [ (COMMUNITY=<community_name>) ]
               (PROTOCOL=decnet)
               (NODE=<nodename>)
               (OBJECT=<objectname>)
             )
             ]
               ... # More addresses
```

According to this listing, the syntax for a tnsnames.ora entry is fairly simple. You first list whatever name you want the listener to be listening for. This name is generally referred to as the net service name. If I have a database named MYDB, I can list it within my tnsnames.ora file as anything I want. The only rule is that I'll have to use exactly the same name when I try to make a connection to the database. For example, I could list my alias as MARLENES_DB, but when I go to connect to the database, I'll have to use that exact name in my connection string, as follows:

```
sqlplus MYSCHEMA/MYPASSWORD@MARLENES_DB
```

So even though my database is named MYDB, I invoke it using the alias, or net service name, that I declared in my tnsnames.ora file.

A Real Tnsnames.ora File

Now, let's look at a real tnsnames.ora file to see how the rest of the descriptors and parameters work. Here's what my tnsnames.ora file looks like with a version 8.1.5 default database named ORC1 and a version 8.0.5 default database named ORCL defined:

```
# D:\ORA8I\NETWORK\ADMIN\TNSNAMES.ORA Configuration
File:D:\ora8i\NETWORK\ADMIN\tnsnames.ora
# Generated by Oracle Net8 Assistant

MARLENES-PC.WORLD.MYDOMAIN.COM =
  (DESCRIPTION =
    (ADDRESS_LIST =
      (ADDRESS = (PROTOCOL = TCP)(HOST = marlenes-pc)(PORT = 1526))
    )
    (CONNECT_DATA =
      (SID = ORC1)
    )
  )

ORC1.WORLD.MYDOMAIN.COM =
  (DESCRIPTION =
    (ADDRESS_LIST =
      (ADDRESS = (PROTOCOL = TCP)(HOST = marlenes-pc)(PORT = 1521))
    )
    (CONNECT_DATA =
      (SID = ORC1)
    )
  )

ORCL.WORLD.MYDOMAIN.COM =
  (DESCRIPTION =
    (ADDRESS_LIST =
      (ADDRESS = (PROTOCOL = TCP)(HOST = marlenes-pc)(PORT = 1526))
    )
    (CONNECT_DATA =
      (SID = ORCL)
    )
  )
```

There are three separate entries in this file. The first and second entries provide connection information using two different aliases for the ORC1 database and two different port numbers—the Oracle standard ports 1521 and 1526. Notice too that in both of the top two entries, the SID information is the same.

Tnsnames.ora Parameters

As with the listener.ora file, you can have a **description_list=** area or just have the **description=** keyword. The **description_list** area is used to define the list of descriptors that are associated with the net service name. If you have more than one address stop that must be made before a connection request can reach its destination, you use the parameter **source_route=** with either YES, NO, ON, or OFF and under the address list, the addresses in the order that they are needed. When would you set **source_route=**YES or ON? When you use the Connection Manager, the request must first go from the client to the Connection Manager and then on to the requested machine. So, for Connection Manager routing, you turn **source_route** on.

Another parameter that must be placed under the description area, if it is used, is **type_of_service**. This parameter specifies the type of service to use for an Oracle Rdb database. The Rdb interface tools use the **type_of_service** parameter. This feature should only be used if the application supports both an Oracle Rdb database and Oracle RDBMS database, and you want the application to randomly choose one database or the other for connections. This parameter is used for load balancing.

Below and within the description area are the **address_list=** and **address=** parameters. The address information can be embedded directly below the **description=** parameter without using **address_list=** at all.

Within the address list area, you list parameters based on the type of protocol you're using. Table 3-7 shows some of the protocols and the parameters you use with them.

Although the parameters **host** and **node** are both used to describe the machine that the database resides on, you must use the correct parameter name for the correct protocol or you won't be able to make the connection successfully. Thus,

Protocol	Parameter
TCP	HOST, PORT
IPC	KEY
DECNET	NODE, OBJECT

TABLE 3-7. *Required Protocol Parameters*

you can't list the protocol as TCP and then add the parameter **node** to describe the machine location.

Within the **description_list** area and under **connection_data=**, you can list any of the parameters shown in Table 3-8.

Parameter	Description
service_name	Identifies the release 8.1 service to access and is usually set to the global database name.
global_name	Identifies the Oracle Rdb database.
instance_name	Identifies the database instance name to access. This is usually the system identifier (SID) and can be found in the init.ora parameter file.
failover_mode	Instructs Net8 to fail over to a different listener if the first listener fails during runtime. Depending upon the configuration, any session or any **select** statements that were in-progress are automatically failed over. Failover_mode supports the subparameters BACKUP, TYPE, and METHOD. Below TYPE are SESSION, SELECT, or NONE, and below METHOD are BASIC and PRECONNECT.
hs	Instructs Net8 to connect to a non-Oracle system.
rdb_database	Identifies the name of the Rdb database.
sdu	Instructs Net8 to optimize the transfer rate of data packets being sent across the network with the session data unit (SDU) size you specify. The default is 2048, and the size should be set in a multiple of the normal transport frame size. The normal transport frame size for Ethernet is 1024, and for efficiency, the sdu for Ethernet should be set to no more than four times 1024.
server	Instructs the listener to use a dedicated connection in a Multi-Threaded Server environment by using the value DEDICATED.

TABLE 3-8. ***connection_data*** *Parameters*

A Bit More About Service Names

A service name is a logical representation of a service, which may include a database name. A service may include more than one instance. When creating a net service name, you must identify a release 8.1 service with a service name. Optionally, you may identify a release 8.1 instance with an instance name. Hmm, how do you do that? First, you can insert the parameters **service_name=** and **instance_name=** in the init.ora file of your database. Then, you can list the values in your tnsnames.ora file like this:

```
net_service_name=
(description =
  (address= (protocol_address_information))
  (connect_data=
     (service_name=service_name)
     (instance_name=instance_name)))
```

In this example, notice how the service name is identified by the **service_name** parameter and the instance name is identified by the **instance_name** parameter.

Sqlnet.ora

I travel a great deal. When I began to travel, my travel agent had me fill out a form that described my travel preferences. Included in my travel profile is information about where I like to sit in a plane, whether I prefer an aisle or a window seat, whether I have any special dietary needs, my credit card number, hotel room preferences, and so on. In other words, when I want to make a travel reservation, I call my agent, and she looks at my profile before she starts to make my travel arrangements so that she can book appropriate accommodations for me.

In a similar way, the sqlnet.ora file acts as a profile on each client machine to tell Net8 how to work on behalf of the client to establish and maintain connections and services on the network. Just as my travel profile enables my travel agent to map out my journeys effectively, the sqlnet.ora profile information maps out the prioritization of naming methods, tracing and logging features, security features, and connections through specific processes.

The sample sqlnet.ora file that is delivered with Oracle's Windows NT 8.1.5 version is huge. In Microsoft Word format, the file is almost 50 pages. Here's the header information stating the goal of this file. The section names in the list that are followed by an asterisk are sections that I added but are not listed in the file header. They are sections that are found in the file.

```
# copyright (c) 1996 by the Oracle Corporation
# NAME
#   sqlnet.ora
# FUNCTION
```

```
#   Oracle Network Client startup parameter file example
# NOTES
#   This file contains examples and instructions for defining all
#   Oracle Network Client parameters. It should be possible to read
#   this file and set up a Client by uncommenting parameter definitions
#   and substituting values. The comments should provide enough
#   explanation to enable a reasonable user to manage his TNS connections
#   without having to resort to 'real' documentation.
# SECTIONS
#   ONames Client
#   Client Cache (ONRSD)*
#   Namesctl
#   Native Naming Adapters
#   Advanced Networking Option Network Security*
#   Oracle Security Server*
#   Sqlnet(v2.x) and Net3.0 Client*
```

I've taken the information that appears in each section and formatted it into separate tables for easier viewing. You'll find the tables of profile parameters in Appendix A. You use the sqlnet.ora file when you are configuring

- Domains
- Preferred Oracle Names servers
- Advanced profile information
- Routing connection requests
- Oracle advanced security,

or when you are prioritizing Net Service Name naming method resolution. We'll look more closely at all of these things in Chapters 4 and 6.

Understanding SNMP

Imagine that you are a weather forecaster. You spend your days and nights monitoring the weather and reporting on what is happening in your area. Based on the information that you gather, you project what you think the weather will do in the next several hours. Although you wish you could change or influence it, you can only monitor and report on what the weather is currently doing and what you think it will do in the near future.

The Simple Network Management Protocol (SNMP) has been designed primarily for database, network, and system administrators to use from a central machine to locate, identify, and monitor databases and applications. SNMP is used more for real-time monitoring of Oracle applications during normal operations and spotting and reporting on potential problems rapidly than for managing or modifying an Oracle system and network. Other tools are designed to set or tune system parameters. Because SNMP does not currently have adequate security to be used for changing system parameters, Oracle SNMP Support is designed to query status but make no changes.

A Look Under the Hood

Looking at SNMP as a standard Internet protocol, you find that there are two kinds of machines involved. The first machine type is a *management station* or *managing node* that queries other network nodes or applications to check their status and activities—sort of like your mother calling you daily to see how you are or what you are doing. The call that a management station performs is called an SNMP poll. Any machine or application that can be polled is referred to as a *managed element.* Please note that when I use the word "application" when talking about SNMP, I'm really referring to a database. Okay, so you have a management station polling managed elements on a network. Hmm, that seems pretty straightforward and easy to understand. Let's look further.

The management station uses software to perform its work. This software is known as a *management framework* or *management platform.* Some examples of SNMP management frameworks that Oracle products can be integrated into are CA Unicenter, HP Open View, IBM Netview/6000, DEC Netview POLYCENTER, Sun SunNet Manager, Tivoli, Novell Network Management System, Bull Integrated System Management, Cabletron Spectrum, and Castle Rock SNMP Network Manager.

Each managed element has a *master agent* that communicates with the management framework. Here's how it works. The management framework sends a request to the master agent via SNMP. The master agent then answers with the appropriate response, again through SNMP. The master agent is performing monitoring tasks on a network machine. What happens if an action that the master agent is watching for occurs? Well, the master agent can transmit a message called a *trap* to a known address outside of the management framework if an event occurs. In this way, actions can be quickly taken to avoid or repair possible problems. A structure called a *Management Information Base* (MIB) is located on each managed element that describes the information that SNMP can obtain.

Along with the master agent on each managed element, there can be one or more *subagents* performing monitoring tasks or interacting directly with one or more databases or programs. Note that just because a machine is part of the network, this doesn't automatically mean there is SNMP support on that machine.

An SNMP master agent may or may not be provided directly with your operating system, and the agent provided may or may not be compatible with the Oracle-supplied subagents. Because each operating system is so different from another, I recommend that you use the information supplied with your specific system to determine what, if anything, you need to do to configure SNMP.

Oracle Enterprise Manager and the Intelligent Agent

This past summer, I decided to plant a vegetable garden. I have just a little plot of land in back of my house, so I kept the scope of my gardening small. I decided to plant three tomato and three bell pepper plants. What I didn't realize initially was that the ground in my backyard is extremely rocky. I had a small hoe and a couple of hand tools when I began to prepare the ground for my plants. In very short order, I realized that my tools would not do the job I needed, so I went to a gardening supply shop and bought more suitable tools to work with. I can't say that I had a really easy time after that, but I can say that the tomatoes were delicious!

Oracle supplies several tools with the basic Oracle installation to help you configure the various aspects of Net8. In the next several chapters, you and I will look at these tools together. Right now, however, I'd like to introduce a tool that you can use to more easily see how your Net8 configuration fits together with your nodes and databases.

This tool, known as the Oracle Enterprise Manager (OEM), is supplied free of charge with your basic purchase of the Oracle database software. Along with the Oracle Network Configuration tools, OEM can help you to get your jobs done more easily.

A Look at OEM

The OEM tool set can only be accessed using a Windows environment on a PC, either using Windows 95, Windows 98, or Windows NT. This tool set was introduced in Oracle version 7 and has been released, with a different version number, for each release of the Oracle RDBMS. For example, Oracle8.0.3 was released with OEM version 1.5, Oracle8.0.5 was released with OEM 1.6, while Oracle8.1.5 has been released with OEM 2.0.4, and Oracle8.1.6 is released with OEM 2.0.5.

I'm going to focus on the features offered in the OEM version 2.0.5 release because it is compatible with the earlier Oracle releases from Oracle7.3 forward and offers the richest set of options currently available.

The Oracle Enterprise Manager tool set is a GUI tool that offers you a way to manage databases from one central PC. But what does the OEM have to do with networking? Well, you use networking to examine the configuration of each of your databases and to perform general database administration tasks. These abilities are provided with the basic tool delivery. Along with the basic tools, Oracle also offers three extra-cost options that enable a DBA to automatically run monitoring tasks and jobs from a remote console to any database on the system. To be able to interact with each database, the server that the database resides on must have an

OEM listener (referred to as an Intelligent Agent or db subagent) running. You can only configure one Intelligent Agent per server, and you must register each of the available databases for that server in the Intelligent Agent's configuration file so that OEM can "discover" each of the available databases. Even if you are not the DBA for your organization, if you perform network configuration, you may be called upon to configure the Intelligent Agents for each of the operating systems that support Oracle databases on your network. Right now, let's look at the part SNMP plays in the OEM world.

SNMP and OEM

Although it does not use SNMP directly, OEM can interact with subagents using the Transparent Network Substrate or non-TNS methods. If SNMP is available on the managed element, the database subagents (Intelligent Agents) can interact with both OEM and the SNMP master agent to communicate problems or convey information.

Figure 3-1 shows a management station with a management framework using SNMP to communicate with a master agent. The master agent talks to a subagent through SNMP, but the subagent is using Net8 to talk to an Oracle database. OEM can communicate with the subagent through the TNS or through a non-TNS protocol. The Intelligent Agent works independently from the databases and any other services.

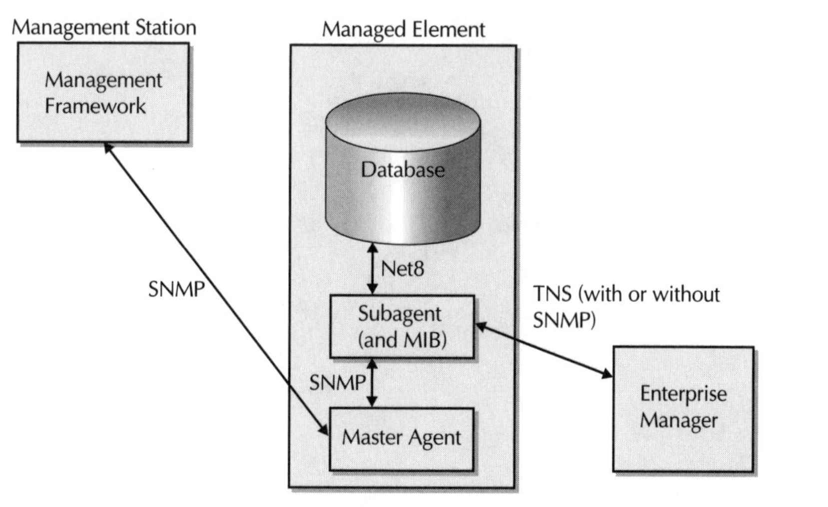

FIGURE 3-1. *Oracle integrated with SNMP components*

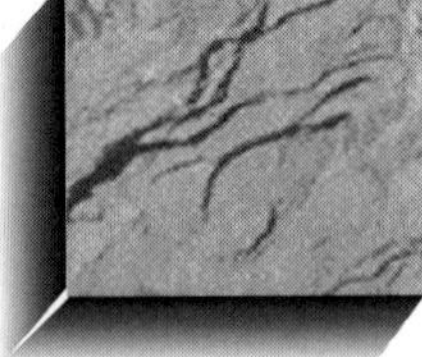

Oracle Names Server

ames are very important. Almost everything in our world has a name. In most cases, the same plant or tree or bird will have both a scientific name and a common name. From the time we're born, we're given one or more names to help make it easier to identify each of us. You may have a formal name that's used by most people you come into contact with as well as a nickname that your close friends and family use. If you've ever had someone mispronounce your name, you know just how much your name is tied to your identity.

In the Oracle world, names are equally important. Each computer in a network will have some form of identification. In most cases, each computer will have an Internet Protocol (IP) address as well as a name assigned. You see, we are so used to referring to things in our world by names that we prefer to use names rather than numbers when we talk about computers and other inanimate things in our computing environment. It's usually much easier for us to remember names than meaningless strings. After all, it's much easier to hit a button that's labeled "Doctor" on your telephone than to recognize the doctor's telephone number.

I remember once visiting a computer installation where each computer's name was written on a large cardboard sign that hung suspended above the computer. If I remember correctly, one group of computers at the facility were named "Groucho," "Harpo," "Chico," and "Karl," while another group were named after the planets in our solar system, and a third group were named after fast-moving animals like "Lynx," "Cheetah," and "Cougar." Of course, from a security standpoint, you don't want to use obvious names that can be easily guessed like ONLINE_DB or PROD1, PROD2.

We also use database, instance, and service names on our computers. In reality, even though we assign pronounceable names to our computers and databases, we could just as easily use meaningless jumbles of letters and numbers, and our computers and databases would continue to function just fine. We, on the other hand, would probably have trouble when we tried to refer to a specific machine or database. Over time, if you assigned an unpronounceable name to a computer, like "AXCZ23B1," you'd probably start to call the computer something like "ax-ees-two-three-bee-one" or just "bee-one" for short. It's human nature to want to use meaningful names to relate to objects in our world.

Thinking about my computer name, AXCZ23B1, what if you have a database with the name SKDL and you want to connect to it? To perform the connection, using the complete address, you have to type something like the following, where MYDBACCT is your username and MYPW is your password:

```
sqlplus  MYDBACCT/MYPW@SKDL.AXCZ23B1.US.COM
```

What happens if you move the database from AXCZ23B1? Your connection string will change. Everyone who has been connecting to the database will have to be informed and will have to modify their connection string in every application that connects to that database. How cumbersome! Without some type of nickname to replace full address resolution, you would have to know the complete address of each machine and database in your network. Now, multiply that complete machine address by many databases and many servers in your environment, and you have a management nightmare.

In this chapter, you'll learn about the Oracle Names server, a distributed naming service provided by Oracle Corporation that enables you to easily support many clients connecting to distributed servers. Just as networks use IP addresses that can be resolved to names, an Oracle Names server can take a connection identifier, like a nickname, and resolve it to a connection descriptor or machine location. I'll tell you more about connection identifiers and descriptors a bit later in this chapter.

Networking in General

In Chapter 2, I talked about the evolution of the computing environment from mainframe to client/server to thin client. To begin our discussion of the Oracle Names server, let's briefly review client/server concepts to ensure that you and I are looking at the concepts from the same perspective.

Different Architectures

In a mainframe environment, both the database server and the application software are housed on the same machine. If there are a large number of users to support, or if there are lower resources than needed on the machine, the resource requirements can easily surpass what's available. In a client/server approach, the applications are moved from the server to the client machines. Thus, the server's resources can be used to support the database requirements while the client machines support the application requirements. However, each time an application is changed, each client's configuration must be changed. Each client must also maintain enough resources to support the application and the client queries.

Thin-client architecture can be used to get around the maintenance and resource issues created by the client/server approach. The difference between a client/server and a thin-client architecture is that the applications are moved off of the clients and placed on a separate machine that can be accessed by all of the client machines. In this way, the client requires a bare minimum of resources, the middle-tier machine absorbs the application resource requirements, and the back-end server is still free to support just the database.

The new machine acts as a facilitator between the clients and the database servers. The middle-tier machine

- Accepts information requests from the clients
- Passes the requests to the appropriate database server, if there's more than one server in the network
- Obtains the response from the server database
- Passes the responses back to the appropriate client

With Oracle8i, Oracle Corporation has introduced products like WebDB that serve their application information directly from the database. This is a hybrid form of architecture similar to that of the original mainframe but which relies on the faster processors and larger memory resources available today. In Chapter 12, we'll look more closely at WebDB and the listener you must configure for communication with this product set.

Where Networking Fits In

The advent and refinement of networking protocols have enabled the shift from mainframes to client/server to thin-client architectures to where we are today with some applications being stored directly to the database. From the introduction of client/server technology forward, we've used Oracle network configuration files such as listener.ora and tnsnames.ora to supply the details necessary to support the underlying network protocols and enable a broader range of distributed communications. Pretty cool!

As you saw in Chapter 3, the listener.ora file provides configuration information for one or more listener processes and details the locations and parameters associated with each listener. The tnsnames.ora file provides a way to translate a service name or alias into the location of an instance.

About Translations

Before we talk further about the tnsnames.ora file and the Oracle Names server, let's play a game. Let's pretend we're spies and we need to communicate in a secret code. To get started, I'm going to give you a coded phrase and a hint, and you get to decode the phrase. Ready? Here's the phrase: "Jvv, evknfibzex tre sv wle!" And your hint: Start with *J* and end with *i*. I'll give you the translation a bit later in the chapter.

Let's consider what you must do to break the code. Obviously, it's a simple substitution code. In other words, I probably wrote a phrase on a piece of paper and then created a key to help guide me in encoding my phrase. Maybe I wrote out the letters of the English alphabet in order from *a* to *z* and then shifted a few letters to the right or left and rewrote the alphabet again, something like this:

```
a b c d e f g h i j k l m n o p q r s t u v w x y z
e f g h i j k l m n o p q r s t u v w x y z a b c d
```

Now, let's say I want to encode the words "Hi there" and send them to you. I look at my key and see that below the *h* is the letter *l*, and below the *i* is the letter *m*. Thus, my first coded word would be "Lm". You code the word "there". Did you come out with "xlivi"? Good job! You should be able to go back and solve the other puzzle without any trouble now.

What you've done in both the quiz and example is translate or resolve one form of a word into another form. The Net8 software uses the tnsnames.ora file in a similar way to look up and resolve instance locations. But, there are several name translation approaches that you can choose from. Let's see what they are and briefly look at each option's advantages and disadvantages.

Name Translation Approaches

There are actually five different approaches that you can implement to resolve connection descriptors: local naming, directory naming, Oracle Names server, host naming, and external naming. In this chapter, we're going to take an in-depth look at Oracle Names, and in Chapter 5, I'll be detailing directory naming. But to have a more complete picture of the available options, I'll briefly describe each option and its advantages and possible drawbacks.

Probably the most commonly used method of name translation is the local naming method because it is relatively straightforward to implement and can be used to resolve net service names across networks that are running different protocols. The possible drawback, as I'll discuss in a bit more detail in the next section, is that it requires modification to each local configuration each time something in the environment changes. Local naming is best suited for simple distributed systems that have infrequent service changes.

With the directory naming method, the names of the services and their connection information are stored in a directory. This method is easy to configure using the supplied tools and provides a centralized storage facility. Changes are made in only one location. This method works best in large, complex networks of over 20 databases that change on a frequent basis. The drawback associated with this method of names serving is that it requires access to a directory server. You'll see why that can be a potential problem in Chapter 5.

The Oracle Names server also provides a centralized approach to storing network names and addresses. Any change made to a server, either new or existing, is made only once in one place to one Oracle Names server and is quickly propagated out to potentially hundreds or even thousands of users. As with directory naming, this method works best in large, complex networks of over 20 databases that change on a frequent basis. The drawbacks of using the Oracle Names server method are that it only supports Oracle services and requires additional setup and administration.

With host naming, an IP address translation mechanism such as the Domain Name Services (DNS), Network Information Services (NIS), or a centrally maintained TCP/IP hosts file is used for names resolution. This method requires minimal user configuration since the user only needs to provide a host name to establish a connection, which eliminates the need for a tnsnames.ora file. However, this method is only available for use in a limited environment. You see, there are a few rules that are enforced: Both the client and server must be using TCP/IP and either DNS, NIS, or an available TCP/IP hosts file. Host naming is best suited for a simple TCP/IP environment that meets the client and server requirements I just mentioned. The last requirement for implementing this environment is that no Oracle Connection Manager features are available since they are not supported by this software configuration.

The final naming method, external naming, lets you load Oracle net service names into a third-party name service product. If you already have an existing name service product, you can load the Oracle net service names into it using the vendor-supplied tools and utilities. This enables you to continue using a tool that you are familiar with. However, the third-party tool usually can't be administered using Oracle's Net8 products.

Potential Problem

Here's a basic but very important rule to remember about the Net8 environment. If you're using the local naming approach, which is the most common form of name translation, each server and each client must have a tnsnames.ora file. Hmm, what happens when you need to add, change, or remove a service name? Well, you're going to have to add, change, or remove it in every single tnsnames.ora file on your system. If you rarely add or remove a database or have very few clients and services, modifying each tnsnames.ora file is not a big deal.

But what if you have a large number of clients or a really dynamic database environment? That could pose a real maintenance nightmare for you! Consider, too, the situation in which some developers or customers require a more customized tnsnames.ora file than the one that's normally distributed. How will you keep track of whose file needs to be modified and whose file doesn't?

Problems really begin to compound when new clients are added to the system and another group within your company is in charge of configuring their systems. Who will determine which tnsnames.ora file should be used? If a new version of the tnsnames.ora file is generated, how will it be propagated throughout the system, and who will do the porting? How can you guarantee that the correct tnsnames.ora file will remain on each client's system? Hmm, there certainly are a lot of issues to think through and resolve, aren't there?

To alleviate many of these problems, Oracle Corporation first developed an application that provides a centralized method of service name resolution known as the Oracle Names server. The second method, introduced with Oracle8i, Release 2, is the Lightweight Directory Access Protocol (LDAP) directory server. As I said earlier, I'll tell you more about LDAP in Chapter 5. For now, let's take a close look at what the Oracle Names server is and how it works.

About the Oracle Names Server

The Oracle Names server is an Oracle Corporation proprietary application that stores the names and addresses of all the services on a network and makes this information available to each client that requests a connection. When you use the Oracle Names server, you no longer have to supply a tnsnames.ora file to each client on your system. When you have to make a change to your Oracle network, you make the change in the Oracle Names server and propagate it to any other Names servers on your system. Therefore, you only need to make each change one time in one place. That certainly sounds like a great way to reduce your administrative tasks, doesn't it?

As with everything in this world, there is a trade-off. The trade-off in this case is that you will have to put more effort and thought up front to implement this feature. Don't let that scare you off, okay? You see, over time, the Oracle Names server has been made more and more user friendly and easier to work with. Let's look at how Oracle Names server works and some of the decisions you have to make before you begin to work with it.

Getting Connection Information

To understand how Oracle Names server works with a client request, let's say you are a teacher and you're sitting at a personal computer that's connected to your school's network. You've just finished grading the latest exam and want to enter the grades for each of your students. There are three different servers on your network, and their connection identifiers are STUDENTS, GRADES, and COURSES. You need to connect using the GRADES identifier. As each database is started on the network, it registers with the Oracle Names server. We'll assume for this discussion that the GRADES service is up and available and has registered with the Oracle Names server.

The application you are using presents a connection request with the connection identifier, GRADES, to the Oracle Names server. The Oracle Names server does a query of either its memory cache or its database repository, depending on how it's been configured, and obtains the necessary information to resolve the connection identifier to a connection descriptor, supplying the same information that you'd get from the tnsnames.ora file:

```
(ADDRESS=
   (PROTOCOL=tcp)
   (HOST= marlenes-pc)
   (PORT=1521))
(CONNECT_DATA
   (SID=grades))
```

It then returns the connect descriptor to your application. In this case, the address supplied by the Oracle Names server says that the listener is on MARLENES-PC, using the TCP/IP protocol, is listening for connection requests on port 1521, and the database SID to use is GRADES.

Transparently to you, the application then presents the connection request to the appropriate listener at the correct address and connects to the service. Figure 4-1 shows a client presenting a connection request with connection identifier to an Oracle Names server, receiving a connection descriptor, and presenting a connection request to the listener on the appropriate machine.

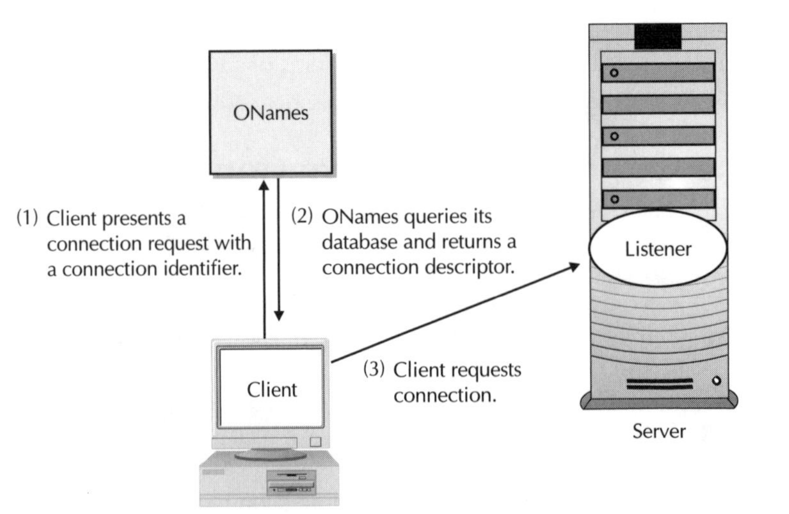

FIGURE 4-1. *Obtaining a connection descriptor from Oracle Names server*

Well, this all seems very straightforward, doesn't it? And it really is! Of course, for the example here, I've only shown one Oracle Names server. Things begin to get a bit more complicated when you introduce more than one Oracle Names server on a network. Let's look at why you might want more than one Oracle Names server and some of the management considerations that you face when you have two or more of them.

Multiple Oracle Names Servers

Under what circumstances do you want to have more than one Oracle Names server on your network? Hmm, that's a good question! The answer, however, is a bit complex.

When I was telling you about how the Oracle Names server processes a request, I skimmed over the fact that the Oracle Names server uses either a memory cache or a database in which it stores the connection identifiers along with the connection descriptors so that it can provide the identifier-to-descriptor resolution. The method used by the Oracle Names server to obtain its information is determined by how you configure it.

If you opt to use a database for the Oracle Names server repository, where does this database come from? Quite simply, you designate one of your current databases or create a separate database in which to store the names and associated information. We'll talk more about how you designate a repository for the Oracle Names information in Part II when we look at configuration tools. For right now, just keep in mind that you have a choice in how the Oracle Names server information is stored. If you decide to have each of your Oracle Names servers store its information in its memory cache, you will be allocating real memory for that purpose. You may find that for your environment it makes more sense to have the Oracle Names servers store their information in one or more databases.

Next, think about the volume of clients you are supporting. If you have, say, 2,000 clients and they all request connections to databases at about the same time, what's going to happen? Well, with only one Oracle Names server to support the requests, you'll probably have a bottleneck and refused connection requests. That tends to produce very unhappy users!

While we're on the subject of supporting users, consider what happens if the computer that supports the Oracle Names server becomes unavailable. You know, someone walking behind the machines in the computer room accidentally trips and pulls out the plug, and the machine crashes. With only one Oracle Names server, you have a single point of failure and potential problems that often become very real.

Therefore, to ensure availability and more rapid response times to support your large volume of clients, at least two Oracle Names servers seem like a logical choice right from the beginning. You have a choice when you add more than one Oracle Names server. You can have both Names servers share the same repository in the same database, or you may decide to have each server on a different machine using a separate database to ensure ease of fail-over in an emergency. You can even have several Oracle Names servers supporting different areas of the network from a few databases. The choices are up to you.

Based on the size of your client base, the number of data centers, the number of instances, and the locations of the computers on your network, you may find that you need several separate Oracle Names servers reading information from and writing information to one or more databases.

But, how do you manage more than one Names server? Ah, that's where the concept of administrative regions comes into play. Let's take a look at what they are.

Administrative Regions

Does the area where you live have a fire and rescue station? Mine does. The physical station is just down the street from my house, but the fire trucks are used to fight fires in a much wider area than just my neighborhood. About ten miles away, there's another station that supports my city as well as another city. Both stations share one central office where dispatchers receive calls and send out the fire trucks. A third city nearby has its own dispatch office. However, all of the cities are in the same county, and they share equipment from all of the fire stations.

Now, let's translate that information to an Oracle Names server community by first saying that an *administrative region* is composed of one or more Oracle Names servers reading from and writing to a single repository. In my example with the fire stations, there are two administrative regions, one with two fire stations and a second region supporting only one fire station.

In Oracle terms, you could equate each fire station with one Oracle Names server and each central dispatch office with one repository. Each Oracle Names server usually gets its information from a specific repository, just as each fire station gets its dispatch requests from a specific central office. However, all of the Names servers belong to the network, just as all of the cities belong to one county. Thus, all of the service addresses are really shared among all of the Names servers, and if one repository becomes unavailable, the Names servers can get the necessary information from another administrative region.

If you decide to implement one or more Oracle Names servers, you'll want to create a plan and identify the administrative regions that you will use. You'll also want to determine one or more Oracle domains; so let's talk about them next.

Domains

First of all, let's see if we can define the word "domain." My pocket dictionary, *The New Merriam-Webster Dictionary*, from 1989, says, "do-main *n* **1**: complete and absolute ownership of land **2**: land completely owned **3**: a territory over which dominion is exercised." Definition 3 looks promising, but let's see what it says about dominion. Included in the definition for dominion is "supreme authority." Using definition 3 and swapping in the definition for dominion, we get "a territory over which supreme authority is exercised." Now, how does this apply to the Oracle Names server?

According to the *Oracle Net8 Administrator's Guide, Release 8.1.6*, "a domain is a logical group of machines and network services." That sounds a bit like our previous definition. Oracle goes one step further though. There can be one or more domains within an administrative region in the Oracle world. You can divide an administrative region into separate logical domains to make administrative tasks easier to implement and track.

All names used within a domain must be unique, but you can use simple names across domains. That means you can have the same service name or database name in two separate domains within your system, just as you can have two different objects with the same name in the same database as long as they belong to different schemas. You can't, however, have two objects with the same name owned by the same schema.

You see, if the objects are owned by different schemas, you can distinguish two objects with the same name since the schema name is tied to the object name. Let's say that you have a table named MYTAB in the NELSON schema and a table named MYTAB in the ROZ schema. Each table is unique because one is really named NELSON.MYTAB and the other is ROZ.MYTAB. But, how would you distinguish one object from the other if they are both owned by the same schema? Since each administrative region has a unique name and each domain has a unique name, objects within each region will be qualified by their domain and administrative region names and will, therefore, be unique.

Like operating system directories, network domains are hierarchical. Unlike operating systems, network and Oracle domains are *logical* rather than physical domains and don't necessarily map out to any actual network or computer hardware. Oracle and network domains are just used as name spaces to ensure that there won't be any name space conflicts. You can declare an administrative region with one or more domains anywhere in your network.

Some operating systems use Domain Name Server (DNS) name spaces, but although they look the same, the domains of an Oracle network are really independent of any DNS name spaces. If it makes your administration easier and less confusing and you want to, you can make your domain names match your DNS name spaces. That's perfectly okay. However, you don't have to make them match if you don't want to.

Storing Oracle Names Data

I mentioned earlier in this chapter that when you configure your Oracle Names servers, you have a choice about where names information will be stored. You can have each Names server store its information in its respective memory cache and replicate the information continuously among all of the Names servers in its region. For smaller environments where all of the services are registered dynamically, this approach makes sense and works well. With this approach, each time a service registers itself with a listener, the information is immediately forwarded to all of the Oracle Names servers in the region.

However, if you have a large or widely distributed environment, you'll probably want to have several administrative regions logging their information to one or more *region databases.* A region database is one that has tables in which Oracle Names server repository data is stored. Each time a service registers with a listener, the information is written to that region database. Periodically, each Oracle Names server will poll the region database for updates. In that way, the Oracle Names servers stay current without having to talk to each other constantly.

Types of Stored Data

So far, I've told you about how the Oracle Names server works and explained some of the associated vocabulary. What I haven't talked about yet is the various types of information that the Names servers store and work with.

Table 4-1, as taken from the *Oracle Net8 Administration Guide, Release 8.1.6,* shows the various types of information stored by the Oracle Names server.

As you can see, some of the data stored in the Oracle Names server is recorded in an automated manner, either through a service registering with the listener or through the listener.ora configuration file itself. The data that you must provide includes database links, aliases, net service names, and non-Oracle and Rdb database information.

More About Global Database Links

When you are dealing with database links through the Oracle Names server, keep in mind that three types of links can be created. Each type of database link enables a different form of data access. Table 4-2 shows the three types of database links and the form of privilege each type allows.

Data	Description
Global database names and addresses	The Oracle Names server retrieves information about the database, including the global database name (database name and domain) and address, from the listener. The address is configured in the listener.ora file, and the global database name is registered during database start-up or statically configured in the listener.ora file. You do not need to register this information.
Other Oracle Names server names and addresses	An Oracle Names server stores the names and addresses of all other Oracle Names servers in the same administrative region. If there is more than one administrative region in a network, the Oracle Names server stores the name and address of at least one Oracle Names server in the root administrative region and each of the immediate subregions. You do not need to register this information.
Net service names	If you register net service names with the Names Control utility or Net8 Assistant, an Oracle Names server stores them. An Oracle Names server also stores gateways to non-Oracle databases and Oracle Rdb databases. (See the discussion of **namesctl** in the last part of this chapter.)
Global database links	Database links allow a database to communicate with another database. The name of a database link is the same as the global database name of the database to which the link points.Typically, only one database link should exist per database.
Aliases	An Oracle Names server stores aliases or alternative service names for any defined net service name, database service, or global database link. Aliases may be registered with the Oracle Names server using either the Names Control utility or Net8 Assistant.
Oracle Connection Managers	An Oracle Names server stores the names and listening addresses of all Oracle Connection Managers on the network. You do not need to register this information.

TABLE 4-1. *Data Stored by Oracle Names Server*

Database Link	Access Type
Private database link in a specific schema of a database	Only the owner can use it.
Public database link for a database	All users in the database can use it.
Global database link in Oracle Names server	Anyone in the network can use it.

TABLE 4-2. *Types of Database Links*

Remember in Chapter 2 when I said I'd tell you more about global database links? Well, it's time to learn more about them now!

Creating a Global Database Link

First of all, let's talk about what a global database link really does. A global database link provides a way to link each database in a network to all of the other databases in that network. Once all of the databases are linked together, any user in the network can access any global object by specifying the global object name in a SQL statement or object definition.

Let's pause for a moment in our discussion about global database links and review just a little about global database names. Remember, a global database name is used to uniquely identify a database and has the following form: database_name.database_domain. For example, let's say that your company's name is XYZ Corporation and that it's a commercial company doing business in the United States. For this example, your database name is SKDL, which is an abbreviation for your company's product, skingwaddles. The assigned Oracle database domain is us.xyzcorp.com. Thus, your global database name would be SKDL.US.XYZCORP.COM.

Okay, back to global database links. To enable a global database link to be set to the global database name, the initialization parameter **global_names** must be set to TRUE in the init.ora file for that database. When the database registers with the listener and the **global_names** parameter equals TRUE, the listener will store the global database name.

Now, let's see what happens if you're using Oracle Names server. Since Oracle Names retrieves the global database name from the listener, a global database link will automatically be registered with the Oracle Names server. You do not have to do anything to register or create this link. But, where did the listener get the global database name? Well, it's the name that you placed in your database's init.ora parameter file as its **service_name**. So, let's follow the thread.

1. In your database init.ora file, you've set **global_names** = TRUE and put your global database name as **service_name** = SKDL.US.XYZCORP.COM.
2. Upon start-up, your database registers itself with the listener.
3. Oracle Names polls the listener for new registrations.
4. Oracle Names receives your global database name from the listener.
5. Oracle Names creates a global database link using your global database name.
6. You verify that the link is working by performing a **select** using the link.

Step 6 is performed using the form

```
select *
  from EMPLOYEE@SKDL.US.XYZCORP.COM;
```

where EMPLOYEE is a globally defined object.

You can also create a global database link yourself by accessing the Names Control utility and entering the link information:

```
$ namesctl
NAMESCTL> register skdl.us.xyzcorp.com -d
(description=(address=(protocol=tcp)(host=skingwad)(port=1521)))
```

In this code example, the **-d** indicates that you want to use a default TCP/IP listening address. The protocol is specified as TCP, while the host machine designated is SKINGWAD, and the port is 1521.

You can use the Net8 Assistant to create a global database link by following the steps listed here:

1. Start the Net8 Assistant by running netasst from $ORACLE_HOME/bin on a UNIX system. Or from Windows NT, choose Start > Programs > Oracle ORACLE_HOME > Network Administration > Net8 Assistant.
2. From the navigator pane, expand the Oracle Names Servers list by clicking on the Navigator plus sign (+).
3. Select the Oracle Names server to which you want to add a global database link.
4. From the list in the right pane, select Manage Data.
5. Click the Links tab and select Add.

6. Enter the global database link name in the DB Link Name field.
7. In the User and Password fields, enter a valid username and password of an account that has privileges to create a global database link for the database.
8. Click Execute to create the link.
9. Choose File > Save Network Configuration.

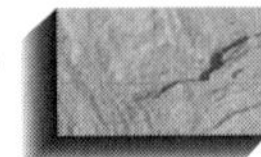

NOTE
*If the **global_names** parameter has been set to TRUE in your initialization parameter (init.ora) file, the name you enter for the global link must be the global database name.*

Oracle Corporation recommends that you have a global database link for each database in your network so that global objects can be shared automatically among the users on your network. However, I recommend that you take great care in deciding what types of information you want globally shared and what objects you are *really* allowing all of the users on your network to access.

Security and Global Database Links

If you do not want to specify a username and password for the global database link that's registered with Oracle Names, you don't need to do any other configuration. However, if you want to ensure that only the users you expect to access global objects are the ones who actually get to them, you need to establish user access control. I'll tell you about database link qualifiers next.

Global database links may be superseded with private and public database links created by individual users. Thus, if you, or a user with the appropriate privileges, create a private or public database link with the same name as the global database link, the Oracle Names server will use your private or public database link to resolve the connection request and will not use the global database link.

About Database Link Qualifiers

In earlier versions of Oracle, it was not uncommon to have several database links in one database. Multiple database links were used to get to multiple schemas in a database or to get to several different databases from one or more schemas in the local database. In Oracle8i, the approach has changed, and Oracle Corporation recommends that you have only one global database link per database. However, they have provided a mechanism, known as link qualifiers, that you can use to create alternate settings for the database username and password credentials so that you can control who has access to specific objects in your various databases. You can have as many link qualifiers as you want in a global database link.

Perhaps you want to control the access to your EMPLOYEE table. You can establish a link qualifier in your skdl.us.xyzcorp.com that requires a specific username and password. I'll show you how to define a link qualifier in the next section.

Once you've defined the link qualifier, you can connect to a remote database with the global database link and link qualifier like this:

```
connect @SKDL.US.XYZCORP.COM@EMPLOYEE
```

When the connection request is processed, the user will be prompted for the appropriate username and password before the connection can be completed.

Adding a Link Qualifier

Although you can use the Names Control utility to register username and password credentials for the global database link, the utility is lacking in global database links functionality; so Oracle Corporation recommends that you use the Net8 Assistant to perform this task instead. To add a username and password to a global database link, follow these steps:

1. Start the Net8 Assistant by running netasst from $ORACLE_HOME/bin on a UNIX system. Or from Windows NT, choose Start > Programs > Oracle HOME_NAME > Network Administration > Net8 Assistant.
2. From the navigator pane, expand the Oracle Names Servers list by clicking on the plus sign (+).
3. Select the Oracle Names server to which you want to add a global database link.
4. From the list in the right pane, select Manage Data.
5. Click the Links tab and select the Add action.
6. Select the DB Qualifiers option at the bottom of the screen.
7. A separate DB Qualifiers window will be displayed. Enter a DB Qualifier in the first box.
8. In the User and Password fields, enter valid username and password credentials for the link, and click OK.
9. Repeat steps 6 through 8 for as many qualifiers as you want to add.
10. Click Execute to modify the link.
11. Choose File > Save Network Configuration to save the changes you've made.

That's all there is to it.

Oracle Naming Models

I started this chapter by talking about names and our human penchant for naming things. Well, things are no different when you use Oracle Names servers. Each object within the network must have a unique name. That includes every database.

You can use two distinct approaches for assigning names to objects in your Oracle Names server network. You can use either the Single Domain Naming model or the Hierarchical Naming model. Hmm, what's the difference? Let's look and see.

Single Domain Naming Model

Well, right off the top, the Single Domain Naming model sounds less complex than the Hierarchical Naming model, and it is. If your network is small and there's no duplication of service or database link names, the Single Domain Naming model will work well for you. Essentially, as the name implies, you have one domain in which you identify all of your database service names and any other information that you are storing in your Oracle Names server. By default in the past Oracle networking versions, the domain name for a single domain has been .WORLD. Although this is no longer a requirement in Net8 and Oracle Names version 8, you may want to continue to use the .WORLD convention to be compatible with your older naming conventions.

To see how this works, let's say that the XYZ Corporation makes several products besides skingwaddles. Let's say that they manufacture ramafrazits and dinglesompters as well. There is a database to house the information for each of these products: purchase orders, parts, supplies, stock orders, shipped parts, and so on. You know, the general accounting information necessary to support a company's products. As I said earlier, skingwaddle information is stored in the SKDL database. Ramafrazits data is stored in the RMFS database, while the DGSS database contains all of the necessary information to support dinglesompters. There are, of course, development and test/quality assurance databases for each of these production databases. Since they are all built on Oracle8i, all of the databases are identified by their service names. (In earlier releases of Oracle, the databases are identified by SIDs rather than service names.)

Now, let's place these databases in a Single Domain Naming environment. In this case, our domain will be called .WORLD. Figure 4-2 shows graphically what our single domain looks like. For identification purposes, the domain name is attached to the service name. Therefore, SKDL would become SKDL.WORLD.

Hierarchical Naming Model

Did you ever try to create a family tree? If you go to draw one, you generally end up with something like Figure 4-3. In this figure, you see a family tree for a family that I made up. If it matches your family tree, I'm really amazed!

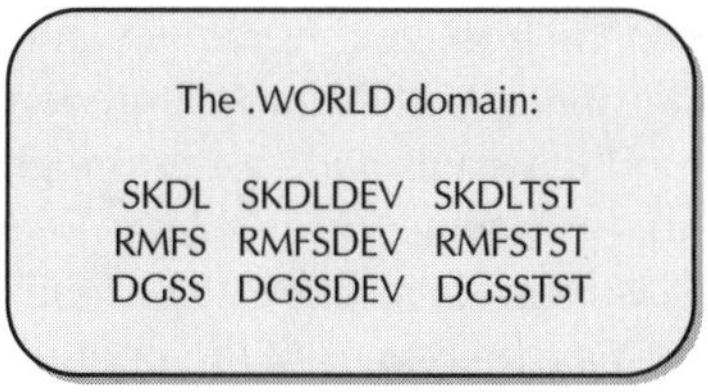

The .WORLD domain:

SKDL SKDLDEV SKDLTST
RMFS RMFSDEV RMFSTST
DGSS DGSSDEV DGSSTST

FIGURE 4-2. *Single Domain Naming method*

As you can see in Figure 4-3, the tree starts with one set of parents. The next level shows the children from this union, and the third level shows the grandchildren. A structure such as this one is hierarchical. One layer or level depends on the next higher level for its existence. Even though there is dependence within the structure, each family unit acts both independently and as part of the larger group. Look at the second and third or lowest level in Figure 4-3. There are two sets of people with the same name: Duwap Tzcn and Pocus Abc. "Ah," you say, "but they're not really the same. One is senior and one is junior." Of course, you're quite right. They really *are* two different people.

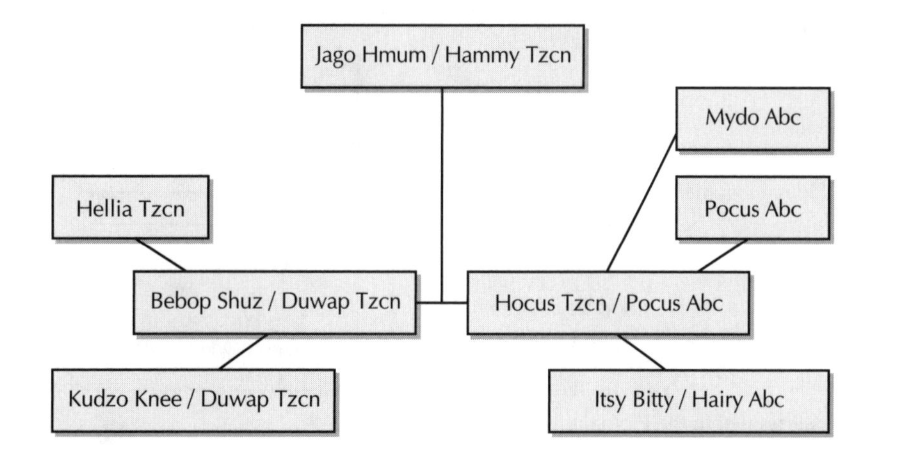

FIGURE 4-3. *A sample family tree*

So a family tree is divided into a hierarchical structure with different family members in different regions of the tree. With Oracle Names servers, you can use a Hierarchical Naming model to divide names into different regions. By dividing a large network into a hierarchical model, you provide for future growth and more flexibility in naming objects. You see, just as we had more than one person with the same name in our family tree, you can have more than one database in a hierarchical structure with the "same" name. And just as the names of the people represented two different family members, each of the database names will represent a different database. Let's see how this works by changing our family tree into a Hierarchical Naming model. Look at Figure 4-4.

In Figure 4-4, you can see that the family members are divided into the domains: Tzcn Family, with three children domains. Where a family member is married, the spouse's name is shown coupled with the family member. There is only one root domain in Figure 4-4, but in your network, there may be more than one logical domain. In this structure, there is room to add more names as new family members are born and room to add new domains below each of the existing

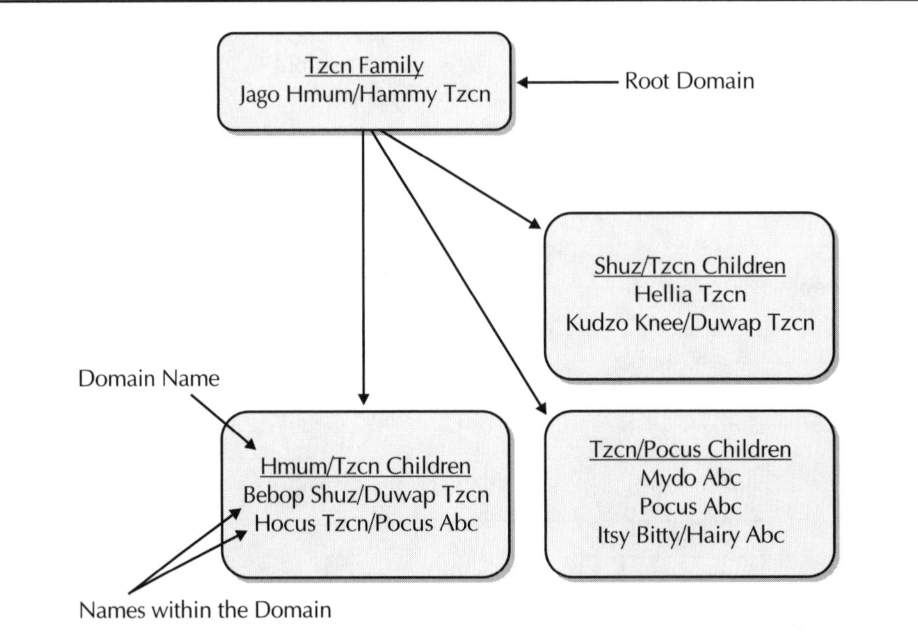

FIGURE 4-4. *Hierarchical domain family tree*

ones as new generations are added. Each domain has a domain name and contains other names within it.

With a Hierarchical Naming method, there are a series of parent-child relationships. You have more room to expand your model, but you have the added burden of tracking which members belong to which domain. A graphical map helps you to see the relationships between the different members of each domain. In earlier versions of the networking tools, you could create a graphical representation of your Oracle Names server model. In Oracle8i, this feature has been removed. You may, however, find it helpful to sketch out a map of your network configuration.

Multiple Administrative Regions

When do you want to use a Hierarchical Naming method instead of a Single Domain Naming method? If you have a very large or widely distributed network, you probably want to distribute the administrative tasks so that each local group can have control over their specific region. The only way you can enable local management of an area of the network and still use Oracle Names servers is by implementing a Hierarchical Naming method. You can then place control of one or more domains under each administrative region and assign people to manage each region.

Think about this issue for a moment. If there are several different domains within different administrative regions and more than one database with the same local name, how does a client know what connection string to use to get to the correct database? Did I hear you say that each client has to qualify each connection request with the complete domain name? Well, you're very close to the right answer. You see, clients are generally assigned to the domain in which most of their name requests are made. The domain a client is assigned to is called the *default domain.* A client can request a network service within its own domain without using the domain name. That is, a client can leave off the "." qualifier, and its own default domain name will be automatically attached to its database service or database link connection request. Let's see how this works.

You have been configured with the default domain US.XYZCORP.COM. When you make a request for the SKDL service without adding any other qualifiers, SKDL will be automatically appended to the default domain name, and the resulting connection request string will be SKDL.US.XYZCORP.COM. If you want to connect to a database in the European domain, EURO.XYZCORP.COM, you must qualify your connection request with the complete domain name since it is not your default domain. Thus, to connect to the European database called SKDL, you'd have to make your connect request SKDL.EURO.XYZCORP.COM.

With a network of multiple administrative regions, you have one root administrative region that contains the root domain and one or more delegated administrative regions that contain one or more domains each. Hmm, that sounds a bit confusing, doesn't it? Let's see if we can make this concept clearer.

Think about your company. If you're in an established company that's been around for many years, you probably have a hierarchy of management. You may have a manager who has a group manager. The group manager has a section leader whose activities are overseen by a section manager. The section head reports to a director or vice president and on up the chain of command. At the highest level of the "food chain" is a single person or group of people who head

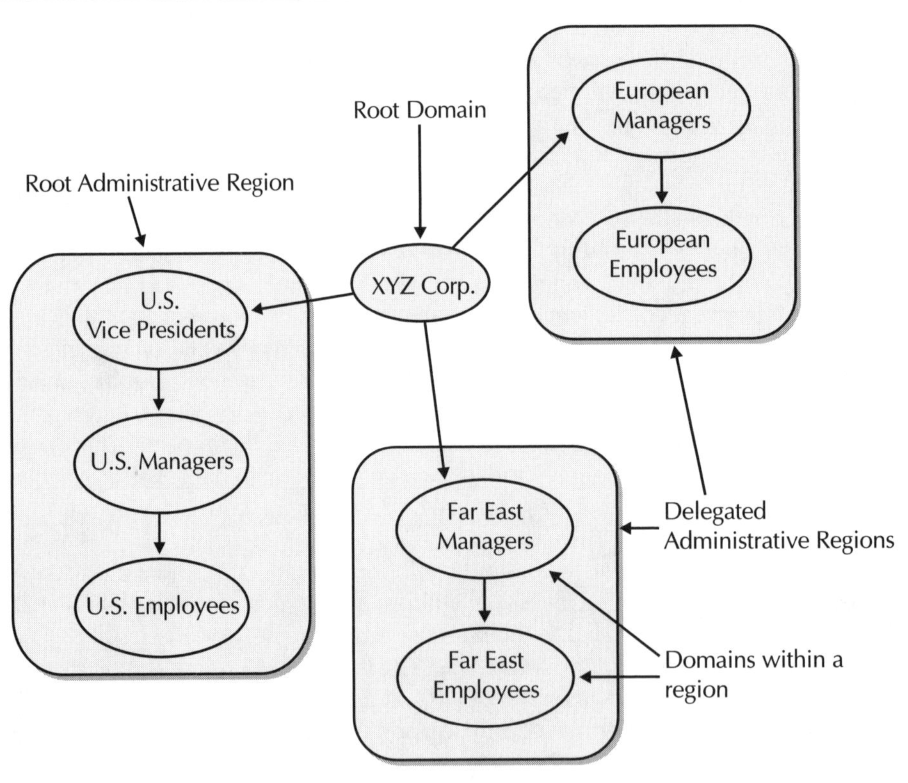

FIGURE 4-5. *Root and delegated administrative regions*

the company. The company head has access to all of the areas or regions. If it makes things easier to understand, think of the root administrative region as the company head and the delegated administrative regions as directors. Let's see how that maps out.

Look at Figure 4-5. As you can see, the XYZ Corporation is represented as the root domain. According to the figure, the location of the root domain is in the United States. The root administrative region, with three domains, is also located in the United States. The three domains are Vice Presidents, Managers, and Employees. There are two delegate regions represented here: One is in Europe and the other is in the Far East. Each delegate region has two domains: a Managers domain and an Employees domain.

The root administrative region will always have at least one domain, but as you can see from Figure 4-5, our root administrative region has more than one domain. In other words, you can divide your network in any way that makes logical administrative sense for you and your company. If you have seven domains, you can have anywhere from one to seven administrative regions.

The root administrative region will also contain the Oracle Names servers in its region as well as the delegated administrative region's Oracle Names servers and domain addresses. Finally, the root administrative region will contain the data definitions for the root region, including all of the database service names, database links, and aliases for the root region.

More About Delegated Regions

Any administrative regions below the root are considered to be delegated administrative regions. The root administrative region will assign administrative responsibility for a domain to a delegated administrative region, although another delegated administrative region can assign administrative responsibility for a domain to a delegated region below it in the hierarchy.

As you would expect, each delegated administrative region stores all of the Oracle Names servers and domains in its region as well as the domain and Oracle Names service information for child regions below it. Of course, the delegated region must store the addresses of the Oracle Names servers in the root region so that it can contact any other region through the root region's information. As with the root administrative region, each delegated administrative region stores all of the data definitions for its own local region, such as database service names, database links, and aliases.

Configuring an Oracle Names Server

By now, you should have determined that either you need service registration data replicated continuously among your Oracle Names servers or you want all of the Oracle Names servers within each region to store their data in an Oracle database.

You should also have decided upon either a Single Domain Naming method or a Hierarchical Naming method. If you've opted to implement a Hierarchical Naming method, have you mapped out the location and name of your root administrative region and its domain? Have you identified all of your delegated administrative regions?

If you answered yes to the preceding questions, you're ready to install the software and begin configuration. To install the software for your specific system, please refer to your platform-specific Oracle Names server installation documentation. Even if you've already installed the Oracle Enterprise Server 8.1.6 software, the probability is that the Oracle Names server software has not yet been installed. To verify whether the necessary software is installed on a UNIX system, go to $ORACLE_HOME/network and search for the namesini.sql file.

```
find ./ -name namesini.sql -print
```

On a Windows NT system, use Windows Explorer and look in the folder ORACLE_HOME\network\names for the namesini.sql file. If you do not find this file on your system, the Oracle Names server software has not yet been installed. If you have an existing Oracle Names server structure, you can run the script namesupg.sql in the same directory to upgrade a version 1 or 2 structure to Net8.

Oracle recommends that you use a dedicated machine as your Oracle Names server with no other services or servers on it. You'll also need to install either the Net8 client software or SQL*Net client software on each client and the Net8 server software or SQL*Net server software on the server.

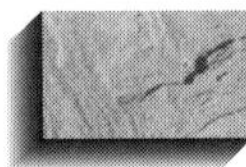

NOTE

If you are using a UNIX machine as your Oracle Names server, the Oracle Universal Installer will not create the necessary $ORACLE_HOME/network/names directory. You must manually create this directory yourself before you begin the configuration.

You have three different tools available to you for configuration and management of your Oracle network: Net8 Assistant, Net8 Configuration Assistant, and Control utilities. Which tool do you use to configure an Oracle Names server? Great question! Let's take a brief look at each of these tools and see if you can decide which one is best suited for use in configuring an Oracle Names server.

Available Configuration and Control Tools

The Net8 Assistant, detailed in Chapters 7 and 8, is a graphical user interface (GUI) tool that you can use to configure and control networking components from one central location. You can use it from either the client or server. Using the Net8 Assistant, you can configure or define the following:

- Listeners.
- Simple names and connect identifiers that can be mapped to connect descriptors. The mapping of simple names and connect identifiers to connect descriptors are stored in either tnsnames.ora, centralized LDAP-compliant directory service, or an Oracle Names server.
- Naming methods to describe the different ways to resolve connect identifiers into connect descriptors.

You can also use the Net8 Assistant to stop, start, tune, or gather statistics for an Oracle Names server, once it's been configured.

The Net8 Configuration Assistant, which I'll tell you much more about in Chapter 9, is used to configure basic network components. When you install the Oracle software, the Net8 Configuration Assistant runs automatically to configure the listener names and protocol addresses, the net service names in the tnsnames.ora file, directory server access, and naming methods the client will use to resolve connect identifiers. You can run the Net8 Configuration Assistant manually in stand-alone mode to configure any or all of these components.

The Control utilities consist of the Listener Control (lsnrctl) utility, which we examined in Chapter 3, the Names Control (namesctl) utility, which we'll look at later in this chapter, and the Connection Manager Control (cmctl) utility, which we'll look at in Chapter 10.

Well, what do you think? Which tool did you choose to configure an Oracle Names server? In reality, that was a trick question, sort of. You see, if you want a simple, basic, default Oracle Names server, you can let the Names server run with no configuration at all! The Oracle Names server will have the name ONAMES_<host> if its name is configured in the names.ora file. By default, ONAMES_<host> will have the default port number 1575 using TCP/IP on the local host or on other well-known addresses that support protocols. So if you have a machine whose host name is MYPC and there's an entry for it in the names.ora file, your default Oracle Names server will be named ONAMES_MYPC.

Storing the Information in a Database

If you've decided to store the Oracle Names resolution information in a database, you need to configure the database server. If the database server is not currently running, start it by connecting to the database as the user INTERNAL. As of Oracle8i, you can use SQL*Plus to perform this task. From the operating system prompt, you type

```
$ sqlplus
SQL> connect INTERNAL/PASSWORD (if you have a password established for INTERNAL)
SQL> startup;
```

Next, while still connected to SQL*Plus, you must create an account with a password. You use this account to house the Names server tables. Decide on a username and password for the account. Let's use NAMES as the username and NAMESPW for the password here. Be sure not to make your password as obvious as I've made mine.

```
    create user NAMES
identified by NAMESPW
   default tablespace USERS
 temporary tablespace TEMP;
```

The script assumes that your database has two tablespaces, one named USERS and one named TEMP.

To create the Oracle Names server tables, you run the script namesini.sql that's located in $ORACLE_HOME/network/admin on a UNIX machine or, on a Windows NT machine, ORACLE_HOME\network\admin\names. To run the script, connect to SQL*Plus as the user you created in the last step and run the script. On a UNIX box, you would connect to SQL*Plus and type the following:

```
connect NAMES/NAMESPW
@$ORACLE_HOME/network/admin/namesini.sql;
```

Now that the tables have been created, you can create the Oracle Names servers using the Net8 Assistant. Aha! That's the tool you use.

Using Net8 Assistant to Create an Oracle Names Server

To create an Oracle Names server, you must first start the Net8 Assistant. On a UNIX machine from $ORACLE_HOME/bin, you type

```
run netasst
```

To start the Net8 Assistant from Windows NT with a $ORACLE_HOME name of OraHome81, you choose

Start > Programs > Oracle OraHome81 > Network Administration > Net8 Assistant.

Figure 4-6 shows the initial screen of the Net8 Assistant with the Oracle Names Servers option selected. Notice the four icons at the upper-left side of the screen. The plus (+) sign turns green when you have selected an option that allows object creation, and a letter *X* indicates you can remove an object. The third icon, a disk with a check mark next to it, indicates that you can test a server or service. The fourth icon is a question mark (?) that you can click to obtain help. Along the top of the screen are four pull-down options: File, Edit, Command, and Help. You can use either the pull-down menus or icons as you proceed through your tasks.

The following steps assume that you have not created an Oracle Names server and that there are no Oracle Names servers already in your environment. If you

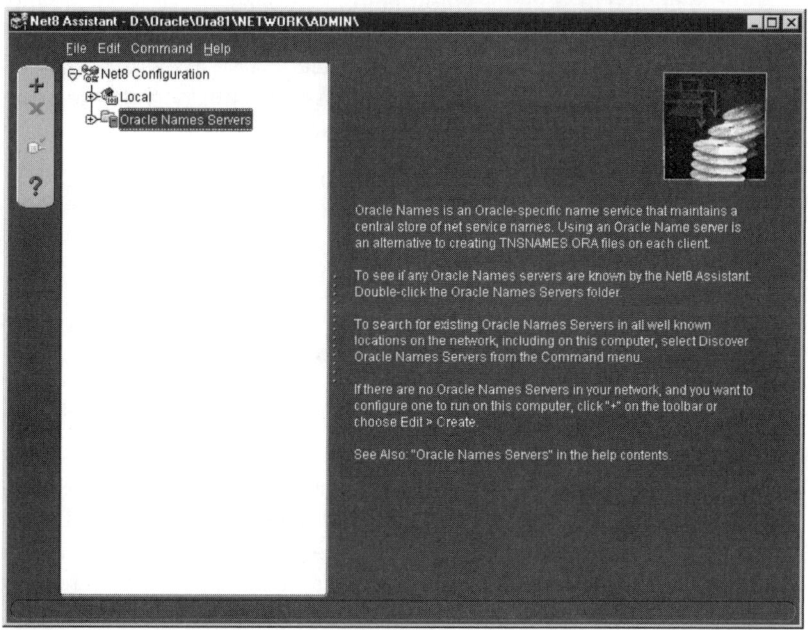

FIGURE 4-6. *Net8 Assistant's initial screen with Oracle Names Servers option selected*

have created one or more Oracle Names servers, your screens will look different from the figures shown here. Once you've started the Net8 Assistant tool, follow these steps:

1. In the navigator pane, select the Oracle Names Servers option.
2. From the pull-down menu, choose Edit > Create, or click on the large green plus (+) button that is displayed in the upper-left side of the Net8 Assistant screen to create a new Oracle Names server. The Names wizard will start. Chapter 7 contains the screen illustrations for the Names wizard.
3. The Names wizard will prompt you for
   - A unique Oracle Names server name.
   - A protocol address for the new Oracle Names server. (With TCP/IP, Oracle recommends using the registered port number 1575.)
   - The choice to store the information in a database or replicate the information among Oracle Names servers. To create a server that will store its information in a database, select "Use a region database." If you are going to use a region database, you must create the necessary database tables before you run the Names wizard.
   - A protocol address for a database's listener. (With TCP/IP, Oracle recommends using the registered port number 1521.)
   - The database user ID that you used to populate the Names server tables, the password you assigned to that account, and service name or SID. In the example, I used NAMES for the username and NAMESPW for the password. My SID name was ORCL.
   - Whether this Oracle Names server is the root administrative region.
4. If you designate this Oracle Names server as the root, the names wizard will complete. If you do not designate this server as the root, the Names wizard will assume this is a delegated administrative region and will prompt you for the local administrative region's domain name and the address of the root administrative region's Oracle Names server. Once you supply this information, the Names wizard will complete.
5. The Oracle documentation says that once the Names wizard completes, you will see the following message:

   "A Names Server, onames_server, has been created with default settings. Use the Configuration Server section to modify the default configuration."

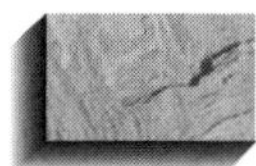

NOTE
I did not receive a completion message, but when I clicked on the Oracle Names Server Navigator minus (-) sign, it became a plus (+) sign. When I then clicked on the Navigator plus sign, my new Oracle Names server was present. (See Figure 4-7 for the screen illustration of a newly created Oracle Names server.)

6. Choose File > Save Network Configuration. You can create more Oracle Names servers by following steps 2 through 6.

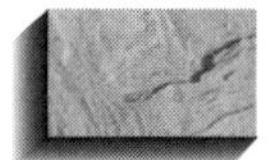

NOTE
The Net8 Assistant does not support creating more than one Oracle Names server on one machine.

Figure 4-7 shows the Net8 Assistant with one configured Oracle Names server.

After you have created your first Oracle Names server or set of servers and exit the tool, you'll find that the Net8 Assistant has created a file called names.ora. At a minimum, the parameters and values shown in Table 4-3 will be present.

You will find a complete list of the names.ora parameters in Appendix C.

Configuring Multiple Domains

If you are using the Hierarchical Naming method and want the region to administer more than one domain, you can use the Net8 Assistant to specify the additional domain or domains by following these steps. These steps assume that you have not exited the tool and are connected to it.

1. In the navigator pane, click on the Oracle Names Servers option.
2. Select the Oracle Names server from which you will administer the domain.
3. From the list in the right pane, select Configure Server.
4. Click the Domains tab.
5. Enter the domain name in the Domain Name field and time-to-live information, and click Add.
6. Repeat step 5 to add more domains.
7. When you are done adding domains, choose File > Save Network Configuration.

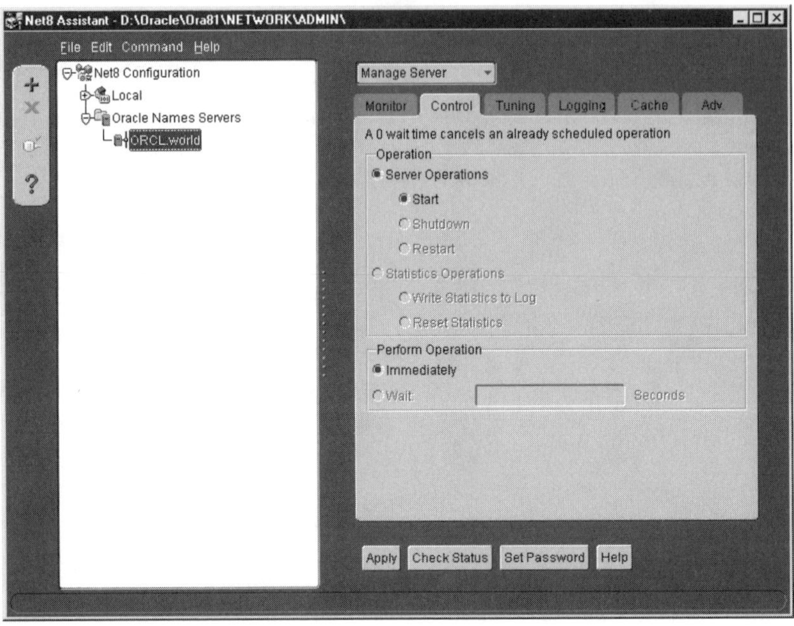

FIGURE 4-7. *The Net8 Assistant navigator screen with one Oracle Names server*

Parameter	**Value**
names.server_name	Oracle Names server name
names.addresses	Oracle Names server listening protocol address
names.admin_region	Database information

TABLE 4-3. *Minimum Contents of the Names.ora File*

The time-to-live information is a number that will be assigned to the parameter **min_ttl**. The default value is 86400.

More About Oracle Names Server Cache Storage

As I mentioned earlier, the last option for Oracle Names server configuration is to store the names resolution information in each Names server cache or memory area and replicate new information among the Oracle Names servers. What I haven't mentioned before is that although the information is stored in each Oracle Names server memory cache, the information is also written periodically to a file on a disk. There are actually three files that store information for the Oracle Names servers. On a UNIX machine, the files are stored in $ORACLE_HOME/network/names, and on Windows NT, you'll find the files in ORACLE_HOME\network\names. Table 4-4 shows the file names and the type of information each file stores.

The only difference in the Oracle Names server creation steps shown earlier occurs while you are using the Names wizard. Instead of choosing "Use a region database," you specify "Don't use a region database."

Starting an Oracle Names Server

Okay, now that you've created at least one Oracle Names server, you need to learn how to start it. You have two choices when starting an Oracle Names server: the Names Control (namesctl) utility or Net8 Assistant.

If you are using the Names Control utility, you have two choices to start a Names server. My, isn't it nice to have choices? You can type the entire command either from the operating system command line or from inside the utility. The only problem with typing the full command at the operating system prompt is that you will start whatever Oracle Names server is set as the default root server for the administrative region. I'll tell you more about this problem in the section about the Names Control utility a little later in the chapter. For now, let's just start the Oracle Names server from inside the tool. To access the tool, at the operating system prompt, type the following:

```
namesctl
```

File Name	Usage
ckcfg.ora	Contains a backup copy of the configuration parameters stored in the ONRS_CONFIG table in the region database.
ckpcch.ora	Contains all current nonauthoritative data that has been retrieved and cached from remote regions and has not yet expired.
ckpreg.ora	Contains all authoritative data for the region. If the Oracle Names server uses a region database, this checkpoint file is a copy of the region data in the tables as of the last reload. This data is used when the Oracle Names server starts if the database is inaccessible. If the server is not using the database, this file is its only persistent storage and is loaded by the Oracle Names server at start-up. The Oracle Names server considers the data in the region checkpoint file to be current if there are no other Oracle Names servers in the region. In this case, the file is kept current as of the last update to the region.

TABLE 4-4. *Oracle Names Server Configuration Files*

As the tool starts, you may see one or more of the following error messages. You can ignore them.

```
NNL-00024: warning: no preferred names servers in SQLNET.ORA
NNL-00018: warning: could not contact default name server
```

Once you have entered the tool, your prompt will change to

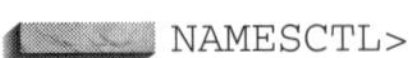

```
NAMESCTL>
```

At the prompt, you can type **start**. The **start** command loads the Oracle Names server into memory and tells it to begin executing. When the Oracle Names server starts, it loads its configuration and data into memory. For an Oracle Names server named ORCL in the ORACLE_HOME OracleOraHome81 with the domain .world, the service name takes the form: OracleOraHome81NamesORCL.world. Figure 4-8 shows the Services screen with the Oracle Names service highlighted.

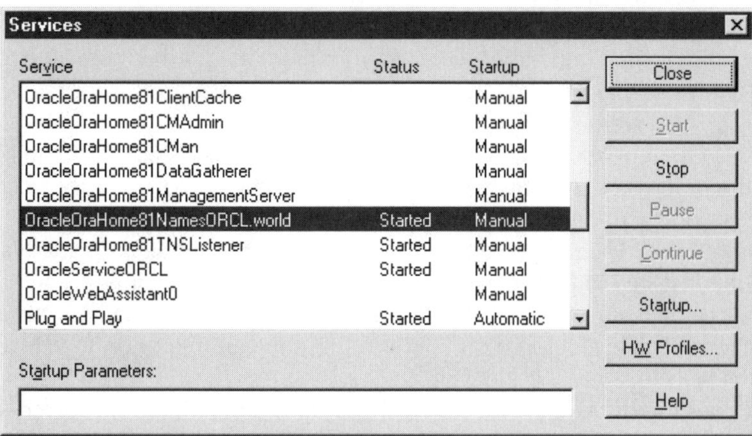

FIGURE 4-8. *The Services screen with the Oracle Names service highlighted*

To start an Oracle Names server using the Net8 Assistant, start the tool as described earlier and follow these steps:

1. In the navigator pane, select the Oracle Names Servers option to expand it.
2. Select the Oracle Names server you want to start.
3. From the list in the right pane, select Manage Server.
4. Click the Control tab.
5. Click Start.
6. Click Apply.

When the server starts, you should see the following message:

```
Server started successfully.
```

If you are using a Windows NT machine, a service is created.

About Discovery

The other day, I discovered that I could look up my stock portfolio information on the Internet. A while ago, my husband discovered that he could make me very happy by occasionally washing the dishes. What are some of the things that you've discovered over the last few weeks? Go ahead, make a list of your recent discoveries. To make your list of discoveries, you either searched your memory or asked someone for help. You might have said to a friend, "Did we make any discoveries over the last few weeks? If so, what were they?"

When a client or another Oracle Names server creates a list of Oracle Names servers, the process of creating the list is called *discovery*. You can use either the Names Control utility or the Net8 Assistant to try to discover the Oracle Names server information. Using either tool, discovery of any individual Oracle Names server is the first step in this process. Next, the located server pings all of the other Oracle Names servers in the area and creates a list of them sorted in order of response time. The list is stored on UNIX in the .sdns.ora file or on Windows NT in the sdns.ora file.

How does the discovery process work? Well, the first file to be searched for preferred Oracle Names server information is sqlnet.ora. The preferred Oracle Names server is either the closest physical server to the client or the one that's available over the least-expensive network link. The next option for discovery is the hard-coded address of a well-known Oracle Names server. This address is hard-coded in both the server and the clients. The last option is to look for a local Oracle Names server configured using TCP/IP on port 1575.

But what happens if you can't find the first Oracle Names server by using one of the three listed approaches? Well, if you are using the Net8 Assistant, you are prompted for the address of a known Oracle Names server. Unfortunately, if you are using namesctl, the utility will fail, and you have to rerun the command specifying the known address.

New Features for Net8 Oracle Names Server

With Oracle Names server version 8, you can either choose to use your current version 1 or version 2 Oracle Names server configuration, or you can incorporate the new features available in Oracle8i, version 8.1.6, Release 2. Among the new features is the use of the Dynamic Discovery option without the restriction of having only a single region or single domain.

Using this release of the Oracle Names server, a service can register itself with any Oracle Names server it can find. Once a service has registered itself, or an administrator has registered the service, its name and address are made available to all of the other Names servers. There are two different ways in which the service information is made available to the other servers: through a region database or stored within an Oracle Names server cache. If the information is stored in an Oracle database, it can be queried by all of the Oracle Names servers. If the service information is stored in an Oracle Names server cache, it's instantly replicated to the caches of the other Oracle Names servers.

In the new Net8 release, a discovery process is used to create a list of Oracle Names servers that a client can contact. This method replaces the manual configuration that was used in prior releases.

If you want to reduce the address lookup time the client spends contacting Oracle Names servers, you can configure the client to run a process that creates a client cache version of the data stored in the Oracle Names server. This cache contains the database addresses, Oracle Names server addresses, and other necessary service information.

Although you can configure the Oracle Names server version 8 without a database to hold topology information, Oracle Corporation recommends that you incorporate topology information in one.

The Oracle Names Control (namesctl) Utility

Just as the Listener Control (lsnrctl) utility is a tool that you run from the operating system prompt to start and control the Oracle listeners, the Names Control (namesctl) utility is used in the same way to start and control one or more Oracle Names servers. And, as with the Listener Control utility, you can issue commands either from the operating system level or from "inside" the tool for the Names Control utility. To access the tool and work within it, at the operating system prompt, you type

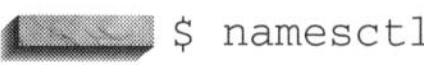

```
$ namesctl
```

If you do not follow the word **namesctl** with a command, you will be logged on to the tool and will see the following prompt:

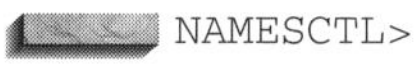

```
NAMESCTL>
```

There are several different forms of commands available for you to use with this utility. They are in the form of

- Operational commands (**stop**, **start**, **restart**, etc.)
- Modifier commands (**set** property)
- Informational commands (**status**, **show** property, and **ping**)
- Command utility commands (**exit**, **quit**, and **help**)

You can use any of these commands to perform basic management tasks on all of your Oracle Names servers from one central location as well as to view and change parameters. I'll tell you more about the various commands you can use with this utility later. Right now, let's look at how to migrate from a local naming method to the Oracle Names server.

Migrating from Tnsnames.ora to Oracle Names Server

Once you have created your Oracle Names server, you can upload your existing tnsnames.ora file. To perform the migration, you can use either the Net8 Assistant or the namesctl utility. In other words, you don't have to reinvent the wheel and retype all of your configuration data manually.

Realistically speaking, it's much easier to perform the migration using the Names Control utility. Here, I'll show you. To upload the tnsnames.ora file to an Oracle Names server using the Names Control utility, you perform the following steps:

1. Invoke namesctl by typing

    ```
    namesctl
    ```

2. From the NAMESCTL prompt, type

    ```
    NAMESCTL> load_tnsnames tnsnames.ora
    ```

See, I told you it was easy!

If you prefer, you can upload the tnsnames.ora file using the Net8 Assistant. As with the manual procedure above, this procedure also assumes that you have already created one or more Oracle Names servers. Here are the steps you use to accomplish this task:

1. Start the Net8 Assistant by running netasst from $ORACLE_HOME/bin on a UNIX system. Or from Windows NT, choose Start > Programs > Oracle HOME_NAME > Network Administration > Net8 Assistant.
2. From the navigator pane, expand the Oracle Names Servers list by clicking on the plus sign (+).
3. Select the Oracle Names server to which you want to upload the tnsnames.ora file.
4. At the top of the right pane is the pull-down list of values: Manage Server, Manage Data, Configure Server. From the list, select the Manage Data option.
5. By default, when you select the Manage Data option, the Net Service Names tab is selected.

6. The Action choices are Query, Add, Remove, and Load. Click Load.
7. In the File field, type the path where your current master tnsnames.ora configuration file is located.
8. Click Execute.
9. Choose the File > Save Network Configuration option.

Namesctl Commands

In Chapter 3, we explored the Listener Control (lsnrctl) utility, and I talked about the associated listener commands. Like the Listener Control utility, the Names Control (namesctl) utility has a group of commands that begin with **set** or **show**. Since these two commands operate in the same way as the Listener Control command, let's look at them first.

Set and Show Commands

Obviously, if you want to see the current value of a configuration setting for an Oracle Names server, you use the **show** command, and if you want to initialize or modify a configuration setting, you use the **set** command. The command qualifiers that are available for use with the **set** command are shown in Table 4-5.

For the most part, the **show** command has the same qualifiers as the **set** command, but there is no **password** qualifier for the **show** command. There are, however, three

Command Qualifier	Description
cache_ checkpoint_ interval	Sets how often all collected information about remote regions is saved in the local cache file whose default value is ckpcch.ora. The time value is in seconds. Minimum: 10 seconds Maximum: 259200 (3 days) Default: 0 (disabled)
default_domain	Sets the domain from which the namesctl client most often looks up name resolution requests, or changes the domain specified by the **names.default_domain** parameter in the sqlnet.ora file. The domain name will be automatically appended to any unqualified net service name or service name.

TABLE 4-5. *Namesctl Command Qualifiers*

Command Qualifier	Description
forwarding_ available	Turns on or off forwarding to remote Oracle Names servers for client name requests. Arguments: ON, OFF, YES, NO Default: OFF
log_file_name	Sets the name for the Oracle Names server's log file. Default: names.log
log_stats_ interval	Changes the frequency with which the statistics are logged to the log file. The time is in seconds. You can specify any valid combination, such as the number of days combined with number of hours, minutes, and seconds; or just the number in hours. Minimum value: 10 seconds Maximum value: no maximum Special value: 0 (which means never reset) Default value: 0 (no logging) Example: set log_stats_interval 129600 set log_stats_interval 1 day 12:00:00 (Both examples set the time to 36 hours.)
NAMESCTL_ trace_level	Sets the level at which the Names Control utility can be traced. Arguments: OFF—Tracing is not set. USER—Tracing is set to identify user-induced error conditions. ADMIN—Tracing is set to identify installation-specific problems. SUPPOR —Tracing is set to a level appropriate for support.
password	Sets the password for privileged namesctl commands, such as STOP, RESTART, RELOAD. **set password** does not change the Oracle Names server's password. It simply sets a namesctl variable that is sent over to the Oracle Names server with any namesctl command and is compared to the value configured on the Oracle Names server. If they match, operations requiring passwords are allowed. The password will always be encrypted when it is sent over the network.

TABLE 4-5. *Namesctl Command Qualifiers (continued)*

Command Qualifier	Description
requests_ enabled	Determines whether the current Oracle Names server will respond to requests. Setting this property to OFF will send refusals to all clients that approach with name resolution requests. This is primarily useful for diagnostics when an Oracle Names server is functioning unexpectedly. Values: ON, OFF
reset_stats_ interval	Changes the time between the statistics being reset to zero or initial values in the current server. Time is in seconds. Minimum value: 10 seconds Maximum value: no maximum Default value: 0 (never reset) (This command works the same way as log_stats_interval.)
save_config_ interval	Saves any changes made by **namesctl set** commands to the names.ora at an interval. Time is in seconds.
save_config_ on_stop	Specifies whether changes made by the **namesctl set** commands are saved to the names.ora file after the namesctl session has ended. The saving of all values occurs right before the namesctl session exits, taking as much care as possible to preserve the formatting, comments, and letter case. Arguments: ON, OFF
server	Sets the name of the Oracle Names server. If there are no arguments presented, the value stored in the **names.preferred_servers** parameter in the sqlnet.ora file will be used. Use this command to switch between multiple servers. The server qualifier can be either an address or the name of a server whose values are currently stored in the Oracle Names server's memory.
trace_file_name	Sets the name for the Oracle Names server's trace file. Default: names.trc

TABLE 4-5. *Namesctl Command Qualifiers (continued)*

Command Qualifier	Description
trace_level	Sets tracing for the Oracle Names server at a specific level. Arguments: OFF—No trace output USER—User trace information ADMIN—Administration trace information SUPPOR —World Wide Customer Support trace information

TABLE 4-5. *Namesctl Command Qualifiers (continued)*

additional qualifiers: status, system_queries, and version. Table 4-6 explains these qualifiers.

Command Qualifier	Description
status	Displays the general status information about the Oracle Names server. Use server names separated by a space to see the status of more than one server.
system_queries	Displays the next occurrence of all system queries. This command is only relevant in a distributed environment and shows the next scheduled time for a system query. Important when an administrator is determining whether to perform a **restart**.
version	Displays the current version and name of the Oracle Names server; very useful in determining the current server.

TABLE 4-6. ***show*** *Command Qualifiers*

The Rest of the Commands

The **set** and **show** commands are just two of the many commands available for use with the Names Control utility. You'll find a very brief description of the rest of the namesctl commands in Table 4-7. For more detailed information, see the *Oracle Net8 Administrator's Guide, Release 8.1.6.*

Command	Description
delegate_domain	Defines a domain as the start of a subregion of the current administrative region.
domain_hint	Enables you to specify domain hints for requests for data from remote regions. A domain hint contains the name of a remote domain and at least one address of an Oracle Names server in that domain. This enables the Oracle Names server to forward the request to a specific address, reducing network traffic. Without a domain hint, an Oracle Names server forwards a request to whatever remote Oracle Names servers it knows, which then forwards the request to the root Oracle Names server in its region. The root Oracle Names server will forward the request to the Oracle Names server that has information on the domain that the request refers to.
dump_ldap	Queries all the authoritative data in a domain or region and exports the data to an LDAP-compliant directory service or into an LDAP Data Interchange Format (LDIF) file, which can later be loaded into a directory.
dump_tnsnames	Writes the names and addresses of all addresses defined in the local region into a tnsnames.ora file.
exit	Exits from the Names Control utility.
flush	Instructs the Oracle Names server to clear all remote region information from its local cache checkpoint file, which has a default of ckpcch.ora.

TABLE 4-7. *Namesctl Commands*

Command	Description
flush_name	Instructs the Oracle Names server to clear a specific region's information from its local cache checkpoint file, which has a default of ckpcch.ora.
help	Provides a list of all the namesctl commands available. In response to one of the **help** commands, namesctl displays help on how to use the command.
list_delegated	Lists all the delegated domains for the root region or a specified domain.
list_domains	Lists all the domains in the root region or subdomains for a specified domain.
list_objects	Lists all the network objects for the root region or a specified domain.
load_ tnsnames	Loads all net service names and addresses defined in one or more tnsnames.ora files into an Oracle Names server.
log_stats	Logs the current set of statistics to the configured log file for that Oracle Names server. The log file has a default of names.log.
password	Sets an encrypted password for privileged Names Control utility commands.
ping	Contacts the current Oracle Names server, or named Oracle Names servers, and displays the request/response time.
query	Retrieves the contents of a network object stored in the Oracle Names server.
quit	Quits the Names Control utility.
register	Registers a network object to an Oracle Names server.
reload	Forces the Oracle Names server to check immediately for data changes in its administrative region. If there are any changes, the Oracle Names server reloads all database service names, net service names, global database links, and aliases.
reorder_ns	Creates the file that lists local Oracle Names servers and their listening addresses.

TABLE 4-7. *Namesctl Commands* (continued)

Command	Description
repeat	Performs **query**, **register**, **timed_query**, or **unregister** multiple times to compute average return rates.
reset_stats	Resets the Oracle Names server statistics to the original values of the Oracle Names server at start-up.
restart	Initiates a reset of an Oracle Names server to its original state at start-up.
set	Lists the available configuration commands that can be set for the current namesctl session.
show	Lists the available commands that can be shown for the current namesctl session. In response to one of the **show** commands, namesctl displays the current setting for that parameter.
shutdown	Stops one or more Oracle Names servers.
start	Loads the Oracle Names service program and starts loading system and local administrative region data.
start_client_cache	Starts the client cache daemon process.
startup	Loads the Oracle Names service program and starts loading system and local administrative region data.
status	Displays statistics for one or more Oracle Names servers as well as many of its internal settings.
stop	Stops one or more Oracle Names servers.
timed_query	Shows all data in the Oracle Names server cache.
unregister	Removes a network object from an Oracle Names server.
version	Displays the current version and name of the Oracle Names server.

TABLE 4-7. *Namesctl Commands* (continued)

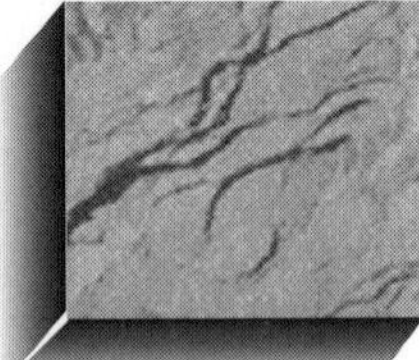

CHAPTER 5

Oracle Internet Directory

I needed to contact the Social Security Administration (SSA) office in my area recently. I opened the telephone book with the white pages and looked in the section with blue pages under the Federal Government listings. Since the telephone directory is set up in alphabetical order, I quickly found that the SSA has both a 1-800 number and a Web page.

From this example, we can surmise that a directory is a mechanism or an object that's used to store information about one or more subjects. Directories that are created with a logical flow, like the telephone book in alphabetical order, enable us to obtain specific information efficiently.

Given the definition of a directory as a mechanism or object in which you store information about one or more objects, what other forms of directories do you have around you right now? If you have a dictionary nearby, you have a directory of words. A recipe book might be considered a directory of recipes. My computer store catalog just arrived, and I consider it to be a directory of items available for purchase. Hmm, how about your TV or cable guide? Two more examples of directories that store many kinds of information together are an encyclopedia and an almanac.

Other than using directories on a computer to store Net8 configuration files, what do directories have to do with networking? Well, in this chapter we're going to look at the new Oracle8i feature called the Oracle Internet Directory (OID). This technology has been developed to comply with the Lightweight Directory Access Protocol (LDAP). I know that sounds a bit intimidating, but don't worry. I'll tell you all about LDAP as well as what the Oracle Internet Directory is, why you might want to use it, and how to perform its initial configuration. Since the Oracle Internet Directory is a very complex tool, telling you *everything* about it in one small chapter is impossible. Therefore, I'd like to give you enough information to get you started and help you to better understand the technology. If you need more in-depth information, I recommend you read the Oracle-supplied documentation, *Oracle Internet Directory Administration Guide, Release 2.0.6*, Part Number A77230-01. So, let's get started on our road to learning about electronic directories.

A Different Kind of Directory

Before we go any further, I want to make one point really clear. When I use the word "directory" in this chapter, I am referring to a specialized electronic database in which very specific information is being stored in a very precise manner. I am *not* referring to a computer directory in which you store files. This can be a very difficult mind-set to get over. If you have been dealing with computers for any length of time, you have learned that files are organized and compartmentalized within your computer for easier and more logical file access. These files are stored in several different computer file systems that are referred to as directories. Each computer directory structure has a name that either hints or openly tells you what that computer directory is storing.

Okay, so now we all know what a computer directory is. But, what do we know about the kind of directory that we're examining in this chapter? Well, in a computer environment, the kind of directory I'm referring to is a specialized database in which you store pieces of information. For example, within your email application, you have a list of friends and their associated email addresses. With some email applications, you can open your address book, type a few letters, and a search routine will locate the names that match the entry you typed. The address book is only available through the email application.

This form of directory lends itself well to any information resource that requires management. One of the common uses for this kind of directory is the storage of machine names, their IP addresses, and the other relevant information about each machine's location for net service name resolution as well as lists of authorized users for each machine and their privilege levels.

Enter, the Database Directory

Now, for a moment, let's consider a relational database. Isn't a relational database a mechanism used to organize and store information? Isn't it really just a set of files containing data and metadata stored in directories that the database engine accesses to provide information that you can manipulate? Well, yes. All of the electronic databases that I've ever encountered have been composed of files in directories. But, remember, we're not talking about computer directories. We're talking about relational databases and directory databases. However, we need to identify the things that set a relational database apart from a directory database.

Relational Database vs. Directory Database

For one thing, the way you interact with a relational database is different from the way you interact with a directory database.

Think about how you use a relational database. Let's say that you are using a database application for your local college. In this database are tables that contain information about the courses the college offers, each student's personal data, the courses in which each student is registered, each student's grades, and enrollment forms. As a student, you can view an enrollment form and sign up for one or more courses or modify your own personal information. You can look up an instructor's course schedule, and you may even be permitted to view your own grades online. As an instructor, you can insert each student's test scores and grades. You can take advantage of the database's relational capabilities to join the grade information with the student's personal data. As an administrative assistant, you can process student enrollments and add, update, or remove course information.

Hmm, so what you're doing is lots of inserts, updates, and a few deletes with some queries thrown into the mix. Granted, if you are looking at documents from a data warehouse, you won't do any data manipulation, but, for the most part, a relational database is used to store, retrieve, insert, update, and delete a large quantity of data items. Thus, I think we can safely say that a relational database is much more write intensive, handling very diverse forms of information. A relational database engine also expects to find its information in very specific areas, in a certain datafile located on a specific machine. The data locations the relational database relies on are stored in its data dictionary.

Now, let's examine a directory database structure. For the most part, when you interact with a directory database, you initially build the database and insert information to it, but once you've loaded the data to the directory database, you spend the majority of your time requesting to see small pieces of information. The information is generally stored in information pairs, like your friend's name and email address. A directory database is more read focused and tends to handle relatively simple transactions. There is little or no relational information stored in a directory database. What do you use to retrieve information from your directory database? In most cases, you use a directory server application to make the data available to you and all of your clients, and you use a client application to query the directory server.

A Look at Directory Servers

Okay, so now we're finally talking about the real main topic of this chapter. It sure took me long enough to get to it, didn't it. Let's start our look at directory servers in general, and then I'll get to Oracle's implementation of an LDAP Directory server. Okay? Oh, by the way, as this chapter is being written, Oracle Corporation is using the term Oracle Internet Directory to refer to their new technology. When I talk about generic LDAP directory server methods, I'll use the term "LDAP Directory server," and when I'm talking about Oracle's specific implementation of a directory server, I'll refer to it as "Oracle Internet Directory."

When we were looking at relational databases, I mentioned that the database expects to find its data in specific locations on specific machines. By contrast, a directory server's information is machine independent. Hmm, what does that mean to you and me?

Think back to the Oracle Names servers in Chapter 4. You have the ability when you create an Oracle Names server to declare that the servers will store their name translation information in their memory cache. If you are using this method of name information storage, as soon as a new name is registered, it's populated to all of the other Oracle Names servers in its region. Well, a directory server application is written to expect to see the same information throughout its environment, regardless of which server it is querying. What happens, though, if a client request can't be fulfilled locally? In that case, the server will either retrieve the requested information or point the client to a location where it can retrieve the information. This, of course, will be done transparently to the client.

Like the Oracle Names server, an LDAP Directory server enables translation of a location request from one form to another. Unlike the Oracle Names server, an LDAP Directory server can provide translations for objects other than Oracle-specific ones. An LDAP Directory server can link people, applications, and resources across machines, networks, and even geographic boundaries.

Let's say that you have spent a lot of time customizing your environment on your personal computer at work. You've got your desktop set up exactly as you want it, and the background and foreground colors are perfect for your temperament. Your environment profile is stored locally on your work PC. When you dial in from home to your network at work, however, your environment profile is not available to you. To set up your home PC in the same format as your PC at work, you have to reinvent the wheel, as it were. Wouldn't it be great to have your machine profile available to you from anywhere in the world? A directory provides the means by which users can access their environment settings from wherever they are.

About LDAP Directory Servers

If you drive an automobile, you know that there are many rules and regulations that you must follow. These rules and regulations tell you the actions you must take under specific circumstances to stay within the legal limits in your country. You may have a law that says that you cannot drive faster than a certain speed when driving by a school or that you must come to a complete stop when you reach a stop sign. You might be permitted to make a right turn after coming to a complete stop when the traffic light is red unless there is a sign posted that tells you not to turn right on red. All of these rules and regulations were created to help keep traffic flowing smoothly and safely.

In Chapters 1 and 2, I told you about various protocols on which Oracle Corporation has based its networking technologies. Remember that protocols are sets of rules that define how data is transported across networks. Just like our rules of the road, protocols are agreed-upon ways of doing things so that traffic on the network can flow smoothly and safely.

One advantage of using an LDAP Directory server is that you have a centralized location for many different forms of information. You can use an LDAP Directory server as a central repository for all of the information on your database network components, user and corporate policies, and even user authentication and security data. By having a single repository, you only need to make changes in one location instead of a potentially huge number of files. You also remove the need to have a tnsnames.ora file on each of your client and server machines. Since the directory stores names for other services, you can connect to different kinds of protocols from one configuration.

There are a few disadvantages to using an LDAP Directory server. For one thing, if you only have one central Directory server and it becomes unavailable, how will your request be answered? What happens if the application you're trying to run is disconnected from the network or partitioned in a way that the Directory server can't be accessed?

Another concern is that your clients are required to have access to the directory, and, therefore, you may have a potential security hole in your system. You see, by providing users access to the LDAP Directory server, you provide a possible way for a hacker to access all of your network component information as well as corporate policy data. I point these concerns out to you so that you will be aware of some of the potential problems as you design and configure your Directory server. If you use careful planning and forethought as you develop your Directory server, you can avoid many of these potential problems.

For example, if you want to guard against the directory being down or unavailable, you can use locally cached data from the time when the information was last read from the Directory server. The very latest changes may not be reflected in the cached data, but at least the majority of the needed information will be available if your server is down.

Okay, I've given you a lot of peripheral information about an LDAP Directory server, but I haven't really explained much about its composition. Let's look at a bit of LDAP history and some of the "rules of the road" to better understand what we're dealing with.

A Little LDAP Directory Server History

Produced by the Internet Engineering Task Force (IETF), the Lightweight Directory Access Protocol (LDAP) is an open Internet standard. Just to name a few of its accomplishments, the IETF is the same body that developed the TCP/IP, DNS, SMTP, NNTP, SNMP, and HTTP protocols.

X.500, which is the OSI directory service, incorporates many fine ideas but proved to be unsuited for implementation and deployment on the Internet. You see, X.500 has proven to be both complex and heavyweight in nature. Thus, implementations of X.500 are hard to use and require more computer resources than the average user has available. LDAP was originally developed to be a lightweight front end for the X.500 Directory Access Protocol. LDAP was designed to provide about 90 percent of the X.500 full functionality at about 10 percent of the resource cost. LDAP provides a simplified approach to directory access by supplying the following features:

- Runs directly over TCP/IP and eliminates the upper-layer overhead of the OSI multilayer communications stack that X.500 uses
- Eliminates X.500 little-used features and redundant operations, greatly simplifying the functionality

- Uses a simple string format for most data elements, while X.500 has more complicated and highly structured representations
- Provides a simplified version of the same rules that X.500 uses for encoding data for network transport

Originally, LDAP was used as a front end for the X.500 protocol. An LDAP client would contact an LDAP server that would, in turn, make its request to an X.500 server. There was still the overhead of dealing with the heavyweight and cumbersome X.500 server at the back end of the request process. Over time, the LDAP model was divorced from the X.500 protocol, and a stand-alone LDAP server was developed. With this model, the LDAP client makes its request directly to the LDAP server and gets an immediate response from that server. By using the LDAP model and eliminating the X.500 portion of the process, LDAP servers can function just like any other lightweight Internet servers with very low overhead and full integration with the Internet environment.

LDAP Models

There are four basic models that fully describe the LDAP operations, storage, and use. The models include

- Information model to define the kind of information that can be stored
- Naming model to define how information in an LDAP directory can be organized and referenced
- Functional model to describe what can be done with the information and how it can be accessed and updated
- Security model to define how information in the LDAP directory can be protected from unauthorized users and actions

Let's take a look at each one of these models to better understand how an LDAP Directory server is assembled and works.

Information Model

How do you describe yourself? Are you tall or short? Are you heavy, average weight, or thin? What color are your eyes and hair? Are you male or female?

If you want to use a directory to store descriptions of you and your friends, each person's description counts as one row or entry. Each entry is composed of attributes such as height, weight, hair color, eye color, and gender. Each attribute has rules associated with it. The rules are referred to as types. For example, the attribute eye color could be a character string type called **eyeColor**. Values are associated with each type. For the attribute **eyeColor**, the type is character string and the values are BLUE, BROWN, BLACK, HAZEL, VIOLET, and so on. So, what do we have here? We actually have an information model for how an LDAP Directory server entry is composed. Let's take a more formal look at this model.

The LDAP Information model defines what kind of information can be stored and is centered on individual entries. Generally, entries relate to concepts or objects in the real world, such as people, organizations, printers, locations, and so on. However, there is no actual requirement demanding that an entry relate to a real-world object. So, now you know that entries are composed of attributes that contain the information to be recorded about the object, and you know that each attribute has a type with one or more values. Figure 5-1 shows the composition of a generic entry with the type and values mapped to its attribute. Next to the generic entry, I've added a copy of the entry with equivalent values for the **eyeColor** attribute and its associated type and values to help you see the definitions more clearly.

Let's consider the type of an attribute a bit more. To determine the kind of information that's allowed to be stored in the value area, you can look at the syntax of the attribute's type. The type also defines how the values behave during a search or other directory operation. For example, let's look at the Common Name attribute, referred to in LDAP as "cn." The cn attribute has a syntax called **caseIgnoreString**. This syntax says that the case of the values will be ignored during comparisons and that the values must be character strings. Thus, the entries JONES, Jones, and jones would all be evaluated as matching. The attribute todayDate has an identical syntax to **caseIgnoreString** but is translated to ignoring any dashes or spaces in the dates during value comparisons. Using this context, the dates 10-02-2000 and 10022000 are viewed as identical.

Attributes can also have constraints applied to them that limit the size, composition, or number of arguments, and so on. For example, an attribute designed to hold a person's credit card number can be restricted to allow only

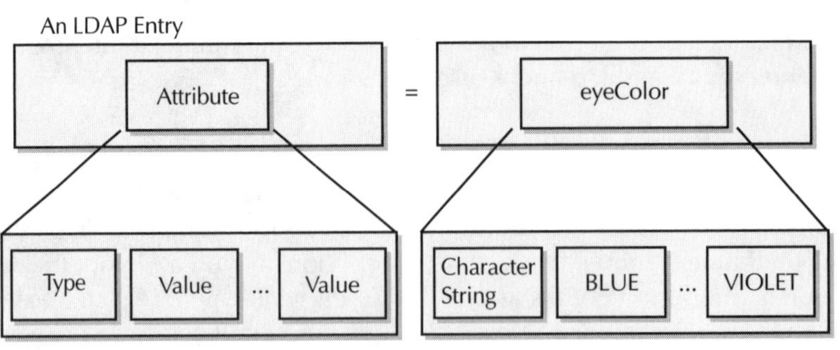

FIGURE 5-1. *LDAP Directory service entry with example*

one value to be input, or an attribute used to hold a document's text could have a maximum number of words allowed to restrict the disk space used for document storage. Content rules are used to define the required or permitted attributes on a per server basis. Instead of using content rules, you can use a special attribute in each entry called an **objectClass**. The **objectClass** defines the type of entry and determines the required and optional attributes. The **objectClass** for PERSON might require the attributes sr (surname) and cn (common name) as well as other attributes. The database equivalent for this form of structure is a schema. To change the current schema for an LDAP structure, you add new object classes to the entry.

Each entry has one special object class, called a *structural* object class, that defines what kind of entry it is. The structural object class cannot be changed. The rest of the object classes are called *auxiliary*. Auxiliary object classes may be added to or deleted from the entry based on any access rules in place. The version 3 LDAP standard contains a special object class called **extensibleObject** used to override any schema rules that are currently in place. Why would you want to permit the schema rules to be overridden? Well, sometimes there is a high resource cost in defining a new schema rule and making both the clients and servers aware of the change. In that case, it's more convenient and far less resource intensive to be able to just override the schema rules and add or remove attributes as needed.

LDAP Version 3 Enhancements

Oh, by the way, as long as I'm talking a bit about version 3 LDAP enhancements, I'd like to mention that the LDAP version 3 standards were adopted in December 1997 by the IETF as the Internet Standard. The new standards provide enhancements that Oracle has taken advantage of. The new standards enable Oracle to use the following features in the Oracle Internet Directory implementation:

- Supports the characters used in every language in the world
- Enables global deployment of a Directory Information Tree across multiple LDAP servers by using a referral mechanism (explained shortly, in the section "LDAP Referrals")
- Implements and supports a standard mechanism for Simple Authentication and Security Layer (SASL) and Transport Layer Security (TLS), which provides LDAP with a comprehensive and extensible framework for data security
- Enables vendors to extend existing LDAP operations through mechanisms called controls
- Enables publishing information useful to other LDAP servers and clients

Naming Model

Back in Chapter 2, I talked about hierarchical structures. Let's revisit the hierarchy chart for the XYZ Corporation shown in Figure 5-2. I've made a minor change to the chart that was shown as Figure 2-5 in Chapter 2, but the rest of this chart should look familiar to you. I've added a top-level entry labeled "XYZCORP."

Although there is no protocol requirement, LDAP Naming model entries are generally displayed in a tree structure that follows a geographical or organizational structure. The structure shown in Figure 5-2 is such a structure. Entries are named according to their position in the hierarchy, and each entry has a Distinguished Name (DN). Each component of the name is called a Relative Distinguished Name (RDN). Each RDN can be composed of one or more attributes from the entry.

To more easily understand the Naming model, consider the way a UNIX or Windows NT file system is structured and named. Think of the RDN as the name of a file on the system. The DN is the fully qualified pathname to that file. For example, look at this file name: D:\Ora816\Oracle\Network\Admin\trace_010500.trc. What part of the file name is the DN, and what part is the RDN? I'll let you think about the answer while we continue to look at the LDAP Naming model.

Just as two files in the same directory can't have the same name, entries with the same parent in an LDAP Directory must have different names. Also, leaf nodes and non–leaf nodes in an LDAP structure can contain information. The term *namespace* is used to refer to the combination of locations that make up a fully qualified path to get to the information you are interested in. In an operating system file structure, the namespace starts at the root or most significant component and proceeds downward to the file name. Thus, the directory path D:\Oracle\Ora81\network\admin is a

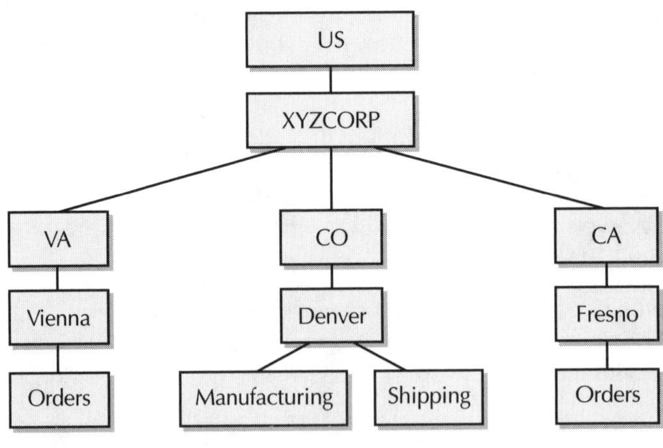

FIGURE 5-2. *Hierarchy chart for the XYZ Corporation, U.S. division*

namespace, and you start at the disk location D: to begin moving through the namespace to a file within the admin directory. In an LDAP structure, the namespace starts at the least significant component and proceeds upward towards the root. Therefore, you start at the cn= location of a common name and work your way up to a root level when working through an LDAP namespace. Before I show you an example of the Naming model, I need to tell you about the separators that are used.

In the file name I showed you earlier, the separators were backward slashes (\), although they could have been forward slashes (/) as well, depending on whether the operating system is UNIX or Windows NT. In LDAP, naming components are separated using commas (,). An LDAP entry might be named "cn=Orders,u=Vienna,st=VA,o=XYZCORP,c=US," where the common name is Orders, the unit is Vienna, the state is Virginia, the organization is XYZCORP, and the country is the United States. This example has the expanded RDNs of "cn=Orders," "u=Vienna," "st=VA," "o=XYZCORP," and DN "o=XYZCORP,c=US." Oh, by the way, in the earlier file name, the DN is "D:\Ora816\Oracle\Network\Admin\," and the RDN is "trace_010500.trc." Did you get it right? Great!

I just realized that this answer might be a bit confusing, so let's go over it more carefully. In the case of a file name, the entire fully qualified pathname could be considered equivalent to one piece of a Distinguished Name entry. Let's pretend that there is a unit called pathname that has the designation "pn." Following the LDAP Naming methods, you would consider the entire pathname as a single component: pn=D:\Ora816\Oracle\Network\Admin. The actual file name becomes cn=trace_010500.trc. If we decide to break the pn component into separate pieces, each individual piece below the root becomes an RDN, and the combination of pieces leading up from the area of interest becomes the DN. The whole point of naming is to ensure unique locations within the structure to enable the LDAP server to locate information quickly and accurately.

A Distinguished Name is really a sequence of Relative Distinguished Name components separated by either commas (,) or semicolons (;). Each RDN component is a set of attribute-value pairs, separated by plus signs (+). Now, what happens if the value itself contains a separator character? Well, in that case, the value must be enclosed in double quotes ("), or the separator character must be preceded by an escape character. The escape character is a backward slash (\). But, what if the value contains a double quote or backward slash? Well, then the character must be preceded with a backward slash. Hmm, following these rules, what would you do with the following: cn=http:\\mywebaddress.com? If you said, "cn=http:\\\\mywebaddress.com," you'd be right. Each backward slash in the common name must be preceded by an escape character backward slash. As a rule, since the naming conventions can get quite complicated, you would do well to stay away from multivalued RDNs and using commas as the separator of choice.

Of course, there is more to the Distinguished Name format than I'm showing here, but this should give you enough information to understand Oracle's implementation of LDAP Directory servers when we get to it later in this chapter.

Functional Model

Now that you know the kind of information that's being stored and the naming conventions and organization, let's look at what you can do with the information that's stored in an LDAP Directory. There are actually nine operations within three areas that you can perform. They are

- Interrogation: Search, compare
- Update: Add, delete, modify, modify RDN
- Authenticate: Bind, unbind, abandon

The interrogation options are used to search the LDAP Directory structure and retrieve information. Based on selection criteria known as a search filter, the search option is used to select information from a defined area of the directory tree. The search option can return a set of attributes, with or without values, for each matching entry that is found. The client can specify how long it is willing to wait for a response from the search. The client can also specify the size or number of entries that are acceptable.

As the heading implies, the update options enable you to add, modify, or remove information from the directory structure. The Modify option can be used to change the attributes and values within an existing entry. You can also add or delete attributes and values. You use the delete option to remove an existing entry. To change the name of an entry, you use the Modify RDN option.

The bind and unbind options under the authentication option lay the groundwork for you to secure information in the directory. The bind option allows a client to prove its identity. To prove its identity, the client provides a DN and a clear-text password. Interestingly enough, the server does not need to prove its identity to the client. In the case where no authentication is required, the client can provide a NULL DN and password. Use the unbind operation to terminate a directory session. The abandon option enables you to cancel an operation during processing. This is very useful if a search operation is taking too much time. LDAP version 3 includes much tighter security implementation, including a two-way authentication between the client and server in which the server must also prove its identity to the client.

Security Model

As we can surmise from the bind and unbind features of the Functional model, security is built around the identity of the clients attempting to access the LDAP Directory. The bind operation is used to provide this information. Once a client is identified, access control information is used to determine whether the client is permitted to access what is being requested. Since the LDAP model does not specify the format or capability of access control, the developer is free to implement the controls that make the most sense for his or her system. If replication of information is required between different implementations, a problem can arise if the access controls used by each implementation do not agree.

LDAP Referrals

When LDAP was used as a front end to the X.500 directory, the back-end directory server was expected to resolve all queries and return the final result or error to the client. If the back-end directory server could not handle the query, it would contact the other servers to ask the question on the client's behalf, referred to as *chaining*. The client remained totally unaware that another server had been involved with obtaining a result to its query.

The chaining model has proven to be far too rigid to be effective for the grassroots Internet philosophy. Thus, a new model, called the *referral* model, has been implemented. In a highly distributed and diverse environment like the Internet, referrals make it easier to deploy LDAP Directory servers. The referral model says that if an LDAP Directory server does not have the requested information, it can refer the client to another LDAP Directory server.

Now that you have some background information about basic LDAP history and models, let's take a look at how Oracle Corporation has implemented and enhanced this technology for use with Oracle databases.

Oracle Internet Directory Overview

Oracle Internet Directory, implemented as an application on Oracle8i, Release 2, combines LDAP version 3 features with the Oracle8i server. There are four components included in the implementation as follows:

- Oracle Directory server
- Oracle Directory Replication server
- Oracle Directory Manager
- Command line administration and data management tools

Using a multitiered architecture directly over TCP/IP, the Oracle Directory server responds to and supports updates to client requests for information about people and resources. The Oracle Directory Replication server, as the name implies, supports replication between LDAP Directory servers. If one server in the replication community is unavailable, a user can access the directory data from another server. The Oracle

Directory Manager is a Graphical User Interface (GUI) administration tool. The Oracle Internet Directory also supports a variety of command line administration and data management tools for manipulating large volumes of LDAP data.

Entries, Attributes, and Object Classes (Oh, My!)

Remember in Chapter 1 when I talked about the ISO OSI standards and the fact that each protocol layer is defined but the implementation of the standards is left up to the individual vendors? Well, the LDAP Directory server standards are no different. Vendors are left to develop code for their product's applications based on their interpretation of the protocol standards.

In talking about the various LDAP Directory server models earlier in this chapter, I talked about the composition of the LDAP Directory server based on the IETF adapted standards. Let's take a look now at Oracle's implementation and interpretation of these standards.

Entries

Did you ever play the game called hopscotch? I used to play it all the time. Get a large piece of sidewalk chalk, and I'll show you how to set up the game. Ready? Here's the way you draw the basic hopscotch shape. Look at Figure 5-3. When you draw the shape, be sure to make each square large enough to hold your entire foot without stepping on the lines around the box. Oh, and be sure to make the boxes large enough to be able to turn around in, on one foot!

To play the game, you choose a playing piece. A fairly round, thick stone will do nicely. You want the stone to be easy to pick up and lightweight but have enough body to be able to throw pretty accurately. You toss the stone into the square

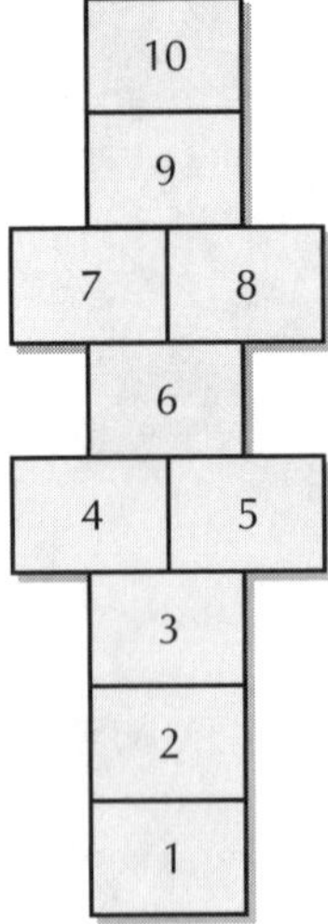

FIGURE 5-3. *Basic shape for hopscotch game*

numbered 1, and then hop into that square, bend over, pick the stone up, and hop back to the starting point, just outside and in front of square number 1. Now, mind you, you mustn't step on any lines while you're doing all of this hopping around, and you have to do this on one foot. Now that you've successfully completed the first round, you next throw your stone into the square marked 2. Continue to hop from square to square, until you reach the square your stone occupies, pick up your stone without falling over or stepping on any lines, turn around, and hop on one foot back to the starting point. Once you pass the number 5 square, as you hop up and back, you can put both feet down in the number 4 and number 5 squares at the same time. This helps give you a bit of rest.

Think about the path that you just took when playing the game. You followed a structured set of movements up and back based on the rules of the game. You entered and exited the squares in an established order and successfully picked up your token, or information, and then returned to your starting point. Great job! Now, let's see how Oracle expects the Oracle Internet Directory to be set up and how the information you need is located.

First of all, each individual collection of information within the directory is called an *entry*, and each entry is identified by a Distinguished Name. Just as each number identifies the square and also supplies the location in our hopscotch game, each Distinguished Name identifies the entry and defines the location of the information for that entry. The collection of entries, along with their associated Distinguished Names, is stored in a directory hierarchy called a *Directory Information Tree* (DIT).

Now, let's go back to our XYZ Corporation structure and see how the DIT would look for two different employees named Bebop Shuz in two different departments. Figure 5-4 shows the DIT with the employee locations.

Given the following information and Figure 5-4, let's see if you can derive the correct Distinguished Name for each employee. Remember that *o* means organization, *c* means country, *ou* is for organizational unit, and *cn* represents the common name.

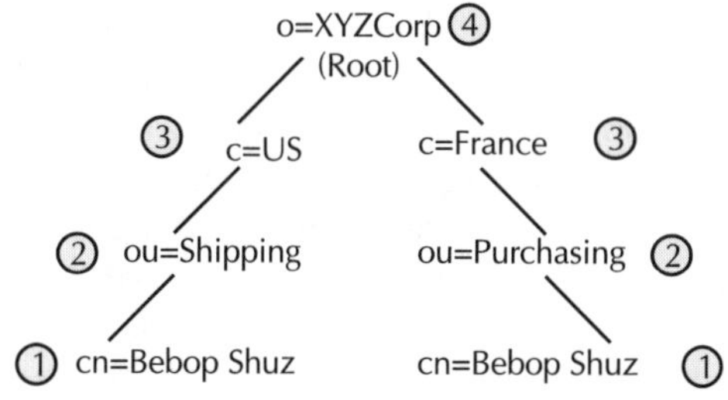

FIGURE 5-4. *Directory Information Tree hierarchy with two employees*

Below the cn level are the attribute values like email address, office location, and so on. Also, keep in mind that it's possible for each level to contain attributes.

When you assemble a Distinguished Name, you begin at the lowest level and work your way upward instead of starting at the root and working down the tree. I've numbered the levels to guide you in assembling the Distinguished Names for the employees. Okay, go ahead and write down your answers. I'll wait.

Here's my answer: cn=Bebop Shuz, ou=shipping, c=US, o=XYZ Corp, and cn=Bebop Shuz, ou=purchasing, c=France, o=XYZ Corp. The lowest DIT component, called the Relative Distinguished Name (RDN), is placed first, at the leftmost position, and then you work your way up the tree to the top, just as you hop from the lowest to the highest number in hopscotch. At each level, the element itself is referred to as an RDN. Thus, the RDN just above the Bebop Shuz entry is the ou value. So, we can say that a Distinguished Name is just a sequence of RDNs separated by commas. To locate the correct entry in the Oracle Internet Directory, you must use the entire DN and not just a single RDN.

In the example in Figure 5-4, there are two employees with the same name, but they are identified uniquely because they are in different organizational units and in different countries. What happens if you have employees with the same names in the same organizational unit? Well, in that case, you must find another way to uniquely identify each of them. You can assign unique identification numbers to them or use their middle names or initials for their common names.

Attributes

When we were looking at the general LDAP Directory server models earlier in this chapter, I mentioned that each entry is made up of attributes and that each attribute consists of an attribute type and one or more values. The attribute type tells you what kind of information is stored. For example, the attribute types for employees could be jobTitle=, salaryAmount=, departmentNumber=, telephoneNumber=, and so on. The values for jobTitle= could be "Manager," "Clerk," "Software Specialist," or "Database Administrator."

Within the Oracle Internet Directory, you can store two kinds of information: application information and operational information. The values that I just listed for the jobTitle attribute are application information. They are information that the client cares about and extracts from the directory structure. Operational information, on the other hand, pertains to the operation of the directory itself. For example, a time stamp for an entry will influence the behavior of the server since the time stamp is referenced each time a refresh of all the directory servers in the system is performed.

You can have attributes with only one value or multiple values. The telephone Number attribute can store more than one value for an employee, such as home number, work number, and cellular number, while a gender attribute will be single valued. If you have established an email group to hold all of the addresses for your sports team, you've created a multivalue attribute.

A set of standard LDAP attributes is available, and Oracle Internet Directory implements all of them. Some of the more common LDAP attributes are shown in Table 5-1.

Oracle Internet Directory also provides several proprietary attributes that can be found in Appendix F of the *Oracle Internet Directory Administrator's Guide, Release 2.0.6.*

Just as a general LDAP Directory server attribute contains both type and value, Oracle Internet Directory attributes contain a type or syntax requirement to describe the nature of the values being stored. The telephoneNumber attribute could have a type that prohibits anything but numbers and dashes to be stored within each value. Another attribute might specify that only characters can be stored or that the data cannot be printed. Oracle Internet Directory supports and implements all of the LDAP standard types and syntax, and you can't add any new ones to your directory.

Attribute	**String**	**Definition**
commonName	cn	Common name of an entry. Example: cn=Anne Smith
domainComponent	dc	Component in a Domain Name System (DNS). Example: dc=uk,dc=acme,dc=com
jpegPhoto	jpegPhoto	Photographic image in JPEG format. The path and file name of the JPEG image you want to include as an entry attribute. Example: /photo/audrey.jpg
organization	o	Name of an organization. Example: o=XYZCORP
organizationalUnitName	ou	Name of a unit within an organization. Example: ou=Server Development

TABLE 5-1. *Common LDAP Attributes Used by Oracle*

Attribute	String	Definition
owner	owner	Distinguished Name of the person who owns the entry. The following is a line in an LDIF file: Example: owner: cn=Anne Smith, ou=Server Development, o= Acme, c=uk
surname	sn	Last name of a person. Example: sn=Smith
telephoneNumber	telephoneNumber	Telephone number. Example: telephoneNumber=(650) 123-4567 or telephoneNumber=650 1234567

TABLE 5-1. *Common LDAP Attributes Used by Oracle* (continued)

When I talked about the LDAP Functional model earlier in this chapter, I mentioned that rules are used to define how attributes are viewed when a search is performed. For example, the values 703-555-1212 and 7035551212 can be viewed as matching depending on what matching rules are applied. Oracle Internet Directory recognizes all of the LDAP standard matching rules and enforces the following rules:

- DistinguishedNameMatch
- caseExactMatch
- caseIgnoreMatch
- numericStringMatch
- IntegerMatch
- telephoneNumberMatch

Object Classes

So far, we've covered entries and attributes. Now, to tackle object classes. You assign one or more object classes when you define a directory entry. An object class contains attributes and is a category of objects. An object class can have both mandatory and optional attributes.

In the case of the object class organizationalPerson, the attributes commonName (cn) and surname (sn) are mandatory, while other attributes like telephoneNumber and streetAddress are available but not required.

Standard LDAP object classes and some proprietary object classes are provided at installation time for the Oracle Internet Directory. You cannot add mandatory attributes to the sets of attributes in the predefined object classes, but you can add optional attributes to an existing object class, define a new object class, or define an object subclass. Huh? What's a subclass?

About the Object Class "top"

My friend Vinnie is the manager of his corporation's baseball team. He has 25 men on his team. The night of a game, Vinnie makes up his starting lineup from his team roster. He lists the 9 men he wants to start the game, including their field positions and their batting order. In Oracle Internet Directory terms, the entire roster of 25 men is the superclass of my personally created object class "baseballTeam." The 9 starting players are a subclass derived from the baseballTeam object class. A subclass inherits all of the attributes of the superclass from which it's derived. Entries in an Oracle Internet Directory may inherit the attributes defined by multiple object classes.

There's one special object class that's called "top." This object class has no superclasses above it, and it's one of the superclasses of every structural object class. Every entry in the directory inherits the attributes in top. For the Oracle Internet Directory, top has one mandatory object class called objectClass. There are several optional attributes as well that I've listed in Table 5-2.

Attribute	Description
orclGuid	Global identification that remains constant if the entry is moved
creatorsName	Name of the object class creator
createTimestamp	Time when the object class was created
orclACI	User-modifiable optional attribute that represents the Access Control List policy information
orclEntryLevelACI	Contains Access Control List directives and is multivalued

TABLE 5-2. *Optional top Object Classes*

There are three types of object classes available: abstract, structural, and auxiliary object classes. Abstract object classes are considered to be virtual object classes, and they can't be the only object class for an entry. Top is an abstract object class and is a superclass for all of the other object classes in the Oracle Internet Directory.

Most of the object classes that make up the Oracle Internet Directory are structural in nature. Structural object classes define what kinds of object classes can be created under a specific object class. For example, a Directory Information Tree structure rule can specify that all objects located directly below the person object class must contain physical feature object classes. Thus, you could not place the address object class directly under the person object class. You could, however, enter gender, hairColor, or eyeColor object classes. Please be aware of the fact that Oracle Internet Directory does not enforce structure rules at this time. You can't help wondering what good the rules are if they aren't enforced. Perhaps, sometime in the future, they will be.

Auxiliary object classes are used to expand the existing list of attributes in an entry when you don't want to redefine an existing object class. Perhaps you've defined an entry as a member of two object classes and you now need to have additional attributes that don't belong in the existing object classes. What are you going to do? Well, you can create an auxiliary object class and place the new object classes in it. Then you can associate this new class with the entry and not impact the existing object classes. For example, you could have an existing object class called horses that included Arabian horses as well as palominos, buckskins, Clydesdales, and paints. You need a class of horses that is comprised exclusively of working breeds. It would not be appropriate to redefine the current object class. Therefore, you can create an auxiliary object class called workHorses.

Subentries and Schemas

Within an Oracle database, the metadata is stored in an area referred to as the data dictionary. The composition of each object, including its name, size, and type, is stored in this area along with much more information. Within the Oracle Internet Directory, metadata like the object classes, attributes, syntaxes, and matching rules is stored within a structure called the dictionary schema. The dictionary schema holds its information in a special class of entry called a subentry. The subentry, in turn, is called subSchemaSubentry, which is part of the LDAP version 3 standards. You modify the subSchemaSubentry to add new object classes and objects. Oracle Internet Directory supports a set of matching rules and syntaxes. You can't add new matching rules and syntax beyond those that the Oracle Internet Directory supports.

Distributing a Directory

In Oracle's early days, the database generally resided on one computer in one centralized location. As database technology and computer software and hardware matured, we gained the ability to distribute our databases over more disks, and now we can distribute a database across computers that are physically placed around the world. Parts of your database might reside on a computer in Paris, France, while other parts might reside on a computer in Paris, Virginia. To anyone using the database, it appears as one logically centralized structure.

In the same way, you can physically distribute your Oracle Internet Directory data onto several servers and still have it appear as one logically centralized entity. There are two advantages to distributing the directory data across servers. By distributing the data, you increase the volume of data that can be stored and decrease the amount of work each individual server must perform. Additionally, you remove a potential bottleneck and can allow subsets of users to continue working should one distributed directory become inaccessible.

To accomplish directory distribution, the directory data is divided into units called naming contexts. Each naming context is actually a subtree that resides on one server and begins with an entry that can serve as the top. The subtree extends down from the top to either leaf entries as ending points or references to subordinate naming contexts. There is no written limit to the size of a naming context, so it can be as small as a single entry or as large as the entire Directory Information Tree.

To distribute a directory, you can use either replication or partitioning. Hmm, what's the difference? Just as the name implies, when you replicate something, you make an exact copy of it. When you partition something, you divide it into pieces. So, you can distribute your directory by copying the same naming context from one machine to another or by dividing it into one or more unique, nonoverlapping naming contexts and placing each naming context on a different machine.

Net8 and Oracle Internet Directory

What do the Oracle listener, Oracle Names server, and Oracle Internet Directory node all have in common? Hmm, good question. If you said, "They are all applications that can run on the Oracle8i server," you'd be partially correct. If you said, "They all communicate using Net8," you'd be absolutely right. You see, an Oracle Internet Directory may or may not be on the same machine as the Oracle database, but either way, it will use Net8 to communicate with the database just as the listener and Oracle Names server will use Net8 for communications. To communicate with an Oracle8i database, OCI and Net8 are used.

About the Components

Look at Figure 5-5. You can see the relationship between LDAP clients and the Oracle Internet Directory as well as the part that Net8 plays in enabling the directory to communicate with the Oracle8i database. LDAP clients make requests to the Oracle Internet Directory server. The server, in turn, connects to the Oracle8i directory and performs a search for the requested information. When the search has completed, the results are returned to the LDAP client through the Oracle Internet Directory server.

Now, let's look at the actual components that are involved. Table 5-3 shows the Oracle Internet Directory components and their descriptions.

By default, the Oracle Internet Directory server is installed with a configuration set entry. Each configuration set entry is called a **configset**. The configset holds the configuration parameters of a specific instance of the directory server. When you issue a start-server or stop-server command from the Oracle Internet Directory Control utility, the command contains a reference to one of these configset entries. The Oracle Internet Directory Monitor executes the request from the oidctl command and uses the information that the configset contains. The default configset that's

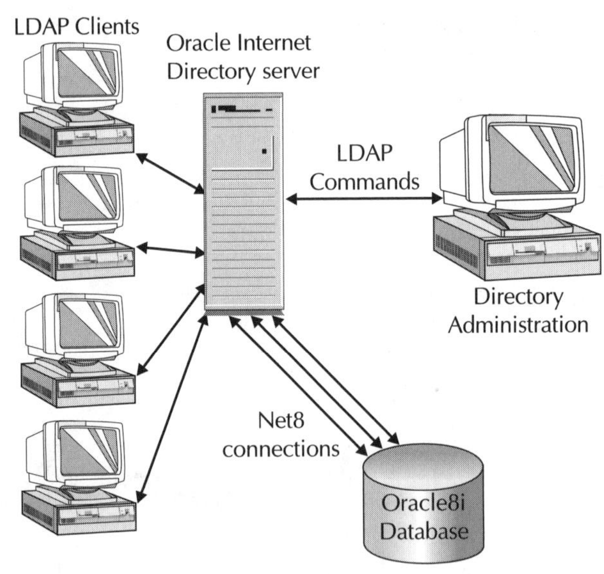

FIGURE 5-5. *Oracle Internet Directory/Net8 communications*

Component	Description
LDAP server instance	Services directory requests through a single Oracle Internet Directory dispatcher process listening at a specific TCP/IP port number (by default, non-SSL port number 389 or SSL port number 636). If you have more than one LDAP server on a machine, each LDAP server instance must listen on a different port. Multiple threads are used by Oracle Internet Directory dispatcher and server processes.
Replication server	Tracks and sends changes to replicated servers in an Oracle Internet Directory system. Only one replication server can be on a node. The Replication server is optional.
Oracle8i database	Stores the directory data. The database can reside on the same node as the servers, or on a separate node. Oracle recommends that you use separate databases for Oracle8i and the Oracle Internet Directory server.
OID Control utility (oidctl)	Used to start or stop directory server instances. The OID Monitor interprets oidctl commands. Oidctl communicates with oidmon by placing message data in OID server tables, including configuration parameters needed to run OID instances.
OID Monitor (oidmon)	Initiates, monitors, and terminates the LDAP server processes. OID Monitor will control a replication server if you choose to install one.

TABLE 5-3. *Oracle Internet Directory Components*

installed is called configset0. By having a preconfigured entry available, you can run the Oracle Internet Directory server immediately upon installation. You can configure new entry sets to customize your environment and can view, add, and modify entries by using either the OID Manager or the supplied command line tools. I'll tell you more about the OID Manager tool later in this chapter.

If a server should abnormally stop running, the OID Monitor will restart the process. Upon starting a server instance, the OID Monitor puts an entry in the directory instance registry and updates the data in a process table. The registry entry and the process table entry are deleted when the OID Monitor shuts the server instance down. Let's say that a server instance has stopped abnormally. When the OID Monitor restarts it, the registry entry will be updated with the new server start time.

There's a file on the system called ORACLE_HOME/ldap/log/oidmon.log in which all OID Monitor activity is logged. The operating system provides the mechanisms that the OID Monitor uses to check the state of the servers.

Following a Client Request

To follow an LDAP client request and see how it's processed, you need to understand the components of the LDAP directory server instance. There's an Oracle Internet Directory dispatcher process that listens at its designated port for LDAP commands. The OID dispatcher process has both a listener and dispatcher mechanism to perform its duties.

When the LDAP directory server starts, server processes are created. You use the configuration parameter **orclserverprocs** to define how many server processes are started. The default is one process. By starting more than one server process, OID can take advantage of multiple processor systems. To process each client's request, a worker thread is used for each operation process. The parameter **orclmaxcc** is used to control the maximum number of database connections that can be spawned as needed from each server process. The default for this parameter is 10.

Okay, so let's see what happens from the time that a client decides to enter a search request.

1. The client enters a search request that may contain one or more of these options:

   - SSL: The Secure Sockets Layer provides encryption and authentication or just encryption. Without SSL, the client request is sent as clear text, which is very easily read by a network sniffer.

   - Type of user: Either a particular user or an anonymous user—the type of user provided will depend on the privileges required to perform the specific function.

   - Filters: Used to narrow the search and can include Boolean conditions like AND, OR, and NOT. Operators like GREATER THAN, EQUAL TO, and LESS THAN can also be used.

2. The client can use either OID Manager or command line tools to issue the command. If the OID Manager is used, a query function in Java Native Interface is invoked. The Java Native Interface, in turn, invokes the C API. If a command line tool is used, a C function in the C API is invoked directly.

3. A request is sent to the directory server instance using the LDAP protocol to connect to the directory.
4. Through a process called *binding*, the directory server authenticates the user and checks the Access Control Lists (ACLs) to make sure the user has the correct privileges to perform the requested search.
5. The search request is converted from LDAP to an Oracle Call Interface (OCI) request by the directory server and sent over Net8 to the Oracle8i database.
6. The Oracle8i database views the request as it would any other request and fetches the information to be sent back up the chain through the directory server, to the C API, and back to the client.

Installing the Oracle Internet Directory

There doesn't seem to be an easy way to find out how to perform the initial installation of the Oracle Internet Directory in the Oracle documentation set, so I'd like to take some time here to talk about, and walk you through, this very important step.

To perform the OID installation, you must use the Oracle Universal Installer. When you are initially prompted with the Available Products option screen, select the third option, Oracle8i Management Infrastructure 8.1.6.0.0. After making your selection, you click the Next button and are presented with the Installation Types wizard screen shown in Figure 5-6.

During the OID installation, if you already have Oracle8i, Release 2, installed on your system, you are prompted to use an existing instance or have the installation create a new one. If you opt to use an existing instance, you are prompted on the next screen to enter the SID for the instance you want to use. Next, you are given the opportunity to decide whether you want the userPassword attribute encrypted. I clicked on No to refuse encryption, so the next screen presented showed me that the Distinguished Name for the area would be "cn=orcladmin." The length of the default password is shown, but the value is not displayed. As you'll see later in this chapter, the default password is "welcome."

The next screen gives you the option to select the approximate number of directory entries that you think will be stored. The values range from less than 10,000 to more than 1,000,000. Finally, you are prompted to affirm the number and type of products that are to be installed, and the actual installation is performed. You can track the progress of the installation by watching the messages that are displayed in the Configuration Tools screen. It's really amazing how easy the installation is once you know how to do it.

Please note that although the installation screen indicates that the installation will require 723 megabytes, far less space will be required if you have already installed other Oracle8i products. The size shown assumes that you are performing a complete Oracle8i installation.

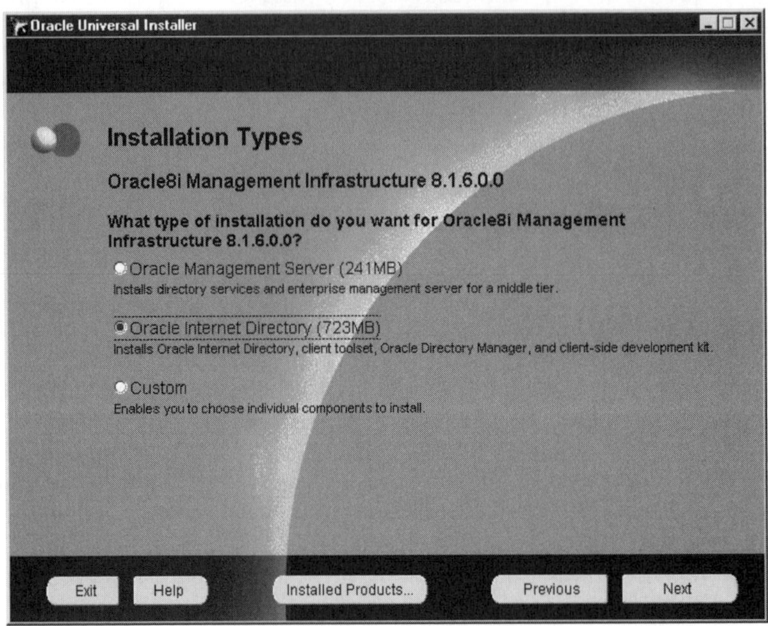

FIGURE 5-6. *Universal Installer Installation Types screen*

Let's take a look now at the OID tool set to see what you can do with your Oracle Internet Directory and how to perform each task.

Oracle Internet Directory Tools

There are several command line tools and one GUI tool that you can use to interact with and administer the Oracle Internet Directory server, as follows:

- Command line tools, interacting with text lines written in LDAP Data Interchange Format (LDIF) files, used for manipulating entries and attributes
- Bulk tools used to load, modify, and delete a large number of entries efficiently and to copy data from the directory information base into an LDIF file for use in bulk data loads
- OID Control utility for starting and stopping the OID server processes
- Catalog Management tool
- OID Database Password utility for setting and changing passwords (default password for an Oracle Internet Directory is "ODS")
- OID Manager GUI tool for OID administration and management

Let's take a look at the options provided by each of these tools.

Command Line Tools

In Chapter 3, we looked at the listener and the Listener Control utility (lsnrctl). To invoke the utility, you had to be at the operating system level—either at the Windows NT DOS prompt or at the UNIX operating system dollar sign ($) prompt. The same approach is used for the Oracle Names server utility, namesctl. For the Oracle Interface Directory server, there are several different command line tools available to provide different types of directory entry management. You can use some tools to affect the direction information individually, or you can use other tools to affect whole groups of information. Other tools are available to enable you to perform directory management tasks. Let's take a look at each of the command line tools first and finish this chapter with an examination of a Graphical User Interface tool, OID Manager, that you can use to perform administrative tasks.

Tools to Manipulate Entries and Attributes

The first set of command line tools we're going to look at are used to manipulate entries and attributes. To use these tools, you create entries using the LDAP Data Interchange Format and place the entries in a text file. The composition of each entry in the file is the Distinguished Name, one or more attribute types, and their values, with one attribute type per line. Table 5-4 contains the command line tool names in LDIF format and their descriptions.

Tool	Description
ldapsearch	Search for directory entries.
ldapbind	Authenticate user/client to a directory server.
ldapadd	Add entries one at a time.
ldapaddmt	Add several entries concurrently by using this multithreaded tool.
ldapmodify	Create, update, and delete attribute data for an entry.
ldapmodifymt	Modify several entries concurrently by using this multithreaded tool.
ldapdelete	Delete entries.
ldapcompare	See whether an entry contains a specified attribute value.
ldapmoddn	Modify the DN or RDN of an entry, rename an entry or a subtree, or move an entry or a subtree under a new parent.

TABLE 5-4. *Command Line Tools in LDIF Format*

Tools to Affect Groups of Entries

You use the second type of command line tools to perform tasks that affect a large number of directory entries. Using these tools you can perform bulk data loads, copy data to a file in LDIF format for bulk loads to another directory, and modify or delete a large number of directory entries. Table 5-5 shows each of these command line tools and the task you can perform with them.

Oracle Internet Directory Control Utility

The OID Control utility is used to start and stop an Oracle Internet Directory server process. The OID Monitor process interprets and executes these commands. Here is the syntax for starting an LDAP server instance:

```
oidctl connect=<NET_SERVICE_NAME> server=OIDLDAPD
instance=<SERVER_INSTANCE_NUMBER> start
```

Keep in mind that the server name is a constant value equal to OIDLDAPD, if you are not using directory replication, and OIDREPLD, if you are using it. The instance number is a number that you arbitrarily assign to the instance. The command **oidctl** is used to activate the OID Control utility. You must supply a service name and instance number. The rest of the available parameters are optional. For an Oracle Internet Directory with the net_service_name of OID1 and the instance number of 2, the command is as follows:

```
oidctl connect=OID1 server=OIDLDAPD instance=2 start
```

Tool	Description
bulkload	Load a large number of entries to Oracle Internet Directory through LDIF files.
ldifwrite	Copy data from the directory information base into an LDIF file. Any LDAP-compliant directory server can read this file. This tool can be used in conjunction with bulkload to create the load file. An ldifwrite file can be used to back up information from all or part of a directory.
bulkmodify	Modify a large number of existing entries at the same time.
bulkdelete	Delete a subtree quickly.

TABLE 5-5. *Bulk Data Command Line Tools*

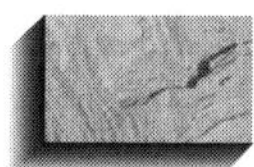

NOTE
When you attempt to start the Oracle Internet Directory process, you may get the error message "NLS_LANG not set in environment. Please set NLS_LANG to the appropriate UTF8 character set." At the operating system prompt, issue this command: set NLS_LANG=AMERICAN_AMERICA.UTF8, and then issue the ***start*** *command again. On one platform, the database had to actually be built with the UTF8 character set before the process would start. On another platform, just setting the NLS_LANG value was enough. At the time of this writing, there is an open issue with Oracle Support about this problem.*

Now, let's look at the parameter descriptions. Table 5-6 shows all of the OID Control utility parameters and their descriptions.

Parameter	Description
net_service_name	The name specified in your tnsnames.ora file, if you have one configured. The file is located in ORACLE_HOME/network/admin.
server	Type of server to start. The valid values are OIDLDAPD and OIDREPLD. The server value is not case sensitive.
server_instance_number	Instance number of the server to start. Valid value range is a number between 0 and 1000.
configset_ number	Configset number used to start the server. If not set, the value defaults to configset0. Valid value range is a number between 0 and 1000.
-p port_num	Specifies a port number during server instance startup. The default port is 389.
-debug debug_level	Specifies a debug level during LDAP server instance startup.
-h host_name	Specifies the host name on which the server runs.

TABLE 5-6. *Parameters for the Oracle Internet Directory Control Utility*

Parameter	Description
-l	Turns replication change-logging on and off with off = -l. If the flag is omitted, replication change-logging is turned on. The values are TRUE and FALSE, and the default is TRUE. This is valid on the directory server only.
-server n	Specifies the number of server processes to start on this port.
start	Starts the server specified in the server argument.
stop	Stops the server specified in the server argument.

TABLE 5-6. *Parameters for the Oracle Internet Directory Control Utility* (continued)

The Catalog Management Tool

To make attributes available for searches, indexes are used within the Oracle Internet Directory. By default, when the OID is installed, to list available attributes for searches, the entry cn=CATALOGS is used. If an attribute has an equality-matching rule, it can be indexed. To make additional attributes available in search filters, you must add entries to the catalog using the Catalog Management tool.

To use the Catalog Management tool, if you are on a UNIX system, you must first unset the LANG parameter. For the Korn shell, you type **unset lang**, and for the C shell, you type **unsetenv lang**. Once you've made your changes, you can reset the LANG value to whatever it was before you began your Catalog Management tool session. You can either add an index or delete an index for the attribute you specify using this tool. The syntax is as follows (I found catalog.sh in ORACLE_HOME\ldap\bin on my Windows NT machine):

```
catalog.sh -connect <NET_SERVICE_NAME> <add|delete> -attr <ATTR_NAME> -file <FILENAME>
```

You can either specify attributes to index one at a time, or you can specify a file name to have all of the attributes in a file indexed. The attributes in the file must be listed one per line. Likewise, you can delete the index from one attribute at a time or from an entire file of attributes.

You must know the correct password for the OID user to successfully run the Catalog Management tool. If you don't furnish the correct password, you will not be able to execute the tool. After you complete your indexing actions, you can reset the value for LANG by typing **set lang=<appropriate_language>**, **export lang** for the Korn shell, and **setenv lang** <appropriate_language> for the C shell.

OID Database Password Utility

When connecting to an Oracle database, the OID uses a password. As mentioned earlier, the default password is ODS. Using the OID Database Password utility, you can change this password. On a UNIX system, the command is as follows:

```
oidpasswd
```

When you activate the OID Database Password utility, you will be prompted for the current password, your choice of new password, and a confirmation of the new password. When you use it, the OID Database Password utility assumes by default that you intend to change the password for the database defined by ORACLE_HOME and ORACLE_SID. If this is not the case, you must use the parameter **connect=<NET_SERVICE_NAME>**.

OID Manager Tool

The only Graphical User Interface tool in the Oracle Internet Director toolbox is the OID Manager tool. Before you can run this tool, you must have a directory server instance running. What does that mean? Well, quite simply, you must first start the OID Monitor daemon before you can start a server instance, and you must have a server instance running before you can start the OID Manager tool. All of this assumes that you have created an Oracle Instance Directory and have the OID software installed on your system. At the end of Chapter 9, you'll find the steps to create an Oracle Internet Directory using the Net8 Configuration Assistant tool.

Starting and Stopping the OID Monitor

To start the OID Monitor, you must first set the appropriate language setting. Set at installation, the default language is AMERICAN_AMERICA. Once you have set the appropriate language, if it's other than the default, you will issue your **start** command at the operating system prompt as follows:

```
oidmon <connect=NET_SERVICE_NAME> <sleep=NUMBER_OF_SECONDS> start
```

The arguments for **connect=** and **sleep=** are optional. The NET_SERVICE_NAME is the one found in your tnsnames.ora file for the OID server. The **sleep** value that you use tells the OID Monitor how many seconds to wait before checking for new requests from the OID Control utility and for restart requests for servers that may have stopped. The **sleep** argument default is 10 seconds. To stop the OID Monitor, you use the same syntax as shown here, but you put "stop" at the end of the command instead of "start."

Once you have the OID Monitor started, you can start the server instance. To accomplish this task, you use the Oracle Internet Directory Control utility just as I described it earlier. After you have the OID Monitor and OID server instance started, you are ready to start and work with the OID Manager tool. Finally!

Oracle Internet Directory Manager Tool

To start the Oracle Directory Manager tool from a Windows NT system, you use the Start > Programs > Oracle <ORACLE_HOME> > Oracle Internet Directory > Oracle Directory Manager option. For a UNIX box, at the operating system prompt, type **oidadmin**. The first time you attempt to connect, you are told that you must connect to a server. Click OK.

You will be prompted for a username and password. Here is the list of appropriate usernames and passwords when you first log on:

- To log in as the superuser to configure SSL features, in the User box, type **cn=orcladmin**.
- To log in anonymously, leave the User box empty.
- If you've already set up the user's entry by using the LDAP command line tools, enter the appropriate username either by using the Browser button or by entering the Distinguished Name in the form cn=<NAME>,ou=< ORGANIZATIONAL UNIT>,o=<ORGANIZATION>,c=<COUNTRY>.

If you established a superuser password during installation, you can enter that password to connect as the superuser. By default, the password for the OID Manager tool is "welcome." If you are logging in anonymously, leave the Password box blank.

Once you've logged in either as the superuser, anonymously, or through an account that you've established, you will see the welcome screen shown in Figure 5-7.

Using the Oracle Directory Manager, you can create object classes, attributes, access control points, and entries, and you can configure entry management. You can refresh entries and subentries and drop indexes. You can create original files and create new files to be exactly like other existing files. You can either use the pull-down menu lists, or you can use the toolbar icons to perform your tasks.

After you've configured your Oracle Internet Directory, you'll see entries for Subtree Access Management, Entry Management, Schema Management, and Audit Log Management. You can perform configuration for Secure Sockets Layer as well as unsecured directory access.

Looking at the toolbar in Figure 5-7, a brief description of each of the icons starting at the leftmost icon, the plug, is given in Table 5-7.

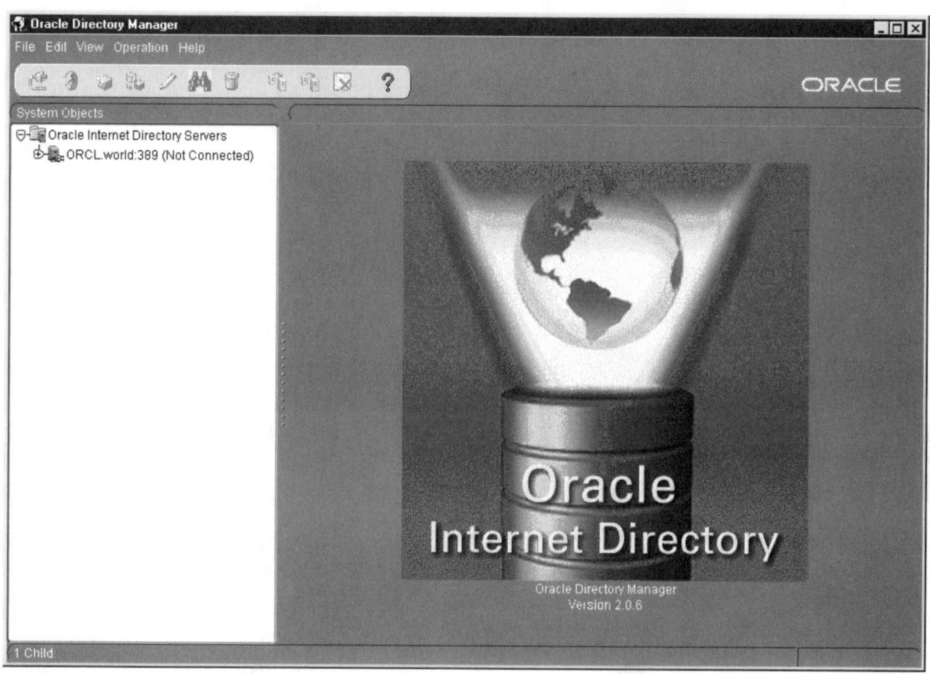

FIGURE 5-7. *Initial screen for the Oracle Directory Manager*

Icon	Description
Plug	Connect/disconnect from a directory server selected in the navigator pane.
Circular Arrow	Refresh or update data for objects stored in memory (other than entries) to reflect changes in the database.
Create	Add a new object.
Create Like	Add a new object using another object as a template.
Pencil	Edit or modify an object.

TABLE 5-7. *Oracle Directory Manager Icons*

Icon	Description
Binoculars	Find or search for an object.
Trash Can	Remove an object.
Refresh Entry	Update data for an entry stored in memory to reflect database changes.
Refresh Subentry	Update the children of entries stored in memory to reflect database changes.
Drop Index	Remove an index from an attribute. You'll be prompted to confirm this action.
Help	Display Help navigator.

TABLE 5-7. *Oracle Directory Manager Icons* (continued)

Research information used for this chapter was obtained from the following book:

1. *LDAP Programming Directory-Enabled Applications with Lightweight Directory Access Protocol,* by Timothy A. Howes, Ph.D and Mark C. Smith, Macmillan Technology Series, 1997.

CHAPTER 6

Planning Your Network

I just bought a great gardening book. Want to plant a garden with me? Hmm, let's see. Should we plant vegetables or flowers or both? I know! Let's plant tomatoes, peppers, lettuce, radishes, carrots, and cucumbers, and we'll be able to make lots of yummy salads. If we plant flowers that are different heights, we'll be able to put lovely bouquets on the table all summer long. Oh, this is going to be such fun! Now, how big should our garden plot be? Where and when should we do our planting? Will we have to plant different types of plants at different times? Do the plants need bright sunlight or partial shade, or do some need more sunlight than others do? What type of soil do we need? How will we water the plants? Are we going to use insecticides? Wow, there sure are a lot of things to think about just to plan how, where, and when we are going to do our planting. And what does all this have to do with networking, anyway?

Normally, the best approach to performing any kind of work is to stop and take some time—a few minutes, a few days, or even weeks—to plan what we are going to do before we actually begin to do any work. By planning first, we get a sense of the scope of our project and in what order to perform our tasks, a definition of what we hope to accomplish, and a determination of what's needed in the way of equipment or other resources. Taking time to plan what we want to do is also a great way to perform sanity checks to ensure that we haven't overlooked anything. What's that you're saying? You never make plans? Well, in reality, we all make some kind of plans somewhere along the line, even if it's planning to make no plans!

When it comes to networking, the wise person (which I know you are) will plan what is needed in the way of both equipment and software, what the client requirements are, and how to implement each installation and configuration step to ensure a successful networking solution. What you do with your network involves just as much careful thought and planning and preparation as how you're going to implement a database or application design or where and how you're going to plant your zucchini.

Creating a Network Plan

Okay, so what kinds of plans do you really need? What must you think about and make decisions about? Granted, when it comes to planning your Oracle networking approach, you are probably not starting from scratch. Most companies have an existing network on which you must base your Oracle networking solution, so you won't have to decide what the underlying network protocols are going to be. Both the underlying network and the applications that you are or will be supporting play into your decisions.

Issues and Considerations

There are many questions that you need to answer to determine what your Oracle network configuration is going to be. Some of the questions may already have been answered in your environment, and not all of the questions presented here will apply to all companies or systems. The questions can be broken down into these general categories:

- Management
- Network
- Server
- Connection
- Backup and recovery

Although no individual category of questions is more or less important than another, there is a somewhat logical flow to the questions. Let's look at each area and the questions that you need to answer.

Management Questions

Within the realm of management are questions that may have their final answers approved by someone who may be higher than you are in the management chain. You may need to confer with your management on these questions, which form the foundation for the rest of the Oracle network solution that you develop. The questions are discussed here in no particular order.

Are You Going to Use a Specific Naming Convention for Listener, Service, and Instance Names?

If you have several different servers with one or more separate listeners on each one, you may want to adopt a naming convention for your listeners, service names, and instance names to more easily identify which databases are being interacted with and from what nodes. It can be very confusing and difficult to verify that you are making database changes on Node A to Database A if you also have a Database A on Nodes B, C, and D.

Since the service names and instance names are listed in the init.ora file for each database and, therefore, read into the database upon database start-up, you can identify the database you're interacting with from an application if you have privileges to perform a query against the V$PARAMETER view. The query you can use to see the name values, with output shown from my 8.1.6 database, is as follows:

```
column NAME format a20
column VALUE format a40
select NAME, VALUE
  from V$PARAMETER
 where NAME in ('instance_name','service_names','db_name');

NAME                 VALUE
-------------------- ------------------
instance_name        orc1
service_names        orc1.world
db_name              orc1
```

There are two interesting things about this query. First, the arguments for the **where** clause are listed in lowercase. That's intentional because the values are stored in the database in lowercase. Second, the value for the service name parameter is plural while the other values are singular.

The lack of consistency is a lesson you should remember because there are many areas where you'll expect consistency in Oracle's naming structures, but you won't find it. This, of course, is a great argument for you to push for consistency in naming your databases, instances, and listeners to avoid confusion about where they are located.

On the other side of naming conventions is the potential for someone outside your organization to figure out or learn your convention and then compromise your system by using the knowledge. For example, if I know that you always use the node name as the beginning of your listener name and then append the word "LIST" and a consecutive number, I may be able to derive your listener name from this information. If I know that your instance naming convention includes the node name, the word "DB" and a consecutive number, I can start to derive your instance names as well.

Let's say that I know your node name is PROD. If this is true, then I know your first listener name on the PROD node will be PRODLIST1, and your first instance will be named PRODDB1. The listener name does not give me much help in trying to "hack" into your system, but the fact that your first instance is now known gives me the ability to attempt to gain access by checking for known usernames within the database, such as SCOTT, DBSNMP, SYSTEM, or SYS. I'll be trying to get in with usernames and passwords that are still set to their default value from the time you created your database.

Naming standards make sense, especially when you maintain multiple databases. There's nothing wrong with setting up naming conventions and following them to ensure consistency and ease of access for your clients, as long as you consider the possible exposure that a naming convention may present to someone intent on accessing your database. In other words, you can use naming standards. Just don't make them too obvious.

What Naming Methods Are You Going to Use—Local Naming, Directory Naming, Oracle Names, Host Naming, External Naming?

This question seems a bit like the previous one, but it's not. In the first question, you are concerned with the form you will use to assign a name to each element in your network. In this question, you are concerned with the way you will support client connections and net service name resolution to your various servers. Let's take a brief look at each of the naming methods listed in the question to help you in making your decision.

When you use local naming, you store the net service names in a local tnsnames.ora configuration file on each of your client machines in the network. The advantage of using individual tnsnames.ora files is that you can configure each file to the individual client's needs and uses. You provide a relatively straightforward way of accessing connection information, and you'll be able to resolve net service names across different kinds of protocols. The disadvantage, as mentioned in Chapter 4, is that you must reconfigure each individual file each time a network change occurs. For example, if you add a new database to your network, you'll have to modify the tnsnames.ora file for every client who needs to access the new database. Likewise, if you remove a database from your system, you'll want to remove the reference from each client's tnsnames.ora file as well. Local naming is recommended for simple, distributed networks with a small number of services that change very little and infrequently and a small number of client machines.

For directory naming, you use the LDAP-compliant directory server (the Lightweight Directory Access Service Protocol that was described in Chapter 5). One advantage of using an LDAP directory server is that you have a centralized location for all of the network names and addresses for your connections, which means you only need to make changes in one location instead of a potentially huge number of files. The directory stores names for other services as well, so you can connect to different kinds of protocols from this configuration. The disadvantage to using an LDAP directory server is that it requires your clients to have access to the directory and, therefore, may provide a potential security hole in your system. The LDAP directory server approach is recommended for systems that have large, complex networks with over 20 databases that change on a frequent basis.

If you choose to use the Oracle Names server, all of the Oracle-specific name services are maintained in a centrally located store of service addresses, as described in Chapter 4. Use of the Oracle Names server makes administration of the Oracle network simpler than local naming because all changes are made in one central location. Even if you are running multiple Names servers, you make the change only once to one server and then repopulate the other servers with the information. The disadvantages are that you can only store names and addresses of Oracle services within the Names servers, and you must perform extra setup and configure steps to establish the initial Oracle Names servers. Like the LDAP directory server, the Oracle Names server is best suited for large, complex networks that support over 20 databases that change on a frequent basis.

With host naming, service names can be stored using an existing IP address translation mechanism such as Domain Name Services (DNS), Network Information Services (NIS), or a centrally maintained TCP/IP hosts file. Although this approach provides minimal user configuration because the user needs to supply only the host name, there are some restrictions you must be aware of. Your client and server must both be using TCP/IP, and they cannot request any Oracle Connection Manager features. This means that you will not be able to connect to a third-party database. Host naming is available in a limited number of environments.

If a third-party naming service is already configured in your environment, you can use external naming to support the storage of Oracle service address information. You'll be able to load the Oracle information into your external tool using utilities that you are already familiar with. This approach, if available, will help you avoid additional configuration.

There is no right or wrong naming method, and you and your management will have to decide what makes the best sense for your organization. Remember too that your decision may not end up "cast in concrete," since you may find after a period of time that your connection needs have changed and your naming method must therefore change as well. One company I worked for started with a local naming method. As the scope and size of the system changed, we realized that we needed to change our naming method as well, and we gradually switched to the Oracle Names server as our solution. With the new emphasis on users being provided with a single sign-on to their systems, they may find that the new LDAP directory server method will make more sense for use in the future.

Who Is Authorized to Make Network Decisions?

At first glance, this question may seem like a "no brainer." I can assure you that it is not! Unless you've identified the management player or players who can support the required costs of implementing one networking approach over another, you may find that you've wasted a lot of time making plans that can't or won't be supported. In a large company, you might find that several people must agree with a decision before you can begin to build your Oracle network. Just as Oracle network traffic may affect everyone on the underlying network, the speed and response of your Oracle queries will be directly affected by all of the other network traffic on your system as well.

By identifying in advance all of the people who must approve your plans, you could save yourself a lot of needless work, upset, and aggravation.

Who Has Final Say over What Configuration and Protocol Support You Are Going to Use?

Like the previous question, this one deals with the identification of the appropriate person to turn to in the event that you cannot obtain consensus from the network players. Knowing who has the final say in making network decisions can help you identify who you need to spend the most time educating. Often, the person with the final say will be someone who is not very knowledgeable about technical details, and you may find that you need to bring that person up to speed before the most effective approach can gain approval.

A word of warning might be appropriate here. I know it's not easy, but try not to get locked into one approach over another too early in the decision-making process. If you lock yourself into one and only one approach, you may find yourself in an awkward position when another approach is suggested and accepted. Try to be flexible, and try to look at all sides of the question before you champion one approach over another. Be sure, too, to prepare a thoroughly understandable and solid case for your choice. Saying, "I think we should go with Choice A because it makes the best business sense" may not be good enough or complete enough to win your solution's approval. Be sure to have several solid reasons for the approach that you are supporting, and make sure that the person with the final say understands the pros and cons of each proposed solution.

Is the Lowest-Cost Option Always the Best?

This question could be reworded to "What are the costs versus administration time versus downtime of your proposed network configuration?" You see, when building proposals for senior management, you must keep in mind that their main concern is not necessarily the lowest-cost option but the option that gives them the best value for their money.

Bear in mind that some methods of building an Oracle network are more expensive than others. For example, let's look at implementing the Oracle Names server versus having many local tnsnames.ora files. As you saw in Chapter 4, ONAMES usually resides on a dedicated machine, while local tnsnames.ora files require no additional hardware. However, the amount of effort involved in maintaining many tnsnames.ora files will soon exceed the cost of additional Oracle Names servers.

The point I'm trying to get across is don't try to make the configuration overly elegant. Always try to create a configuration that will meet the requirements of the system, but don't go overboard.

What Will You Do if a Newer/Better Release of the Oracle Product Set Comes out While You're Developing Your Applications?

I received an electronic message from someone whose company began their development process under one version of Oracle and is now having second thoughts about their decision because a newer, touted-to-be-better product set has just been made available. The reality in the Oracle world is that there will almost always be a "later, greater" version of Oracle software just over the horizon.

Deciding in advance how or when you are going to embrace a newer Oracle version requires careful consideration and forethought.

Each new version brings with it many new features that sound appealing and build on older available features. At a recent conference, I heard someone say, "Of course, you *always* want to be on the newest, latest release of the Oracle product set!" But, do you? Does it make sense to automatically go to the latest released version of the RDBMS? What considerations should you examine before you make a decision to migrate to a newer version of the Oracle products?

The first consideration that comes to my mind is this: Will your current operating system version support the newest version of Oracle? When a company I worked for upgraded from version 7.1.5 to 7.3.2.3.2 on Alpha OpenVMS, we had to upgrade our operating system from V6.2 to V7.1. We also were required to migrate our Oracle Financials application from V9.4.2 to V10.6. This is viewed as a "triple whammy"—operating system, RDBMS, and application version upgrades all at the same time. Very ugly! Our networking approach required some fairly substantial changes as well. With a triple whammy, new and unforeseen problems are likely, and it's often extremely difficult to determine the cause of a problem.

Hesitant to do three upgrades at once, we were able to convince Oracle that we needed an interim solution. We ended up with an interoperability patch that enabled us to upgrade our operating system first and then upgrade the RDBMS and applications software later. However, we had to rework our Oracle networking approach before we could even use the patch. Troubleshooting problems that we encountered as we upgraded our network caused some delays that impacted our overall schedule. Like a picture puzzle, each part of your system relies on the other pieces to fit together properly and support each other in order for your system to function effectively. When you modify one piece, several others may be affected in a minor or very major way.

Another consideration to weigh when deciding whether to go to a new release is the stability of the new Oracle version. I've worked with Oracle products for a long time, and I have yet to see a major release that is completely stable from the beginning. Even interim releases can develop major problems. The bottom line is that you don't know what possible major problems you might be heading into if you migrate immediately to the newest release of Oracle. I've found it beneficial to call Oracle's support line and ask what the known bugs, problems, and patch sets are before I begin an upgrade to a new release.

When contemplating an upgrade or migration, you want to try to determine with your development staff what new features are being offered that you absolutely "can't live without." Do the risks involved with bringing new software into your shop outweigh the new features? Do the newest features being touted even work yet? Are the newest features actually mature enough to be of benefit to your organization? When the ability to perform snapshots was first introduced, a development team I worked with embraced the idea and struggled long and hard to implement this new feature effectively. If they had waited for a later version, they would have had a much easier time of it, because the later version brought a tremendous maturity to the feature. This is not uncommon in any software release. The first attempt at implementing a new feature might not play out exactly as you or your developers expect it to.

Another thing to think about is your potential fallback position. If you migrate to a new operating system version—to support a new Oracle version—to support a new application version, will you be able to get back to where you were before you started the first change? Will your recovery be as simple as rolling back to a previously saved configuration, or will you have to rebuild your system? How long can your system be unavailable during upgrade and fallback? What impact will it have on your users? Exactly how are you going to perform your migration/upgrade? You may want to devote an entire set of disks on your production system to practicing your upgrade. You'll want to do several dry runs during which you can perform timed tests to ensure that when you do the *real* upgrade, there will be no surprises. Many companies rent an equivalent set of computers for a "practice run" before attempting their upgrade in their production environment.

Keep in mind, too, that some applications rely on third-party layers, such as Encina's Transaction Monitor. You must ensure that all third-party software is compatible with the version of Oracle that you're upgrading to. Also, application code often adds in links to Net8 and other libraries, and the entire application may have to be recompiled. Given that some systems contain hundreds or even thousands of programs, the recompile and bind procedures can sometimes run into several days.

Determining which release of the software is the right one for you can be daunting. If you decide that you really must have the newest features being offered, how much time can your area devote to implementing and testing of the version before moving it into your production environment? Try to determine in advance what networking impacts you are going to encounter. To help ensure success in launching your new applications, you need to make a decision about how you will handle newer or patch releases while your development team is implementing and testing their application. Will you be able to continue maintenance on the existing system and integrate those changes into the new one? Will you have to "freeze" the production environment, making only emergency changes? If so, how long can you keep the environment static?

Network Questions

The most obvious network questions are "Which underlying protocol are you going to use?" and "Will the machines you choose be able to support the volume of network traffic that you expect?" Both of these are really good questions.

You are probably not the person who knows what type of hardware would be required to handle the expected network loads. Hardware sizing is not always easy. If possible, enlist the system and/or network management to help you in this area. Your system or network management people generally understand the network load and can determine what hardware is sufficient to meet the load requirements.

In most companies, however, one or both of these network questions have already been answered, and some form of network currently exists. Whether the network protocol choice is one that Oracle supports may be a bigger consideration. Determining that Oracle does not support the protocol your company is using may result in a change in the approach you'll use to connect your machines.

Determining whether a specific machine will be able to support the volume of network traffic you expect is a much more difficult question to answer. The machine's processing characteristics must be taken into account as well as the physical wiring that's being used to support and interconnect the network.

Let's take a look at the network considerations that you must examine.

What Protocols Does Oracle Support?

Oracle's protocol support includes the bequeath program, Inter-Process Communications (IPC), Named Pipes, LU6.2, SPX, TCP/IP, and TCP/IP with SSL. See Chapter 2, Table 2-6 to review these protocols.

To verify that the specific version your network supports is compatible with Oracle's protocol support, call Oracle World Wide Support or check with your Oracle sales consultant. You may find that your network has an earlier network version than the one Oracle currently supports. If this is the case, you will have to decide whether you want to upgrade your network or downgrade the version of Oracle that you are initially going to use. If you are running a later network version than Oracle's, you will have to decide whether you want to downgrade your network or wait for a version of Oracle that is compatible with your current network version. Since Oracle Corporation tends to work closely with the latest protocol versions, it's much rarer for you to be ahead of Oracle.

What Protocol(s) Are You Going to Support?

Along with the underlying network protocols, you need to decide which Oracle protocols you'll be using. If you are supporting development using Java-based applications, you'll want to ensure that you can support the JDBC drivers and OCI interface as well as SQLJ, the Common Object Request Broker Architecture (CORBA), and Enterprise Java Beans (EJBs). All of these products will rely on network support to work properly.

As I discussed in Chapter 2, EJB and CORBA clients use a different communication stack from the one used by Net8 clients. Therefore, if your developers decide to use EJBs and CORBA clients, you'll have to configure GIOP as the presentation layer.

Oracle documentation supplies in-depth information about these features and what you need to do to support them. I'm mentioning them here because they are network considerations that you must determine before you begin your Oracle network configuration tasks.

Is Your Cabling Robust Enough to Handle the Network Load?

I talked about bandwidth in Chapter 1, but let's review the definition here. Each different physical wiring cable can accommodate a different amount of network traffic, so the rate at which data will travel around the network depends on how much data the smallest cable can carry. Remember that the speed at which a cable can carry data is referred to as its bandwidth and that different parts of a network can have different bandwidths.

Now, consider that your connection and networking speed are only as good as the amount of traffic the narrowest cable on your system can carry. If you have a very narrow cable, your bandwidth for the network becomes as slow as that area. Imagine you're out for a drive on a six-lane, high-speed highway that suddenly narrows to two lanes because some lanes are blocked off for road repairs. The traffic was able to flow very quickly but must now slow down to allow the cars to merge into those two lanes. Once you get beyond the blockage, you can pick up speed again, but the damage has been done. Your overall speed has been reduced because of the road narrowing, even though it did eventually widen again.

For an effective network plan, identify any machines that process more slowly than others as well as any areas that might present network traffic slowdowns.

What Are the Locations (IP Addresses) of the Server(s)?

This question is important from several different perspectives. If you have a Domain Names Server that supplies translations from IP addresses to machine names, you will be able to rely on it to translate your machine locations for you. If you do not have a translation mechanism within your network protocol, you must include the IP addresses in your Oracle Names server definitions or your Oracle network configuration files.

By determining in advance your machine IP addresses and whether your network supplies address-to-name translations, you can save time as you configure and test your network. If you have several servers with multiple databases on each one, making a chart of the machine IP address and name along with the database, service, and instance names can be quite helpful both to document your systems and to guide you as you perform configuration tasks. A simple spreadsheet might contain the information shown in Table 6-1.

Using Table 6-1, you can easily see the machines with their IP addresses. You can quickly tell which databases, instances, and service names are associated with each machine. If you have decided to use either local naming methods or Oracle

Machine Name	IP Address	Database(s)	Instance Name(s)	Service Name(s)
MYHOST01	122.233.23.10	PRDFN1	PRDFN1	MYPROD1
		PRDAP1	PRDAP1	MYPROD2
		PRDHR1	PRDHR1	MYPROD3
MYHOST02	122.233.23.11	TSTFN1	TSTFN1	MYTST1
		TSTAP1	TSTAP1	MYTST2
		TSTHR1	TSTHR1	MYTST3
MYHOST03	122.233.23.12	DEVFIN1	DEVFIN1	MYDEV1
		DEVAP1	DEVAP1	MYDEV2
		DEVHR1	DEVHR1	MYDEV3
		DEVHR2	DEVHR2	MYDEV4
MYHOST04	122.233.23.13	QA01	QA01	MYQA

TABLE 6-1. *Mapping Machine Names to IP Addresses with Databases, Instances, and Servers*

Names server, this map can help you confirm that you have not missed defining any instances as you perform your configuration tasks.

What Port Numbers Are You Going to Use?

The first step in determining what port numbers to assign to each instance or service is to look at your current network configuration files and see what ports are already in use on your system. As mentioned in Chapter 3 in Table 3-3, Oracle has registered several ports with specific purposes assigned. You must ensure that you do not configure your listeners or Web Request Brokers, and so on, to listen on a port that has been assigned to another process for another purpose.

If you are using load balancing with multiple listeners, predetermining your listener ports makes the job of doing the actual configuration much easier. Regardless of the complexity of your Oracle network, if you decide on the port numbers you're going to use in advance, you'll be sure that your plan is clear and you will have documented your network. You can add a column to Table 6-1 to include port number assignments. Your map will then look like the one in Table 6-2.

In Table 6-2, the port numbers 1521 and 1526 have each been assigned to two different nodes. As long as the listeners are on different machines, you can assign the same port number to each listener. You can even assign more than one port to each listener. If you have more than one listener on a machine, you want to be sure

Machine Name	IP Address	Port	Database(s)	Instance Name	Service Name
MYHOST01	122.233.23.10	1521	PRDFN1	PRDFN1	MYPROD1
			PRDAP1	PRDAP1	MYPROD2
			PRDHR1	PRDHR1	MYPROD3
MYHOST02	122.233.23.11	1521	TSTFN1	TSTFN1	MYTST1
			TSTAP1	TSTAP1	MYTST2
			TSTHR1	TSTHR1	MYTST3
MYHOST03	122.233.23.12	1526	DEVFIN1	DEVFIN1	MYDEV1
			DEVAP1	DEVAP1	MYDEV2
			DEVHR1	DEVHR1	MYDEV3
			DEVHR2	DEVHR2	MYDEV4
MYHOST04	122.233.23.13	1526	QA01	QA01	MYQA

TABLE 6-2. *Mapping Information with Port Numbers Added*

that each listener is assigned to a different port number to reduce possible listener contention.

The map shown in Table 6-2 gives you a fairly complete picture of your Oracle network plan. To complete the picture, you need to add your naming method for each machine if you are using more than one method, and the protocol or protocols you've decided on.

Server Questions

Now that you've determined your naming method, naming conventions, protocols, and port designations, it's time to consider what listener approach you are going to use. There are several decisions you must make in the server arena. Let's look at some of the questions you need to answer to continue planning your Oracle network configuration.

Are You Going to Use Multi-Threaded Server (MTS), Dedicated Servers, or Prespawned Dedicated Servers?

As you saw in Chapter 2 and in Figure 2-4, the Multi-Threaded Server option can be used to enable Net8 to support multiple client connections through a single dispatcher process. Because a single dispatcher can support multiple user requests, in networks where a large volume of user connections must be supported, MTS can be a wonderful solution for reducing the use of system resources on a per-connection basis.

If, however, you're running huge, single-connection batch processes to load information into a data warehouse, dedicated server processes may make more sense. With dedicated servers, you have the choice of precreating or prespawning the connections before a connection request has been received, or spawning the dedicated server process at the time a request is received. If you decide to prespawn dedicated server processes, the connections will be available immediately upon request. However, once the processes have been spawned, they remain available throughout the entire life of the listener. In other words, if you prespawn ten dedicated server connections and use only two of them, the resources used by the other eight processes are wasted and remain unavailable to the system until the listener is shut down. If you opt to have dedicated processes created as they are requested, your clients will have to wait while the process is started. Each time a client disconnects from a dedicated server connection that is not prespawned, the resources are reclaimed by the system. What happens when you have more connections requested than you have prespawned processes? Well, Oracle will simply begin to create dedicated processes on request, reclaiming resources as they disconnect, until you are back to the original number of prespawned processes.

On the one hand, you can support many clients on a few Multi-Threaded Server connections, or you can support fewer clients on dedicated server connections. However, if you are using MTS, you will have difficulty telling who is connected to which operating system process. On the other hand, if you decide to use dedicated server connections, you must choose whether or not to prespawn, and possibly waste the resources for, multiple dedicated server connections.

NOTE
At least one dispatcher process must be configured and started for each network protocol that the database clients will use with MTS.

If You Use MTS, Will You Allow Overrides for Dedicated Server Connections?

Okay, let's assume you've decided to configure your system to use the Multi-Threaded Server option. Will you always want connections to go through a dispatcher? Maybe or maybe not! Let's think about that huge data warehouse information load again. Hmm, this really does look like a job that's more suited for a dedicated connection, doesn't it? Why?

To answer that question, you must think about how a Multi-Threaded Server dispatcher is designed to work. Remember that the concept behind the dispatcher's ability to support multiple users is the assumption that each user will have some thinking or pausing time between each request. In that way, several users' requests can be interspersed. Now, let's think about our huge data load. There are no pauses involved. There's just a steady stream of inserts or updates or deletes. Therefore, for this task, a dedicated server makes sense.

You'll have to look at the types of transactions that are going to be supported on your system to decide whether you need to allow for the creation of some dedicated server connections along with your MTS scheme. You may also want to consider scheduling your large data loads at times when your user interactions are lightest, and starting dedicated processes to support those data loads. Remember that any existing connections on your system will not be disconnected if you stop and start your listener process. Therefore, depending on your processing requirements, you may decide to stop your MTS processes at a specific time and start dedicated processes for your backups and large batch data loads. This raises the question: Are connections that are made through the MTS stopped when you stop the MTS? To answer this question, let's take a few minutes to examine what's really going on when you use MTS.

The Multi-Threaded Server process flow is as follows:

- The client requests a connection.
- The listener detects the connection and passes back an address of the most lightly loaded dispatcher.
- The client then connects directly to the dispatcher.
- The dispatcher places the request on an incoming "request" queue, which is held in the SGA.
- The next available shared server process will get the request from the queue and process it.
- When the shared process is complete, the result is placed on an outgoing "response" queue.
- The dispatcher reads the entry on the response queue and returns the result to the calling client.

The **alter system set...** clause in conjunction with the **mts_servers** and **mts_dispatchers** parameters allows you to add more shared server processes or dispatchers. They also allow you to terminate existing shared server processes after their current calls finish processing and to terminate existing dispatcher processes for a specific protocol after their current user processes disconnect from the instance.

Thus the answer to the question posed above is that connections made via MTS will not disconnect if you stop the MTS process because the MTS process will not actually stop until the current transactions are completed. I guess the MTS processes could be "killed" by you or the operating system, but I strongly suggest *not* killing them.

Are You Going to Support Multiple Listeners?

Each time a connection request to the database is made, the listener hands the request off to a dispatcher or dedicated server process. Each request entails a certain amount of resource overhead to fulfill. In other words, each request takes a certain amount of processing time. If you have one listener and a large number of connection requests, what's going to happen? Well, you could end up with a backlog of requests, an overburdened listener, and delays in fulfilling all of the requests. Hmm, sounds like you're going to end up with some pretty unhappy clients if response times are slow. How can you get around this bottleneck and improve connection times? You can create multiple listener processes and enable connection pooling and/or load balancing. We'll talk more about connection pooling and load balancing under "Connection Questions." For now, let's talk about the steps you have to take to create more than one listener.

Think back to Chapter 3. When you were looking at the commands that had to be changed to create a second listener, you were really learning how to perform part of the configuration task. One of the things you have to decide on is a different port number from the one your current listener is using. You might want to dedicate a specific range of port numbers for use in creating more listeners for your busy system. Next, you'll need to decide on an appropriate name. Once you've decided on the name and port number for your new listener, you must edit your listener.ora file to add your new listener to the configuration. Finally, you must decide how many databases or clients each listener will support. After you've identified the databases that you want to assign to each listener, you can edit your tnsnames.ora file(s) or your Names server configuration to modify the port assignments according to your plan. Remember that any command procedure you use to start or shut down your listeners must be modified to include the new listener(s) and all listeners must be started and stopped by name.

Connection Questions

There are many different approaches that you can use when considering how you are going to enable clients to connect to your database through your network. If you have a low number of client connections, you may opt for dedicated connections via one listener. If, however, you have an Internet Web site or other system with very heavy traffic, you'll probably want to take advantage of some of the more elegant solutions Oracle offers, such as connection pooling.

Here are some questions to ponder in the connection arena.

Should Your Plan Include Increasing the Listener Queue Size?

As you go through your network evaluation and create your network plan, you may realize that you are going to be experiencing heavy volumes of traffic. One step that you can include in your plan is deciding on the size of the listener queue that you are going to enable. If you expect the listener to handle large volumes of connection requests, one action that you can take is to specify a connection queue to handle listener processing. This will enable the listener to dynamically handle large numbers of connection requests concurrently. To enable a connection queue, you'll need to specify a queue size using the parameter **queuesize=** and an integer value. While you are planning your network, you can decide whether or not to activate a listener queue and what size to make the value.

Currently, you can only enable a listener queue if you are using TCP/IP or DECnet. The default queue size is operating system dependent. For Solaris and Windows NT 4.0 Workstation, the default queue size is set to 5, while for Windows NT Server, the default value is 20. But, what does queue size really mean, and when and how should you use it?

Client connections coming into the listener are almost immediately spawned off. If a listener gets, say, ten connection requests at the same time, the listener keeps a backlog of connection requests. The backlog is in the form of a first in/first out (FIFO) queue. The maximum number of entries on this queue is determined by the **queuesize=** parameter. If the queue is full and another request comes in, the client will receive the error message ORA-12541: No Listener.

Thus, for systems that receive a large number of simultaneous connection requests at any point in time, increasing the size of the queue will allow the listener to have a larger backlog and avoid the ORA-12541 message.

Are You Going to Use Connection Pooling?

Imagine for a moment that you're reading an absorbing book when the telephone rings. You answer and find that your friend is calling to say hello and visit. While you two are talking, your friend, who has the telephone feature "call waiting," hears a click on the line and asks you to hold on while she checks to see who else is calling. While you're waiting, you go back to reading your book. When your friend returns, you continue your conversation. Your friend was able to maintain and talk to two different connections on one phone line. In much the same way, connection pooling allows one dispatcher process to support more than one client connection at the same time. Let's see what connection pooling is and how it works.

If you've decided to use Multi-Threaded Server, you must decide whether to enable connection pooling. Connection pooling, like call waiting, enables the sharing, or pooling, of a dispatcher's set of connections among several client processes. Thus, the number of physical network connections to a Multi-Threaded Server is maximized. That sounds great, but how does it work? Oracle uses a timeout mechanism to temporarily release a transport connection that has been idle for a specific amount of time—sort of like your friend clicking the telephone receiver to see who's on the line. While the current connection is temporarily released, connection pooling makes the physical connection available for another incoming client call. The logical connection for the idle process isn't released; so when the idle process has more work to do, the physical connection is reestablished with the dispatcher, just as you continue your phone conversation when your friend returns.

Are You Going to Use Connection Load Balancing?

Hmm, what's the difference between connection pooling and connection load balancing? Well, you've just learned how connection pooling works. Let's see what's different about connection load balancing.

If you are a parent, you probably already know quite a bit about what's involved in balancing the distribution of a bag of candy among your children. If you're not careful, each child will be convinced that he or she did not get a fair share. If you enable connection balancing, connection requests will be evenly distributed among the available listeners, just as your candy was evenly distributed among your children.

In connection pooling, you must have MTS turned on and configured, while with connection load balancing, you must have multiple listeners configured. If you have multiple listeners and turn connection load balancing on by setting the parameter **load_balance** to ON in the tnsnames.ora file, a client can randomize its requests to several listeners. By using load balancing, you enable the connection load to be distributed among more than one listener so that no listener is carrying a heavier load than the others.

Your network plan should include whether you are going to implement connection load balancing and how many listeners you plan to configure to support this feature.

Are You Going to Use Timer-Initiated Disconnects, and if so, How Long Can a Process Remain Idle Before It's Considered Timed Out?

In earlier versions of Oracle networking, occasionally a process would be disconnected at the client side but remain connected from the server side. In other words, the Oracle networking process didn't notify the Oracle server that it was disconnecting. This occurred frequently when the client was on a PC and the PC was rebooted. The client connection was disconnected, but the server never seemed to realize that the client was gone. The result of this was that sometimes disconnected processes continued to use resources inside the database. These processes could be very difficult to remove unless the database, and sometimes even the operating system, was shut down and restarted.

In later versions of Oracle networking, timer-initiated disconnect or dead connection detection is available. If a client disconnects abnormally and timer-initiated disconnect detection is activated, Net8 will automatically identify connections that have been left hanging. If an abnormal disconnect is identified, the database can be forced to automatically roll back uncommitted transactions and locks that are being held by the user of the disconnected process.

Let's see how timer-initiated disconnect works. To begin, a small probe packet is sent from the server to the client at specific, predefined intervals, usually once every several minutes. If all is well, the probe packet is accepted. However, if the process has been disconnected, the send operation generates an error because the client connection isn't there to receive it. When an error occurs, the server process terminates the connection and performs the necessary cleanup.

To enable timer-initiated disconnect, you must add the parameter **sqlnet.expire_time=**, with a value in minutes, to your sqlnet.ora file. You cannot use dead connection detection on bequeathed connections.

If you decide to enable timer-initiated disconnects, here are a couple of considerations to keep in mind:

- Probe packets generate additional network traffic that might cause performance degradation on the network.
- On some operating systems, additional server processing may be required to enable the listener to distinguish connection-probing events from other normal events that occur on the system. The additional processing may cause performance degradation on the network.

Backup and Recovery Questions

No matter how proactive you are or how careful you are with your machines and connection hardware, eventually you'll encounter a problem or catastrophic event that will make your system unavailable for normal user–machine interaction. I don't want to sound negative, but in case of an emergency like hardware or software failure, human error, or a natural catastrophe like a major storm, flood, or fire, what are you going to do?

All good plans should include contingency planning. Let's look at questions you'll want to address in your network plan.

If You Can't Get to Your Computer Room, What Will You Do?

I like beginning with worst-case scenarios, so let's take a look at the most horrible situation I can think of. A mad bomber has chosen your company site as a target and has exploded a series of bombs. The building that houses your computer room and all of its equipment has been totally destroyed. You are told that you will not be able to get near what's left of the building for at least a week, and the equipment within the building is completely gone. Really scary though, huh! Granted, most disasters aren't quite this drastic, but you need to think through the "unthinkable" and begin to implement a plan that will ensure your ability to recover your network and its data.

In this scenario, you must look at how you are going to re-create your entire computer center at another location. You will need to replace your hardware, re-create your network, and recover your software and applications. You need to determine what information you must have to implement effective networking from a new location, and you must ensure that copies of your applications software as well as your vendor-supplied code are kept up-to-date and available in a storage container away from your computing center.

How Effective Is Your Backup and Recovery Strategy?

Your ability to recover your network and databases is only as solid as your backup and recovery strategies. Most people spend a lot of time thinking about and implementing database backups but forget to consider and capture their network configuration files to ensure that they can easily recover their network if necessary.

Be sure that you have effective copies of all your network files and that you can read the media on which the backups are saved. It's an awful feeling to discover at the worst possible moment that the backups you've been relying on can't be read by the hardware or software that you now have available to you. You'll want to test any backup strategies that you implement to ensure that you can read and use the backups. A database administrator I know periodically "loses" a file or two on his system by copying them to a different directory and deleting them from their original location just to have his data center staff prove that they can recover the missing files quickly and effectively.

You must keep in mind that the tape heads you are using to write data to tape might be out of alignment when the tape is written. If that is the case, when you go to read those tapes, the tape heads will have to be in the same *misalignment* for them to be read successfully, or you won't be able to read them.

What Other Network Lines Will You Need to Re-create?

Along with planning the re-creation of your computer facility, you must determine what other data feeds you have that will need to be duplicated. For example, if you have a direct network line established to another company, like a bank with a line to the Federal Reserve, what will you have to do to re-create that connection at a contingency site? In other words, you need to plan not only for your normal connections, but also for any other necessary connections that must be in place for your company to do "business as usual."

In a Failure Situation, How Are You Going to Handle IP Addresses?

Your company may choose to have a complete standby system available at another site to enable rapid disaster recovery. If you have a perpetually current copy of your system at another location, you must decide how and when you will switch to the standby site. You should map out how you will switch your IP address pointers from one location to another.

You must also plan all possible connection scenarios that you will need to implement. For example, think of your data center as the center of your universe. Now, think of all the various connections coming into and going out of that center, like a star with various points of light. Place yourself in the middle and picture how all of the networking is accomplished. Next, consider what IP addresses you will need and how you must implement them if your data center shifts from its central point to one of the end locations.

These days, with the availability of the Internet, it's potentially easier to move from one location to another, but you must still be prepared with a map of how you are going to re-create your site.

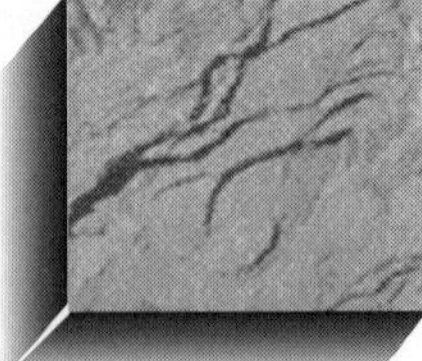

PART II

Using the Configuration Tools

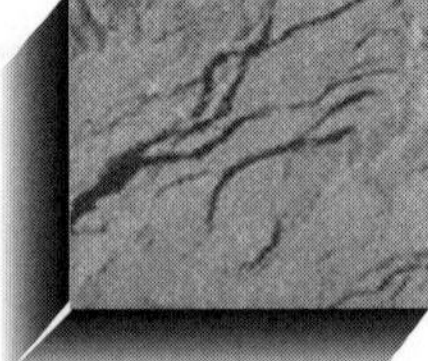

CHAPTER 7

Using Net8 Assistant—Local Options

In Chapter 6, we planned a garden. Well, I just went out to our garden site and began to prepare the ground. I was using a small, handheld tool, and guess what. The ground that we set aside for a garden is filled with rocks and very hard, claylike soil. It's going to be impossible to use my current garden tools to get our garden plot into usable shape. I'm afraid that we'll need a ground tiller and lots of bags of peat moss, topsoil, and cow manure. I'll run down to the garden supply shop later today and get the things we'll need to get this garden going. I just hope we don't strain our backs bending over to pull all of those rocks out of the ground.

In the meantime, let's talk about tools. Having the right tools to accomplish a job sure can make your life easier. Don't you think so? Just think how easily we could dig up that garden plot if we had a power-driven rotary tiller. Why, I bet we'd have the job done in almost no time at all. If we had some sturdy shovels and hoes, I'm sure we'd get the job done, but I also know it would take us much longer with much more effort involved. The bottom line is that, no matter what job you set out to perform, there is always more than one way to accomplish your task. However, having just the right tool will help you get the job done more quickly and efficiently.

In the next four chapters, I'm going to tell you about three different tools that Oracle Corporation provides free to you with the delivery of your database software. The three tools are GUI (Graphical User Interface) in nature, and you can run them in either a Windows or UNIX environment. To run the tools from UNIX, you run netasst from any UNIX window, providing the DISPLAY environment variable points to a workstation capable of running X11/motif applications. The UNIX host must have X11 and Java libraries installed as well. To set the DISPLAY value, you append ":0.0" to the end of your machine's IP address. For example, if your IP address is 196.123.45.678, your DISPLAY value will be 196.123.45.678:0.0. In addition, the workstation IP address must be authorized by the machine hosting the netasst executable, usually granted via the **xhost** command.

The three tools are

- The Net8 Assistant discussed in this chapter and Chapter 8
- The Net8 Configuration Assistant examined in Chapter 9
- The Connection Manager described in Chapter 10

These three tools, along with the Listener Control utility, which was described in Chapter 3, and the Oracle Names Control utility that you learned about in Chapter 4 make up Oracle's toolbox for network configuration, control, and management.

Before we begin our examination of the Net8 Assistant, I'd like to give you some basic information about this tool so you'll know when and how to use it.

Net8 Assistant Basics

Hmm, where should we begin? In Chapter 4, I told you that you use the Net8 Assistant to configure and control networking components from one central location. You can use it from either the client or the server. Using the Net8 Assistant, you can configure or define the following:

- Listeners.
- Simple names and connect identifiers that can be mapped to connect descriptors. The mapping of simple names and connect identifiers to connect descriptors is stored using one of the following methods: tnsnames.ora, centralized LDAP-compliant directory service, or an Oracle Names server.
- Naming methods to describe the different ways to resolve connect identifiers into connect descriptors.

You can also use the Net8 Assistant to stop, start, tune, or gather statistics for an Oracle Names server, once it's been configured.

Now, that all sounds terrific, but before you can perform any of these tasks, you need to start the tool. So, let's talk about how to start the Net8 Assistant.

Using Net8 Assistant

On a UNIX system from $ORACLE_HOME/bin, you start the Net8 Assistant by typing the command

```
netasst
```

On a Windows NT system, when you install the Oracle8i, Release 2 software, the default logical disk suggested by the Universal Installer is the disk with the most available space. When I performed my installation, D: was the disk selected. The default directory path suggested by the Installer for my system was D:\Oracle\Ora81. Therefore, because I accepted the default value suggested by the Installer, my ORACLE_HOME value became OracleOra81. Because I asked to have the demonstration database created, I was prompted for my choice of a name. I cleverly selected ORCL.

I'm sharing this information with you to help you understand the naming convention Oracle uses for your Start > Programs entries. When I select the Start > Programs options, the entry for my Oracle access is shown as Oracle-OraHome81. There are many options shown under this main heading. One of these options is Network Administration. Thus, to start the Net8 Assistant from Windows NT, I choose

Start > Programs > Oracle-OraHome81 > Network Administration > Net8 Assistant

If you choose a different directory pathname for your installation of the Oracle software, you'll see a different entry in your Start > Programs menu.

Once you start the Net8 Assistant, you'll see the basic tool screen, as shown in Figure 7-1.

You can resize any of the screens that are displayed. If you resize the Help screen, for example, you can read all of the information without having to scroll up and down within the window.

Let's take a close look at the initial screen and talk about the various features that are available to you to work with this tool.

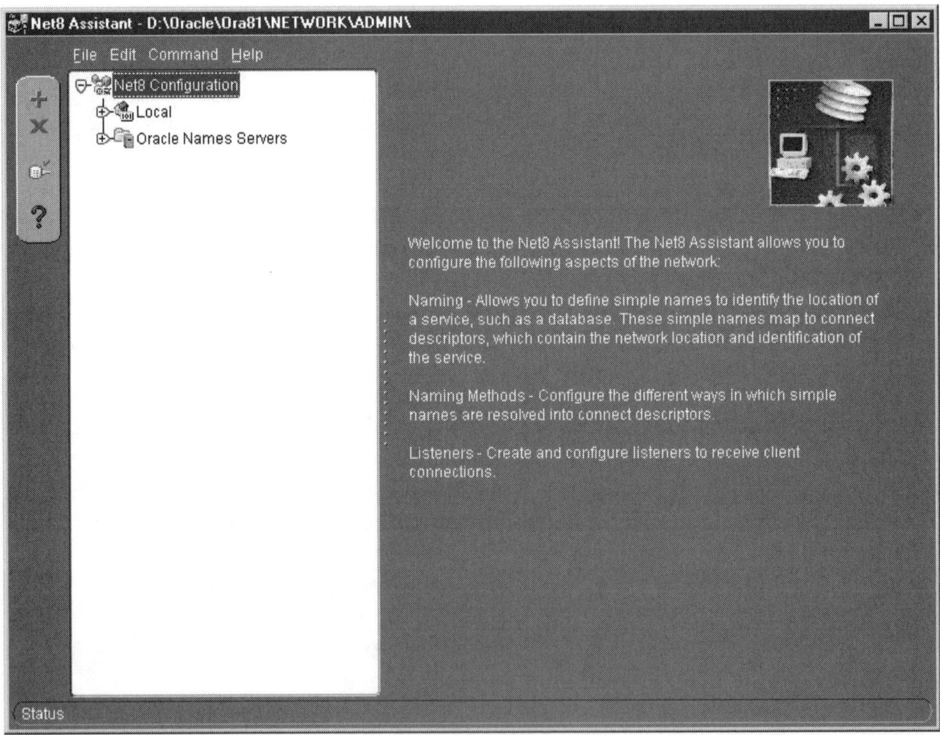

FIGURE 7-1. *The initial Net8 Assistant screen*

Basic Screen Features

When you enter the Net8 Assistant, at the very top of the screen you can see the name of the tool and the directory that the tool is pointing to. If there is no visible directory path, don't worry. That just means you haven't specified one for the tool to access yet.

Directly below these headings is a set of pull-down menu options. Let's "walk" through them and see what options you have available. The menu headings are File, Edit, Command, and Help.

Hmm, that's odd. The words File and Help have their first letter underlined. Does that mean there is a key I can press to access these menu options? I just pressed the F key, but nothing happened. I know, let's try the CTRL key along with the F key. Nope, that didn't work either. How about the ALT key and the F key? Wow! That worked really well. You see, when you press the ALT key, the cursor moves to the leftmost pull-down menu option. In our case, the ALT key moves us to the File option. Pressing the F key will display the options in the menu and highlight the first one. Once you can see the menu options, you can use either the mouse or the UP and DOWN ARROW keys to move to the option you want to use. Once you've selected the option you're interested in, you can either click the left mouse button or press the ENTER key to activate the option. When a letter in an option is underlined, you can press that letter to execute the option.

Oh, by the way, if a menu option is unavailable, it will appear as a dark gray color. We refer to an unavailable option as being "grayed out." If an option is available, it will be black and you'll be able to select the option by clicking on it or using the UP or DOWN ARROW key to reach it. If a value is grayed out, you won't be able to access it.

As with any Windows screen display, there are three buttons on the top right side of the screen:

- An Underline icon to minimize the screen but not exit from the tool or option
- A Screen icon to change the screen from its current size to full-screen mode
- An X icon to close the screen and exit the tool or option

Pull-Down Menu Options

The options available from the File pull-down menu are

- Open Network Configuration…
- Save Network Configuration
- Save As…

- Revert to Saved Configuration
- Exit   Alt+F4

The letter *x* in Exit is underlined. I've already explained how to use the ALT, then F, then X keys to perform an Exit. The key combination ALT+F4 is a shortcut to close the screen and exit the tool immediately. The plus sign indicates that the first key must be held down while the second key is pressed.

Two of the options in the File menu have three dots after their entry in the list. The three dots are used to indicate that there is more involved than just selecting the option. When you choose the Open Network Configuration option, you are prompted for the directory in which the desired configuration is located. The Save As option will prompt you for a directory location as well.

The Edit pull-down menu offers the options

- Create…
- Delete
- Rename…

Initially, these options will be grayed out because you have not yet selected anything that would activate them.

From the Command pull-down menu, you can

- Test Service…
- Discover Oracle Names Servers
- Reload All Names Servers

Because you have not yet selected an action that would activate any of these options, they will also be grayed out initially.

The Help pull-down menu offers

- Contents
- Search for help on…
- About Net8 Assistant

The Help options are available immediately. Let's take a closer look at the Help options.

Help Options

If you select the Contents option, the Help Navigator screen appears. Figure 7-2 shows the initial Help Navigator screen.

Like the initial Net8 Assistant screen, the Help Navigator screen has a set of pull-down menus: File, View, Tools, and Help. The File pull-down menu offers the selections:

- Display (initially grayed out)
- Display to New Window (initially grayed out)
- Print Tree Ctrl+R
- Print Topics Ctrl+T
- Close
- Exit Ctrl+X

FIGURE 7-2. *The initial Help Navigator screen*

The View pull-down menu offers the options to view

- Contents
- Index
- Search
- Expand (initially grayed out)
- Collapse (initially grayed out)
- Expand All (initially grayed out)
- Collapse All (initially grayed out)

The Tools pull-down menu option, shown in Figure 7-3, is Help Preferences and enables you to change the Language Group from the default of Western European to any one of 11 other languages. You can also change the HTML Character Encoding from Western European (ISO 8859-1) to Roman (Mac), Western European (Windows), or Western European (PC). At the bottom of the Help Preferences screen is a check box that enables you to make your selections the default values. Once you've selected your preferences, you can select OK, or if you haven't changed anything or don't want to save your changes, you can click Cancel to close the screen.

The final pull-down menu option is Help. Your options under Help are

- Help on Help...
- About...

I'll let you explore these options on your own.

FIGURE 7-3. *The Help Preferences screen*

Help Navigator Icons and Tabs

Below the pull-down menu options on the Help Navigator screen are two text icons and three tabs. The text icons are interesting because they are not immediately available. If you move your mouse pointer over the first icon, the word Display appears, while moving your mouse pointer over the second icon will present the words Display in New Window.

By default, the Contents tab is displayed, but you can also see an Index tab and a Search tab. Look at the Contents window. You see that there is a book icon with the words NetAssistant Help next to it. The book is closed and there is a plus sign (+) to the left of the book. The plus sign indicates that there are more entries below this entry. Let's click on the plus sign and see what happens. Wow! The book icon now shows an open book, and there are now seven other books displayed below the initial one. Each book has a plus sign next to it. The available book Help options are

- Net8 Assistant Overview
- Net8 Assistant Environment
- Directory
- Local
- Oracle Advanced Security
- Oracle Names Servers
- Glossary

I'm not going to go through all of the Help documentation here. I'll let you explore the documentation set yourself. I would like to point out, though, that once you've highlighted the initial NetAssistant Help entry, if you look at the View pull-down menu, you'll find that you can now use the Expand and Expand All options. Once you've expanded any of the Help Navigator tree, the Collapse and Collapse All options will also become available.

When you choose the Index tab, you see three distinct areas. The first area has the instruction "Type the first few letters of a word" and a place for you to type letters. The second section has a list of keywords, and the third area is titled "Select a topic and click Open," with an empty area.

When you type letters into the first section of the Index tab screen, the options in the second screen change to display the words that match the letters you are typing. Any documentation that corresponds with the displayed topics will be visible in the third section. Figure 7-4 shows the topics that are available for the entry "listener." that is entered in the top area of the Index screen.

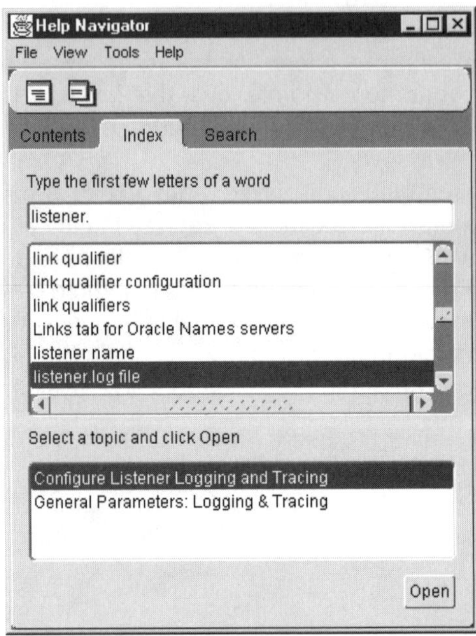

FIGURE 7-4. *The Index tab with letters typed in*

Once you've found the documentation for the topic in which you are interested, you can click on the topic in the third section of the screen. If you click twice on the documentation entry, or click on the Open button, another window will open to display the Help information. Oh, by the way, once you've selected a topic, you'll find that both the Display and Display in New Window options are now available. However, neither icon seems to display the document contents differently. All of the approaches that I tried—double-clicking on the entry, clicking on the Open option, clicking on the Display icon, or clicking on the Display in New Window icon—resulted in the document information being displayed in a new window.

The third tab is labeled Search. At the top of this screen is the instruction to "Type the words for which you want to search" and an area in which you can type words. Next to the word entry area is a button labeled Search. You can choose to make the search case-sensitive by clicking on the Case-sensitive check box. Below the check box are radio buttons labeled "Search for" with the options

- All of these words
- Any of these words
- This Boolean expression

At the bottom of the screen is a Results area labeled "Results: Select a topic and click Open." Figure 7-5 shows the Search tab with the results of a search using the word "Listener." At the very bottom of the screen are the words "Found 68 topics."

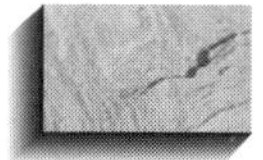

NOTE
You should look at the entire screens as you work with any of the Oracle-provided tools. Watch for additional information that may be available.

To exit the Help Navigator, you can either select the File > Close or File > Exit options, press the CTRL key and X key at the same time, or simply click on the X icon at the top right side of the screen.

Net8 Assistant Navigator Area

Now that we've examined the pull-down menus at the top of the Net8 Assistant screen, let's look at the rest of the screen as a whole. On the far left side of the screen are four icons: a large plus sign (+), a large X, a small disk with a blue

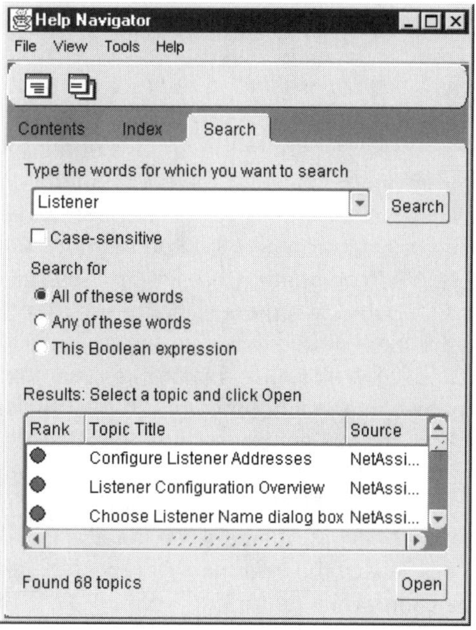

FIGURE 7-5. *The Search tab with the results of a search*

connector and a check mark above the connector, and a question mark (?). When the Create option is available, the plus sign will turn from gray to green. When you are able to delete something, like a service or listener, the X will turn from gray to red to show that the entity can be removed. When you place your mouse cursor over the disk, the words Test Service... appear, and when you move your mouse cursor over the question mark, it becomes larger, and the word Help appears.

Next to the four icons is the Net8 Configuration Navigator tree with a plus sign next to it to indicate that there are options below the highest level. We'll expand the navigator next. Right now, though, look at the right side of the screen. There's a welcome note and some brief informational text to explain that you can use the Net8 Assistant to configure naming, naming methods, and listeners. At the bottom of the screen is an area in which you will see status messages.

As you expand the navigator tree and make selections, different options will appear on the right side of the screen to provide either information or configuration options. Let's go ahead and expand the navigation tree. Hmm, how do you do that? There are actually two ways to expand the tree. You can either click twice on the words Net8 Configuration or click once on the small plus sign that's directly to the left of the Network icon next to the Net8 Configuration words. When you expand the tree, you see the options

- Local
- Oracle Names Servers

Each of these options has a plus sign to its left as well, to indicate that there may be more options below. In this chapter, I'll tell you about all of the options under Local, and in Chapter 8, I'll tell you about the options under Oracle Names Servers.

Let's take a look at the welcome text for the Local option. When you click once on the Local option, you see text that tells you this option allows you to configure network elements in the configuration files located in your ORACLE_HOME/ network/admin directory. You can change the directory by selecting Open Network Configuration from the File pull-down menu. The information goes on to explain that you can configure the local profile that determines how the core Net8 software will operate. The sqlnet.ora file will house this profile. The next action you can take is to configure simple names in a local configuration file. The simple names that are used to map to connect descriptors are housed in the tnsnames.ora file. The final option under the Local information is for configuring one or more listeners on the current host. The configuration will be placed in the listener.ora file.

When you expand the Local option, the three options Profile, Service Naming, and Listeners become visible, but the informational message remains the same. There is no further expansion available for the Profile option, but on my system there are plus signs beside the other two options. Why is that? Well, quite simply, when I was telling you the steps to follow to upload the tnsnames.ora file to the

Net8 Assistant in Chapter 4, I was actually performing the task, so my default listener configuration is already loaded into my version of the Net8 Assistant. When we look at the Oracle Names Server option next, we'll already have a configured Oracle Names server for the same reason. I configured one when I was mapping out the steps in Chapter 4 for the Names server creation as well. Anyway, take a look at Figure 7-6 to see the expansion of the navigation tree so far.

When you click once on the Oracle Names Servers option, the initial informational screen is displayed. The information says that you can configure Oracle Names to store net service names as an alternative to creating a tnsnames.ora file on each client. You are also told how to activate a search for all known Oracle Names servers in all well-known places on your network, as well as how to activate creation of a new Oracle Names server. Figure 7-7 shows the completely expanded navigation tree with the Oracle Names service information.

Now that we've covered the basic structure of the Net8 Assistant tool, let's go back to the Local option and walk through how to actually use each option to perform network configuration. Ready? Let's go!

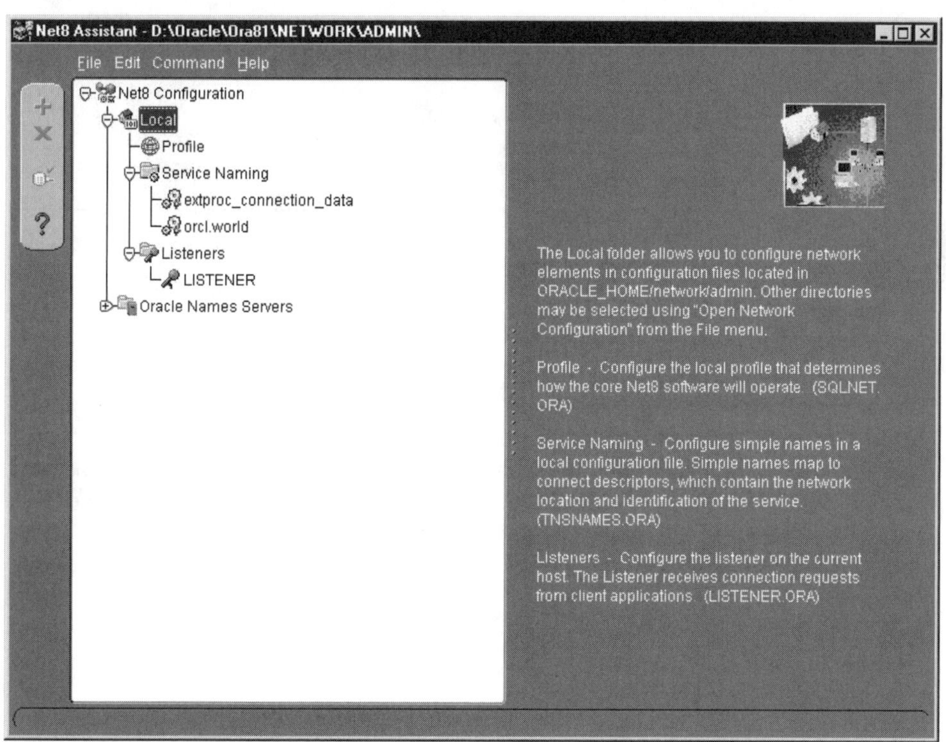

FIGURE 7-6. *The Net8 Assistant Local tree expanded*

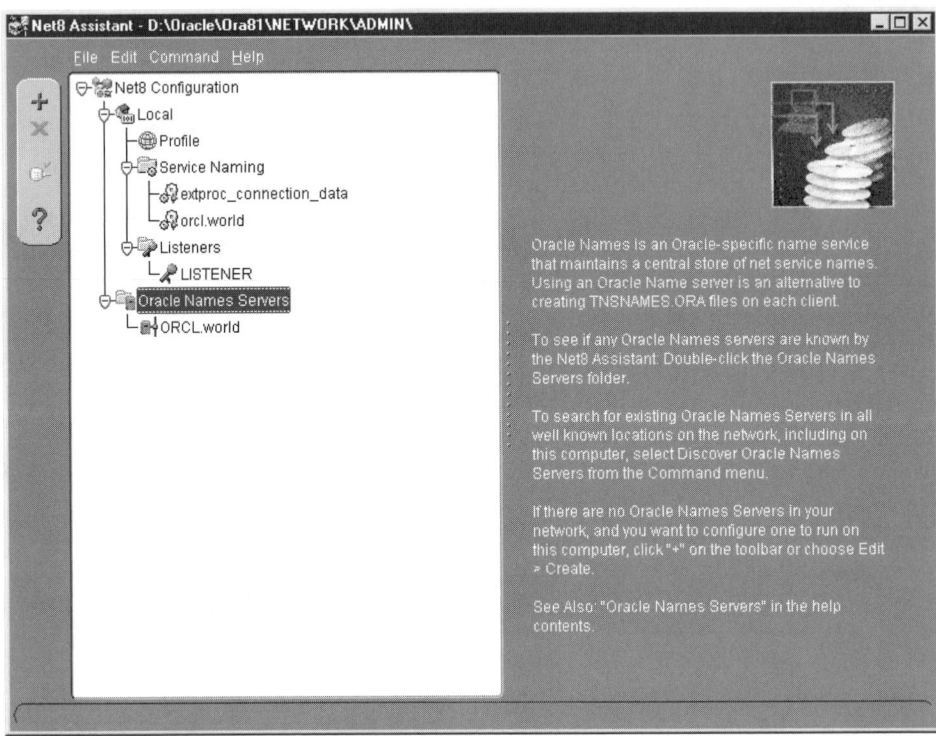

FIGURE 7-7. *Net8 Assistant's completely expanded navigation tree*

Local Configuration Options

To start our exploration of how to use the configuration options, let's begin with the top option in the Local configuration area and work our way through all of the available options in each section. When you click and expand the Local area of the Net8 Configuration navigator tree, the first option you encounter is Profile. Let's think about what a profile is and what it is used for.

Profile Configurations

A friend of mine recently bought a new house. He had a lot of help from the real estate agent he chose. You see, in our area, there are now several different types of real estate agents that you can deal with. There are seller brokers who represent the person or people who are selling their property, buyer brokers who do not list properties but work strictly with the buyer to locate just the right property, and dual brokers who list properties and also work with buyers. My friend used a buyer broker who filled out a profile of the things my friend was looking for in a house and then helped him and his family find the right house for them.

In the same way that my friend's broker used a profile to help keep track of my friend's housing requirements, Oracle uses profiles to keep track of your preferences for how you want to enable and configure Net8 features on both the client and server machines in your environment.

The file that contains profile information is sqlnet.ora. Appendix B shows all of the available parameters that you can use for the Net8 configuration to declare things like

- The default domain you want to have appended to a client connection request when the client doesn't specify one
- In what order you want Net8 to look when trying to resolve a presented name. You can specify "look in the tnsnames.ora file first, Oracle Names server second, etc."
- Whether to enable logging and tracing features for problem tracking and resolution
- How you want parameters for external naming to be configured
- The preferred path for connection routing
- Configuration of Oracle Advanced Security

Well, now that you know some of the profile information you can declare, let's get to work and do some profile configuration.

When you click on the Profile option, a pull-down selection area and three tabs appear on the right side of the Net8 Assistant screen. The pull-down options are as follows:

- Naming
- General
- Preferred Oracle Names Servers
- Oracle Advanced Security

At the bottom of the right side is a Help button that you can use to obtain additional information about each specific tab for each option. I recommend that you take the time to look at the help for each option as you examine the areas. There's a lot of great information to help you configure your system more effectively.

Profile—Naming Method Tabs

There are three tabs associated with the Naming category: Methods, Oracle Names, and External. Under the Methods tab are two areas. As you can see from Figure 7-8, the first area displays the available naming methods, labeled Available Methods, while the second area displays the methods that have been selected and the order in which they should be used. This area is labeled Selected Methods. Notice that there are four action buttons available. The first button has a greater-than sign (>) to indicate that you can select and move an available method over to the selected methods area. The next button has a less-than sign (<) to indicate that you can remove a selected method. The third button is labeled Promote, while the fourth button is labeled Demote. You can use these two buttons to rearrange the order of the methods Net8 will use when attempting to resolve a presented name. The current order tells Net8 to look first in the tnsnames.ora file, second to go to the Oracle Names server, and third to check for a Host Naming method. If Net8 fails to resolve the name after accessing each of these methods, an error occurs and an error message is displayed.

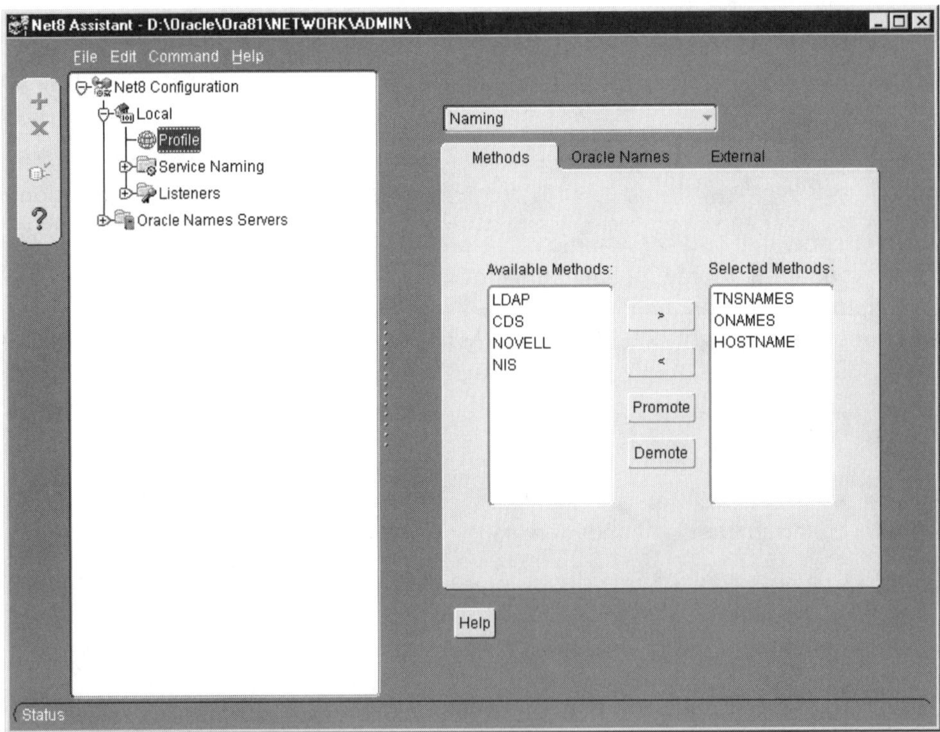

FIGURE 7-8. *Profile Naming Methods screen*

The second Naming tab is Oracle Names. The options under this tab let you declare a default domain name to be used when no domain is specified. You can also declare how long Net8 should wait between attempts to resolve a name (Maximum Wait Each Attempt) and how many times it should try the resolution (Attempts Per Names Server). The value for Maximum Wait Each Attempt is a number of seconds between 1 and 600. This number is used to tell Net8 how long to wait before attempting the request with the next Oracle Names server. The Attempts Per Names Server is a number between 1 and 5 that defines how many attempts will be made before an error is allowed to occur. These values are entered within the Resolution Persistence area.

The final area of this tab is the Performance area. Using this area, you can specify the Maximum Open Connections that this specific client can have, using a value between 3 and 64 with a default value of 3. The other parameter in this area is Initial Preallocated Requests. This parameter is used to preallocate an initial number of messages in the specific client's message pool, using a value between 3 and 256. The default value for this parameter is 10. Unless you have a really overburdened Oracle Names server, you should not change the default value for Initial Preallocated Requests. Figure 7-9 shows the options and appearance of the Oracle Names tab.

The final tab in the Naming area, External, enables you to define where Net8 should resolve new service names for external naming methods. The options are Cell Directory Service used in a Distributed Computing Environment (CDS/DCE); NetWare Directory Service (NDS), also known as Novell Directory Services (NDS); and Sun Microsystems' Yellow Pages client-server protocol, called Network Information Services (NIS). Each of these methods is used to distribute configuration information between computers in a network. Figure 7-10 shows the available areas for the External tab.

You can supply a valid DCE cell name (prefix) in the Cell Name field for this area. In our example,

```
/../subsys/oracle/names
```

has been entered.

If you are using the NetWare, aka Novell, Directory Services, you can enter a Name Context to describe where the database object is located. The way you enter the naming context will determine the service name for use in the connect string. You can use either a full or partial name. Let's say that your database object name is SKWL.US.XYZCORP.COM, as it was in Chapter 4 when I was talking about global database names and global database links. If you are using the NetWare Directory Services, you can specify for the Name Context the value US.XYZCORP.COM; then the client would need to supply only the database object name SKWL.

To configure the profile for Network Information Services, you enter the directory location of the special file that contains the database service name.

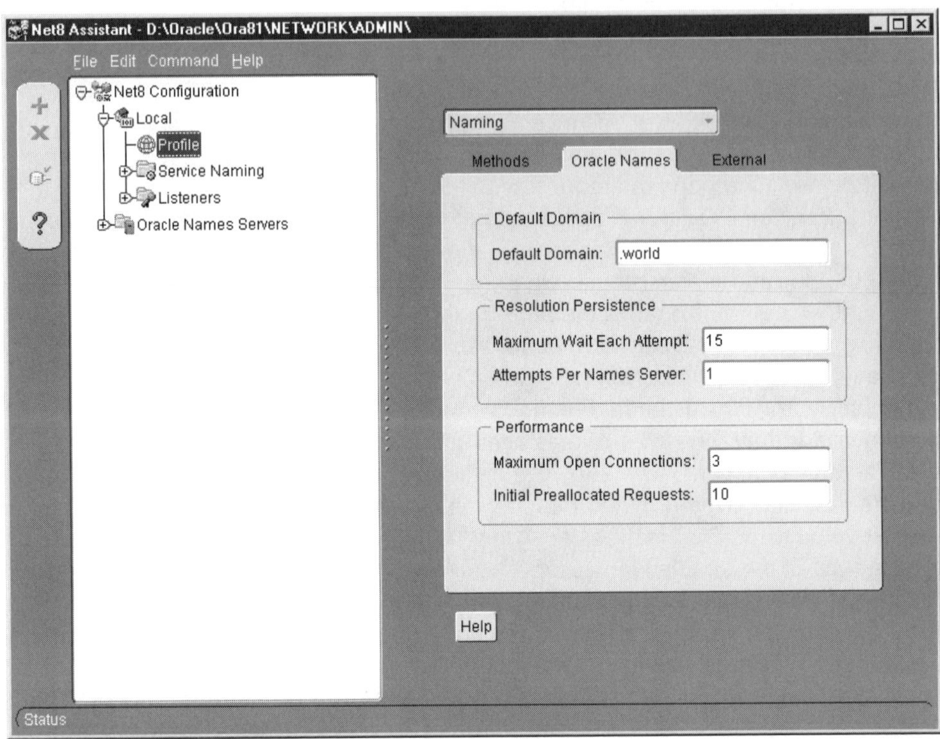

FIGURE 7-9. *Profile Naming Oracle Names screen*

Profile—General Tabs

There are four general profile tabs available: Tracing, Logging, Routing, and Advanced. Before we talk about the tabs available under the General option, I'd like to clarify something that I just realized might not be clear to you. When I talk about tracing, logging, routing, and the Advanced option, I'm talking about them from the perspective of the specific machine that you are currently configuring. Therefore, if you are connected to a machine named MARLENES-PC and you're performing tracing, logging, routing, or advanced configuration, you're creating and saving the configuration profile information to be used specifically for the MARLENES-PC machine. Okay, now let's look more closely at each of these General options.

Within the Tracing tab are areas you can use to establish Client Information tracing and Server Information tracing. You want to enable tracing if you are having a network problem and are trying to determine where the problem is coming from. Client tracing is used to keep track of the actions that the client performs during

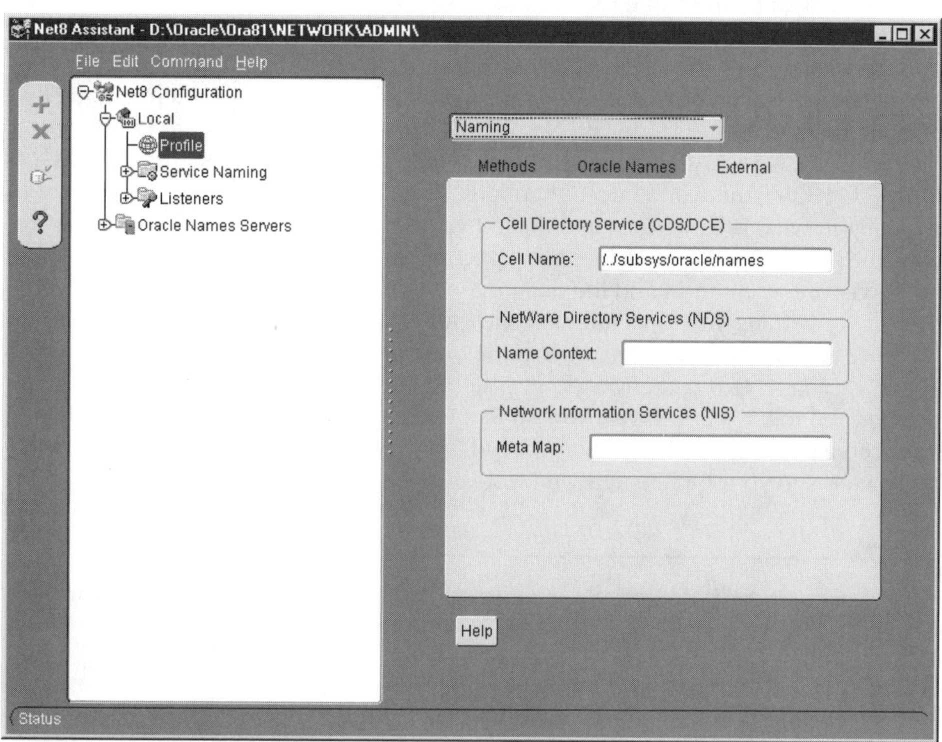

FIGURE 7-10. *Profile Naming External tab*

a network connection. Likewise, server tracking is used to capture the actions that the server performs during a network connection.

For both options, the Trace Level values are

- OFF: Tracing is disabled. This is the default setting.
- USER: Tracing at a level to identify user-induced errors.
- ADMIN: Tracing at a level to identify installation-specific problems.
- SUPPORT: Tracing at a level appropriate for Oracle support evaluation.

Each level produces a more detailed degree of information that you can use for tracking client and/or server Oracle network problems.

To enable client and/or server tracing, you select a level from the Trace Level options and then supply a directory location where you want the trace information to be written and a file name for the trace information file. In Figure 7-11, you can see the General Tracing tab with the Client Information Trace Level set to ADMIN and the partial string for the directory location: D:\Oracle\Ora81\Network\trace. I've entered a Trace File name and requested that the file names be kept unique by clicking on the Unique Trace File Name box. The default trace location for trace files on UNIX is $ORACLE_HOME/network/trace and for a Windows platform is ORACLE_HOME\network\trace. Therefore, in reality, I made more work for myself by filling in what is really the Net8 default value for the trace file destination. By the way, the default Trace File names are sqlnet.trc for the client and svr_<pid>.trc for the server. If these names and the default directory locations are acceptable to you, then the only thing you have to change to enable tracing is the trace level.

Why and when do you enable logging on your client or server? If an error occurs during a Net8 operation, don't you want to know about it? Well, logging enables you to track and save errors so that you can evaluate them. You can also track service activity and other statistics so that you can determine the traffic flow and patterns in your Oracle network. Instead of giving you fine-grained activity

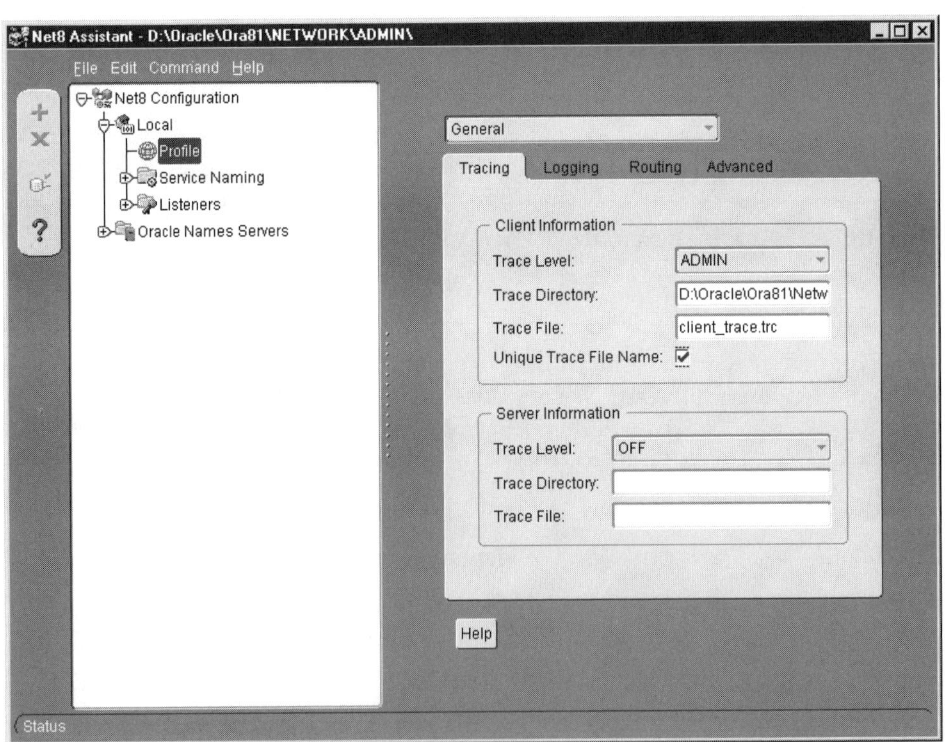

FIGURE 7-11. *Profile General Tracing tab*

information like tracing does, logging gives you overall information about the successful or unsuccessful process connections.

You can use the Logging tab shown in Figure 7-12 to declare the directory location and file name that you want to use. The default directory location for logging on a UNIX platform is $ORACLE_HOME/network/log and for a Windows platform is ORACLE_HOME\network\log. For the client, the Log File name defaults to sqlnet.log. For the server, there is only the Log Directory location. The default log file name is used on the server.

As you can see in Figure 7-13, under the Routing tab are two check boxes. When you check either of the check boxes, you're telling Net8 to *always* route all of this specific machine's requests in this defined way.

The first option is to always create a dedicated process for all of the network sessions from this client. Remember that a dedicated server process is committed to one session only and exists for the entire life of that session. This declaration will override any Multi-Threaded Server configuration because the connection will carry the parameter **server**=DEDICATED in the connect descriptors. Hmm, what are the

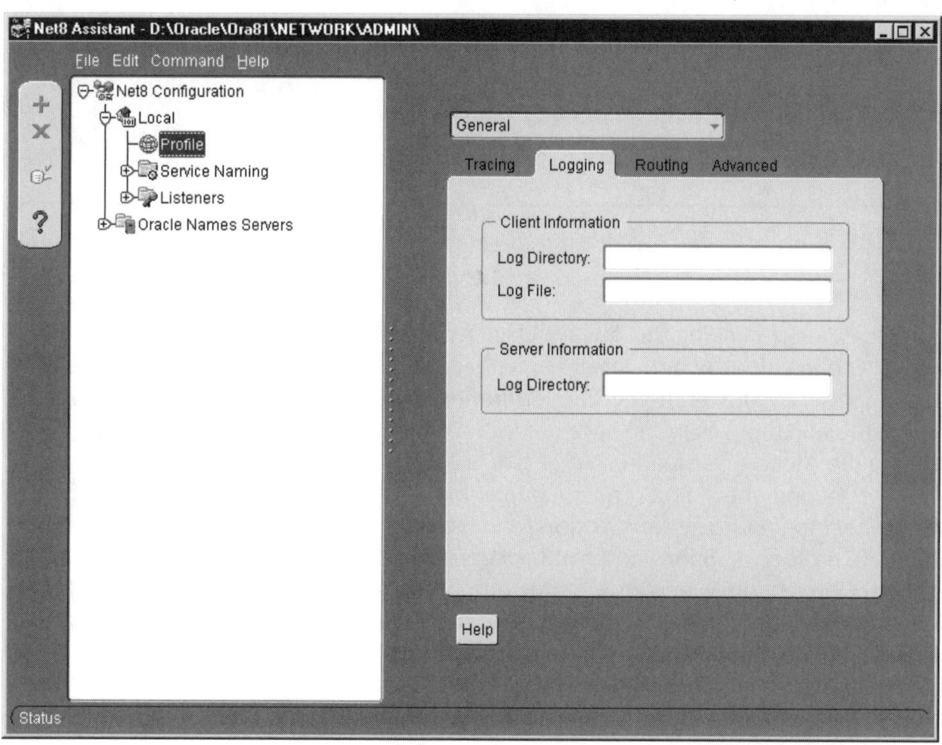

FIGURE 7-12. *Profile General Logging tab*

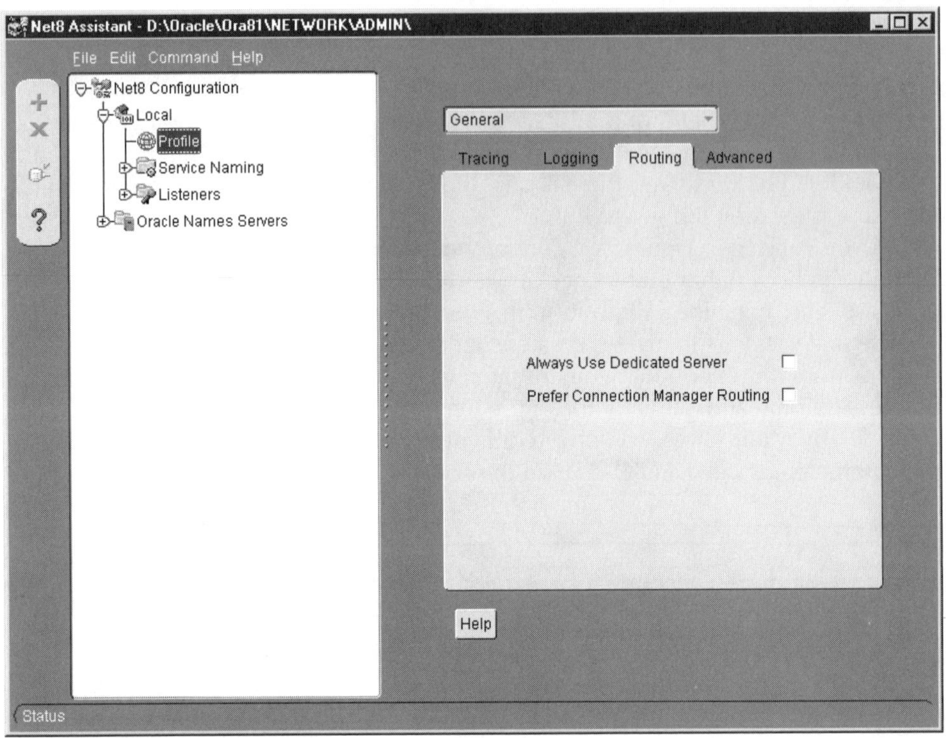

FIGURE 7-13. *Profile General Routing tab*

ramifications of clicking the Always Use Dedicated Server check box? Well, this client's connections will be faster using this option, but dedicated connections can make the server slower. If you are performing massive database transactions with very little idle time, as in the case of large data loads from a batch or cron job, setting the Always Use Dedicated Server is appropriate.

The second check box, Prefer Connection Manager Routing, instructs Net8 to try to connect to an Oracle Connection Manager whenever possible. Concentration, multiple protocol support, and Net8 access control are some of the things that the Oracle Connection Manager provides support for. The network configuration for a client whose connections resolve to the Oracle Connection Manager are specially marked. To get these special connections to be used and preferred over other connections, you choose the Prefer Connection Manager routing check box. I'll tell you more about the Oracle Connection Manager in Chapter 10.

In Figure 7-14, you can see the Advanced tab for the General option. The parameters and check boxes in this tab can be used to declare advanced profile

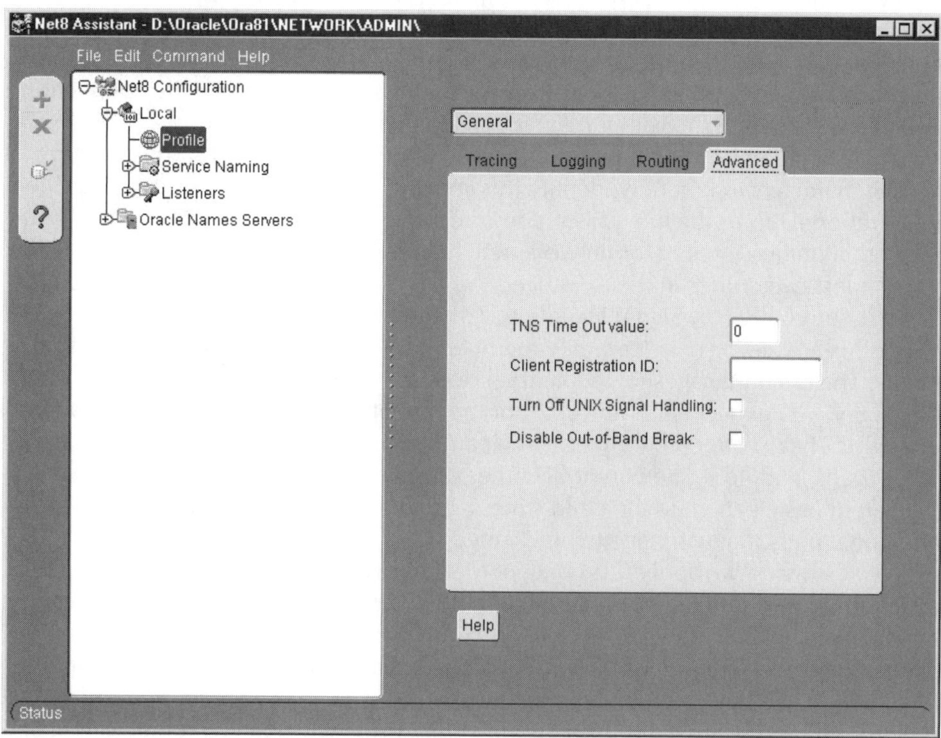

FIGURE 7-14. *Profile General Advanced tab*

information for either a client or server machine. Again, when you set parameter values in this or the other General tabs, you are configuring the profile information for the specific machine you are logged in on.

Did you ever fall asleep while you were watching television? There you were, snoozing away, while the television played on with no one watching it. Or, how about all the times you walked out of a room to do something and forgot to turn the television off? Wouldn't it be wonderful to have the television configured to check at specific intervals to see if you are asleep or out of the room and turn itself off if you're not watching it? Granted, the electricity that you'd save per night is very little, but, over time, if enough televisions were shutting themselves off when people left the room or fell asleep, we might save a substantial amount of resources.

Well, we don't have the technology quite yet to have your television automatically sense your state and respond accordingly. However, in the Oracle networking world, you can use the TNS Time Out value, shown in Figure 7-14 as the first area of the Advanced tab, to declare how frequently Net8 should send out a probe to verify that the client-server connection is still active. After this parameter, which can only be used from the server, is set, when a probe is sent, if a client has terminated abnormally or a connection is no longer in use but still being held open, an error will occur. When an error occurs, the server will terminate the connection and free the resources for other connections to use.

The Client Registration ID is a unique identifier consisting of a string with up to 128 characters to uniquely identify this specific client. The listener uses the Client Registration ID in its log file. This is a terrific way to give each Oracle client in your network a unique identity for network activity tracking.

The last two entries in the Advanced tab are check boxes. The first check box is labeled Turn Off UNIX Signal Handling. To understand what happens when you check this box, let's consider family members. Consider a child playing with finger paints. The child manages to get paint all over everything while creating a picture. Generally, you expect either the child or the parent of that child to clean the paint up, right? That is, after all, only fair. In cleaning up the excess finger paints from the table, walls, and floor, the parent becomes covered with finger paint. Even though the parent has cleaned up the child's mess, the parent has generated some additional mess that will have to be cleaned up as well.

Now, how do we apply this concept to signal handlers? Well, first of all, a client application spawns a server process internally through the bequeath protocol as a child process. Think of this as our child making a finger paint picture. The client application becomes responsible for cleaning up the child process when it completes. Okay so far. We have a client application spawning a server process as a child process with an obligation to clean up the child process when it completes its task. In other words, someone's going to clean up the finger paints when the child finishes making a picture. The process that handles the cleanup becomes defunct after its cleanup task is completed. Whoever did the cleanup is now covered with finger paint. Signal handlers are responsible for cleaning up these defunct processes. The signal handler is going to complete the cleanup chores.

When you check Turn Off UNIX Signal Handling, you tell Net8 to pass the child process cleanup to the UNIX initialization process. Clicking this option means that you disable the signal handlers. Huh? Let's look just a bit closer at how this works.

The UNIX init process always has a process identification value (PID) of 1 and is used for two main purposes:

- The init process is invoked by the UNIX kernel at the end of the bootstrap procedure. The init process reads system-dependent initialization files, such as /etc/rc*, and brings the system to a certain state.
- The init process becomes the parent process of any orphaned child processes. For example, when a process that has child processes terminates and does not wait for child processes to terminate, the child processes become orphaned and are inherited by the init process.

This is standard UNIX SVR4. User-defined exit handles can be configured via the UNIX function atexit(0) to handle process termination as well. You can allow the init process or the parent process to perform the cleanup. If you decide to have the parent process perform the cleanup, it must be able to handle all termination signal interrupts, which requires that you perform additional coding. To summarize, if you check the option Turn Off UNIX Signal Handling, you allow the init process to handle process terminations. If you do not check the option, you make it the parent's responsibility to handle process termination. It is usually better to allow the init process to handle these types of situations. After all, that's one of the reasons the init process exists.

The second check box is labeled Disable Out-of-Band Break. If out-of-band breaks are enabled, a client can cancel an operation while it is processing. When you disable out-of-band breaks, you are requiring all submitted requests to run to completion. This option is usually checked when the underlying transport being used by the client does not support out-of-band breaks.

Profile—Preferred Oracle Names Server Tab

If you are running one or more Oracle Names servers, you need to locate each of them on the network so that client machines can obtain information from them. The order in which you list them will determine which one the client attempts to contact first. Remember that under the Command pull-down menu on the left side is the command Discover Oracle Names Servers. If you use that option, the Names servers will be listed in order from fastest response time to slowest. The entries are stored on a UNIX platform in the file .sdns.ora, while for a Windows platform, the list is stored in the file sdns.ora. Keep in mind that the Oracle Names servers you record in the Preferred list will override the order in which they are entered in the Discover list. If you use the Discover feature after you have entered values in the Preferred Oracle Names Servers area, you may want to go back and remove the entries from the Preferred profile.

There's only one tab under the Preferred Oracle Names Server option, as you can see in Figure 7-15. If I had not already configured an Oracle Names server, no tabs would be available because there would be no Oracle Names server to declare as preferred.

There's something different about this screen. Can you see what it is? Well, instead of having just a Help button at the bottom of the right side, there are now three buttons: New, Delete, and Help. I think these buttons are self-explanatory, don't you?

There's also a pull-down menu for the Protocol area. I'll pull the menu down and see what choices you have for Protocol entries. For each protocol option, there are appropriate parameters for you to enter. Table 7-1, taken directly from the Net8 Assistant Help screen for protocol parameters, shows the protocols and associated parameters. In some cases, more than one parameter is required. In those cases,

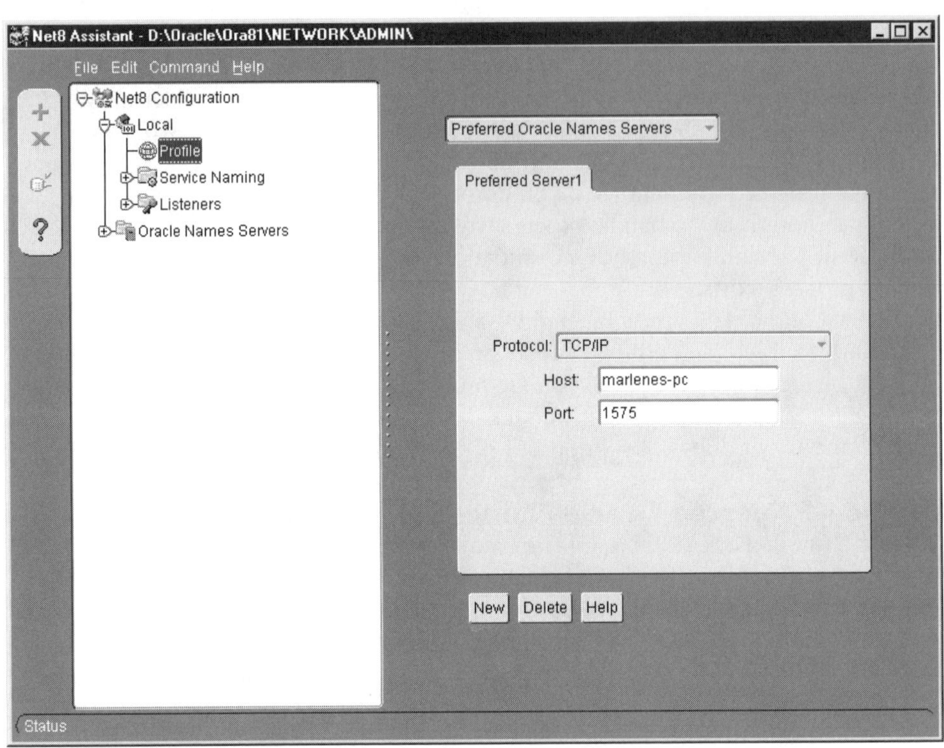

FIGURE 7-15. *Profile Preferred Oracle Names Servers Preferred Server screen*

you'll see more than one entry for a specific protocol. Since both TCP/IP and TCP/IP with SSL require the same parameters, I've listed them together.

For this example, I've used the TCP/IP protocol with my machine name, MARLENES-PC, and the associated port number of 1575.

Profile—Oracle Advanced Security Tabs

Oracle8i, Release 2 is built with the ability to support many third-party vendor authentication adapters. Cool! Um, what's an authentication adapter? To answer that question, but without going into too much detail right now, think about how you prove that you are who you say you are. When you walk up to someone at a party, for instance, you say, "Hi, my name is...," and you tell the person your name to introduce yourself. Usually, just saying your name is enough. The person you're talking to accepts your name without question. Now, when you go to apply for a driver's license for the first time, you have to produce more proof that you are who you say you are. Your word is not enough. You must show a birth certificate or

Protocol	Parameter	Description
IPC	key	Indicates a way of identifying the server. Oracle Corporation recommends using the name of the service.
Named Pipes	server	Identifies the name of the Oracle8i database.
Named Pipes	pipe	Identifies the pipe name used to connect to the server (the same PIPE keyword you specified on the server with Named Pipes). This name can be any name.
SPX	service	Defines the name of the TNS-based application on the network.
TCP/IP and TCP/IP with SSL	host	Identifies the host name of the server.
TCP/IP and TCP/IP with SSL	port	Identifies the listener port number.

TABLE 7-1. *Protocols and Their Required Parameters*

other form of identification. Once you have your driver's license, you can generally use it to identify yourself. If you decide to travel to another country, you take your birth certificate and two pictures of yourself, and you apply for a passport. Once you have your passport, you can travel to other countries. Your passport is now your proof that you are you.

Okay, fine. But, how do you prove that you are you over the telephone? To verify your identification over the telephone, you generally have to be able to give some predefined information, such as your mother's maiden name or your Social Security number and your address and telephone number. The person you are dealing with can't see you but can see what your answers should be. If you're making a purchase, the person will usually just accept your charge card number, its expiration date, and your name and address as proof of your identity.

Things get more complicated when you are using a computer and must prove you are you. There are several products, referred to in the Net8 Assistant as methods, available to enable you to authenticate your identity from your computer. Among them are Kerberos, CyberSafe, SecurID, RADIUS, Identix, and NTS. I mention these particular products because they are the ones that Oracle supports and that you can configure from the Advanced Security option. Let's see what the last Profile option offers.

The tabs for Oracle Advanced Security are Authentication, Other Params, Integrity, Encryption, and SSL. Figure 7-16 shows the initial screen with the Authentication tab values.

There are five available products and one selected. Each product or method requires a different set of parameters. Appendix B lists the parameters available for each of the products. There are four action buttons between the Available Methods and the Selected Methods: Add (>), Remove (<), Promote, and Demote. Using these buttons, you can add and change the order of more than one method. Once you have entered the methods that are appropriate based on the products that you have installed, you use the second tab, Other Params, to input the appropriate parameters for the methods that you're using. Figure 7-17 shows the Authentication Service with Kerberos(V5) selected and the parameters that are associated with this product. Of the available authentication services, Kerberos and RADIUS require multiple parameters, while NTS and SecurID don't require any, and Identix and CyberSafe require one parameter each. I'll let you explore the parameters for these products yourself. Remember that the Help available for each of these products will guide you through configuration, as will the product documentation itself.

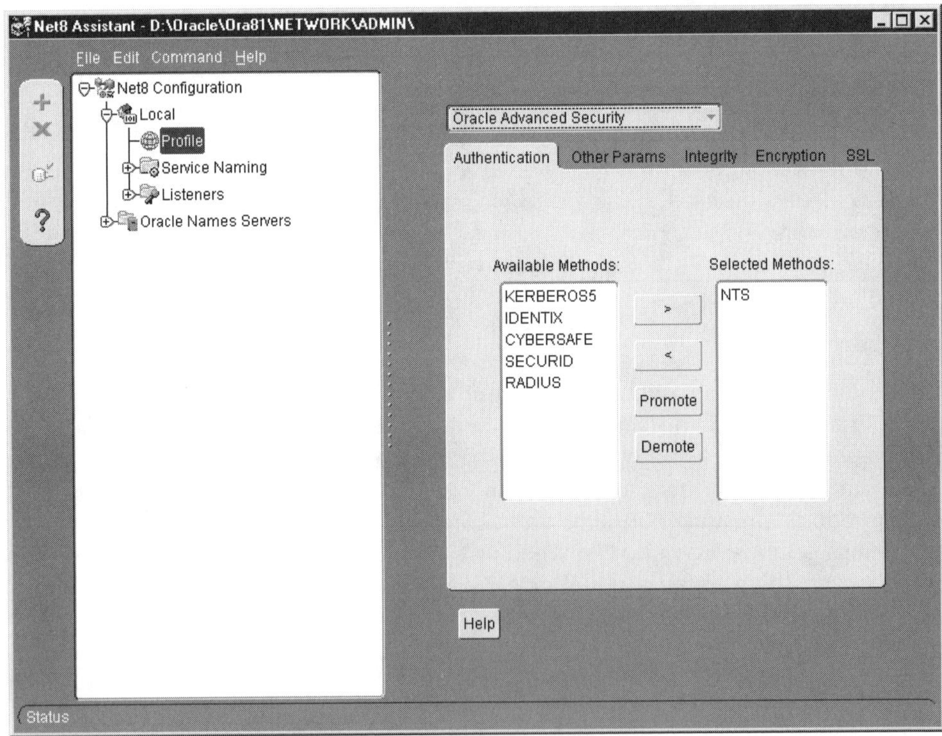

FIGURE 7-16. *Profile Oracle Advanced Security Authentication tab*

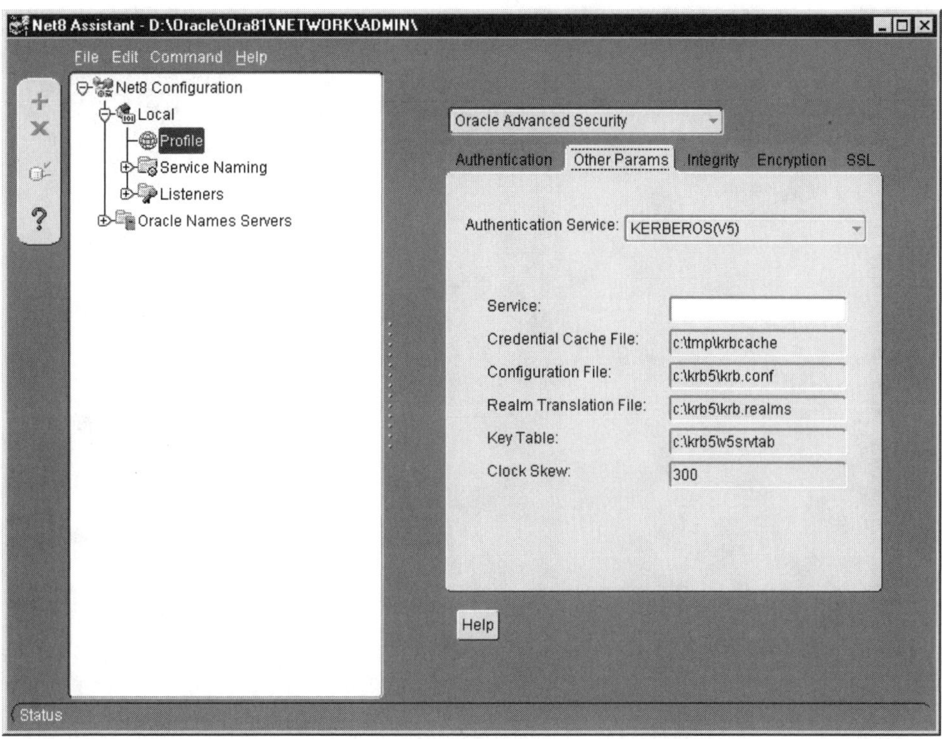

FIGURE 7-17. *Profile Oracle Advanced Security Other Params tab*

The Integrity tab, shown in Figure 7-18, has two options: a Server check box with Checksum Level and a Client check box with Checksum Level. But, what's this used for? If I send you a message, how do you know that you got everything I sent? In Chapters 1 and 2, we learned that messages are broken into numbered packets and sent with a checksum value in each packet's header. When the packets are received, the checksum for each packet is verified to ensure that the packet arrived with the same contents it was sent with, and the entire message is reassembled according to the packet numbers. The Integrity tab enables you to configure checksumming for each of the authentication methods that you have available. Table 7-2 shows the available values for both the client and server with a brief description.

The rule that doesn't show up in Table 7-2 is that in all cases, there must be a compatible checksum algorithm on each side of the connection. Now, assuming there is a matching algorithm on both sides, here are the different ramifications that come with each of these options.

In all of these scenarios, we'll assume that I want to make a connection to your side. Okay? Let's go. If I set my side to Required and you set your side to Accepted,

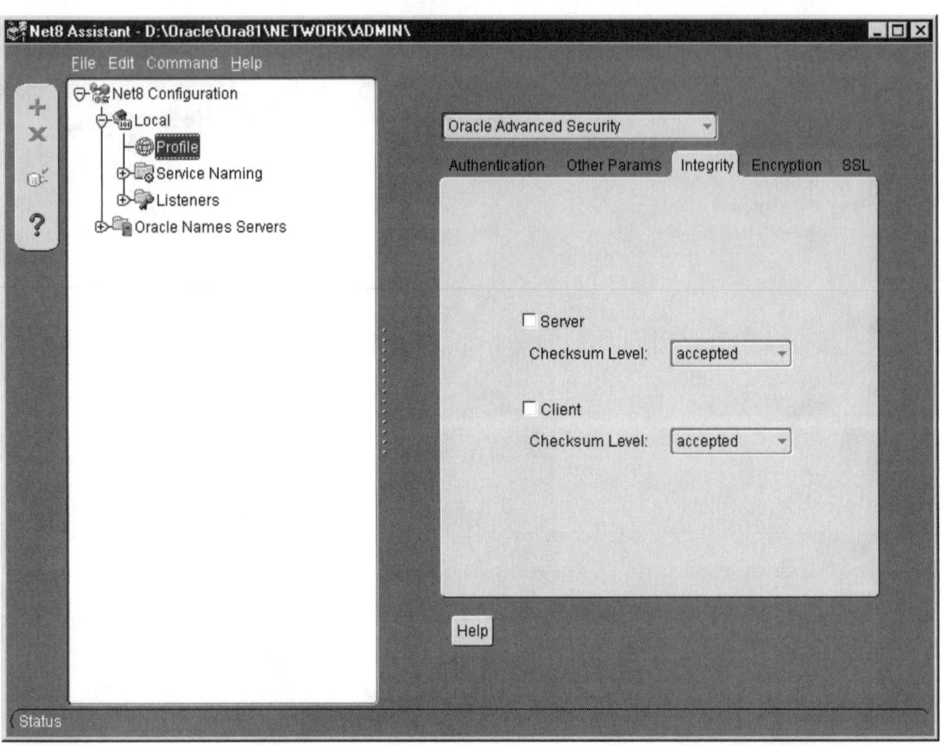

FIGURE 7-18. *Profile Oracle Advanced Security Integrity tab*

the connection will fail because I don't just *want* checksumming, I'm *requiring* it. If I set my side to Requested, the connection will work if you have your side set to Accepted, Requested, or Required. If I set my side to Accepted, I'm saying that I don't really want the security service but I'll accept it if you set your side to Required or Requested and our algorithms match. Interestingly enough, Rejected doesn't work quite the way you'd expect it to. If I set my side to Rejected, I'm saying that I don't want to use the security service but that I still want to make the connection to your side. If you specified Required, the connection will fail. However, if you specified Requested, Accepted, or Rejected, the connection will go through without error and without using the security service. See Chapter 13 for more about these values.

The next Oracle Advanced Security tab is Encryption. The two Encryption options on the pull-down menu are Client and Server. In Figure 7-19, you can see that the Server option has been selected. The Encryption Type, like the Integrity types, are accepted, rejected, required, and requested. There's an encryption seed composed of a random set of characters on which encryption will be based and five

Value	Definition
Required	Turn on the security service or do not make the connection.
Requested	Turn on the security service if the other side enables it.
Accepted	Turn on the security service if the other side wants it.
Rejected	Do not turn on the security service even if the other side wants it.

TABLE 7-2. *Integrity Tab Checksum Levels for Client and Server*

different levels of encryption available. As shown in Figure 7-19, no encryption methods have been selected.

The final tab for the Oracle Advanced Security option is SSL (Secure Sockets Layer). SSL, an industry standard protocol, provides authentication, encryption, and data integrity for both clients and servers. Figure 7-20 shows the SSL tab. It looks

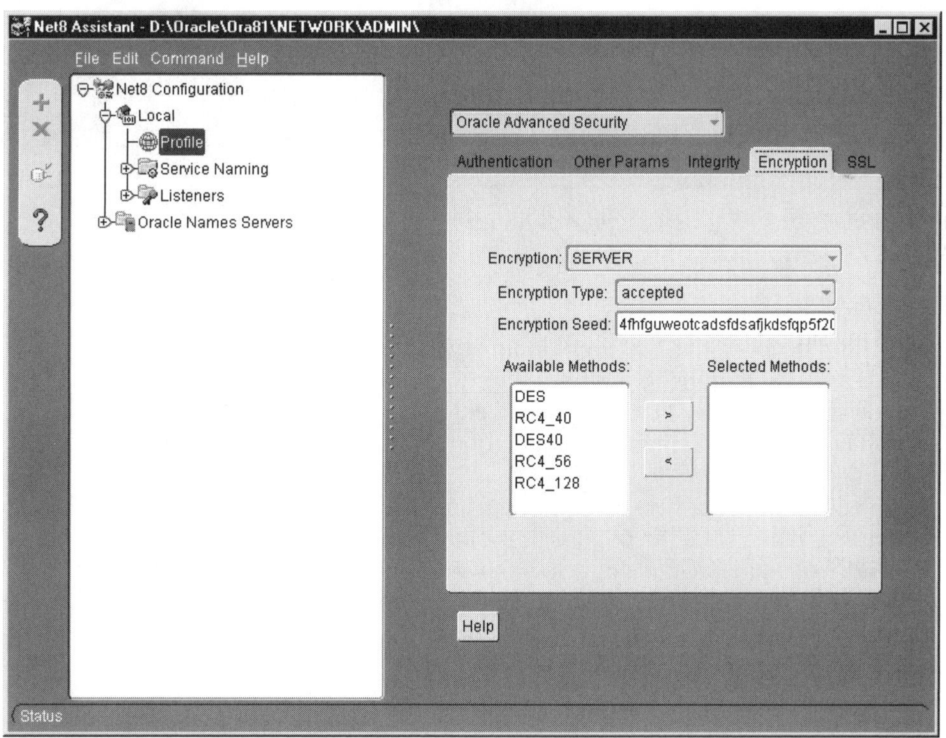

FIGURE 7-19. *Profile Oracle Advanced Security Encryption tab*

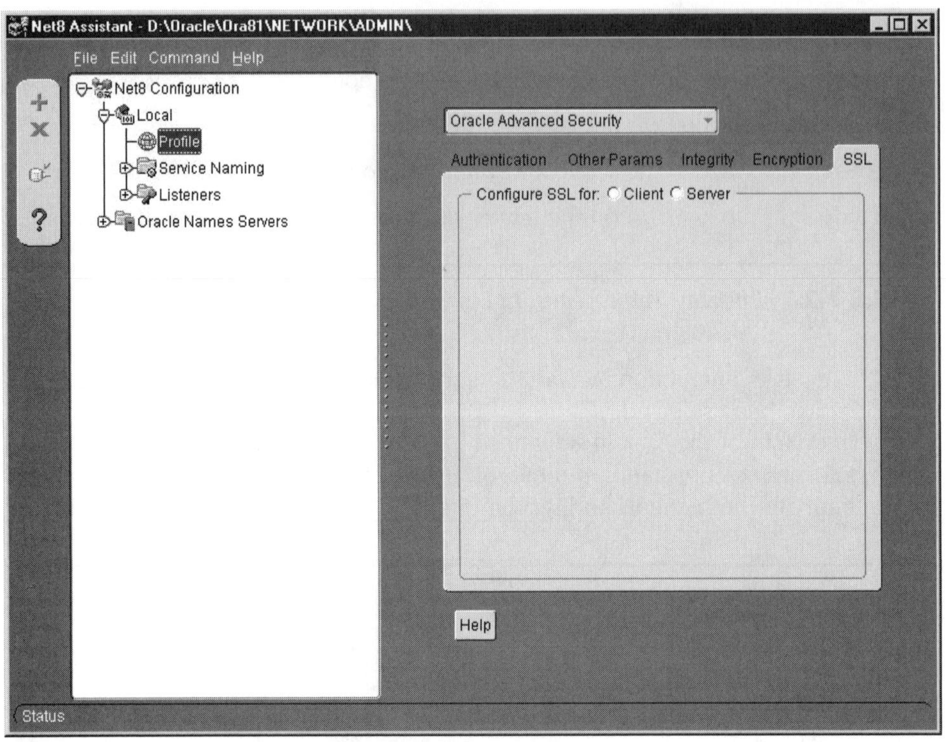

FIGURE 7-20. *Profile Oracle Advanced Security SSL tab*

really simple, doesn't it? You would think that all you have to do is select one of the options and you're done. Not so.

You see, once you click on either Client or Server, a new screen is displayed, as seen in Figure 7-21, and more configuration information is required. I've clicked on the Server option.

The only difference between the client and server screen options is that the client screen does not include the bottom check box indicating that client authentication is required. You must declare a directory in which your security wallet will be kept. By default, six cipher suites have been installed. Figure 7-22 shows the options that are presented when you click on the Add button. If you click on the Show US Domestic Cipher Suites, 13 options appear.

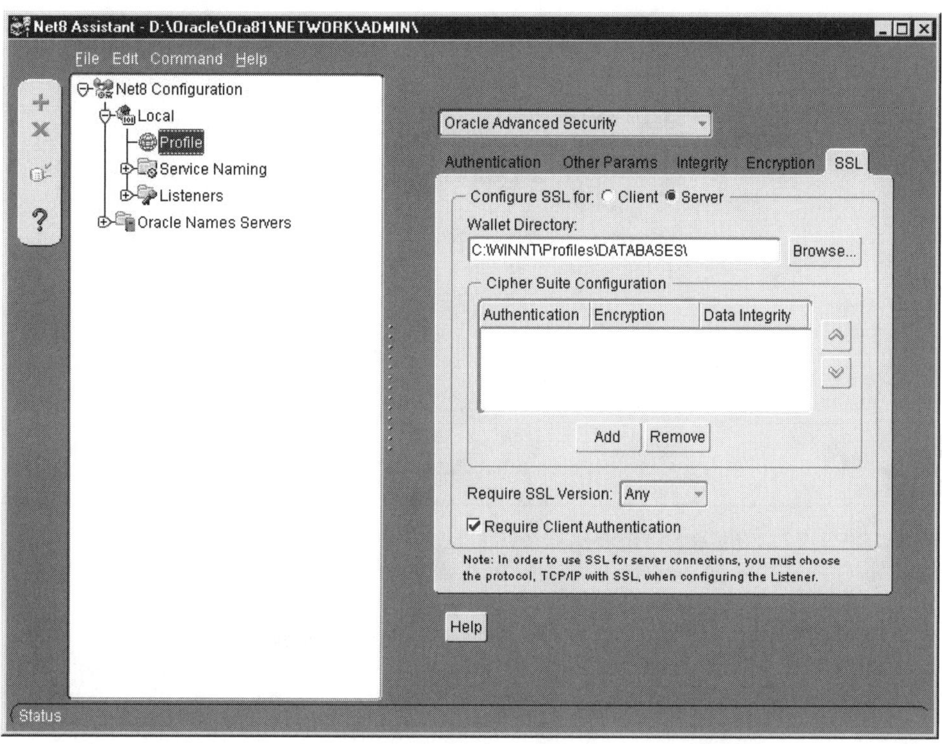

FIGURE 7-21. *Profile Oracle Advanced Security SSL Server screen*

There are two options in the SSL Version pull-down: Any or 3.0. Oh, and just above the Help button is a note to remind you that you must specify TCP/IP with SSL when you configure your listener, or SSL will not be available.

Service Naming Configuration

In the area where I live, there are several different routes that I can take to get to the grocery store. I can stay on the often-crowded main streets, or I can take a set of side streets that I call "my shortcut." I prefer to use my shortcut when the traffic is heaviest, even though it's about a quarter of a mile longer. You see, I've learned that my shortcut will get me to my destination much more quickly.

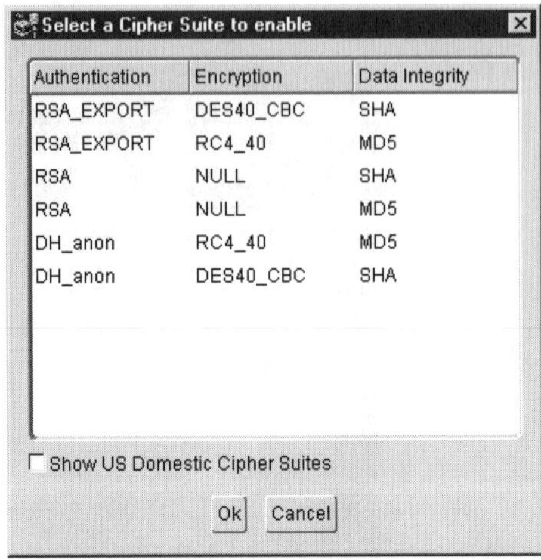

FIGURE 7-22. *Select a Cipher Suite to Enable screen*

I'm also rather lazy and prefer to type as few words as possible to accomplish a task. Therefore, I prefer to use nicknames or aliases when I want to connect to a database or service. I've got my local naming method set up to enable me to type a simple net service name and let the naming method translate that name into the necessary connect string. Rather than type the entire connection string like

```
connect NELSON/NELPW@SKWL.XYZCORP.US.COM
```

I would much prefer to type

```
connect NELSON/NELPW@SKWL
```

and let the software resolve the simple name into the required information to complete the requested connection.

In this section, I'll tell you how you can set up your local naming method to perform connection resolutions. I'd like to point out at the start that if you used any version of the Net8 Easy Config tool supplied with earlier versions of Oracle, you'll find that Net8 Easy Config has been added as the Service Naming option for the Net8 Assistant. If you know how to use the Net8 Easy Config tool, you may want to just skim through this section.

Look at Figure 7-23, which shows the initial Service Naming screen. There's some very helpful initial information to get you started. The large plus sign (+) at the far left side of the screen turns green when you click on the Service Naming

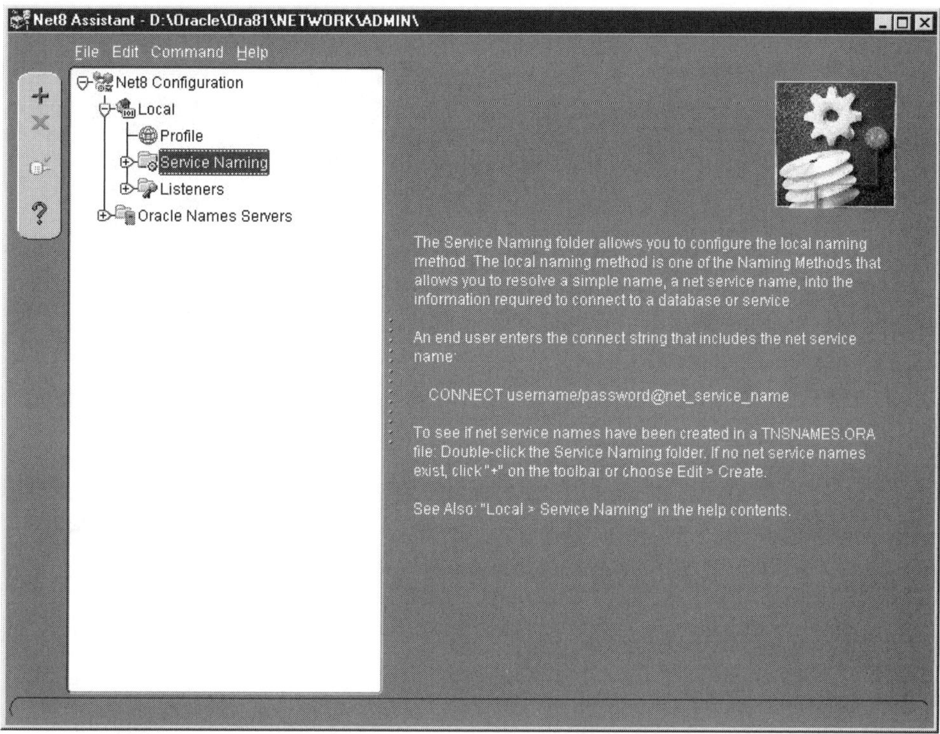

FIGURE 7-23. *Local Service Naming initial screen*

option in the navigation tree, indicating that you can create net service names. The top-level pull-down menu also has the Create option enabled.

When you click the plus sign or select Edit > Create, the Net Service Name Wizard Welcome screen, shown in Figure 7-24, appears. As you can see from the figure, I've already filled in the Net Service Name, the abbreviation for Skingwaddle database.

When you move to the next screen, you are prompted to select the appropriate network protocol used for your database. Your choices, as shown in Figure 7-25, are TCP/IP, TCP/IP with SSL, SPX, Named Pipes, or IPC. I've selected TCP/IP.

In the third wizard screen, you are prompted for protocol settings that are appropriate for the specific protocol you chose in the Protocol screen. If you look closely at Figure 7-26, you'll see that the information is TCP/IP specific and the entries are for the name of the computer machine on which the database resides and the associated listener port number. If I had chosen a different protocol, I would have

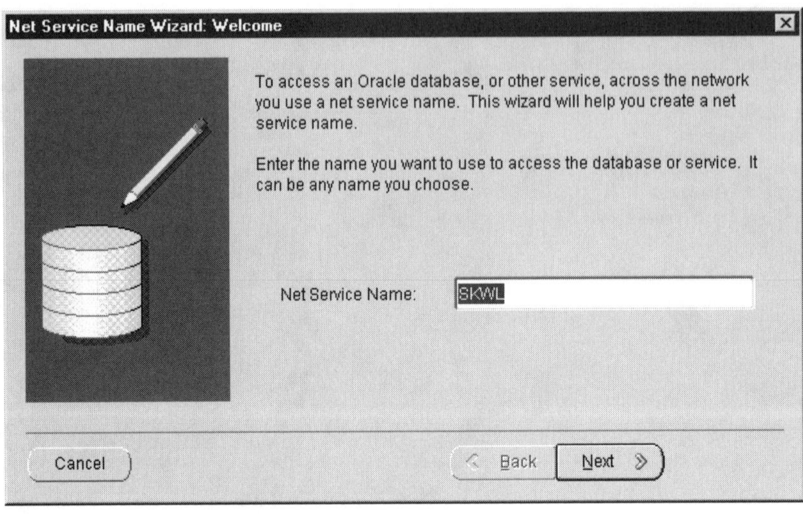

FIGURE 7-24. *Net Service Name Wizard Welcome screen*

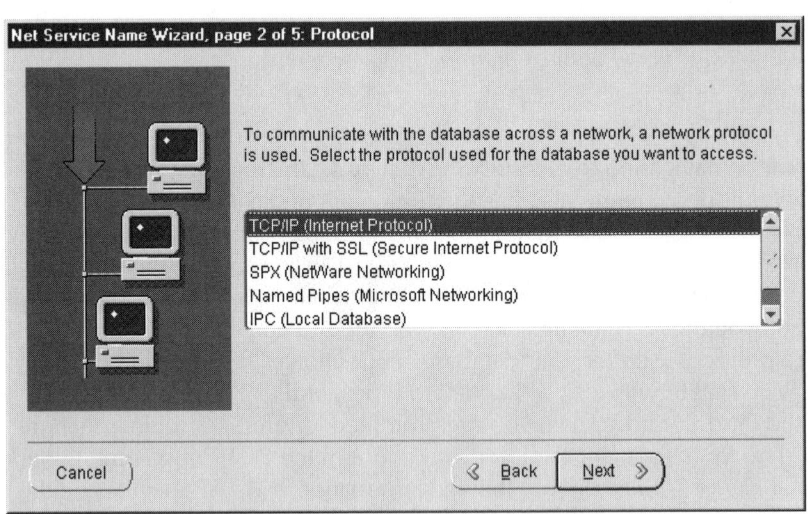

FIGURE 7-25. *Net Service Name Wizard Protocol screen*

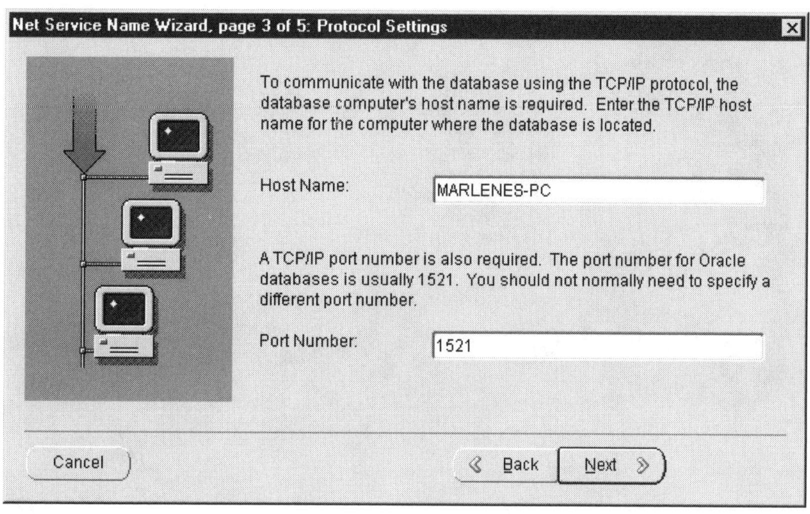

FIGURE 7-26. *Net Service Name Wizard Protocol Settings screen*

seen a screen with prompts for configuration information that's appropriate for the protocol I chose. For example, if you choose SPX, you'll be prompted for the SPX Service Name, while the choice of Named Pipes would have resulted in your being asked for both the Server Name and a Pipe Name. For IPC, you are prompted for IPC Key Value.

Once you've filled in the required protocol settings information and clicked the Next button, you see the screen shown in Figure 7-27. I've already filled in the Service Name for the Skingwaddle database. Notice, though, that I filled in the entire domain name, not just the nickname. The choices for Oracle8i Connection Type are Database Default, Shared Server, or Dedicated Server. I've accepted the Database Default option.

Once you've specified the values for this screen and clicked the Next button, you see the screen shown in Figure 7-28. This screen offers you the chance to test your ability to connect to the specified service. By performing the test, you can ensure that you've configured your new net service name correctly.

If you perform the test successfully, you'll see the results, as shown in Figure 7-29. You can control the account that the Test attempts to log on to by clicking on the Change Login button.

Once you complete your test and exit the Test screen, if you are satisfied with the results, you can click on the Finish button. When you click Finish, your new service will appear in the Service Naming navigation tree, and you'll see the

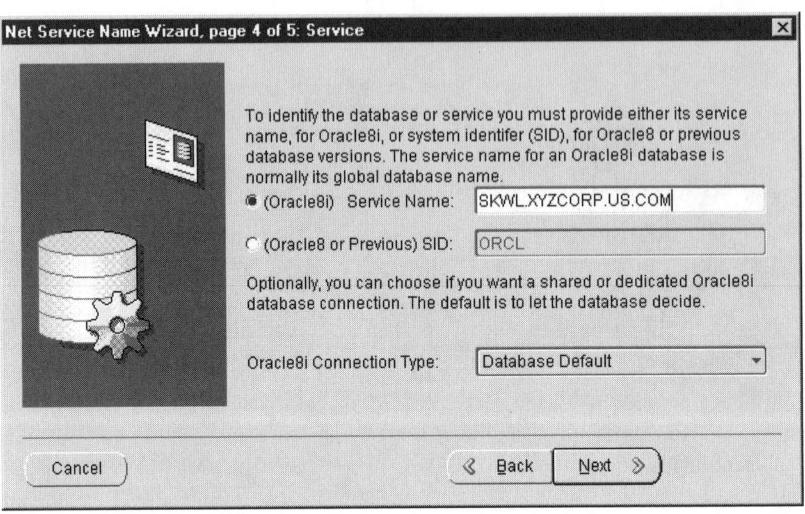

FIGURE 7-27. *Net Service Name Wizard Service screen*

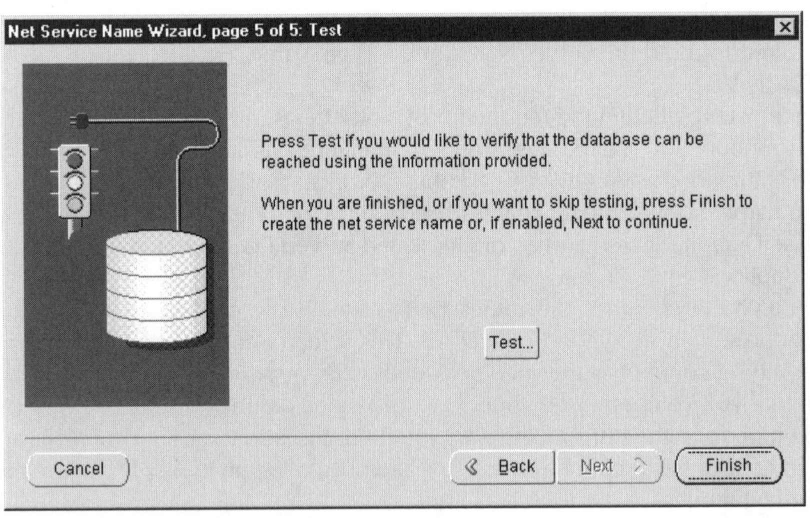

FIGURE 7-28. *Net Service Name Wizard Test screen*

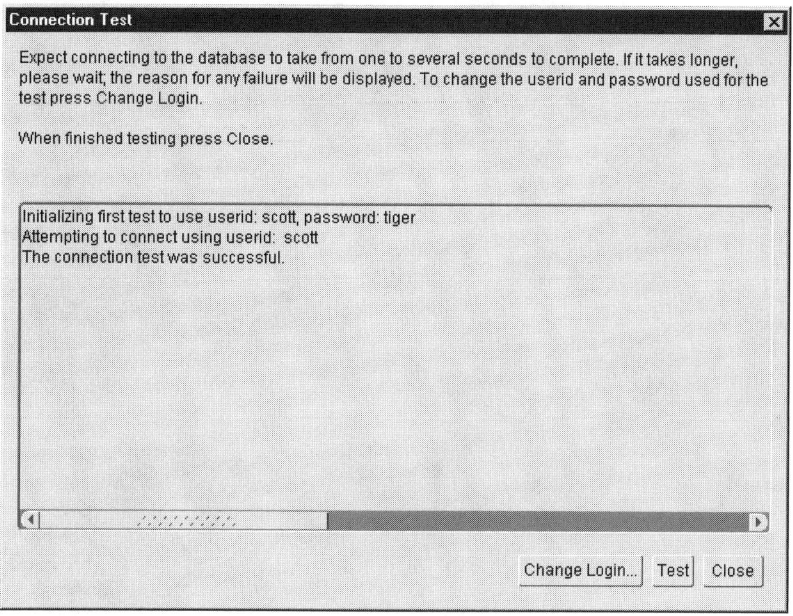

FIGURE 7-29. *Connection Test screen with successful results*

parameter information shown in Figure 7-30. The information summarizes all of the values that I used when I created the net service name.

If you select the Advanced option in the Service Identification area, another screen will be displayed in which you can enter additional service information. Figure 7-31 shows this screen.

Using the Advanced Service Options screen, you can configure Oracle Rdb settings and indicate that you want the service to be used for heterogeneous services.

Listeners Configuration

As with the Service Naming option, when you click on the Listeners option of the Net8 Assistant navigation tree, you see a general information screen with helpful information, and the large plus sign turns green. Figure 7-32 shows the Listeners initial screen. Let's walk through a listener creation.

Listening Locations Option

When you click on the green plus sign or select Edit > Create from the pull-down menu, the Choose Listener Name screen, as shown in Figure 7-33, appears. I've inserted the name LIST1 for our new listener.

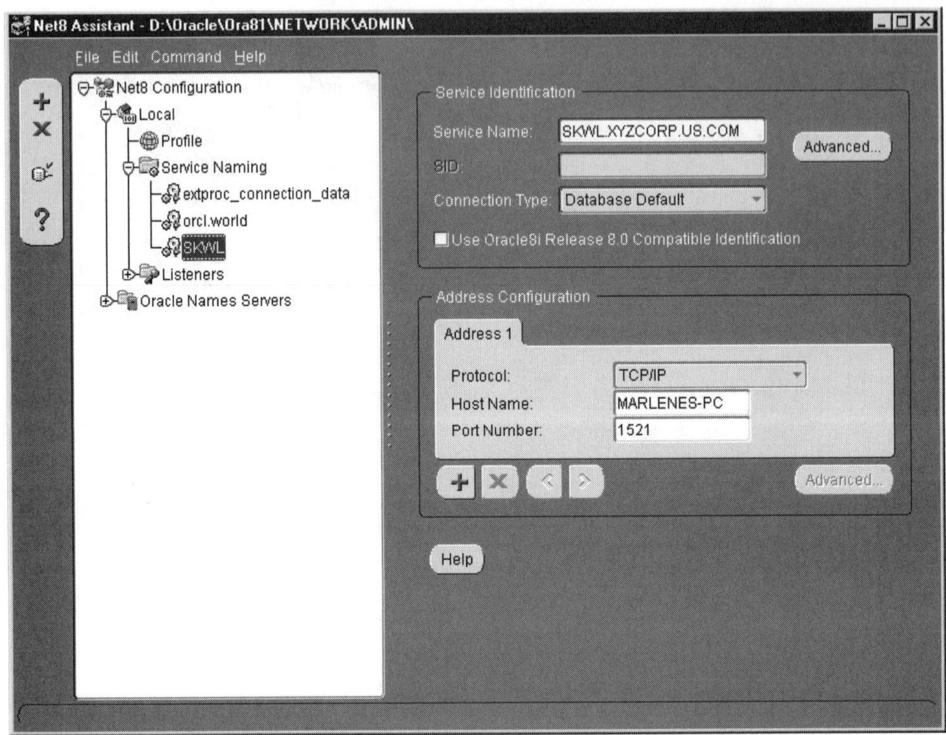

FIGURE 7-30. *Service Naming screen with SKWL service configuration*

FIGURE 7-31. *Advanced Service Options screen*

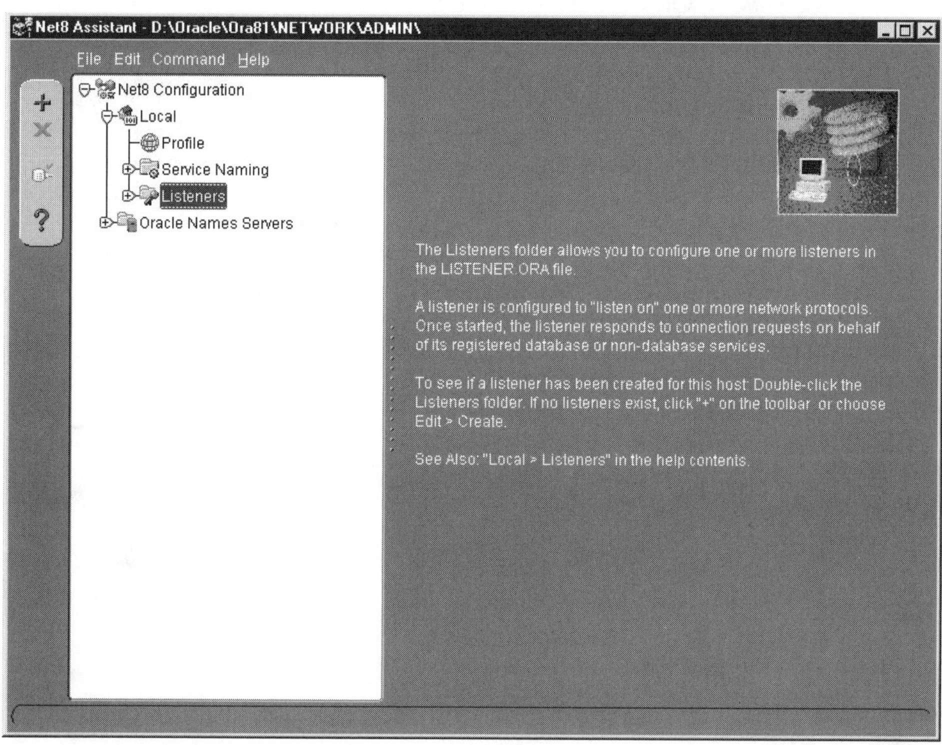

FIGURE 7-32. *Listeners initial screen*

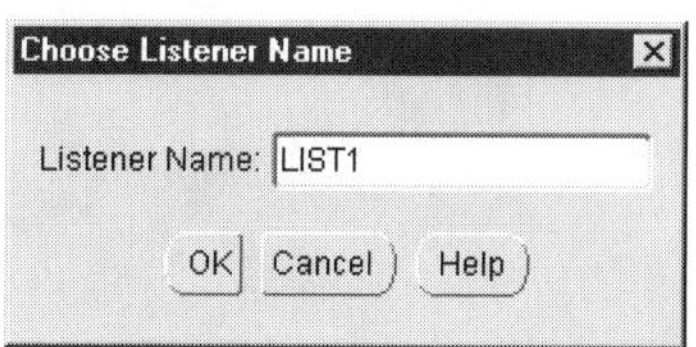

FIGURE 7-33. *Choose Listener Name screen*

When you click on OK, your new listener is placed in the Listeners navigation tree, and you are presented with various options to continue the listener configuration activity. Figure 7-34 shows the new listener's initial screen.

At the upper-right area of the screen is a pull-down menu with Listening Locations selected. The other options in this menu are General Parameters, Database Services, and Other Services. The middle of the screen informs you that there are no listening locations configured. You are instructed to press the Add Address button at the bottom of the screen. Along with the Help button, there is also a Remove Address button.

After clicking the Add Address button, a default Address1 tab appears. It contains the information that was inserted when my original listener was created by the system when I installed my software. Figure 7-35 shows the default values for the Address1 tab.

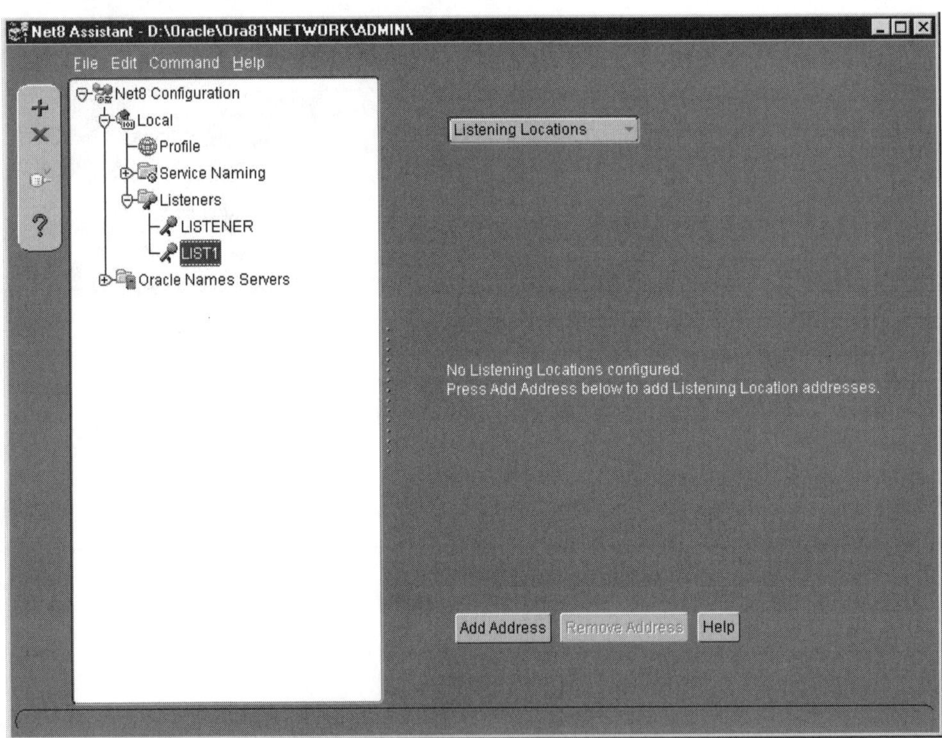

FIGURE 7-34. *Listeners LIST1 initial screen*

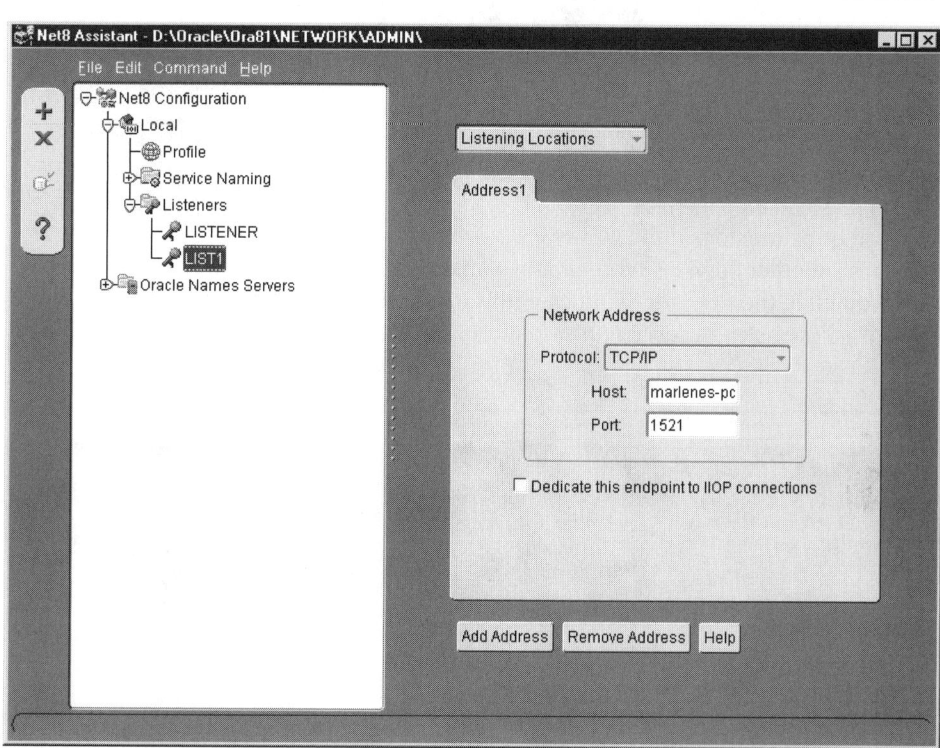

FIGURE 7-35. *Listeners LIST1 address information*

If you click on the Add Address button again, a second tab will be created with the same information that is in the Address1 tab but with the port number removed. The Protocol options are the same as for the Service Naming options. If you already have a listener defined that is using the specified port number and attempt to move on to the General Parameters option, you will receive an error notification. The notification tells you that you already have a listener configured to use the displayed port and that you must choose another port number before you can continue your configuration. I changed my port number for LIST1 to 1526 and then selected the General Parameters option.

Listeners General Parameters Option

There are three tabs associated with the General Parameters option: General, Logging & Tracing, and Authentication. Figure 7-36 shows the General tab selected and the available parameters that you can set for your new listener.

The Listener Name appears to be grayed out because it has a gray background instead of a white one, and it is. You cannot change the Listener Name once you've chosen it. To change the Listener Name, you must remove and re-create it. Almost all of the other parameters in the General Parameters tab are documented in Chapter 3 except for Register Services with Oracle Names and the SNMP Contact Information.

If you click the Register Services with Oracle Names option, when the listener starts, it will register its service information with the Oracle Names servers.

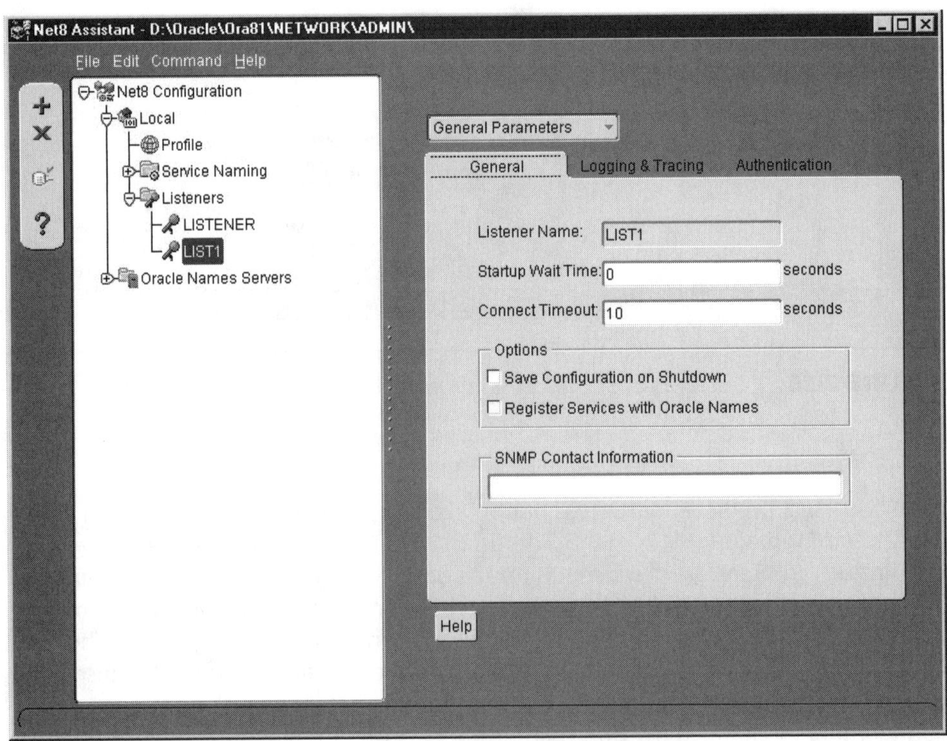

FIGURE 7-36. *Listeners General Parameters General tab*

The information that you can add in the SNMP Contact Information area is written to the snmp.ora file for use with the Oracle Enterprise Manager. You can make this information anything you want. However, the usual information added here is the client's username and/or administrator's name. In the interest of saving space, please look back to Chapter 3 for explanations of the other parameters shown here.

As the name implies, the Logging & Tracing tab shown in Figure 7-37 is the area in which you can configure logging and tracing activities for your new listener.

By default when logging is enabled, the logs on a UNIX platform will go to $ORACLE_HOME/network/log, while the logs for a Windows platform will be written to the ORACLE_HOME\network\log location. Also by default, the log will be written to a file name that matches the listener name with the extension of .log.

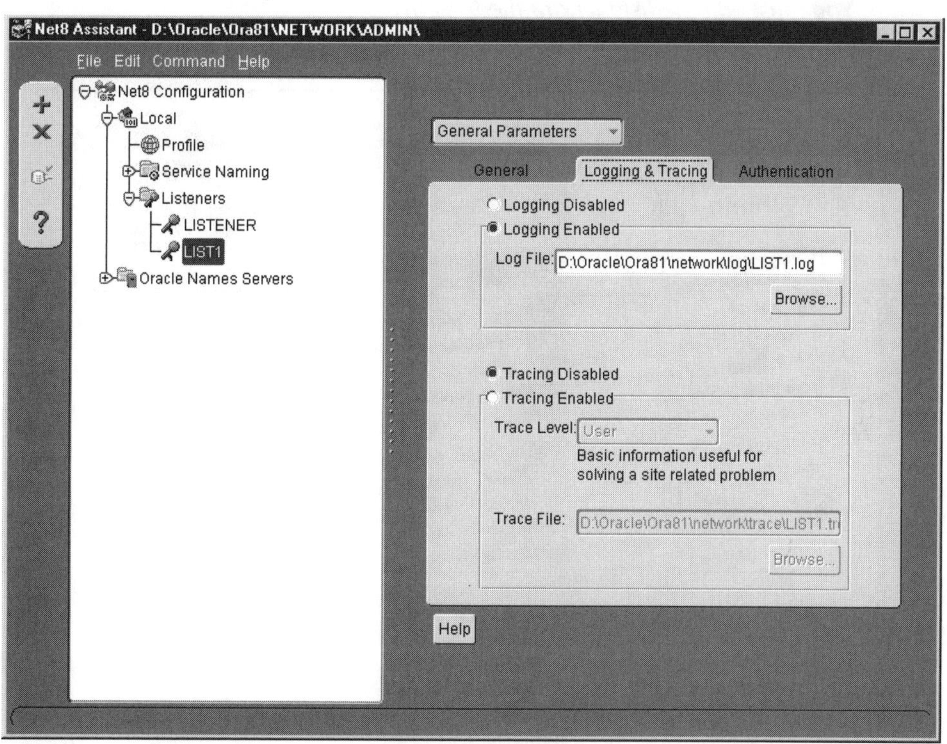

FIGURE 7-37. *Listeners General Parameters Logging & Tracing tab*

If you enable tracing, by default the trace files for a UNIX platform will go to $ORACLE_HOME/network/trace, and for a Windows platform, they will go to ORACLE_HOME\network\trace. The default file name for the trace file will be the listener name with a .trc extension.

The Authentication tab, shown in Figure 7-38, is where you can establish a password for your new listener. You can make the password anything you want, or you can choose not to impose password protection for the listener.

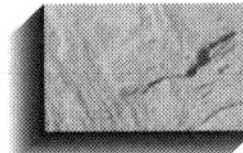

NOTE
There is a known problem in Version 8.1.6 that is fixed in 8.1.7. When you select "Save Network Configuration", the logging and tracing information that you have entered is **not** *saved to the appropriate file. You must edit the listener.ora file to activate logging and tracing in Version 8.1.6.*

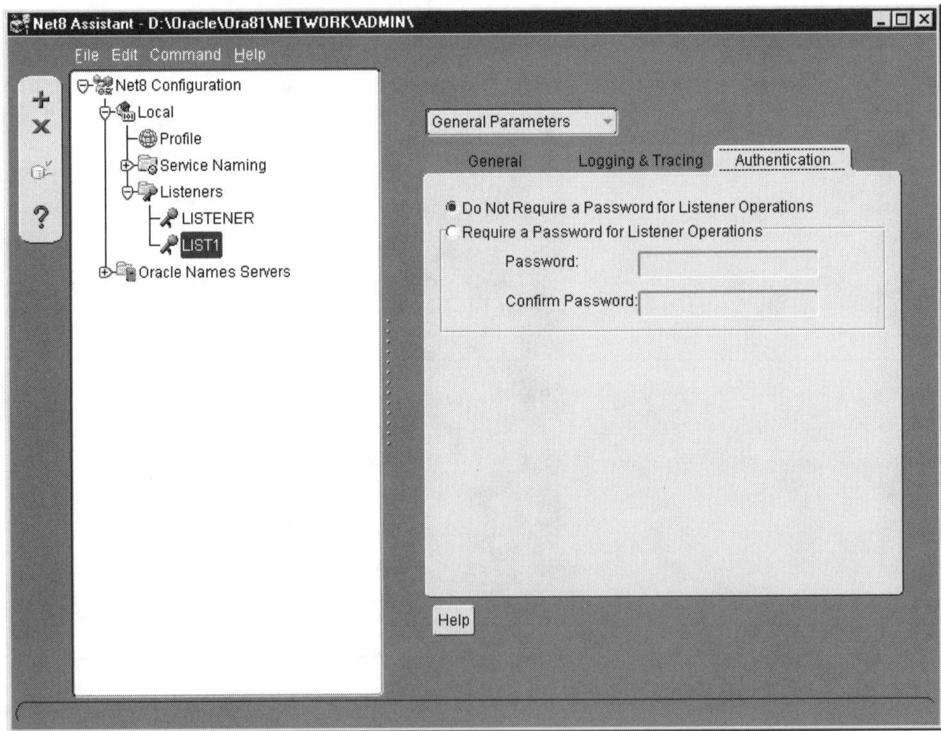

FIGURE 7-38. *Listeners General Parameter Authentication tab*

Listeners Database Services Option

When you first choose the Database Services option, the message that is displayed tells you there are no database services explicitly configured for this listener. As you can see from Figure 7-39, you are also told that databases for Oracle8i will register themselves with the listener upon start-up. You can use this option, however, to manually configure databases that are running earlier versions of Oracle.

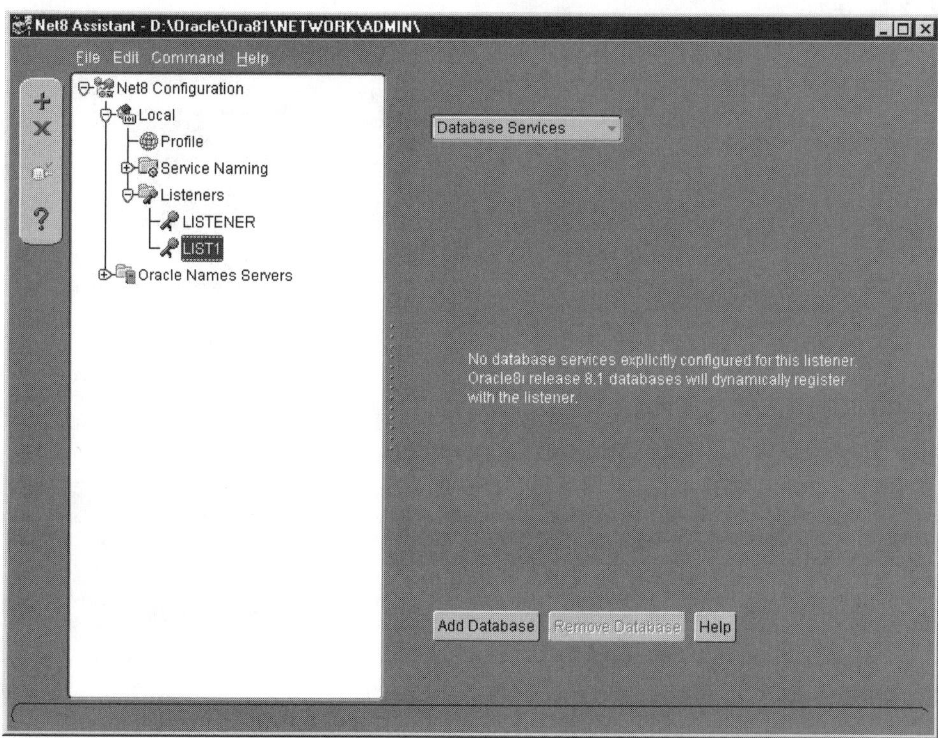

FIGURE 7-39. *Listeners Database Services option*

For completeness, I have included the Add Database screen, Figure 7-40, for you to see so that you will be familiar with its appearance if you have to manually configure a database for an earlier Oracle version.

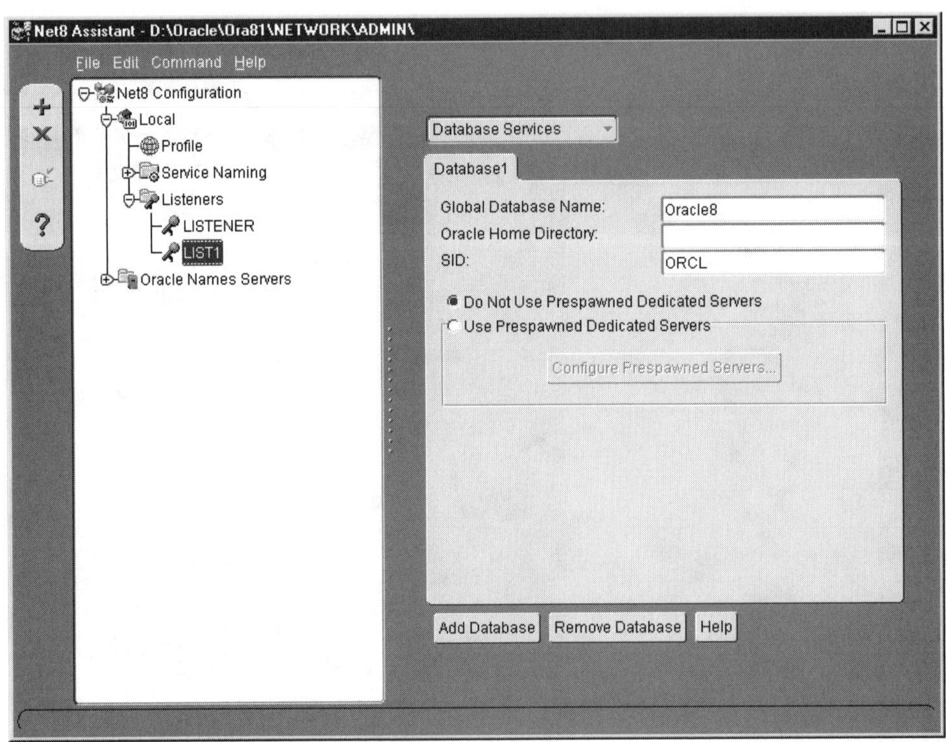

FIGURE 7-40. *Listeners Database Services Database1 tab*

Listeners Other Services Option

The last configuration area for the Listeners option is Other Services. As you can see from Figure 7-41, there are no other services explicitly configured for this listener. However, services may dynamically register with the listener.

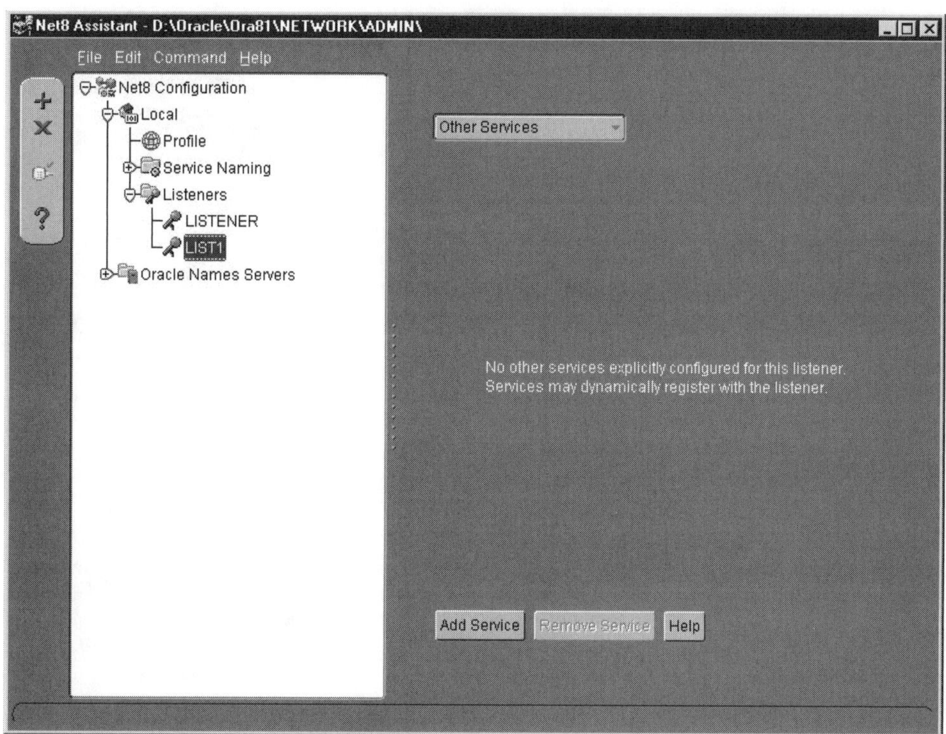

FIGURE 7-41. *Listeners Other Services option*

Using this option, you can specify nondatabase services from which you want the listener to receive connection requests. The services can include external procedures or heterogeneous services. Again, for completeness, in Figure 7-42, I've included the parameters that you fill in to configure a nondatabase service.

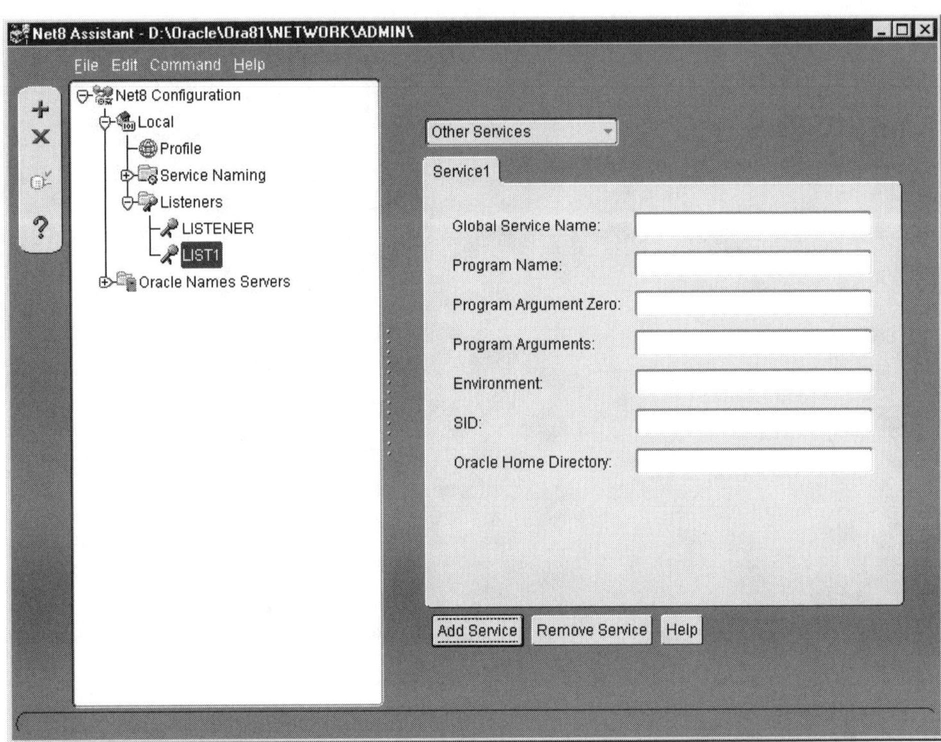

FIGURE 7-42. *Listeners Other Services Service1 tab*

CHAPTER 8

Using Net8 Assistant—Oracle Names Server Options

In Chapter 4, I went into great detail about why, when, and how you create an Oracle Names server. I listed the steps to create a global database link as well. In this chapter, I'd like to show you what each of the screens looks like for the Oracle Names servers so that you can relate them to the documentation that I provided in Chapter 4. Without further ado, let's take a look at the Oracle Names servers screens.

Creating and Configuring Oracle Names Servers

When you initially click on the Oracle Names Servers entry in the Net8 Assistant navigator tree, you see an overview of information, and the plus sign at the left side of the screen turns from gray to green, indicating that you can create an Oracle Names server. Figure 8-1 shows the initial screen.

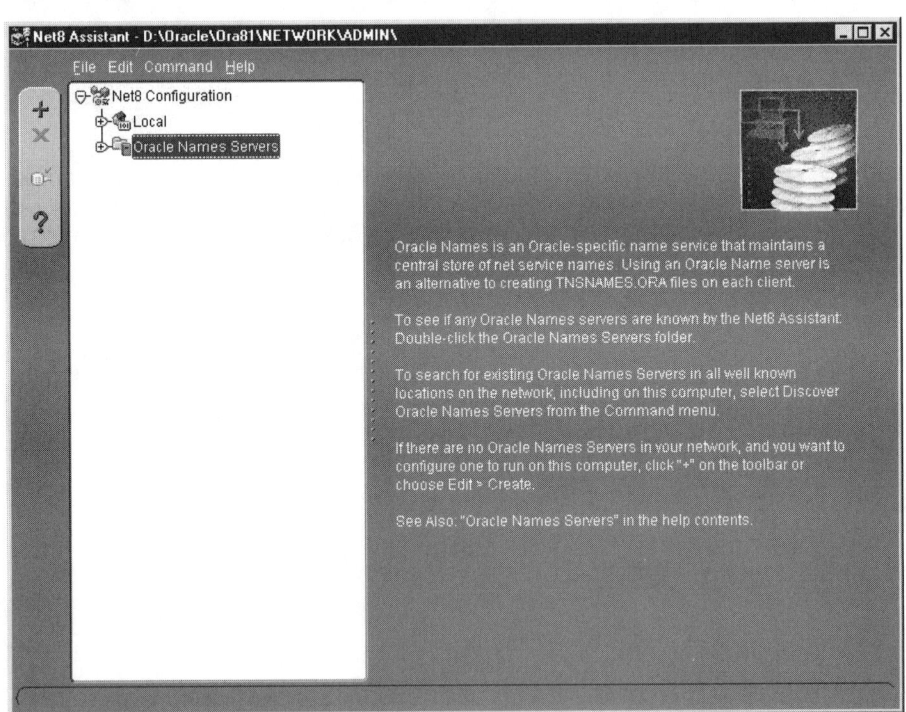

FIGURE 8-1. *Oracle Names Servers initial screen*

Along with an overview of what an Oracle Names server is, the initial screen explains that you can perform a network search in all well-known locations for Oracle Names servers by selecting the Command pull-down menu option Discover Oracle Names Servers. You also are informed that you can create a new Oracle Names server by either clicking on the large plus sign at the left side of the screen or selecting the Edit > Create menu option.

Creating a New Oracle Names Server

Remember how, in Chapter 4, I walked you through the steps to create an Oracle Names server. Well, as I was providing the steps, I was also performing the tasks to ensure that I was giving you the correct instructions. Now, I have an Oracle Names server created. Net8 Assistant does not provide any way to remove it. However, the following steps will delete an Oracle Names server from a Windows NT system. I have tried this set of actions, and the procedure works. I've only tested this with a region root database, and I believe that complications could arise if the Oracle Names server is not a region root. The steps that you can use to remove a region root Oracle Names server from a Windows NT machine are as follows:

1. Remove or rename the $ORACLE_HOME/network/admin/names.ora file.
2. Delete the NT Service from the registry using **regedit**, and delete the key \HKEY_LOCAL_MACHINE\SYSTEM\CurrentControlSet\Services\ <Existing_name_of_NTNames server>.
3. If the Oracle Names server was storing configuration details in a database, then drop the following tables from the Oracle Names server database user: NMO_MASTER, ONRS_SERIAL, ONRS_REGION, and ONRS_CONFIG.
4. Rerun $ORACLE_HOME\Network\Names\namesini.sql.
5. Reboot your machine. A new Oracle Names server can be created.

Now that I've removed the old Oracle Names server from my system, let's review the steps I used to perform the initial creation. I'm going to bring the steps over from Chapter 4, so if they seem hauntingly familiar, they should. Well, here goes.

The following steps assume that there are no Oracle Names servers already in your environment. If you have created one or more Oracle Names servers, your screens will look different from the figures that are shown here. Once you've started the Net8 Assistant tool, follow these steps:

1. In the navigator panel, select the Oracle Names Servers option.
2. To create a new Oracle Names server, choose Edit > Create from the pull-down menu, or click on the large green plus (+) button that is displayed in the upper-left side of the Net8 Assistant screen. The Names wizard will start. Chapter 7 contains the screen illustrations for the Names wizard.

3. The Names wizard will prompt you for
   - A unique Oracle Names server name.
   - A protocol address for the new Oracle Names server. (With TCP/IP, Oracle recommends using the registered port number 1575.)
   - A decision on whether to store the information in a database or replicate the information among Oracle Names servers. To create a server that will store its information in a database, select "Use a region database." If you are going to use a region database, you must create the necessary database tables before you run the Names wizard. Decide which database is going to hold the Oracle Names server information and create a new database user who will own the Oracle names tables. From the new user's account, run $ORACLE_HOME\Networks\Names.ini to create the appropriate tables.
   - A protocol address for a database's listener. (With TCP/IP, Oracle recommends using the registered port number 1521.)
   - The database user ID that you used to populate the Names server tables, the password you assigned to that account, and service name or SID. In the example, I used NAMES for the username and NAMESPW for the password. The SID name I used was ORCL.
   - A decision on whether this Oracle Names server is the root administrative region.
4. If you designate this Oracle Names server as the root, the Names wizard will complete. If you do not designate this server as the root, the Names wizard will assume that this is a delegated administrative region and will prompt you for the local administrative region's domain name and the address of the root administrative region's Oracle Names server. Once you supply this information, the Names wizard will complete.
5. Choose File > Save Network Configuration.

NOTE
The Net8 Assistant does not support creating more than one Oracle Names server on one machine.

Manage Server Options

Now that we have an Oracle Names server to work with and configure, let's walk through the various screens and see what options you have and how to use them.

Manage Server Control Tab

By default after you have an Oracle Names server created, when you click on the expansion (+) sign next to the Oracle Names Servers option in the navigation tree, Manage Server tabs are displayed, with the second tab, Control, visible. The assumption is that you want to start, shut down, or restart the available Oracle Names server. Figure 8-2 shows the Manage Server Control tab.

The other options on the Manage Server pull-down menu are Manage Data and Configure Server.

The Control tab options enable you to interact directly with your Oracle Names server. After you select the Start option, you must click on the Apply button at the bottom of the right-hand panel. If the Names server starts successfully, a small Message screen appears with the message "Server started successfully." You acknowledge the message by clicking on the OK button.

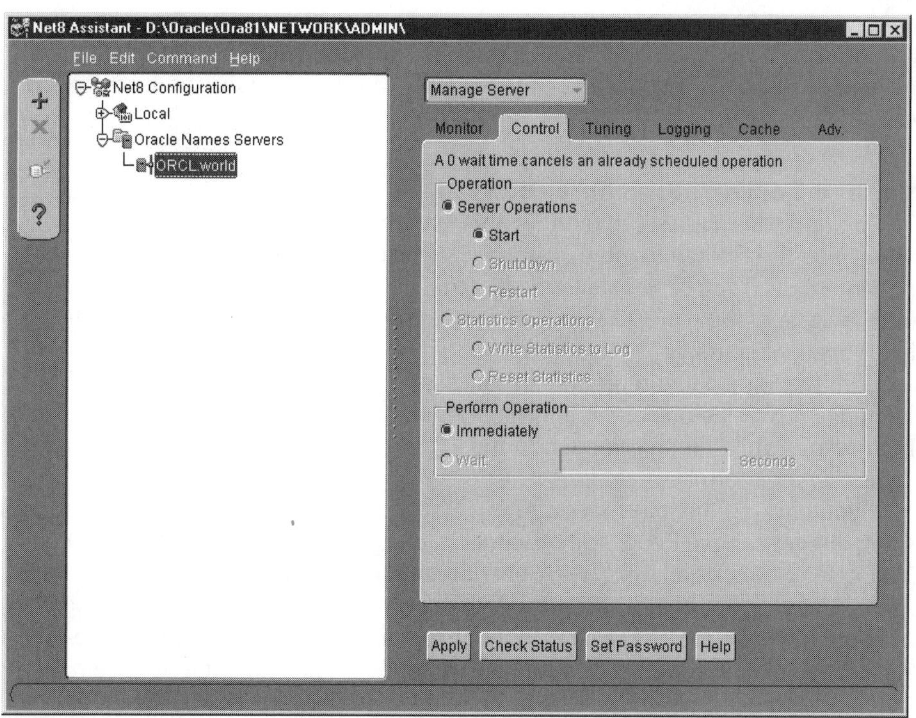

FIGURE 8-2. *Manage Server Control tab*

Once the Names server has started, other options that were grayed out become available. You can shut down or gather and display statistics for the current Oracle Names server. When you click on the Statistics Operations option, the Write Statistics to Log and Reset Statistics options become available. After you have selected one of these options, you can have the operation performed immediately by clicking on the appropriate option under Perform Operation. You can schedule the operation to be performed at another time by selecting Wait and entering a time in seconds that the operation is to be delayed.

When you select Write Statistics to Log and click on Immediately, and you have not declared a log location, the statistics are written to a file in the $ORACLE_HOME/network/log on a UNIX platform and to ORACLE_HOME\network\log on a Windows machine. The default file name is names.log. Once the statistics have been written to the file, the Message box appears with the information "Server saved statistics to the log file." You acknowledge the message by clicking the OK button.

Notice the two additional buttons at the bottom of the screen besides Apply and Help—Check Status and Set Password. When you click on the Check Status button in the initial release of Oracle8i, Release 2, no action occurs. If you have already established a password for the Oracle Names server and you want to perform server operations, you must set the password before you can interact with the Names server. When you click the Set Password button, you are prompted to enter the password.

Manage Server Monitor Tab

The Monitor tab enables you to view information about your Oracle Names server. You use this tab to view on-screen statistics quickly. Figure 8-3 shows the Monitor tab with server statistics displayed. You can use the Refresh button at the bottom of the panel to view the most current statistics. The information that is available through the on-screen monitoring is the same information that's stored in the log file if you request statistics generation from the Control tab. The difference is that the on-screen information is divided into small groups of isolated information, while the information in the log file is the complete group of Oracle Names server information.

If you click on the Information About Statistics option, the information displayed is Requests Received, Requests Forwarded, Foreign Data Items Cached, and Region Data Reload Check Failures. The "Schedule of Operations for" selection has three options: Server, Statistics, and Cache. When you click on each option, you see the schedule for when the next action in that category will occur, or you see the phrase "not set" where appropriate. The Refresh button is available next to the Help button for this screen.

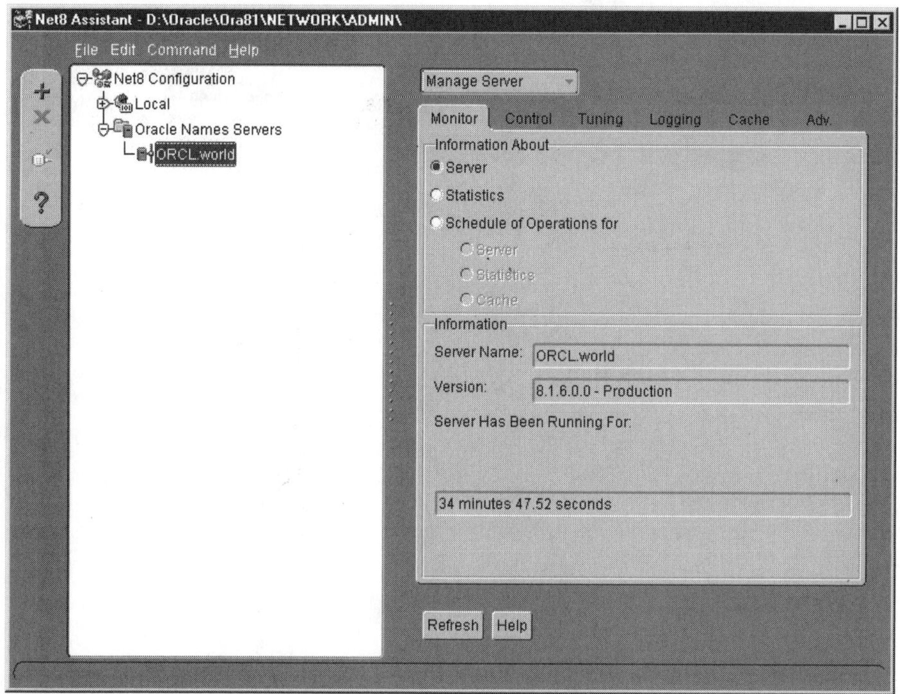

FIGURE 8-3. *Manage Server Monitor tab*

Manage Server Tuning Tab

You can use the Tuning tab to set tuning values for a currently running Oracle Names server, but the values you set are only valid for the current session. In other words, once the Oracle Names server is stopped and restarted, the tuning values you changed in the last session will be reset to their default values. Figure 8-4 shows the Tuning tab.

The Cache Checkpoint Interval is a time, in seconds, that specifies the time interval at which your Oracle Names server will write a copy of its cached information to a checkpoint file on disk. The checkpoint file name defaults to ckpcch.ora, and the minimum value you can use is 10 seconds. The maximum value is 3 days.

With a minimum value of 10 seconds and a maximum value of 3 days, the Statistics Reset Interval specifies the time during which the Oracle Names server will accumulate collected statistics.

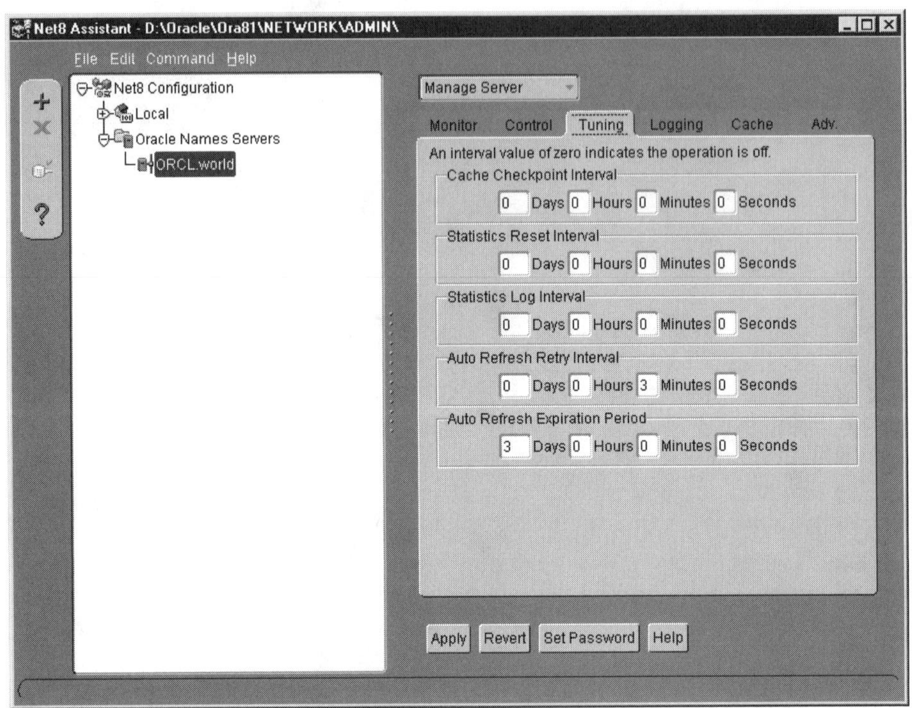

FIGURE 8-4. *Manage Server Tuning tab*

The Statistics Log Interval has a minimum value of 10 seconds and no maximum value. This parameter displays the time between statistical dumps to the log file. The value must be smaller than the Statistics Reset Interval, or the Statistics Log Interval will never log the statistics. The default log file name is names.log.

The Auto Refresh Retry Interval, with a minimum of 1 minute and a maximum of 1 hour, specifies the amount of time in which the Oracle Names server will retry an autorefresh if one fails. The Auto Refresh Expiration Period is the amount of time the Oracle Names server is to wait before attempting to get remote region Oracle Names server address information. The default, which is also the minimum, is 60 seconds.

At the bottom of the right panel is the Help button along with the Apply, Revert, and Set Password buttons.

Manage Server Logging Tab

The Logging tab enables you to declare specific directories and file names for your Oracle Names server logs and trace files. Logging is automatically enabled, while tracing can be enabled or disabled. If you enable tracing, you have the choice of three different trace levels: User, Admin, and Dev. You set User-level tracing to attempt to capture user-induced errors. The Admin tracing level identifies installation-specific problems. The Dev level is not quite as obvious. The level sets tracing that is appropriate for developers. Figure 8-5 shows the Logging tab.

Manage Server Cache Tab

As the name implies, the Cache tab lets you perform various cache operations either immediately or after a specified delay (in seconds). The actions that you can take, as shown in Figure 8-6, are as follows:

- Flush Foreign Region Data: Flushes all remote region data from the local cache checkpoint file.
- Reload From Region Database: Forces an immediate check for data changes in the region databases and, if there are changes, reloads all of the information into the region checkpoint file.

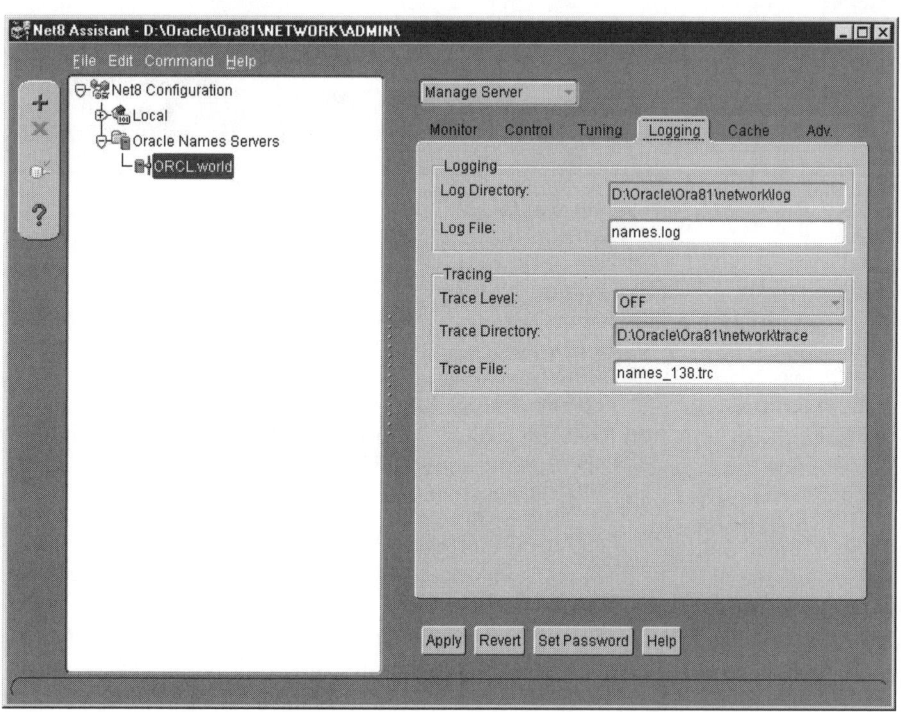

FIGURE 8-5. *Manage Server Logging tab*

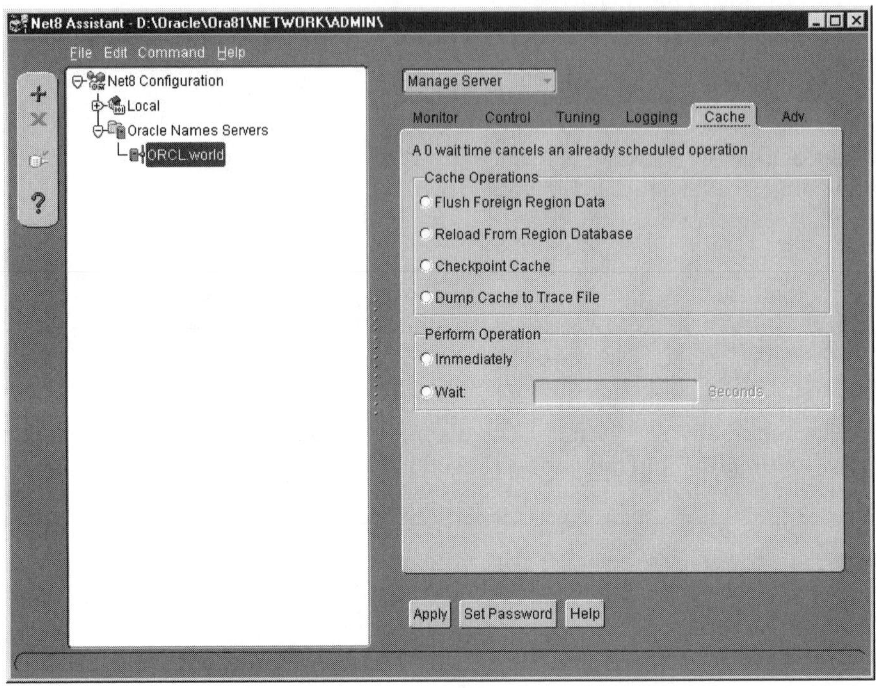

FIGURE 8-6. *Manage Server Cache tab*

- Checkpoint Cache: Forces the Oracle Names server to write its cache information to its checkpoint file. This operation must specify a wait time since it cannot be performed immediately.
- Dump Cache to Trace File: Forces the Oracle Names server to dump its cache information to its trace file. This operation must specify a wait time since it cannot be performed immediately.

The buttons at the bottom of the screen are Apply, Set Password, and Help.

Manage Server Adv. Tab

The final tab in the Manage Server option, the Adv. tab, is shown in Figure 8-7. The Oracle Names server not only collects information from other Names servers but

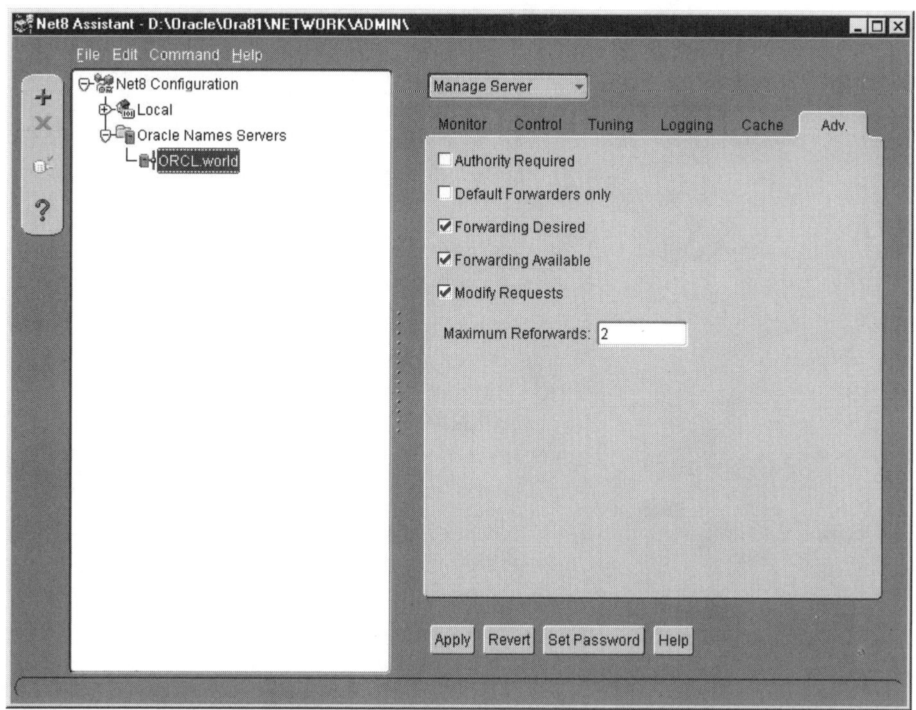

FIGURE 8-7. *Manage Server Adv. tab*

also relays information to other Names servers. The Adv. tab enables you to configure how the Oracle Names server is going to respond to requests from other Names servers in remote administrative regions. Table 8-1 shows the parameters and their descriptions for the Adv. tab.

The available buttons are Apply, Revert, Set Password, and Help.

Manage Data Options

There are five tabs in the Manage Data option. They are Net Service Names, Aliases, Links, Topology, and Adv. I'll start with an overview of the Net Service Names tab, and we can go from there.

Parameter	Description
Authority Required	Enables your current Oracle Names server to collect information from a remote Oracle Names server. If this option is not selected, the current Names server will respond to the client request without forwarding the request to the remote region Names server.
Default Forwarders Only	Restricts forwarding of queries to only those Oracle Names servers that are listed as default forwarders.
Forwarding Desired	Instructs the Oracle Names server to provide remote Names server address locations to clients. If this option is not selected, the current Oracle Names server will have to connect to the remote Names server on behalf of the client instead of the client being forwarded to the appropriate Names server.
Forwarding Available	Tells the Oracle Names server to forward client requests to the appropriate remote Names server. If a client has no access to the network outside of the local domain and this option is disabled, the client will not be able to resolve names.
Modify Requests	Disables any operations that modify data in the Oracle Names server's region.
Maximum Reforwards	Maximum number of times (between 1 and 5) that the Oracle Names server will attempt to forward a client request to a remote Names server before allowing it to fail. Default value is 2.

TABLE 8-1. *Manage Server Adv. Tab Parameters*

Manage Data Net Service Names Tab

Figure 8-8 shows the initial Manage Data screen with the Net Service Names tab displayed.

Many of the tabs for the Oracle Names Servers options are different from any other screens we've seen so far. In these screens, you have a choice of actions that

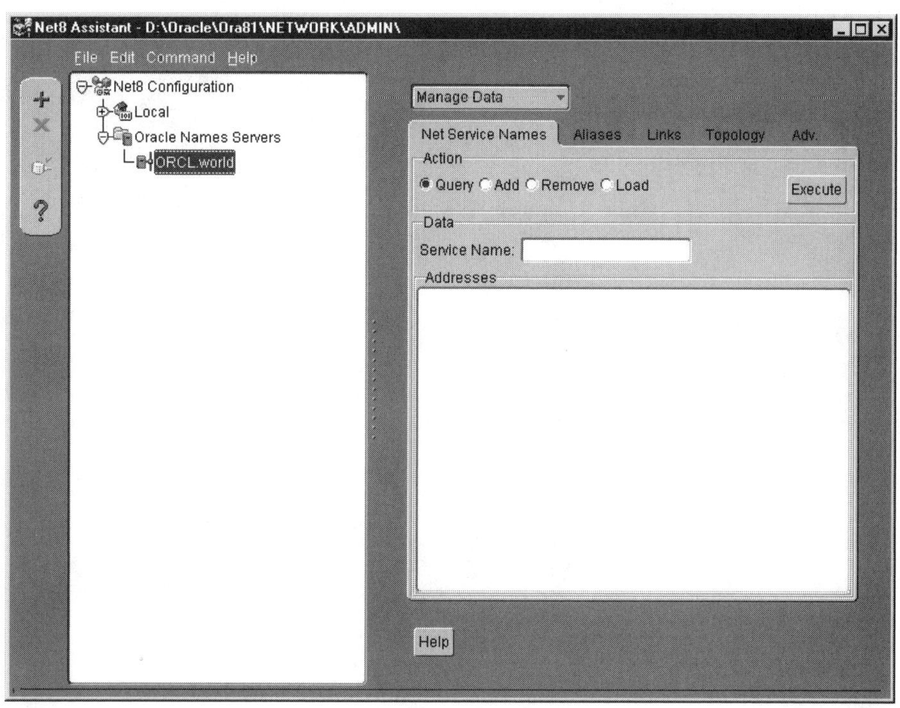

FIGURE 8-8. *Manage Data Net Service Names tab*

you can perform by selecting an Action item and then clicking on the Execute button. The actions that you can choose from are Query, Add, Remove, and Load. You use this tab's options to load your tnsnames.ora file information into your Oracle Names server. Since I've already performed this action, let's see what information we get when I select Query and click on the Execute button. Well, that didn't work. I got an error message telling me that I had to enter a valid service name. Okay, let's try again with a service name entered. Ah, that's better. Figure 8-9 shows the results of the query.

Now that we've successfully performed a query, let's look at the Add option. When you select Add, the screen changes, and you are presented with the same

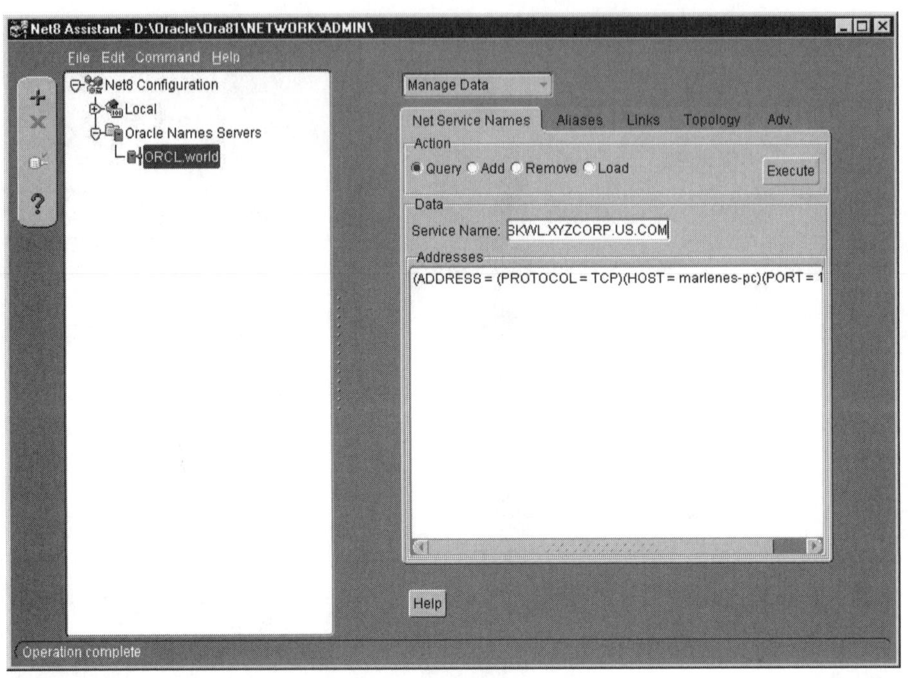

FIGURE 8-9. *Manage Data Query results*

information prompts that you had in the Local Service Naming area. Based on the protocol you choose, you are prompted to fill in appropriate information. Figure 8-10 shows the information required to add a TCP/IP net service name.

The Advanced option in the lower-right side of the screen brings up the same screen we saw in Figure 7-31 in Chapter 7.

The Remove option enables you to delete a net service name, and the Load option lets you browse your computer directories for the tnsnames.ora file to load.

Manage Data Aliases Tab

The Aliases tab for Manage Data offers Query, Add, and Remove actions along with an Execute button. Figure 8-11 shows the Aliases tab with the Add option selected.

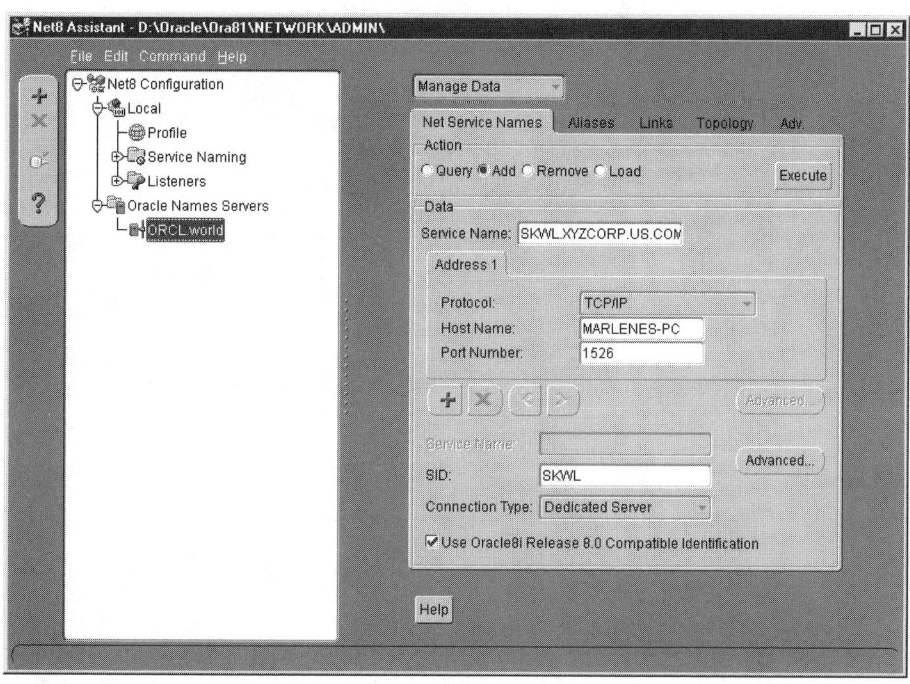

FIGURE 8-10. *Net Service Names Add option for TCP/IP*

Hmm, I wonder what a "canonical name" is. Guess I'd better look at the Help screen for that word. Oh, I see. You enter either the net service name, database service name, or database link in this field. Well, that makes sense. Of course, the Help screen doesn't really explain what a canonical name is, but at least we now know what information is expected. You enter the alias or nickname you want to use, such as SKWL, in the Alias Name area, and then enter the location resolution in the Canonical Name area, for example, SKWL.XYZCORP.US.COM.

Manage Data Links Tab

The Links tab information was covered in the discussion of global database links in Chapter 4, so I won't spend much time on it here. Figure 8-12 shows the Links screen with the Add option selected.

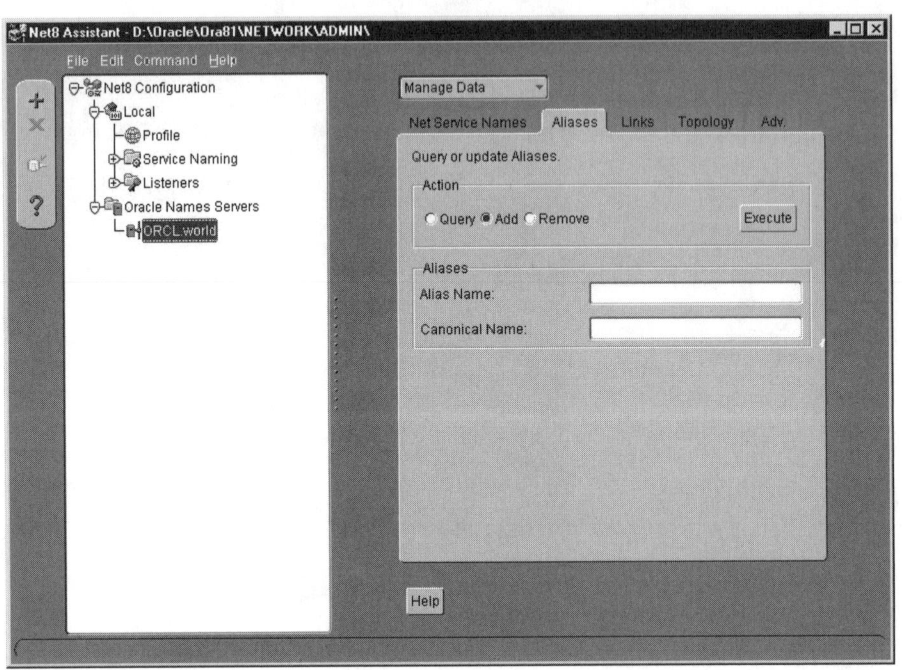

FIGURE 8-11. *Manage Data Aliases tab*

Oh, look at the DB Qualifiers button at the bottom of the screen. You click on this to add database qualifiers to your global database link, as described in Chapter 4.

Manage Data Topology Tab

The Topology tab enables you to delegate domains or provide domain hints. Figure 8-13 shows the Topology tab. By delegating domains within an Oracle Names server region, you create a hierarchy of Names servers that should serve their administrative region more efficiently.

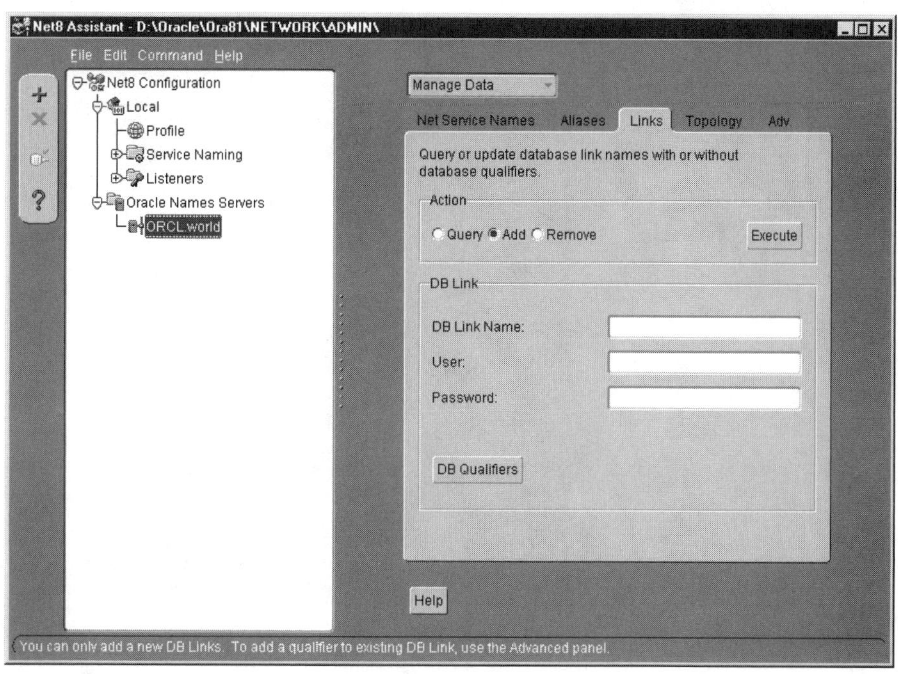

FIGURE 8-12. *Manage Data Links tab*

Let's pause for a moment and think about what happens by default when a client requests a connection that is for a remote location in a remote region. The client request comes to its local Oracle Names server, which in turn forwards the request to whatever remote Oracle Names server the local one knows about. The receiving Names server forwards the request to its region-specific root Oracle Names server. In turn, the root server will forward the request to the Oracle Names server that has information about the domain the request refers to. Wow, isn't that a lot of work? Now, think about how much work is involved if there are a large number of requests of the same remote region. If you do have a remote region that is being heavily requested by local clients, you can configure a domain hint.

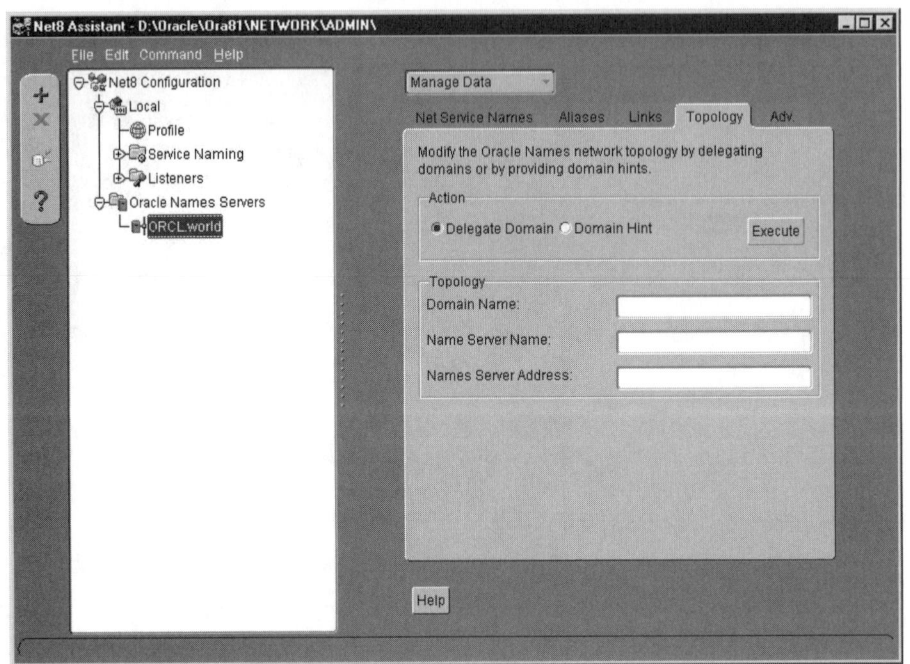

FIGURE 8-13. *Manage Data Topology tab*

The hint will include the domain name and at least one address of an Oracle Names server in that domain. Now, when a request comes in, the local Oracle Names server can use the domain hint to locate the correct remote Oracle Names server directly.

The only available button at the bottom of the Topology tab screen is the Help button.

Manage Data Adv. Tab

The Adv. tab in the Manage Data area, shown in Figure 8-14, enables you to Query, Add, or Remove specific network objects, referred to as records. There are several different record types that may exist on your system. They are shown in Table 8-2.

Configure Server Options

There are five tabs in the Configure Server options area. They are General, Address, Domains, Database, and Adv. Let's see what each of them provides for you.

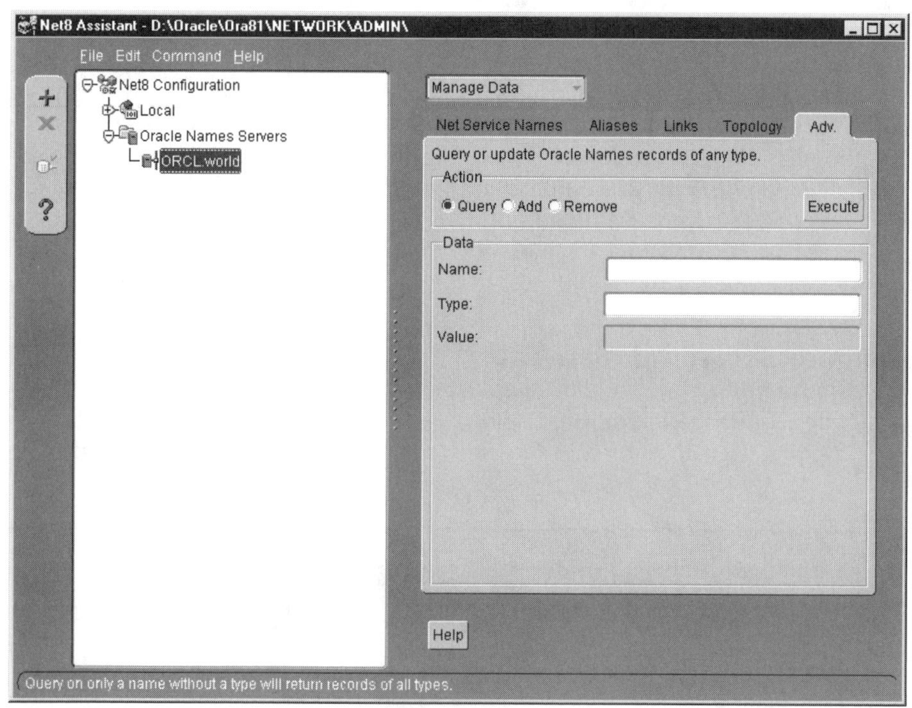

FIGURE 8-14. *Manage Data Adv. tab*

Record Type	Description
-A.SMD	Network addresses, including database service addresses and net service names
-CNAME.SMD	Aliases for any network object
-DL.RDMBS.OMD	Global database links
-DLCR.RDBMS.OMD	Link qualifiers
-NS.SMD	Oracle Names servers and addresses
-V1ADD.NPO.OMD	SQL*Net Version 1 connect string

TABLE 8-2. *Manage Data Adv. Tab Record Type Values*

Configure Server General Tab

The General tab of the Configure Server option enables you to set a password or change an existing Oracle Names server password. Figure 8-15 shows this screen. If you have established a password for your Oracle Names server, the General tab will indicate that a password has been set but will not display the password. Keep in mind, too, that the password is encrypted.

Why would you want to set a password for your Oracle Names server? Quite simply, to prevent anyone from performing privileged operations such as starting or stopping the listener or Oracle Names server from either the Net8 Assistant or the Names Control (namesctl) utility.

Configure Server Address Tab

An Oracle Names server, like a listener, listens for client requests on one or more specific, designated port addresses. Using the Address tab, you can either assign or modify a port designation for your Oracle Names server. If you use the Names

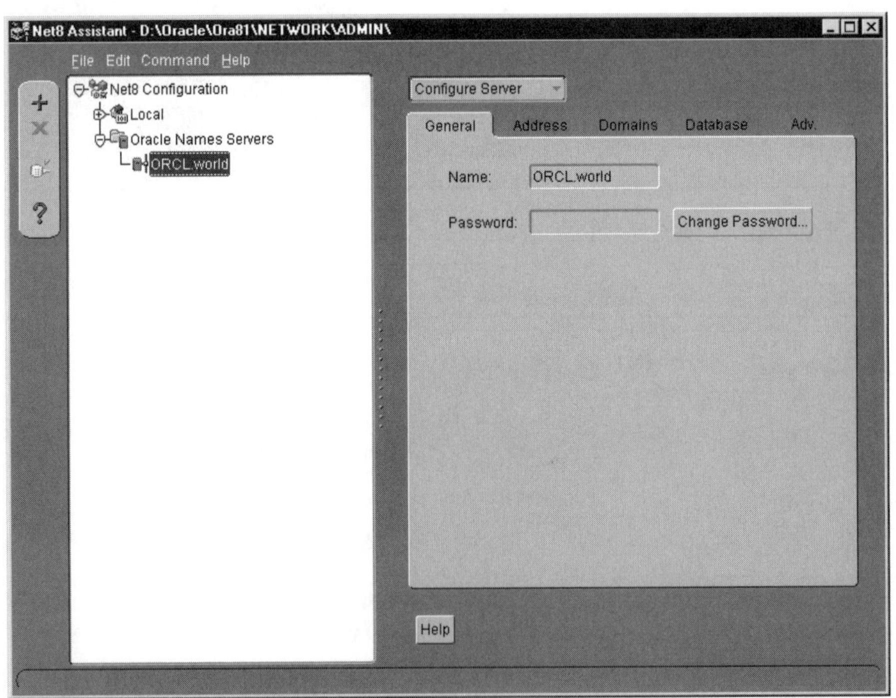

FIGURE 8-15. *Configure Server General tab*

wizard to create your Oracle Names server, there will be an address already configured when you select the tab. Since I created my Oracle Names server using the Names wizard, Figure 8-16 shows the Address tab with address information already assigned.

As with other screens that we've seen where a protocol type is involved, the parameters associated with each protocol type will be displayed or requested based on the protocol that you select. For this tab, you have the options to Add, Remove, or Change the protocol parameter values. The address changes will be reflected in the display area in the middle of the right panel. There is a Help button at the bottom of the screen.

Configure Server Domains Tab

If you need to modify domain information for the Oracle Names server's local administrative region, you can use the Domains tab. However, the Domains tab can only be used and the information modified if the domain is not in the root region. Figure 8-17 shows the Domains tab with information for the current Oracle Names server.

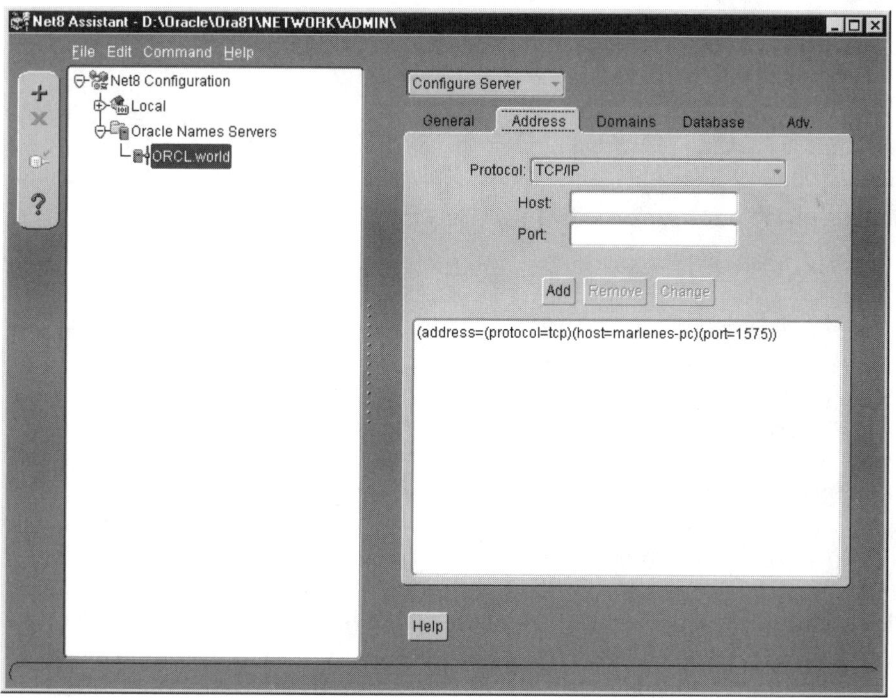

FIGURE 8-16. *Configure Server Address tab*

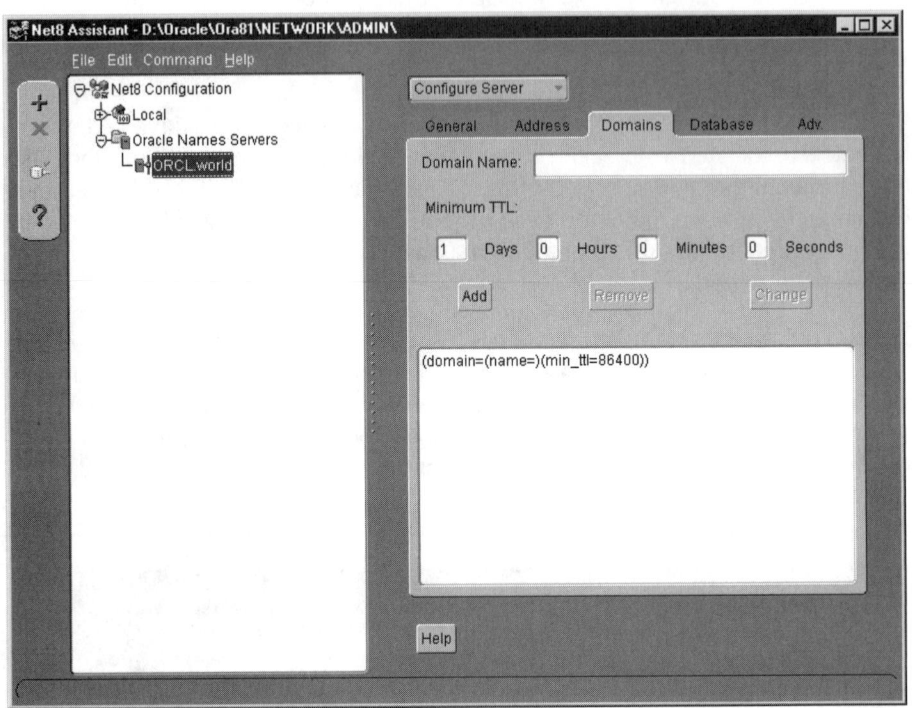

FIGURE 8-17. *Configure Server Domains tab*

You enter the name of the domain you want to change the parameter for and modify the Minimum TTL. Hmm, what is the TTL? This parameter tells the Oracle Names servers the length of time that the information sent from this Names server is to be viewed as valid. Once the time expires, the remote Names servers must request the data again from this Oracle Names server. The default value is 1 day, expressed in seconds. Even if you enter a number of days, the tool will display the value in seconds. To add an initial value or a second, third, or additional value, you simply enter a time and click on Add. If a time value is already displayed, you can click on the displayed information and then type in whatever time value you want. Once you've entered the new time value, click on the Change button. If you want to remove the displayed value entirely, click on the displayed value, and then click on the Remove button. There is a Help button at the bottom of the screen.

Configure Server Database Tab

I talked in Chapter 4 about the difference in storing Oracle Names server information in a region database or in an Oracle Names server's local cache. The Database tab enables you to declare and modify where the Names server is going to store its information. As you can see from Figure 8-18, I've opted to store my Oracle Names server information in a region database.

If you select the option No Region Database, the service replication data will be continuously replicated among the Oracle Names servers. If you choose the Region Database option, you either fill in the protocol selection options with their associated sets of arguments, or they will already be filled in, based on whether or not you used the Names wizard to create the Oracle Names server. In the center of the right panel are the plus sign (Add button), *X* (Remove button), less than (Promote button), and greater than (Demote button). But only the Add button is active. If you

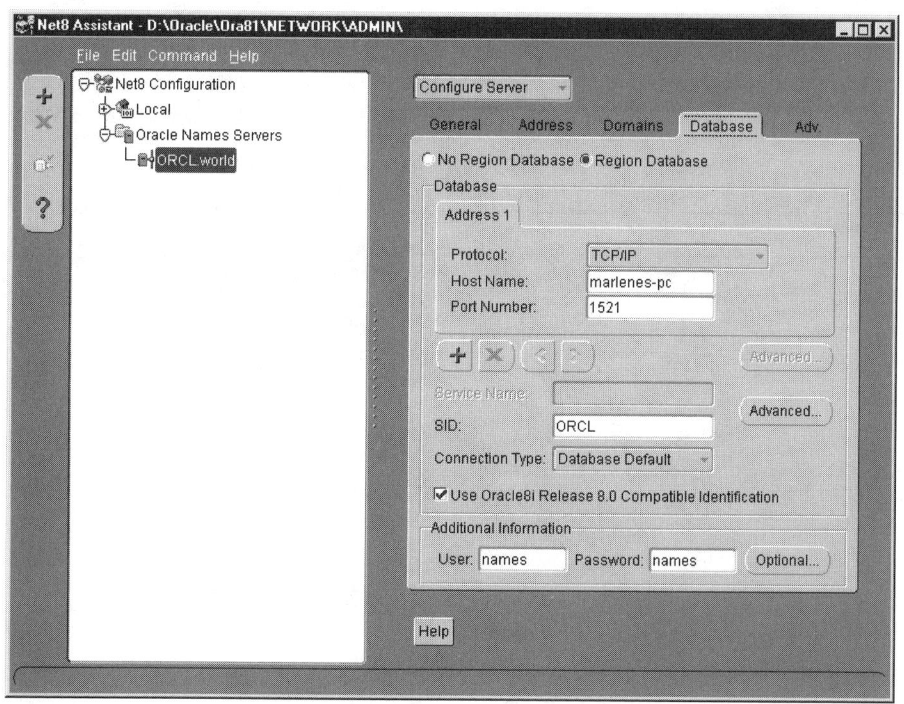

FIGURE 8-18. *Configure Server Database tab*

click the Add button, another Database tab will display, and the other three buttons become active. The Advanced button at the side of the other buttons will produce an Address List Options screen on which you can define rules to control source routing, connect-time failover, and client load balancing.

If you're configuring this Names server to connect to a version 8.1 database, enter a service name. If you're using an earlier version of Oracle, enter an Oracle System Identifier (SID). The Advanced button in this area will enable you to input Additional Service Settings such as Session Data Unit, whether to use Heterogeneous Services, and Oracle Rdb Settings. Figure 8-19 shows the Advanced Service Options. The Advanced Service option is used to convey additional information about non-Oracle database interaction. Therefore, the prompts refer to "heterogeneous" services. This is the area that you use to configure your Oracle Rdb or other databases.

Next, for the Connection Type (shown in Figure 8-18), you can declare whether connections to this address are to be dedicated server, Multi-Threaded Server, or are to rely on whatever the database has been configured to use. If you click on the Use Oracle8i Release 8.0 Compatible Identification option, you must fill in an SID value.

The one thing that I am not very happy about is that both the username and password that I established for my database Oracle Names server repository are displayed on this screen. Look at the Optional button next to the Username and

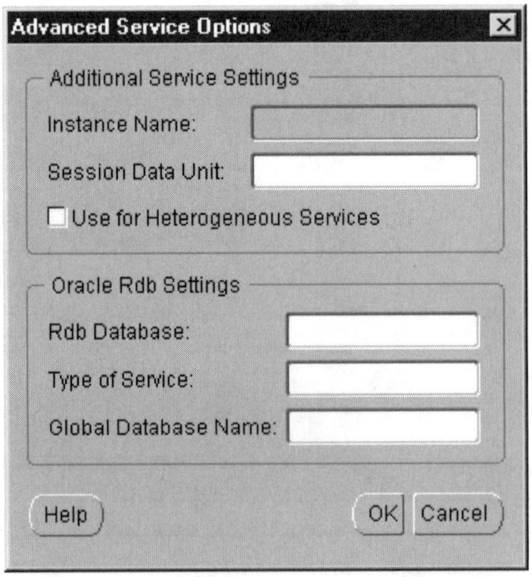

FIGURE 8-19. *Advanced Service Options*

Password display. If you click on this button, a separate screen is displayed with tuning options for the database. Through this screen, you can define the following refresh settings:

- Refresh from Database: How often the region database should be refreshed with information
- Retry Interval: How long to wait for a response
- Retry Expiration: How long to wait before terminating the retry attempt

Configure Server Adv. Tab

There are three types of checkpoint files that can be declared for an Oracle Names server: cache checkpoint file, config checkpoint file, and region checkpoint file. Using the Adv. tab of the Configure Server option, you can declare the location for each of these files. You can also declare the directory locations and names for the Oracle Names server log and trace files. Figure 8-20 shows the Adv. tab.

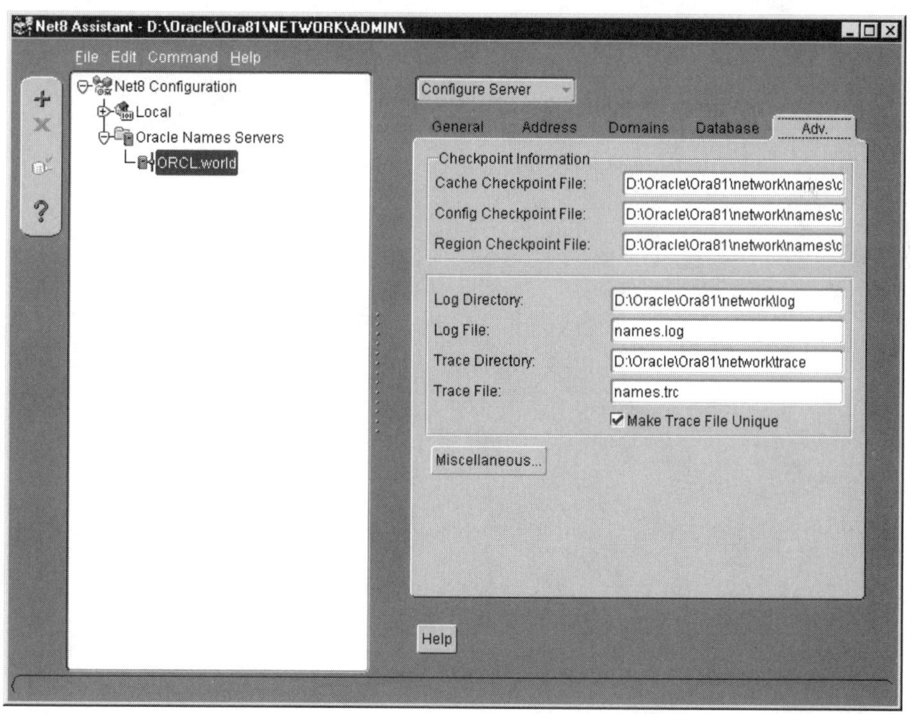

FIGURE 8-20. *Configure Server Adv. tab*

The default directory location for all of the checkpoint files for a UNIX system is $ORACLE_HOME/network/names/, while on a Windows system, the default location is ORACLE_HOME\network\names. The cache checkpoint file is used to store the names and addresses that are cached from both the local administrative region and remote regions. The config checkpoint file stores configuration information similar to the information stored in a names.ora file. If the Oracle Names server should shut down unexpectedly, this file will be used to provide configuration information at restart. The region checkpoint file is a local copy of the administrative region information.

We've already covered the log and trace file locations and names in earlier sections, so I'll just tell you about the option Make Trace File Unique. If you select this option, a process identifier is appended to the name of each trace file. In this way, several trace files can be retained. If you want to track differences from one trace file to another for an Oracle Names server, select this option. If you want all of the trace information to be stored in one central file, do not select this option.

Towards the bottom of the right panel is a button labeled Miscellaneous. Using this option, you can define the Max Open Connections option, with 10 as the default, the Message Pool Start Size, again with 10 as the default, the Auto Refresh Expiration Period, which defaults to 3 days, and the Auto Refresh Retry Interval, which defaults to 3 minutes.

There is a Help button at the bottom of the right panel.

CHAPTER 9

Using Net8 Configuration Assistant Options

id you ever notice how different people perform the same task in different ways? For example, even though we have a dishwasher, when I wash dishes, I place a stopper into the sink drain, squirt some liquid dishwashing soap into the sink, pour in lots of hot water, and then put the dishes in to soak before I actually wash them. I then wash the dishes, and after I've washed them all, I dry them and put them away. I always feel like there aren't enough dishes to make running the dishwasher worthwhile.

My husband, on the other hand, puts all of the dirty dishes into the sink first, turns on the hot water, applies dishwashing soap to a clean sponge, and washes each individual dish using the sponge and hot water. Once he's washed each dish, he puts it into the dishwasher, and then he runs the dishwasher to rewash them. My mother puts all of the dirty dishes directly into the dishwasher.

Just as we each have different methods and procedures for performing a task, Oracle supplies us with different tools that we can use to perform the same task. In Chapter 7, I showed you how to use the Oracle Net8 Assistant to configure a listener, different naming methods, and local net service names. In this chapter, I'm going to show you how to use the Net8 Configuration Assistant to perform the same tasks.

Bundled into some of the activities we covered in the Net8 Assistant chapter were directory service access configurations. Using the Net8 Configuration Assistant, you can easily configure this facility since it's offered as a separate configuration feature.

If a screen, or set of screens, is repeated in more than one configuration activity, I'll just display the screen once and then reference it later. To save a bit of space and keep you from having to constantly shuffle through pages to see the appropriate screen, if a screen is very easily described, I will not show a screen print of it. Okay? Let's get our exploration of the Net8 Configuration Assistant under way then.

Net8 Configuration Assistant Overview

Remember when we accessed the Net8 Assistant for the first time in Chapter 7? When we activated the tool, all of the options were displayed on one screen, and you could interact with any of the options directly from the navigator panel. The Net8 Configuration Assistant is not the same in appearance or interactions since this tool is strictly a wizard-based utility. That means you can choose an option, and then the wizard screens will guide you through performing the task by prompting you for required information. Often, based on the information you supply, different wizard options will be displayed. For example, if you run the wizard to configure a listener and you specify that the listener will use TCP/IP, you'll be prompted for a port number. However, if you specify the listener will use SPX, you'll be prompted for a standard SPX service name. I'll talk more about the various options you have and what responses they require as we go through the various wizard screens.

In Figure 9-1, you can see the Net8 Configuration Assistant Welcome screen. There are four options listed with a radio button before each option. The radio buttons are used to ensure that only one option will be chosen from this screen.

The four options you can choose from are as follows:

- Listener configuration: Create, delete, modify, or rename a listener.
- Naming Methods configuration: Create, delete, or modify the following naming methods: Local naming (LOCAL), Directory naming (LDAP), Oracle Names (ONAMES), Host naming (HOST), Novell Directory Services (NDS), Network Information Service (Sun NIS), or Cell Directory Service (DCE CDS) on the server and, where appropriate, in the client's tnsnames.ora file.
- Local Net Service Name configuration: Create, delete, modify, rename, or test connectivity of a local net service name from a tnsnames.ora file.
- Directory Access Service configuration: Create the LDAP-compliant directory server structure necessary to support either directory naming to centrally administer connect identifiers or enterprise user security for use with the Oracle Advanced Security product.

As we did with the Net8 Assistant, let's take each available option and walk through all of the choices that you can make.

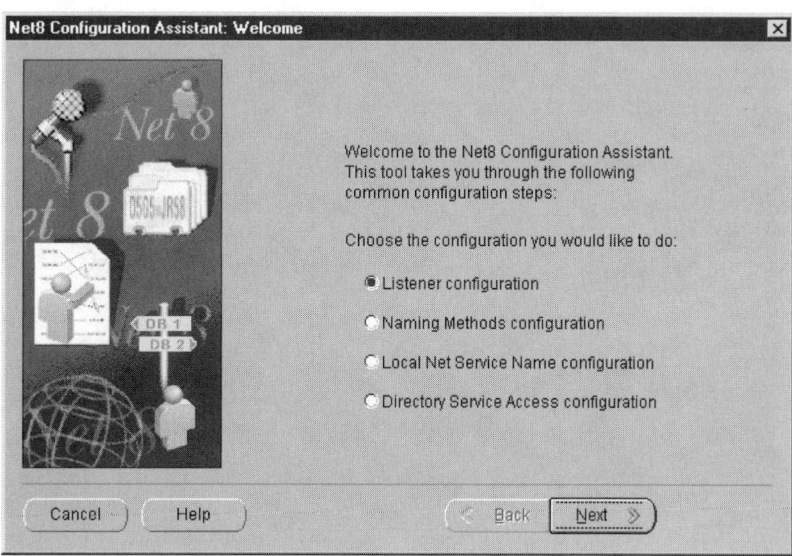

FIGURE 9-1. *Net8 Configuration Assistant Welcome screen*

Listener Configuration

As I mentioned above, you have the option to add, modify, delete, or rename a listener. Once you select Listener from the Welcome screen, you see the screen shown in Figure 9-2. Let's walk through each option and see the screens that you work with and the information you are expected to supply for each operation. We'll start by adding a listener.

Add a Listener

Well, since it just makes sense to want to have a name for your new listener, the first prompt you encounter when creating a new listener is for its name. I've chosen to call our new listener LIST1. Pretty clever, huh. Figure 9-3 shows the prompt screen with our new listener name filled in.

Once you've declared the name for your listener, you are prompted to select one or more protocols over which your listener accepts connections. I've selected TCP/IP but could select any other or all of the protocols listed. Oracle Corporation suggests that you use as few protocols as necessary to keep your configuration as simple as possible. Figure 9-4 shows the protocol selection screen with TCP/IP selected.

The next screen that you see will be based on the protocol selection you made. Since I chose TCP/IP, we are prompted for the port number. We're given the choice of using the standard port number 1521 or changing the port number. Since our current listener, using the default name LISTENER, listens on port 1521, I've chosen to change the port number to 1526. Figure 9-5 shows the selection.

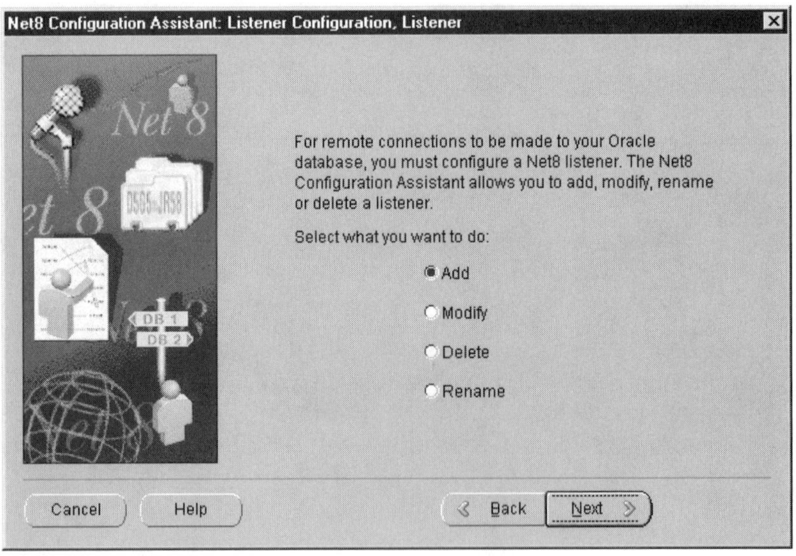

FIGURE 9-2. *Listener Configuration, Listener screen*

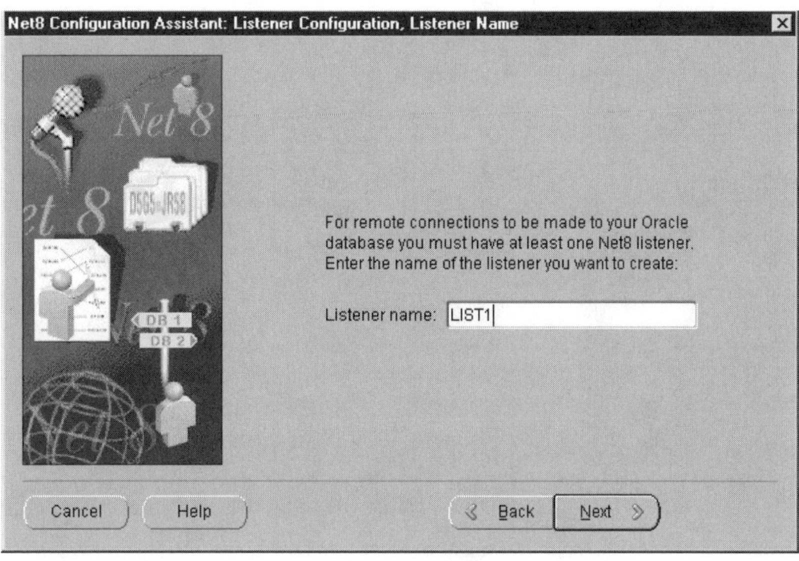

FIGURE 9-3. *Listener Configuration, Listener Name screen*

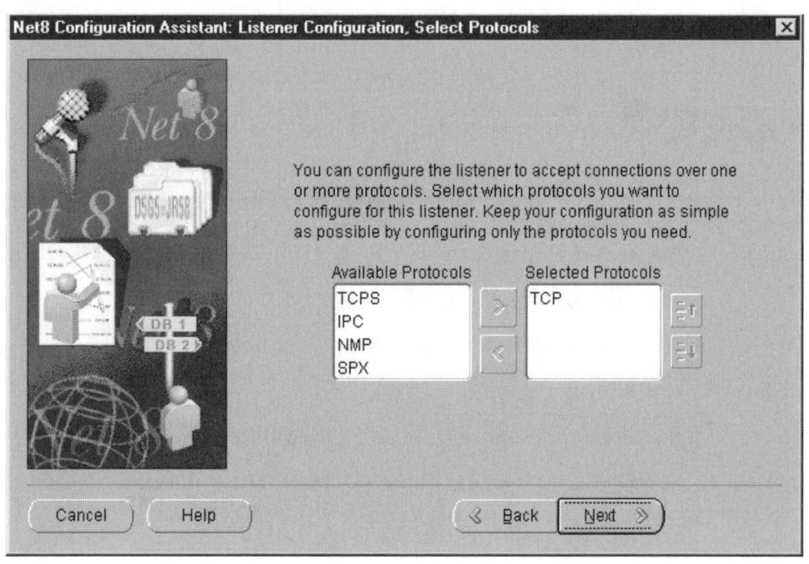

FIGURE 9-4. *Listener Configuration, Select Protocols screen*

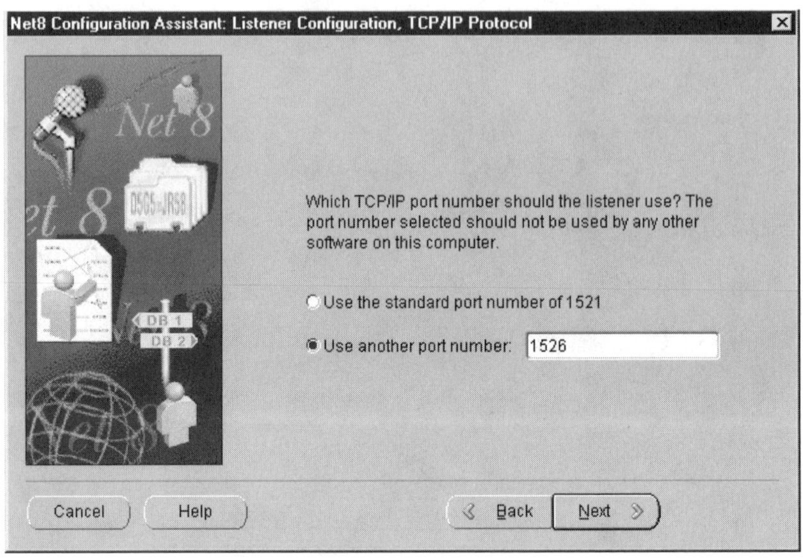

FIGURE 9-5. *Listener Configuration, TCP/IP Protocol screen*

Now, let's go back and see what parameters, if any, you must fill in for each of the other protocol choices. Table 9-1 shows each of the protocols and its required parameter. Where applicable, I've added the default value for the parameter.

Once you've entered the required parameter for the protocol you have selected, you are given the option to create more listeners. Figure 9-6 shows the More Listeners? prompt screen.

Protocol	**Required Parameters**
TCP/IP	Port number (Default: 1521)
IPC	IPC key value for database you want to access
TCP/IP SSL	Port number (Default: 2484)
NMP	Standard pipe name (Default: ORAPIPE)
SPX	Standard SPX service name (Default: Host machine name with _lsnr affixed to end of name)

TABLE 9-1. *Listener Configuration Protocols and Parameters*

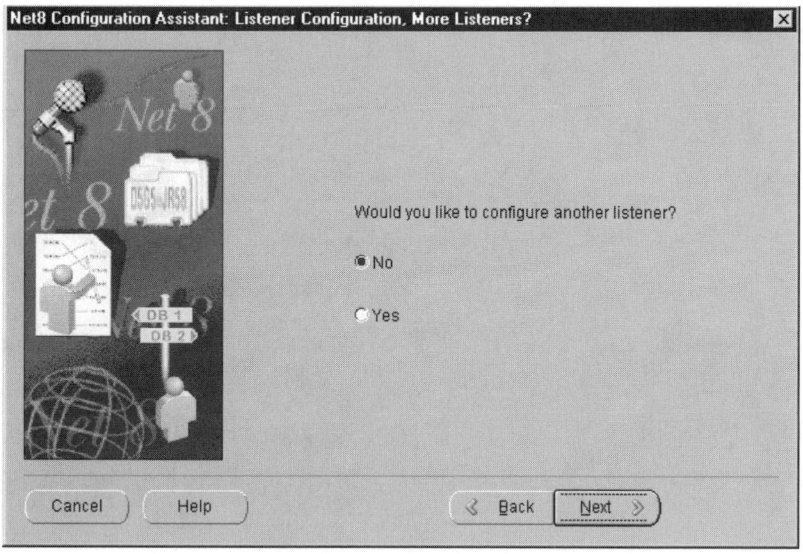

FIGURE 9-6. *Listener Configuration, More Listeners? screen*

I selected No for the More Listeners? prompt and was then prompted to select a listener to start. You can see that I have two options for listeners to start in Figure 9-7. My options are my original listener, LISTENER, and our newly created listener, LIST1.

Once a listener has been selected to start and the listener has been started, a final screen with the message "Listener configuration complete!" is displayed. The Next button takes you back to the Net8 Configuration Assistant Welcome screen.

Modify a Listener

The next listener activity that we'll explore is Modify. Our task will be to change the port number of the LIST1 listener from 1526 to 1525 just to have a goal in mind as we walk through the Modify screens.

As you would expect, the first Modify screen prompts you for the name of the listener you want to modify. As planned, I've selected our new listener, LIST1. Figure 9-8 shows the Select Listener screen.

After selecting the name of the listener to modify, the Select Protocols screen shown in Figure 9-4 is displayed with the same default protocol option, TCP, selected. You are not shown the current protocol of the listener you are modifying. Therefore, you must keep track of the original listener settings as you move through the Modify screens to make meaningful changes. We don't want to add or remove any protocols, so we'll just click on the Next button and move on to the next option.

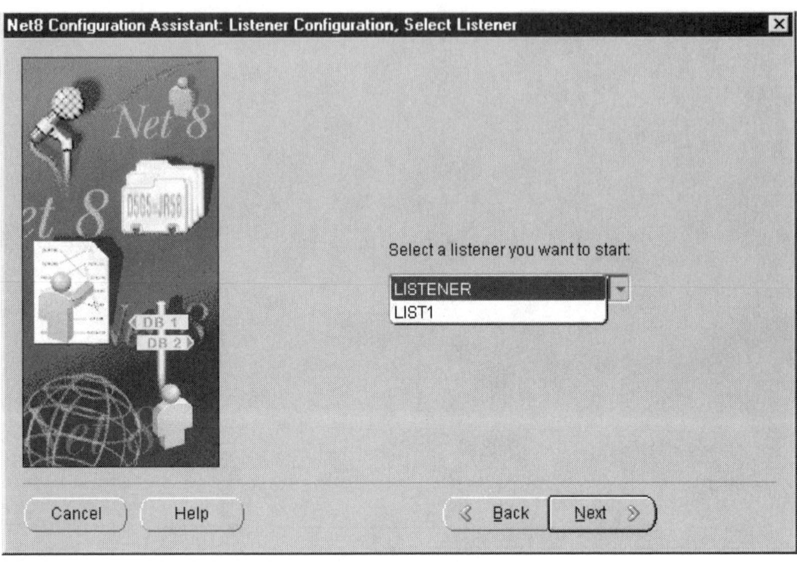

FIGURE 9-7. *Listener Configuration, Select Listener (start) screen*

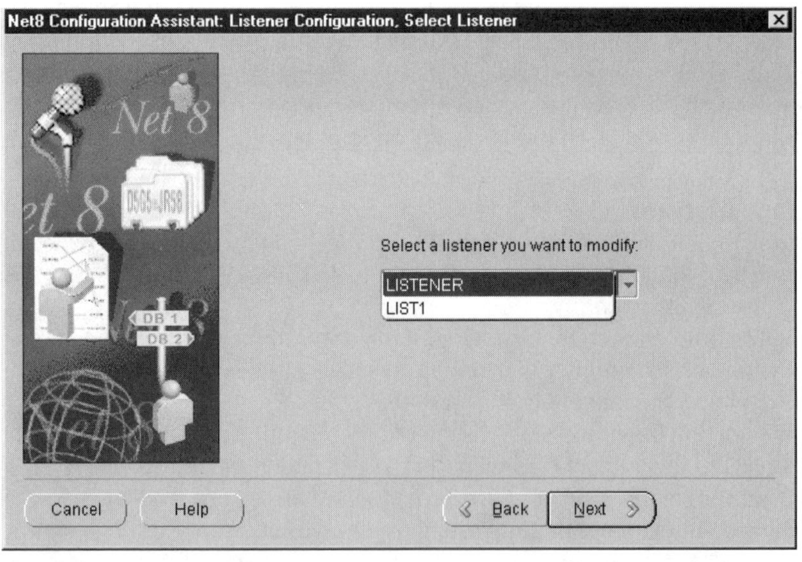

FIGURE 9-8. *Listener Configuration, Select Listener (modify) screen*

The same TCP/IP Protocol screen we saw in Figure 9-5 is displayed with the same default, port 1521, selected. As with the previous screen, you are not shown the current port setting that was chosen when LIST1 was created. Once we change the port number from 1521 to 1525, as we set out to, the More Listeners? screen shown in Figure 9-6 is displayed. If you've inadvertently selected a value that is in use by another listener or if the listener you chose to modify is currently running, an error message like the one shown in Figure 9-9 is displayed with the option to continue with the configuration or not. If you opt not to continue, you are returned to the Listener Protocol screen to make another selection. If you decide to continue with the modification, the change will not take effect until the listener you modify is stopped and restarted. If you've chosen a port that is being used by another listener, you'll need to change the port number of the listener that you are currently working with or shut down the other listener and change its port number. You see, two listeners can't listen on the same port at the same time. Wow! Just think of the confusion that could cause.

Finally, the Listener Configuration, Done screen is displayed. When you click on the Next button, the Net8 Configuration Assistant Welcome screen appears.

Rename a Listener

Although the next option on the Listener Configuration screen is Delete, let's walk through the Rename option first so that we can continue to work with our new listener, LIST1, and leave our currently running listener, LISTENER, alone. We'll rename our current LIST1 listener to LIST2. Okay?

After choosing the Rename option from the Listener screen, the Select Listener screen is displayed. We saw this screen in Figure 9-8, but the instruction above the name has been changed from "Select a listener you want to modify:" to "Select a listener you want to rename:". We'll select LIST1. The Rename Listener screen shown in Figure 9-10 is displayed with the prompt to change the listener name. As you can see in Figure 9-10, I've already changed the name from LIST1 to LIST2.

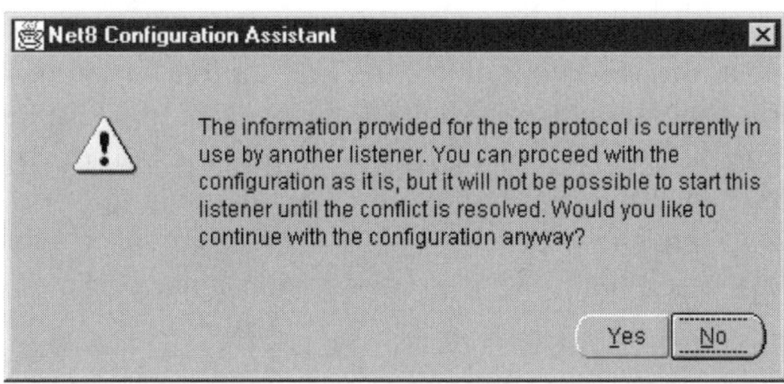

FIGURE 9-9. *Net8 Configuration Assistant warning message screen*

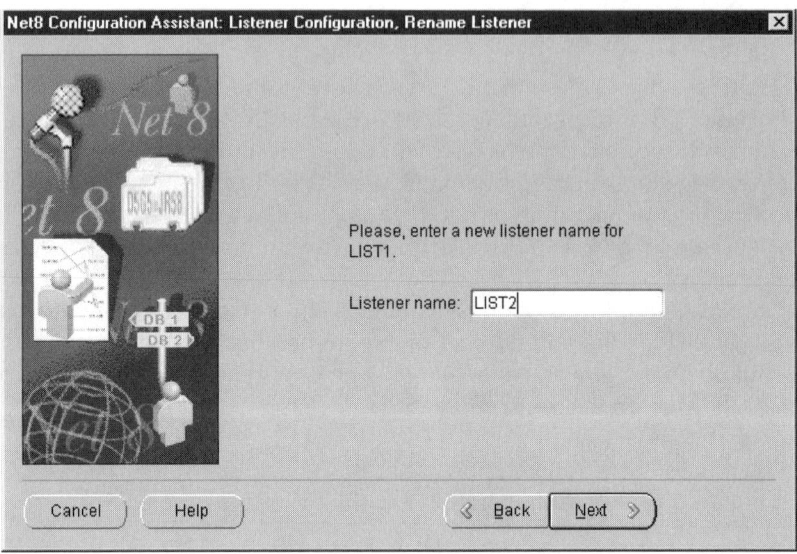

FIGURE 9-10. *Listener Configuration, Rename Listener screen*

Be aware that until you stop the listener and restart it, the Listener Control utility status option will still show the old name.

After clicking on the Next button, a confirmation screen is displayed with the message "Listener was renamed to LIST2." When you again click on the Next button, the "Listener configuration complete!" screen is displayed. Another click of the Next button brings you back to the Net8 Configuration Assistant Welcome screen.

Delete a Listener

The final activity that you can perform from the Listener Configuration options screen is to Delete a listener. We'll delete the listener that's currently named LIST2.

As you would expect by now, the Select Listener screen is displayed with the prompt "Select a listener you want to delete:" and the pull-down menu with our choices of LISTENER and LIST2 available. Once you've selected a listener name, a message screen is immediately displayed. The message screen, as shown in Figure 9-11, asks if you really want to delete the listener LIST2.

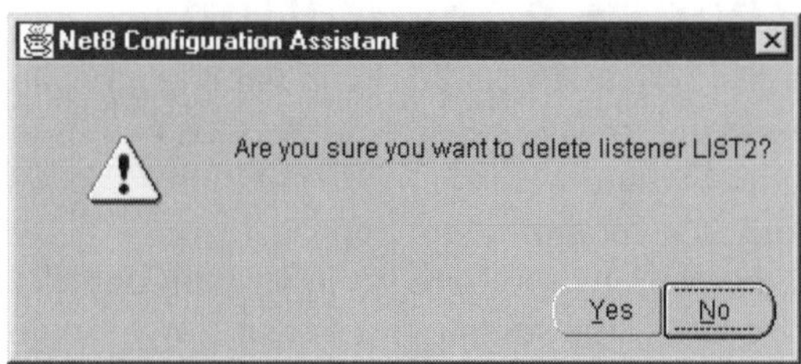

FIGURE 9-11. *Listener Configuration, Delete Listener confirmation screen*

My technical editor, Ian Fickling, noticed on Windows NT that when you delete a listener, the listener is not removed from the services. If you delete a listener that is running, the NT services window shows you that the service is still running. To completely remove a listener from existence on NT, you must perform the following steps:

1. Stop the NT service by choosing Start > Settings > Control Panel > Services. Select the appropriate listener service, and click on the Stop button.
2. Open the Net8 Configuration Assistant and select the listener that you want to remove.
3. Choose to delete option either by clicking on the large, red letter X on the upper-right side of the left panel or by using the pull-down menu.
4. Using **regedit,** remove the service name by deleting the following key: HKEY_LOCAL_MACHINE\SYSTEM\CurrentControlSet\Services\ <*OraServiceName*>.

Oh, and adding a new listener with the name of a previously deleted listener is okay.

You must confirm your decision to delete this listener before any other action occurs. After clicking the Yes button, a screen is displayed with the message "Listener LIST2 was deleted." As with the Modify and Rename wizards, when you click on the Next button, the "Listener configuration complete!" screen is displayed. A final click on the Next button brings you back to the Net8 Configuration Assistant Welcome screen.

Naming Methods Configuration

A great deal of effort and activity in dealing with Net8 centers around how you want the Oracle networking tools to resolve net service names into the necessary information to locate and connect to an Oracle database or other service. In other chapters, we've looked at several different approaches.

When you select the Naming Methods configuration option from the Net8 Configuration Assistant Welcome screen, the screen shown in Figure 9-12 is displayed. The text on the screen says that recommended naming methods have been preselected, but, as you can see from the screen print, there are no preselected values entered.

NOTE
After you select and configure one or more naming methods, if you need to modify the parameters for any one of them, you must use the Net8 Assistant to make your modifications.

Table 9-2 shows the various Naming Methods options and parameters required or information supplied by the tool.

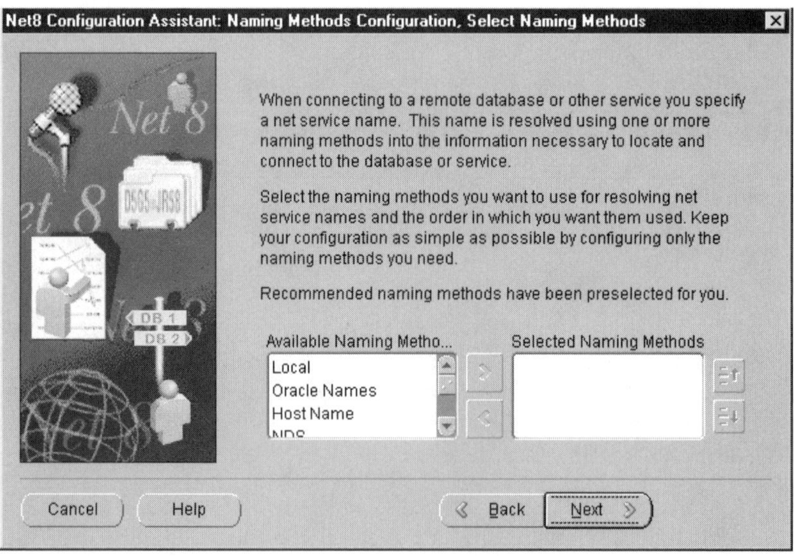

FIGURE 9-12. *Naming Methods Configuration, Select Naming Methods screen*

Naming Method	Parameters or Other Information
Local	No other parameters required
Oracle Names	No other parameters required
Host Name	Informational: says that each time you add a database service, you must separately make an entry in the TCP/IP host name resolution system
Novell Directory Services (non-LDAP)	The NDS name context to be used for net service names resolution in either the form <database or service name>.<domain> or cn=<service name>.ou=<domain.<etc>
Sun's Network Information System (NIS)	The name of the special file that contains the meta map database service names
Distributed Computing Environment's Cell Directory Service (DCE CDS)	Cell name used in resolving the net service names

TABLE 9-2. *Naming Methods and Required Parameters or Other Information*

Once you have completed selecting one or more naming methods and supplying the other required parameters, you see the Naming Methods Configuration, Done screen with the message "Naming Methods configuration complete!" When you click the Next button again, you are returned to the Net8 Configuration Assistant Welcome screen.

Net Service Name Configuration

If you've worked with earlier versions of Net8, you know that there was a tool called Net8 Easy Config that enabled you to create, modify, delete, or test net service names. Each action that you took wrote or removed or modified entries in the tnsnames.ora file for the machine on which you were working. You accessed Easy Config through its own entry in the Start > Programs > Oracle Networking options.

As we saw in Chapter 7, Net8 Easy Config is now bundled with the Net8 Assistant. It is also bundled with the Net8 Configuration Assistant. Although I already showed you the screens for this option in Chapter 7, I'd like to review them here for completeness.

When you select the Local Net Service Name configuration option from the Net8 Configuration Assistant Welcome screen, the initial Net Service Name Configuration screen is displayed. Figure 9-13 shows this screen.

As you can see from Figure 9-13, the available actions that you can take from the initial screen are Add, Modify, Delete, Rename, and Test. Let's take a look at each option in more detail.

Add a Net Service Name

When you select the Add option from the initial Net Service Name Configuration screen, you are prompted for the version of the database that you want to connect to. Figure 9-14 shows you the Database Version screen with the default value of an Oracle8i database or service selected.

After you click on the Next button, you are prompted to enter the Oracle8i database or service name. The text also tells you that this value is usually the global database name. Figure 9-15 shows the Service Name screen with the Skingwaddle global database name entered.

The next screen prompts you for the network protocol that will be used to support connections for this service. Figure 9-16 shows four of the five options available. The only option that is not visible from this figure is SPX.

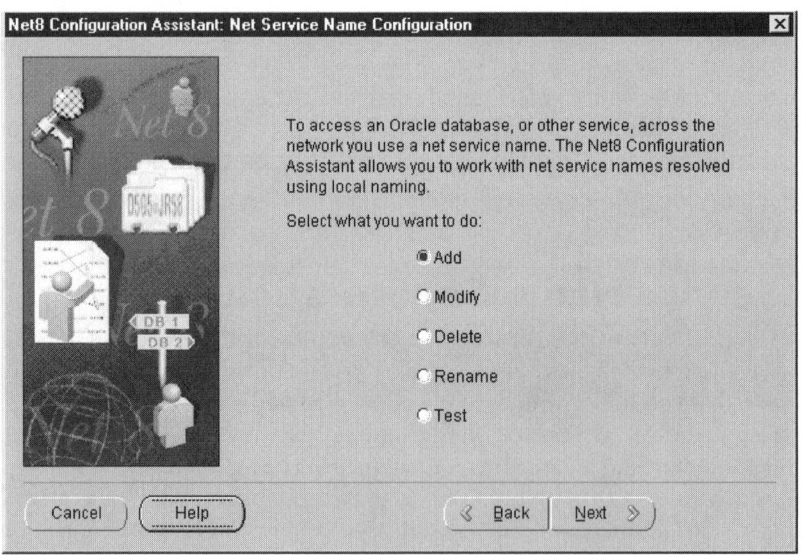

FIGURE 9-13. *Net Service Name Configuration initial screen*

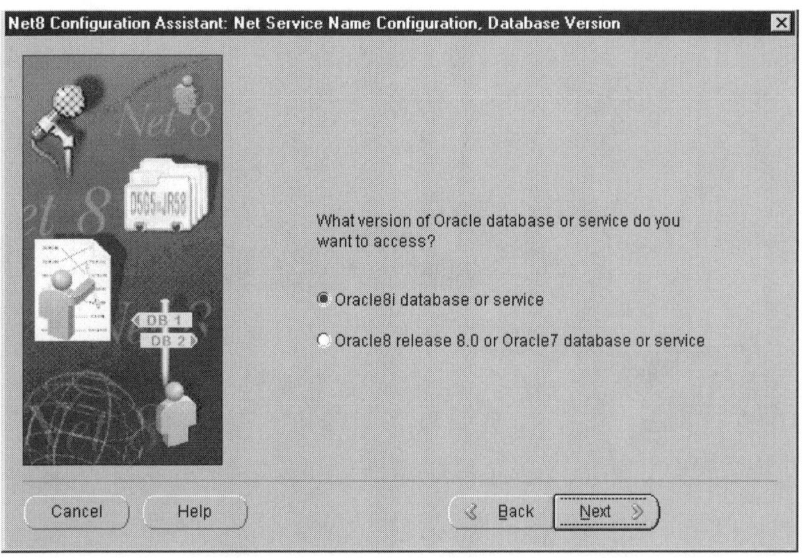

FIGURE 9-14. *Net Service Name Configuration, Database Version screen*

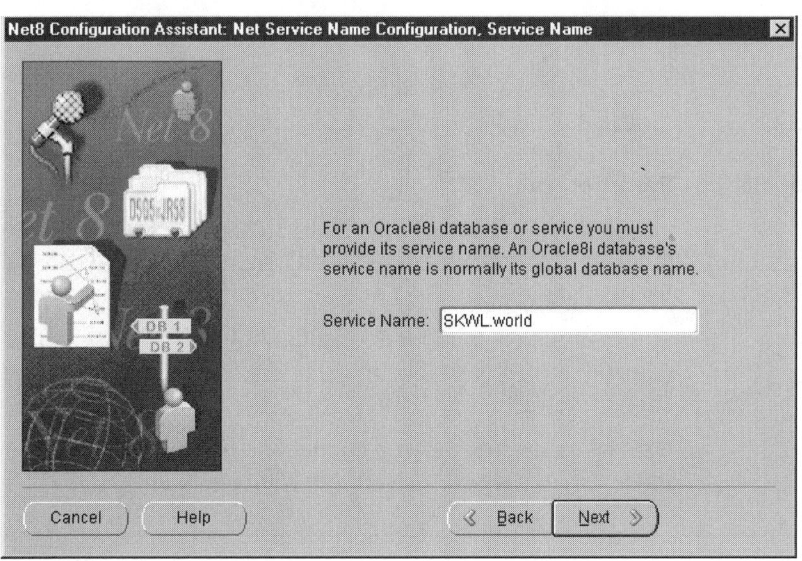

FIGURE 9-15. *Net Service Name Configuration, Service Name screen*

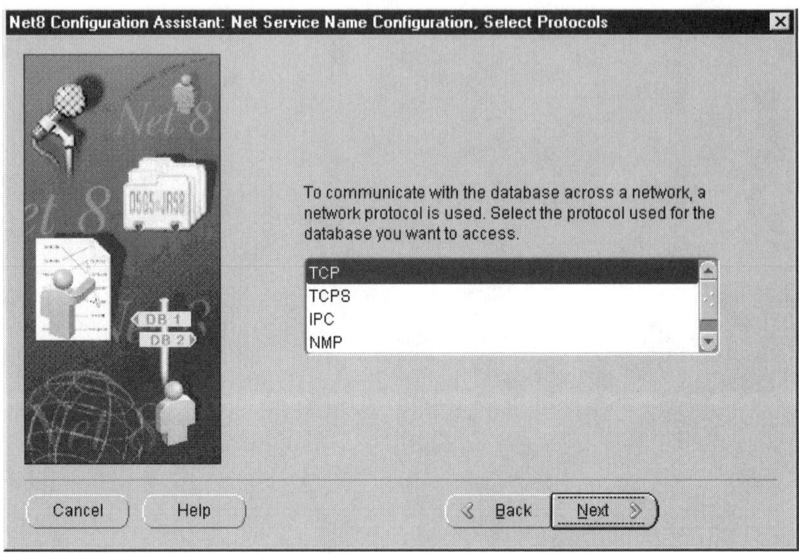

FIGURE 9-16. *Net Service Name Configuration, Select Protocols screen*

Table 9-3 shows the parameters you are prompted for based on the protocol selection you make.

Protocol	Parameters
TCP	Host name, Port number (Default: 1521), Test service connection (Default: No), Net service name (Default: Previously entered Service Name)
TCPS	Host name, Port number (Default: 2484), Test service connection (Default: No), Net service name (Default: Previously entered Service Name)
IPC	IPC key value, Test service connection (Default: No), Net service name (Default: Previously entered Service Name)

TABLE 9-3. *Net Service Name Configuration Protocol Options with Parameters/Actions*

Protocol	Parameters
NMP	Computer name (Default: Current machine name), Pipe name (Default: ORAPIPE), Test service connection (Default: No), Net service name (Default: Previously entered Service Name)
SPX	SPX service name (Default: <current machine name with _lsnr>), Test service connection (Default: No), Net service name (Default: Previously entered Service Name)

TABLE 9-3. *Net Service Name Configuration Protocol Options with Parameters/Actions* (continued)

Since TCP/IP was the protocol chosen from the Select Protocols screen, the next prompt is for Host Name and a port number on which the listener will be listening for connection requests. Figure 9-17 shows this request screen. I've already specified that my machine, MARLENES-PC, is to be used and that my listener uses port 1521.

Now that you've entered all of the required information for the net service, you are prompted to accept or reject the option to perform a connection test. The default, as shown in Figure 9-18, is not to perform the test.

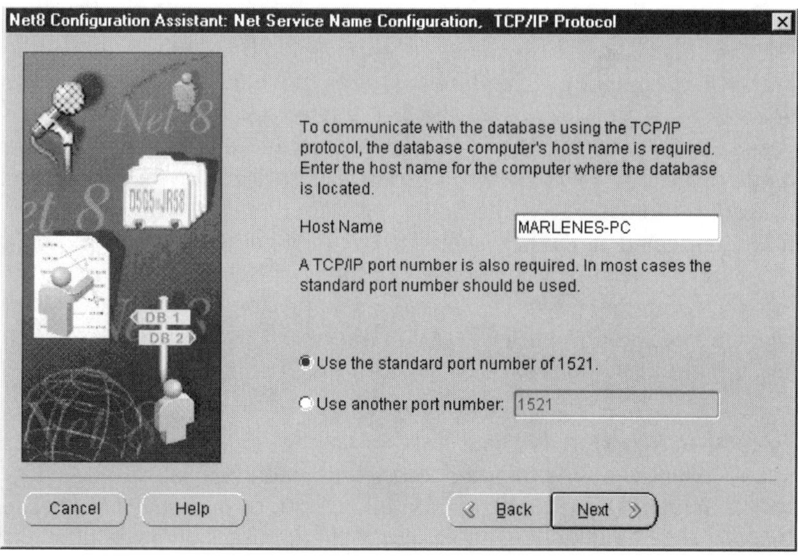

FIGURE 9-17. *Net Service Name Configuration, TCP/IP Protocol information screen*

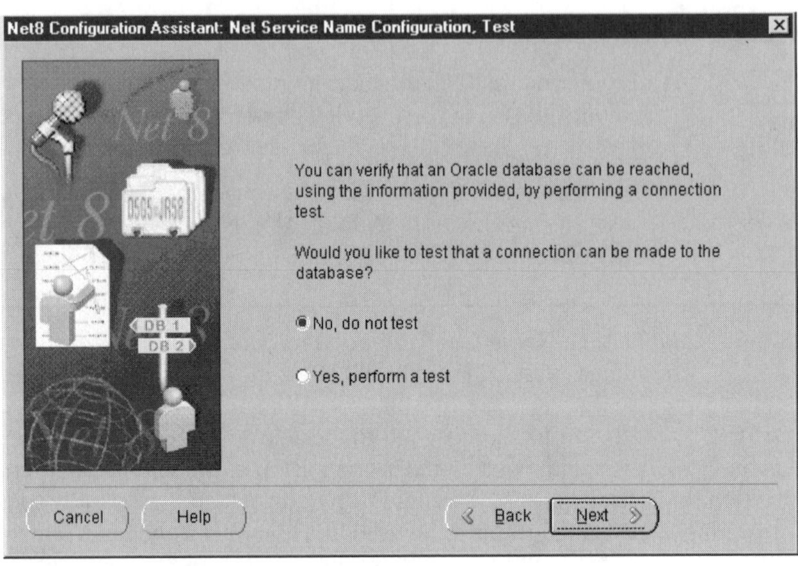

FIGURE 9-18. *Net Service Name Configuration, Test options screen*

If you decide to perform a test of the net service, the Test screen is displayed with both the information about the connection test and the results. If the test is not successful, you can either use the Back button to move through the previous screens to make corrections, or continue by clicking on the Next button. When you move forward, you are prompted to enter a name for your net service. The value defaults to the name of the service you entered earlier. Figure 9-19 shows the Net Service Name screen.

You are prompted on the next screen to decide whether you want to configure another net service name. If you choose No, the final Net Service Configuration screen displays with the message "Net service name Configuration Complete!" Clicking on the Next button returns you to the Net8 Configuration Assistant Welcome screen.

Modify a Net Service Name

The first action that you are prompted to perform when you select the Modify option from the Net Service Name Configuration initial options is to select the net service name you want to modify. Figure 9-20 shows the options that are available from my configuration. I'll choose to modify the Skingwaddle net service name.

As with the Add option, the next screen asks for the version of the database or service you want to access. You can see a copy of this screen in Figure 9-14. You are prompted for the service name, as I showed in Figure 9-15 earlier. In this case,

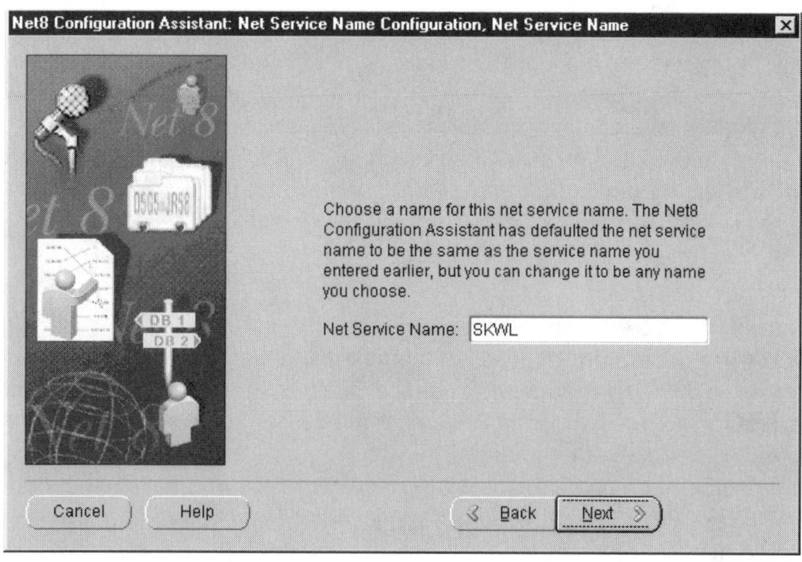

FIGURE 9-19. *Net Service Name Configuration, Net Service Name screen*

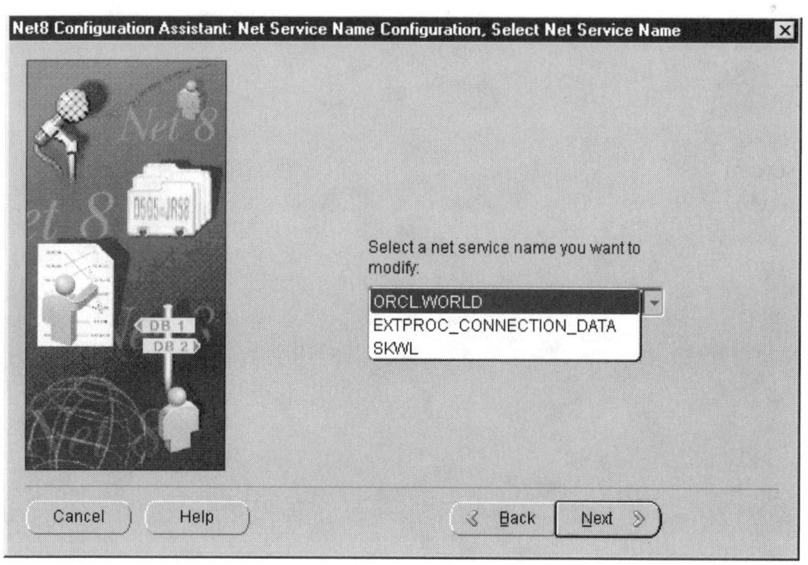

FIGURE 9-20. *Net Service Name Configuration, Select Net Service Name screen*

I entered the database name SKDL where I had initially used the name SKWL. As with the listener modifications earlier, you are not shown any of the values that were entered previously, so you must keep track of what those values were in order to make meaningful changes.

Once you've entered the appropriate service name, you are prompted for the appropriate protocol and its associated parameters. You are prompted to test or not test your service, modify another net service name, and, finally, the Configuration Completed screen is displayed. You can then return to the Net8 Configuration Assistant Welcome screen.

Rename a Net Service Name

As with the listener options earlier, I'm taking the Net Service Name options slightly out of order so that I can continue to use the Skingwaddle entry in my examples. The next option we'll cover is the Rename option.

When you select the Rename option, you are prompted to choose a net service name to rename. I'll rename the SKWL service back to SKDL, just to show you how a rename works. After selecting the net service name to rename, you are prompted to enter the new net service name, as shown in Figure 9-21. As you can see from the figure, I have not yet modified the net service name.

After modifying the name and clicking the Next button, the Net Service Name Renamed screen is displayed with the message "The net service name was renamed

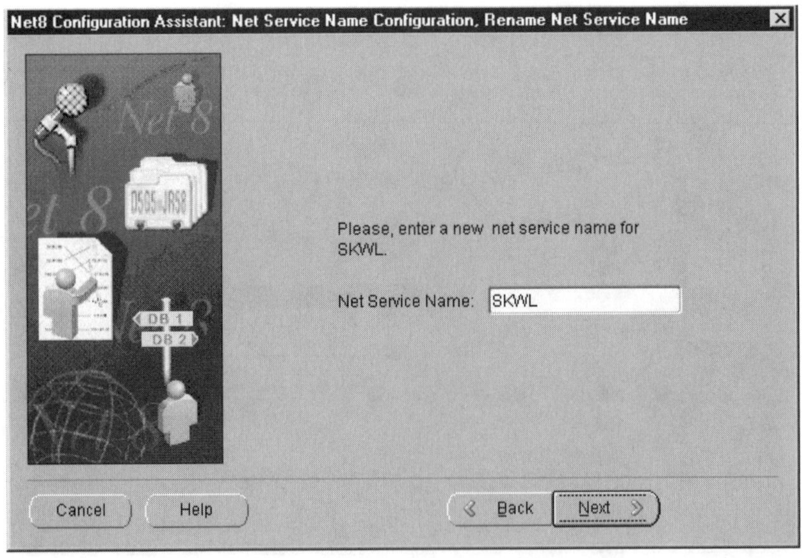

FIGURE 9-21. *Net Service Name Configuration, Rename Net Service Name screen*

to SKDL." The next click of the Next button brings you to the Net Service Name Configuration, Done screen with the message "Net service name Configuration Complete!" Clicking the Next button returns you to the Net8 Configuration Assistant Welcome screen.

Test a Net Service Name

The Net Service Name Test option first prompts you for the name of a net service you want to test. I've chosen SKDL. Keep in mind that your net service name test will only work if the underlying service or database that you want to connect to is started and available. Figure 9-22 shows the test screen with a successful test completed. Notice that you can change the login name and password that are to be used for the test if your database or service does not have a SCOTT account available with the password TIGER, which are the default username and password used for a connection test.

As with all of the other actions, when you complete the test and click the Next button, the Net Service Name Configuration, Done screen is displayed with the message "Net service name Configuration Complete!"

Delete a Net Service Name

For the final option, deleting a net service name, you are prompted to select the net service name to delete. Once you've selected the net service name, you are prompted to confirm that you really want to delete the name. The message "Are

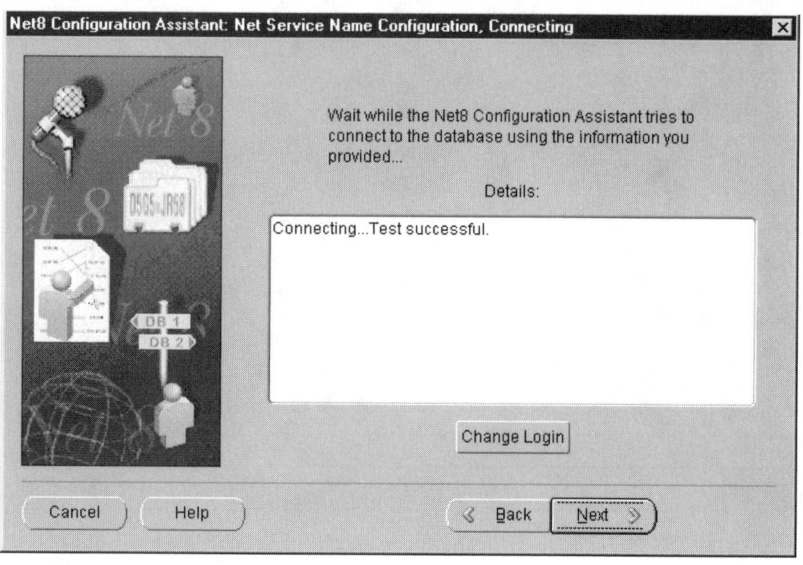

FIGURE 9-22. *Net Service Name Configuration test screen*

you sure you want to delete net service name <net service name>?" is displayed with Yes and No buttons. After you select the Yes button, you see the Net Service Name Deleted screen with the message "The net service name <net service name> was deleted." And, as always, a screen with the message "Net service name Configuration Complete!" is displayed. Clicking the Next button will bring you back to the Net8 Configuration Assistant Welcome screen.

Directory Service Access Configuration

In Chapter 5, you learned about the Lightweight Directory Access Protocol (LDAP) structure used to support the Oracle Internet Directory. In this part of the chapter, we're going to examine the options available through the Net8 Configuration Assistant to help you configure both the client and server to support directory service access.

After selecting the Directory Service Access configuration option from the Net8 Configuration Assistant Welcome screen, you see the first Directory Service Access screen, as shown in Figure 9-23.

Hmm, that's interesting. Notice that two of the options are grayed out. That means they are not available initially.

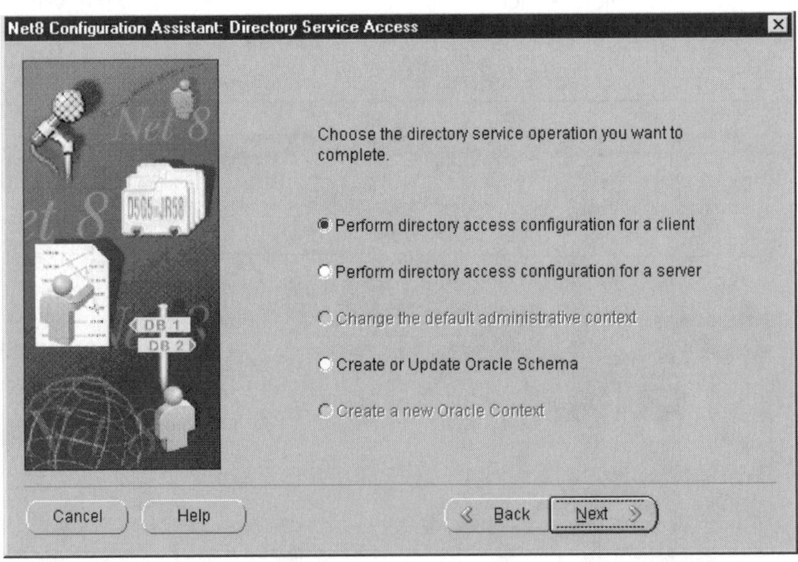

FIGURE 9-23. *Directory Service Access initial screen*

Perform Directory Access Configuration for a Client

Configuring the first option on the Directory Service Access screen enables a client to look up entries in the directory. A client will not be able to modify or add entries to a directory though. Once you've selected the option to perform a directory access configuration for a client, you are prompted to select the directory type. I must point out before we get too far into this configuration attempt that if you have not already installed an Oracle schema that defines the Oracle entries and their attributes that can exist in the directory, you will not be able to successfully configure directory access for a client.

Figure 9-24 shows the screen with the available values. You can declare that the Directory Type will be either an Oracle Internet Directory, a Novell Directory Service, or a Microsoft Active Directory. Although it is listed as an option, the first release of Oracle8i, Release 2 does not support a Novell Directory Service.

For this example, I've selected the Oracle Internet Directory. Figure 9-25 shows the next screen with prompts to fill in the parameters for Hostname, Port, and SSL Port. By default, the values for Port (389) and SSL Port (636) are displayed.

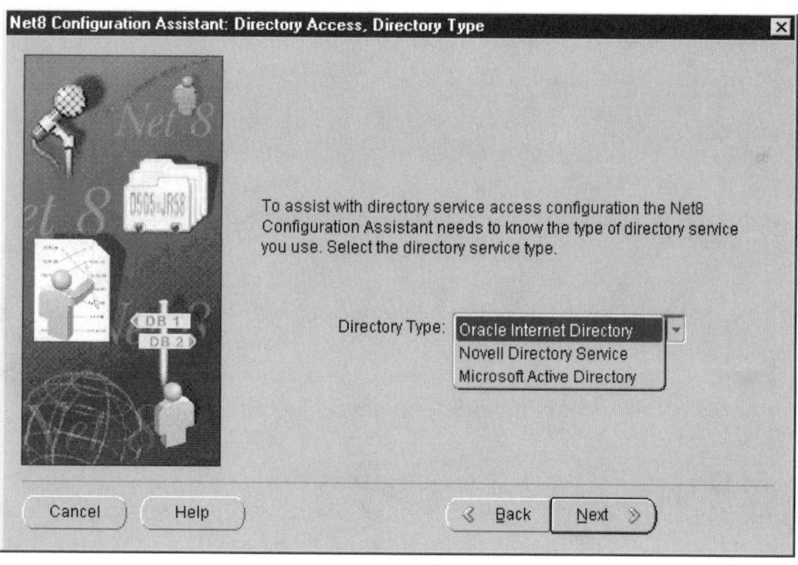

FIGURE 9-24. *Directory Access, Directory Type screen*

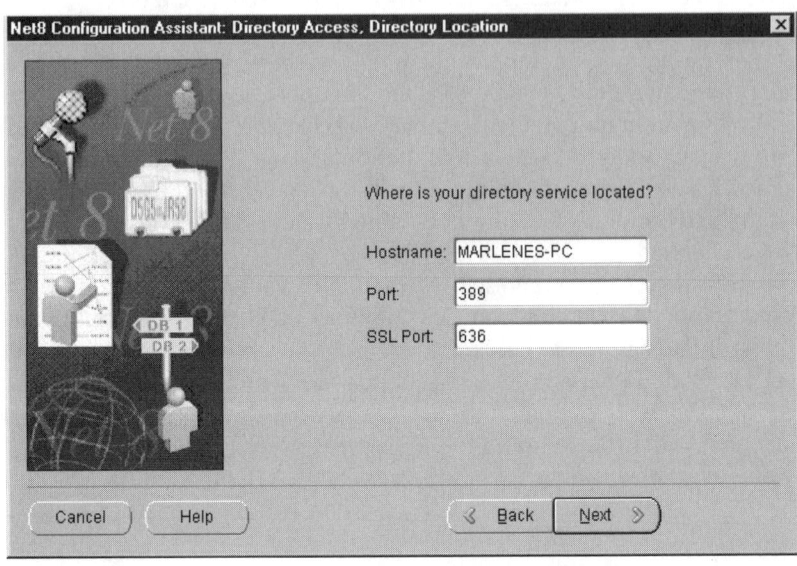

FIGURE 9-25. *Directory Access, Directory Location screen*

After you complete the parameter inputs and click on the Next button, a connection to the requested directory is attempted. If the connection cannot be completed, the error message shown in Figure 9-26 is displayed.

Although it is not supported in the initial Oracle8i, Release 2 version, for the Novell Directory Service option, you are prompted for the same parameters with the same default values as for the Oracle Internet Directory. For the Microsoft Active Directory option, you are only prompted for a Hostname value.

After a successful connection is made, you are prompted for the type of directory your client is using, the location of the directory, and the administrative context from which this client can look up connection identifiers.

Perform Directory Access Configuration for a Server

The second option on the Directory Service Access screen enables a directory server to add, modify, and look up entries in the directory. The same initial screen as shown in Figure 9-24 is used to obtain the necessary information to make a connection. Once the connection is established, you must furnish the type of directory, specify the directory location, and fill in the administrative context from which the server can access and create Oracle entries. If an Oracle Context doesn't yet exist in the directory, you'll be prompted to create one. An Oracle Context

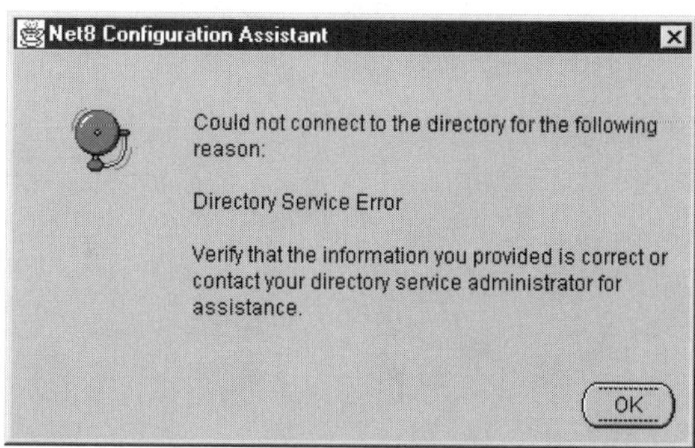

FIGURE 9-26. *Net8 Configuration Assistant Directory Service error screen*

(cn=OracleContext) is the root of a directory subtree where all relevant information about Oracle software is kept.

The Net8 Configuration Assistant verifies that the Oracle schema is created in the directory. You are prompted to create the schema if it doesn't already exist or is an older version. There are three different groups that an authenticated user can be placed in if the Oracle Context is created successfully. The groups are as follows:

- OracleDBCreators (cn=OracleDBCreators,cn=OracleContext)
- OracleNetAdmins (cn=OracleNetAdmins,cn=OracleContext)
- OracleSecurityAdmins (cn=OracleSecurityAdmins,cn=OracleContext)

Users in the OracleDBCreators and OracleNetAdmins can use Oracle Database Configuration Assistant to create a database service and Net8 Assistant to create net service names or modify Net8 attributes of database services or net service names. Other users can be added to these groups by the directory administrator. To create net service entries in a directory, you must be a member of the OracleNetAdmins group. By default, the authenticated user that created the Oracle Context during directory access on the server is a member of this group.

The Create or Update Schema option on the Directory Service Access screen enables you to create or update the Oracle schema in the directory.

Once you've created the net service name for the directory server, you must edit the sqlnet.ora file to make LDAP the first naming method. You do this by setting **names.directory_path**=LDAP. You can also use the Net8 Assistant Naming Methods option under Profiles to set LDAP as the first naming method.

CHAPTER 10

Connection Manager

It's a beautiful day today! I have tickets for a ball game. Want to come along? I just love professional ball. It's always so exciting, and my favorite team is playing. So, let's go! Okay, here we are at the stadium. Wow, is it big. Hmm, I wonder where our seats are. Oh, there's an usher. Let's ask him for directions. We have to take that escalator over there and go up to the second level. Well, that was easy. Now, help me look for Section 372. The section numbers are above the entryways along this corridor. Ah, here's our section, but where are our seats? Let's ask this usher for some help. She said we just go down the stairs over there to Row C and find seats number 1 and 2. Aren't these seats terrific? We can really see all of the action from here. I sure hope my team wins! I brought some peanuts. Want any?

Let's consider the route we just took to get to our stadium seats and the ushers who helped us along the way. Each of the ushers in the stadium works as a human router, routing the fans to their assigned seats within the ballpark. In networking terminology, a *hop* is defined as one leg of a journey taken by a packet from router to router in order to reach its destination. So, if we are talking in networking terminology and think of ourselves as packets, when we reached the first usher and asked for and received directions, we began our first hop on our journey to our seats. When we reached the second attendant, we completed our first hop and began our second. Thus, our trip from the first attendant to our assigned seats took two hops.

In the same way, the Oracle Connection Manager acts as a router to send client connection requests either to their next hop or to their requested database server destination. Unlike the stadium ushers who basically provide routing support, directing fans to their seats, the Oracle Connection Manager offers clients that are routed through it several different options, including connection concentration, Net8 access control, and multiprotocol features. In this chapter, we'll examine the various features of the Oracle Connection Manager, and I'll tell you how to configure and use this tool.

Oracle Connection Manager Overview

What makes the Oracle Connection Manager different from the Oracle Names server? Why would you use one over the other? In reality, the two tools are very different. Oracle Names servers inform a client of the address where it has to connect, for example, the host machine name, listening port number, and a database identifier (SID or service name). Oracle Names servers do not tell the client how to get to a connection location. Oracle Names servers can be thought of as a phone book. A phone book gives you a person's address but does not give you directions on how to get to the location. Oracle Connection Manager can assist in the directions and take advantage of connection concentration, access control, and multiprotocol support. Let's look at these three components of the Oracle Connection Manager.

Oracle Connection Manager Processes

Composed of two processes and a utility, the Oracle Connection Manager listens for incoming client connection requests and initiates connection requests to destination services. The two processes are the Oracle Connection Manager Gateway process (CMGW) and the Oracle Connection Manager Administrative process (CMADMIN). The utility, called the Oracle Connection Manager Control utility (cmctl), provides administrative access to CMADMIN and CMGW. Here's a brief overview of the CMGW and CMADMIN processes. I'll tell you much more about the cmctl utility at the end of this chapter.

Oracle Connection Manager Gateway Process

The CMGW process initially registers with the CMADMIN process and acts as a hub for the Oracle Connection Manager. By default, CMGW listens, using TCP/IP on port 1630, for incoming connection requests. It initiates connection requests to listeners from clients and relays data between clients and servers. CMGW also responds to requests made by the cmctl utility.

The Connection Manager Administrative Process

The multithreaded CMADMIN process is responsible for all of the administrative issues. CMADMIN listens on port 1830 by default, processes CMGW registration, and registers source route addressing information about CMGW and listeners. CMADMIN also answers cmctl requests and identifies each listener that is serving at least one database instance. CMADMIN can use Oracle Names servers to perform the following tasks:

- Locate local Oracle Names servers
- Monitor registered listeners
- Maintain client address information
- Periodically update the Oracle Connection Manager's cache of available services
- Handle source route information about CMGW and listeners

Oracle Connection Manager Connection Concentration

In Chapter 3, I talked about using Multi-Threaded Servers (MTS) to reduce the number of connections between clients and a server. MTS is wonderful if you use Net8 between an Oracle client and server. You can use the Oracle Connection

Manager to multiplex or funnel multiple client network sessions through a single transport protocol connection to an MTS destination. This is known as *connection concentration*, and it reduces the demand on resources. By using connection concentration, you can maintain multiple connections between two processes and enable the server to use fewer connection end points for incoming requests. Thus, when you use connection concentration, you increase the total number of network sessions that a server can handle. Carrying this idea one step further, if you use multiple Connection Managers, you can enable thousands of concurrent users to connect to a server. Figure 10-1 shows several clients connecting to the Connection Manager with only one actual connection from the Connection Manager machine to the database server. By using the Connection Manager and Multi-Threaded Server, the number of supported connections increases geometrically.

Net8 Access Control

At the beginning of this chapter, I mentioned that the Oracle Connection Manager provides three different features: connection concentration, Net8 access control, and multiple protocol support. In this section, I'll tell you about Net8 access control.

I was in Las Vegas recently and ate at a wonderful dinner buffet. I was with three other people, and after we paid for our meals, we stood in a line to be directed to

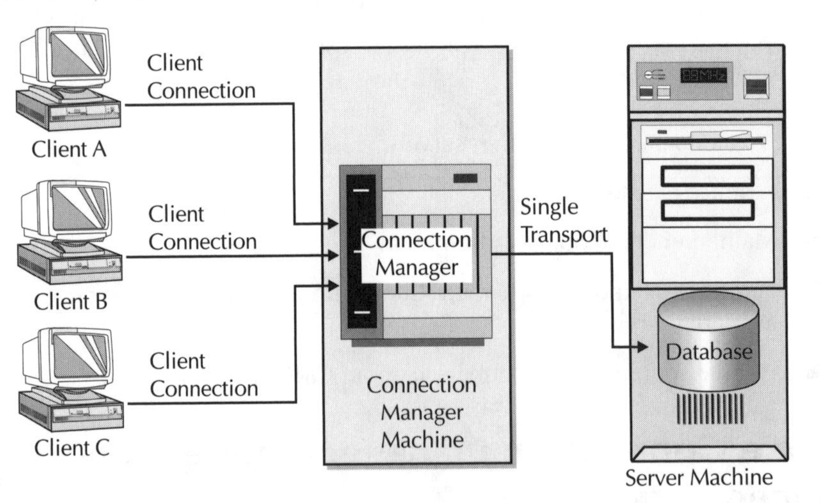

FIGURE 10-1. *Oracle Connection Manager connection concentration*

our table. The hostess verified that we had paid for our meals and asked for the number of people in our party and whether we wanted to sit in the smoking or nonsmoking section. She then directed us to another person who showed us to our table. Figure 10-2 shows the restaurant's table access flow.

As you can see, we went from the cashier to the hostess and then were directed to either the smoking or nonsmoking section, where we were directed to a specific table. I've marked our assigned table with an *X*. The journey to our table was based on several filtering rules that helped to determine the location of an appropriate table for us. Let's see if we can determine some of the filtering rules that were used:

1. All clients must pay for their meal before being seated.
2. There must be a known number of people designated to be seated on a per table basis.
3. The members of a party must agree to sit in the same section, either smoking or nonsmoking.
4. There must be an empty table available in the selected section.

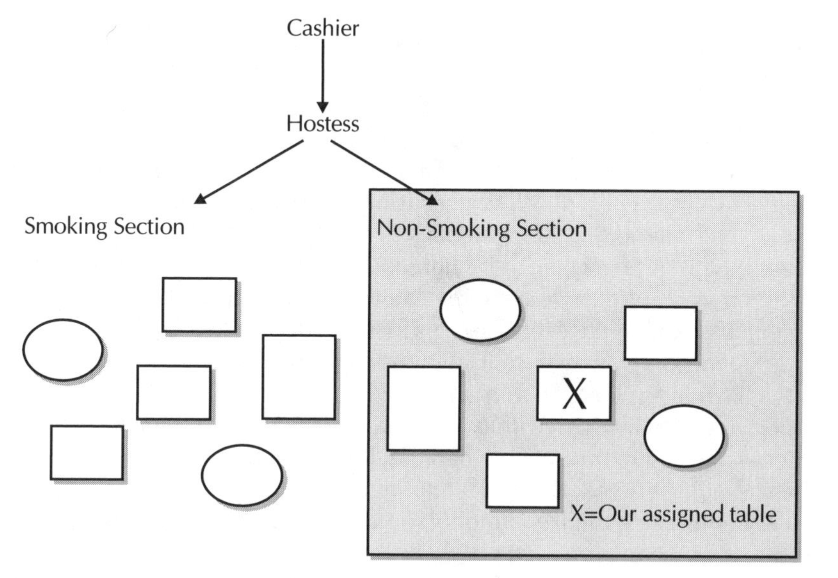

FIGURE 10-2. *Restaurant seating arrangement*

Did you think of any other rules?

You can specify filtering rules to enable the Oracle Connection Manager to control client access to designated servers in a TCP/IP environment. The filtering rules that you specify are used to restrict specific clients from accessing a server based on the designated criteria. You can base the restricting criteria on any of the following:

- Source host names or IP addresses for clients
- Destination host names or IP addresses for servers
- Destination database service name

Although the first two criteria are stated in the plural, you can use singular host names or IP addresses. You add your filtering rules to the cman.ora file. I'll tell you more about cman.ora a bit later in this chapter.

Multiprotocol Support

My neighbor who lives just across the street from me is new to the United States and does not speak any English yet. If I want to ask her a question, I must ask her husband who speaks both English and his wife's language. He, in turn, asks his wife my question and translates the answer so that I can understand it.

In versions of Oracle prior to Net8, a tool called the MultiProtocol Interchange was used to establish communication links between otherwise incompatible network protocols through the use of network communities. Each machine in a community communicated with the others in its community via a single protocol. For example, you might have a network with a community of UNIX servers using TCP/IP and a community of Compaq OpenVMS servers using DECnet. To transfer database requests from one community to another using SQL*Net2, you used a MultiProtocol Interchange, just as I use my neighbor's husband to establish communications between his wife and myself. In other words, the MultiProtocol Interchange was used to establish database links between otherwise incompatible network protocols. In Net8, the Oracle Connection Manager replaces the MultiProtocol Interchange.

Although Net8 can traverse as many network protocol stacks as you can install and support, the actual nodes within your network may impose hardware, memory, and/or operating system restrictions that may limit the protocols you can make available to Net8. As an example of how multiprotocol support works, Figure 10-3 shows SPX clients using the IPX protocol to talk to a database using TCP/IP.

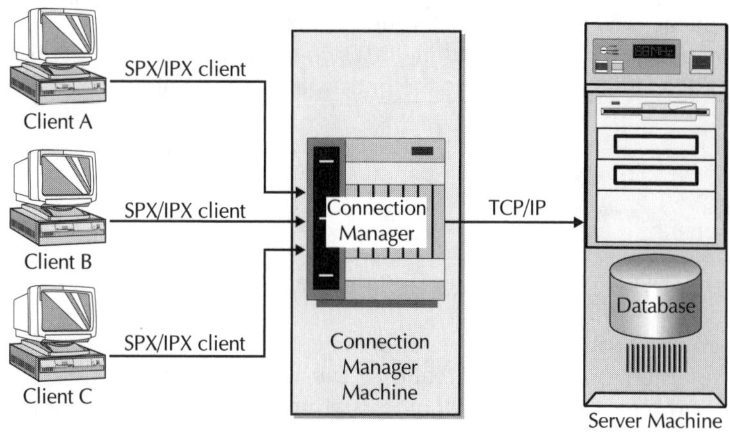

FIGURE 10-3. *Oracle Connection Manager multiprotocol support*

Configuring the Oracle Connection Manager

Once you've determined that you need one or more Oracle Connection Managers, you must begin the configuration process. If you look in the directory $ORACLE_HOME/network/admin/samples on UNIX, or ORACLE_HOME\network\admin\samples on Windows NT, you find a sample file called cman.ora. You can use this sample file as a guide to help you configure your Oracle Connection Manager processes. You cannot use either the Net8 Assistant or Net8 Configuration Assistant to configure the Oracle Connection Manager. You must manually edit the cman.ora file to complete this task.

Let's begin our discussion by examining parts of the sample cman.ora file now.

Cman.ora

Just as the Net8 listener has a listener.ora file and tnsnames.ora file in which you place listener configuration parameter values, and the Oracle Names server has an oname.ora file, the Oracle Connection Manager has a configuration file called cman.ora that is used for its configuration variables.

The initial entries in the sample cman.ora file are comments explaining the syntax and usage of each available parameter. Below the commented area is a complete sample configuration. I've included the first two lines of the sample configuration here. The only value that I added to the lines was my host name, MARLENES-PC.

```
#
# cman's listening addresses
#
cman = (ADDRESS_LIST=
(ADDRESS=(PROTOCOL=tcp)(HOST=marlenes-pc)(PORT=1630)(QUEUESIZE=32)))
cman_admin = (ADDRESS=(PROTOCOL=tcp)(HOST=marlenes-pc)(PORT=1830))
```

As the comment above the code states, the entries define the address on which the processes listen for connection requests. The first entry is for the CMGW process, and the second is for the CMADMIN process. The port numbers used are the default values. If you intend to have the processes listen using the TCP/IP protocol on their default ports, you do not need to include these two lines. However, for ease of maintainability, you will probably want to include them anyway. If you include them, you won't have to go hunting later to confirm the ports that these processes are using. Because the CMGW process performs all of the Oracle Connection Manager basic functions, you can run it without running the CMADMIN process.

Now, let's take a look at the other parameters that you can include in the cman.ora file. Table 10-1 contains the four Oracle Connection Manager parameters and, with the exception of cman_profile, their values.

Parameter	**Description**
cman	Specifies the listening addresses for the Oracle Connection Manager gateway process, CMGW. Default: cman=(address=(protocol=tcp)(host=<local_host>)(port=1630))
cman_admin	Specifies the listening addresses for the Oracle Connection Manager administrative process, CMADMIN. Default: cman_admin=(address=(protocol=tcp)(host=<anyhost>)(port=1830))
cman_profile	Sets parameters related to the Oracle Connection Manager. (See Tables 10-2 and 10-3.)

TABLE 10-1. *Cman.ora Parameters*

Parameter	Description
cman_rules	Sets the filtering rules for the network access control portion of Oracle Connection Manager. To establish a filtering rule, you use the following parameters with appropriate values to instruct the Oracle Connection Manager either to accept or reject connections for the applicable source, destination, and database combination. SRC—Source host name or IP address of session request in dot notation DST—Destination server host name or IP address in dot notation SRV—Database server SID ACT—Accept or reject incoming requests with the previous characteristics

TABLE 10-1 *Cman.ora Parameters* (continued)

Two parameters listed in Table 10-1 are of special interest to us. They are cman_profile and cman_rules. Since there are only four values in the cman_rules area, I listed them in Table 10-1. However, there are quite a few profile variables available to refine the way each Oracle Connection Manager behaves, so I've listed the variables and their definitions in Table 10-2 and their default and range of values in Table 10-3. I've included a sample profile so that you can see how one looks.

As I said, you can further define your Oracle Connection Manager's individual behavior by creating a profile using the variables and their values listed in Tables 10-2 and 10-3. Here is an example of a cman profile. You place the profile in the cman.ora parameter file after the cman and cman_admin definitions.

```
cman_profile=
    (parameter_list=
        (maximum_relays=512)
        (log_level=1)
        (relay_statistics=yes)
        (remote_admin=yes)
        (show_tns_info=yes)
        (use_async_call=yes)
        (authentication_level=0)
        (tracing=yes)
        (trace_timestamp=yes)
        (trace_filelen=100)
        (trace_fileno=2))
```

Parameter	Definition
answer_timeout	Determines the number of seconds that Oracle Connection Manager uses to time out the protocol handshake associated with an incoming connection request.
authentication_level	Determines the level of security the Oracle Connection Manager can enforce: 1 = Reject connect requests that are not using the Oracle Advanced Security option Secure Network Services (SNS). 0 = Do not check for SNS between client and server.
log_level	Determine the level of logging: 0 = No logging performed 1 = Basic reporting 2 = RULE_LIST matching lookup reporting 3 = Relay blocking reporting 4 = Relay I/O counts reporting
max_freelist_buffers	Determines the maximum number of buffers that TNS keeps in its freelist for later reuse instead of returning them to the operating system after a relay is closed.
maximum_connect_data	Limits the connect data string length of the incoming connection requests.
maximum_relays	Determines the maximum number of concurrent connections that Oracle Connection Manager supports.
relay_statistics	Determines whether I/O statistics are recorded.
remote_admin	Determines whether remote access to an Oracle Connection Manager is allowed.
show_tns_info	Determines whether TNS information is to be recorded.
tracing	Determines whether tracing is enabled for the Oracle Connection Manager.
trace_directory	Specifies the trace directory. You must set this parameter to a nondefault location if you plan to use the TRACE_FILELEN or TRACE_TIMESTAMP parameters.
trace_filelen	Specifies the size of the trace file in kilobytes (KB). When the size is met, the trace information is written to the next file. The number of files is specified with the TRACE_FILENO parameter.
trace_fileno	Specifies the number of trace files for tracing. When this parameter is set along with the TRACE_FILELEN parameter, trace files are used in a cyclical fashion.
trace_timestamp	Adds a timestamp in the form of dd-month-yyyy hh:mm:ss to a trace event in the trace file.
use_async_call	Determines whether Oracle Connection Manager uses asynchronous functions while in the answering or calling phase of establishing a Net8 connection.

TABLE 10-2. *Cman_profile Parameters*

Parameter with Default Value	Values
answer_timeout=0	0–n
authentication_level=0	0 | 1
log_level=0	0–4
max_freelist_buffers=0	0–10240
maximum_connect_data=1024	257–4096
maximum_relays=128	1–2048
relay_statistics=NO	[YES | TRUE | ON | 1 | NO | FALSE | OFF | 0]
remote_admin=NO	[YES | TRUE | ON | 1 | NO | FALSE | OFF | 0]
show_tns_info=NO	[YES | TRUE | ON | 1 | NO | FALSE | OFF | 0]
tracing	[YES | TRUE | ON | 1 | NO | FALSE | OFF | 0]
trace_directory=$ORACLE_HOME/network/trace on UNIX ORACLE_HOME\network\trace on Windows NT	A directory location
trace_filelen=unlimited	Size of file in kilobytes
trace_fileno=1	Number
trace_timestamp=NO	[YES | TRUE | ON | 1 | NO | FALSE | OFF | 0]
tracing=NO	[YES | TRUE | ON | 1 | NO | FALSE | OFF | 0]
use_async_call=YES	[YES | TRUE | ON | 1 | NO | FALSE | OFF | 0]

TABLE 10-3. *Cman_profile Default and Range of Values*

The final entry in the cman.ora sample is the notation that you can use cman as a firewall proxy on TCP/IP if you establish cman_rules. Here's the code to define a cman_rules entry. This code is included in the cman.ora sample file.

```
#
#===========================================================================
# cman is used as a fire wall proxy on TCP, IF AND ONLY IF "cman_rules" exists
#===========================================================================
#
#cman_rules = (rule_list=
#               (rule=(src=skdl)(dst=x)(srv=x)(act=accept))
#          )
```

In the example, the cman_rules parameters tell the Oracle Connection Manager to accept all transmissions from the SKDL server. The *x* is a wildcard notation that means any destination to any server from SKDL should be accepted. The other option for the variable **act** is REJECT. By default, when you've enabled cman_rules, cman follows the principle that anything not expressly permitted is prohibited, so make sure you don't shoot yourself in the foot by neglecting to explicitly permit actions that you want to allow.

Configuring Oracle Connection Manager Connection Concentration

To enable connection concentration, you must first configure the Oracle Connection Manager following the information presented in the previous section. Once you've configured the Oracle Connection Manager, you configure the server and then the client. Since you've already learned how to configure the Oracle Connection Manager, let's go straight to server and client configuration, shall we?

In order to support connection concentration, the destination server must be configured to run with the Multi-Threaded Server (MTS) option. You must also have multiplexing turned on. You can accomplish both of these tasks using the Oracle Database Configuration Assistant. If you do not want to use the tool, you can set the parameter **mts_dispatchers** in the server database's init.ora parameter file. The following code sample shows you how to declare the protocol and turn multiplexing on:

```
mts_dispatchers="(protocol=TCP) (multiplex=ON)"
```

There are several other MTS parameters that can be set. However, these are the only values that must be set to support connection concentration. Let's look at the options you have for arguments for both **protocol** and **multiplex** in Table 10-4.

Okay, so now you've configured the server. It's time to configure the client. To create client support, you have to create two addresses: one for the Oracle Connection Manager and the other for the listener. The configuration will vary depending on the naming method you are using.

For Local and Directory Naming methods, you must create an address list in which the first address is for the Oracle Connection Manager and the second address is for the listener. To ensure that the client will connect first to the Oracle Connection Manager and second to the listener, you must set the parameter **source_route=** YES. You have to modify the tnsnames.ora file to tell the connection request that Oracle Connection Manager is to be used. Here's a copy of the parameters you need to include and the format to include them in:

```
skdl=
 (description=
   (source_route=yes)
   (address=
     (protocol=tcp)
     (host=cman-pc)
     (port=1630))
 (address=
   (protocol=tcp)
   (host=marlenes-pc)
   (port=1521))
 (connect_data=
 (service_name=skdl.xyzcorp.us.com)))
```

The section that's been added to make this specifically configured for the Oracle Connection Manager is the area just below **description=** and includes the values for **source_route**, **protocol**, **host**, and **port**. The designation CMAN-PC is the name of the machine that is being used as the Oracle Connection Manager machine. If I

Parameter	**Description**
protocol (pro or prot)	The network protocol (TCP in the example) for which the dispatcher generates a listening end point.
multiplex (mul or mult)	Used to enable connection concentration. If 1, ON, YES, TRUE, or BOTH is specified, then connection concentration is enabled for both incoming and outgoing network connections. If IN is specified, the connection concentration is enabled for incoming network connections from the client. If OUT is specified, the connection concentration is enabled for outgoing network connections. If 0, NO, OFF, or FALSE is specified, then connection concentration is disabled for both incoming and outgoing network connections.

TABLE 10-4. *Connection Concentration Protocol and Multiplex Commands*

were using MARLENES-PC as the Oracle Connection Manager machine, that name would be entered for the **host** value. The first **address** is the Oracle Connection Manager machine, while the second address is the location of the database. From the first address, the Oracle Connection Manager connects to the database service through the listener.

If you're using Oracle Names servers, things are a bit easier. You see, listener and Oracle Connection Manager information is automatically passed to the Oracle Names server. From the client side, the parameter **use_cman**=TRUE must be placed in the sqlnet.ora file. This parameter must also be placed in the sqlnet.ora file for each Oracle Names server machine.

Configuring Oracle Connection Manager Multiprotocol Support

As with the last set of tasks to configure the connection concentration, to begin the configuration for multiprotocol support, you must first configure the Oracle Connection Manager. Keep in mind that any protocol supported by Oracle can be used to listen for connection requests by an Oracle Connection Manager. Also, without multiprotocol support, an SPX client cannot connect to a server using TCP/IP. However, with the Oracle Connection Manager, the SPX client can connect to the Oracle Connection Manager, and, in turn, the Connection Manager can connect to the server using TCP/IP.

Once you've configured the Oracle Connection Manager, you must configure the client. In this case, the configuration is almost identical to the configuration steps used in the connection concentration described in the previous section. The only difference is that the variables in the tnsnames.ora file entry change slightly, as shown here:

```
skdl=
 (description=
   (source_route=yes)
   (address=
     (protocol=spx)
     (service=cman))
 (address=
   (protocol=tcp)
   (host=marlenes-pc)
   (port=1521))
 (connect_data=
 (service_name=skdl.xyzcorp.us.com)))
```

The only change is in the section that shows the **protocol**=SPX and **service**=CMAN.

Configuring Oracle Connection Manager Access Control

In addition to the standard configuration for the Oracle Connection Manager, to configure for access control, you must add cman_rules to the cman.ora file to reflect the access that you want to ACCEPT or REFUSE. The values for cman_rules are shown in Table 10-1. Remember that the letter *x* is used as a wildcard value either to allow all access or refuse all access from a specific machine, to a specific machine, or both. Let's review the syntax for declaring the cman_rules values now:

```
cman_rules=
 (rule_list=
    (rule=
      (src=marlenes-pc)
      (dst=skdl-pc)
      (srv=skdl.us.xyzcorp.com)
      (act=accept))
    (rule=
      (src=196.123.45.67)
      (dst=196.123.46.78)
      (srv=mydb)
      (act=reject)))
```

In this example, I've included multiple rules by adding each entry under a distinct **rule=** area. In the first rule, any connection request coming from MARLENES-PC to the SKDL platform to connect to the SKDL.XYZCORP.US.COM database is to be accepted. For the second rule, any connection request coming from platform 196.123.45.67 to the MYDB database on platform 196.123.46.78 is to be refused. Okay, that completes the Oracle Connection Manager configuration. Now, you must configure the client.

The client configuration starts out the same as we saw in both the connection concentration and multiprotocol support for a Local Naming or Directory Naming method. You create an address list in which the first address is to the Oracle Connection Manager and the second address is for the listener. Again, the **source_route** parameter must be set. For the Oracle Names server, you just have to add **use_cman**=TRUE to the sqlnet.ora file. Oh, by the way, if you're using more than one Oracle Connection Manager in the connection path, you can't use Oracle Names to perform the client connections.

Oracle Connection Manager Control Utility

Once you complete all of the configuration tasks, how do you stop, start, and control the Oracle Connection Manager processes? Oracle provides a utility called cmctl (Connection Manager Control) that you can use to interact with the processes. As with the Listener and Names Control utilities, you run cmctl from the operating system level by typing

```
cmctl <command> <process_type>
```

The commands that you can use are shown in Table 10-5. The process_type argument is the name of the process on which the command is being executed. You

Parameter	Definition
accept_connections	Enables or disables Oracle Connection Manager to accept new connections. If set to OFF, it will not affect existing connections. Default: ON Values: ON I OFF
close_relay	Enables a connection identified by relay number to be shut down. A value of ALL immediately shuts down all connections. Use with caution. Default: None Values: relay_num I ALL
help	Provides a list of all the cmctl commands available. If used in conjunction with a parameter, displays help on how to use the command.
shutdown	Shuts down the Oracle Connection Manager processes using one of the following arguments: NORMAL (default)—No new connections will be accepted, and the Oracle Connection Manager terminates after all existing connections close. ABORT—The Oracle Connection Manager shuts down immediately, closing down all open connections. [cman]—You can use this argument after NORMAL or ABORT, but both NORMAL and ABORT implicitly use this argument so you don't really have to.

TABLE 10-5. *cmctl Commands (* Indicates More Parameters Associated with This Command)*

Parameter	Definition
start	Starts Oracle Connection Manager. cman (default)—Starts both CMGW and CMADMIN processes. cm—Starts the CMGW process.
stats	Displays statistical information for the Oracle Connection Manager. cman (default)—Displays statistics for the CMGW and CMADMIN processes. cm—Displays statistics for the CMGW process. The following statistics are displayed with the argument COMPAT or VERBOSE. I've added an explanation for each argument. TOTAL_RELAYS (COMPAT)—Total number of connections handled. (VERBOSE)—Total number of connections successfully established by the Oracle Connection Manager since it started. ACTIVE_RELAYS (COMPAT)—Number of currently a ctive relays. (VERBOSE)—The number of currently active connections. MOST_RELAYS (COMPAT)—Peak active relays. (VERBOSE)—The maximum number of concurrent connections ever held by the Oracle Connection Manager since it started. OUT_OF_RELAY (COMPAT)—Total refusals due to max_relays exceeded. (VERBOSE)—Total number of connect request refusals due to out-of-relay since the Oracle Connection Manager started. TOTAL_REFUSED (COMPAT)—Total number of connections refused. (VERBOSE)—Total number of connect request refusals since the Oracle Connection Manager started.

TABLE 10-5. *cmctl Commands (* Indicates More Parameters Associated with This Command)* (continued)

Parameter	Definition
status	Displays basic status information, including version, start time, and current statistics used with the argument process_type: cman (default)—Displays status information for both the CMGW and CMADMIN processes. cm—Displays status information for the CMGW process.
stop	Shuts down Oracle Connection Manager immediately, prompting you if there are open connections using the process_type: cman (default)—Stops both CMGW and CMADMIN processes. cm—Stops the CMGW process.
stopnow	Shuts down Oracle Connection Manager immediately, closing down all open connections without warning. cman (default)—Stops both CMGW and CMADMIN processes. cm—Stops the CMGW process.
version	Displays the current version and name of the cmctl utility.
quit	Exits the cmctl utility and is identical to the **exit** command.
exit	Exits the cmctl utility and is identical to the **quit** command.
set*	Lists the available configuration commands that can be set for the current cmctl session.
show*	Lists the available commands that can be shown for the current cmctl session. In response to one of the **show** commands, cmctl displays the current setting for that parameter.

TABLE 10-5. *cmctl Commands (* Indicates More Parameters Associated with This Command)* (continued)

have two recommended choices for process_type: **cman** to affect both CMGW and CMADMIN or **cm** to affect only the CMGW process. Although there is a third option, **adm**, available through the cmctl utility, Oracle recommends that this process_type not be used. They also recommend that you use **cm** only to reserve resources. The following command can be used to start *both* the CMGW and CMADMIN processes:

```
cmctl start cman
```

To access the tool and enter commands at the cmctl> prompt instead of the operating system prompt, you type

```
cmctl
```

This command brings you to the cmctl> prompt. From there, you can enter commands. Figure 10-4 shows a DOS screen print of the cmctl utility accessed from the cmctl> prompt. I've also typed **help** to show you the options that are available within the tool.

Use the **close_relay** command with caution. You see, from the time you use the **show relay** command to the time you issue the **close_relay** command, the same relay may have been reused by another connection.

There are four parameters under the **set** command. They are shown in Table 10-6.

Under the **show** command, there are six commands, as shown in Table 10-7.

If you modify an Oracle Connection Manager parameter using the **set** command, the change will only remain in effect until you exit your current cmctl session. You cannot save parameter settings to the cman.ora file.

Oh, by the way, Oracle recommends that you use **shutdown** rather than **stop** and **stopnow** since **shutdown** offers all the functionality of **stop** and **stopnow** in a cleaner manner.

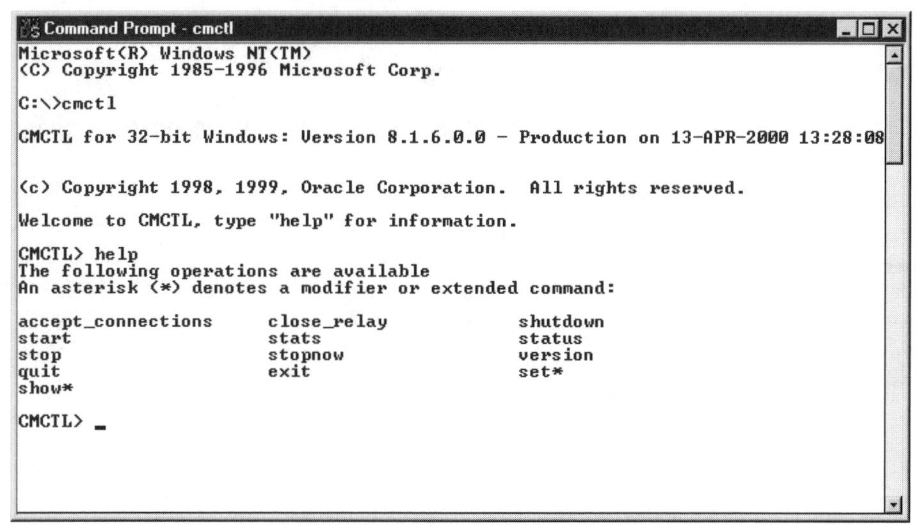

FIGURE 10-4. *cmctl command prompt with help values*

Parameter	**Definition**
authentication_level	Sets the level of security for the Oracle Connection Manager using the <level> argument with one of the following values: 0 (default) = No authenticating is required for client connections. 1 = Rejects connections that are not employing Secure Network Service (SNS) to perform client authentication.
Displaymode	Changes the output of the following commands: **start**, **stats**, **status**, **stop**, or **version**. Used with the following arguments: COMPAT (default)—Displays output that is compatible with older versions of Oracle Connection Manager. VERBOSE (recommended)—Displays a formatted and descriptive output.
log_level	Sets the log level for the Oracle Connection Manager using one of the values, 0 through 4, as follows: Level 0 (default) = No logging Level 1 = Basic reporting Level 2 = RULE_LIST matching lookup reporting Level 3 = Relay blocking reporting Level 4 = Relay I/O counts reporting
relay_statistics	Turns statistic collection pertaining to the I/O of connections of the Oracle Connection Manager ON or OFF. If set to ON, will display the following information: Number of IN bytes Number of OUT bytes Number of IN packets Number of OUT packets

TABLE 10-6. *cmctl **set** Command Parameters*

Parameter	Definition
address	Lists the listening protocol address of the Oracle Connection Manager that is set in the cman.ora **cman** parameter.
all	Displays the output for the **address**, **profile**, and **rules** commands.
displaymode	Shows the current display mode used for the **start**, **stats**, **status**, **stop**, and **version** commands and is used with the arguments: COMPAT (default)—Displays output that is compatible with older versions of Oracle Connection Manager. VERBOSE—Displays a formatted and descriptive output.
profile	Lists the current parameter settings for the Oracle Connection Manager. Information is obtained from the **cman_profile** parameter in the cman.ora file and any changes made with the **set** command.
relay	Displays the current status of a selected relay (connection) or all active relays for the Oracle Connection Manager. Using the argument ACTIVE, you see a list of all of the active relays. If you enter a specific relay by entering the number of the relay as an argument, you see the following information: Relay number Source address (client-side end point) Destination address (server-side end point) Number of IN bytes Number of IN packets Number of IN DCD probes Number of OUT bytes Number of OUT packets Number of OUT DCD probes
rules	Lists the current Net8 access rules used by the Oracle Connection Manager.

TABLE 10-7. *cmctl* ***show*** *Command Parameters*

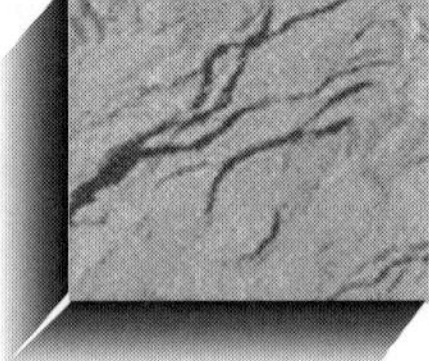

CHAPTER 11

Supporting Large Networks

h, dear. I just got a call from my mother. She's on her way over here, and there are papers, books, clothes I just took out of the dryer, and magazines all around the living room. Can you help me quickly gather everything up to put away? Boy, is it hard to carry more than a certain amount of clothes or magazines at one time. Maybe if we shift things from one hand to the other or rest the articles against the inside of our arms between the elbow and wrist, we can carry more at once. Hey, I have an even better idea to help speed up our cleaning. Let me get my laundry basket. We can gather all of the articles together and put them in the basket and then just move the basket from one room to another. I can actually put the things away later, and, for now, the room will look neat and tidy. Whew, that was a close call, but the living room certainly does look better now, doesn't it? Thanks so much for your help!

If I had been alone and trying to straighten the living room quickly, I would have had to put forth much more effort, and it would have taken me twice as much time. By dividing the workload, we were able to do the same amount of work with less individual effort in a much shorter time. Pretty cool, huh.

Just as we pooled our resources to make short work of our task at hand, there are many Net8 features that you can use to help make the most of the resources available on your machine to support more work with less effort. In this chapter, I'm going to tell you about several of the Net8 features and how you can use them to optimize your Oracle network. We'll be looking at Multi-Threaded Server configuration, load balancing, connection pooling, connection concentration, and prespawned dedicated servers. I've mentioned all of these topics very casually before in this book, but I'm going to give you a much more in-depth view of each feature in this chapter. We can start our exploration with a quick look at large networks in general. I'm going to spend most of this chapter talking about the Multi-Threaded Server since it's one of the best ways to get the most out of your operating system resources, especially if you are using Windows NT as your server.

If you envision supporting a large network with a high number of concurrent connections, there are many options available to you through Net8 to support your environment. Here is a list of available actions you can take to increase the number of connections that you can support, even if you have more limited resources:

- Enable Multi-Threaded Server (MTS)
- If MTS is enabled, enable connection pooling, connection concentration, and/or client load balancing
- Prespawn dedicated servers

Now, the first question to ask yourself is "What makes sense in your environment?" Then you want to think about what's really right for you and your company? Every one of the options sounds great, but what, if anything, are the drawbacks and trade-offs? Let's take a close look at each of these options to help you decide what makes sense for you.

Enable Multi-Threaded Server

Let's take just a bit of time to review what we covered in Chapter 2 about Multi-Threaded Server processes. You learned that the steps to start an MTS process are as follows:

1. Start the Net8 listener. The listener configuration, stored in the listener.ora file, determines the port or ports that are used to listen for connection requests.
2. Each database that is going to be made available is started and registers itself with the listener process. In this way, the listener knows what services and instances are available at any given moment.
3. When the database starts, if the appropriate configuration parameters are present in the initialization file, init.ora, dispatchers are started. Each dispatcher listens on the address to which it has been assigned. When the dispatcher is started, its address is registered with the listener. The dispatcher either will attempt to register with the listener at its default listener address or will use the listener's network name that is specified in the database init.ora file. The listener's network name can resolve to more than one address if multiple listeners are being used.
4. Once the dispatchers are registered, the listener can redirect incoming connection requests to the dispatchers. Remember that if the databases are started before the listener in Oracle8i, the databases will register successfully with the listener but MTS connections will be refused, and all connections will be made as dedicated connections.
5. Using the listener network address, the clients connect to the listener. The listener validates the connection request to determine whether the request may be serviced. If it can't be serviced, the listener refuses the network session. If it can, the listener issues a redirect message to the client. This message contains the network address of the least-used dispatcher.
6. Using the dispatcher network address provided, the client dissolves the network session to the listener and establishes a network session to the dispatcher.

7. Once the connection has been established, the dispatcher updates the listener with the new load value. In this way, the listener will be able to balance the incoming network session requests between dispatchers running on the same protocol.

8. The dispatcher places the information request on the Shared Server request queue and the request is picked up and processed. The reply is placed on a response queue for the dispatcher to return to the client who made the request. The client disconnects from the dispatcher.

9. Once a client disconnects from a dispatcher, the dispatcher remains available. The shared servers can process incoming requests. If a request sits on the queue for too long, new shared servers can be started up to the maximum number specified in the init.ora parameter file. In this way, it's possible for different requests from the same client to be processed by more than one shared server.

Take a look at Figure 11-1 to see the flow of a client's connection request in a Multi-Threaded Server environment. You can see the process flow for the first nine steps listed here. The client disconnection, step 8, is not shown in Figure 11-1.

Why Use Multi-Threaded Servers?

When you work at a computer, do you type steadily for hours at a time? I know that I don't. I stop to think about what I'm going to type next. If I'm filling out a form to order something over the Internet, I stop to get my wallet out so that I can look up my charge card number. I know of people who leave their computers connected to the database from the time they get to work in the morning until the time they leave work in the evening. Sometimes, they even forget to log off when they leave and remain logged on all night—unless, of course, their processes are killed off when nightly backup procedures run.

As you saw earlier in this section, when you create a connection to a server using Net8, there are specific steps that are performed. Each of these steps takes time and uses an amount of computer resources. Regardless of the amount of real resources that are available on your machine, eventually, if enough connections are made and left connected, the machine will reach its resource limits, and the next connection request that is presented will be refused.

Now, let's say you are running an Internet site. Your site has a large traffic volume, and thousands of orders are placed each day. Each order is recorded in an Oracle database. If you are relying on individual, dedicated Net8 connections, there's a very real possibility that your machine can run out of resources and customers will be turned away or won't be able to execute an order on your system. I suspect that the CEO of your company will be very unhappy to learn that the site does not

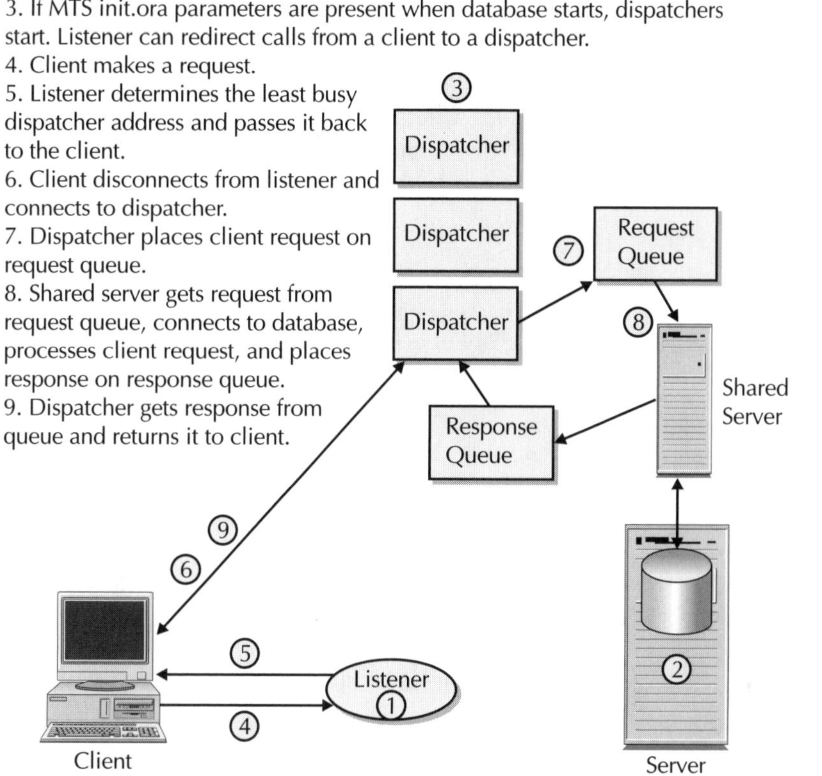

1. Listener is started.
2. Databases are started.
3. If MTS init.ora parameters are present when database starts, dispatchers start. Listener can redirect calls from a client to a dispatcher.
4. Client makes a request.
5. Listener determines the least busy dispatcher address and passes it back to the client.
6. Client disconnects from listener and connects to dispatcher.
7. Dispatcher places client request on request queue.
8. Shared server gets request from request queue, connects to database, processes client request, and places response on response queue.
9. Dispatcher gets response from queue and returns it to client.
3
Dispatcher
Dispatcher
Dispatcher
7
Request Queue
8
Shared Server
Response Queue
9
6
5
Listener
1
4
2
Client
Server

FIGURE 11-1. *Multi-Threaded Server connection flow*

support customers who want to make a purchase! So, what's the answer to this problem? I think you can answer that question easily based on the topic we're discussing here. If you answer, "Multi-Threaded Server," you are correct.

Because MTS enables more than one client to use a single Net8 connection, more users can be supported with less resource expended per connection request. Let's review the process. When the database is started, a number of dispatchers are created with virtual connections to a pool of shared server processes. As client requests are received, a dispatcher places each of the incoming network session requests on a common queue. As each shared server process becomes idle, it picks up the next request in the queue. Figure 11-2 shows the Multi-Threaded Server architecture. As you can see, even though five clients are shown in Figure 11-2, only two dispatchers are needed to handle all of them. Notice, too, that there are only three shared server processes connected to the database to perform the actual queries on behalf of the clients.

Since the shared server processes are only started once, the additional overhead of creating each client connection is eliminated. Each client actually uses less memory, so memory requirements are reduced. Process management requirements are also reduced. Because of these reductions, more users can be supported at the same time. Pretty cool, huh!

NOTE
Adding MTS to a system with few connections (<200) or low activity will probably have a detrimental effect on performance. MTS is designed to make better use of resources for heavily loaded systems.

When MTS is used, Oracle moves the User Global Area (UGA) portion of the Process Global Area (PGA) into the shared pool. The UGA contains user session information, sort areas, and private SQL areas. Usually the largest portion of the UGA is the sort area, which is specified by the init.ora parameter **sort_area_size**. Without MTS, each client process reserves the sort area size regardless of whether or not that process is going to perform a sort. By using MTS, the area reserved for sorting is created on the server as part of the shared or large pool and can be used by all processes. This eliminates the need for all clients to reserve sort work areas.

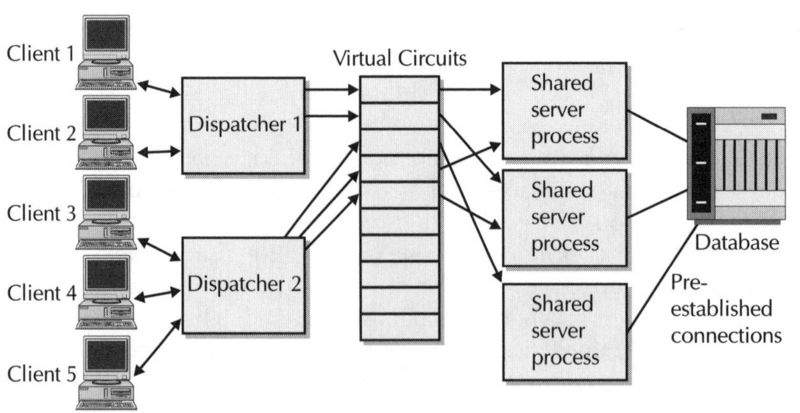

FIGURE 11-2. *Multi-Threaded Server architecture*

The downfall of moving the UGA into the shared pool is that the shared pool must be increased to allow for this sorting activity. Don't worry though. You do not increase the shared pool by the number of clients multiplied by the sort area size, so you don't have to increase the size of the shared pool as much as you might initially think. You see, by shifting your system's sorts to the server SGA, you're getting better overall usage of memory throughout your network. The book *Oracle8 Advanced Tuning and Administration*, by Aronoff, Loney, and Sonawalla, suggests increasing the shared SQL area by one half of the total SGA size. This is a good initial value when you first migrate to MTS; however, when Oracle introduced the parameter **large_pool_size** with Oracle8, they recommended using the large pool rather than the shared pool for the UGA. The following queries can be used to help determine the correct setting or to help you determine whether you need to increase the setting, if you've already set the **large_pool_size** parameter value.

```
select sum(VALUE) || 'Bytes' "Total memory for all sessions"
  from V$SESSTAT, V$STATNAME
 where upper(NAME) = 'SESSION UGA MEMORY'
   and V$SESSTAT.STATISTIC# = V$STATNAME.STATISTIC#;

select sum(VALUE)|| 'Bytes' "Total Max. memory for all sessions"
  from V$SESSTAT, V$STATNAME
 where upper(NAME) = 'SESSION UGA MEMORY MAX'
   and V$SESSTAT.STATISTIC# = V$STATNAME.STATISTIC#;
```

The results will be something like the following:

```
Total memory for all sessions
-----------------------------
157125 Bytes

Total Max. memory for all sessions
------------------------------
417381 Bytes
```

The result of the first query indicates that the memory currently allocated to all sessions is 157,125 bytes. The result of the second query indicates the sum of the maximum sizes of the memories for all sessions is 417,381 bytes.

You can use the result of either of these queries to determine how much larger to make the large or shared pool if you use a Multi-Threaded Server. The first value is likely to be a better estimate than the second one unless nearly all sessions are likely to reach their maximum allocations at the same time. You must keep in mind, though, that if the sessions are connected to dedicated server processes, this memory is part of the memory of the UGA; while if the sessions are connected to shared server processes, this memory is part of the shared pool or SGA.

Enabling Multi-Threaded Server Processes

There are many parameters available that you can use to configure MTS. To enable MTS, you must put, at a minimum, the parameter **mts_dispatchers** in the init.ora file for the database that you want to use MTS with. You must include one or more of the first three parameters shown in Table 11-1. In other words, although I show each of the first three entries with an equal sign (=), you can have one, two, or all three of these values in the **mts_dispatchers** entry. The point is that you must have at least one of these values associated with the entry. This table shows the various attributes for the parameter **mts_dispatchers**. Sample syntax for this parameter is as follows:

```
mts_dispatchers="(address=(<protocol>)(<host>)(<port>)(<number of
dispatchers>)(<number of connections>))"
```

With values included, the sample looks like this:

```
mts_dispatchers="(address=(protocol=TCP)(host=MARLENES-PC)(port=5001))
(dispatchers=2)(connections=10)"
```

In this example, I've included all of the first three attributes, but only one of them is required, and you are free to choose whether you are going to include one, two, or all three of them. After the first three attributes shown here, the rest of the attributes in Table 11-1 are optional. Remember that the **mts_dispatchers** values must be surrounded by double quotation marks and enclosed in parentheses.

Attributes	Description
"(**address**=<value>)"	Network protocol address of the end point on which the dispatchers listen.

TABLE 11-1. ***mts_dispatchers*** *Parameter Arguments*

<table>
<tr><th>Attributes</th><th>Description</th></tr>
<tr><td>"(description= <value>)"</td><td>Network description of the end point on which the dispatchers listen, including the IP address.</td></tr>
<tr><td>"(protocol=<value>)"</td><td>Network protocol for which the dispatcher generates a listening end point.</td></tr>
<tr><td>connections (con or conn)</td><td>Maximum number of network connections to allow for each dispatcher.</td></tr>
<tr><td>dispatchers</td><td>Initial number of dispatchers to start.
Default: 1</td></tr>
<tr><td>listener</td><td>An alias for the listener(s) with which the pmon process registers dispatcher information. Specify a value for this only if the listener is local and uses a nondefault port or protocol or if the listener is on a different node.</td></tr>
<tr><td>multiplex</td><td>Enables Oracle Connection Manager's connection concentration feature.
Values:
1|ON|YES|TRUE|BOTH—Enables connection concentration for both incoming and outgoing connections.
IN—Connection concentration only enabled for incoming network connections from clients.
OUT—Connection concentration only enabled for outgoing network connections to clients.
0|NO|OFF|FALSE—Disables connection concentration for both incoming and outgoing network connections.</td></tr>
</table>

TABLE 11-1. ***mts_dispatchers*** *Parameter Arguments* (continued)

Attributes	Description
pool	Enables Oracle Connection Manager's connection pooling feature. Values: A number—Enables connection pooling for both incoming and outgoing network connections. The number specified is the timeout in ticks for both incoming and outgoing network connections. ON|YES|TRUE|BOTH—Enables connection pooling for both incoming and outgoing network connections. Default timeout value: 10 ticks—Used for both incoming and outgoing network connections. IN—Enables connection pooling for incoming network connections. Default timeout value: 10 ticks—Used for incoming network connections. (IN can also be assigned a timeout in ticks value, such as (IN=20). If the numeric value of a specified timeout is 0 or 1, the default value of 10 ticks is used.) OUT—Enables connection pooling for outgoing network connections. Default timeout value: 10 ticks—Used for outgoing network connections. (OUT can also be assigned a timeout in ticks value, such as (OUT=20). If the numeric value of a specified timeout is 0 or 1, the default value of 10 ticks is used.) NO|OFF|FALSE—Disables connection pooling for both incoming and outgoing network connections.
service	Service name(s) that the dispatchers register with the listener. Default: The value(s) specified for the init.ora parameter **service_names**.
session (**ses** or **sess**)	Maximum number of network sessions to allow for each dispatcher.

TABLE 11-1. ***mts_dispatchers*** *Parameter Arguments* (continued)

Attributes	Description
ticks	Size of a network tick in seconds. When multiplied by the **pool** timeout value, supplies the total connection pool timeout value. Default: 15 seconds—For a fast network, a tick size of about 1 second is recommended. For a slow network, a tick size of about 3 or 4 seconds is recommended.

TABLE 11-1. ***mts_dispatchers*** *Parameter Arguments* (continued)

The other parameters that you can include in your database init.ora parameter file are shown in Table 11-2.

To establish MTS, perform the following steps:

1. Stop the database.
2. Modify the init.ora file for the appropriate database to include the following parameters:
   mts_dispatchers="(address=(<protocol>)(<host>))(<number of dispatchers>)(<number of connections>)"
   mts_max_dispatchers=<max number of dispatchers>
   mts_servers=<number of shared servers to start>
   mts_max_servers=<max number of shared servers>
   mts_service=<SID or value that was used for the **service_names** parameter in the init.ora file>
   mts_listener_address=<address of the TNS listener>

Parameter	Description
mts_max_dispatchers	Maximum number of dispatchers
mts_servers	Number of shared servers to start
mts_max_servers	Maximum number of shared servers
mts_service	SID name
mts_listener_address	Address of the TNS listener

TABLE 11-2. *Other init.ora MTS Parameters*

3. Restart the database.

For example, let's say you want to set up a Multi-Threaded Server environment on the host machine called MARLENES-PC using a port that is not the standard default port of 1521 or 1526. You initially want two dispatchers to be started and made available, and you do not want more than ten dispatchers to be running at the same time. The initial number of servers to start is two, and the maximum number of servers is to be four. The database to be connected to is SKDL, which is located on the host called NELSONS-PC, listening on port 1521. Here are the init.ora entries for this configuration:

```
mts_dispatchers="(address=(protocol=TCP) (host=MARLENES-PC) (port=5001)) (dispatchers=2)"
mts_max_dispatchers=1
mts_servers=2
mts_max_servers=4
mts_service=SKDL
mts_listen_address="(address=(protocol=TCP)(host=NELSONS-PC)(port=1521))"
```

Well, that's all pretty clear and straightforward, but how in the world do you know how many dispatchers you are going to need? Hmm, good question. Let's see if I can help you to determine the right number to use.

Determining the Right Number of Dispatchers to Specify

As you just saw, the number of dispatchers to start when the instance is started is controlled by the value that you use for the **dispatchers** attribute. The value that you put for this attribute is the minimum number of dispatchers that will ever be started for the instance. Thus, if you start too many dispatchers to begin with, you will waste resources because the excess dispatchers will remain running until the instance is shut down and the value is adjusted. This also means that if you do not initially start enough dispatchers as a minimum, you will take the time and performance hit of starting more dispatchers almost immediately to accommodate the extra client connection requests that are received. If you have not specified enough dispatchers initially, you must explicitly change the number by issuing an **alter system** command to increase the number of dispatchers. You can increase the number of dispatchers up to the number that is specified in the **mts_max_dispatchers** parameter.

To determine the appropriate values for the **dispatchers** attribute, you must consider three criteria:

- Any operating system limit on the number of connections that each process can maintain

- The performance you want from your database
- How many connections each network protocol requires

NOTE
Oracle Corporation strongly recommends not using more than one dispatcher per 1000 connections in a Windows NT environment. This is a much higher value than has been used in earlier releases.

Once you've determined the values for the operating system limit per process, you can use the following formula to calculate the number of dispatchers to start when the instance is started, per network protocol.

```
number of dispatchers = ceil (maximum number of concurrent sessions/connection per
dispatcher)
```

In this equation, **ceil** is used to indicate that you take the result of dividing the maximum number of concurrent sessions that you expect by the connections per dispatcher and round that number up to the next higher number. For example—and this really is just a made-up example—let's say you expect to have a maximum of 5000 concurrent sessions connected using TCP/IP. Each process can support 1500 connections per process. Let's also say that you have 3000 concurrent sessions using SPX, and each process can support 1000 connections per process. Using the formula above, you would have

```
number of dispatchers for TCP/IP = ceil(5000/1500)
number of dispatchers for TCP/IP = ceil(3.33333)
number of dispatchers for TCP/IP = 4
```

Now, using the formula again for the SPX calculations, the value comes out to 3. Here's how you'd specify these values in the init.ora file:

```
mts_dispatchers="(protocol=TCP)(dispatchers=4)(connections=1500)"
mts_dispatchers="(protocol=SPX)(dispatchers=3)(connections=1000)"
```

Of course, depending on the performance you get from these values, you may need to adjust the number of dispatchers that you use. Also, over time, the values you've used for your calculations can change; so, periodically, you should go back and verify whether the values you are using are still valid or require adjustments. You can read more about tuning the Multi-Threaded Server in Chapter 21 of *Oracle8i Designing and Tuning for Performance, Release 2 (8.1.6)* in the Oracle online documentation set.

You have two choices in how you establish dispatcher addresses. You can either force dispatchers to use one specific IP address by hard-coding the address into the **mts_dispatchers** statement as follows,

```
mts_dispatchers="(address=(protocol=TCP)(host=198.254.38.17))(dispatchers=4)"
```

or you can start multiple dispatchers at once and force the exact location that each dispatcher is listening on by specifying the port numbers within the init.ora file. Bear in mind that you must use adjacent ports to accomplish this. Here's an example to help make this concept clearer:

```
mts_dispatchers="(address=(protocol=TCP) (host=198.254.38.17) (port=6100))
(dispatchers=2)"
mts_dispatchers="(address=(protocol=TCP) (host=198.254.38.17) (port=6101))
(dispatchers=1)"
```

By default, if MTS is configured, all clients will be passed to one or more dispatchers for request processing. But what if you have a client that's going to be doing steady inserts or updates to rows in a table, like a batch data load? It certainly wouldn't make sense to have that client connected through MTS. So, what do you have to do to enable a specific client to connect to a database through a dedicated process? Well, if you want to ensure that a specific client always connects to the database through a dedicated server process, you can modify the sqlnet.ora file for that client and set the following parameter:

```
use_dedicated_server=ON
```

When you set **use_dedicated_server**=ON, the parameter (**server**=DEDICATED) is added to the **connect_data** section of the connect descriptors used by the client. Oh, and setting **use_dedicated_server**=ON will override any other **server**= value you may have already set for that client. You can also edit the tnsnames.ora file to add (**server**=DEDICATED) in the **connect_data** area. If you always want a client to use a dispatcher, you can put (**server**=SHARED) in the **connect_data** area of the tnsnames.ora file for that client.

Resolving Contention Issues Caused by MTS

If you are using MTS, you may see a slight degradation in performance with features like Bfiles, parallel execution, internode parallel execution, and hash joins. You see, these features can potentially prevent a session from migrating to another shared server because they haven't stored all of the user state information in the User Global Area (UGA). In some cases, these processes have left some of their user state information in the Process Global Area (PGA) space instead. Remember that a single user can have more than one query handled by more than one shared server during a single session. Well, if part of the user state is stored in the PGA instead of the UGA, the part stored in the PGA becomes inaccessible to the shared servers, and the user session can remain nonmigratable. What this all boils down to is that if a user is taking advantage of any of the above-listed features and has multiple queries, she may not be able to take advantage of MTS, and the shared server that's supporting her becomes unavailable to any other user.

Now, although the specific user's performance may not show any problems, your other users may end up with a problem because one of your shared servers has become unavailable for multiple processing purposes. Therefore, if users in your environment are using Bfiles, parallel execution, internode parallel execution, and/or hash joins, you may need to either configure and use more shared servers to balance the amount of processing that can be done concurrently or have the users connect via a dedicated server process.

But how are you going to detect contention problems? Well, Oracle provides several views that show you different areas of MTS performance statistics. The views I'm going to tell you about are shown in Table 11-3. I'll describe each view, and then we can look at how you can use them to help you determine the performance of your Multi-Threaded Server environment.

View	Description
V$DISPATCHER	Provides general dispatcher information
V$DISPATCHER_RATE	Provides statistics for current, average, and maximum values for several dispatcher areas
V$QUEUE	Shows the amount of time, in hundredths of a second, that requests and responses have been waiting in a queue for processing
V$SHARED_SERVER	Displays the number of shared servers currently running
V$MTS	Provides summary MTS connection information

TABLE 11-3. *V$ Views for Contention Resolution*

V$DISPATCHER View

This view provides general information about your dispatcher processes. Table 11-4 shows the columns in the view and their description.

Column	Description
NAME	Name of the dispatcher process
NETWORK	Network address of this dispatcher
PADDR	Process address
STATUS	Status of the dispatcher Values: WAIT—Idle SEND—Sending a message RECEIVE—Receiving a message CONNECT—Establishing a connection DISCONNECT—Handling a disconnect request BREAK—Handling a break TERMINATE—In the process of terminating ACCEPT—Accepting connections (no further information available) REFUSE—Rejecting connections (no further information available)
ACCEPT	Whether this dispatcher is accepting new connections Values: YES or NO
MESSAGES	Number of messages processed by this dispatcher
BYTES	Size in bytes of messages processed by this dispatcher
BREAKS	Number of breaks occurring in this connection
OWNED	Number of circuits owned by this dispatcher
CREATED	Number of circuits created by this dispatcher
IDLE	Total idle time for this dispatcher in hundredths of a second
BUSY	Total busy time for this dispatcher in hundredths of a second
LISTENER	The most recent Oracle error number the dispatcher received from the listener
CONF_INDX	Zero-based index of the **mts_dispatchers** configuration used by this dispatcher

TABLE 11-4. *V$DISPATCHER View*

As you can see, the V$DISPATCHER view provides general information about each of your dispatchers. The areas to watch to help detect dispatcher process contention are your dispatcher busy rates and the amount of time each dispatcher is waiting for responses in the response queues. You can use V$DISPATCHER to evaluate the IDLE and BUSY times for each dispatcher. You must have the **select any table** system privilege to view these values. The SYS and SYSTEM accounts both have this privilege.

You must record your statistics during peak workloads. If you try to evaluate your statistics over the time that your database is up rather than during only the times that your database is under load, your statistics will be skewed, and you won't get a clear picture of dispatcher performance. Average the amount of time your dispatchers are busy over the workload period. If a dispatcher for a specific protocol is busy more than 50 percent of the time, consider increasing the number of dispatchers for that protocol.

V$DISPATCHER_RATE View

The V$DISPATCHER_RATE view provides statistics about the dispatcher processing. This view contains statistics on current (prefixed "cur_"), average (prefixed "avg_"), and maximum (prefixed "max_") values for several categories. The current values show you statistics for the current session. The average values, as the name implies, are the averages of the statistics gathered since the collection period started, while the maximum values show you the highest value that was reached in that category since the collection period started. Table 11-5 shows you the composition of the V$DISPATCHER_RATE view.

Column	Description
NAME	Name of the dispatcher process.
PADDR	Address of the dispatcher process.
CUR_LOOP_RATE	Rate at which the dispatcher has been iterating through its dispatching loop, reported over the past TTL_LOOPS, in iterations/SCALE_LOOPS.
CUR_EVENT_RATE	Rate at which the dispatcher has been processing dispatcher events, reported over the past TTL_LOOPS, in events/SCALE_LOOPS. Such dispatcher events include network events and shared server requests.

TABLE 11-5. *V$DISPATCHER_RATE View*

Column	Description
CUR_EVENTS_PER_LOOP	Average number of events the dispatcher has been processing in each iteration through its dispatching loop, reported over the past TTL_LOOPS, in events/iteration.
CUR_MSG_RATE	Rate at which the dispatcher has been relaying messages between clients and shared servers, reported over the past TTL_MSG, in messages/SCALE_SVR_BUF.
CUR_SVR_BUF_RATE	Rate at which the dispatcher has been relaying buffers to shared servers, reported over the past TTL_SVR_BUF, in messages/SCALE_SVR_BUF.
CUR_SVR_BYTE_RATE	Rate at which the dispatcher has been relaying data to shared servers, reported over the past TTL_SVR_BUF, in bytes/SCALE_SVR_BUF.
CUR_SVR_BYTE_PER_BUF	Average number of data types in each buffer relayed to shared servers, reported over the past TTL_SVR_BUF, in bytes/buffer.
CUR_CLT_BUF_RATE	Rate at which the dispatcher has been relaying buffers to clients, reported over the past TTL_CLT_BUF, in buffers/SCALE_CLT_BUF.
CUR_CLT_BYTE_RATE	Rate at which the dispatcher has been relaying data to clients, reported over the past TTL_CLT_BUF, in bytes/SCALE_CLT_BUF.
CUR_CLT_BYTE_PER_BUF	Average number of data bytes in each buffer relayed to clients, reported over the past TTL_CLT_BUF, in bytes/buffer.
CUR_BUF_RATE	Rate at which the dispatcher has been relaying buffers to either clients or shared servers, reported over the past TTL_BUF, in bytes/SCALE_BUF.
CUR_BYTE_RATE	Rate at which the dispatcher has been relaying data to either clients or shared servers, reported over the past TTL_BUF, in bytes/SCALE_BUF.

TABLE 11-5. *V$DISPATCHER_RATE View* (continued)

Column	Description
CUR_BYTE_PER_BUF	Average number of data bytes in each buffer relayed to either clients or shared servers, reported over the past TTL_BUF, in bytes/buffer.
CUR_IN_CONNECT_RATE	Rate at which the dispatcher has been accepting incoming client connections, reported over the past TTL_IN_CONNECT, in connections/ SCALE_IN_CONNECT.
CUR_OUT_CONNECT_RATE	Rate at which the dispatcher has been establishing outbound connections, reported over the past TTL_OUT_CONNECT, in connections/ SCALE_OUT_CONNECT.
CUR_RECONNECT_RATE	In a connection pooling setup, the rate at which clients have been reconnecting to the dispatcher, reported over the past TTL_RECONNECT, in reconnections/SCALE_RECONNECT.
MAX_LOOP_RATE	Maximum rate at which the dispatcher has ever iterated through its dispatching loop, reported in iterations/SCALE_LOOPS, over the dispatcher's lifetime excluding the past TTL_LOOPS.
MAX_EVENT_RATE	Maximum rate at which the dispatcher has ever processed dispatcher events, reported in events/SCALE_LOOPS, over the dispatcher's lifetime excluding the past TTL_LOOPS.
MAX_EVENTS_PER_LOOP	Maximum number of events the dispatcher has ever processed in one iteration through its dispatching loop, reported in events/iteration, over the dispatcher's lifetime.
MAX_MSG_RATE	Maximum rate at which the dispatcher has ever relayed messages between clients and shared servers, reported in messages/SCALE_MSG, over the dispatcher's lifetime excluding the past TTL_MSG.

TABLE 11-5. *V$DISPATCHER_RATE View* (continued)

Column	Description
MAX_SVR_BUF_RATE	Maximum rate at which the dispatcher has ever relayed buffers to shared servers, reported in buffers/SCALE_SVR_BUF, over the dispatcher's lifetime excluding the past TTL_SVR_BUF.
MAX_SVR_BYTE_RATE	Maximum rate at which the dispatcher has ever relayed data to shared servers, reported in bytes/SCALE_SVR_BUF, over the dispatcher's lifetime excluding the past TTL_SVR_BUF.
MAX_SVR_BYTE_PER_BUF	Maximum number of data bytes the dispatcher has ever relayed in one buffer to a client, reported in bytes/buffer, over the dispatcher's lifetime.
MAX_CLT_BUF_RATE	Maximum rate at which the dispatcher has ever relayed buffers to either clients or shared servers, reported in buffers/SCALE_CLT_BUF, over the dispatcher's lifetime excluding the past TTL_CLT_BUF.
MAX_CLT_BYTE_RATE	Maximum rate at which the dispatcher has ever relayed buffers to clients, reported in bytes/SCALE_CLT_BUF, over the dispatcher's lifetime excluding the last TTL_CLT_BUF.
MAX_CLT_BYTE_PER_BUF	Maximum number of data bytes the dispatcher has ever relayed in one buffer to a client, reported in bytes/buffer, over the dispatcher's lifetime.
MAX_BUF_RATE	Maximum rate at which the dispatcher has ever relayed buffers to either clients or shared servers, reported in buffers/SCALE_BUF, over the dispatcher's lifetime, excluding the past TTL_BUF.
MAX_BYTE_RATE	Maximum rate at which the dispatcher has ever relayed data to either clients or shared servers, reported in bytes/SCALE_BUF, over the dispatcher's lifetime excluding the past TTL_BUF.

TABLE 11-5. *V$DISPATCHER_RATE View* (continued)

Column	Description
MAX_BYTE_PER_BUF	Maximum number of data bytes the dispatcher has ever relayed in one buffer to either a client or a shared server, reported in bytes/buffer, over the dispatcher's lifetime.
MAX_IN_CONNECT_RATE	Maximum rate at which the dispatcher has ever accepted incoming client connections, reported in connections/SCALE_IN_CONNECT, over the dispatcher's lifetime excluding the past TTL_IN_CONNECT.
MAX_OUT_CONNECT_RATE	Maximum rate at which the dispatcher has ever established outbound connections, reported in connections/SCALE_OUT_CONNECT, over the dispatcher's lifetime excluding the past TTL_OUT_CONNECT.
MAX_RECONNECT_RATE	In a connection pooling setup, the maximum rate at which clients have ever reconnected to this dispatcher, reported in reconnections/SCALE_RECONNECT, over the dispatcher's lifetime excluding the past TTL_RECONNECT.
AVG_LOOP_RATE	Historical average rate at which the dispatcher has iterated through its dispatching loop, reported in iterations/SCALE_LOOPS, over the dispatcher's lifetime excluding the past TTL_LOOPS.
AVG_EVENT_RATE	Historical average rate at which the dispatcher has processed dispatcher events, reported in events/SCALE_LOOPS, over the dispatcher's lifetime excluding the past TTL_LOOPS.
AVG_EVENTS_PER_LOOP	Historical average number of events the dispatcher has processed in one iteration through its dispatching loop, reported in events/iteration, over the dispatcher's lifetime excluding the past TTL_LOOPS.

TABLE 11-5. *V$DISPATCHER_RATE View* (continued)

Column	Description
AVG_MSG_RATE	Historical average rate at which the dispatcher has relayed messages between clients and shared servers, reported in messages/SCALE_MSG, over the dispatcher's lifetime excluding the past TTL_MSG.
AVG_SVR_BUF_RATE	Historical average rate at which the dispatcher has relayed buffers to shared servers, reported in buffers/SCALE_SVR_BUF, over the dispatcher's lifetime excluding the past TTL_SVR_BUF.
AVG_SVR_BYTE_RATE	Historical average rate at which the dispatcher has relayed data to shared servers, reported in bytes/SCALE_SVR_BUF, over the dispatcher's lifetime excluding the past TTL_SVR_BUF.
AVG_SVR_BYTE_PER_BUF	Historical average number of data bytes per buffer the dispatcher has relayed to shared servers, reported in bytes/buffer, over the dispatcher's lifetime excluding the past TTL_SVR_BUF.
AVG_CLT_BUF_RATE	Historical average rate at which the dispatcher has relayed buffers to clients, reported in buffers/SCALE_CLT_BUF, over the dispatcher's lifetime excluding the past TTL_CLT_BUF.
AVG_CLT_BYTE_RATE	Historical average rate at which the dispatcher has relayed data to clients, reported in bytes/SCALE_CLT_BUF, over the dispatcher's lifetime excluding the past TTL_CLT_BUF.
AVG_CLT_BYTE_PER_BUF	Historical average number of data bytes per buffer the dispatcher has relayed to clients, reported in bytes/buffer, over the dispatcher's lifetime excluding the past TTL_CLT_BUF.
AVG_BUF_RATE	Historical average rate at which the dispatcher has relayed buffers to either clients or shared servers, reported in buffers/SCALE_BUF, over the dispatcher's lifetime excluding the past TTL_BUF.

TABLE 11-5. *V$DISPATCHER_RATE View* (continued)

Column	Description
AVG_BYTE_RATE	Historical average rate at which the dispatcher has relayed data to either clients or shared servers, reported in bytes/SCALE_BUF, over the dispatcher's lifetime excluding the past TTL_BUF.
AVG_BYTE_PER_BUF	Historical average number of data bytes per buffer the dispatcher has relayed to either clients or shared servers, reported in bytes/buffer, over the dispatcher's lifetime excluding the past TTL_BUF.
AVG_IN_CONNECT_RATE	Historical average rate at which the dispatcher has accepted incoming client connections, reported in connections/SCALE_IN_CONNECT, over the dispatcher's lifetime excluding the past TTL_IN_CONNECT.
AVG_OUT_CONNECT_RATE	Historical average rate at which the dispatcher has established outbound connections, reported in connections/SCALE_OUT_CONNECT, over the dispatcher's lifetime excluding the past TTL_OUT_CONNECT.
AVG_RECONNECT_RATE	In a connection pooling setup, the historical average rate at which clients have reconnected to this dispatcher, reported in reconnections/SCALE_RECONNECT, over the dispatcher's lifetime excluding the past TTL_RECONNECT.
TTL_LOOPS	Time-to-live for "loops" samples, reported in hundredths of a second. Default: 10 minutes
TTL_MSG	Time-to-live for "messages" samples, reported in hundredths of a second. Default: 10 seconds
TTL_SVR_BUF	Time-to-live for "buffers to servers" samples, reported in hundredths of a second. Default: 1 second

TABLE 11-5. *V$DISPATCHER_RATE View* (continued)

Column	Description
TTL_CLT_BUF	Time-to-live for "buffers to clients" samples, reported in hundredths of a second. Default: 1 second
TTL_BUF	Time-to-live for "buffers to clients/servers" samples, reported in hundredths of a second. Default: 1 second
TTL_IN_CONNECT	Time-to-live for "inbound connections" samples, reported in hundredths of a second. Default: 10 minutes
TTL_OUT_CONNECT	Time-to-live for "outbound connections" samples, reported in hundredths of a second. Default: 10 minutes
TTL_RECONNECT	Time-to-live for "reconnections" samples, reported in hundredths of a second. Default: 10 minutes
SCALE_LOOPS	Scale for "loops" statistics, reported in hundredths of a second. Default: 1 minute
SCALE_MSG	Scale for "messages" statistics, reported in hundredths of a second. Default: 1 second
SCALE_SVR_BUF	Scale for "buffers to servers" statistics, reported in hundredths of a second. Default: 1/10 second
SCALE_CLT_BUF	Scale for "buffers to clients" statistics, reported in hundredths of a second. Default: 1/10 second
SCALE_BUF	Scale for "buffers to clients/servers" statistics, reported in hundredths of a second. Default: 1/10 second

TABLE 11-5. *V$DISPATCHER_RATE View* (continued)

Column	Description
SCALE_IN_CONNECT	Scale for "inbound connections" statistics, reported in hundredths of a second. Default: 1 minute
SCALE_OUT_CONNECT	Scale for "outbound connections" statistics, reported in hundredths of a second. Default: 1 minute
SCALE_RECONNECT	Scale for "reconnections" statistics, reported in hundredths of a second. Default: 1 minute

TABLE 11-5. *V$DISPATCHER_RATE View* (continued)

Now that you have seen the composition, I bet you would like to know how to use this view. Before I tell you how to evaluate the contents of the view, I'd like to suggest that you gather statistics over a period of time during both light and heavy processing loads so that you can get a feel for your system load patterns. Once you feel comfortable with looking at the contents of this view and your overall load pattern, you can begin to take actions. If you don't have several days to spend gathering values to find out what your projected system loads are going to be, you can set up load simulations and periodically poll the V$DISPATCHER_RATE view to gather statistics. Here's what to do.

To determine your dispatcher performance, query the view and compare the current values with the maximums. Are the current values near the average and below the maximum values? Does your present system throughput seem to provide adequate response times? If so, your MTS environment is probably close to optimally tuned.

Consider reducing the number of dispatchers you have if the current and average rates are significantly below the maximum values. Likewise, if you see that the current and average rates are close to the maximums, you should increase the number of dispatchers that you have configured.

V$QUEUE View

There is a third view that you will find of interest as you work to determine your dispatcher performance. This is the V$QUEUE view. Table 11-6 shows the columns of the V$QUEUE view.

Column	Description
PADDR	Address of the process that owns the queue.
TYPE	Type of queue: COMMON (processed by servers), DISPATCHER.
QUEUED	Number of items in the queue.
WAIT	Total waiting time, in hundredths of a second, for all responses that have ever been in the queue. Divide by TOTALQ for average wait per item.
TOTALQ	Total number of responses that have ever been in the queue.

TABLE 11-6. *V$QUEUE View*

You can query V$QUEUE occasionally while your application is running to see the response queue activity for the dispatcher processes. You can use the following query, found in Chapter 21 of the *Oracle8i Designing and Tuning for Performance, Release 2* documentation.

```
select CONF_INDX INDEX,
decode (sum(TOTALQ), 0, 'NO RESPONSES', sum(WAIT)/sum(TOTALQ) || ' HUNDREDTHS OF
SECONDS') "AVERAGE WAIT TIME PER RESPONSE"
  from V$QUEUE Q, V$DISPATCHER D
 where Q.TYPE = 'DISPATCHER'
   and Q.PADDR = D.PADDR
 group by CONF_INDX;
```

The query returns the average time that a response waits in each response queue for a dispatcher to route it to a user process. Let's look at sample output from this query to help understand more clearly what you will be looking at:

```
INDEX    AVERAGE WAIT TIME PER RESPONSE
-------- ------------------------------
0        .2145041 HUNDREDTHS OF SECONDS
1        .1372035 HUNDREDTHS OF SECONDS
2        NO RESPONSES
```

Hmm, this output looks confusing, doesn't it? Well, the response is telling you that a response for the first dispatcher's value waits in the queue an average of 0.21 hundredths of a second, while for the second dispatcher, the average wait on the queue is 0.14 hundredths of a second. There are no responses waiting for the third dispatcher. If you see the average wait times increasing, you may want to add more dispatchers for that protocol to handle the workload.

You can also use the V$QUEUE view to look at the average wait time per request on the queue before it is processed. Here's the query you can use with sample output:

```
select decode(TOTALQ,0,'No Requests', WAIT/TOTALQ||' HUNDREDTHS OF SECONDS')
"AVERAGE WAIT TIME PER REQUESTS"
  from V$QUEUE
 where TYPE = 'COMMON';

AVERAGE WAIT TIME PER REQUEST
-----------------------------
.061423 HUNDREDTHS OF SECONDS
```

In this example, you can see that a request waits about 0.06 hundredths of a second before processing.

V$SHARED_SERVER View

You can determine how many shared servers are currently running by querying the V$SHARED_SERVER view. Table 11-7 shows the columns contained in this view.

Column	Description
NAME	Name of the server
PADDR	Server's process address
STATUS	Server status Values: EXEC—Executing SQL WAIT (ENQ)—Waiting for a lock WAIT (SEND)—Waiting to send data to user WAIT (COMMON)—Idle; waiting for a user request WAIT (RESET)—Waiting for a circuit to reset after a break QUIT—Terminating
MESSAGES	Number of messages processed
BYTES	Total number of bytes in all messages
BREAKS	Number of breaks
CIRCUIT	Address of circuit currently being serviced

TABLE 11-7. *V$SHARED_SERVER View*

Column	Description
IDLE	Total idle time in hundredths of a second
BUSY	Total busy time in hundredths of a second
REQUESTS	Total number of requests taken from the common queue in this server's lifetime

TABLE 11-7. *V$SHARED_SERVER View* (continued)

After looking at the composition of this view, you can use the following query to show how many shared servers are currently running in your environment:

```
select COUNT(*) "SHARED SERVER PROCESSES"
  from V$SHARED_SERVER
 where STATUS != 'QUIT';
```

The results of this query would look something like the following:

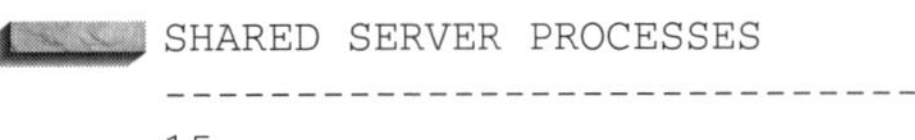

```
SHARED SERVER PROCESSES
-----------------------------
15
```

When you start your database, the number of servers specified by the parameter **mts_servers** is started. This value is the minimum number of shared servers that Oracle will keep running for the time the database is running. As processing continues, shared servers will automatically be added by Oracle as they are needed up to the value specified by **mts_max_servers**. By default, if you haven't specified a value for **mts_max_servers**, the value will be 20 if **mts_servers** is less than or equal to 10. If a value greater than 10 is used for **mts_servers**, **mts_max_servers** will default to two times the **mts_servers** value. If you find that processing is slow or the maximum number of servers is always running, you must shut the database down to increase the minimum and maximum number of shared servers that Oracle can use for that database. Remember that performance can degrade if there are not enough shared servers to support the number of requests that are being received.

V$MTS View

To gain usable information from the V$MTS view, you must first determine the value that your database is using for the parameter **mts_max_servers**. You can find this value by logging on to your database as SYS or SYSTEM or INTERNAL and typing the command **show parameters mts_max_servers**. Once you have the value for **mts_max_servers**, you can use the V$MTS view to see the high-water mark for the shared servers. Table 11-8 shows the columns in the V$MTS view.

Let's pause for a moment to think about what is really going on when you have MTS enabled. Client requests enter the system. A dispatcher accepts the client request and places it on a request queue. The shared server process then performs the data access and passes back the information to the dispatcher via a queue. The dispatcher forwards the data to the client process. If, however, there are not enough shared servers to handle the volume of client queries, the queue backs up and the requests take longer to process. So, before you go looking at the queue waits, you really want to look at whether you are running out of shared servers.

First, you need to determine how much memory each shared server is using. On a UNIX system, you can use the **ps** utility to gather this information. You also need the amount of free RAM available for your system. Once you have these two pieces

Parameter	Description
MAXIMUM_CONNECTIONS	The highest number of virtual circuits in use at one time since the instance started. If this value reaches the value set for the MTS_CIRCUITS initialization parameter, consider raising the value of MTS_CIRCUITS.
MAXIMUM_SESSIONS	The highest number of Multi-Threaded Server sessions in use at one time since the instance started. If this reaches the value set for the MTS_SESSIONS initialization parameter, consider raising the value of MTS_SESSIONS.
SERVERS_STARTED	Cumulative number of shared servers that have been started; does not include those started during startup.
SERVERS_TERMINATED	Cumulative number of shared servers that have been terminated since the instance started.
SERVERS_HIGHWATER	The highest number of servers running at one time since the instance started. If this value reaches the value set for the MTS_MAX_SERVERS initialization parameter, consider raising the value of MTS_SERVERS.

TABLE 11-8. *V$MTS View*

of information, you can divide the amount of free RAM by the size of a shared server to determine how many more shared servers your system can support. Of course, you may not want to use all of your available memory for shared servers, but at least you'll have a better understanding about how much higher you can go.

A good rule of thumb is to set your value for **mts_servers** to a little higher than the number of shared servers you need for average processing load on your system. Generally, set **mts_max_servers** to just a little higher than the number of shared servers that you need to support your heaviest workload. Gradually adjust these numbers to find the most effective values for your environment. If processes start to be swapped out because of the shared server value, back off the number until swapping stops, or buy more physical memory for your system.

Enabling Connection Pooling, Connection Concentration, and/or Client Load Balancing

Let's think about the process the listener goes through to determine which dispatcher it will pass a client request. The listener evaluates each dispatcher load by the number of connections it is currently supporting. As each connection completes and disconnects, the dispatcher notifies the listener so that the current number of active connections for that dispatcher can be recalculated and tracked. This approach is known as *connection load balancing.* If there is more than one dispatcher or more than one node, the listener will take into consideration both the dispatcher load and the number of connections on the node to determine which node and dispatcher to use for a client request.

But how does a dispatcher support multiple users at the same time? Although I covered this earlier in the book, let's review it here. If a client's connection is idle for a specific length of time, a timeout mechanism is used to temporarily release the client's transport connection while maintaining a logical connection between the dispatcher and the client.

Once the dispatcher has released the client's transport connection, the dispatcher can make the now freed physical connection available for a new incoming request. When the idle client becomes active again, the dispatcher reestablishes a physical connection on the client's behalf.

Remember, though, that connection pooling and load balancing can only be used on the server and only if the Multi-Threaded Server option is configured and available. You can also use the Oracle Connection Manager to multiplex or funnel multiple client network sessions through a single transport protocol connection to an MTS destination. This is known as *connection concentration,* and it reduces the demand on resources. By using connection concentration, you can maintain multiple connections between two processes and enable the server to use fewer connection end points for incoming requests. Thus, when you use connection concentration, you increase the total number of network sessions that a server can handle. Carrying this idea one step further, if you use multiple Connection Managers, you can enable thousands of concurrent users to connect to a server. By using the Connection Manager and Multi-Threaded Server, the number of supported connections increases geometrically.

To enable the connection pooling feature, you must use the attribute **pool**, and you can use any of these optional attributes: **connections**, **sessions**, and **ticks** in the **mts_dispatchers** parameter, as explained in Table 11-1. Let's go back to the example I used earlier when I showed you how to calculate the number of initial dispatchers you need. Modifying that example to enable one dispatcher to support 5000 connections with 1500 sessions each over TCP/IP, and 3000 connections with 1000 sessions each over SPX, here's how you enable connection pooling:

```
mts_dispatchers="(protocol=TCP)(dispatchers=1)(pool=ON)(tick=1)(connections=5000)
(sessions=1500)"
mts_dispatchers="(protocol=SPX)(dispatchers=1)(pool=ON)(tick=1)(connections=3000)"
```

You can also configure a pool of MTS dispatchers to support a specific client request. Let's say you have heavier traffic to the order area for skingwaddles than to any other area. You can configure a general dispatcher to support all of the general connections to the SKDL database and one specifically to support the skingwaddles orders in the SKDL database. Here's how you can accomplish this task:

```
service_name=SKDL.XYZCORP.US.COM
instance=SKDL
mts_dispatchers="(protocol=TCP)"
mts_dispatchers="(protocol=TCP)(service=ORDERS.SKDL.XYZCORP.US.COM)"
```

Prespawn Dedicated Servers

I've spent a lot of time telling you about Multi-Threaded Servers and how to configure and work with and tune them. However, there are other options available for you to use to help improve connection performance if you feel that MTS is not quite right for your environment. For example, you can use prespawned dedicated servers to handle your client connection needs.

I touched briefly on prespawned dedicated servers in Chapter 6. Let's review what was said earlier in the book and take a closer look at this option here. With dedicated servers, you have the choice of precreating, or prespawning, connections to the database before any connection requests have been made, or spawning each dedicated server process at the time a request is received.

Overview of Prespawned Dedicated Server Processes

If you decide to prespawn dedicated server processes, you will take an initial resource hit as each connection starts, but the connections will be available immediately when they are needed. The problem with this is that once the processes have been spawned, they remain available throughout the entire life of the listener. Therefore, if you prespawn ten dedicated server connections and use only two of them, the resources used by the other eight processes are wasted and remain unavailable to the system until the listener is shut down.

If you decide to have dedicated processes created as they are requested, your clients will have to wait while the requested process is started. Each time a client disconnects from a dedicated server connection that is not prespawned, the resources are reclaimed by the system. What happens when you have more connections requested than you have prespawned processes? Oracle will simply begin to create dedicated processes on request, reclaiming resources as they disconnect, until you are back to the original number of prespawned processes.

Let me summarize the advantages of using prespawned dedicated servers. With this feature, you reduce the amount of time it takes for each client request to make a connection because you've eliminated the need to create a dedicated server for each new request. Since the prespawned dedicated server processes remain available for the life of the listener, you provide better use of allocated memory and system resources by recycling servers without having the overhead of shutting down and re-creating server processes. This option is great for networks where MTS is not supported or where creation of new server processes is slow and resource intensive.

NOTE
Prespawned dedicated servers are not available for Windows NT.

Configuring Prespawned Dedicated Server Processes

Now that you are completely convinced that you want to use them, how do you establish prespawned dedicated server processes? Can you guess what you have to do? I've given you a hint already because I've mentioned that they are started when you start the listener. Therefore, you should be able to guess that you must place the appropriate parameters in the listener.ora file. But what are the appropriate parameters? Let's take a look. Table 11-9 shows the parameters that you can use to enable this feature.

You can either manually modify the listener.ora file to enter the appropriate parameters, or you can use the Net8 Assistant to enable prespawned dedicated server processes. The entries in your listener.ora file will be similar to the following:

```
sid_list_listener=
(sid_list=
```

```
(sid_desc=
 (global_dbname= SKDL.world)
 (sid_name= SKDL)
 (oracle_home=D:\Oracle\Ora81
 (prespawn_max=25)
 (prespawn_list=
  (prespawn_desc=
   (protocol=TCP)
   (pool_size=4)
   (timeout=5))))))
```

Parameter	Description
PRESPAWN_MAX	The maximum number of prespawned dedicated servers that the listener can create. This number must be at least as many as the sum of the pool size for each protocol. Set this value to a large number so that prespawned dedicated servers are always available for new connections.
PROTOCOL	The protocol on which the listener creates prespawned dedicated servers.
POOL_SIZE	The number of unused prespawned dedicated servers for the listener to maintain on the selected protocol. Choose a number that is greater than 0 but no greater than the PRESPAWN_MAX value. The value should be about what you expect the average number of connections to be at any given time.
TIMEOUT	Time in minutes that an inactive prespawned dedicated server process waits for the next connection. The value should be greater than 0. A value of 0 enables an inactive shadow process to continue indefinitely, thus wasting machine resources. Set a short timeout value. The timeout is activated only after a prespawned dedicated server process has carried a connection and been disconnected. In other words, prespawned dedicated servers that are waiting for their first connection do not time out.

TABLE 11-9. *Listener.ora Parameters to Enable Prespawned Dedicated Server Processes*

In this example, the maximum number of prespawned server processes that can be used is set to 25. The minimum number of prespawned processes that will be started is 4, and the time that a process will wait for a new connection is five minutes. Remember that the timeout value only applies after the prespawned process has been used once. Until then, the timeout value has no effect on the process.

PART III

Oracle Networking and the Internet

CHAPTER 12

About the WebDB Listener

When you were a kid, did you ever dream about what your occupation would be when you grew up? I always wanted to be a woodworker. I love to work with my hands and love to build things. Do you? Of course, I've tried my hand occasionally at putting a bookshelf together and have had very good results, but when I tried to carve a piece of wood and make something even remotely recognizable, I didn't do very well at all. The good news is that I can build wonderful databases and have been known to build a few really beautiful software applications.

If you also enjoy building things, Oracle Corporation has a terrific tool that you can use to build enterprise portals to the Internet. Since you've already read the title to this chapter, you know that I'm about to introduce you to Oracle's browser-based software known as WebDB. But, what you may not know is that I'm not going to tell you very much about WebDB itself. I intend to focus primarily on a piece of the WebDB tool set known as the WebDB listener. Yep, that's right. WebDB comes with its own listener, and you need to know how to install and configure it in order for the rest of the WebDB product set to work properly. I must warn you, though, that Oracle is currently working on a new listener that is tentatively named the Oracle Internet Listener. The new listener will be based, from what I've been told, on the Apache listener software. Since the new listener may not be available for a while, I want to tell you as much as I can about the current WebDB listener. Okay? Let's get started then.

NOTE
This chapter is based on Oracle WebDB Version 2.2, which was the most current release available at the time of publication. Since then, Oracle WebDB 3.0 Production has been released as well as a beta version of WebDB, renamed "Internet Portal."

About WebDB

Although I intend to spend most of this chapter telling you about the WebDB listener, you would probably think I was remiss if I didn't give you at least a basic understanding of what WebDB is and how it works.

I recently sat in a half-day workshop where the WebDB product set was overviewed. I found it a bit confusing because I didn't see how the pieces fit together. I hope that I can tell you about all of the WebDB components more clearly.

When you hear the word "portal," what do you think of? I think of an old *Star Trek* episode where Captain Kirk and a few of the crew stepped through a huge circular portal and ended up in another place at a much earlier time in history. They had quite an adventure before they found their way back to their original place and time. With that show in mind, I'd be tempted to say that a portal is a doorway or entry point through which you can travel to various other places of interest. In reality, when you hear someone say that she is building an enterprise portal, you can pretty safely assume that she is developing an Internet Web site as an entryway to a company's information area. Did you ever notice how, periodically, there are buzzwords that all of the technology people we encounter have latched on to? A "Web-based portal" seems to be one of those phrases currently in use.

A Look at WebDB Features and Listener

WebDB contains several different features that make it a really easy product for less technical people to use to produce interactive Web applications. One of the most interesting aspects of WebDB is that everything that is generated to describe and run an application is stored directly to a database. Because everything is saved within a database, WebDB provides a centralized environment for management, monitoring, tuning, protection, and maintenance of the applications and data by trained Oracle professionals like you and me.

Anyone who has been granted the correct privileges can add or manage content within a WebDB application without knowing how to write sophisticated programs. In fact, you don't even have to know how to program in Perl, HTML, Java, SQL, or C. The tool does all of the language translation for the user. In this way, people can communicate with each other both rapidly and globally.

Now that I've sold you on the wonderful aspects of WebDB, I think I should tell you that this product is an extra-cost item that does not come bundled with your standard Oracle software purchase. However, it has so many neat features that I think you should at least be aware of the product set.

The WebDB listener is a lightweight HTTP Web server that enables you to build and deploy PL/SQL-based Web applications and serve static files. Bundled with the WebDB listener is a PL/SQL gateway that functions in a similar manner to the Oracle Application Server PL/SQL Cartridge with a bit more functionality. This means that Database Access Descriptors (DADs) are used to capture the database connection information for an application and to resolve URLs to the correct PL/SQL procedures that have been requested.

If you already have a Web server and don't want to use WebDB's server, you can install the WebDB cartridge or the WebDB Common Gateway Interface instead. The Oracle-supplied installation documentation for WebDB tells you how to perform these installations.

Installing the WebDB Listener

Normally, when you perform an Oracle software installation, you are shown the amount of space that the software is projected to use on your system. When you install WebDB 2.2.0.0.5, you are not shown any space allocation requirements. On my Windows NT machine, the installation took about 100 megabytes of disk space. However, the majority of the WebDB installation resides in your designated database.

The WebDB installation documentation tells you that part of the installation is performed with the regular listener and database shut down and part is performed with the database up and running. This makes sense since you can't store the

WebDB schema to a database that is not online and running. The documentation also tells you to create a new Oracle home for the WebDB installation. Whether or not you create a new directory to house the WebDB files, you are prompted for a company name and Oracle home directory to use. The default Oracle home directory that's displayed is your registered Oracle home directory name and location. If you accept these values, you'll be prompted to go back and enter a different location and directory name. If you enter a directory name and location that do not currently exist on your system, the installation software will automatically create the directory for you.

You are given the choice of performing a typical or custom installation. I selected the recommended typical installation. The majority of the installation is very straightforward. Keep in mind though that the WebDB installation is going to create a network directory of its own, with its own configuration files and listener information. Let's pick up the installation from the beginning of the WebDB listener installation. Ready?

Before You Begin Installation

Before you begin your WebDB installation, I recommend that you open the installation documentation that comes on the WebDB disk. The documentation supplies you with the information that you need to effectively get started, including the fact that you must have the SYS password available to you and enough space within the tablespace you are planning to use to support each WebDB Web site you intend to run. You must also have administrative privileges on the machine from which you are planning to run WebDB. I'm not going to cover all of the installation requirements here because there are different requirements for different platforms, and the total tool installation is a bit outside the scope of this book. However, having said that, I will tell you that along with deciding what directory name and location you are going to use, you must determine the port on which you want the WebDB listener to perform its listening duties.

The default port for the listener is 80. If this port is not being used for any other purpose, the installation documentation recommends that you use 80 as your port number. Because browsers and Web servers use port 80 to communicate, by using this port number for your WebDB listener, you enable URLs to be entered without the need to enter a port number. Keep in mind, though, that UNIX systems usually reserve port numbers below 1024 as system ports. Therefore, on a UNIX system, if you use port 80, you may end up needing root privilege to run the WebDB listener. I should tell you that the installer tells you the Web listener *must* be started by root.

To determine what ports are currently in use on your machine, you can enter the command **netstat –a**. Figure 12-1 shows a sample output from my Windows NT machine.

As you can see from the illustration, there are many ports assigned or currently in use, but port 80 is not among them. Therefore, when I performed my WebDB installation and configuration, I used that port number, as you will see in the screen prints I made. I'll show you the steps I took to install the WebDB listener very soon.

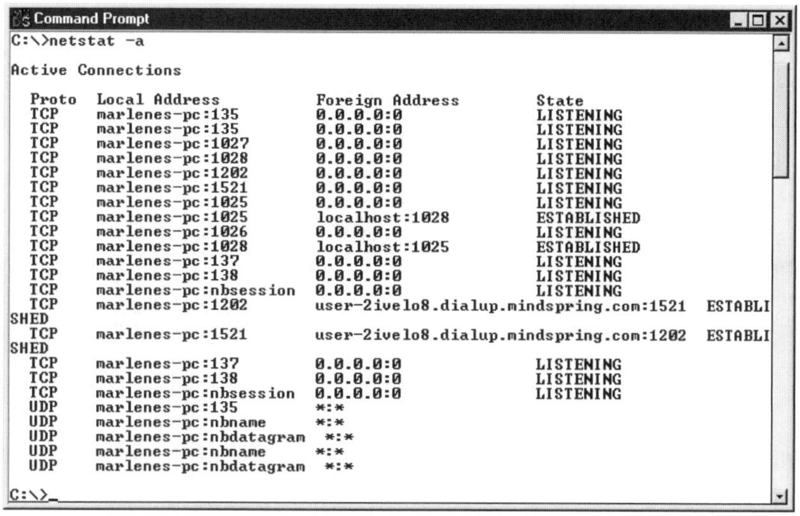

```
C:\>netstat -a

Active Connections

  Proto  Local Address          Foreign Address        State
  TCP    marlenes-pc:135        0.0.0.0:0              LISTENING
  TCP    marlenes-pc:135        0.0.0.0:0              LISTENING
  TCP    marlenes-pc:1027       0.0.0.0:0              LISTENING
  TCP    marlenes-pc:1028       0.0.0.0:0              LISTENING
  TCP    marlenes-pc:1202       0.0.0.0:0              LISTENING
  TCP    marlenes-pc:1521       0.0.0.0:0              LISTENING
  TCP    marlenes-pc:1025       0.0.0.0:0              LISTENING
  TCP    marlenes-pc:1025       localhost:1028         ESTABLISHED
  TCP    marlenes-pc:1026       0.0.0.0:0              LISTENING
  TCP    marlenes-pc:1028       localhost:1025         ESTABLISHED
  TCP    marlenes-pc:137        0.0.0.0:0              LISTENING
  TCP    marlenes-pc:138        0.0.0.0:0              LISTENING
  TCP    marlenes-pc:nbsession  0.0.0.0:0              LISTENING
  TCP    marlenes-pc:1202       user-2ivelo8.dialup.mindspring.com:1521  ESTABLI
SHED
  TCP    marlenes-pc:1521       user-2ivelo8.dialup.mindspring.com:1202  ESTABLI
SHED
  TCP    marlenes-pc:137        0.0.0.0:0              LISTENING
  TCP    marlenes-pc:138        0.0.0.0:0              LISTENING
  TCP    marlenes-pc:nbsession  0.0.0.0:0              LISTENING
  UDP    marlenes-pc:135        *:*
  UDP    marlenes-pc:nbname     *:*
  UDP    marlenes-pc:nbdatagram  *:*
  UDP    marlenes-pc:nbname     *:*
  UDP    marlenes-pc:nbdatagram  *:*

C:\>_
```

FIGURE 12-1. *In-use port report*

Oh, can you feel the tension and excitement building? I, for one, can hardly wait to show you the installation steps!

If you choose a typical installation, the components shown in Table 12-1 will be installed to support WebDB on your system.

Component	Description
WebDB 2.2	Software that enables you to create a Web site based on an Oracle database
WebDB Listener 2.2	Allows you to use your Web browser to access the database
PL/SQL Web Toolkit 4.0.8	Allows you to write Web-enabled applications
Required Support Files 8.0.5.1	Files required by the WebDB listener
SQL*Loader 8.0.5	Installed in the Oracle home where you install WebDB
SQL*Plus 8.0.5	Installed in the Oracle home where you install WebDB

TABLE 12-1. *WebDB Software Components Used in a Typical Installation*

If you opt to perform a custom installation, all it means is that you can install the WebDB tools and WebDB listener during separate installations. Since this book is specifically Oracle8i based, I selected the Oracle8i option. This option assumed that I was installing WebDB locally. If you are installing WebDB in an earlier version, you are prompted for whether the installation is local or remote.

WebDB Listener Installation Steps

Well, the magic moment has arrived. Here are the steps I used and the associated screen prints to perform the WebDB installation. I'm picking the installation up at the beginning of the WebDB listener installation and configuration. The documentation tells you to have the database up and running and then tells you that the installation tool will prompt you to shut the database down while you leave the installation running. Later in the installation process, the tool instructs you to start the database back up while the installation is still running.

The first WebDB installation screen used to begin the listener configuration is shown in Figure 12-2.

As you can see, you are prompted for the SYS password, TNS names alias, host machine name, and WebDB listener port number. When you type the SYS password, it will remain hidden from view, and an asterisk (*) is displayed for each letter that you type. The TNS names alias is the service name that you are using or the database in which the installation will store the WebDB schema. The host machine name is the

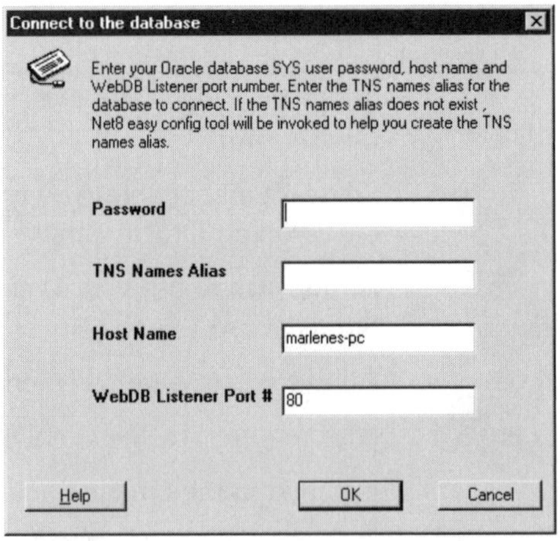

FIGURE 12-2. *"Connect to the database" information screen*

name or IP address of the machine on which the database resides, and the port number defaults to 80. You can, of course, use another port number.

If you enter a TNS names alias that is not currently in the WebDB home directory network configuration file, you receive the warning message displayed in Figure 12-3. You are told that the Net8 Easy Config wizard is going to start so that you can create the appropriate entry.

Since the Net8 Easy Config tool is not shipped with Oracle8i, Release 2, I have not shown you the tool screens yet. Let's "walk through them" now.

Net8 Easy Config Wizard

The first screen you see, shown in Figure 12-4, is the Service Name wizard welcome screen. As you can see, I've entered the database service name, SKDL.world, which I want to use for the new service. By default, there are a number of example services configured and present when you start the tool.

Oh, I forgot to mention that when the wizard started, I was notified that there were comments found in the current file, and I was prompted to accept the fact that information might get overwritten or moved to another location within the file. This is a normal Net8 Easy Config message. Since this was the first time I was opening the file, I accepted the action. However, if I had already performed manual configuration within the file, I would have hesitated to accept the override since my manual configuration could be overwritten. It has been my experience with lower versions of this product that manual configuration entries sometimes do disappear after a Net8 Easy Config session. I just mention this so you'll be aware of the possibility if you use this tool for future WebDB service name configuration and you've entered any service names manually.

In the next screen, you are prompted for your network protocol type. Since you are given the option to test the network connection later in this wizard, you should have the database running and available by the time you get to this screen. Figure 12-5 shows the network protocol registration screen.

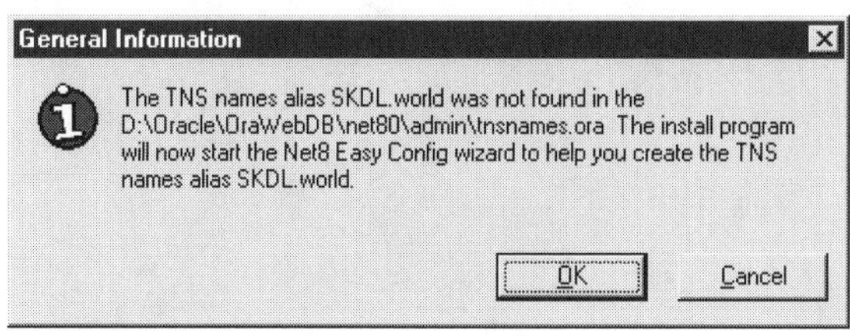

FIGURE 12-3. *TNS names General Information screen*

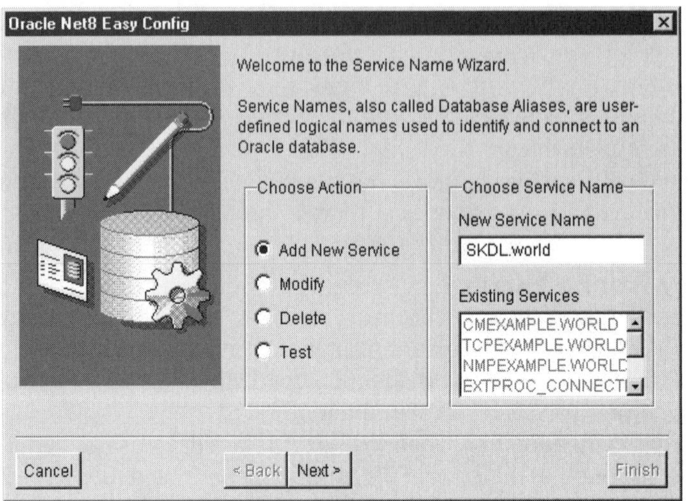

FIGURE 12-4. *Net8 Easy Config Service name welcome screen*

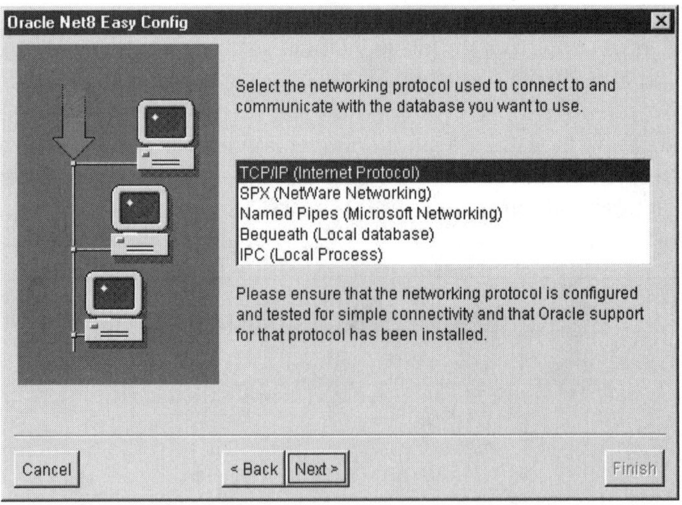

FIGURE 12-5. *Net8 Easy Config network protocol screen*

For the next step in the service name creation, you are prompted for the host machine name and port number on which the standard listener machine is listening. As you can see in Figure 12-6, I've entered my machine name, MARLENES-PC, and the port number on which my network listener is listening.

The next step in the process of creating a service name entry is to enter the name of the database that you are going to use to store your WebDB schema and tool information. Figure 12-7 shows the wizard screen on which you enter the database information. I've entered SKDL for my database.

As you've seen with the other Oracle Net8 configuration tools, the next screen enables you to test the service name to ensure that you can connect to the location in question. Figure 12-8 shows the screen from which you launch the test. Since you've already seen the test screens before in Chapters 6 and 8, I won't show them here again.

The next screen you see is a "thank you" screen with the prompt to click on the Finish button to complete the service name creation task. Figure 12-9 shows this screen.

The WebDB installation resumes with a notice that you have successfully created the TNS names alias. Once you have completed the TNS names alias

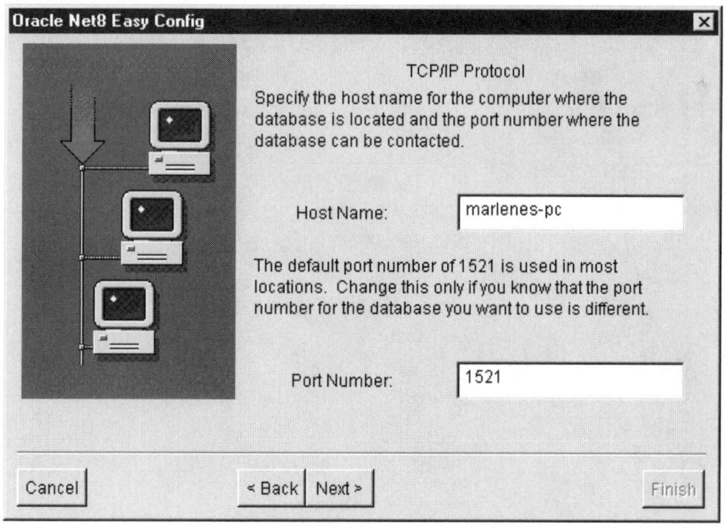

FIGURE 12-6. *Net8 Easy Config host and port information screen*

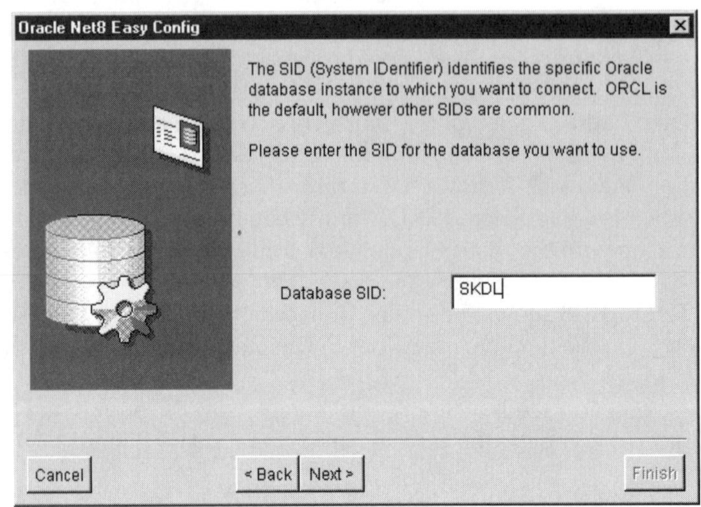

FIGURE 12-7. *Net8 Easy Config database information screen*

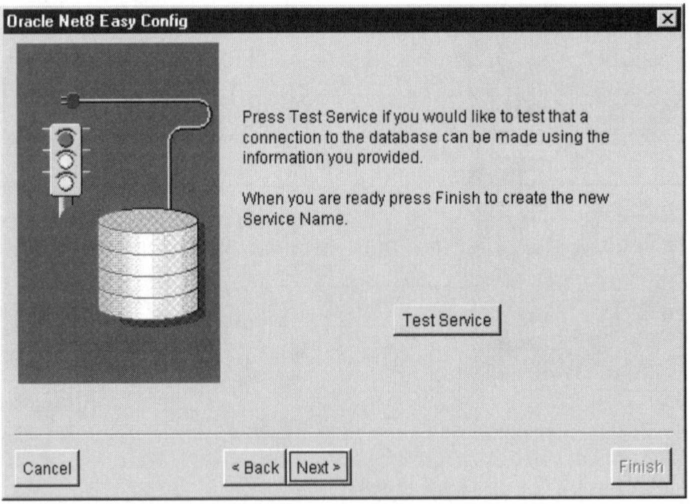

FIGURE 12-8. *Net8 Easy Config test service screen*

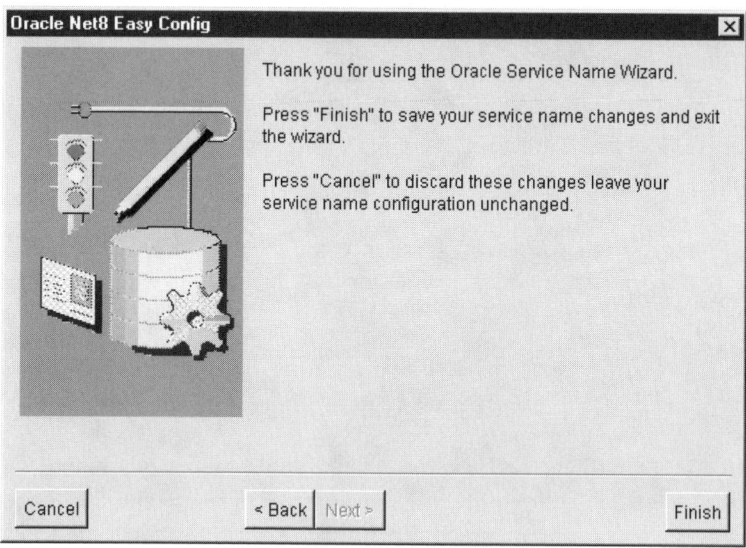

FIGURE 12-9. *Net8 Easy Config thank you/finish screen*

configuration, you are presented with the environment screen prompting you for the WebDB schema location, default tablespace, temporary tablespace, and document tablespace locations. Figure 12-10 shows this screen with the default values that are used. Notice that you can use the pull-down option on each tablespace listed to select another tablespace. You must ensure that for each tablespace you select, you have enough space to support the required areas. Oracle recommends that each tablespace have at least 25 megabytes to 30 megabytes of space available for WebDB's use. Figure 12-10 shows the WebDB schema and tablespace selection screen.

The next screen you will see is an informational screen telling you that the password for your WebDB user is WEBDB. Since the screen only has one line that says, "Note that the password for WEBDB is WEBDB," there really isn't much need to show you this screen.

Having acknowledged the password for the WebDB schema, you are then prompted to add any languages besides English, which is automatically installed. Figure 12-11 shows the screen that you will see with some of the other available languages.

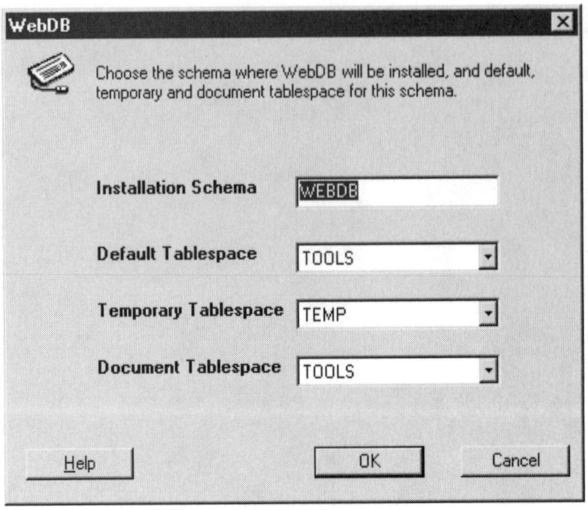

FIGURE 12-10. *WebDB schema and tablespace selection screen*

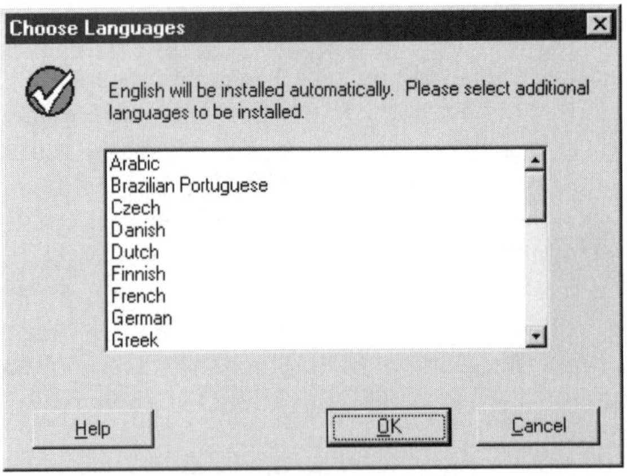

FIGURE 12-11. *WebDB installation Choose Languages screen*

After you've selected any languages besides English that you want WebDB to be able to use, you receive the following message to acknowledge: "Oracle WebDB 2.2 installation will start now. You cannot cancel during this process. Do you want to continue?" Your response choices are Help, Yes, or No. The default value is Yes.

The actual installation process runs for a while before you see the "installation complete" screen that will be similar to, but not exactly like, the screen shown in Figure 12-12.

The really important pieces of information on this screen are the username/password and the listener modification location information. Notice that the very bottom of the graphic text is chopped off. Based on the location for the gateway.htm file, I am assuming that the listener.htm file is located at http://marlenes-pc:80/admin_/listener.htm. Let's start my Internet Explorer browser and go to that location and see what's there. Okay?

After Installation Actions

I must be honest with you. After I performed my WebDB initial installation, I got hungry, shut down my machine, and went to lunch. I didn't continue working. Since I have my services on my Windows NT machine set to "manual" mode, I have to go start my listener and database services. It will only take me about a minute.

Hmm, while I was starting my services, I noticed that I now have two new services available. Can you guess what they are? One is set to start automatically and is labeled "Oracle WebDB Listener." It was already running when I went to start my database and listener. The other service, which was set on manual start, is labeled "OracleOraWebDBClientCache80." We'll have to look into what that

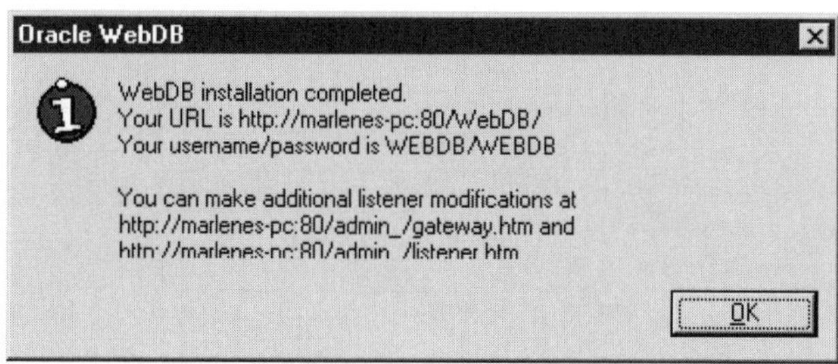

FIGURE 12-12. *WebDB "installation complete" screen with important information*

service does in a little while. Right now, I'll start my browser and access the HTML page that was listed in the final WebDB installation screen shown in Figure 12-12. Wow! The location I typed in was http://marlenes-pc/WebDB/admin_/listener.htm, and Figure 12-13 shows the page that was displayed. Now, remember that since I defined my listener port as 80, which is the default port for Internet browsers and listeners, I don't have to specify the "80" in my URL.

As you can see from the scroll bar, there's more information on the page than is being displayed on the screen. The page contains various environment configuration parameters and their current settings for the WebDB listener. The page is divided into several sections, as shown in Table 12-2.

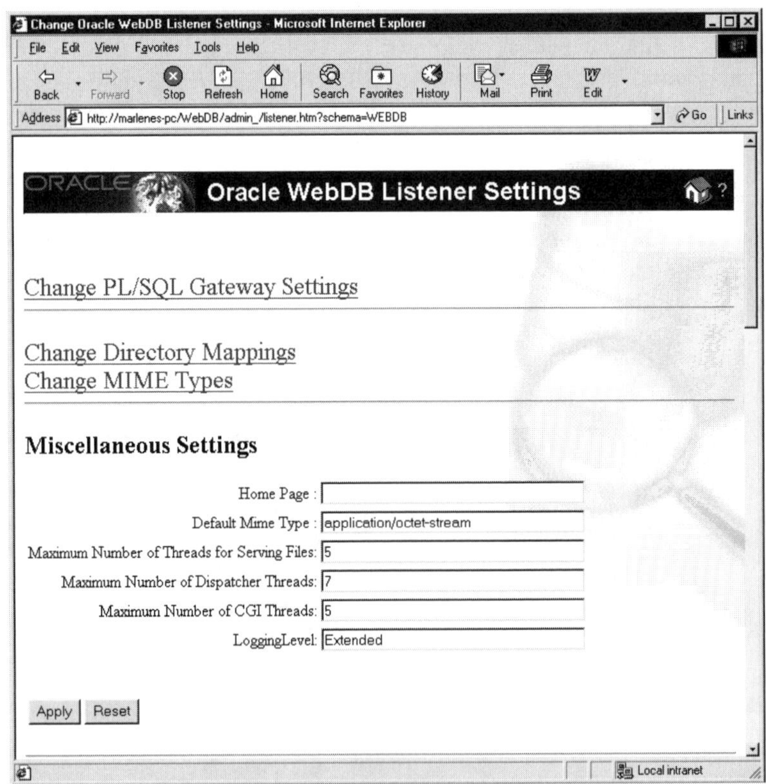

FIGURE 12-13. *Oracle WebDB Listener Settings page*

Section	Components
Miscellaneous Settings	Home page location, default MIME type, maximum number of dispatcher threads for serving files, maximum number of dispatcher threads, maximum number of CGI threads, and logging level
Directory Mappings	Physical directory locations and virtual directories
CGI Directory Mappings	Physical directory locations and virtual directories
MIME Types	By default, 17 MIME types listed with their file extensions, with room to define several more (see Table 12-3)

TABLE 12-2. *Oracle WebDB Listener Settings Page*

In Table 12-2, there are two references: directory mapping and CGI mapping. Hmm, what's the difference? Well, according to my technical reviewer, Ian Fickling, directory mappings are used in conjunction with the Oracle WebDB listener. The CGI directory mappings have to be configured if you're going to use WebDB with a Web server/CGI interface, like Netscape or Microsoft, instead of the WebDB listener. The scope of this chapter is the WebDB listener. However, there is a lot of information about CGI on the Internet. The following links are good references:

- http://www.cgi-resources.com
- Http://www.bignosebird.com
- http://www.cgi-free.com
- http://www.cgiforme.com

The default MIME types are shown in Table 12-3.

MIME Type	Extension
audio/x-wav	.wav
text/html	.htm I .html

TABLE 12-3. *MIME Types and Associated File Extensions*

MIME Type	Extension
image/jpeg	.jpg I .jpeg I .JPG
image/gif	.gif I .GIF
text/plain	.txt I .jsg I .1st
application/pdf	.pdf
application/powerpoint	.ppt I .PPT
application/msword	.doc I .dot I .DOC I .DOT
application/x-tar	.tar I .TAR
application/zip	.zip
text/edi	.edi
application/excel	.xls I .XLS
x-world/x-vrml	.vrml
application/x-gzip	.gz I .Z
application/x-director	.dcr
application/oracle-magic	.yyy
application/oracle-video	.mpi I .mpg I .osf

TABLE 12-3. *MIME Types and Associated File Extensions* (continued)

Now, let's go over to the PL/SQL Gateway page and see what's there. Figure 12-14 shows a piece of this page. As you can see, the page includes the global settings for the Database Access Descriptor (DAD) and database access descriptor settings information for the database that I used to house my WebDB schema. Notice that the username and password are not filled in for the database access descriptors.

By default, the configuration file for WebDB is stored in a file called wdbsvr.cfg in the directory <WebDB_home>\listener\cfg.

Starting and Stopping the WebDB Listener

If you are running more than one WebDB listener, you must start and stop the listeners manually from the command line prompt or from a batch job. If you want to ensure

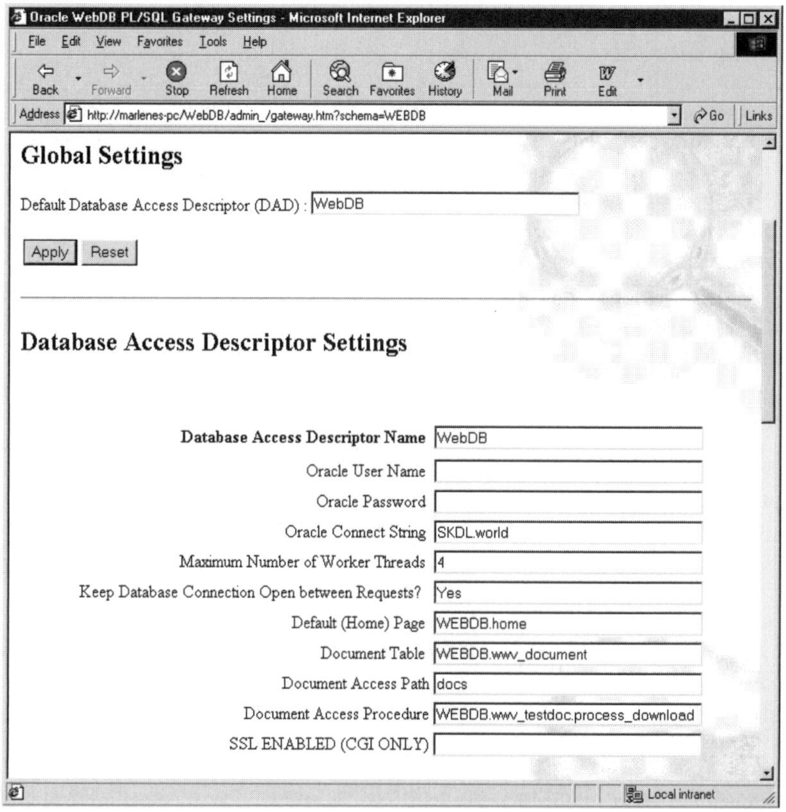

FIGURE 12-14. *Oracle WebDB PL/SQL Gateway Settings screen*

that you are starting and stopping the WebDB listener(s) yourself, you must go to the services screen and reset the WebDB listener service from automatic to manual. To accomplish this task, choose Start > Settings > Control Panel > Services, and move the scroll bar down until you see the entry for the WebDB listener. Select the entry and select the Startup button. From the Startup screen, choose Startup Type – Manual, and then select OK. Close the Services and Control Panel screens. Once you have ensured that the WebDB listener startup is set to manual, you can start and stop the WebDB listener from the command line prompt by opening a DOS window and issuing the appropriate start or stop command as follows:

```
wdblsnr <host> <port> start
wdblsnr <host> <port> stop
```

Unlike the other Listener Control utility, if you just type **wdblsnr**, you will not see a list of commands displayed. Using my configuration, the commands look like the following example:

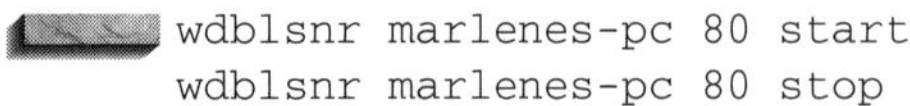

```
wdblsnr marlenes-pc 80 start
wdblsnr marlenes-pc 80 stop
```

Here's some additional information for WebDB on UNIX. As mentioned earlier, the WebDB listener must be initiated by root. To allow root to start the listener, the following environment variables must be set: WV_GATEWAY_CFG and LD_LIBRARY_PATH. For example, using Korn shell (ksh), and with the assumption that root always has the $ORACLE_HOME environment variable set, to define the variables, you'd type something like the following:

```
$ export WV_GATEWAY_CFG=$ORACLE_HOME/webdb/listener/cfg/wdbsvr.app
$ export LD_LIBRARY_PATH=$ORACLE_HOME/webdb/lib:$LD_LIBRARY_PATH
```

Now, if the webdb/lib directory is not set, you will receive the message

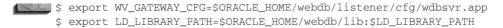

```
ld.so.1: wedlsnr: fatal libclntsh.so.1.0: open failed. No such directory
```

Also, when you issue the following syntax, it's a good idea to run the Web listener in the background; so place an ampersand (&) after a blank space at the end of the command.

```
wdblsnr <host> <port> [start|stop]
```

For example, if you want to start the Web listener that will run on MARLENES-PC on port 80 in background mode, you type the following at the operating system prompt:

```
wdblsnr marlenes-pc 80 start &
```

You can even add **nohup** to the command. That way, if the shell that started the listener is terminated, the listener will continue to execute. The command **wdblsnr** does not automatically run in the background the same way as **lsnrctl** does.

NOTE
Do not try to alter the owner and permissions of ***weblsnr*** *so that it is owned by root and runs with root permission, and then try and execute it from the ORACLE UNIX ID. This approach does not work.*

Running Multiple Virtual Hosts

You can set up WebDB to run multiple instances of the WebDB listener, referred to as multiple virtual hosts, on the same machine. By running the WebDB listener from the command line, you can start more than one instance of the listener. In the following example, two instances of the listener are started using two different Web addresses. One instance of the listener is bound to www.marlenesite.com and the other to www.nelsonsite.com.

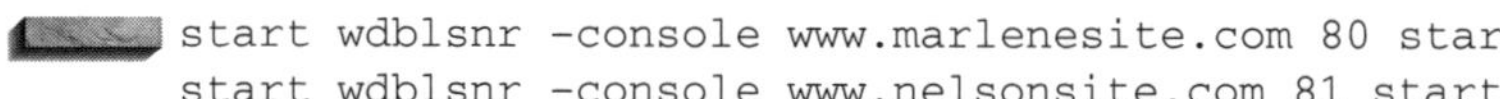

```
start wdblsnr -console www.marlenesite.com 80 start
start wdblsnr -console www.nelsonsite.com 81 start
```

If you start the WebDB listener from the Windows NT services screen, you can only run one listener. The configuration file is defined by the variable **wv_gateway_cfg**, and this variable can only hold one value if you use the services screen. To get around this problem and run more than one listener, you can write a script to establish the correct environment variable and read the appropriate configuration file before starting an instance of the listener. A simple batch file, which starts the two instances of the listener used just now, would look like the following:

```
SET WV_GATEWAY_CFG=D:\Oracle\OraWebDB\listener\cfg\wdbsvr.app
start wdblsnr -console www.marlenesite.com 80 start
SET WV_GATEWAY_CFG=D:\Oracle\OraWebDB\listener\cfg\wdbsvr2.app
start wdblsnr -console www.nelsonsite.com 81 start
```

If you edit the registry using **regedit** on Windows NT, you can have the batch file run automatically at start-up. You want to add the pathname for the location of the batch file to the following registry location. Go to

```
\HKEY_LOCAL_MACHINE\SOFTWARE\Microsoft\Windows\CurrentVersion\Run
```

Once you are at this location, select Edit and create a new string value pair. Since the name is arbitrary, choose something meaningful like "WebDB Listener," and make the data value the location of the command file to be run when the system starts.

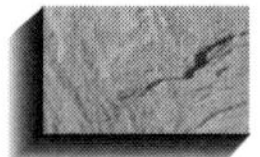

NOTE

As I've mentioned in other chapters, editing the Windows NT registry is risky at best. Therefore, be sure to make a backup copy of the registry before you make any changes or additions to it.

How to Access Static Files

At the beginning of this chapter, in the initial overview of WebDB, I mentioned that you could access static files using the WebDB listener. Why would you want to do this? Well, you may want to launch another WebDB application from a static HTML page. To accomplish this task, you must modify the listener's virtual directory mapping to point the appropriate URLs to your local file system.

Remember when I showed you the WebDB Listener Settings page in Table 12-2? Well, if you look at this table, you'll see that one of the configuration areas enables you to map a physical directory location to a virtual directory. You can access the page by starting your Web browser and going to the page located at http://<your host : port>/admin_/listener.htm. In my example, the location is http://marlenes-pc:80/admin_/listener.htm. Figure 12-15 shows the screen print for this location for the directory mapping area. Although there appear to be two directory mapping areas on the screen, you are really only mapping one physical directory location to one virtual directory location.

Notice the instruction just above the Physical Directory/Virtual Directory area, which tells you to be sure to end each entry with a slash. To use the WebDB listener to access static files, perform the following steps:

1. Copy the static files that you want to access to a directory location of your choice.
2. Type the name of the directory location you have moved the files to in the Physical Directory field.
3. Type a short name to associate to the physical directory in the corresponding Virtual Directory field, and click Apply.

That sounds really easy, doesn't it? The only qualification on this action is that the file has to be of a type recognized by the listener's MIME type settings as shown in Table 12-3. Look through the settings that are available. To add a MIME type to the current settings, enter the string for the MIME type in the left column of the MIME Types area and enter the appropriate file extensions in the right column. To verify that the WebDB listener can recognize the new directory mapping, you can test it from your browser by accessing the file, using the following syntax:

```
http://<server_name>:<port>/<directory>/<filename>
```

Since I'm sure by now that you're sick of hearing about Windows NT tests, here's the approach that Ian used to successfully test this from his UNIX environment. For some example htm files, he copied the files in his directory, $ORACLE_HOME/webdb/listener/cfg/*.htm, to his /tmp/testhtm directory. In the

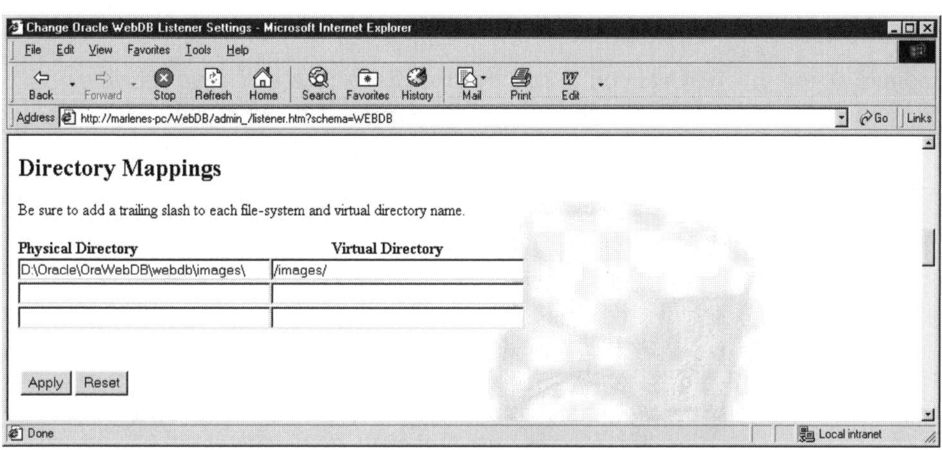

FIGURE 12-15. *WebDB listener Directory Mappings page*

WebDB listener configuration for directory mappings, he mapped /tmp/testhtm/ to /testhtm/. He found that he could then use a Web browser to see the HTML document http://avenger:80/testhtm/dbdown.htm.

Examining the Configuration Parameters

Although editing the configuration files manually is recommended only for advanced WebDB users, I think that you should at least see what each of the parameters is within each of the configuration files. Therefore, I'd like to show you the parameters with a brief description of each.

Remember that there are two different parameter files: wdbsvr.app and wdbsvr.cfg. Table 12-4 shows the parameters available in the wdbsvr.app file.

Parameter	Description
[WVGATEWAY]	Marks the start of the gateway section.
defaultDAD	Specifies a path that points to the default DAD. If the end user types a WebDB URL without specifying the DAD name, the home page for the default DAD will be displayed. Default: WebDB

TABLE 12-4. *Wdbsvr.app Parameters*

Parameter	Description
administrators	Allows you to specify those users who will have access to WebDB's administration pages (gateway.htm, listener.htm). By default, this is set to "all," which permits any user to access these pages. To enforce security on these pages, type a comma-separated list of users (administrators). For example: administrators = user1,user2,user3@webdb Only the users who log on as user1, user2, and user3 with the correct password can access the gateway settings page on the WebDB host (using a connect string, like @webdb). Default: All
adminPath	The virtual directory location containing the gateway files. For example, the end user can type the following to display the gateway page: http://myhost/WebDB/admin_/gateway.htm?schema=WEBDB, where /admin_ is the adminPath Default: /admin_/
debugModules	Used to generate complete logging information. This parameter is enabled only when a problem is encountered and logging information is required by an Oracle representative to help resolve the problem. Default: Commented
[DAD_WebDB]	Marks the start of the first Database Access Descriptor (DAD) section. In this case, the DAD is named "WebDB." The WebDB's URL is based on this DAD name. You can change this name by typing a new name. Default: WebDB
connect_string	Type the tnsnames alias if you are using a remote database. Leave this parameter blank if the database is local. Default: Blank
password	Refers to the Oracle database account password. The password is typically set at WebDB installation, but you can change it by typing a new password for this parameter. **Note**: There should always be an Oracle username and password for PUBLIC Web site DADs. This enables public users to access the WebDB site without having to log on. Default: Blank

TABLE 12-4. *Wdbsvr.app Parameters* (continued)

Parameter	Description
username	Refers to the Oracle database account username. The username is typically set at WebDB installation or during creation of new WebDB sites. You can change it by typing a new name for this parameter. Default: WebDB
default_page	Refers to the WebDB default home page. You can change it by typing a new name for this parameter. Default: webdb.home
document_table	(For DADs related to the WebDB Site Builder features only.) Type the name of the database table to be used for storing uploaded files. The default value for this parameter is based on the name of the schema in which you created the WebDB site. Default: webdb.www_document
document_path	(For DADs related to the WebDB Site Builder features only.) Type a path in the URL for the current installation that is used to indicate a document being referenced. The default value for this parameter is based on the name of the schema in which you created the WebDB site. Default: Docs
document_proc	(For DADs related to the WebDB Site Builder features only.) Type the procedure that will be used to upload and download documents. Default: Based on the name of the schema in which you created the WebDB site. For example: webdb.wwv_testdoc.process_download
after_proc	To execute a particular stored procedure after execution of any other stored procedure. For example: after_proc = webdb.show_footer This stored procedure would display the footer after a stored procedure is executed. Default: Commented (null)
before_proc	To execute a particular stored procedure before execution of any other stored procedure. For example: before_proc = webdb.show_header This stored procedure would display the header before a stored procedure is executed. Default: Commented (null)

TABLE 12-4. *Wdbsvr.app Parameters* (continued)

Parameter	Description
reuse	Allows you to choose whether, after processing one URL request, the database connection should be kept open to process future requests. In most configurations, specify Yes for maximum performance. Default: Yes
conmax	Type the number of simultaneous connections allowed to the database that will be used to service applications. **Tip**: You'll need to adjust this number depending on your server, its capacity, and the number of connected users. As a rule of thumb, set this number between 5 and 10 at a medium-sized installation (approximately 200 users). Default: 4

TABLE 12-4. *Wdbsvr.app Parameters* (continued)

For each WebDB site, three DADs are created: public, private, and administrator. You must configure each DAD section according to the information shown in Table 12-4.

Table 12-5 shows the parameters available in the wdbsvr.cfg file.

Parameter	Description
[SERVER]	Marks the start of the Server section.
HomePage	Refers to the WebDB default home page. You can change it by typing a new name for this parameter. **Note**: The setting for this parameter overrides the default DAD setting in the gateway configuration file, wdbsvr.app.

TABLE 12-5. *Wdbsvr.cfg Parameters*

Parameter	Description
DefaultMimeType	Displays the MIME type that is used by the listener when a MIME type for a given URL request can't be determined. Default: Application/octet-stream
LoggingLevel	Displays how much logging information will be captured by logging files located in the listener log directory. You can use this information for debugging purposes and for performance analysis. You may want to test the following Logging Level settings to determine how much logging information you want to capture: NONE, STANDARD, TEST, ETEST, EXTENDED, ERROR, DEBUG, EDEBUG Default: EXTENDED
MaxCGIThreads	Not used for WebDB CGI. This parameter is currently used by Oracle Reports. Default: 5
MaxFileThreads	Displays the number of threads that serve static files off the file system. As a rule of thumb, increasing the number of threads improves performance, although this is contingent on operating system limitations. Default: 5
MaxDispatcherThreads	Displays the number of threads used to dispatch HTTP requests. As a rule of thumb, increasing the number of threads improves performance, although this is contingent on operating system limitations. Default: 7
MaxQueueSize	Connection requests from clients are queued up to a maximum queue size. This parameter determines the maximum length of the queue for pending connections on the listener socket. If a connection request arrives and the listener queue is full, the client receives an error, "Connection Refused." Default: 64

TABLE 12-5. *Wdbsvr.cfg Parameters* (continued)

Parameter	Description
ReceiveTimeOut	This parameter determines the number of seconds the listener will wait to receive data from across the network before it signals a timeout. This parameter should be configured according to your network connection. If you have a really slow network connection, you may want to increase this parameter so that the listener waits longer before timing out. For example, to set the timeout to two minutes, add the following line: ReceiveTimeOut=120 Default: 60 (seconds)
OnlyClient	This parameter can be used to restrict access to the WebDB listener so that only a specific client can access it. This parameter can be set to a specific IP address, and only a client having that specific IP address will have access to the listener. For example, setting this value to the following, OnlyClient=144.25.84.254, will restrict access so that only a client with an IP address of 144.25.84.254 can access the listener.
[DirMaps]	Marks the start of the directory mapping section. It is used to map virtual directories specified in your WebDB URL to physical directories on the file system.
[CGIDirMaps]	Marks the start of the CGI directory mapping section; currently used with Oracle Reports and Oracle Forms.
[MIMETypes]	Marks the start of the MIME types section. Each line contains the type of file and the file extension(s) that WebDB recognizes. WebDB MIME types are used when returning content to the browser as a result of a URL request. Default: All the MIME types are shown in Table 12-3.

TABLE 12-5. *Wdbsvr.cfg Parameters* (continued)

Troubleshooting WebDB Listener Problems

Unfortunately, the only symptom you may get when there's a WebDB listener problem is a very cryptic error message from the browser. The message may be completely meaningless but will serve to let you know that there is a problem. As with the Net8 listener troubleshooting procedures recommended in Chapter 14, using a step-by-step approach to determine what's really wrong can save you a great deal of time in the long run.

Generally, problems encountered by the WebDB listener are caused by conflicts with other software that is running on the same machine. By default, the WebDB home page address is http://<your machine name>:<port>/webdb/, where **webdb** is the DAD for your WebDB installation. Remember, if you defined port 80 for your WebDB listener, the port number can be eliminated.

Now, for machines that are not on your network, it's possible that host name resolution might not tell the browser to look on your local machine until after a network DNS lookup has timed out.

The most obvious problem you may encounter is that either the WebDB listener has not actually been installed or the listener hasn't been started and isn't currently running. To verify that the WebDB listener is installed and running, on a Windows NT server, look in the Services dialog box and verify that there is an entry for Oracle WebDB Listener and that the service is marked as started. For a UNIX system, check for the system process, wdblsnr.

Now, just because the WebDB listener appears to be installed and running, do not assume that the listener is really functioning properly. To verify that the listener is really able to process URL requests, use your browser and see if you can reach the following URL without receiving a timeout error: http://<your machine>:<port>/admin_/gateway.htm. If your browser does time out, there's a very good chance that the WebDB listener has been configured to listen on a port that's being used by another process. Since several different Web listeners are generally configured to listen on port 80, if you've chosen that port number and another listener is using it, your WebDB listener may not be able to access the port, and the browser attempt will fail. In any event, it can't hurt to restart the WebDB listener and attempt to access it again.

If there doesn't seem to be any conflict with port assignments and the listener is functioning properly, you should see the WebDB PL/SQL Gateway Settings page. If you don't see this page, there could be a problem with the syntax you used to define a DAD. You see, the Keep Database Connection Open selection is case sensitive. This parameter requires that the first letter be capitalized. Something as simple as the response in all caps or all lowercase can keep the WebDB listener from performing properly.

CHAPTER 13

The Oracle Advanced Security Option

I have a very personal question to ask you. What makes you feel secure? Having a steady job, a little money in the bank for emergencies, enough food in the refrigerator to feed you and your family for several days, a car that is in good mechanical shape, a comfortable place to live? All of the conditions I've just listed are very subjective. The elements that help to make you feel very secure might not give me the same sense of security because we each have different needs and different frames of reference. Even the word "security" can mean different things to you than it does to me.

Now, think about what computer security means to you. Do you think of your hardware behind locked doors in a separate room that only select people can access? Or is computer security represented in your mind by the words "firewall," "RSA or DES encryption," or a specific brand of software like Kerberos, CyberSafe, or RADIUS? And what place do biometrics like scanning a person's fingerprints, facial features, or eyes and then comparing the obtained images with those kept on file for system access have in your security world? With the introduction of eCommerce and business-to-business (B2B) Internet access, has the word "security" taken on a whole new meaning in your life?

In this chapter, you and I are going to look at the Oracle Advanced Security product suite. This product set was formerly two different software packages: Oracle Advanced Networking Option and the Secure Network Services. Please keep in mind that this product set comes as an extra-cost item to you. License to use the Oracle Advanced Security products is not included with your basic Oracle8i, Release 2 bundle. Also, you must have licensed and installed the Oracle8i Enterprise Edition since Oracle Advanced Security and its components are not available with Oracle8i Standard Edition.

I'm including the information on this product set to give you an opportunity to learn about its features and to give you a better understanding of how Oracle uses Net8 for security purposes.

Overview of the Oracle Advanced Security Products

I have another question for you. This one isn't personal at all. Which of these actions do you think is safer: placing an order for goods using your telephone, placing an order for goods using the Internet, or making a purchase in person using your charge card? Oh, you don't ever use a charge card? Wonderful!

Well, in reality, any one of these options is about as safe as any other. The problem isn't usually placing the order or making the purchase. The security problem is introduced in the way your personal information is protected on the company's server or the actions that the person who processes your charge card takes! Even if your card is never completely out of your sight, you may still be at risk. You see, any time you make a purchase with your VISA, MasterCard, American Express, Discover, or other brand of charge card, you are enabling anyone who holds your card to make an extra imprint of it or copy the charge card number after you have left the establishment.

In a recent newspaper article, it was reported that a woman in New York was arrested for copying charge card information into her handheld personal assistant. The woman worked at a restaurant, and each time she processed a customer charge, she swiped the card twice, once into the company charge card machine and once into her personal assistant. The only reason she was caught is that the customer watching her thought he detected her swiping the card more than once and reported the action to the restaurant manager.

Now that I've convinced you never to make a charge card purchase again, here are some other computer-related security risks that you should consider. As you've seen throughout this book, data is broken into formatted packets and moved from one computer over a network of cables, routers, and possibly insecure landlines, via microwave and satellite links or other equipment, to its destination. There is a risk that someone will intercept the packets and either view or modify the data within them. The reality is that you can eavesdrop pretty easily on network traffic using a network sniffer if you have one available and know how to use it.

Just as the employee at the restaurant could potentially steal your identity using your charge card information, a user on a computer can falsify an identity to gain access to private company information. In a widely distributed computing environment, it's possible for a connection request to be intercepted and routed to a terminal masquerading as the server you are attempting to reach.

Now, let me ask you this: How many different passwords do you have to use in your daily work life? Gee, I'm just full of questions for you, aren't I. At the height of my database management activities, I had over 40 different passwords to remember. Of course, we used a system that helped make it easier for me to remember each server, database, and account password I had to keep track of, but things still got a bit confusing every once in a while. Users are generally asked to remember more than one password to access different applications with which they interact. What are the most common things that a user will do when faced with remembering multiple passwords? Here's my list:

- Write them down on post-it notes and stick them in an "inconspicuous" place, like the side of their terminal screen or inside their desk drawer
- If they select their own passwords, use the same password or slightly different variations of the same word for every account
- If they select their own passwords, use easily guessed words, like names of family members or pets or fictional characters

And, of course, the most obvious thing a user can do with complicated passwords: Forget them! The last action requires the most effort on the part of administrators and support staff. According to an article I read in an airline magazine, the entire employee base in San Diego County's city of Oceanside log on to their computers with a fingerprint scanner rather than username and password. Why did the city implement this method of computer access? Well, quite simply, the employees kept forgetting their passwords, and the management of their system was being steadily impacted. An employee is not likely to forget or lose his or her fingerprint. If you are a season pass holder for Disney World in Orlando, Florida, access to the park is geared to your fingerprint, and in Texas and Arizona, about 180 automatic teller machines (ATMs) employ face-recognition biometric devices to enable customers to access their funds at grocery and convenience stores. You can expect to see the same kind of machines in casinos in Nevada as well. If you aren't already doing so, you may soon be able to access your own Compaq laptop or notebook computer with a scan of your finger. Amazing technology for unique feature recognition is just around the corner.

If people can access your data as it moves from one place to another on your network, they can just as easily modify that data to your detriment and their advantage. For example, let's say that you are performing a bank transaction where you are transferring $100 from your checking to your savings account. Someone accessing your transaction could change the amount from $100 to $10,000 and have the transaction written to their account instead of yours.

Any of the activities I've mentioned here, from identity theft to user carelessness, can compromise your computer systems and the data you are charged with protecting.

Oh, the Language That They Use

To begin our exploration of the Oracle security suite, let's look at some general security terminology so that we can be sure we understand the jargon. What I'm going to do is list the words that are most often used and give you a brief explanation of each one. Table 13-1 shows the words and their description. I've tried to show the words that I think are the most commonly used and potentially misunderstood. A few of the descriptions presented here were taken from the *Oracle Advanced Security Administrator's Guide, Release 8.1.6.*

Now that you've seen some of the jargon, let's take a look at the security options offered within the Oracle Advanced Security products to help you protect your company's data assets.

Term	Explanation
Access Control List (ACL)	Grants levels of access on data for specific clients or groups of clients.
Algorithm (used for security)	A computer program used to implement an encryption and decryption method.
Authentication	Verification of a user, device, or other entity before allowing access to resources within a computer system.
Authorization	Permission to access an object or set of objects within an operating system or database. Permission can be granted to a specific user, program, or process. Within an Oracle database, permission is granted through roles or as individual grants.
Certificate	Electronic certification that the entity's name, identifying information, and public key are valid and actually belong to the entity. A certificate is signed by a trusted identity like a certificate authority. A certificate usually contains information about the authority that issued it as well as a serial number, expiration date, and information about the rights, uses, and privileges associated with the certificate.
Certificate authority	A trusted third party that certifies that other entities are who they say they are. When a certificate authority generates a certificate, the authority verifies the user's identity and that the user is not on the certificate revocation list. The certificate authority signs the certificate using its private key. The certificate authority has its own certificate and public key that it publishes for servers and clients to use to verify signatures that have been made by the certificate authority. Certificate authorities can be external or internal to a company.

TABLE 13-1. *Common Security Terms*

Term	Explanation
Certificate revocation list (CRL)	A list of all entities whose certificates have expired or been revoked.
Cipher suite	A set of authentication, encryption, and data integrity algorithms used for exchanging messages between network nodes. During an SSL handshake, for example, the two nodes negotiate to see which cipher suite they will use when transmitting messages back and forth.
DES	U.S. Data Encryption Standard.
Digital signature	Created when a public key algorithm is used to sign a message and assures that the document is authentic, has not been forged by another entity, has not been altered, and cannot be repudiated by the sender.
HTTPS	Hypertext Transfer Protocol using the Secure Sockets Layer as a sublayer under the HTTP application layer.
Identity	Combination of public key and other public user identification data, such as an email address, that establishes an entity as who it claims to be.
MD5	An algorithm that assures data integrity by generating a unique, 128-bit cryptographic message digest value from the contents of a file. If as little as a single bit value in the file is modified, the MD5 checksum for the file will change. Forgery of a file in a way that will cause MD5 to generate the same result as that for the original file is considered extremely difficult.

TABLE 13-1. *Common Security Terms* (continued)

Term	Explanation
Network authentication service	A means for authenticating clients to servers, servers to servers, and users to both clients and servers in distributed environments. It is a repository for storing information about users and the services on different servers to which they have access, as well as information about clients and servers on the network, and can be a physically separate machine, or a facility co-located on another server within the system.
Public-key encryption	The sender encrypts a message using the public key of the receiver. The received message is decrypted using the receiver's private key.
Public/private key pair	A set of two mathematically related numbers. One is called the public key and the other is called the private key. The public key is usually made widely available, while the private key is kept available only to the key owner. The receiver, using the private key, can decrypt the message. A message encrypted with a public key cannot be decrypted with the same public key.
Secure Hash Algorithm	An algorithm that produces a 160-bit message digest from any message of less than 264 bits in length. This is slightly slower than MD5 but considered more secure against brute-force collision and inversion attacks.
Secure Sockets Layer (SSL)	An industry standard protocol for securing network connections. SSL provides authentication, encryption, and data integrity using public key infrastructure.

TABLE 13-1. *Common Security Terms* (continued)

Term	Explanation
Service ticket	Trusted information used to authenticate a client to a service.
Session key	A key shared by at least two parties, usually a client and a server.
Smart card	A device similar to a credit card with an embedded integrated circuit read by a hardware device at a client or server. The smart card generally stores a username and password for user identification.
Wallet	A storage mechanism used to manage security credentials for a user. A *wallet* implements the storage and retrieval of credentials used with various cryptographic services.
Wallet resource locator	A directory path that provides all of the information necessary to locate a specific wallet.
X.509	An ISO data format in which public keys can be signed.

TABLE 13-1. *Common Security Terms* (continued)

A Look at Oracle Advanced Security Features

The Oracle Advanced Security option offers many features that enable you to protect your company's valuable data. These features include the ability to transmit and receive data in an encrypted form using either RSA or DES encryption. Before you even ask, let me tell you about these forms of encryption.

In Chapter 4, I used a very simple cypher to introduce the idea of net service names translation. Remember that you listed the letters of the alphabet once, beginning with the letter *a*, and then shifted a certain number of letters over and again wrote the alphabet below the original entries. The pattern looked like this:

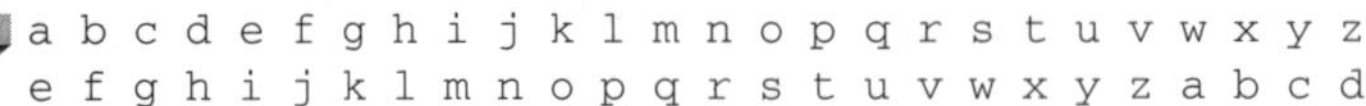

```
a b c d e f g h i j k l m n o p q r s t u v w x y z
e f g h i j k l m n o p q r s t u v w x y z a b c d
```

This is called a simple substitution code because you substitute one letter for another in your message. It's not only very easy to use but also very easy to break. I believe that you had no trouble decoding the message I gave you back in Chapter 4.

Since computers can be programmed to easily solve encryption methods that are much more complex than this, more and more difficult encryption schemes have been developed to help maintain data privacy. The two most popular approaches, available through the Oracle Advanced Security option, are RSA and DES encryption.

RSA, DES, MD5, and SSL Features

What do you think is the best approach you can use to help keep an encryption method effective? How about if the key could be randomly generated each time you needed to encrypt something? Having a constantly changing encryption key would help thwart thieves from easily stealing your data. RSA encryption uses an algorithm called the RSA Data Security RC4 encryption algorithm. This computer program uses a secret, randomly generated key that is unique for each user session. By changing the encryption key each time a session begins, all network transmissions between the client and server for the session should be protected. The client and server can either request or require that encryption be used. The performance penalty for the overhead of encrypting and decrypting any transmission between the client and server is listed as minimal.

When an encryption algorithm is applied to a message, the key that is used can be 40 bits, 56 bits, or 128 bits in length. Obviously, the longer the encryption key, the more difficult it is to compromise the encrypted message. The U.S. government has laws restricting the shipment of software that provides more than 40-bit and 56-bit implementations. Therefore, Oracle provides an export version that complies with these requirements.

Now, what's the difference between RSA encryption and DES encryption? Well, basically, the U.S. Data Encryption Standard (DES) is required for use by financial and many other institutions. The current standard is a 56-bit encryption key, but there is a 40-bit encryption key provided for backward compatibility.

Okay, so you, as the client, have your message being encrypted when you send it, decrypted at the server, the response encrypted from the server, and decrypted when you receive it. That's all well and good, but how can you be sure that the message wasn't tampered with in transit? How can you prove that it wasn't intercepted and replayed before you or the server received it? Great questions!

The action of examining packets as they flow through a network is commonly referred to as *packet sniffing,* although the more formal reference is to communication line and local area network monitoring. Packet sniffing is designed to be passive and noninvasive. Read that as "invisible." So, just looking at a packet does not change the checksum of that packet. However, intercepting and retransmitting with changed data will generate a new checksum for the new data in a packet.

Remember that normal packet checksums are calculated and included at level 2, the data-link control level, of the OSI model. You can see the layers of the OSI model in Chapter 1, Table 1-3. These checksums are most frequently provided in the hardware. Checksums, typically referred to as cyclic redundancy check or CRC, are used for error identification—that is, to verify the integrity of the data in the packet. The transmitter generates the CRC as it sends the data, and appends the CRC to the end of the packet. The receiver, including a line monitor or LAN sniffer, recalculates a CRC as it reads the data and compares its calculated CRC with the one in the data. If the checksums fail to match, the data very likely has errors or has been tampered with.

To ensure that a message isn't tampered with in any way, Oracle Advanced Security features enable a cryptographically secure message digest to be generated and attached to the message. The message digest is generated using the MD5 algorithm to create a cryptographic checksum. This checksum is different from the normal, standard checksum that the hardware layer generates and is included with each packet that is sent across the network. If any of the packets are tampered with, the checksum won't match the packet contents.

Use of the Secure Hash Algorithm (SHA) is allowed through the Oracle Advanced Security Secure Sockets Layer feature. The SHA option is slightly slower than MD5, but the message digest that it produces is larger. Thus, the message is more secure against brute-force collision and inversion attacks.

Authentication

If I say to you, "Prove who you are," what would you do? If you were at home, you would probably produce a driver's license with your picture on it, a birth certificate, credit card, library card, passport, or some other document that has your name and possibly a picture on it. Since at the time I ask you to prove who you are, I can see you, my verification of your identity becomes as easy as comparing your features with any picture you show me. If you don't produce a picture, verifying your identity becomes a bit more problematic. I'm forced to accept whatever documents you have as proof and take your word for your claim to be who you say you are. Again, because I can look directly at you, I can try to gauge if you are being truthful as you produce your documents.

Let's move our scene to a computer environment. Since you are now at one computer anywhere in the world and I'm at another computer probably somewhere else, I can't look at you or your paperwork to verify that you are who you say you are. If we are both on the same network, behind a firewall, I can probably accept your identity at face value and just think to myself that since you were able to gain access to a computer on our network, you are probably who you claim to be.

However, you could be entering my system from the Internet outside of my closed network and without a firewall. In that case, I really have no absolute way of knowing that you are you. The most common form of authentication method in use today is that of username and password. If they are sent over the network as clear text, the chance that they could be intercepted and used by a third party is pretty high. Oracle Advanced Security, Release 8.1.6 provides authentication through Oracle authentication adapters. These adapters support various third-party authentication services like Kerberos, RADIUS, and so forth. We'll look more closely at these products a bit later in this chapter.

About Single Sign-On

Earlier in this chapter, I asked you how many passwords you are currently keeping track of. Wouldn't it be great to be able to say, "Oh, just one." A feature that's available in the Oracle Advanced Security product set, called single sign-on, enables users to authenticate themselves once with a centralized authentication mechanism and then access multiple accounts without having to authenticate themselves again.

Oracle supports several third-party products that provide single sign-on capabilities within your system. Table 13-2 shows these products with a brief description of each one.

Product	Description
Secure Sockets Layer (SSL)	SSL is an industry standard protocol for securing network connections that provides authentication, data encryption, and data integrity. SSL contributes to a public key infrastructure (PKI). SSL is used to secure communications from any client or server to one or more Oracle servers or from an Oracle server to any client. You can use SSL alone or with other authentication methods, and you can configure SSL to require server authentication only, or both client and server authentication.
Remote Authentication Dial-In User Service (RADIUS)	RADIUS is a client/server protocol that enables remote authentication and access using a variety of authentication mechanisms such as token cards, smart cards, and biometrics.
Kerberos and CyberSafe	Used with Oracle Advanced Security, these products provide single sign-on and centralized password storage, database link authentication, and enhanced PC security. Kerberos is a trusted third-party authentication system that relies on shared secrets and assumes that the third party is secure. CyberSafe TrustBroker is a commercial Kerberos-based authentication server.

TABLE 13-2. *Third-Party Authentication Methods*

Product	Description
Smart cards (RADIUS compliant)	A device similar to a credit card with an embedded integrated circuit read by a hardware device at a client or server. The smart card generally stores a username and password for user identification. Because a smart card reader located at the client workstation reads it, a user can log in from any workstation equipped with a smart card reader.
Token cards (SecurID or RADIUS compliant)	Token cards look like a small calculator and have a keypad. Some token cards dynamically display a one-time-use password synchronized with an authentication server. Other forms of token cards work on a challenge-response basis. The server presents a challenge. The user enters the challenge into the token card and presses a key. The token card furnishes a response that the user types in to the server.
Biometric authentication (Identix or RADIUS compliant)	Identix biometric authentication is used to communicate fingerprint-based authentication data between the authentication server and client. This form of authentication is used on both the clients and Oracle servers. Other RADIUS-compliant biometric authentication devices can be integrated with Oracle Advanced Security to authenticate Oracle users.
Bull Integrated System Management (ISM)	Offered by Bull Worldwide Information Systems, this product provides a variety of management tools for system administrators. However, this authentication method is only available on AIX platforms.

TABLE 13-2. *Third-Party Authentication Methods* (continued)

User Authentication

Before we get into authentication, let's take a look at how a user is authenticated by a network authentication server. Here are the steps that are followed:

1. A user attempts to access a server by requesting authentication services. The user provides some form of identification to prove his or her identity.
2. The server authenticates the user and passes a ticket or credential back to the client. The credential is usually stored in the user's wallet in a directory on the user's system or in a central, known directory location. The ticket may or may not contain an expiration date and/or time.
3. When the user requests connection to an Oracle database, the user's credentials are passed to the Oracle server.
4. The server sends the credentials back to the authentication server to confirm that they are valid.
5. The Oracle server is notified if the authentication server accepts the credentials.
6. If the credentials are valid, the Oracle server performs the requested task. If the credentials are not accepted, the Oracle server denies access to the client.

That's pretty straightforward and understandable once you understand all of the underlying terminology and technology, isn't it? Now, let's look at the Oracle Advanced Security architecture.

Authentication vs. Authorization

So far, we've looked at ways in which you can prove your identity. Once you've successfully proven that you are who you claim to be, what happens? Well, just because you've established who you are, you haven't yet proven that you have a right to access a specific server or database. And even after you prove you have the right to access a system, there still must be methods in place to determine what information you are allowed to input, see, modify, or remove.

Oracle8i already provides the standard features of roles and privileges to control user authorization to data within an Oracle database. However, using the authentication methods supported by Oracle Advanced Security, these features are significantly enhanced. On a Solaris platform, for example, Oracle Advanced Security supports distributed computing environment (DCE) authorization. It's true that DCE does have a reputation for being difficult to administer. However, its security features are extremely reliable, which is why DCE is used, in conjunction with Encina, in many banking systems.

In Chapter 5, I told you about the Lightweight Directory Access Protocol (LDAP) and Oracle's implementation of it through the Oracle Internet Directory. You can integrate Oracle Advanced Security with LDAP version 3–compliant directories to deploy the Oracle Internet Directory for user management and authorization storage and retrieval. Be sure you understand the licensing dos and don'ts that are involved with using the two products together. Some things are covered under a single license, while others are not.

Examining the Oracle Advanced Security Architecture

Think back to Chapter 2 when we explored Oracle's implementation of the OSI model. From both the client and server sides, Oracle Advanced Security includes adapters that integrate below the Net8 interface and allow transparent access to the security features without changes or rewrites to existing applications. Basically, what this means is that configuration for the security option is performed below the application layers and, therefore, is transparent to the users and application writers. In reality, you configure Oracle Advanced Security by placing configuration parameters in your sqlnet.ora file. Appendix A at the back of this book shows the range of parameters that you can use to configure sqlnet.ora to support the various security products.

To review just a little, Table 13-3 shows Oracle's general implementation of the OSI model for Net8 for the client side.

Notice that the Net8 layer is broken into three layers: Network Interface (NI), Network Routing (NR)/Network Naming (NN)/Network Authentication (NA), and the Transparent Network Substrate (TNS). When you implement Oracle Advanced Security, three more areas are added to the Net8 layer, as shown in Table 13-4.

It seems pretty obvious to me, but I'm going to say this anyway. If you intend to use an authentication area product like Kerberos or CyberSafe, you must have the products installed on your system in order to configure them for Oracle Advanced Security. Table 13-5 shows the associated products for each of the authentication tools that you may want to use.

If you intend to use Oracle Advanced Security, Release 8.1.6 with an earlier version of Oracle, the only problem you will encounter is that the security

Stack Layer	Description
Oracle-side Programmatic Interface (OPI)	Responsible for responding to each of the possible messages sent by the client-side Oracle Call Interface (OCI). For example, an OCI request to fetch 25 rows would have an OPI response to return the 25 rows once they have been fetched.
Two-Task Common	Resolves character set differences between the sender and receiver.
Net8 (consists of three layers)	Network Interface (NI)—Hides the underlying network protocol and media from the client application. Network Routing (NR)/Network Naming (NN)/Network Authentication (NA)—Takes care of routing the data to its final destination. Transparent Network Substrate (TNS)—Takes care of generic communications such as sending and receiving data.
Oracle Protocol Adapter	Thin layer of code that insulates Net8 from the underlying network protocol.
Network-Specific Protocol	Stack of layers that translates the SQL statement into packets to transmit across the network.

TABLE 13-3. *Oracle's Implementation of the OSI Layers for Net8*

functionality defaults to the earlier release, so you may not have the most current security features available for your system's use.

Setting Up Your Sqlnet.ora Configuration File

In order to enable Oracle Advanced Security, you must put the parameter **sqlnet.authentication_services=** in your sqlnet.ora file with an appropriate value. For example, if you want to enable CyberSafe on your system, the parameter would look like the following:

```
sqlnet.authentication_services=(CYBERSAFE)
```

Area	Feature
Encryption	DES, RSA
Authentication	Kerberos, SecurID, RADIUS, CyberSafe, Indentix
Data integrity	MD5

TABLE 13-4. *Additional Areas in the Oracle Advanced Security Net8 Layer*

Authentication Tool	System/Version Requirements
CyberSafe TrustBroker	CyberSafe GSS Runtime Library, version 1.1 or later, installed on both the machine that runs the Oracle client and the machine that runs the Oracle server. CyberSafe TrustBroker, release 1.2 or later installed on a physically secure machine that runs the authentication server. CyberSafe TrustBroker Client, release 1.2 or later installed on the machine that runs the Oracle client.
Kerberos	MIT Kerberos Version 5, Release 1.1. The Kerberos authentication server must be installed on a physically secure machine.
SecurID	ACE/Server 3.3 or higher running on the authentication server.
Identix Biometric	Identix hardware and driver installed on each Biometric Manager station and client.

TABLE 13-5. *System/Version Requirements for Authentication Tools*

Authentication Tool	System/Version Requirements
RADIUS	A RADIUS server that is compliant with the standards in the Internet Engineering Task Force (IETF) RFC #2138, Remote Authentication Dial-In User Service (RADIUS) and RFC #2139 RADIUS Accounting. To enable challenge-response authentication, you must run RADIUS on a platform that supports the Java Native Interface as specified in release 1.1 of the Java Development Kit from JavaSoft.
SSL	A wallet that is compatible with the Oracle Wallet Manager version 2.1. Wallets created in earlier releases of the Oracle Wallet Manager are not forward compatible.

TABLE 13-5. *System/Version Requirements for Authentication Tools* (continued)

Again, you want to be sure that the necessary products are installed on your system before trying to enable Oracle Advanced Security.

Guarding Against a Security Breach

When you enable Oracle Advanced Security, you want to ensure that the init.ora parameter **remote_os_authent** is set to FALSE. This parameter, if set to TRUE, allows someone using a nonsecure protocol like TCP to gain access to your database without performing a system-authorized login. Hmm, what does that mean?

Well, normally, you have several different options for gaining access to your database. You can create a telnet session, log in to the operating system using a username and password, and connect to the database from the operating system session by supplying another username or password. From a telnet session, you can also take advantage of a mechanism that has been referred to as "OPS$" (pronounced "ops-dollar"). Using the OPS$ approach, you declare a database account as **identified externally**. That nomenclature tells Oracle to allow the account to access the database as long as access is attempted from an operating system account with the same name that someone has successfully logged on to. Oracle accepts the operating system authentication in lieu of database authentication. The mechanism was called OPS$ because, originally, you had to preface the account with these letters. For example, an account for NELSON **identified externally** would have to be created with the username "OPS$NELSON."

To get around having to use the OPS$ nomenclature, you set the parameter to a null value by entering **os_authent_prefix=**"" in your init.ora parameter file. Since you can only create usernames of 30 characters or less in an Oracle database, Oracle Corporation strongly recommends that you set this parameter to null, as shown here, if you are going to use externally identified accounts. Of course, you can set the **os_authent_prefix=** value to any string you want. However, if you already have accounts that are externally identified and rely on a specific string, you won't want to pull the rug out from under them by changing the string or setting it to a null value.

Now that you have a bit of background about externally identified users, what's the problem with **remote_os_authent**, and why do you want to be sure that it's set to FALSE? Well, normally, when you want to use Net8 to access a database, you present a username and password. To use Net8 to make a database connection, you type something like the following,

```
sqlplus NELSON/OHSOSILLY@SKDL
```

or you enter the values in a dialog box from a client machine. If you have set the parameter **remote_os_authent** = TRUE and have a database account with the same username as the client machine name, a user attempting to gain access to your database from that machine does not have to present a username or password for authentication. So, if you have a client machine named MARLENES-PC and you create a database account called MARLENES-PC and have **remote_os_authent** set to TRUE in your init.ora parameter file for the database, anyone who has access to the MARLENES-PC machine can access your database with, possibly, very high privileges. Pretty ugly, huh.

Establishing Encryption

In Chapter 7, we looked at the various Net8 Assistant screens and the values that you can configure using this tool. Because it was out of context in that chapter, I'd like to just briefly review the approach that you can use to establish encryption on your client and server machines.

Following the instructions in Chapter 7, you can bring up the Net8 Assistant main menu screen. From there, select the Local option and click on Profile. From the right-side pull-down options, select Oracle Advanced Security. Once you've selected the Oracle Advanced Security option, you can see the tabs for the security features. They are Authentication, Other Params, Integrity, Encryption, and SSL. The screens are all shown and explained in Chapter 7. To establish the client or server encryption type, you set the encryption level, an encryption seed, and the method that you want implemented, such as DES, RC4-40, DES40, RC4-56, and, in the United States, RC4-128.

There are four encryption values that you can use to negotiate whether encryption and integrity features are to be turned on or off. They are, in order of increasing security, REJECTED, ACCEPTED, REQUESTED, and REQUIRED. REJECTED is the minimum amount of security you can have between a client and server communication, while REQUIRED is the maximum. The default value is ACCEPTED. Table 13-6 shows the values and their translations.

Now, let's look at the *truth table* shown in Table 13-7. To read a truth table, you look at the option on the left side and then look at the meaning along the top line. Where the two values intersect, you can see whether security is enabled. Hmm, that explanation sounded a bit confusing to me, and I'm the one who said it. Let me see if I can explain it using the table as the example to make things clearer. The label that may be a bit confusing is the "Client/Server" at the top-left corner of the table. This label is intended to indicate that the Client values are along the side of the table and the Server values are along the top.

NOTE
When the values are both set to ACCEPTED, cryptography and data integrity are not enabled. The value defaults to OFF.

Value	Translation
REJECTED	Does not enable the security service, even if the other side has required the service. If you specify this option, which disallows security, and the other side requires security, the connection will terminate with an ORA-12650 error. If the other side has enabled any other option besides REQUIRED, the connection will continue without enabling the security service.

TABLE 13-6. *Encryption Values and Their Meanings*

Value	Translation
ACCEPTED	If the other side specifies REQUIRED or REQUESTED, this value enables the security service. The other qualification for enabling security with this option is that an algorithm match be found. If the other side has set the option to REQUIRED and there is no algorithm match, the connection terminates with an ORA-12650 error. If the other side is set to REQUESTED and no algorithm match is found, or if the other side is set to ACCEPTED or REJECTED, the connection continues without error, but no security service is enabled.
REQUESTED	Enables security service if the other side allows it. If the other side is set to ACCEPTED, REQUESTED, or REQUIRED, the security service is enabled. With any of these options, there must be a matching algorithm as well on the other side. If there is no matching algorithm and the other side specifies REQUIRED, the connection will fail.
REQUIRED	Enables or completely disallows the connection. If the other side specifies REJECTED or there is no matching algorithm, the connection fails.

TABLE 13-6. *Encryption Values and Their Meanings* (continued)

Client/Server	REJECTED	ACCEPTED	REQUESTED	REQUIRED
REJECTED	OFF	OFF	OFF	Connection fails
ACCEPTED	OFF	OFF	ON	ON
REQUESTED	OFF	ON	ON	ON
REQUIRED	Connection fails	ON	ON	ON

TABLE 13-7. *Encryption Security Service Chart*

According to the chart, if the server has enabled REQUIRED and the client has specified REJECTED, what happens? To determine the answer to that, begin on the server side and put your finger on the word REQUIRED. Now, look at the entries along the side and find the location of the client's REJECTED option. It's the first entry in the top line. Follow along the column until the REJECTED option intersects with the server's REQUIRED value. What's the result? If you said, "Connection fails," you understand how to read the truth table. Let's try one more to make sure you feel comfortable with this. The server side has specified REQUESTED, and the client side has specified REQUIRED. What is the result? Did you answer that security is turned on? Great! I think you've got it.

You can enable encryption, data integrity, and the other Oracle Advanced Security features using the Net8 Assistant. See Chapter 7 for detailed instructions and screen prints for establishing values for this option, but remember that this is an extra-cost option and you must be licensed to use it.

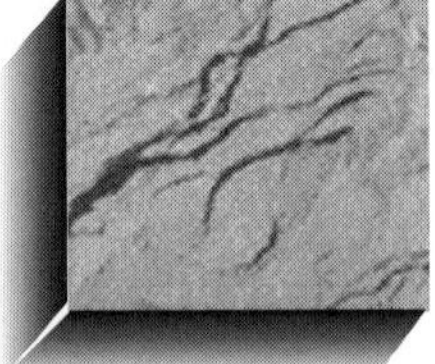

PART IV

Troubleshooting

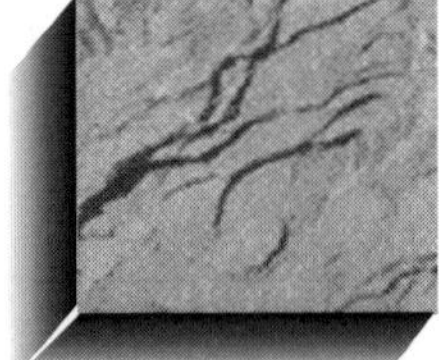

CHAPTER 14

Diagnosing Net8 Problems

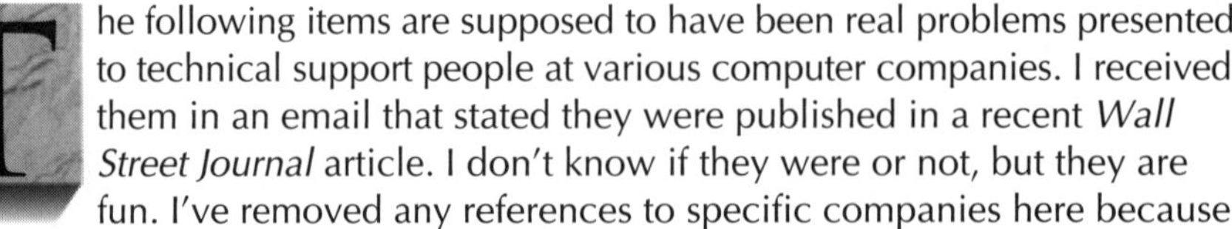

The following items are supposed to have been real problems presented to technical support people at various computer companies. I received them in an email that stated they were published in a recent *Wall Street Journal* article. I don't know if they were or not, but they are fun. I've removed any references to specific companies here because I've heard several of these attributed to more than one computer vendor.

Reported Technical Support Calls

1. A computer company is considering changing the command "Press any key" to "Press the Enter key" because of the flood of calls asking where the "any" key is.
2. A technical support person had a caller complain that her mouse was hard to control with the dust cover on. The dust cover turned out to be the plastic bag the mouse was packaged in.
3. A technician received a call from a man complaining that the system wouldn't read word-processing files from his old diskettes. After troubleshooting for magnets and heat failed to diagnose the problem, it was found that the customer had labeled the diskettes and then rolled them into the typewriter to type the labels.
4. Another customer was asked to send a copy of her defective diskettes. A few days later a letter arrived from the customer along with Xeroxed copies of the diskettes.
5. A technician advised a customer to put his troubled floppy back in the drive and close the door. The customer asked the technician to hold on and was heard putting the phone down, getting up, and crossing the room to close the door to his office.
6. Another customer called to say he couldn't get his computer to fax anything. After 40 minutes of troubleshooting, the technician discovered that the man was trying to fax a piece of paper by holding it in front of the monitor and pressing the "Send" key.
7. Yet another customer called to complain that his keyboard no longer worked. He had cleaned it by filling his tub with soap and water and soaking the keyboard for a day, then removing all the keys and washing them individually.

8. A technician spoke to a customer who was enraged because his computer had told him he was "bad and an invalid." The technician explained that the computer's "bad command" and "invalid entry" responses shouldn't be taken personally.

9. An exasperated caller couldn't get her new computer to turn on. After making sure the computer was plugged in, the technician asked her what happened when she pushed the power button. Her response was, "I pushed and pushed on this foot pedal and nothing happened." The "foot pedal" turned out to be the mouse.

10. A customer called support to say her brand-new computer wouldn't work. She said she unpacked the unit, plugged it in, and sat there for 20 minutes waiting for something to happen. When asked what happened when she pressed the power switch, she asked, "What power switch?"

11. This guy calls in to complain that he gets an "Access Denied" message every time he logs in. It turned out he was typing his username and password in capital letters. Tech Support: "OK, let's try once more, but use lowercase letters." Customer: "Uh, I only have capital letters on my keyboard."

Aside from being comical, what do these blurbs have in common? They all deal with people attempting to solve a problem based on either a lack of knowledge, faulty assumptions, or misinterpretation of a message they've received. I don't know about you, but I've occasionally suffered from all of these deficits over the course of my career. And it's very easy to reach the wrong conclusions when you are in the throes of trying to solve a problem that has made your operating system, database, or network unavailable.

General Troubleshooting Guidelines

I think that we all tend to get a bit ruffled when we are under pressure to solve a problem quickly, and it's very easy to get locked into one way of thinking or one specific approach before you have enough information to begin to resolve your problem. Therefore, I'd like to make what I consider to be a very important suggestion right here at the beginning of the troubleshooting chapter: *Never assume anything*! Along those same lines, I'd like to suggest that you keep your Net8 configuration as simple as possible for maintainability. If you have to transfer support from yourself to someone else, the less complicated your environment is, the more easily someone else will be able to pick up where you've left off. You should also document your Net8 environment and keep your documentation up-to-date. I know that it's generally boring and not always easy to keep documentation available and up-to-date. In fact, it's much less fun than almost anything else I can think of. However, having an environment that others can support will free you to more easily pursue other growth opportunities.

In this chapter, I'll give you some steps that you can follow when you are faced with what appears to be a Net8 problem, and approaches you can use to try to solve the problems. I've used these techniques for years and found them to be very helpful. I hope that you'll find them to be effective as well.

Rules You Can Follow

Last night, I couldn't sleep, and I'm afraid I may not be able to sleep tonight either.

What was your reaction to my statement? Did you immediately think of things that you've done to help you sleep? If we were standing together right now, would you tell me you're sorry to hear that I had a problem, or would you begin to make suggestions about things I can do to help me sleep better tonight?

The impulse is generally to begin making suggestions, isn't it? You might say that when you can't sleep you drink a glass of warm milk or read a really boring book or play cards or surf the Internet. Right?

If you remember my earlier suggestion, you will not assume anything, and you might ask me why I couldn't sleep. If you did ask, I'd tell you that there was a cat outside my bedroom window yowling most of the night.

Ah, now that you have some further information, you can see my problem from a different perspective and begin to look at alternate solutions for me to try. With your added insight, you can suggest that I look up the telephone number of the animal control officer in my area or purchase a pair of really sturdy earplugs to use in case the cat comes back. It's amazing how one little detail about a situation can make you see it in a completely new light and send you down an entirely different path towards a solution.

Therefore, aside from recommending that you not assume anything and that you keep things as simple as possible, I'd like to offer these general problem-solving suggestions as well:

- Try to isolate the problem yourself. If a user reports a problem, try to re-create it yourself. If you can, you will probably save yourself time, since you won't have to keep calling back every time you want the user to try something. Also, you will probably get to the root of the problem much faster, and even if you don't resolve the problem yourself, you will be able to describe the problem much better to Oracle Support and be able to tell them what you've tried.

- Be sure you are treating the real problem and not just a symptom.
- Ensure you have all of the available facts.
- Don't be afraid to ask questions.
- Be willing to say, "We don't have enough information yet to draw a conclusion."
- Don't be afraid to change direction or look for an alternate solution.
- Keep all of the available troubleshooting tools in mind (log and trace files, people who are expert in systems administration or network administration, Oracle Worldwide Support, etc.).
- Always try to keep the person who reported a problem informed of the progress you've made. If they can find other things to work on, people generally don't mind too much that it might take a long time to resolve a problem. What they do mind is being kept in the dark.
- Whenever possible, try to give accurate estimates on how long it will take to fix the problem. Keep in mind that it's always better to overestimate and finish early than to underestimate and have to explain "unexpected" delays. Setting your users' expectations on the side of taking longer can really pay off. Unfortunately, things tend not to get fixed as quickly as we would like them to.

While troubleshooting Net8 problems, I've found that there seem to be some errors that crop up repeatedly. My technical reviewer, Ian Fickling, says, "When a system has been working for some time and then suddenly stops working, I often find that it's due to someone somewhere changing a configuration file. A quick way to determine this possibility is to check the dates of the configuration files. A date rather close to 'now' is good cause to look at what has changed by comparing the altered configuration file to the configuration file that was backed up prior to this latest change." This is really terrific advice that I highly recommend.

Here are a few suggestions to keep in mind as we look at some of the problems you might encounter after you've installed, configured, and performed any initial debugging. This section assumes that your installation of Net8 has been functioning well for a while. I'll tell you how to troubleshoot a new installation later in this chapter.

- Be sure the problem is really Net8 and not a general network problem.
- See if you can perform a loopback while logged in directly to the server.
- If a loopback works, test to see if you can connect from a client to the server via Net8.

- If configuring the listener, check listener.ora for mismatched parentheses or syntax errors.
- Check for misdefined tnsnames.ora entries (wrong host name, wrong instance name).
- Verify that the port number is the same in listener.ora and tnsnames.ora for the connection.
- Check the log and trace files for insights into errors that you receive.

Now that you have some objectives in mind, here are some steps you can take to narrow the scope and increase your knowledge about the problem that's been reported to you or that you encountered.

Isolating the Problem

All too often, you receive a call from a user claiming that the "database is down" or that "Oracle is broken." Before you begin to check into the problem, get as much detailed information as you can. Don't be afraid to ask questions, but do try to keep your voice and manner gentle. After all, you don't want your poor user to feel like the Spanish Inquisition has just been revived. You can ask questions like the ones shown in Table 14-1. The table also lists the information you hope to gain from asking the question. You may have to ask the same question more than once or in different ways to gain the information you need to help you begin to solve the problem. Your goal is to determine the real problem and find an effective solution quickly but accurately. The more immediate information you can get about the problem, the better your chance of fulfilling these goals will be.

Question	Information Gained
Which database or application were you trying to access (if you have more than one database or application)?	Database and/or application name and server name. Often a user won't know what database is involved, only what job they were trying to do.
Were you logged in to that database today? What time?	A time frame for the problem.
If not, when was the last time you logged in successfully?	A time frame for the problem.

TABLE 14-1. *Troubleshooting Questions and the Information Gained*

Question	Information Gained
What error message, if any, do you see? Is there a number associated with the message?	The error message and number can indicate whether it's an Oracle, operating system, or network problem.
Have you changed your password recently?	Often, users will change passwords and then forget that they made the change.
What steps have you taken already?	Sometimes users will try different actions to overcome the problem they are having. You are looking for steps they've already taken so that you don't repeat the process. You may be able to suggest an action that they have not thought of that will enable them to connect.
Have you been able to connect to any other database or server today?	Whether the problem is their machine or a specific server or network area.
Have you had any recent trouble with your computer?	A problem with their computer could result in a problem with a connection to a specific database or node, or indicate a client hardware problem.
Have any new products been installed on your computer recently?	A network driver can be overwritten when a new product is installed.
Have any products been upgraded on your computer recently?	A network driver can be overwritten when a product is upgraded.
Can others in your department access the database you are trying to reach?	This could be either a specific user problem or a department-wide problem.
Have one or more files been replaced on your computer recently?	A newer tnsnames.ora file can be overwritten when a directory or a subset of files within a directory is restored.

TABLE 14-1. *Troubleshooting Questions and the Information Gained* (continued)

If you have a large number of databases and applications, you may find it useful to have a chart in front of you indicating what applications connect to which database. That way, if a user says, "I'm having a problem connecting to the accounting database," you will know almost immediately which database has the potential problem.

If it looks like there is a problem connecting to the database, your approach is to first verify that the database is running and then determine whether or not you can connect to it, directly and remotely.

Is the Database Up?

You can confirm that the database is running by checking for the existence of the detached Oracle processes on your UNIX or Compaq OpenVMS system. If your server is a Windows NT machine, you can verify that the Oracle executable is running by using either the CTRL+ALT+DEL keys or a right-click with the mouse within the task bar to access the Task Manager. Check for the presence of oracle.exe for Oracle8i or oracle8.exe for Oracle8 process. Of course, if you are running more than one Oracle database on the system, you must be sure to check for the detached processes for the specific database in question.

Okay, so now you know that the processes are out there. However, it is possible for the database to be down with both the Windows NT service and the Oracle executable running. For example, if someone has brought down the database using **svrmgrl** and issued a **shutdown immediate**, **shutdown abort**, or **shutdown normal** command, you may find that the Windows NT service and Oracle executable are still running. Because it is not always possible to telnet to a Windows NT system, log on to your Windows NT system directly in a privileged mode and use either SQL*Plus or the Server Manager command **svrmgrl** and **connect internal** to access the database directly. Enter a command such as **show sga**. If the output shows something like the following, then the database is up:

```
Total System Global Area                    40396044 bytes
Fixed Size                                     70924 bytes
Variable Size                               23470080 bytes
Database Buffers                            16777216 bytes
Redo Buffers                                   77824 bytes
SVRMGR>
```

For UNIX, telnet to the server and use **svrmgrl** to **connect internal** and issue the **show sga** command. If all is well, then the database is up. If you receive an error during this test, it's possible your environment variables are incorrect or an Oracle detached process such as PMON has died and was unable to restart. Issuing the following command will show you the detached processes. I've included the command and a sample output here.

```
ps -ef | grep ora | grep -v grep

oracle  2387    1  0 21:03:11 ?       0:00 /free/oracle/products/815/bin/tnslsnr
LISTENER -inherit
oracle  2299    1  0 20:23:13 ?       0:00 ora_pmon_orcl
oracle  2301    1  0 20:23:14 ?       0:00 ora_dbw0_orcl
```

```
oracle  2303     1  0 20:23:14 ?        0:00 ora_lgwr_orcl
oracle  2305     1  0 20:23:14 ?        0:01 ora_ckpt_orcl
oracle  2307     1  0 20:23:14 ?        0:06 ora_smon_orcl
oracle  2309     1  0 20:23:14 ?        0:00 ora_reco_orcl
oracle  2311     1  0 20:23:15 ?        0:00 ora_s000_orcl
oracle  2313     1  0 20:23:15 ?        0:00 ora_d000_orcl
```

Once you've confirmed that the database is, indeed, up and running, you must begin the process of determining where the problem really lies.

NOTE
*With Oracle8i, you can use SQL*Plus to perform all the features of the svrmgr command line. You can issue the command* ***sqlplus*** *and connect as* ***internal****.*

Is the Database Available to Nonprivileged Users?

Of course, the next logical question to ask is, "Is the database in restricted mode?" At the risk of posing a security breach, I'd like to share a secret with you. Ready? Okay, here goes: I always keep a nonprivileged account within each database that I manage. I usually call the user for this account something recognizable as a "dummy" account. I use the name of a household item like DISH with a password that's easy to remember by association like WASHER or RAG. The only privilege I give this account is **create session**. For those of you who do not work as database administrators but would like to know this, the syntax for the user creation is as follows:

```
create user DISH identified by RAG
default tablespace USERS temporary tablespace TEMP;
grant CREATE SESSION to DISH;
```

In this statement, I'm using tablespaces named USERS and TEMP. You want to ensure that the tablespaces you declare in your user creation statement are valid tablespace names. Of course, you must have a database account with enough privilege to create a user, or request that the DBA create the nonprivileged user for you.

Remember that you are currently connected directly to the server. Your next goal is to determine whether a nonprivileged user can connect to the database. Therefore, you can use the bequeath process to attempt your connection to the database. At this point, you are not yet ready to determine whether a network problem is involved. By performing these first few quick steps before trying to solve a network problem that may not exist, you can save time and possible unnecessary effort in the long run.

To connect to the database through your nonprivileged account, type

```
sqlplus DISH/RAG
```

where DISH is the username and RAG is the password. If the database is not in restricted mode, you should see a connection header like the following:

```
SQL*Plus: Release 8.1.6.0.0 - Production on Tue May 2 14:34:38 2000
(c) Copyright 1999 Oracle Corporation.  All rights reserved.

Connected to:
Oracle8i Enterprise Edition Release 8.1.6.0.0 - Production
With the Partitioning option
JServer Release 8.1.6.0.0 - Production

SQL>
```

Your screen's appearance will vary depending on what version of Oracle you are using and what options you have installed. The important point here is that the connection worked. So, let's see what we've learned so far:

- The database is up and running.
- The database is not in restricted mode.
- A nonprivileged user can access the database from the operating system level without use of network technologies.

What you have not verified yet is whether the listener, Oracle Names server, and Connection Manager are up and available. Let's check these components next.

Is There a Problem with the Listener, Oracle Names Server, or Connection Manager?

Each of the Control utilities for the network support tools listed here includes a **status** or **stats** command. You can use the command line utilities for the tools that are available on your system to verify that the listener, Oracle Names server, and Connection Manager are available. Here are the commands you can use one at a time to verify that the tools are running:

```
lsnrctl status <LISTENER_NAME>
namesctl status <NAMES_SERVER_NAME>
cmctl stats
```

If any of the processes you use is not running, you've found your problem. If, however, they are up and running, you still must ensure that you can make a successful connection. To test the listener, you can perform a loopback test. I'll tell you how to perform this test in the next section.

To verify that you can reach a specific database server through the Oracle Names server, you can connect to the namesctl and issue the following command:

```
NAMESCTL> ping <MACHINE_NAME>
```

For the machine MARLENES-PC, you type

```
NAMESCTL> ping MARLENES-PC
```

If it is successful, the **ping** command returns the amount of time it takes to contact the Oracle Names server and return an acknowledgment. If it's not successful, make sure that the Oracle Names server you are **ping**ing is really up and running. To review starting and stopping an Oracle Names server, look at Chapter 4.

Performing a Loopback

Assuming that the listener is available, the next step in the troubleshooting process is to determine whether you can connect to the database using Net8. To determine this, you will perform what's known as a *loopback*. You want to perform the loopback while you are still logged on to the server through your telnet session. Using the SKDL instance, here are the steps to follow:

1. Ensure that your current session environment variables are pointing to the correct instance by typing **env | grep ORACLE_SID** on UNIX. For Windows NT at the DOS prompt, you can type **Set ORACLE_SID=SKDL** to ensure that you are pointing to the correct instance.
2. To perform the loopback, type **sqlplus DISH/RAG@SKDL**.
3. If you connect successfully to the database, type **exit**.

If you cannot successfully connect to the database, you know that something in your Net8 environment is the problem. With this result, you can now turn your full attention to solving the problem you have with your listener. I'll tell you how to work through listener problems in depth a bit later in this chapter.

To follow the easiest troubleshooting path first, let's assume that you have connected successfully to the database from your loopback test. You have proven that you can get from the server to the server via Net8.

Making a Client/Server Connection

Keep in mind, the earlier ping that I showed you was a "NAMESCTL> **ping**," which will ping one or more Oracle Names servers. Before you try to make a client/server connection, ensure that the client can perform a **ping** as described earlier so that you can reach the machine you are trying to access. After you are sure you can reach the machine, your next test is to attempt to connect from a client to the server. If you have a client machine in your office that has the Net8 client software installed and a properly configured tnsnames.ora file, try to connect from your machine to the database via Net8. If you are successful, the problem may be the network. Here are some of the possible problem areas that you can consider:

- Physical network cabling between the client machine and the database
- A hardware problem within the network
- Improper configuration of the client hardware or software
- Server resources are intermittently depleted, thus the server cannot support the volume of connection requests

Unless you are the resident network administrator, you probably won't be able to do much about the first two items listed above, or the hardware side of the third one. You can check the client software and verify that the supporting files have not been overwritten with incorrect information. How could the files get overwritten? If the client had a problem that required recovery of a disk, the files could easily be overwritten with potentially out-of-date ones.

If the problem is an intermittent lack of server resources, your system administrator can provide you with more insights into this area. As I tell you about the various Net8 error numbers and their associated messages, you'll see some that indicate server resources may be falling too low to support the volume of connections requested.

Understanding Logs, Trace Files, and Error Messages

Before we get into demystifying the Oracle Net8 error messages found in the log and trace files, I'd like to make a request. I'd like you to keep in mind at all times when working with Net8 problems that the error messages presented in the Net8 log and trace files may not accurately convey what the *real* problem is. In other words, because Net8 encounters an underlying network error and must report it, the error messages that are available to Net8 may not describe the real problem that was encountered. Therefore, the messages can sometimes be very misleading, confusing, or inaccurate. Of course, this is true in other areas of Oracle, but it's particularly true in the networking arena.

Some of the information that appears here can be found in one form or another in the last section of the Oracle online documentation in Chapter 12 of the *Net8 Administrator's Guide, Release 8.1.6*. I have also included pieces of information that I found on Oracle's Support Web site at http://www.oracle.com/support/oracleinstall/networking/net8.htm. The information found there is installation specific, but many of the errors highlighted can occur when you change the listener.ora or tnsnames.ora file to add, modify, or remove an instance.

Getting the Listener to Work

Do you have a brother or sister? If you have siblings, are they older, younger, or do you have some that are older and some younger? I have an older sister named Judith, and when we were young, every time something went wrong, we were both very quick to blame each other. "She did it!" was a common cry around our house. I'm amazed that my parents actually correctly determined who was the guilty party the majority of the time. As we grew older, we began to realize that pointing fingers and blaming others does not solve problems. (Of course, we don't bite, kick, or scratch each other any more either, thank goodness.)

At the risk of sounding just a little preachy, what I'm trying to say here is that when a problem arises with your system, try not to point fingers or look for someone or something else to blame. Instead, try to find the real cause and come up with solutions. If you can do that, you'll go far in your career.

Now, having said that, let's look at the areas where problems can develop and how to correctly diagnose and fix them. Let's see. The first area I mentioned where things can go wrong is on the server. The second area is on the client, and the third area is within the network itself. In all three areas, things can go wrong with the software, hardware, or both.

All of the steps that I mention in the first part of this chapter assume that the Net8 software has been installed and configured correctly and has been running successfully for some amount of time. Let's back up and look at the things that can fail and ways to fix them in a new Net8 installation and configuration. For the first problem-solving exercise, let's assume that the Oracle Names server and Connection Manager are not being used.

Listener.ora Problems

The first action you take, after you've installed the Oracle software and created one or more databases, is to attempt to start the Net8 listener. By default, as I mentioned in Chapter 3, the listener's name is LISTENER and its default password is ORACLE. In Chapter 7, I showed you how to configure the listener using the Net8 Assistant.

Once the listener has been configured, you're only halfway through the process because you must also ensure that the tnsnames.ora file contains an entry for each net service name that you are using to connect to an instance. You can review how to create a net service name by looking in Chapter 7.

Debugging in the Real World—Step by Step

One of the last actions that you take when creating a net service name is to test the connection. For this exercise, I configured a listener named LIST1. I defined LIST1 to listen using the TCP/IP protocol on my host named MARLENES-PC. I've created the listener to listen using port 1525. Next, I created a new net service name called SKDL.world and assigned it to use the listener on port 1525. After I specified the service name, SKDL, I was given the option to test the connection. I clicked the Test button. Figure 14-1 shows the results of the test. It failed. What in the world did I do wrong?

Working Through Error ORA-12541

Let's see, I got an "ORA-12541: TNS: no listener" error message. Hmm, I wonder if the new listener is running. Guess I'd better check and see. How can I check to see if the listener is running? I'm using a Windows NT operating system, so I can look in my Services window. There, I used Start > Programs > Settings > Control Panel and opened the Services window. Figure 14-2 shows that there is no service running for a LIST1 listener. In fact, there's no service entry for this listener.

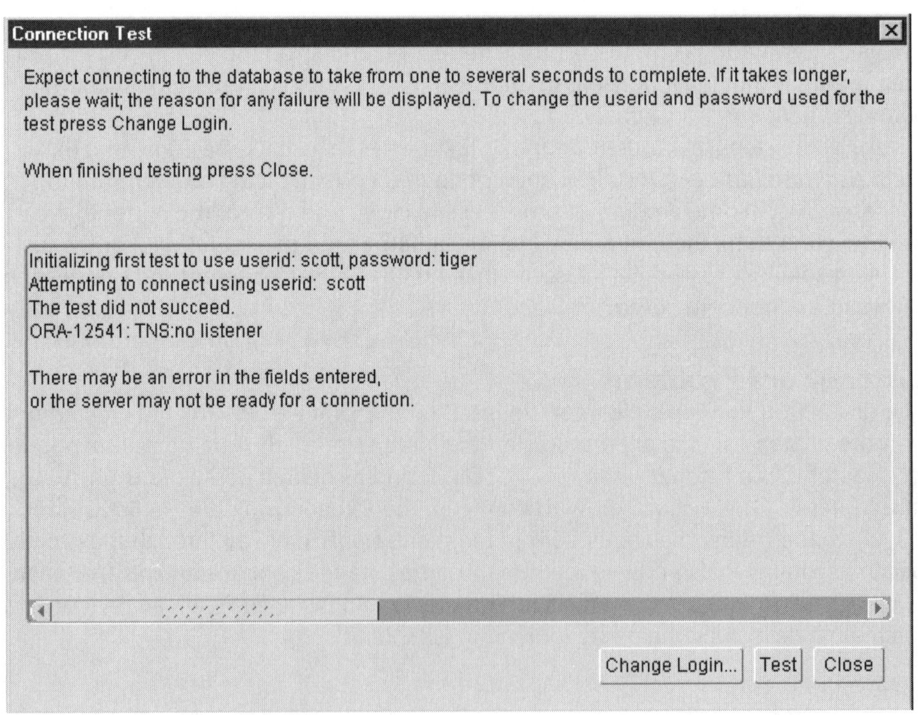

FIGURE 14-1. *Connection test results—first try*

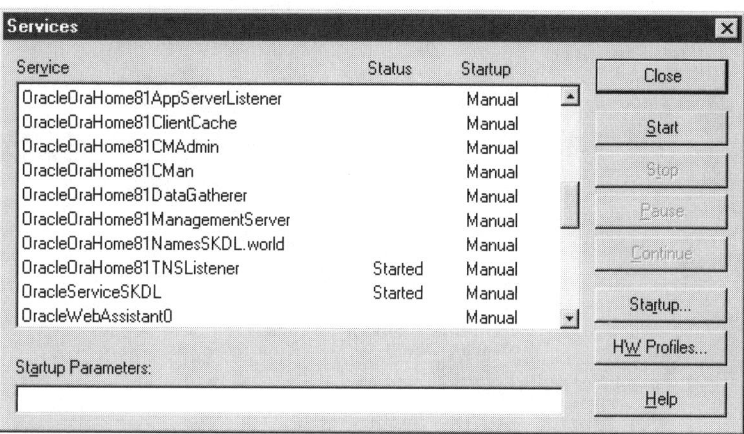

FIGURE 14-2. *Services window with no LIST1 service*

If, however, I am using a UNIX system, I can use the Listener Control utility to check whether or not the new listener, LIST1, is running. Think about how you would perform this task.

I wonder what I should do next. I know, I'll use a DOS prompt window and the Listener Control utility to start the new listener. There. I issued the Listener Control utility command as follows:

```
lsnrctl start LIST1
```

If you look at Figure 14-3, you'll see that I initially got an error number 1060 because there was no existing service entry. However, the necessary listener.ora file was present in the correct directory, so the listener started successfully. Hurray! Oh, by the way, to check the status of the listener on either UNIX or Windows NT using the Listener Control utility, you use the command **lsnrctl status** <listener_name>. The following script will quickly show you the status of all running listeners on your UNIX system:

```
for loop in `ps -ef|grep tnslsnr|grep -v grep|awk '{print $9}'`
do
   lsnrctl status $loop
done | more
```

I'm sure that if we check the Services window again, we'll find that the service to start the new listener is now present. Want to take a look? Figure 14-4 shows the current appearance of the Services window with the new listener entry and the new listener started.

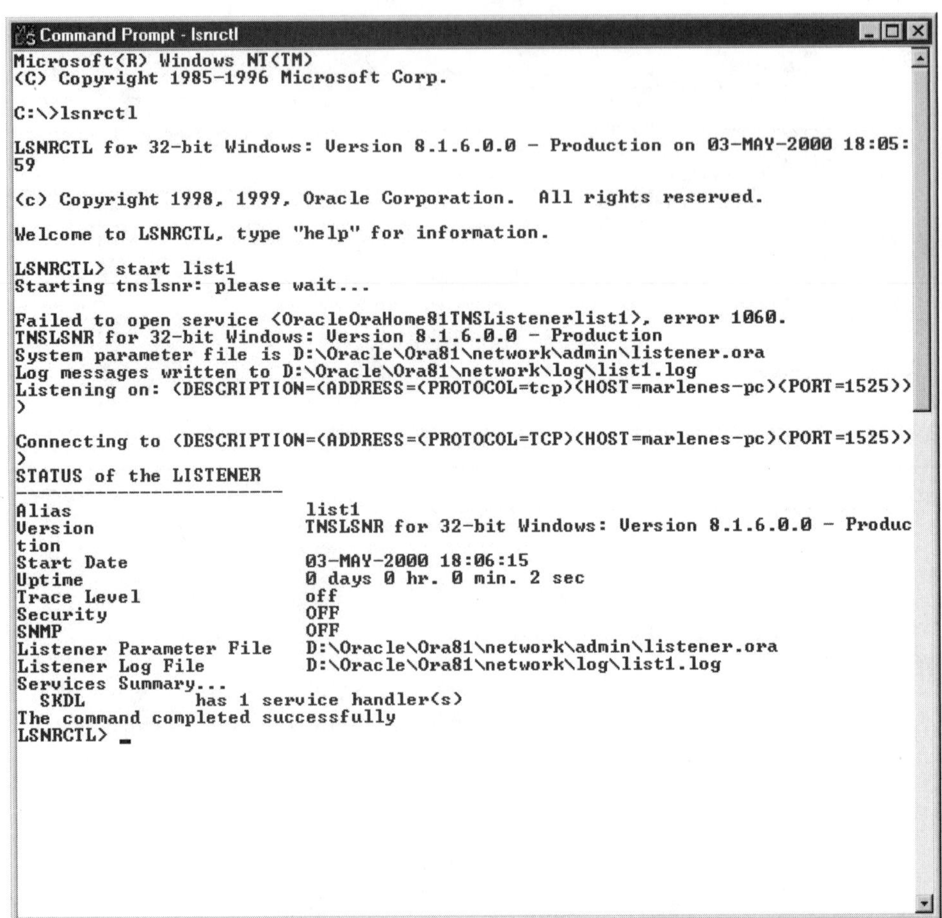

```
Command Prompt - lsnrctl
Microsoft(R) Windows NT(TM)
(C) Copyright 1985-1996 Microsoft Corp.

C:\>lsnrctl

LSNRCTL for 32-bit Windows: Version 8.1.6.0.0 - Production on 03-MAY-2000 18:05:
59

(c) Copyright 1998, 1999, Oracle Corporation.  All rights reserved.

Welcome to LSNRCTL, type "help" for information.

LSNRCTL> start list1
Starting tnslsnr: please wait...

Failed to open service <OracleOraHome81TNSListenerlist1>, error 1060.
TNSLSNR for 32-bit Windows: Version 8.1.6.0.0 - Production
System parameter file is D:\Oracle\Ora81\network\admin\listener.ora
Log messages written to D:\Oracle\Ora81\network\log\list1.log
Listening on: (DESCRIPTION=(ADDRESS=(PROTOCOL=tcp)(HOST=marlenes-pc)(PORT=1525))
)

Connecting to (DESCRIPTION=(ADDRESS=(PROTOCOL=TCP)(HOST=marlenes-pc)(PORT=1525))
)
STATUS of the LISTENER
------------------------
Alias                     list1
Version                   TNSLSNR for 32-bit Windows: Version 8.1.6.0.0 - Produc
tion
Start Date                03-MAY-2000 18:06:15
Uptime                    0 days 0 hr. 0 min. 2 sec
Trace Level               off
Security                  OFF
SNMP                      OFF
Listener Parameter File   D:\Oracle\Ora81\network\admin\listener.ora
Listener Log File         D:\Oracle\Ora81\network\log\list1.log
Services Summary...
  SKDL            has 1 service handler(s)
The command completed successfully
LSNRCTL> _
```

FIGURE 14-3. *DOS command prompt window with* ***lsnrctl***

Working Through Error ORA-12514

Now that the new listener has been started, let's try the connection test again. I'll use the pull-down menu option under Commands to perform a connection test. Figure 14-5 shows the test results.

Ouch! The connection test failed again. This time there's an "ORA-12514: TNS: listener could not resolve SERVICE_NAME given in connect descriptor" error. Well, at least we've gotten past the ORA-12541 error. The error message says that there's something wrong with the service name. Let me go look and see what I've done wrong. Oops, I misspelled the instance name. How careless of me! This is one of the easiest mistakes to make but one of the easiest to correct as well. Let me correct the spelling and run the test again. Nope, it still failed. What *am* I doing

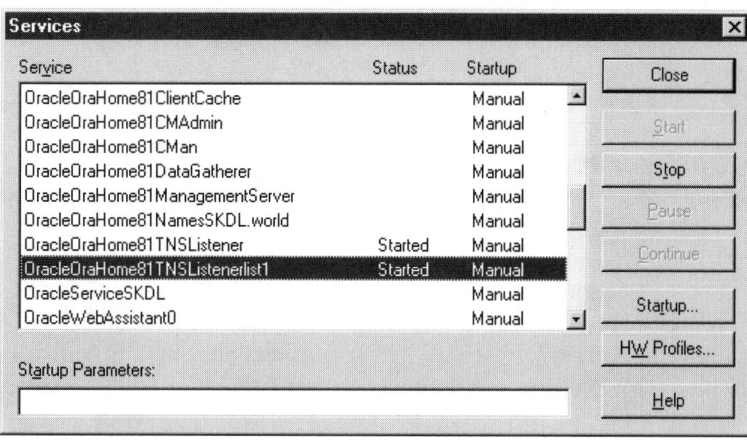

FIGURE 14-4. *Services window with LIST1 service started*

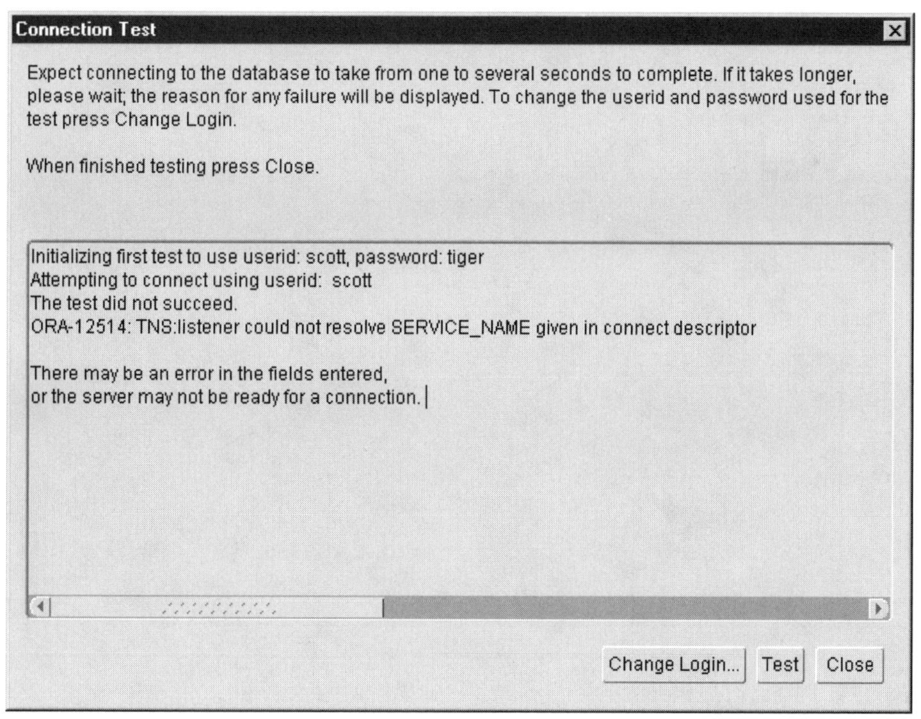

FIGURE 14-5. *Connection test results after starting the listener*

wrong? Oh, I see. I've left off the domain name for the service name. I'll just add the domain name .WORLD to the service name and try the test again. Figure 14-6 shows the test results.

Hurray! The test worked.

Manual Configuration Problems and Solutions

Now, what have you learned from all of this? Well, first of all, you've learned the meaning of two Net8 error messages and how to look for solutions to the problems they identify. You've also learned that when you get one problem fixed, you may discover that there's another one to be corrected below the first one. That's a very common situation. Do I sense an unasked question bubbling around in your mind? Are you wondering just how I knew what was wrong and where to look for possible solutions? That, in my opinion, would be a very good thing for you to be wondering.

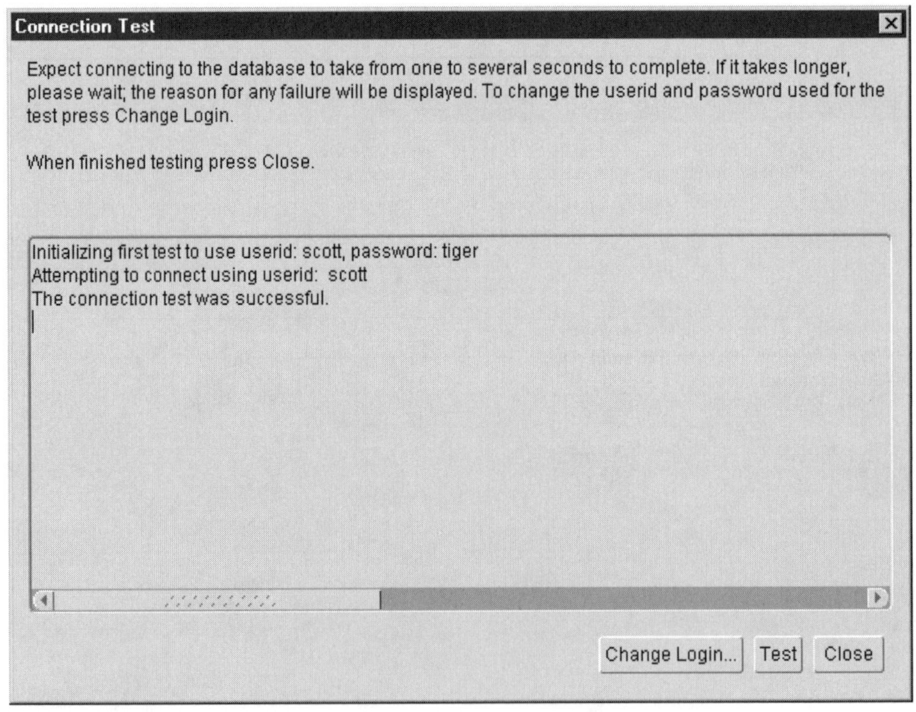

FIGURE 14-6. *Connection test results—success at last*

Part of Net8 problem solving is understanding the pieces that must be in place for the listener to start successfully, and part of the process, quite truthfully, is solving the same problems so many times that you begin to get an instinct about where to look. I don't know about you, but I tend to make the same mistake over and over. After a while, I know what I am likely to have done wrong. The error messages can sometimes guide you to solutions, as they did in this example. However, as I mentioned earlier, the messages can sometimes be misleading as well.

What happens if you decide not to use the Net8 Assistant to configure the listener and net service names? Although the Net8 Assistant is a wonderful tool to use, there may be some reason why you do not have it available to you. In that case, you can make a copy of the sample listener.ora file and modify it to create an initial listener. You can also copy the tnsnames.ora sample file and modify your copy to include the net service names that you need for your environment. You'll find sample files in Chapter 3 as well as on your system in $ORACLE_HOME/network/admin/samples on UNIX or ORACLE_HOME\network\Admin\Samples on Windows NT.

One problem I've encountered frequently when manually configuring the listener is using one port number assignment, like 1521, in the listener.ora file and then forgetting which number I used and using another port number, like 1526, in the tnsnames.ora file. Although you can have one listener listening on more than one port number, it's impossible for two different listeners to listen on the same port number. Therefore, be very careful about how you assign port numbers if you are using more than one listener.

Mismatched parentheses have often proved to be a very difficult problem to correct. If you look back at Chapter 3, you'll see that there are a number of opening "(" and closing ")" parentheses for each entry in the file. Keeping track of how many are opened and ensuring that each open parenthesis has a matching closing parenthesis in the correct location can be a little daunting. I've used the method of holding up one finger for each open parenthesis as I count them and putting one of the raised fingers down as I encounter each ending parenthesis. If I have one or more fingers left pointing up when I reach the last closing parenthesis, I know I'm missing that many matching closing parentheses. Another technique is to indent each set of parentheses so you can easily see where one is missing. Below is a listener.ora file. Are there any missing parentheses? If so, where should the missing parentheses go?

```
LISTENER =
  (ADDRESS_LIST =
        (ADDRESS=
          (PROTOCOL= IPC)
          (KEY= oracle.world))
        (ADDRESS=
          (PROTOCOL= TCP)
          (Host= marlenes-pc)
```

```
          (Port= 1526))
STARTUP_WAIT_TIME_LISTENER = 0
CONNECT_TIMEOUT_LISTENER = 10
TRACE_LEVEL_LISTENER = 0
SID_LIST_LISTENER =
  (SID_LIST =
    (SID_DESC =
      (GLOBAL_DBNAME = marlenes-pc)
      (SID_NAME = ORCL)))
PASSWORDS_LISTENER = (oracle)
```

There is one parenthesis missing. Did you find the correct location for the missing parenthesis? The open parenthesis in ADDRESS_LIST is missing its closing parenthesis. Where should the missing one be placed? If you said, "Directly after the two closing parentheses after the value 1526," you'd be correct.

The third problem I've periodically encountered is having the underlying network protocol configured incorrectly to support Oracle's Net8 implementation. This problem is very network-product dependent and beyond the scope of this chapter.

Let's talk just a bit more about the location of the Net8 configuration files. You see, when you attempt to connect to an instance, there is a specific order in which Net8 performs its search for its supporting files. Just as a reminder, the files that Net8 needs in order to function properly are listener.ora, tnsnames.ora, and sqlnet.ora. Net8 will begin its search in the working directory where the application is executed. This means that if your application is run from a directory called D:\Ora81\Oracle\MyApps\, Net8 will begin looking for the configuration files in that location. If they are not found there, Net8 will look in the location defined by the environment variable TNS_ADMIN. If you can't find a definition for this variable on your Windows NT machine, check the registry. There may not be a definition for this variable on your system.

If TNS_ADMIN is undefined, the $ORACLE_HOME/network/admin directory on UNIX will be checked, or ORACLE_HOME\network\Admin will be searched on Windows NT. To verify that there is a valid value for ORACLE_HOME on your system, you can use the command **env | grep ORACLE_HOME** for a UNIX system, or check the registry on Windows NT.

By having the TNS_ADMIN variable defined in the registry, you allow all of the Oracle and Net8 products to view only one tnsnames.ora. This significantly simplifies updating Net8.

Please do *not* edit the registry unless you are familiar with making changes there. Any mistake could corrupt your Windows NT operating system. Be sure to make a backup of your registry before you begin the following steps. Having warned you sufficiently, here are the steps that you can follow to define TNS_ADMIN in your registry:

1. To create an entry in the Windows NT registry, you must use the **regedt32** feature. To access this feature, you use Start > Run and enter the command **regedt32** in the Open area.
2. When you enter the Registry Editor, select the entry HKEY_LOCAL_MACHINE. Double-click on the SOFTWARE option. (Notice the little plus sign (+) on the folder icon. Once you double-click the left mouse button, you see the list of software that is installed on your machine in the right window.)
3. Double-click on the ORACLE option. Under ORACLE you will find one or more "homes" called HOME0, HOME1, and so on. HOME0 is the home of the first product installed. HOME1 will be the second product installed, and so on. You want to set up the TNS_ADMIN in every home option. If you have Oracle8.1.5 installed, you must also place an entry for the LOCAL variables into every home except for the actual v8.1.5 database home itself.
4. Click on HOME*x* (for example, HOME0).
5. Click on Edit at the top of the box.
6. Click on Add Value and type the following in the Add Value box: Value Name: **TNS_ADMIN**, Data Type: **REG_SZ**. When you click the OK button, the String Editor box will appear. In the String Editor box, type the following: String: **D:\Oracle\ora81\network\admin** or the appropriate location for your listener.ora and tnsnames.ora files.
7. If you have Oracle v8.1.5 installed, click on Edit again.
8. Click on Add Value and type the following in the Add Value box: Value Name: **LOCAL**, Data Type: **REG_SZ**. When you click on the OK button, the String Editor box will appear. In the String Editor box, type the following: String: <alias for 8.1.5 database>. A string example would be **DB815**.
9. Repeat the above steps for each HOME*x*.
10. Exit the registry.

Guidelines for Debugging the Most Common Errors

In this section, I'd like to present several of the most common errors that you may encounter while working with Net8. Table 14-2 lists the errors that we'll be looking at and the message text associated with each one. Just below the message text, I've included one or more of the problems that can cause each of these errors.

Error Number	Message
ORA-12154	TNS: could not resolve database name Cause: Net8 could not find the database name specified in the connect string defined as an alias in the tnsnames.ora file.
ORA-12198	TNS: could not find path to destination Cause: The client is not able to find the desired database.
ORA-12203	TNS: unable to connect to destination Cause: This is a generic error message with several potential causes. The first possible cause to check is that the incorrect Oracle protocol for the selected networking protocol is installed. A missing protocol support driver usually produces the following errors in the sqlnet.log or any client trace file: ORA-12203, ORA-12538, and ORA-00508.
ORA-12224	TNS: no listener Cause: The connection request could not be completed because the listener is not running.
ORA-12500	TNS: listener failed to start a dedicated server process Cause: This is a more generic error message identifying one or more of four possible problem areas as follows: Problems with linking and permissions Lack of resources Failure to start a dedicated process on the server An operating system environment that is incorrectly set up
ORA-12533	TNS: illegal ADDRESS parameters Cause: The protocol-specific parameters in the **address** section of the designated connect descriptor in your tnsnames.ora file are incorrect.
ORA-12545	TNS: name lookup failure Cause: The listener on the remote node cannot be contacted.

TABLE 14-2. *Net8 Error Messages and Their Causes*

Error Number	Message
ORA-12560	TNS: protocol adapter error Cause: The listener was unable to start a process connecting the user to the database server.
ORA-12571	TNS: packet writer failure Cause: An error occurred during a data send.
ORA-03113	TNS: End of file on communication channel Cause: An unexpected end of file was processed on the communication channel. This may be an indication that the communications link has gone down, at least temporarily. It could also indicate that the server has gone down.
ORA-03121	TNS: No interface driver connection—function not performed Cause 1: A SQL*Net version 1 prefix was erroneously used in the connect string. This prefix takes the form T:, X:, or P:. Example: sqlplus nelson/hot_shot@T:marlenes-pc:skdl Cause 2: Only the username and password were specified from a client machine that had no local Oracle database installed.

TABLE 14-2. *Net8 Error Messages and Their Causes* (continued)

Now that you've had a chance to look at the errors in general, let's look at them in more detail. I'll try to supply you with enough information so that you at least get a feeling for what has gone wrong, and I'll suggest one or more actions that you can take to begin to resolve each problem.

TNS-12154: TNS: Could Not Resolve Database Name

On the surface, this error seems clear and easy to repair. However, as you will see when you encounter a TNS-12154, there are many reasons why the database name might not be able to be resolved. Speaking from my own past experience, this particular error can be very frustrating to track down. You see, it can sometimes be difficult to determine which tnsnames.ora file Net8 is using if you have multiple $ORACLE_HOME directories. To make matters worse, in versions of the Oracle RDBMS earlier than v8.1.5, the Oracle Enterprise Manager supports its own copy of the networking software and configuration files. Net8 sees two tnsnames.ora files in different directories and gets confused. You, on the other hand, may not realize that there are two configuration files. Therefore, your troubleshooting work becomes compounded.

Keep in mind too that you can end up in a situation where you are only using one listener.ora file and one tnsnames.ora file and get an ORA-12154 error for what seems to be no apparent reason. I spent several days recently trying to resolve this error and, thanks to the help of two wonderful and patient Oracle employees, Peter Povinec and Pierre Baudin, finally discovered that I had defined an Oracle Names server, and the sqlnet.ora file showed the following entry:

```
NAMES.DIRECTORY_PATH= (ONAMES)
```

You see, with this entry in the file, Net8 won't look for or use your tnsnames.ora file. Once I changed the entry to the following, my ORA-12154 error disappeared:

```
NAMES.DIRECTORY_PATH= (TNSNAMES,ONAMES)
```

One approach to solving the problem that this error identifies is to perform a search of all of your Oracle directories to determine whether there is more than one copy of the tnsnames.ora file on your system. Oracle recommends that you use the highest-level version of the listener for your Net8 communications. This approach should work well for you unless you are running versions of the RDBMS that are lower than v7.3.4.

As listed in Chapter 12 of the Oracle8i, Release 2 *Net8 Administrator's Guide*, the steps that you can take when working through a TNS-12154 error are as follows:

1. Verify that a tnsnames.ora file exists.
2. Verify that multiple copies of the tnsnames.ora file do not exist on your system. If you do find multiple copies, put a unique entry into each one to help you determine which file Net8 is using.
3. In the tnsnames.ora file, verify that the net service name specified in your connect string is mapped to a connect descriptor.
4. Verify that there are no duplicate copies of the sqlnet.ora file.
5. If you are using domain names, verify that your sqlnet.ora file contains a **names.default_domain** parameter. If this parameter does not exist, you must specify the domain name in your connect string.

6. If you are not using domain names, and this parameter exists, delete it or disable it by commenting it out.
7. If you are connecting from a login dialog box, verify that you are not placing an "@" symbol before your connect net service name in the Host string box.
8. Activate client tracing and reexecute the operation.

ORA-12198: TNS: Could Not Find Path to Destination

This error message indicates that the client could not locate the database to which it wants to establish a connection. You can get this message if you have not correctly entered the service name you want to reach. Thus, your first step is to verify that you typed the service name correctly and that you used the name exactly as it appears in your tnsnames.ora file. The other things to verify are as follows:

- The net service name in the **address** parameter area of your tnsnames.ora file is correct.
- The tnsnames.ora file is located in the correct directory.
- The listener is running on the server that you are trying to reach.
- You have not placed an "@" symbol before your connect net service name if you are using a login box to perform your connection.

TNS-12203: TNS: Unable to Connect to Destination

This error is generic in nature and may hide underlying secondary problems. Because it's used as a multipurpose error message, you may have a harder time finding the real reason that you've received it. You see, you first have to determine which problem this error message really represents before you can begin to correct anything. The first thing you want to do when you receive this error message is to check your latest sqlnet.log file for secondary ORA messages. You'll find this file in $ORACLE_HOME/network/log on UNIX and on a Windows platform, in ORACLE_HOME\network\log. Later I'll show you how to read the log and trace files. If you decide, after analyzing the log file, that there are no secondary errors, see if one of the scenarios listed in Table 14-3 fits your situation. I've listed the reasons that you might receive a TNS-12203 error message and the actions you can take to correct each situation.

Cause	Action
The installed Oracle protocol does not match the underlying network protocol.	1. Check the sqlnet.log or client trace file for underlying error numbers. If you are missing a protocol-support driver, you should see ORA-12203, ORA-12538, and/or ORA-00508 error messages. 2. On a UNIX system, from $ORACLE_HOME/bin, run the **adapters** program to verify that you have the appropriate Oracle protocol installed. You should see a list of installed Net8 transport protocols such as IPC, TCP/IP, BEQueath, SSL, and RAW.
An invalid net service name was supplied in the connect string.	Verify that the net service name supplied in your connect string exists in your tnsnames.ora file and the address information for that net service name is valid. Ask yourself the following questions: Have I supplied the correct host or service name? Have I supplied the correct port number?
Net8 could not find the connect descriptor specified in the tnsnames.ora file.	After verifying that the database is running, check the following: 1. Verify that the listener is running. Enter **lsnrctl status** <LISTENER_NAME>. If you are using the default listener name, LISTENER, you don't have to include the listener name in the query. 2. If the listener is not running, use the command **lsnrctl start** <LISTENER_NAME>. 3. Be sure that the tnsnames.ora file is in the correct location.
The destination system's listener is not listening.	Verify that the remote system's listener is running as shown in the last entry.

TABLE 14-3. *TNS-12203 Error Message Causes and Actions*

Cause	Action
There are underlying network transport problems.	Use the utilities supplied with your networking protocol to verify that the protocol itself is functional. For example, with TCP/IP, try to **ping** the remote system.
The tnsnames.ora file is not in the proper directory.	The default directory location for the listener.ora, tnsnames.ora, and sqlnet.ora files is $ORACLE_HOME/network/admin on a UNIX system and ORACLE_HOME\network\Admin on a Windows NT system. If you have placed your files in another location, such as /etc on a UNIX system, ensure that the environment variable TNS_ADMIN is pointing to that location.
The clients and server machine values for the (HOST=server_name) parameter for TCP/IP addresses, or the (SERVICE=tns_application) parameter for SPX addresses, are not consistent.	Ensure the values for these parameters are the same on the server and client. For TCP/IP, make sure the **host** parameter in listener.ora on the server and in the tnsnames.ora file on the client point to the same name, or at least to names that are then translated to the same IP address by each system. This is especially important for servers with multiple IP addresses assigned to the various network interfaces on the server. For SPX setups, the name must be the same on the server and client workstations.
The Net8 software couldn't find the ORACLE_HOME directory.	Verify that ORACLE_HOME\bin is present within your path. The default ORACLE_HOME for Oracle8i on Windows NT is Oracle\Ora81\bin.

TABLE 14-3. *TNS-12203 Error Message Causes and Actions* (continued)

If you have been successfully making Net8 connections and have suddenly begun to receive TNS-12203 error messages that you can find no cause for, as a last resort, according to the Oracle Support Web site, you can try reinstalling Net8 and the TCP/IP adapter. Reinstall? Why in the world would you want to do this?

If you're on a Windows NT machine and have recently installed a new product or upgraded an existing product (Oracle's or another vendor's), it's possible for an area of the registry to become overwritten or corrupted in some way. You may begin to have products fail that have been working correctly over a period of time. By reinstalling Net8 and the TCP/IP adapter, necessary registry information will be reinserted, thus correcting the problem.

In the case where multiple versions of Oracle have been installed on Windows NT and things have gotten into a complete mess, you may find it necessary to uninstall the Oracle software first. On occasions, the Oracle installer will not uninstall. Sometimes you have to use the brute force method to uninstall. Please realize that if you have a valuable database that you are able to access successfully, you will want to back up the database or otherwise protect it before you attempt to completely uninstall and reinstall Oracle.

The following steps will accomplish the uninstall/reinstall tasks:

1. Stop all Oracle NT services.
2. Delete the following keys from the registry:

   HKEY_LOCAL_MACHINE/SOFTWARE/ORACLE

   HKEY_LOCAL_MACHINE/SYSTEM/CurrentControlSet/SERVICES/Oracle*
3. Delete the Oracle directories from disk.
4. Remove all Oracle-related system variables.
5. Remove references to Oracle directories from the PATH.

By completely removing all references to Oracle from your machine, you are performing a new install. Again, if you have a database of value, you should take appropriate steps to protect it before performing any of the steps listed here. This is a very drastic measure.

ORA-12224: TNS: No Listener

The cause listed in the message for this error is that the connection couldn't be completed because the listener is not running or doesn't exist. However, the real problem that causes this error message to be displayed may be that the destination address that was supplied does not match one of the addresses used by the listener.

For example, if you have configured a listener to listen for connection requests on port 1521 and the **port** parameter in your tnsnames.ora specifies **port**=1525, you will get this error message. Now, isn't that intuitively obvious?

The other possibility you should consider when working through this problem is that you could be dealing with a version compatibility issue. In other words, the version of the client software might not be compatible with the version you are running on the server or vice versa. If you are dealing with two different versions of the Oracle connection software, you should contact Oracle Support to verify what the certified versions are and their compatibility.

ORA-12500: TNS: Listener Failed to Start a Dedicated Server Process

On a UNIX client, a TNS-12500 error message is almost always caused by a linking problem with the executable you are trying to use, such as SQL*Plus. The other possibilities are all server related and can be as follows:

- Lack of resources
- Failure to start a dedicated process on the server
- An operating system environment that is incorrectly set up

Client TNS-12500 Troubleshooting The first step you should take when addressing this problem is to check linking to make sure the appropriate protocol adapter is linked with the application being used. To accomplish this task on a UNIX system, you first go to the $ORACLE_HOME/bin directory. There is a program there called **adapters**. You must run the adapters program on the executable being run. Huh? What does that mean?

To explain what I just said, it may be easier to just show you an example. Let's say that you are trying to run SQL*Plus and receive this error message. You go to the $ORACLE_HOME/bin directory and type in the following command:

```
adapters sqlplus
```

You should see output similar to but not necessarily exactly like the following display:

```
Net8 Protocol Adapters linked with SQL*Plus are:
BEQ Protocol Adapter
IPC Protocol Adapter
TCP/IP Protocol Adapter
RAW Protocol Adapter

Net8 Naming Adapters linked with SQL*Plus are:
Oracle TNS Naming Adapter
Oracle Naming Adapter
```

Hmm, what should you do if you don't see any output? If you do not see any output under the "Protocol Adapters" section, your platform is probably using shared libraries. If that's the case, it means that the network code is being dynamically loaded. If your system is using shared libraries, you can locate the shared library that is used by the client. Typically, that library is the libclntsh.so library located in $ORACLE_HOME/lib. However, locating shared libraries is really platform specific. For example, on a Solaris machine, typing the command

```
$ ldd sqlplus
```

may show the following results:

```
libclntsh.so.1.0 => /u2/app/oracle/product/V816/lib/libclntsh.so.8.0
```

Ah. Now that you know where the shared library is located, go to that directory or use the fully qualified file name and try the **adapters** command on the shared library.

If your platform does not use shared libraries but there is no output, try to **grep** for the protocol symbol in the executable manually. For example, if you are using TCP/IP and are trying to run SQL*Plus, use this command:

```
nm sqlplus | grep nttini
```

You see, **nttini** is the symbol for TCP/IP in both SQL*Net v2 and Net8. Each protocol has its own symbol. Table 14-4 shows some of the other protocol symbols that you can use to show what adapters are installed and linked on your system.

If you still do not get any output, manually relink the executable. Well, that's easy to say, but how do you go about relinking them? Before you begin to relink the executable for any product, you should always make a copy of the current executable to ensure that you can go back to it if necessary. Also, before you relink anything, especially the "oracle" executable, be sure to shut down the database. Okay, let's get linking.

Protocol Adapter	Symbol
TCP/IP	nttini
DECNET	ntdini
LU 6.2	ntlini
SPX	ntsini
IPC	ntusini
BEQ	ntpini

TABLE 14-4. *Protocol Adapter Symbols*

Using SQL*Plus as an example, if you have the privilege to perform these actions on your system, you can go to the $ORACLE_HOME/sqlplus/lib directory and execute the following commands:

```
make -f ins_sqlplus.mk
install
```

When you run these commands, your executable should be linked with a protocol adapter, and your connection should now work.

If you are still getting the TNS-12500 error, another area that you can check on your machine is the definitions for the variables ORACLE_HOME and ORACLE_SID. You may want to make sure the variable LD_LIBRARY_PATH is set correctly as well. I've had trouble many times because this variable was not set or not set properly in my environment. You can also add or change the parameter AUTOMATIC_IPC in the sqlnet.ora file and set its value to OFF.

UNIX Server TNS-12500 Troubleshooting Now, let's take a look at the problems that can cause you to get a TNS-12500 on a UNIX server. In the first part of this section, you saw that there could be a problem when an *application* executable is not linked correctly with an adapter protocol. In this part of the section, we're looking at a linking problem with the *listener* or the *Oracle* executable. Permissions or environment settings can cause this error message to be reported on a UNIX server as well.

To determine whether the problem is that the listener is not properly linked, you can go to the $ORACLE_HOME/bin directory and run the **adapters** command that we looked at earlier. This time, however, you'll run the command on tnslsnr, as follows:

```
adapters tnslsnr
```

You should see output similar to the following:

```
Net8 Protocol Adapters linked with tnslsnr are:
BEQ Protocol Adapter
IPC Protocol Adapter
TCP/IP Protocol Adapter
RAW Protocol Adapter

Net8 Naming Adapters linked with tnslsnr are:
Oracle TNS Naming Adapter
Oracle Naming Adapter
```

Just as you learned earlier, if you do not see any output under the "Protocol Adapters" section, your platform is probably using shared libraries, and the network code is being dynamically loaded. The task of locating the shared library has already been explained, and Table 14-4 shows the protocol adapters and their symbols for performing the verification actions, so I won't repeat these steps here.

If you still do not get any output and you have the correct privileges on your operating system, try manually relinking the Net8 executable. Go to the $ORACLE_HOME/network/lib directory and execute the following commands:

```
make -f ins_network.mk
install
```

Oh, by the way, on Oracle8.1.5 and higher, at the operating system prompt, you can simply type **relink network**.

After you've successfully linked the network executable to the protocol adapter, your connection should work. Okay, that takes care of how to link the network executable, but what about the Oracle executable?

Well, to link the Oracle executable, go to $ORACLE_HOME/bin and run the **adapters** command using the argument "oracle" instead of "tnslsnr." Follow the same steps as above. If you find that you have to relink the Oracle executable, from the $ORACLE_HOME/rdbms/lib directory, execute the commands

```
make -f ins_rdbms.mk
install
```

Notice that for each of these links, you are going to a different directory area and relinking a different executable. Again, for an Oracle8i system, at the operating system prompt, you can just type **relink oracle**.

If you are still having problems, check the permissions on the tnslsnr and Oracle executables. To do this, go the $ORACLE_HOME/bin directory and type

```
ls -l tnslsnr
```

You should see the following output:

```
-rwsr-xr-x oracle dba
```

If you type

```
ls -l oracle
```

you should see the same output. If you see that the permissions are different, you can change them with the following commands:

```
chmod 4755 tnslsnr
chmod 4755 oracle
```

When you use the **chmod** command, you are telling UNIX to change the mode of protection on the specified file. The numbers are the amount of privilege that you are allowing. Each number is positional, and each position is a different area of privilege. For reference, the UNIX permissions are in the following order: User, Group, and Other. The letter *"r"* represents the read permission and has a value of 4. The letter *"w"* represents the write permission and has a value of 2, while the letter *"x"* grants the permission to execute and has a value of 1.

The values can be added together. Thus, a permission value 6 is 4+2, or read and write. When you see four digits specified in a **chmod** command (as shown in Table 14-5), the leftmost digit has a special meaning.

If the owner of a file or executable is not the oracle account, you can change the owner by using the following command:

```
chown oracle tnslsnr
chown oracle oracle
```

NOTE
Some UNIX operating systems only allow you to use the change owner command if you have root privileges.

Letter	Number	Used for a File	Used for a Directory
r	4	Grant read permission to file.	Grant ability to list directory contents.
w	2	Grant write permission to file.	Grant ability to add and remove files from the directory.
x	1	Grant execute permission.	Grant ability to **cd** into the directory.
SUID	2	Program will run with the permission of the owner of the file.	n/a
SGID	4	Program will run with the permission of the group ID of the file.	Newly created files in the directory will inherit the same group ID as the directory.
SVTX	1	n/a	To delete the file, the user must own either the file or the directory.

TABLE 14-5. *UNIX File and Directory Privileges*

Once you've changed the privileges or owner, you need to restart the listener and database instance so that the changes to the executables will take effect. As we did above, you'll want to verify that your environment variables are set correctly for ORACLE_HOME, ORACLE_SID, and LD_LIBRARY_PATH.

Troubleshooting Intermittent TNS-12500 Errors If you are getting TNS-12500 errors intermittently, you probably have a lack of resources on your server. Now, having said that, I must warn you that finding the resource that is being depleted may not be an easy task. Let's take a look at the resource that may be getting depleted and what you can do to help alleviate the problem, as shown in Table 14-6.

Resource	Action
The init.ora **processes** parameter could be set too low.	Increase the value for **processes** in init.ora.
UNIX kernel parameters may be too low to support the number of processes or users.	Increase the values for **nproc** or **maxuprc** (operating system–specific values).
Swap space may be inadequate.	Increase the swap space.
The tracing feature, **Otrace**, may be enabled.	By default, **Otrace** is enabled. **Otrace** can cause many problems. To disable this feature, perform the following steps: Shut down the Oracle database. Go to $ORACLE_HOME/otrace/admin. 1. Delete all files with a .dat extension. 2. Restart the Oracle database. To prevent new entries to the trace files, you can do two things: 1. Set the environment variable EPC_DISABLED=TRUE in the profile or login file for the user account that owns the Oracle software. This prevents tracing from direct connections on the server. 2. Add the clause (ENVS='EPC_DISABLED=TRUE') to the SID_DESC clause of the SID_LIST clause in the listener.ora file. This prevents tracing from client connections.

TABLE 14-6. *Depleted Resource and Actions to Take*

Resource	Action
There are not enough system resources to support the number of concurrent connection requests.	Enable Multi-Threaded Server. To establish MTS, perform the following steps: 1. Stop the database. 2. Modify the init.ora file for the appropriate database to include the following parameters: mts_dispatchers="(address=(<protocol>)(<host>)(<number of dispatchers>)(<number of connections>))" mts_max_dispatchers=<max number of dispatchers> mts_servers=<number of shared servers to start> mts_max_servers=<max number of shared servers> mts_service=<SID name> mts_listener_address=<address of the TNS listener> 3. Restart the database. Example: mts_dispatchers="(address=(protocol=TCP)(host=MARLENES-PC)(port=5001))(dispatchers=2)" mts_max_dispatchers=10 mts_servers=2 mts_max_servers=4 mts_service=SKDL mts_listen_address="(address=(protocol=TCP)(host=NELSONS-PC)(port=1521))"

TABLE 14-6. *Depleted Resource and Actions to Take* (continued)

Windows NT TNS-12500 Troubleshooting Problems can arise on a Windows NT system if the userid of the process that installed and started Oracle and the listener was Administrator. Just as you have a separate account for Oracle on a UNIX or OpenVMS system, you should have a separate Oracle account on a Windows NT system in which you install Oracle and its related products. To verify that the services are running and owned by the Oracle user, go to Start > Settings > Control Panel > Services and verify that the Oracle services are present and running.

Look at the OracleOraHome81TNS<listener_name> for Oracle8i, Release 2, or OracleService<sid> entry for Oracle8.1.5 to see if the service is set to start automatically or manually and whether or not it is running. Keep in mind that Oracle versions earlier than Oracle8i will have both an OracleService<sid> and OracleStart<sid> entry. These services should be started. If they are not, click on the Start button on the right side of the dialog box to start them. If you are using Windows NT as an Oracle server, be sure that the services are set to start automatically on system start-up.

Another problem you can encounter is that the SID shown for OracleService on the server does not match the value shown in the server's listener.ora file or does not match the value shown in the client's tnsnames.ora file.

While we're looking at the services, click on your entry for the listener and click on the Startup button. You should see a dialog box similar to the one shown in Figure 14-7.

Make sure that the listener is logged on as the option System Account. If it is not, click on the System Account radio button. Once you make this change, you must make sure that you stop and start the listener for the new value to take effect.

If all else fails, you may simply want to try restarting your instance.

Troubleshooting Intermittent Windows NT TNS-12500 Errors On a Windows NT system, it is much easier to run out of real system resources rapidly. If you are having intermittent TNS-12500 error messages, try to increase the amount

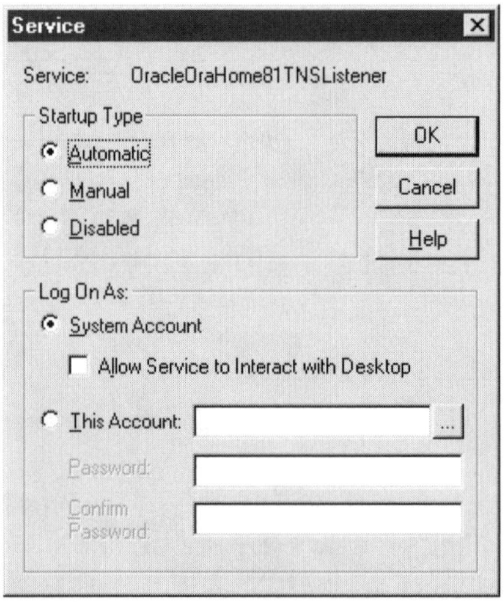

FIGURE 14-7. *Services startup box*

of memory available to the system by either removing unnecessary processes or increasing the amount of physical memory. You can also relieve the symptoms, at least temporarily, by increasing the amount of swap space you have available.

Just as the **Otrace** tracing feature can be a problem for a UNIX server, it can be a problem on Windows NT as well. Be sure to disable **Otrace**. To disable **Otrace**, perform the following steps:

1. Stop the Oracle database.
2. Go to the ORACLE_HOME\Otrace\admin directory.
3. Delete all files with a .dat extension.
4. Restart the Oracle database.

To prevent new entries from being written to the trace files, perform the following two steps:

1. Set the environment variable EPC_DISABLED=TRUE in the registry for the user account that owns the Oracle software. This prevents tracing from direct connections on the server.
2. Add the clause (ENVS='EPC_DISABLED=TRUE') to the SID_DESC clause of the SID_LIST clause in the listener.ora file. This prevents tracing from the client connections.

The parameter **processes** may be too low in your init.ora file as well.

ORA-12533: TNS: Illegal ADDRESS Parameters

This problem is very easy to understand and repair. If you receive an ORA-12533 error message, it means that the **address** section in your tnsnames.ora file for the connection you are trying to make has a problem. Look closely at the protocol-specific parameters that are listed in the tnsnames.ora file for your connection, and correct the error.

ORA-12545: TNS: Name Lookup Failure

Although the error message is a bit misleading in my opinion, the problem is a relatively simple one. You see, the reason that you get an ORA-12545 is that the listener on the remote server cannot be contacted. There are two reasons for this problem. Either there is a mismatch in the **address** area of the client's tnsnames.ora file or the listener.ora file, or there is an error in this area of the associated file.

The other reason that you can receive this error is if the listener on the remote server is not running. Therefore, you need to verify that the listener has been started.

ORA-12560: TNS: Protocol Adapter Error

This error is like several of the others we've already looked at. All this error message is really saying is that the listener was unable to start a process connecting the user to the database server. To determine what the real problem is, you need to turn on tracing and try the operation again. This time, when the connection fails, you can look in the trace file and get a better perspective on what's really going wrong. Keep in mind that when I say, "Turn on tracing," I'm talking about the Net8 network tracing facility and not Otrace.

ORA-12571: TNS: Packet Writer Failure

The cause for this error is not usually visible to the user. You see, an error occurred during the time that a data send was occurring. To better see what's really happening, you need to turn on tracing and try the operation again. This time, when the connection fails, you can look in the trace file to better see what's really going wrong. If the error persists, you will need to contact Oracle Support for more help.

ORA-03113: TNS: End of file on Communication Channel

The underlying reason that you receive the error messages TNS-12571 and/or ORA-03113 is pretty much the same. Either message indicates that the connection is being terminated prematurely. This can be caused in part if there is a long distance between the client and server. One potential solution for this problem is to increase the value for TCP/IP reconnect attempts in the Windows NT registry.

As with any action involving the registry, this should not be tried at home, or without a net! What I mean by that is, when you interact with the registry, there is a good chance that you can cause more damage than good. I would suggest that you approach any dealings with the registry with great caution. Be sure to make a backup of the registry before you change anything. Okay? Thanks!

Having warned you sufficiently (I hope!), here's what you can do. Increase the retransmission setting on the Windows NT client by editing the registry. You will add the key TcpMaxDataRetransmissions (REG_DWORD) and set the value for this key to 15. In Douglas Adams's wonderful book *Hitchhiker's Guide to the Galaxy*, there is some terrific advice: "Don't panic!" I'm going to walk you step-by-step through the actions you need to take to add this key. Ready? Here we go.

1. Click on the Start menu and select the Run option.
2. In the Run dialog box, type **regedt32** in the Open field and press ENTER. You use **regedt32** instead of **regedit** so that you can add a key instead of just look at or remove registry information.
3. In the View menu at the top of the screen, make sure that "Tree and Data" is selected.

4. Find the window labeled "HKEY_LOCAL_MACHINE on Local Machine" and double-click on the folder labeled SYSTEM. Figure 14-8 shows the Registry Editor with the HKEY_LOCAL_MACHINE window and the SYSTEM entry selected.
5. Double-click on the folder labeled CurrentControlSet.
6. Double-click on the folder labeled Services.
7. Double-click on the folder labeled Tcpip.
8. Click on the folder labeled Parameters.
9. Select Add Value from the Edit menu.
10. In the Value Name field, type **TcpMaxDataRetransmissions**.
11. Using the drop-down list, change the Data Type to REG_DWORD.
12. Click OK.
13. In the DWORD Editor dialog box, type **15** in the Data field and make sure the Hex radio button is selected.
14. Click OK.

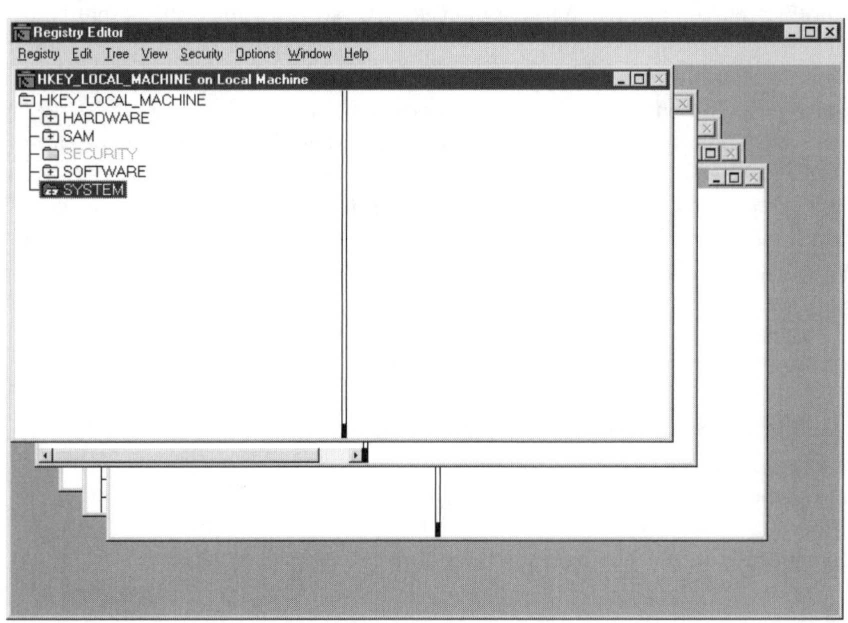

FIGURE 14-8. *Registry Editor with HKEY_LOCAL_MACHINE selected*

You should see the new parameter added to the data window. If not, repeat the steps.

On Windows 95, increase the retransmission setting on the Windows 95 client by editing the registry and adding the key MaxDataRetries (REG_DWORD) with a value of 15. The steps that you follow are almost the same as for Windows NT. You use **regedit** instead of **regedt32**, however. Now, follow the same steps as listed above until you get to step 7. Let's pick up at step 7, and I'll list the steps that you follow from there.

7. Double-click on the folder labeled vxd.
8. Click on the folder labeled MSTCP.
9. From the Edit menu, select New and then String Value.
10. A highlighted field is displayed that reads "New Value #1." Type **MaxDataRetries** and press ENTER.
11. Right-click on the new entry, MaxDataRetries, and select Modify.
12. In the Value Data field, type **15**.

You should see the new parameter added to the data window. If not, repeat the steps.

Another reason that you can get the ORA-03113 error message is that Net8 tried to transmit the packet five times before it detected the network was down. Five is the default value for packet transmission attempts for TCP/IP on Windows 95 and Windows NT. The other side to this problem is that the server may not be receiving the last packet being sent. The error number 54 translated as "connection reset/network is busy" will be returned if this is the case. When this error is received, Net8 assumes that the server is down and closes the connection. Now, just because this error is received does not mean that the server isn't down, so be sure to verify whether the communications link has gone down, at least temporarily, or that the server is actually up and running.

If you need more help or information about troubleshooting this problem, consult your operating system–specific documentation.

ORA-03121: No Interface Driver Connection—Function Not Performed

If you have erroneously used an older-style SQL*Net v1 prefix, you can get this error message. Obviously, the solution to this problem is not to use any of the following prefixes in a Net8 connection string:

- T:
- X:
- P:

Another reason that you may receive this error message is that only the username and password were specified from a client machine that had no local Oracle database installed. To correct this situation, be sure that the complete, required connect string is entered.

Understanding Net8 Log and Trace Files

Are you allergic to anything? I have a rather uncommon allergy to pepper—the food seasoning. I'm not bothered at all if I eat the vegetable, but even a little black or white pepper sprinkled on food causes me to have a reaction. It was very difficult to determine what was causing my reaction because I never use this seasoning on my food when I cook and I never add it to foods before I eat. How did I finally determine what was causing me problems? Well, since I only reacted to foods when I was eating in a restaurant, whenever I ate something and reacted to it, I immediately asked for the ingredients that had been used in my food preparation. I kept track of the ingredients that had been used, and over the course of several weeks, I was able to determine that the only thing that was consistently used as an ingredient was pepper. I then made the deciding test. I intentionally added pepper to a food that I had eaten most of without a reaction, and the pepper caused a reaction. I have found that, as long as I do not get food seasoned with pepper, I am fine.

Now, let's think about my approach. Each time a specific event occurred, I noted that I had a problem. I wrote down what I thought might be the cause and, eventually, was able to correlate the information and reach a diagnosis of my problem and implement a successful solution. The key that enabled me to succeed was that I kept a log of the events that precipitated my problem. Net8 essentially takes the same actions. When a problematic event occurs, the event is noted in a log file. Net8 also supplies tracing information so that you can see what was happening before the problem occurred.

In this part of the chapter, I'm going to guide you through using the Net8 log and trace files to help you to determine and resolve Oracle networking problems that occur on your system.

Examining Log Files

By default, if you have not specified where Net8 should place log files on your system, they will be located in $ORACLE_HOME/network/log on a UNIX system and ORACLE_HOME\network\log on a Windows NT system. On a client machine, if a log file is generated, it will be placed in the user's current working directory.

Now, keep in mind that as Net8 encounters errors or takes actions, each event is appended to the log file. There are times when the error messages that you receive on your terminal screen do not really supply enough information for you to know where to begin your search for a solution. The Net8 log file provides additional information for a network or database administrator to use to help troubleshoot and solve the problem.

But, what's in a Net8 log file? Oh, glad you asked! As the listener processes connection requests, any errors that are encountered are written to the log file. Remember back in Chapter 2 when I told you about the protocol stack that Oracle uses? Well, Net8 keeps an error stack that shows the state of the software at various layers. However, errors cannot be captured unless you ensure that logging remains enabled on clients or Oracle Names servers. Since only administrators, or any other accounts that have been granted the appropriate privileges to perform the tasks, have the ability to replace or erase log files, you can control this process. Swell! But that doesn't really answer the question posed earlier, does it. Okay, you now know that the error log contains all errors. For the listener, the log also contains audit trail information about every client connection request and most of the listener control commands that have been issued.

Hmm, if the log file is storing all of this information, can you think of a possible problem that can occur? If you said that the file could potentially get very large, you were correct. If you enable the log file to capture information at the Admin or Support level, you should monitor the size of this file to ensure that it does not become too large and unwieldy.

Let's Look at a Log File

I have just started my listener. I've defined my listener to have the default listener name LISTENER, and, at least this time, the listener has started with no errors. Here's the information that has been stored in the listener log file:

```
TNSLSNR for 32-bit Windows: Version 8.1.6.0.0 - Production on 12-MAY-2000 19:36:57
(c) Copyright 1998, 1999, Oracle Corporation.  All rights reserved.

System parameter file is D:\Oracle\Ora81\network\admin\listener.ora
Log messages written to D:\Oracle\Ora81\network\log\lsnr.log
Trace information written to D:\Oracle\Ora81\network\trace\lsnr.trc
Trace level is currently 16

Listening on: (DESCRIPTION=(ADDRESS=(PROTOCOL=tcp)(HOST=marlenes-pc)(PORT=1521)))
TIMESTAMP * CONNECT DATA [* PROTOCOL INFO] * EVENT [* SID] * RETURN CODE
```

Now, let's see. We don't have any errors, so there isn't much information stored here, is there? You can see the version of the RDBMS being used and the date and time that the listener was started. The location of the listener system configuration file that was used, the log file, and trace file are captured. That's really helpful because you can be sure, if there is more than one listener file on your system, which file Net8 was looking at when the listener was started. Of course, if you've stored your log and trace files to a nondefault location and you forget where you've put them, you'll have to do a search of your system to find them since you won't be able to look in the log file. You can also see the protocol that was declared, the host machine name or IP address used, and the port number the listener is listening on. The trace level that was specified is also recorded. The last line in the entry looks kind of confusing, doesn't it? Let me display it again so we can talk about it more easily.

```
TIMESTAMP * CONNECT DATA [* PROTOCOL INFO] * EVENT [* SID] * RETURN CODE
```

There, that's better. Hmm, it seems pretty meaningless. Can you tell me what it might be used for or why it's in the listener.ora file? You can think about this while you look at the next listing.

Now, let's look at two examples of the information that is saved to the log file when an error occurs. Here's a section of error log listings from my listener.ora file:

```
TNSLSNR for 32-bit Windows: Version 8.1.6.0.0 - Production on 10-MAY-2000 04:20:29
(c) Copyright 1998, 1999, Oracle Corporation.  All rights reserved.

System parameter file is D:\Oracle\Ora81\network\admin\listener.ora
Log messages written to D:\ORACLE\Ora81\network\log\lsnr.log
Trace information written to D:\ORACLE\Ora81\network\trace\lsnr.trc
Trace level is currently 6

Listening on: (DESCRIPTION=(ADDRESS=(PROTOCOL=tcp)(HOST=marlenes-pc)(PORT=1521)))
TIMESTAMP * CONNECT DATA [* PROTOCOL INFO] * EVENT [* SID] * RETURN CODE
10-MAY-2000 04:20:31
(CONNECT_DATA=(CID=(PROGRAM=)(HOST=)(USER=theriml1))(COMMAND=status)(ARGUMENTS=64
(SERVICE=LISTENER)(VERSION=135290880)) * status * 406
NNC-00406: name "LISTENER_marlenes-pc" does not exist
 NNC-00406: name "SKDL.world" does not exist
  NNC-00406: name "PLSExtProc" does not exist
10-MAY-2000 04:21:10 * service_register * SKDL * 0
10-MAY-2000 04:21:40
(CONNECT_DATA=(CID=(PROGRAM=)(HOST=)(USER=theriml1))(COMMAND=status)(ARGUMENTS=6
(SERVICE=LISTENER)(VERSION=135290880)) * status * 406
NNC-00406: name "LISTENER_marlenes-pc" does not exist
 NNC-00406: name "SKDL.world" does not exist
  NNC-00406: name "PLSExtProc" does not exist
10-MAY-2000 04:24:08 * service_died * SKDL * 12547
TNS-12547: TNS:lost contact

TNSLSNR for 32-bit Windows: Version 8.1.6.0.0 - Production on 10-MAY-2000 10:14:24

(c) Copyright 1998, 1999, Oracle Corporation.  All rights reserved.

System parameter file is D:\Oracle\Ora81\network\admin\listener.ora
Log messages written to D:\Oracle\Ora81\network\log\lsnr.log
Trace information written to D:\Oracle\Ora81\network\trace\lsnr.trc
Trace level is currently 6

Listening on: (DESCRIPTION=(ADDRESS=(PROTOCOL=tcp)(HOST=marlenes-pc)(PORT=1521)))
TIMESTAMP * CONNECT DATA [* PROTOCOL INFO] * EVENT [* SID] * RETURN CODE
TNS-01155: Incorrectly specified SID_LIST_listener parameter in LISTENER.ORA
```

```
NL-00305: the specified path name does not exist
No longer listening on:
(DESCRIPTION=(ADDRESS=(PROTOCOL=tcp)(HOST=marlenes-pc)(PORT=1521)))
```

There certainly is a lot going on here, isn't there? Let's break this listing down a bit and see if we can figure out what's going on. There are really two distinct entries from two different time periods with different error numbers. I'm going to go ahead and list a few lines I'd like to call your attention to within the error listing first. All right?

```
TIMESTAMP * CONNECT DATA [* PROTOCOL INFO] * EVENT [* SID] * RETURN CODE
10-MAY-2000 04:20:31
(CONNECT_DATA=(CID=(PROGRAM=)(HOST=)(USER=theriml1))(COMMAND=status)(ARGUMENTS=64
(SERVICE=LISTENER)(VERSION=135290880)) * status * 406
```

Oh, that's the same line I showed you earlier, but this time, there's more information below it. Do you see what the line is used for now? Yup, that's right! Its purpose is to be used as a header for the information that follows. If you go back through the error example, you'll find that sometimes the data that follows is coordinated with the header, and sometimes it isn't. There's a second header that you can receive as well. Take a moment to look back at the error listing, and see if you can find the second header and its associated contents. Notice that the header information in brackets ([]) may not be present in the listing that follows the header. This is true of the piece of listing I extracted. There's a time stamp and connection information but no protocol data. The event information is present, but the SID data isn't. The status code is 406. Before I tell you what was really wrong with my environment and what I did to fix it, I'd like you to decide what the errors are and think about what approach you'd use to attempt to repair the problems. Okay?

Network Layers and Error Messages

There are several different layers that the Net8 interface interacts with. Each layer has an abbreviation associated with it. Table 14-7 shows the abbreviations and their associated layer or layers.

Initials	Description
NR	Network Routing
NN	Network Naming (Oracle Names server)
NS	Network Session (main and secondary layers)
NA	Native Services, including Network Authentication (NA) and Network Encryption (NAE)
NT	Network Transport (main, secondary, and operating system layers)

TABLE 14-7. *Net8 Network Interface Layers*

Now, when an error occurs, knowing the layer that Net8 was interacting with can help you to identify what the error is and how to resolve it. In the error messages I displayed first, the abbreviations are all NNC. Thus you can pretty easily determine that they are all related to the Network Naming layer. Since the indication is that the Oracle Names server is involved, you can check for problems with name resolution and connection configuration. You can also check to see if your listener is running. Notice that the error messages are repeated twice, but the second time, you get closer to the heart of the problem. You can see that the listener "died" and the connection was lost. Well, that narrows the field down quite a bit, doesn't it. In this case, the listener did "drop out" and the connection was lost. Go ahead and map out what you would do to resolve this error.

As to the second error, well, let's see. There is no abbreviation NL listed, so I think we can assume that we're dealing with a general Network Layer error. The real error number we are interested in is the "TNS-01155: Incorrectly specified SID_LIST_listener parameter in LISTENER.ORA" error. What do you think about this one? I think it's time to go back to the listener.ora file and see what might be wrong with the **sid_list**_LISTENER parameters.

With a little practice, you should be able to tell what layer of the Net8 interface you're dealing with and have a better general idea of what the problem is. Remember, if you're having a lot of trouble troubleshooting and resolving the problem, don't waste an excessive amount of time. Call Oracle Support.

Examining Trace Files

By default, if you have not specified where Net8 should place log files on your system, they will be located in $ORACLE_HOME/network/trace on a UNIX system and ORACLE_HOME\network\trace on Windows NT. In Oracle8i, Release 2 v8.1.6.0.0, there is a problem with the Net8 Assistant. When you create a listener and enable tracing, the tool does not write the parameters to the listener.ora file. Therefore, to enable tracing, you must manually edit the listener.ora file and put the following parameters in with the correct information for your system:

```
TRACE_LEVEL_<lsnr_name> = <support_level>
TRACE_FILE_<lsnr_name> = <file_name>
TRACE_DIRECTORY_<lsnr_name>=<directory path>
```

Here are the entries in my listener.ora file for these parameters:

```
TRACE_LEVEL_LISTENER = SUPPORT
TRACE_FILE_LISTENER = LSNR
TRACE_DIRECTORY_LISTENER=D:\Oracle\Ora81\network\trace
```

In this example, my listener name is LISTENER, and the file will be named lsnr.trc. The file will be located in the directory D:\Oracle\Ora81\network\trace.

Please keep in mind that when you enable tracing on your system, the process can be very resource intensive. Therefore, you really only want to enable tracing if you are having a problem with your listener that you can't solve in any other way. Also, be sure to turn tracing off as soon as you can after resolving the problem.

Trace Files and Parameters

When tracing is enabled, each Net8 component produces its own trace file. Table 14-8 shows the different files and the type of information that each contains.

As I mentioned earlier, you can place the configuration parameters to enable listener connection tracing in your listener.ora file. However, there are configuration parameters that you can set in your other Net8 configuration files to enable capture of information about client, server, Oracle Names server, or Oracle Connection Manager processes. To capture client or server information, you can enable the parameters shown in Table 14-9 in your sqlnet.ora file on the client or server or both.

There are also some optional tracing parameters that you can add to your sqlnet.ora file to enable the **tnsping** utility. **Tnsping** is used to determine whether or not a service can be reached on a Net8 network. The parameters are **tnsping.trace_level** and **tnsping.trace_directory**. Just as you can set a trace level using either a number or character value, you can set the **tnsping.trace_level** to a number between 0 and 16 or the character values OFF, USER, ADMIN, or SUPPORT. The

File Name	Description
sqlnet.trc	Client
svr_<pid>.trc	Server
listener.trc	Listener
names.trc	Oracle Names server
cman_<pid>.trc on UNIX cman<pid>.trc on Windows NT	Oracle Connection Manager CMGW gateway process
cmadm_<pid>.trc on UNIX cmadm<pid>.trc on Windows NT	Oracle Connection Manager CMADMIN administrative process

TABLE 14-8. *Trace Files and Their Information Type*

Parameter in Sqlnet.ora	Description
trace_level_client	Indicates the level of detail the trace facility records for the client. The trace level value can be either a value within the range of 0 to 16 (where 0 is no tracing and 16 represents the maximum amount of tracing) or a value of OFF, ADMIN, USER, or SUPPORT. OFF (equivalent to 0)—Provides no tracing USER (equivalent to 4)—Traces to identify user-induced error conditions ADMIN (equivalent to 6)—Traces to identify installation-specific problems SUPPORT (equivalent to 16)—Provides trace information for troubleshooting information for support
trace_directory_client	Establishes the destination directory for the client trace file. By default, the client directory is $ORACLE_HOME/network/trace on UNIX and ORACLE_HOME\network\trace on Windows NT.
trace_file_client	Sets the name of the log file for the client. By default the log name is sqlnet.trc.
trace_unique_client	Determines whether or not a unique trace file is created for each client trace file. If the value is set to ON, a process identifier is appended to the name of each trace file generated so that several can coexist. If the value is set to OFF, when a new trace file is created for a client, it overwrites the existing file. This parameter creates unique trace files named sqlnet<pid>.trc.

TABLE 14-9. *Sqlnet.ora Trace Parameters*

Parameter in Sqlnet.ora	Description
trace_level_server	Indicates the level of detail the trace facility records for the server. The trace level value can be either a value within the range of 0 to 16 (where 0 is no tracing and 16 represents the maximum amount of tracing) or a value of OFF, ADMIN, USER, or SUPPORT. OFF (equivalent to 0)—Provides no tracing USER (equivalent to 4)—Traces to identify user-induced error conditions ADMIN (equivalent to 6)—Traces to identify installation-specific problems SUPPORT (equivalent to 16)—Provides trace information for troubleshooting information for support.
trace_directory_server	Establishes the destination directory for the server trace file. By default, the server directory is $ORACLE_HOME/network/trace on UNIX and ORACLE_HOME\network\trace on Windows NT.
trace_file_server	Sets the name of the trace file for the server. By default the log name is svr_<pid>.trc.

TABLE 14-9 *Sqlnet.ora Trace Parameters* (continued)

meanings are the same as shown in Table 14-9 for the parameter **trace_level_server**. For **tnsping.trace_directory**, you enter the destination directory for the **tnsping** trace file.

As you saw earlier, you set the trace level, file name, and trace directory location for the listener in the listener.ora file. The Oracle Names server has the same type of parameters available to enable tracing, but the names are **names.trace_directory**, **names.trace_file**, and **names.trace_level**. There is one additional Oracle Names parameter called **names.trace_unique**. If this parameter is set to ON, a unique file name is created for each trace session. That way, you can have multiple trace files in the same directory. The process identifier for the process performing the trace is appended to the file name. The file name will have the form names<pid>.trc.

For cman.ora, the parameters are **tracing** and **trace_directory**. If **tracing** is set to YES, CMGW creates a trace file called cman_<pid>.trc on UNIX or cman<pid>.trc on Windows NT. The value for **trace_directory** establishes the destination directory for the trace file.

Understanding the Output

In 1993, I lived in Germany for several months. I really loved being there, but I didn't know how to speak the native language very well. I wanted to buy a map of the city I was living in. I used a German phrase book to learn how to ask where the location of the city maps was. I practiced really hard to be able to say my phrase just right. Gathering all of my courage, I entered the local bookstore and asked in my best attempt ever where the city maps were located. I must have succeeded in asking my question perfectly because the shop attendant answered quickly and walked away. I stood there in shock realizing that I did not have a clue what the translation was to the answer he had just given me. I had spent all of my time learning to ask the question and none of my time learning to understand the answer I received.

I was far too embarrassed to ask again in English so I walked out of the store and down the street to another shop where I saw maps for sale. I asked the clerk for a city map. This time, I asked my question in English and was successful in getting the map I wanted. The point here is that you can gather all of the trace information in the world, but if you do not understand what you are reading, the trace files won't do you a bit of good.

Okay, now that you've added the trace-enabling parameters to the appropriate file to trace the actions of a specific area, let's see if I can help you to understand the answers you'll get. Trace files provide you with insights into the flow of packets between network nodes. They can help you determine which component of Net8 is really failing. Finally, they will provide error codes that can help you determine the root cause of your problem.

Viewing Packets

As you learned at the beginning of this book, information is sent from place to place on a network using packets. Net8 performs its functions the same way. If you specify a trace level of SUPPORT, you can view the actual contents of the Net8 packets on your system. To better understand the meaning of the codes that you'll see, look at Table 14-10, which shows the Net8 packet keywords and the type of packets they represent.

Keyword	Description
NSPTCN	Connect
NSPTAC	Accept
NSPTRF	Refuse
NSPTRS	Resend
NSPDA	Data
NSPCNL	Control
NSPTMK	Marker

TABLE 14-10. *Net8 Packet Keywords*

When a problem occurs with the connection, an error code is logged to the trace file. The error message will have a prefix of <ERROR> or <FATAL>. Let's look at a typical trace file and see what the error output looks like:

```
nspsend: entry
nspsend: plen=244, type=6
ntpwr: entry
ntpwr: exit
-<ERROR>- nspsend: transport write error
nspsend: error exit
nserror: entry
-<ERROR>- nserror: nsres: id=0, op=65, ns=12541, ns2=12560; nt[0]=511, nt[1]=61,nt[2]=0
-<ERROR>- nsopen: unable to open transport
nricdt: Call failed...
nricdt: exit
-<ERROR>- osnqper: error from nricall
-<ERROR>- osnqper: nr err code: 12203
-<ERROR>- osnqper: ns main err code: 12541
-<ERROR>- osnqper: ns (2) err code: 12560
-<ERROR>- osnqper: nt main err code: 511
-<ERROR>- osnqper: nt (2) err code: 61
-<ERROR>- osnqper: nt OS err code: 0
osnqme: entry
osnqme: reporting nr (1) error: (12203) as rdbms err (12203)
osnqme: exit
-<ERROR>- onstns: Couldn't connect, returning 12203
nricall: Exiting NRICALL with following termination result -1
nricall: exit
osnqme: entry
osnqme: reporting nr (1) error: (12203) as rdbms err (12203)
osnqme: exit
-<ERROR>- onstns: Couldn't connect, returning 12203
-<ERROR>- osnqper: error from nricall
```

This is an actual error message. Can you tell which error is being returned through the packets and protocol stack? If you said an ORA-12203, you'd be correct. If you find the most recent NS error code, you'll be able to more efficiently evaluate the problem since the session layer controls the connection. The most important error messages are usually at the bottom of the file and will be more likely to reflect the most recent errors and the source of the problem.

There is an error tool on UNIX called **oerr** that can provide more information about Net8 return codes. You can invoke the tool by typing the following:

```
oerr tns error_number
```

Oracle also provides a tool called the Trace Assistant to help you understand the information provided in your trace files. You can only use the Trace Assistant if you have enabled level 16, or SUPPORT, tracing. To run the Trace Assistant, use the following command syntax:

```
trcasst <options> filename
```

Figure 14-9 shows the options available for this tool. To get more information about how to translate the information that this tool provides, look in the Oracle *Net8 Administrator's Guide, Release 8.1.6* in Chapter 12 under the section "Evaluating Net8 Traces."

```
Command Prompt
Microsoft(R) Windows NT(TM)
(C) Copyright 1985-1996 Microsoft Corp.

C:\>trcasst

Trace Assistant Utility for 32-bit Windows: Version 8.1.6.0.0 - Production on 15
-MAY-2000 00:38:40

(c) Copyright 1997 Oracle Corporation.  All rights reserved.

TNS-04202: Trace Assistant Usage ERROR: Not enough arguments

Usage: trcasst [options] <filename>
               [options]  default values are: -odt -e -s
               <filename> is always the last argument
   Options can be zero or more of the following:
   -o    Enables display of SQL*Net and TTC information
         After the -o the following options can be used:
          c or d for summary or detailed SQL*Net information respectively
          u or t for summary or detailed TTC information respectively
          q displays SQL commands (used together with u)

   -s    Enables display of statistical information
   -e    Enables display of error information
         After the -e, zero or one error decoding level may follow:
          0 or nothing, translates NS error numbers
          1 displays NS error translation plus all other errors
          2 displays error number without translation

C:\>
```

FIGURE 14-9. *DOS Window with Trace Assistant tool options*

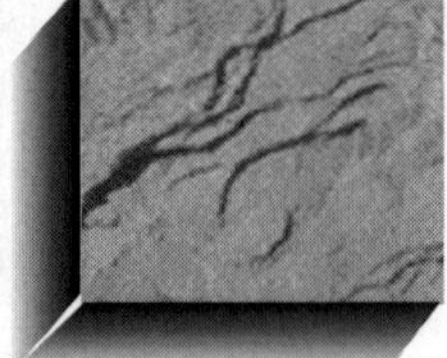

APPENDIX A

Sqlnet.ora Parameters

here are many parameters available for each of the Net8 configuration files. In this appendix, you will find definitions of the parameters used in the sqlnet.ora file on a profile-by-profile basis. I will include the default values and, where appropriate, an example in the Description column.

Keep in mind that each version of Net8 may have different parameters or different default values for any parameter that is used. Therefore, you will always want to verify, looking at the delivered Oracle document set, what the values are for the parameters you use.

OName Client Profile

The parameters for the ONames Client profile are displayed in Table A-1.

Parameter	Description
names.dce.prefix	Specifies the DCE cell name (prefix) to use for name lookups. Default: /.:/subsys/oracle/names Example: names.dce.prefix=/.:/subsys/oracle/names
names.default_domain	Indicates the domain from which the client most often requests names. When this parameter is set to the default domain name (for example, US.ACME), the domain name will be automatically appended to any unqualified name in an ONames request (query, register, deregister, etc). Any name that contains an unescaped dot (.) will not have the default domain appended. Simple names may be qualified with a trailing dot (for example, "rootserver."). Default: null Example: names.default_domain = world

TABLE A-1. *ONames Client Profile Information*

Parameter	Description
names.directory_path	Sets the (ordered) list of naming adapters to use in resolving a name. The default is as shown for 3.0.2 of sqlnet onward. The default was (TNSNAMES, ONAMES) before that. The value can be presented without parentheses if only a single entry is being specified. The parameter is recognized from version 2.3.2 of sqlnet onward. Acceptable values include TNSNAMES—tnsnames.ora lookup ONAMES—Oracle Names HOSTNAME—Use the host name (or an alias of the host name) NIS—NIS (also known as "yp") CDS—OSF DCE's Cell Directory Service NDS—Novell's Netware Directory Service Default: TNSNAMES, ONAMES, HOSTNAME Example: names.directory_path=(value is operating system dependent)
names.initial_retry_timeout Range: 1–600 seconds	Determines how long a client will wait for a response from a Names server before reiterating the request to the next server in the preferred_servers list. Value is in seconds. Default: 15 (operating system dependent) Example: names.initial_retry_timeout=30
names.max_open_connections Range: 3–64	Determines how many connections an ONames client may have open at one time. Clients will ordinarily keep connections to servers open once they are established until the operation (or session in namesctl) is complete. A connection will be opened whenever needed unless the maximum are already open, in which case the least recently used connection will be closed before the new connection is opened. Minimum is 3 and maximum is 64. Default: 10 Example: names.max_open_connections=10

TABLE A-1. *ONames Client Profile Information* (continued)

Parameter	Description
names.message_pool_start_size Range: 3–256	Determines the initial number of messages allocated in the client's message pool. This pool provides the client with preallocated messages to be used for requests to ONames servers. Messages that are in the pool and unused may be reused. If a message is needed and no free messages are available in the pool, more will be allocated. Default: 10 Example: names.message_pool_start_size=10
names.nis_meta_map	Specifies the file to be used to map NIS attributes to an NIS mapname. Default: sqlnet.maps Example: names.nis.meta_map=sqlnet.maps
names.nds.name.context	Specifies the naming context in the NDS tree where the database object resides. Default: none Example: cn=Payroll.o=Oracle
names.preferred_servers	Specifies a list of ONames servers in the client's region; requests will be sent to each ADDRESS in the list until a response is received, or the list (and number of retries) is exhausted. Addresses of the following form specify that messages to the Onames server should use Oracle Remote Operations (RPC): (description = (address=(protocol=tcp)(host=nineva)(port=1383)) (connect_data=(rpc=on))) Default: ADDR_LIST (operating system dependent) Example: names.preferred_servers = (address=(protocol=ipc) (key=n23)) (address_list = (address=(protocol=tcp) (host=nineva)(port=1383)) (address=(protocol=tcp) (host=cicada)(port=1575)))

TABLE A-1. *ONames Client Profile Information* (continued)

Parameter	Description
names.request_retries Range: 1–5	Specifies the number of times the client should try each server in the list of preferred_servers before allowing the operation to fail. Default: 1 Example: names.request_retries=2

TABLE A-1. *ONames Client Profile Information* (continued)

Namesctl Profile

Table A-2 shows the parameters for the Namesctl profile.

Parameter	Description
namesctl.internal_encrypt_password Range: T/F	When TRUE, namesctl will not encrypt the password when it is sent to the Names server. This would enable an unencrypted password to be set in names.ora:names.server_password. Default: False Example: namesctl.internal_encrypt_password = False
namesctl.internal_use Range: T/F	If TRUE, namesctl will enable a set of internal undocumented commands. All internal commands are preceded by an underscore (_) in order to distinguish them as internal. (See text after table.) Default: False Example: namesctl.internal_use=True
namesctl.no_initial_server Range: T/F	If TRUE, namesctl will suppress any error messages when namesctl is unable to connect to a default Names server. Default: False Example: namesctl.no_initial_server=False

TABLE A-2. *Namesctl Profile*

Parameter	Description
namesctl.noconfirm Range: T/F	When TRUE, namesctl will suppress the confirmation prompt when sensitive operations (stop, restart, reload) are requested. This is quite helpful when using namesctl scripts. Default: False Example: namesctl.noconfirm=True
namesctl.server_password	Automatically sets the password for the Names server in order to perform sensitive operations (stop, restart, reload). The password may also be set manually during a namesctl session using **set password**. Default: NULL Example: namesctl.server_password=mangler
namesctl.trace_level Range: {OFF, USER, ADMIN, 0–16}	Indicates the level at which namesctl is to be traced. Available values: 0 or OFF—No trace output 4 or USER—User trace information 10 or ADMIN—Administration trace information 16 or SUPPORT—World Wide Customer Support trace information Default: OFF (0) Example: namesctl.trace_level=ADMIN
namesctl.trace_file	Indicates the output file from a namesctl trace session. Default: namesctl.trc Example: namesctl.trace_file=namesctl.trc
namesctl.trace_directory	Indicates the directory to which trace files from a namesctl trace session are written. Default: $ON/trace Example: namesctl.trace_directory= /oracle/network/trace
namesctl.trace_unique	Indicates whether each trace file has a unique name, allowing multiple trace files to coexist. If the value is set to ON, a process identifier is appended to the name of each trace file generated. Default: False Example: namesctl.trace_unique=True

TABLE A-2. *Namesctl Profile* (continued)

The parameter **namesctl.internal_use**=TRUE is set if undocumented parameters are turned on. The following commands are enabled. No detail is given on what these commands do or what the asterisk next to some of them indicates. The parameters all begin with an underscore to distinguish them as parameters and indicate that they are internal.

_add_data	_create_name	_delete_name
_full_status	_ireplace_data	_newttl_name
_pause	_remove_data	_rename_name
_replace_data	_start	_walk*

There is also a set of Names server variables that may be set when namesctl is in internal mode:

_authority_required	_auto_refresh*	_cache_checkpoint_interval
_cache_dump	_default_autorefresh_expire	_default_autorefresh_retry
_default_forwarders_only	_forwarding_desired	_max_reforwards
_modify_ops_enabled	_next_cache_checkpoint	_next_cache_flush
_next_stat_log	_next_stat_reset	_reload
_request_delay	_restart	_shutdown

Native Naming Adapters Profile

Table A-3 shows the parameters for the Native Naming Adapters profile.

Parameter	Description
names.dce.prefix	Specifies the DCE cell (prefix) to use for name lookup. Default: /.:/subsys/oracle/names Example: names.dce.prefix = /.:/subsys/oracle/names
names.nds.name_context	Specifies the default NDS name context in which to look for the name to be resolved. Default: Operating system dependent Example: names.nds.name_context = personnel.acme

TABLE A-3. *Native Naming Adapters Profile*

Parameter	Description
names.nis.meta_map	Specifies the file to be used to map NIS attributes to an NIS mapname. Currently unused. Default: sqlnet.maps Example: none provided

TABLE A-3. *Native Naming Adapters Profile* (continued)

Sqlnet Kerberos Profile

The parameters that you use for the Kerberos profile are shown in Table A-4.

Parameter	Description
sqlnet.authentication_services Range: A single value or a list from {beq, none, all, oss, kerberos5, cybersafe, securid, identitx}	Enables one or more authentication services. To enable authentication via the Oracle Security Server, use (beq, oss). If the Advanced Networking Option has been installed with Kerberos5 support, use (beq, kerberos5) to enable authentication via Kerberos. Default: none Example: sqlnet.authentication_service=oss
sqlnet.kerberos5_cc_name Range: any valid pathname	The Kerberos credential cache pathname. Default: /tmp/krb5cc_<uid> Example: sqlnet.kerberos5_cc_name=/tmp/mycc
sqlnet.kerberos5_clockskew Range: any positive integer	The acceptable difference in the number of seconds between when a credential was sent and when it was received. Default: 300 Example: sqlnet.kerberos5_clockskew=250
sqlnet.kerberos5_conf Range: any valid pathname	The Kerberos configuration pathname. Default: /krb5/krb.conf Example: sqlnet.kerberos5_conf=/tmp/mykrb.conf
sqlnet.kerberos5_realms Range: any valid pathname	The Kerberos host name to realm translation file. Default: /krb5/krb.realms Example: sqlnet.kerberos5_realms=/tmp/mykrb.realms

TABLE A-4. *Sqlnet Kerberos Profile*

Parameter	Description
sqlnet.kerberos5_keytab Range: any valid pathname	The Kerberos secret key file. Default: /etc/v5srvtab Example: sqlnet.kerberos5_keytab=/tmp/myv5srvtab

TABLE A-4. *Sqlnet Kerberos Profile* (continued)

Advanced Networking Option Authentication Adapters Profile

The parameters for the Advanced Networking Option Authentication Adapters profile are shown in Table A-5. There are several parameters required to configure CyberSAFE to validate the identity of clients. A service principal, as required in the first description in Table A-5, is created on the CyberSAFE TrustBroker Master Server to aid in client validation.

Parameter with a Value	Description
Parameters used with CyberSAFE adapter: sqlnet.authentication_gssapi_service	The CyberSAFE service principal. Default: none Example: HYPERLINK mailto:sqlnet.authentication_gssapi_service= acme/asriniva.us.oracle.com@US.ORACLE. COM
Parameters used with Identix adapter: sqlnet.identix_fingerprint_method	The Identix authentication server method. Default: none (must be oracle) Example: sqlnet.identix_fingerprint_method=oracle
sqlnet.identix_fingerprint_database	The Identix authentication server TNS alias. Default: none Example: sqlnet.identix_fingerprint_database=ofm

TABLE A-5. *Advanced Networking Option Authentication Adapters for CyberSAFE and Identix*

Parameter with a Value	Description
sqlnet.identix_fingerprint_database_user	The Identix authentication service well-known username. Default: none Example: sqlnet.identix_fingerprint_database_user= ofm_client
sqlnet.identix_fingerprint_database_password	The Identix authentication service well-known password. Default: none Example: sqlnet.identix_fingerprint_database_password =ofm_client

TABLE A-5. *Advanced Networking Option Authentication Adapters for CyberSAFE and Identix* (continued)

Advanced Networking Option—Radius Adapter Profile

The profile parameters for the Radius Adapter are shown in Table A-6.

Parameter with a Value	Description
sqlnet.radius_authentication=localhost	Need to specify the location of the Radius server.
sqlnet.radius_authentication_port=1654	Need to specify the port address of the Radius server.
sqlnet.radius_accounting=off	If your Radius server supports accounting, you can enable it.
sqlnet.radius_challenge_response=off	Turn on/off challenge response.
sqlnet.radius_challenge_keyword=challenge	If you use activcard, enter activcard keyword to request a challenge from Radius server. If you use something else, enter challenge.
sqlnet.radius_authentication_interface= DefaultRadiusInterface	Enter the name of the client interface you want to use for challenge response.
sqlnet.radius_secret= $ORACLE_HOME/security/radius.key	Where the secret file is located.

TABLE A-6. *Radius Adapter Profile (No Syntax or Defaults Provided)*

Advanced Networking Option for Network Security

For the Advanced Networking Option for Network Security, the parameters follow. Because the parameters have the same default value and four possible values, I've listed them in a different format. First, the parameters are

- sqlnet.crypto_checksum_client
- sqlnet.crypto_checksum_server
- sqlnet.encryption_client
- sqlnet.encryption_server

These four parameters are used to specify whether a service (such as crypto-checksumming or encryption) should be active. Each parameter defaults to ACCEPTED.

Each of the above parameters can have one of four possible values shown in Table A-7. Descriptions of the values are also displayed here. See Chapter 13 for more information about the Oracle Advanced Security option.

Value	Description
ACCEPTED	The service will be active if the other side of the connection specifies REQUESTED or REQUIRED and there is a compatible algorithm available on the other side; it will be inactive otherwise.
REJECTED	The service must not be active, and the connection will fail if the other side specifies REQUIRED.
REQUESTED	The service will be active if the other side specifies ACCEPTED, REQUESTED, or REQUIRED and there is a compatible algorithm available on the other side; it will be inactive otherwise.
REQUIRED	The service must be active, and the connection will fail if the other side specifies REJECTED or if there is no compatible algorithm on the other side.

TABLE A-7. *Values for the Advanced Networking Option for Network Security*

The following parameters control which algorithms will be made available for each service on each end of a connection:

- sqlnet.crypto_checksum_types_client
- sqlnet.crypto_checksum_types_server
- sqlnet.encryption_types_client
- sqlnet.encryption_types_server

The value of each of these parameters can be either a parenthesized list of algorithm names separated by commas or a single algorithm name. Each example given here is a form of encryption algorithm representing a different degree of encryption. The higher the value (like the difference between 40, 56, and 128), the more complex the encryption algorithm is. Encryption types can be RC4_40, RC4_56, RC4_128, DES or DES40. (Encryption defaults to all the algorithms.) Crypto_checksum types can be MD5. (Crypto_checksum defaults to MD5.)

The last parameter within this profile is the sqlnet.crypto_seed. This is the value upon which the rest of the encryption process will be based. The default seed value is displayed here:

```
sqlnet.crypto_seed ="4fhfguweotcadsfdsafjkdsfqp5f201p45mxskdlfdasf"
```

Oracle Security Server Profile

This will probably all change for V8.1.6, but for 8.1.5 the profile values for the Oracle Security Server parameters are shown in Table A-8.

Parameter with a Value	Description
oss.source.my_wallet	The method for retrieving and storing my identity. Default: platform specific. The UNIX default is $HOME/oracle/oss. Example: oss.source.my_wallet= (source= (method=file) (method_data= /dve/asriniva/oss/wallet))

TABLE A-8. *Oracle Security Server Profile*

Parameter with a Value	Description
oss.source.location	The method for retrieving encrypted private keys. Default: Oracle method, oracle_security_service/oracle_security_service@oss Example: oss.source.location = (source= (method=oracle) (method_data= (sqlnet_address=andreoss)))

TABLE A-8. *Oracle Security Server Profile* (continued)

SQLNet(V2.x) and Net3.0 Client

Table A-9 contains a list of parameters available in the sqlnet.ora file with the designation of "available in" and a version value.

The use of the name Net3.0 instead of Net8 is intentional. Originally, Net3 was supposed to follow SQLNet 2 as the next version name, and the documentation and original versioning that was released followed this convention. However, with the release of Oracle8 for production, the network version name was changed to be more easily recognized as a part of Oracle8. Thus, the name Net8 came into being. To be consistent with Oracle's actual release names, Net3.0 is used for the specific parameters shown in Table A-9.

In the following descriptions, the term "client program" could mean either sqlplus, svrmgrl, or any other OCI program written by users.

Parameter	Purpose	Default/Range of Values
trace_level_client **Supported since: V3.0	Indicates the level at which the client program is to be traced.	Default: OFF (0) Possible values: {OFF, USER, ADMIN, 0–16} 0 or OFF—No trace output 4 or USER—User trace information 10 or ADMIN—Administration trace information 16 or SUPPORT—Oracle World Wide Support trace information

TABLE A-9. *Sqlnet.ora Parameters with the Version in Which They Were Released*

Parameter	Purpose	Default/Range of Values
tnsping.trace_directory **Supported since: V2.3.3	Indicates the directory to which the execution trace from the tnsping program is to be written.	Default: $ORACLE_HOME/network/trace Possible values: Any valid directory pathname
automatic_ipc **Supported since: V2.3.2	Forces a session to use or not to use IPC addresses on the client's node.	Default: OFF Possible values: {ON, OFF}
bequeath_detach **Supported since: V2.1	Turns off signal handling on UNIX systems. If signal handling is not turned off and client programs written by users make use of signal handling, they could interfere with Sqlnet/Net3.	Default: NO Possible values: {YES, NO}
sqlnet.client_registration **Supported since: V2.0	Sets a unique identifier for the client machine. This identifier is then passed to the listener with any connection request and will be included in the audit trail.	Default: OFF Possible values: The identifier can be any alphanumeric string up to 128 characters long.
trace_directory_client	Indicates the name of the directory to which trace files from the client execution are written.	Default: $ORACLE_HOME/network/trace Possible values: Any valid directory path with write permission
trace_file_client	Indicates the name of the file to which the execution trace of the client is written.	Default: $ORACLE_HOME/network/trace/cli.trc Possible values: Any valid file name
trace_unique_client	Gives each client trace file a unique name to prevent each trace file from being overwritten by successive runs of the client program.	Default: OFF Possible values: {ON, OFF}

TABLE A-9. *Sqlnet.ora Parameters with the Version in Which They Were Released* (continued)

Parameter	Purpose	Default/Range of Values
log_directory_client	Indicates the name of the directory to which the client log file is written.	Default: $ORACLE_HOME/network/log Possible values: Any valid directory pathname
log_file_client	Indicates the name of the log file from a client program.	Default: $ORACLE_HOME/network/log/sqlnet.log Possible values: This is a default value; you cannot change this.
log_directory_server	Indicates the name of the directory to which log files from the server are written.	Default: $ORACLE_HOME/network/trace Possible values: Any valid directory path with write permission
trace_directory_server	Indicates the name of the directory to which trace files from the server are written.	Default: $ORACLE_HOME/network_trace Possible values: Any valid directory path with write permission
trace_file_server	Indicates the name of the file to which the execution trace of the server program is written.	Default: $ORACLE_HOME/network/trace/svr_<pid>.trc, where <pid> stands for the process ID of the server on UNIX systems Possible values: Any valid file name
trace_level_server	Indicates the level at which the server program is to be traced.	Default: OFF (0) Possible values: {OFF, USER, ADMIN, 0–16} Available values: 0 or OFF—No trace output 4 or USER—User trace information 10 or ADMIN—Administration trace information 16 or SUPPORT—Oracle World Wide Support trace information

TABLE A-9. *Sqlnet.ora Parameters with the Version in Which They Were Released* (continued)

Parameter	Purpose	Default/Range of Values
use_dedicated_server	Forces the listener to spawn a dedicated server process for sessions from this client program.	Default: OFF Possible values: {OFF, ON}
use_cman	Tells the listener that Oracle Connection Manager is being used.	Default: FALSE Possible values: {TRUE, FALSE}
tnsping.trace_level	Indicates the level at which the server program is to be traced.	Default: OFF (0) Possible values: {OFF, USER, ADMIN, 0–16} Available values: 0 or OFF—No trace output 4 or USER—User trace information 10 or ADMIN—Administration trace information 16 or SUPPORT—Oracle World Wide Support trace information
sqlnet.expire_time	Indicates the time interval for sending a probe to verify that the client session is alive (this is used to reclaim wasteful resources on a dead client).	Default: 0 minutes Possible values: 0–any valid positive integer! (in minutes) Recommended value: 10 minutes
disable_oob	Disables out-of-band breaks if the underlying transport protocol (TCP, DECnet, etc.) does not support out-of-band breaks.	Default: OFF Possible values: {ON, OFF}

TABLE A-9. *Sqlnet.ora Parameters with the Version in Which They Were Released* (continued)

APPENDIX B

Names.ora Parameters

he parameters for the names.ora file are displayed within this appendix. I've used a tabular format to help make the parameters easier to read and follow. In Appendix A, I listed the Oname Client profile parameters that are placed in the sqlnet.ora file. The parameters listed here are server specific and are placed in the names.ora file. Chapter 4 contains information about the location and use of these parameters.

Table B-1 contains the available names.ora parameters for Oracle8i, Release 2. Wherever possible, I've added the default value and an example of the parameter's usage.

Parameter	Description
names.addresses	Lists the protocol address(es) on which the Oracle Names server listens. Any valid ADDRESS or ADDRESS_LIST is allowed. Default: names.addresses= (address=(protocol=tcp) (host=oranamesrvr0) (port=1575)
names.admin_region	Describes the data source for an administrative region. If set, this parameter defines a database as a repository for information. If this parameter is not set, replication of data between Oracle Names server caches. Default: Null Example: names.admin_region= (region= (description= (address=(protocol=tcp) (host=marlenes-pc) (port=1575))) (connect_data= (service_name=xyzcorp.us.com)) (userid=NELSON) (password=RINGADING) (refresh=172800) (retry=2700) (expire=8700) (version=34619392))
names.authority_required	Determines whether system queries require authoritative answers. Default: FALSE Example: names.authority_required=true

TABLE B-1. *Names.ora Parameters*

Parameter	Description
names.auto_refresh_expire	Specifies the amount of time in seconds the Oracle Names server caches other regions' database server addresses, which have been obtained through the names.domain_hints parameter. At the end of this interval, the Oracle Names server issues a query to the other regions' database servers to refresh the address. Default: 600 seconds Acceptable Values: 60–1209600 seconds Example: names.auto_refresh_expire=1200000
names.auto_refresh_retry	Specifies the interval in seconds that the Oracle Names server retries the Oracle Names servers on its domain hint list. Default: 180 Acceptable Values: 60–3600 Example: names.auto_refresh_retry=180
names.cache_checkpoint_file	Specifies the name and path of the file to which the Oracle Names server writes its checkpoint file. Default: $ORACLE_HOME/network/names/chpcch.ora on UNIX ORACLE_HOME\network\names\ckpcch.ora on Windows NT Example: names.cache_checkpoint_file= D:\Oracle\Ora81\network\names\cacheck.ora
names.cache_checkpoint_interval	Indicates the interval in seconds in which an Oracle Names server writes a checkpoint of its stored data to a checkpoint file. Each Oracle Names server can periodically write its cached data to a file to protect against start-up failures. Default: 0 (disabled) Acceptable Values: 10–259200 seconds (3 days) Example: names.cache_checkpoint_interval=24
names.config_checkpoint_file	Specifies the name and path of the file used to checkpoint Oracle Names server configuration settings. Default: $ORACLE_HOME/network/names/ckpcfg.ora on UNIX ORACLE_HOME\network\names\ckpcfg.ora on Windows NT Example: names.config_checkpoint_file=D:\Oracle\Ora81\ network\names\configck.ora

TABLE B-1. *Names.ora Parameters* (continued)

Parameter	Description
names.connect_timeout	Limits the amount of time in seconds the Oracle Names server waits for the connection from a client to complete. Default: 3 seconds Acceptable Values: 1–600 seconds Example: names.connect_timeout=8
names.default_forwarders	Address list of other Oracle Names servers that are used to forward queries. Example: names.default_forwarders=(forwarder_list=(forwarder=(name=adminroot1.com)(address=(protocol=tcp) (port=4200)(host=marlenes-pc))))
names.default_forwarders_only	When set to TRUE, the Oracle Names server forwards queries only to those Oracle Names servers listed as default forwarders with the names.default_forwarders parameter.
names.domain_hints	Lists the names, addresses, and domains of all servers in one or more remote regions. Enables the Oracle Names server to know about other regions' Oracle Names servers. This includes at least the root region for all Oracle Names servers that are not in the root region. Other regions can be provided as optimization requires. Example: names.domain_hints= (hint_desc=(hint_list= (hint= (name=adminroot1.com)(address=(protocol=tcp)(host=marlenes-pc)(port=4200)))))
names.domains	List of domains in the server's local region, as well as the default time to live (TTL) for data in those domains. Example: names.domains=(domain_list=(domain=(name=adminroot1.com) (min_ttl=86400))(domain=(name=com)(min_ttl=8640)))
names.forwarding_available	If set to ON, the Oracle Names server forwards client request to remote Oracle Names server. If set to OFF, clients without access to the network outside the local domain are unable to resolve names. Default: ON Values: ON | OFF Example: names.forwarding_available=OFF

TABLE B-1. *Names.ora Parameters* (continued)

Parameter	Description
names.forwarding_desired	If set to TRUE, the Oracle Names server provides remote Oracle Names server address location information to clients. This way, clients are redirected to the appropriate Oracle Names server. If set to FALSE, the Oracle Names server connects to the remote Oracle Names server on behalf of clients. Default: TRUE Values: TRUE I FALSE Example: names.forwarding_desired=TRUE
names.keep_db_open	Specifies whether or not to attempt to keep the TNS connection to the region database open between operations. If set to FALSE, the connection is closed after each load, reload, or reload-check. Default: TRUE Values: TRUE I FALSE Example: names.keep_db_open=FALSE
names.log_directory	Specifies the destination directory where the log file for Oracle Names server operational events are written. Default: $ORACLE_HOME/network/log on UNIX ORACLE_HOME\network\log on Windows NT Example: names.log_directory=D:\Oracle\Ora81\network\names
names.log_file	Indicates the name of the output file to which Oracle Names server operational events are written. The file name extension is always .log. Do not enter an extension for this parameter. Default: NAMES Example: names.log_file=onames
names.log_stats_interval	Specifies the number of seconds between full statistical dumps in the log file. Default: 0 (OFF) Acceptable Values: 10 seconds and beyond Example: names.log_stats_interval=12
names.log_unique	If set to TRUE, the log file names are unique and do not overwrite existing log files. Default: FALSE Values: TRUE I FALSE Example: names.log_unique=TRUE

TABLE B-1. *Names.ora Parameters* (continued)

Parameter	Description
names.max_open_connections	Specifies the number of connections that the Oracle Names server can have open at any given time. The value is generated as the value 10 or the sum of one connection for listening, five for clients, plus one for each remote domain defined in the local administrative region, whichever is greater. Default: Calculated based on entered data Acceptable Values: 2–64 Example: names.max_open_connections=52
names.max_reforwards	Specifies the maximum number of times the server attempts to forward an operation. Default: 2 Acceptable Values: 1–15 Example: names.max_reforwards=4
names.message_pool_start_size	Determines the initial number of messages allocated in the server's message pool that are used for incoming or outgoing forwarded messages. Default: 10 Acceptable Values: 3–256 Example: names.message_pool_start_size=15
names.no_modify_requests	If set to TRUE, the server refuses any operations that modify the data in its region. Default: FALSE Values: TRUE | FALSE Example: names.no_modify_requests=TRUE
names.no_region_database	If set to TRUE, the server does not look for a region database. Default: FALSE Values: TRUE | FALSE Example: names.no_region_database=TRUE
names.password	Sets an encrypted password for an Oracle Names server so that certain privileged operations, such as STOP, RESTART, and RELOAD, used from the namesctl utility are secure. If this parameter is set with the Net8 Assistant, the password is encrypted. A clear-text password can be made manually. If the password is clear-text, ensure the namesctl.internal_encrypt_password parameter in the sqlnet.ora file is set to FALSE. Default: None Example: names.password=625926683431aa55

TABLE B-1. *Names.ora Parameters* (continued)

Parameter	Description
names.region_checkpoint_file	Specifies the name and path of the file used to checkpoint region data (for example, domain addresses, database addresses of Oracle Names servers in the local region). Default: $ORACLE_HOME/network/names/ckpreg.ora on UNIX ORACLE_HOME\network\names\ckpreg.ora on Windows NT Example: names.region_checkpoint_file=D:\Oracle\Ora81\network\names\regionck.ora
names.reset_stats_interval	Specifies the number of seconds during which the statistics collected by the Oracle Names servers should accumulate. At the frequency specified, they are reset to zero. Default: 0 (never reset statistics) Acceptable Values: 0–10 seconds Example: names.reset_stats_interval=5
names.save_config_on_stop	If set to TRUE, the Oracle Names server saves its runtime configuration settings back into the names.ora file. Any parameters, which were modified through namesctl set operations, replace prior names.ora settings. Default: FALSE Values: TRUE | FALSE Example: names.save_config_on_stop=TRUE
names.server_name	Each Oracle Names server is uniquely identified by a name. All configuration references to a particular Oracle Names server use this name. Default: ONAMES_<onames_server> Example: names.server_name=namesrv1.xyzcorp.us.com
names.trace_directory	Indicates the name of the directory to which trace files from an Oracle Names server trace session are written. Default: $ORACLE_HOME/network/trace on UNIX ORACLE_HOME\network\trace on Windows NT Example: names.trace_directory=D:\Oracle\Ora81\network\admin\trace

TABLE B-1. *Names.ora Parameters* (continued)

Parameter	Description
names.trace_file	Indicates the name of the output file from an Oracle Names server trace session. The file name extension is always .trc. Default: NAMES Example: names.trace_file=onames
names.trace_func	Enables internal mechanism to control tracing by function name. Default: FALSE Values: TRUE I FALSE Example: names.trace_func=TRUE
names.trace_level	Indicates the level at which the Oracle Names server is to be traced. Default: OFF Values: OFF—No trace output USER—User trace information ADMIN—Administration trace information SUPPORT—World Wide Customer Support trace information Example: names.trace_level=ADMIN
names.trace_unique	Indicates whether each trace file has a unique name, allowing multiple trace files to coexist. If the value is set to ON, a process identifier is appended to the name of each trace file generated. Default: ON Values: ON I OFF Example: names.trace_unique=ON

TABLE B-1. *Names.ora Parameters* (continued)

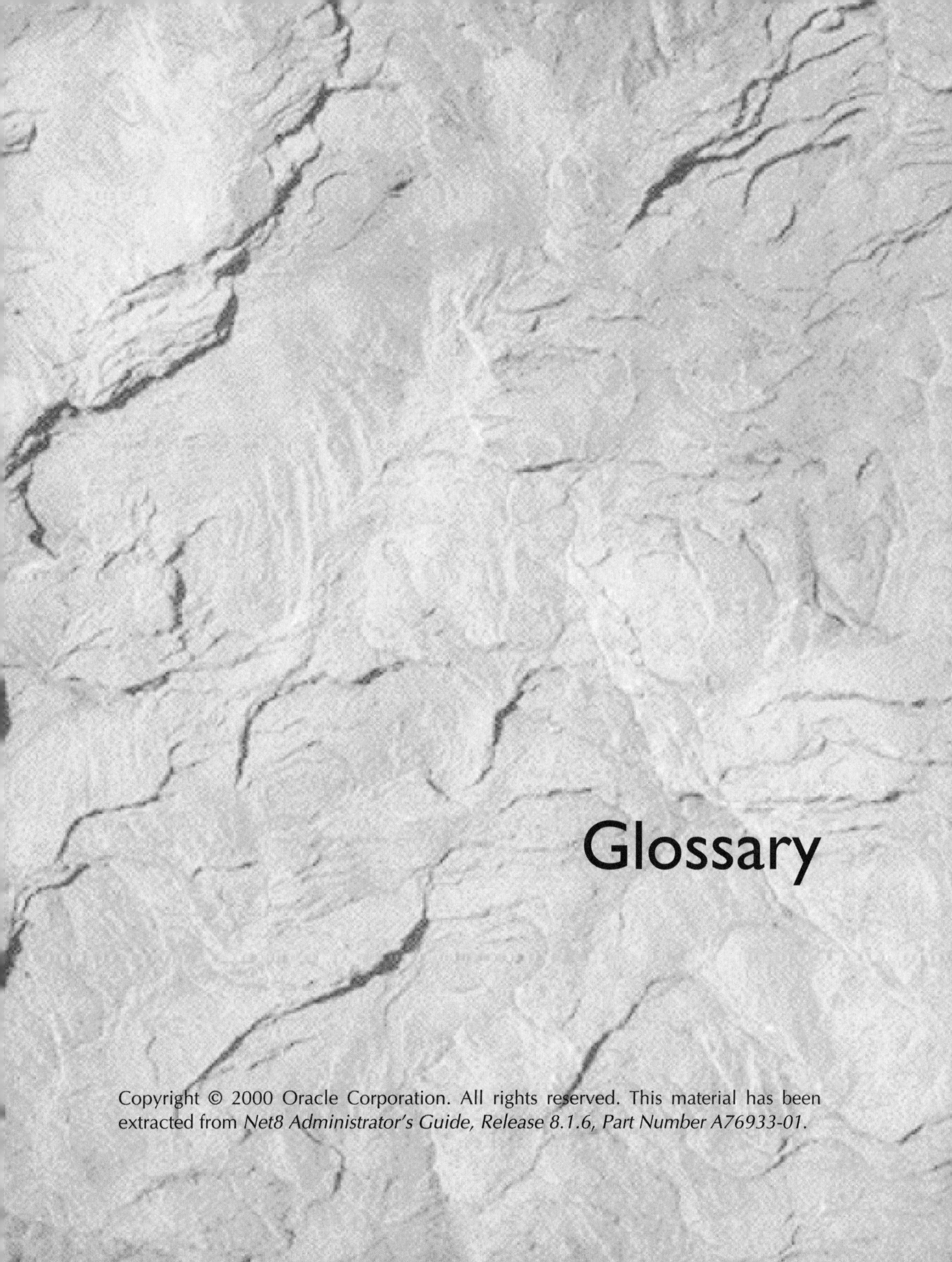

Glossary

A

Access Control List (ACL) The group of access directives that you define. The directives grant levels of access to specific data for specific clients and/or groups of clients.

ACL See Access Control List (ACL).

access control See Net8 access control.

address A unique network location used to identify a network object, such as a listener address, Oracle Connection Manager, or Oracle Names server. Addresses have a specific format and must be unique.

administrative context A directory entry under which an Oracle Context resides. An administrative context can be a directory naming context. During directory access configuration, clients are configured with an administrative context in the directory configuration file (ldap.ora). The administrative context specifies the location of the Oracle Context in the directory whose entries a client expects to access.

administrative region An organizational entity for administering Net8 network components. Each administrative region includes:

- One or more domains
- One or more Oracle Names servers
- One or more databases and listeners

alias An alternative name for an existing network object. Once an alias is created, it is resolved to the same name as the initial network object. An Oracle Names server stores aliases for any defined net service name, database server or database link.

API See Net8 Open.

ASCII character set Stands for American Standard Code for Information Interchange character set, a convention for representing alphanumeric information using digital data. The collation sequence used by most computers with the exception of IBM and IBM-compatible computers.

attribute A piece of information that describes some aspect of an entry. An entry comprises a set of attributes, each of which belongs to an object class. Moreover, each attribute has both a type—which describes the kind of information in the attribute—and a value—which contains the actual data.

authentication method A security method that enables you to have high confidence in the identity of users, clients, and servers in distributed environments. Network authentication methods can also provide the benefit of single sign-on for users. The following authentication methods may be supported, depending on whether or not Oracle Advanced Security is installed:

- CyberSafe
- SecurID
- RADIUS
- Identix
- Kerberos
- SSL
- Windows NT native authentication

B

Bequeath protocol If the listener and server exist on the same node, the listener may create or spawn dedicated servers as connect requests are received. Dedicated servers are committed to one network session only and exist for the duration of that network session. The sequence of events that occur when the listener creates a dedicated server process and passes or "bequeaths" control of a network session to it.

C

cache Memory that stores recently-accessed data to so that subsequent requests to access the same data can be processed quickly.

CDS Cell Directory Services. See Cell Directory Services (CDS).

Cell Directory Services (CDS) An external naming method that enables users to transparently use Oracle tools and applications to access Oracle8i databases in a Distributed Computing Environment (DCE) environment.

central administration An Oracle Names network where network management consists of one administrative region for the entire network. With central administration, all Oracle Names servers know about one another and about all the services in the network. Contrast with delegated administration.

client A user, software application, or computer that requests the services, data, or processing of another application or computer. In a two-task environment, the client is the user process. In a network environment, the client is the local user process and the server may be local or remote.

client load balancing Load balancing, whereby a client can randomly choose between the listeners for its connect requests if more than one listener services a single database. This randomization enables all listeners to share the burden of servicing incoming connect requests.

client profile The properties of a client, which may include the preferred order of naming methods, client and server logging and tracing, the domain from which to request names, and other client options for Oracle Names and Oracle Advanced Security.

client-server architecture Software architecture based on a separation of processing between two CPUs, one acting as the client in the transaction, requesting and receiving services, and the other as the server that provides services in a transaction.

cman.ora file A configuration file that specifies protocol addresses for incoming requests and administrative commands, as well as Oracle Connection Manager parameters and Net8 access control rules.

configuration files Files that are used to identify and characterize the components of a network. Configuration is largely a process of naming network components and identifying relationships among those components.

connect data A portion of the connect descriptor that defines the destination database service name or Oracle System Identifier (SID). In the example below, SERVICE_NAME defines a database service called `sales.us.acme.com`:

```
(description=
(address= (protocol=tcp)(host=sales-pc)(port=1521)
(connect_data=
   (service_name=sales.us.acme.com)))
```

connect descriptor A specially formatted description of the destination for a network connection. A connect descriptor contains destination service and network route information.

The destination service is indicated by using its service name for Oracle release 8.1 database or its Oracle System Identifier (SID) for Oracle release 8.0 or version 7 databases. The network route provides, at a minimum, the location of the listener through use of a network address.

connect identifier A net service name or service name, that resolves to a connect descriptor. Users initiate a connect request by passing a user name and password along with a connect identifier in a connect string for the service to which they wish to connect, for example:

```
CONNECT username/password@connect_identifier
```

connect-time failover A client connect request is forwarded to a another listener if first listener is not responding. Connect-time failover is enabled by service registration, because the listener knows if an instance is up prior to attempting a connection.

connection An interaction between two processes on a network. Connections are originated by an initiator (client), who requests a connection with a destination (server).

connection concentration A feature of Oracle Connection Manager that consolidates multiple connection requests from clients to establish a single connection to a server in order to conserve server resources.

connection load balancing Load balancing, whereby the number of active connections among various instances and dispatchers for the same service are balanced. This enables listeners to make their routing decisions based on how many connections each dispatcher has and on how loaded the nodes that the instances run.

connection pooling A resource utilization and user scalability feature that enables you to maximize the number of physical network connections to a multi-threaded server. A feature of Oracle Connection Manager that consolidates multiple connection requests from clients to establish a single connection to a server in order to conserve server resources.

connection request A notification sent by an initiator and received by a listener that indicates that the initiator wants to start a connection.

connect string Information the user passes to a service to connect, such as user name, password and net service name. For example:

```
CONNECT username/password@net_service_name
```

D

data packet See packet.

database administrator (DBA) (1) A person responsible for operating and maintaining an Oracle Server or a database application. (2) An Oracle username that has been given DBA privileges and can perform database administration functions. Usually the two meanings coincide. Many sites have multiple DBAs.

database link A network object stored in the local database or in the network definition that identifies a remote database, a communication path to that database, and optionally, a username and password. Once defined, the database link is used to access the remote database.

A public or private database link from one database to another is created on the local database by a DBA or user.

A global database link is created automatically from each database to every other database in a network with Oracle Names. Global database links are stored in the network definition.

See also global database link, private database link, and public database link.

decentralized administration See delegated administration.

dedicated server A server that requires a dedicated server process for each user process. There is one server process for each client. Net8 sends the address of an existing server process back to the client. The client then resends its connect request to the server address provided. Contrast with multi-threaded server (MTS).

default domain The domain domain within which most client requests take place. It could be the domain where the client resides, or it could be a domain from which the client requests network services often. Default domain is also the client configuration parameter that determines what domain should be appended to unqualified network name requests. A name request is unqualified if it does not have a "." character within it.

delegated administration A Net8 network where network management is delegated to one or more administrative regions below the root administrative region. Also referred to as distributed or decentralized administration. Contrast with central administration.

delegated administrative region A region hierarchically below the root administrative region. Any region other than the root administrative region.

destination The client that is the endpoint of a connection. The initiator of the connection requires some data or service of the destination.

Directory Information Tree (DIT) A hierarchical tree-like structure in a directory sever of the Distinguished Names (DNs) of the entries.

directory naming A naming method that resolves a database service or net service name to a connect descriptor, stored in a central directory server.

A directory provides central administration of database services and net service names, reducing the work effort associated with adding or relocating services. Although net service names can be configured to alias a service, the directory can refer to a database service directly without using a net service name. To further aid with configuration ease, the database service is automatically added as an entry to the directory during installation.

directory naming context A subtree which is of significance within a directory server. It is usually the top of some organizational subtree. Some directories only allow one such context which is fixed; others allow none to many to be configured by the directory administrator.

directory sever A LDAP-compliant directory server that is accessed with the Lightweight Directory Access Protocol (LDAP). A directory can provide centralized storage and retrieval of database network components, user and corporate policies preferences, user authentication and security information, replacing client-side and server-side localized files.

dispatcher A process that enables many clients to connect to the same server without the need for a dedicated server process for each client. A dispatcher handles and directs multiple incoming network session requests to shared server processes. See also multi-threaded server (MTS).

Distinguished Name (DN) Name of entry in a directory sever. The DN specifies where the entry resides in the LDAP directory hierarchy, much the way a directory path specifies the exact location of a file.

distributed administration See delegated administration.

distributed processing Division of front-end and back-end processing to different computers. Net8 supports distributed processing by transparently connecting applications to remote databases.

domain Any tree or subtree within the Domain Name System (DNS) namespace. Domain is most commonly used to refer to a group of computers whose host names share a common suffix, the domain name.

Domain Name System (DNS) Domain Name System (DNS) is a system for naming computers and network services that is organized into a hierarchy of domainss. DNS is used in TCP/IP networks to locate computers through user-friendly names. DNS resolves a friendly name into an IP address, which is understood by computers.

For Net8, DNS translate the host name in a TCP/IP address into an IP address.

domestic domains The set of domains that are managed within a given administrative region. Domains are only domestic relative to a region; they are never domestic in any absolute sense. Also referred to as local domains.

DNS Domain Name System. See Domain Name System (DNS).

E

error message A message from a computer program informing you of a potential problem or condition preventing program or command execution.

enterprise role An enterprise role is analogous to a regular database role, except that it spans authorization on multiple databases. An enterprise role is a category of roles that define privileges on a particular database. A enterprise role is created by a Database Administrator of a particular database. An enterprise role can be granted or revoked to one or more enterprise users. The information for granting and revoking these roles is also stored in the directory. In addition to creating global roles, a Database Administrator can also grant roles and privileges to a database schema. Everyone sharing a schema gets these local roles and privileges in addition to the enterprise roles.

Each enterprise user has a unique identity across an enterprise. Enterprise users connect to individual databases via a schema. Enterprise users are assigned enterprise roles which determine their access privileges on databases.

enterprise user Each enterprise user has a unique identity across an enterprise. Enterprise users connect to individual databases via a schema. Enterprise users are assigned enterprise roles which determine their access privileges on databases.

entry The building block of a directory, it contains information about an object of interest to directory users.

external naming A net service name resolution that uses a supported third-party naming service, such as NIS or NDS.

external procedures Functions or procedures written in a third-generation language (3GL) that can be called from PL/SQL code. Only C is supported for external procedures.

F

failover See connect-time failover.

firewall support See Net8 access control.

flat naming model An Oracle Names infrastructure in which there is only one domain. All names must be unique within that domain.

foreign domains The set of domains not managed within a given administrative region. Domains are only foreign relative to a region; they are not foreign in any absolute sense. A network administrator typically defines foreign domains relative to a particular region to optimize Names Server caching performance.

G

General Inter-ORB Protocol (GIOP) A presentation layer type that is used in Java option connections to provide messaging.

global database link A database link that links each database in a network to all other databases. This enables any user of any database in the network to specify a global object name in a SQL statement or object definition. An Oracle Names server can store global database links.

A database link that links each database in a network to all other databases. This enables any user of any database in the network to specify a global object name in a SQL statement or object definition.

global database name The full name of the database which uniquely identifies it from any other database. The global database name is of the form "database_name.database_domain", for example, `sales.us.acme.com`.

The database name portion, `sales`, is a simple name you wish to call your database. The database domain portion, `us.acme.com`, specifies the database domain in which the database is located, making the global database name unique.

When possible, Oracle recommends that your database domain mirror the network domain.

The global database name is the default service name of database, as specified by the SERVICE_NAMES parameter in the initialization parameter file.

H

Heterogeneous Services An integrated component that provides the generic technology for accessing non-Oracle systems from the Oracle server. Heterogeneous Services enables you to:

- Use Oracle SQL to transparently access data stored in non-Oracle systems as if the data resides within an Oracle server.
- Use Oracle procedure calls to transparently access non-Oracle systems, services, or application programming interfaces (APIs), from your Oracle distributed environment.

hierarchical naming model An infrastructure in which names are divided into multiple hierarchically-related domains. For Oracle Names, hierarchical naming model can be used with either central or delegated administration.

host naming A net service name resolution that enables users in a TCP/IP environment to resolve net service names via their existing name resolution service. This name resolution service might be Domain Name System (DNS), Network Information Service (NIS) or simply a centrally maintained set of `/etc/hosts` files. Host Naming enables users to connect to an Oracle server by simply providing the server computer's host name or host name alias. No client configuration is required to take advantage of this feature. This method is recommended for simple TCP/IP environments.

I

initialization parameter file File that contains information to initialize the database and instances.

instance An instance of the running Oracle8i software referencing the database. When a database is started on a database server (regardless of the type of computer), Oracle allocates a memory area called the System Global Area (SGA) and starts one or more Oracle processes. This combination of the SGA and the Oracle processes is called an instance. The memory and processes of an instance efficiently manage the associated database's data and serve the database users. You can connect to any instance to access information within a parallel server database.

Inter-ORB Protocol (IIOP) An implementation of General Inter-ORB Protocol (GIOP) over TCP/IP or TCP/IP with SSL for connections to Oracle8i JServer.

Interprocess Communication A protocol used by client applications the reside on the same node as the listener to communicate with the database.

IIOP Clients Clients that use the General Inter-ORB Protocol (GIOP) presentation to access the Java option. These clients include:

- Enterprise JavaBeans (EJBs)
- CORBA Servers
- Java Stored Procedures

IP address Used to identify a node on a network. Each machine on the network is assigned a unique IP address, which is made up of the network ID, plus a unique host ID. This address is typically represented in dotted-decimal notation, with the decimal value of each octet separated by a period (for example 144.45.9.22).
See Interprocess Communication.

J

Java Database Connectivity (JDBC) Drivers Drivers that provide Java programmers access to an Oracle database.

K

keyword-value pair The combination of a keyword and a value, used as the standard unit of information in connect descriptors and many configuration files. Keyword-value pairs may be nested; that is, a keyword may have another keyword-value pair as its value.

L

LDAP Lightweight Directory Access Protocol. The framework of design conventions supporting industry-standard directory severs.

LDAP Data Interchange Format (LDIF) The set of standards for formatting an input file for any of the LDAP command line utilities.

ldap.ora file A file created by the Net8 Configuration Assistant that contains the following directory access information:

- Type of directory
- Location of the directory
- Default administrative context the client or server will use to look up or configure connect identifiers for connections to database services

The `ldap.ora` file resides in `$ORACLE_HOME/network/admin` on UNIX platforms and ORACLE_HOME`\network\admin` on Windows platforms.

link qualifier A qualifier appended to a global database link to provide alternate settings for the database user name and password credentials. For example, a link qualifier of `emp` can be appended to a global database link of `sales.us.acme.com`.

listener A process that resides on the server whose responsibility is to listen for incoming client connection requests and manage the traffic to the server.

Every time a client (or server acting as a client) requests a network session with a server, a listener receives the actual request. If the client's information matches the listener's information, the listener grants a connection to the server.

listener.ora file A configuration file for the listener that identifies the:

- Listener name
- Protocol addresses that it is accepting connection requests on
- Services it is listening for

The `listener.ora` file typically resides in `$ORACLE_HOME/network/admin` on UNIX platforms and ORACLE_HOME`\network\admin` on Windows NT.

An Oracle release 8.1 databases does not require identification of the database service because of service registration. However, static service configuration is required for an Oracle release 8.1 databases if you plan to use Oracle Enterprise Manager.

Listener Control Utility (LSNRCTL) A utility included with Net8 to control various listener functions, such as to start, stop, and get the status of the listener.

load balancing A feature by which client connections are distributed evenly among multiple listeners, dispatchers, instances, and nodes so that no single component is overloaded.

Net8 supports client load balancing and connection load balancing.

local naming A net service name resolution that locates network addresses by using information configured and stored on each individual client's tnsnames.ora file. Local naming is most appropriate for simple distributed networks with a small number of services that change infrequently.

location transparency A distributed database characteristic that enables applications to access data tables without knowing where they reside. All data tables appear to be in a single database, and the system determines the actual data location based on the table name. The user can reference data on multiple nodes in a single statement, and the system automatically and transparently routes (parts of) SQL statements to remote nodes for execution if needed. The data can move among nodes with no impact on the user or application.

logging A feature in which errors, service activity, and statistics are written to a log file. The log file provides additional information for an administrator when the error message on the screen is inadequate to understand the failure. The log file, by way of the error stack, shows the state of the software at various layers.

See also tracing.

loopback test A connection from the server back to itself. Performing a successful loopback verifies that Net8 is functioning on the server side.

LU6.2 protocol Logical Unit Type 6.2. A protocol enables an Oracle application on a PC to communicate with an Oracle database. This communication occurs over an System Network Architecture (SNA) network with the Oracle database on a host system that supports Advanced Program-to-Program Communication (APPC) architecture.

M

map Files used by the Network Information Service (NIS) `ypserv` program to handle name requests.

Microsoft's Active Directory A LDAP-compliant directory service included with the Windows 2000 Server. It stores information about objects on the network, and makes this information available to users and network administrators. Active

Directory also provides users access to resources on the network using a single logon process.

Active Directory can be configured as a directory naming method to store service information that clients can access.

MTS See multi-threaded server (MTS).

multi-protocol support A feature of Oracle Connection Manager that enables a client and server with different networking protocols to communicate with each other. This feature replaces functionality previously provided by the Oracle Multi-Protocol Interchange with SQL*Net version 2.

multi-threaded server (MTS) A server that is configured to allow many user processes to share very few server processes, so the number of users that can be supported is increased. With MTS configuration, many user processes connect to a dispatcher. The dispatcher directs multiple incoming network session requests to a common queue. An idle shared server process from a shared pool of server processes picks up a request from the queue. This means a small pool of server processes can server a large amount of clients. Contrast with dedicated server.

multiplexing Combining multiple sessions for transmission over a single transport connection in order to conserve the operating system's resources. See also connection concentration

N

names.ora file A configuration file that contains parameter settings for an Oracle Names server.

Named Pipes protocol A high-level interface protocol providing interprocess communications between clients and servers (distributed applications). Named Pipes enables client/server conversation over a network using Named Pipes.

naming method The method used by a client application to resolve a connect identifier to a connect descriptor when attempting to connect to a database service. Net8 provides five naming methods:

- local naming
- directory naming

- host naming
- Oracle Names
- external naming

naming model The set and structure of domains within which names can be allocated.

In a flat naming model, there is a single domain.

In a hierarchical naming model, the highest level is the root domain, and all other domains are hierarchically related.

NDS authentication An authentication method that enables a client single login access to a multi-server and multi-database network under a single NDS directory tree.

NDS See Novell Directory Services (NDS).

net service name A simple name for a service that resolves to a connect descriptor. Users initiate a connect request by passing a user name and password along with a net service name in a connect string for the service to which they wish to connect:

```
CONNECT username/password@net_service_name
```

Depending on your needs, net service names can be stored in a variety of places, including:

- Local configuration file, `tnsnames.ora`, on each client
- Directory server
- Oracle Names server
- External naming service, such as NDS, NIS or CDS

Net8 Oracle's remote data access software that enables both client-server and server-server communications across any network. Net8 supports distributed processing and distributed database capability. Net8 runs over and interconnects many communications protocols. Net8 is backward compatible with SQL*Net version 2.

Net8 access control A feature of Oracle Connection Manager that sets rules for denying or allowing certain clients to access designated servers. Also known as firewall support.

Net8 Assistant A graphical user interface tool that combines configuration abilities with component control to provide an integrated environment for configuring and managing Net8. It can be used on either the client or server.

You can use Net8 Assistant to configure the following network components:

- Naming: Define connect identifiers and map them to connect descriptors to identify the network location and identification of a service. Net8 Assistant supports configuration of connect descriptors in local `tnsnames.ora` files, centralized LDAP-compliant directory service, or an Oracle Names server.
- Naming Methods: Configure the different ways in which connect identifiers are resolved into connect descriptors.
- Listeners: Create and configure listeners to receive client connections.

Net8 Configuration Assistant A post-installation tool that configure basic network components after installation, including:

- Listener names and protocol addresses
- Naming methods the client will use to resolve connect identifiers
- Net service names in a `tnsnames.ora` file
- Directory server access

Net8 Open The application program interface (API) to Net8 that enables programmers to develop both database and non-database applications that make use of the Net8 network already deployed in their environment. Net8 Open provides applications a single common interface to all industry standard network protocols.

network A group of two or more computers linked together through hardware and software to allow the sharing of data and/or peripherals.

network administrator The person who performs network management tasks such as installing, configuring, and testing network components. The administrator typically maintains the configuration files, connect descriptors and service names, aliases, and public and global database links.

network character set As defined by Oracle, the set of characters acceptable for use as values in keyword-value pairs (that is, in connect descriptors and configuration files). The set includes alphanumeric upper- and lowercase, and some special characters.

Network Information Service (NIS) Sun Microsystems' Yellow Pages (yp) client-server protocol for distributing system configuration data such as user and host names between computers on a network.

Network Interface (NI) A network layer that provides a generic interface for Oracle clients, servers, or external processes to access Net8 functions. The NI layer handles the "break" and "reset" requests for a connection.

See listener.

network object Any service that can be directly addressed on a network; for example, a listener or a Oracle Names server.

network protocol See Oracle Protocol.

Network Program Interface (NPI) An interface for server-to-server interactions that performs all of the functions that the OCI does for clients, allowing a coordinating server to construct SQL requests for additional servers.

network service In an Oracle application network, a service performs tasks for its service consumers; for example, a Names Server provides name resolution services for clients.

Network Session (NS) NS is a session layer types that is used in typical Net8 connection to establish and maintaining the connection between a client application and server.

NI Network Interface

NIS Network Information Service. See Network Information Service (NIS).

NN Network Naming (Oracle Names)

node A computer or terminal that is part of a network.

Novell Directory Services (NDS) A distributed computing infrastructure that stores information about network resources on your network. NDS provides easy network access regardless of the user's physical location or the location of needed resources.

Using NDS, you can simplify network administration by using objects to represent any network resource in the network file system.

NPI See Network Program Interface (NPI).

NR Network Routing

NS Network Session. See Network Session (NS).

NT Network Transport. See transport.

O

object class A named group of attributes. When you want to assign attributes to an entry, you do so by assigning to that entry the object classes that hold those attributes.

All objects in the same object class share the same attributes.

OCI Oracle Call Interface. See Oracle Call Interface (OCI).

OPI See Oracle Program Interface (OPI).

Open Systems Interconnection (OSI) A model of network architecture developed by ISO as a framework for international standards in heterogeneous computer network architecture.

The OSI architecture is split between seven layers, from lowest to highest: 1 physical layer, 2 data link layer, 3 network layer, 4 transport layer, 5 session layer, 6 presentation layer, 7 application layer. Each layer uses the layer immediately below it and provides a service to the layer above.

Oracle Advanced Security A product that provides a comprehensive suite of security features to protect enterprise networks and securely extend corporate networks to the Internet. Oracle Advanced Security provides a single source of integration with network encryption and authentication solutions, single sign-on services, and security protocols. By integrating industry standards, it delivers unparalleled security to the network.

Oracle Call Interface (OCI) An application programming interface (API) that enables you to create applications that use the native procedures or function calls of a third-generation language to access an Oracle database server and control all phases of SQL statement execution. OCI supports the datatypes, calling conventions, syntax, and semantics of a number of third-generation languages including C, C++, COBOL and FORTRAN.

Oracle Connection Manager A router through which a client connection request may be sent either to its next hop or directly to the database server. Clients who route their connection requests through a Connection Manager can then take advantage of the connection concentration, Net8 access control, or multi-protocol support features configured on that Connection Manager.

Oracle Connection Manager Control Utility (CMCTL) A utility included with Net8 to control various functions, such as to start, stop, and get the status of the Oracle Connection Manager.

Oracle Context A RDN of `cn=OracleContext`, under which all Oracle software relevant information is kept, including entries for directory naming and enterprise user security.

There may be one or more than one Oracle Context in a directory. An Oracle Context can be associated with a directory naming context.

Oracle Database Configuration Assistant A tool that enables you to create, delete, and modify a database.

Oracle Internet Directory A directory service implemented as an application on the Oracle release 8.1 database. It enables retrieval of information about dispersed users and network resources. It combines Lightweight Directory Access Protocol (LDAP) Version 3, the open Internet standard directory access protocol, with the high performance, scalability, robustness, and availability of the Oracle8i Server.

Oracle Names An Oracle directory service made up of a system of Oracle Names servers that provide name-to-address resolution for each Net8 service on the network.

Oracle Names Control Utility (NAMESCTL) A utility included with Oracle Names to control various functions for Oracle Names servers, such as to start, stop, and get the status of an Oracle Names server.

Oracle Names server A server that uses Oracle Names to store a service's network address along with its simple name so that client applications can request connections with simple names, rather than lengthy addresses.

Oracle Program Interface (OPI) A networking layer that is responsible for responding to each of the possible messages sent by OCI. For example, an OCI request to fetch 25 rows would have an OPI response to return the 25 rows once they have been fetched.

Oracle Protocol A set of rules that defines how data is transported across networks. There are several industry standard transport protocols, such as TCP/IP and SPX.

Oracle Rdb A database for Digital's 64-bit platforms. Because Oracle Rdb has its own listener, the client interacts with Rdb in the same manner as it does with an Oracle database.

Oracle schema (as it relates to LDAP) A set of rules that determine what can be stored in directory sever. Oracle has its own schema that is applied to many types of Oracle entries, including Net8 entries. The Oracle schema for Net8 entries includes the attributes the entries may contain.

Oracle System Identifier (SID) A name that identifies a specific instance of a running pre-release 8.1 Oracle database. For any database, there is at least one instance referencing the database.

For pre-release 8.1 databases, SID was used to identify the database. The SID was included in the part of the connect descriptor in a tnsnames.ora file, and in the definition of the listener in the listener.ora file.

ORACLE_HOME An alternate name for the top directory in the Oracle directory hierarchy on some directory-based operating systems.

OSI Open Systems Interconnection. See Open Systems Interconnection (OSI).

Oracle8i JServer Provides support for Java stored procedures, JDBC, SQLJ, Common Object Request Broker Architecture (CORBA), and Enterprise JavaBeans (EJBs) in the Oracle8i database.

P

packet A block of information sent over the network each time a connection or data transfer is requested. The information contained in packets depends on the type of packet: connect, accept, redirect, data, etc. Packet information can be useful in troubleshooting.

parameter Information passed to a program, command, or function, such as a file specification, a keyword, or a constant value.

password A string (word or phrase) used for data security and known only to its owner. Passwords are entered in conjunction with an operating system login ID,

Oracle username, or account name, in order to connect to an operating system or software application (such as the Oracle database). Whereas the username or ID is public, the secret password ensures that only the owner of the username can use that name, or access that data.

PMON process A process monitor database process that performs process recovery when a user process fails. PMON is responsible for cleaning up the cache and freeing resources that the process was using. PMON also checks on dispatcher (see below) and server processes and restarts them if they have failed. As a part of service registration, PMON registers instance information with the listener.

preferred Oracle Names server The Oracle Names server(s) preferred by a client for names resolution; usually the Oracle Names Server that is physically closest to the client, or available over the least expensive network link.

presentation layer The presentation layer manages the representation of information that application layer entities either communicate or reference in their communication. Example of session layers are Two-Task Common (TTC) and General Inter-ORB Protocol (GIOP).

prespawned dedicated server Prespawned dedicated server processes are prestarted by the listener before any incoming connection requests. They improve the time it takes to establish a connection on servers where multi-threaded server (MTS) is not used or not supported on a given machine. They also use allocated memory and system resources better by recycling server processes for use by other connections with shutting down and recreating a server.

private database link A database link created by one user for his or her exclusive use.

See also database link, global database link, and public database link.

profile A collection of parameters that specifies preferences for enabling and configuring Net8 features on the client or server. A profile is stored and implemented through the `sqlnet.ora` file.

protocol address An address that identifies the network address of a network object.

When a connection is made, the client and the receiver of the request, such as the listener, Oracle Names server or Oracle Connection Manager, are configured with identical protocol addresses. The client uses this address to send the connection request to a particular network object location, and the recipient "listens" for requests on this address. It is important to install the same protocols for the client and the connection recipient, as well as configure the same addresses.

protocol stack Designates a particular presentation layer and session layer combination.

public database link A database link created by a DBA on a local database which is accessible to all users on that database.

See also database link, global database link, and private database link.

R

RDBMS Relational Database Management System

RDN See Relative Distinguished Name (RDN).

Relative Distinguished Name (RDN) The local, most granular level entry name. It has no other qualifying entry names that would serve to uniquely address the entry. In the example, `cn=sales,dc=us,dc=acme,dc=com`, `cn=sales` is the RDN.

region See administrative region.

region database Tables in an Oracle database that store Oracle Names information.

root administrative region The highest level administrative region in a distributed installation. The root administrative region contains the root domain.

root domain The highest level domain in a hierarchical naming model.

RPC Remote Procedure Call

S

Secure Sockets Layer (SSL) An industry standard protocol designed by Netscape Communications Corporation for securing network connections. SSL provides authentication, encryption, and data integrity using public key infrastructure (PKI).

Sequenced Packet Exchange (SPX)

service handler A service handler can be a multi-threaded server dispatcher, dedicated server, or prespawned dedicated server.

service registration A feature by which the PMON process automatically registers information with a listener. Because this information is registered with the listener, the `listener.ora` file does not need to be configured with this static information.

Service registration provides the listener with the following information:
Service registration provides the listener with information about:

- Service names for each running instance of the database
- Instance names of the database
- Service handlers (dispatchers and dedicated servers) available for each instance

This enables the listener to direct a client's request appropriately.

- Dispatcher, instance, and node load information

This load information enables the listener to determine which dispatcher can best handle a client connection's request. If all dispatchers are blocked, the listener can spawn a dedicated server for the connection.

service replication A process that fully replicates a directory system on the network. New services need to register with only one Names Server. The service replication process automatically distributes the new registration to all other active Names Servers on the network.

service name A logical representation of a database, which is the way a database is presented to clients. A database can be presented as multiple services and a service can be implemented as multiple database instances. The service name is a string that is the global database name, a name comprised of the database name and domain name, entered during installation or database creation. If you are not sure what the global database name is, you can obtain it from the combined values of the SERVICE_NAMES parameter in the initialization parameter file.

The service name is included in the connect data part of the connect descriptor.

session layer The session layer provides the services needed by the presentation layer entities that enable them to organize and synchronize their dialogue and manage their data exchange. This layer establishes, manages, and terminates network sessions between the client and server. An example of a session layer is Network Session (NS).

SID Oracle System Identifier. See Oracle System Identifier (SID).

SID_LIST_listener_name A section of the listener.ora that defines the Oracle System Identifier (SID) of the database served by the listener. This section is only valid for version 7.x and version 8.0 Oracle databases, as release 8.1 instance information is now automatically registered with the listener. Static configuration is also required for other services, such as external procedures and heterogeneous services, and some management tools, including Oracle Enterprise Manager.

SPX protocol Sequenced Packet Exchange protocol. A protocol known for high performance and acceptance among many major network management systems, in particular, Novell Advanced NetWare.

SQL*Net Net8's precursor. An Oracle product that works with the Oracle Server and enables two or more computers that run the Oracle RDBMS or Oracle tools such as SQL*Forms to exchange data through a network. SQL*Net supports distributed processing and distributed database capability. SQL*Net runs over and interconnects many communications protocols.

sqlnet.ora file A configuration file for the client or server that specifies:

- Client domain to append to unqualified service names or net service names
- Order of naming methods the client should use when resolving a name
- Logging and tracing features to use
- Route of connections
- Preferred Oracle Names servers
- External naming parameters
- Oracle Advanced Security parameters

The `sqlnet.ora` file typically resides in `$ORACLE_HOME/network/admin` on UNIX platforms and `ORACLE_HOME\network\admin` on Windows platforms.

SSL Secure Sockets Layer. See Secure Sockets Layer (SSL).

System Global Area (SGA) A group of shared memory structures that contain data and control information for an Oracle instance.

system or topology data Data used by the Oracle Names server to control regular functioning or communicate with other Oracle Names servers. Includes interchanges, root region's Oracle Names servers, and any delegated regions' Oracle Names servers.

T

TCP/IP protocol Transmission Control Protocol/Internet Protocol. The de facto standard Ethernet protocol used for client/server conversation over a network.

protocol TCP/IP with Secure Sockets Layer. A protocol that enables an Oracle application on a client to communicate with remote Oracle databases through TCP/IP and SSL (if the Oracle database is running on a host system that supports network communication using TCP/IP and SSL).

Thin JDBC Driver Thin JDBC driver is Oracle's Type 4 driver designed for Java applet and Java application developers. The JDBC driver establishes a direct connection to the Oracle database server over Java sockets. Access to the database is assisted with a lightweight implementation of Net8 and Two-Task Common (TTC).

TNS See Transparent Network Substrate (TNS).

tnsnames.ora file A configuration file that contains net service name mapped to connect descriptors. This file is used for the local naming method. The `tnsnames.ora` file typically resides in `$ORACLE_HOME/network/admin` on UNIX platforms and `ORACLE_HOME\network\admin`.

tracing A facility that writes detailed information about an operation to an output file. The trace facility produces a detailed sequence of statements that describe the events of an operation as they are executed. Administrators use the trace facility for diagnosing an abnormal condition; it is not normally turned on.

See also logging.

Transparent Application Failover (TAF) A runtime failover for high-availability environments, such as Oracle Parallel Server and Oracle Fail Safe, that refers to the failover and re-establishment of application-to-service connections. It enables client applications to automatically reconnect to the database if the connection fails, and optionally resume a SELECT statement that was in progress. This reconnect happens automatically from within the Oracle Call Interface (OCI) library.

Transparent Network Substrate (TNS) A foundation technology, built into Net8, Oracle Connection Manager and Oracle Names, that works with any standard network transport protocol.

transport A networking layer that maintains end-to-end reliability through data flow control and error recovery methods. Net8 uses Oracle Protocols for the transport layer.

TTC Two-Task Common. See Two-Task Common (TTC).

Two-Task Common (TTC) TTC is a presentation layer type that is used in typical Net8 connection to provide character set and data type conversion between different character sets or formats on the client and server.

U

user name The name by which a user is known to the Oracle Server and to other users. Every username is associated with a password, and both must be entered to connect to an Oracle database.

UPI User Program Interface

virtual circuit A piece of shared memory used by the dispatcher for client database connection requests and replies. The dispatcher places a virtual circuit on a common queue when a request arrives. An idle shared server picks up the virtual circuit from the common queue, services the request, and relinquishes the virtual circuit before attempting to retrieve another virtual circuit from the common queue.

well-known Oracle Names server Addresses for one or more Oracle Names servers hardcoded into both the Oracle Names server and its clients. Oracle Names servers then become available at these well known addresses, so that clients do not need to be told, by way of configuration files, where to find the server.

Windows NT native authentication An authentication method that enables a client single login access to a Windows NT server and a database running on the server.

Index

D

E

F

G

J

K

L

M

N

P

Q

R

S

U

V

W

X

☐ YES! Please send me a FREE subscription to *Oracle Magazine*. ☐ NO

To receive a free bimonthly subscription to *Oracle Magazine*, you must fill out the entire card, sign it, and date it (incomplete cards cannot be processed or acknowledged). You can also fax your application to **+1.847.647.9735. Or subscribe at our Web site at www.oracle.com/oramag/**

SIGNATURE (REQUIRED) X ______ **DATE** ______

NAME ______ TITLE ______

COMPANY ______ TELEPHONE ______

ADDRESS ______ FAX NUMBER ______

CITY ______ STATE ______ POSTAL CODE/ZIP CODE ______

COUNTRY ______ E-MAIL ADDRESS ______

☐ From time to time, Oracle Publishing allows our partners exclusive access to our e-mail addresses for special promotions and announcements. To be included in this program, please check this box.

You must answer all eight questions below.

1 What is the primary business activity of your firm at this location? *(check only one)*

- ☐ 03 Communications
- ☐ 04 Consulting, Training
- ☐ 06 Data Processing
- ☐ 07 Education
- ☐ 08 Engineering
- ☐ 09 Financial Services
- ☐ 10 Government—Federal, Local, State, Other
- ☐ 11 Government—Military
- ☐ 12 Health Care
- ☐ 13 Manufacturing—Aerospace, Defense
- ☐ 14 Manufacturing—Computer Hardware
- ☐ 15 Manufacturing—Noncomputer Products
- ☐ 17 Research & Development
- ☐ 19 Retailing, Wholesaling, Distribution
- ☐ 20 Software Development
- ☐ 21 Systems Integration, VAR, VAD, OEM
- ☐ 22 Transportation
- ☐ 23 Utilities (Electric, Gas, Sanitation)
- ☐ 98 Other Business and Services ______

2 Which of the following best describes your job function? *(check only one)*

CORPORATE MANAGEMENT/STAFF

- ☐ 01 Executive Management (President, Chair, CEO, CFO, Owner, Partner, Principal)
- ☐ 02 Finance/Administrative Management (VP/Director/ Manager/Controller, Purchasing, Administration)
- ☐ 03 Sales/Marketing Management (VP/Director/Manager)
- ☐ 04 Computer Systems/Operations Management (CIO/VP/Director/ Manager MIS, Operations)

IS/IT STAFF

- ☐ 07 Systems Development/ Programming Management
- ☐ 08 Systems Development/ Programming Staff
- ☐ 09 Consulting
- ☐ 10 DBA/Systems Administrator
- ☐ 11 Education/Training
- ☐ 14 Technical Support Director/ Manager
- ☐ 16 Other Technical Management/Staff
- ☐ 98 Other ______

3 What is your current primary operating platform? *(check all that apply)*

- ☐ 01 DEC UNIX
- ☐ 02 DEC VAX VMS
- ☐ 03 Java
- ☐ 04 HP UNIX
- ☐ 05 IBM AIX
- ☐ 06 IBM UNIX
- ☐ 07 Macintosh
- ☐ 09 MS-DOS
- ☐ 10 MVS
- ☐ 11 NetWare
- ☐ 12 Network Computing
- ☐ 13 OpenVMS
- ☐ 14 SCO UNIX
- ☐ 24 Sequent DYNIX/ptx
- ☐ 15 Sun Solaris/SunOS
- ☐ 16 SVR4
- ☐ 18 UnixWare
- ☐ 20 Windows
- ☐ 21 Windows NT
- ☐ 23 Other UNIX ______
- ☐ 98 Other ______
- 99 ☐ **None of the above**

4 Do you evaluate, specify, recommend, or authorize the purchase of any of the following? *(check all that apply)*

- ☐ 01 Hardware
- ☐ 02 Software
- ☐ 03 Application Development Tools
- ☐ 04 Database Products
- ☐ 05 Internet or Intranet Products
- 99 ☐ **None of the above**

5 In your job, do you use or plan to purchase any of the following products or services? *(check all that apply)*

SOFTWARE

- ☐ 01 Business Graphics
- ☐ 02 CAD/CAE/CAM
- ☐ 03 CASE
- ☐ 05 Communications
- ☐ 06 Database Management
- ☐ 07 File Management
- ☐ 08 Finance
- ☐ 09 Java
- ☐ 10 Materials Resource Planning
- ☐ 11 Multimedia Authoring
- ☐ 12 Networking
- ☐ 13 Office Automation
- ☐ 14 Order Entry/Inventory Control
- ☐ 15 Programming
- ☐ 16 Project Management
- ☐ 17 Scientific and Engineering
- ☐ 18 Spreadsheets
- ☐ 19 Systems Management
- ☐ 20 Workflow

HARDWARE

- ☐ 21 Macintosh
- ☐ 22 Mainframe
- ☐ 23 Massively Parallel Processing
- ☐ 24 Minicomputer
- ☐ 25 PC
- ☐ 26 Network Computer
- ☐ 28 Symmetric Multiprocessing
- ☐ 29 Workstation

PERIPHERALS

- ☐ 30 Bridges/Routers/Hubs/Gateways
- ☐ 31 CD-ROM Drives
- ☐ 32 Disk Drives/Subsystems
- ☐ 33 Modems
- ☐ 34 Tape Drives/Subsystems
- ☐ 35 Video Boards/Multimedia

SERVICES

- ☐ 37 Consulting
- ☐ 38 Education/Training
- ☐ 39 Maintenance
- ☐ 40 Online Database Services
- ☐ 41 Support
- ☐ 36 Technology-Based Training
- ☐ 98 Other ______
- 99 ☐ **None of the above**

6 What Oracle products are in use at your site? *(check all that apply)*

SERVER/SOFTWARE

- ☐ 01 Oracle8
- ☐ 30 Oracle8*i*
- ☐ 31 Oracle8*i* Lite
- ☐ 02 Oracle7
- ☐ 03 Oracle Application Server
- ☐ 04 Oracle Data Mart Suites
- ☐ 05 Oracle Internet Commerce Server
- ☐ 32 Oracle *inter*Media
- ☐ 33 Oracle JServer
- ☐ 07 Oracle Lite
- ☐ 08 Oracle Payment Server
- ☐ 11 Oracle Video Server

TOOLS

- ☐ 13 Oracle Designer
- ☐ 14 Oracle Developer
- ☐ 54 Oracle Discoverer
- ☐ 53 Oracle Express
- ☐ 51 Oracle JDeveloper
- ☐ 52 Oracle Reports
- ☐ 50 Oracle WebDB
- ☐ 55 Oracle Workflow

ORACLE APPLICATIONS

- ☐ 17 Oracle Automotive
- ☐ 35 Oracle Business Intelligence System
- ☐ 19 Oracle Consumer Packaged Goods
- ☐ 39 Oracle E-Commerce
- ☐ 18 Oracle Energy
- ☐ 20 Oracle Financials
- ☐ 28 Oracle Front Office
- ☐ 21 Oracle Human Resources
- ☐ 37 Oracle Internet Procurement
- ☐ 22 Oracle Manufacturing
- ☐ 40 Oracle Process Manufacturing
- ☐ 23 Oracle Projects
- ☐ 34 Oracle Retail
- ☐ 29 Oracle Self-Service Web Applications
- ☐ 38 Oracle Strategic Enterprise Management
- ☐ 25 Oracle Supply Chain Management
- ☐ 36 Oracle Tutor
- ☐ 41 Oracle Travel Management

ORACLE SERVICES

- ☐ 61 Oracle Consulting
- ☐ 62 Oracle Education
- ☐ 60 Oracle Support
- ☐ 98 Other ______
- 99 ☐ **None of the above**

7 What other database products are in use at your site? *(check all that apply)*

- ☐ 01 Access
- ☐ 02 Baan
- ☐ 03 dbase
- ☐ 04 Gupta
- ☐ 05 IBM DB2
- ☐ 06 Informix
- ☐ 07 Ingres
- ☐ 08 Microsoft Access
- ☐ 09 Microsoft SQL Server
- ☐ 10 PeopleSoft
- ☐ 11 Progress
- ☐ 12 SAP
- ☐ 13 Sybase
- ☐ 14 VSAM
- ☐ 98 Other ______
- 99 ☐ **None of the above**

8 During the next 12 months, how much do you anticipate your organization will spend on computer hardware, software, peripherals, and services for your location? *(check only one)*

- ☐ 01 Less than $10,000
- ☐ 02 $10,000 to $49,999
- ☐ 03 $50,000 to $99,999
- ☐ 04 $100,000 to $499,999
- ☐ 05 $500,000 to $999,999
- ☐ 06 $1,000,000 and over

If there are other Oracle users at your location who would like to receive a free subscription to *Oracle Magazine*, please photocopy this form and pass it along, or contact Customer Service at +1.847.647.9630

Form 5

OPRESS